48: *American Poets, 1880-1945*, Second Series, edited by Peter Quartermain (1986)

49: *American Literary Publishing Houses, 1638-1899*, 2 parts, edited by Peter Dzwonkoski (1986)

50: *Afro-American Writers Before the Harlem Renaissance*, edited by Trudier Harris (1986)

51: *Afro-American Writers from the Harlem Renaissance to 1940*, edited by Trudier Harris (1987)

52: *American Writers for Children Since 1960: Fiction*, edited by Glenn E. Estes (1986)

53: *Canadian Writers Since 1960*, First Series, edited by W. H. New (1986)

54: *American Poets, 1880-1945*, Third Series, 2 parts, edited by Peter Quartermain (1987)

55: *Victorian Prose Writers Before 1867*, edited by William B. Thesing (1987)

56: *German Fiction Writers, 1914-1945*, edited by James Hardin (1987)

57: *Victorian Prose Writers After 1867*, edited by William B. Thesing (1987)

58: *Jacobean and Caroline Dramatists*, edited by Fredson Bowers (1987)

59: *American Literary Critics and Scholars, 1800-1850*, edited by John W. Rathbun and Monica M. Grecu (1987)

60: *Canadian Writers Since 1960*, Second Series, edited by W. H. New (1987)

61: *American Writers for Children Since 1960: Poets, Illustrators, and Nonfiction Authors*, edited by Glenn E. Estes (1987)

62: *Elizabethan Dramatists*, edited by Fredson Bowers (1987)

63: *Modern American Critics, 1920-1955*, edited by Gregory S. Jay (1988)

64: *American Literary Critics and Scholars, 1850-1880*, edited by John W. Rathbun and Monica M. Grecu (1988)

65: *French Novelists, 1900-1930*, edited by Catharine Savage Brosman (1988)

66: *German Fiction Writers, 1885-1913*, 2 parts, edited by James Hardin (1988)

67: *Modern American Critics Since 1955*, edited by Gregory S. Jay (1988)

68: *Canadian Writers, 1920-1959*, First Series, edited by W. H. New (1988)

Documentary Series

1: *Sherwood Anderson, Willa Cather, John Dos Passos, Theodore Dreiser, F. Scott Fitzgerald, Ernest Hemingway, Sinclair Lewis*, edited by Margaret A. Van Antwerp (1982)

2: *James Gould Cozzens, James T. Farrell, William Faulkner, John O'Hara, John Steinbeck, Thomas Wolfe, Richard Wright*, edited by Margaret A. Van Antwerp (1982)

3: *Saul Bellow, Jack Kerouac, Norman Mailer, Vladimir Nabokov, John Updike, Kurt Vonnegut*, edited by Mary Bruccoli (1983)

4: *Tennessee Williams*, edited by Margaret A. Van Antwerp and Sally Johns (1984)

5: *American Transcendentalists*, edited by Joel Myerson (1988)

Yearbooks

1980, edited by Karen L. Rood, Jean W. Ross, and Richard Ziegfeld (1981)

1981, edited by Karen L. Rood, Jean W. Ross, and Richard Ziegfeld (1982)

1982, edited by Richard Ziegfeld; associate editors: Jean W. Ross and Lynne C. Zeigler (1983)

1983, edited by Mary Bruccoli and Jean W. Ross; associate editor: Richard Ziegfeld (1984)

1984, edited by Jean W. Ross (1985)

1985, edited by Jean W. Ross (1986)

1986, edited by J. M. Brook (1987)

1987, edited by J. M. Brook (1988)

Concise Series

The New Consciousness, 1941-1968 (1987)

Colonization to the American Renaissance, 1640-1865 (1988)

Canadian Writers, 1920-1959
First Series

Dictionary of Literary Biography • Volume Sixty-eight

Canadian Writers, 1920-1959
First Series

7567

Edited by
W. H. New
University of British Columbia

A Bruccoli Clark Layman Book
Gale Research Company • Book Tower • Detroit, Michigan 48226

Manufactured by Edwards Brothers, Inc.
Ann Arbor, Michigan
Printed in the United States of America

Library of Congress Cataloging-in-Publication Data

Canadian writers, 1920-1959. First series / edited by William
H. New.
    p. cm—(Dictionary of literary biography; v. 68)
    "A Bruccoli Clark Layman book."
    Includes index.
    ISBN 0-8103-1746-X
    1. Canadian literature—20th century—History and
criticism. 2. French-Canadian literature—20th century—
History and criticism. 3. Canadian literature—20th century—Bio-bibliography. 4. French-Canadian literature—
20th century—Bio-bibliography. 5. Authors, Canadian—
20th century—Biography—Dictionaries. 6. Authors,
French-Canadian—20th century—Biography—Dictionaries. I. New, William H. II. Series.
PR9186.2.C34 1988   88-724
810'.9'0052--dc19   CIP

Contents

Contents

Plan of the Series

. . . Almost the most prodigious asset of a country, and perhaps its most precious possession, is its native literary product–when that product is fine and noble and enduring.

Mark Twain*

The advisory board, the editors, and the publisher of the *Dictionary of Literary Biography* are joined in endorsing Mark Twain's declaration. The literature of a nation provides an inexhaustible resource of permanent worth. We intend to make literature and its creators better understood and more accessible to students and the reading public, while satisfying the standards of teachers and scholars.

To meet these requirements, *literary biography* has been construed in terms of the author's achievement. The most important thing about a writer is his writing. Accordingly, the entries in *DLB* are career biographies, tracing the development of the author's canon and the evolution of his reputation.

The purpose of *DLB* is not only to provide reliable information in a convenient format but also to place the figures in the larger perspective of literary history and to offer appraisals of their accomplishments by qualified scholars.

The publication plan for *DLB* resulted from two years of preparation. The project was proposed to Bruccoli Clark by Frederick G. Ruffner, president of the Gale Research Company, in November 1975. After specimen entries were prepared and typeset, an advisory board was formed to refine the entry format and develop the series rationale. In meetings held during 1976, the publisher, series editors, and advisory board approved the scheme for a comprehensive biographical dictionary of persons who contributed to North American literature. Editorial work on the first volume began in January 1977, and it was published in 1978. In order to make *DLB* more than a reference tool and to compile volumes that individually have claim to status as literary history, it was decided to organize volumes by topic, period, or genre. Each of these freestanding volumes provides a biographical-bibliographical guide and overview for a particular area of literature. We are convinced that this organization–as opposed to a single alphabet method–constitutes a valuable innovation in the presentation of reference material. The volume plan necessarily requires many decisions for the placement and treatment of authors who might properly be included in two or three volumes. In some instances a major figure will be included in separate volumes, but with different entries emphasizing the aspect of his career appropriate to each volume. Ernest Hemingway, for example, is represented in *American Writers in Paris, 1920-1939* by an entry focusing on his expatriate apprenticeship; he is also in *American Novelists, 1910-1945* with an entry surveying his entire career. Each volume includes a cumulative index of subject authors and articles. Comprehensive indexes to the entire series are planned.

With volume ten in 1982 it was decided to enlarge the scope of *DLB*. By the end of 1986 twenty-one volumes treating British literature had been published, and volumes for Commonwealth and Modern European literature were in progress. The series has been further augmented by the *DLB Yearbooks* (since 1981) which update published entries and add new entries to keep the *DLB* current with contemporary activity. There have also been *DLB Documentary Series* volumes which provide biographical and critical source materials for figures whose work is judged to have particular interest for students. One of these companion volumes is entirely devoted to Tennessee Williams.

We define literature as the *intellectual commerce of a nation:* not merely as belles lettres but as that ample and complex process by which ideas are generated, shaped, and transmitted. *DLB* entries are not limited to "creative writers" but extend to other figures who in their time and in their way influenced the mind of a people. Thus the series encompasses historians, journalists, publishers, and screenwriters. By this means readers of *DLB* may be aided to perceive litera-

*From an unpublished section of Mark Twain's autobiography, copyright © by the Mark Twain Company.

ture not as cult scripture in the keeping of intellectual high priests but firmly positioned at the center of a nation's life.

DLB includes the major writers appropriate to each volume and those standing in the ranks immediately behind them. Scholarly and critical counsel has been sought in deciding which minor figures to include and how full their entries should be. Wherever possible, useful references are made to figures who do not warrant separate entries.

Each *DLB* volume has a volume editor responsible for planning the volume, selecting the figures for inclusion, and assigning the entries. Volume editors are also responsible for preparing, where appropriate, appendices surveying the major periodicals and literary and intellectual movements for their volumes, as well as lists of further readings. Work on the series as a whole is coordinated at the Bruccoli Clark Layman editorial center in Columbia, South Carolina, where the editorial staff is responsible for accuracy of the published volumes.

One feature that distinguishes *DLB* is the illustration policy–its concern with the iconography of literature. Just as an author is influenced by his surroundings, so is the reader's understanding of the author enhanced by a knowledge of his environment. Therefore *DLB* volumes include not only drawings, paintings, and photographs of authors, often depicting them at various stages in their careers, but also illustrations of their families and places where they lived. Title pages are regularly reproduced in facsimile along with dust jackets for modern authors. The dust jackets are a special feature of *DLB* because they often document better than anything else the way in which an author's work was perceived in its own time. Specimens of the writers' manuscripts are included when feasible.

Samuel Johnson rightly decreed that "The chief glory of every people arises from its authors." The purpose of the *Dictionary of Literary Biography* is to compile literary history in the surest way available to us–by accurate and comprehensive treatment of the lives and work of those who contributed to it.

The *DLB* Advisory Board

Foreword

DLB 68: Canadian Writers, 1920-1959, First Series is the third of five *DLB* volumes devoted to the writers of Canada who use English or French as their main language of artistic expression. (Canada is officially bilingual, but a large number of writers publish in languages other than these two.)

The first two published volumes, *Canadian Writers Since 1960,* first and second series, include authors whose careers were effectively established during the decades of the 1960s and 1970s. This volume, and its companion second-series volume (in preparation), cover the preceding decades, beginning with the 1920s.

Between World War I and 1959 Canadian literature went through approximately four evolutionary changes. They had to do with the nature of image and the power of image to "represent" national experience; the relation of class, economics, and social change; voice and the articulation of the "marginal" experience of women, regions, and ethnic minorities; and the abstraction of language and the rejection of "representative" presumptions about art and society.

Like other nations in 1918, Canada was deeply affected by the realities of the war in which it had just fought. A "war to end all wars," World War I did not usher in a golden age; it stimulated change instead: industrialization, urbanization, alterations in the status quo. Women voted. The ethnic mix altered. Individuals acquired automobiles and telephones. Cities grew. People began to celebrate the new Canada that had emerged from the war–a *separate* signatory to the Treaty of Paris (though the country had entered the war automatically as part of the British Empire), a separate member of the League of Nations, and, in 1931, a separate member of the newly formed British Commonwealth. People also began to reject any aspect of the society that maintained the familiar norms of power and cultural value. Hence many new "national" organizations and institutions developed–from popular magazines (*Chatelaine, Canadian Bookman*), to national clubs (the Native Sons of Canada), to academic and reflective journals (*Le Nigog, Canadian Forum*)– some of them involved in cultural boosterism. At the same time, writer John Glassco led the way

for antinationalist sentiments, turning his back on his established family and heading off to attach himself to the literary coteries in Paris, to live as hedonistic and bohemian a life as health and inclination permitted.

In Quebec, which had politically resisted the war for the entire duration, writers were still largely engaged in celebrations of the soul of the land; the school of "littérature du terroir" had been established in the 1890s and still attracted poets and short-story writers in the 1920s. In English Canada the school of nature writers (Charles G. D. Roberts and Ernest Seton, with Grey Owl [Archibald Stansfeld Belaney] and Roderick Haig-Brown to follow) continued to exert its literary presence and to attract a popular following. Sentimentality and historical romance (as in the work of Frederick Niven, Robert de Rocquebrune, Léo-Paul Desrosiers, and Philip Child) continued in vogue. But by 1921 there were already many changes underway. Such writers as Jessie Georgina Sime were asserting the independence of women's voices in art and society and at the same time using fiction to probe the life of the urban poor. Others were upsetting the conventions of formal style by using vernacular speech as a literary norm, condemning war and social hypocrisy, and attacking the very institutions (church, state) upon which civilization was presumed to rest, but which were now equated with social and moral decay. Albert Laberge's *La Scouine,* for example, was in 1918 denounced for its anticlericalism and immorality. But it was a critique of a system of values that did not take into account its own involvement in civil disarray. As the years progressed the critical attitude Laberge's novel expressed became the more dominant literary voice.

One of the most striking agents of attitudinal change in the 1920s was painting. In the late 1920s and early 1930s such writers as Robert Choquette (in *Metropolitan Museum,* 1931) and Alfred DesRochers were drawing on analogues in American art for symbols of change in society; A. J. M. Smith and F. R. Scott (who as students founded the influential *McGill Fortnightly Review* in 1925) responded to the imagists, to T. S. Eliot, and to the Toronto-based painters known as the

Group of Seven. The Group of Seven, formally founded in 1920, included such painters as Lawren Harris, Arthur Lismer, Frederick Varley, and J. E. H. MacDonald. Associated with them were Tom Thomson and (on the west coast) Emily Carr. Carr looked to the art of the native Indians for a different "art-spirit," one that would break Canadian art free from European models. Harris was a theosophist abstractionist. For all their differences, the Group of Seven, using bolder colors and stronger lines than Canadian landscape painters before them, substantially shaped Canadian taste in art for several decades to come. Their influence on literature was significant too: just as the Seven wanted to "see" place more accurately, so did the poets they influenced (Smith, Scott) want to "sing" place by means of an authentically local speech.

Whereas Smith and others went on to celebrate the "objectivity" of image, Scott involved himself more directly in the social arena. Liberal reformer, he made no apology for subjective engagement. Lawyer, teacher, social activist, he used his poetic gifts to satirize the emptiness of the "social register" and the passing fad. Scott was, moreover, by the 1930s, at the forefront of legal challenges to the restrictive Quebec laws enacted by Premier Maurice Duplessis and to the national legislation that still limited the rights of women.

By the 1930s, in response to depression, drought, sporadic civil unrest (from the Winnipeg Strike in 1919 to the Bloody Sunday riots in Vancouver in 1935), and other forces, Canadian governments were instituting legislation to deal with clear social problems. For many, however, their efforts were not enough. There were calls from the Theatre of Action and other left-wing groups (and journals: *New Frontier, Masses*) for more attention to the homeless and the jobless; at the same time there were literary calls from the radical right for exclusion of non-Europeans from Canada and for a revolution to bring a Catholic autocracy into power. By far the majority of writers was left-leaning in the 1930s–though not all were as partisan as Dorothy Livesay and Earle Birney, who, until World War II changed political perspectives once again, embraced Marxist and Trotskyist causes. Miriam Waddington (like Livesay) became a social worker. Ted Allan fought in the Spanish civil war with Dr. Norman Bethune, who later went on to become a hero of Mao's Revolution in China and a model for Hugh MacLennan's character Jerome Martell in

The Watch That Ends the Night. Winnipeg-born George Woodcock, poet, critic, man of letters, was a pacifist, intellectual anarchist, and civil libertarian, one of a group of intellectuals in England during these decades (with George Orwell and others), who after his return to Canada in 1948 had a substantial effect on the course of criticism and social commentary.

In fiction, by the 1930s, social realism was in fashion, displacing at last the attachment to the wilderness romance. Such writers as Claude-Henri Grignon, Robert Stead, Ringuet (Philippe Panneton), Raymond Knister, Jovette-Alice Bernier, and Martha Ostenso focused on the grimmer realities of rural life, disputing the clichés of bucolic arcadia and habitant peasant happiness. In the scenes they portrayed, women had to resist becoming victims of men and power, immigrants had to assess their real position in the social hierarchy. Félix-Antoine Savard continued the attack on the "triple alliance" of clergy, capitalist, and civil politician. Raymond Knister, too, in his landmark 1928 anthology, *Canadian Short Stories*, drew attention to the changes that were taking place in prose style as well. The writers who emerged in the 1920s (Knister, Morley Callaghan, and others, all influenced by the American writer Sherwood Anderson) were experimenting with a vernacular style, using it to promote a nonestablishment point of view. While sympathetic and influential critics (for example, B. K. Sandwell, editor of *Saturday Night*) were quick to recognize what was going on in the new fiction but slow to appreciate it, English prose style in Canada after Knister and Callaghan would not ever be quite the same again. In French, in contrast, stylistic conventions–simple past tense, omniscient narrator–did not change significantly until the 1940s.

The English-Canadian literary establishment was more willing to accept Frederick Philip Grove at face value than to value Callaghan. Grove was a European immigrant who wrote sagas of prairie life that many called "naturalistic." Grove himself claimed to have come of noble stock, not incidentally giving a certain social cachet to his work. The fictions Grove perpetuated in the name of autobiography, the frauds and masks that were later found to be an intrinsic part of his life, constitute fragments in one of the most fascinating biographical stories in Canadian literary history. But it was Callaghan, Ernest Hemingway's one-time colleague on the *Toronto Star,* who won international praise. For his pared-back vignettes of provincial ambition and urban decay, his rhythmically controlled insights into moral desire and human limitation, Callaghan found acceptance in such avant-garde magazines as *transition* and *This Quarter* and a secure niche in Canadian letters.

One of the other developments of the 1930s was the establishment of a national broadcasting system, the CBC (with a French counterpart called Radio-Canada). Rapidly the medium became a forum for the discussion of ideas, for the communication of values and perspectives from region to region, as well as an opportunity for literary artists. While at first the CBC was an arbiter of received standards (anglophone actors adopted a "mid-Atlantic" accent), the ordinary Canadian speaking voice quickly won out as the norm. Radio drama developed as an art form in its own right, Andrew Allan, Robert Choquette, Gratien Gélinas, Roger Lemelin, W. O. Mitchell, Earle Birney, and Dorothy Livesay being among the many writers to adapt the medium to their own purposes. Radio drama was even, to many critics, more interesting than contemporary writing for the stage by such playwrights as Robertson Davies, James Reaney, Gwen Pharis Ringwood, and John Coulter. With Robert Weaver's involvement in the CBC, another genre found a home in radio. Weaver set up such programs as *CBC Wednesday Night* and *Canadian Short Stories*. Actively Weaver encouraged writers to write short fiction (in many respects he can claim to have "discovered" Hugh Garner, Alice Munro, Norman Levine, and others), and he arranged to have their works read on the air. The revolution that Callaghan began, marrying speech rhythm with fictional form, acquired further momentum in this new medium.

Film, too, had an impact on literature. P. K. Page was one of a score of writers who worked for the National Film Board when it came into existence in the early 1940s. The Film Board's well-earned reputation for documentary perhaps clarifies the character of the writing that attracted critical attention over the next ten years. Documentary (in that it fastened on empirical problems), this writing was also acutely subjective, shaped, as it were, by the cinematic lens, concerned with the perceiving eye. Many of the most important poets to emerge at this time used observation—with a perceiving "I" as persona or narrator—to invite readers to participate in a social dialogue.

Such poetry was also a vehicle for criticizing the status quo. Another war brought new discontent in tow. "Dieppe" became a watchword for social resentment of Britain's imperial presumptions. Quebeckers resisted conscription once again. P. K. Page created verbal portraits of psychological case studies. Raymond Souster, influenced by W. W. E. Ross, observed poverty with dispassionate judgment. Dorothy Livesay drew attention to discrimination, A. M. Klein to anti-Semitism and the limits of provinciality. Ralph Gustafson, Louis Dudek, Alain Grandbois, James Reaney, Robert Charbonneau: all devised separate systems (involving myth, music, mechanical media, drawing on the critical and historical theories of Northrop Frye, Harold Adams Innis, Lionel Groulx, and Marshall McLuhan) to separate art from society or to claim the connection between the two. There were many new journals: *Preview* and *First Statement* (editorially at odds until they were united as John Sutherland's *Northern Review*), *La Relève*, Robert Weaver's *Tamarack Review*, Alan Crawley's *Contemporary Verse* (after which Dorothy Livesay later named her journal *CV/II*), and the several journals, including *Delta*, edited by Dudek and Souster. In them, and in the numerous new anthologies, the voices of literary coteries sounded, took stances, disputed, thrived. The dominant English-language poetic voice was that of Irving Layton–passionate, proud, idiosyncratic, ironic, iconoclastic, bawdy, shrewd, tender, wry. All these adjectives apply. Consciously setting himself apart from the provinciality he perceived in both anglophone and francophone traditions in Canada (the one, in his terms, angloprotestant and life-denying, the other Jansenist and infatuated with martyrdom), he celebrated his own Jewishness, his links with a separate tradition, as the agency of vitality that could transform the present age. A critic of the status quo, he courted conventional displeasure. Masks were Layton's métier. Coming to recognize the self was what he demanded of his readers; hence his poetry issued challenges, with which many were unwilling to comply.

In francophone Quebec the dominant voices were those of Hector de Saint-Denys Garneau and his cousin Anne Hébert. Acutely private, highly symbolic, they represent the very kind of self-preoccupation Layton found limiting, though (after Saint-Denys Garneau's death) Hébert embarked on a much more critical, self-enfranchising engagement with language. Her works (from *Le Tombeau des rois*, 1953, through her stories and plays, to such novels as *Les Fous de Bassan*, 1982) celebrate her female freedom from male norms of language and the conventional shapes of Quebec history. As for many subsequent women writing in Quebec, freedom exists in the power over choice, even if choice always means some form of enclosure.

In anglophone Canada the literary status quo to which Layton objected consisted of imitative forms: the historical romances of E. J. Pratt, the "realistic" allegories of Hugh MacLennan, the ironies of Robertson Davies, the historical conservatism of Donald Creighton, the now-established lyricism of Scott, Smith, and Douglas LePan. Theirs was an angloprotestant, centralist version of Canada, nudging toward biculturalism. (MacLennan's 1945 novel *Two Solitudes* gave this vision of Canada a name.) But while these changes were under way, Quebec was moving toward the separatism that was to occupy the 1960s and 1970s, the ethnic minorities in Canada were starting to preempt biculturalism (announcing the reality of multiculturalism instead), and writers were beginning to declare the separation of art from a direct, mimetic relation with society altogether.

Germaine Guèvremont, Gabrielle Roy, Joyce Marshall, Ethel Wilson, Sinclair Ross, Henry Kreisel: in the works of all these writers there was still a strong sense of the empirical bases of art. Their art was "about" people in time and place. But in every case the angle of representation was as important to the reader's connection with the work of art as was the fact of representation itself. Ross manipulated first-person narrative in *As For Me and My House* (1941), for example, to contrive an ambivalent portrait of resentment and desire. Ethel Wilson broke stylistic "rules" to invite the reader into an ironic reading of her surface text, disclosing the violence that is an inherent part of the life women lead. Roy drew on experience. The world was changing again.

There were comedic satires (Paul Hiebert's *Sarah Binks* [1947], most notably), and there were fantasies (Catherine Anthony Clark's books for children). There were rhythmic experiments, including the expressionist writings of Herman Voaden and the vorticist works of Bertram Brooker. There were symbolic stories such as those of Ernest Buckler and the part-Montagnais narrative artist Yves Thériault. By and large, however, the "mythic departures" from reality went unnoticed until later decades. It was, for example, not until the 1970s that there was a substan-

tial readership sympathetic to Howard O'Hagan's *Tay John* (1939). Even less was there in English Canada a readership ready for the stream-of-consciousness of Elizabeth Smart or for the Joycean play of A. M. Klein's fiction. And the Earle Birney that was appreciated at the time was the early lyrical poet, reminiscent of Robert Frost; the later Birney, anarchist of literary form, was yet to be heard from.

The year 1959 constitutes a terminus for this volume, as well as for its companion, because it was a year in which several changes are, with hindsight, clearly observable. The Canada Council (formed in 1958 on a recommendation by the Massey Commission) was beginning its mandate, to assist in financing artistic composition, publication, performance, and research. New journals came into existence in 1959–*Canadian Literature*, *Liberté*, *Prism*–serving the academic study of Canadian literature as a discipline. In 1959, moreover, three novels appeared that indicate a kind of literary crossroads: MacLennan's romantic, traditional *The Watch That Ends the Night*, a narrative elegy, full of sadness and hope; Mordecai Richler's raucous, ironic *The Apprenticeship of Duddy Kravitz*, an exposé of the limitations of received social norm; Sheila Watson's *The Double Hook*, a work of high modernism in which the text takes precedence over empirical referent. Many of the writers covered in this volume or its companion continued to publish long after 1959; they are included here because their reputations were established by this date, even though (as with Hébert, Birney, Livesay, for example) their subsequent careers often turned their writings in provocative new directions.

It must also be added that 1959 is a more appropriate terminus date for anglophone than it is for francophone writing. In Quebec the "significant moments of change" that hindsight recognizes occurred in 1948, 1953, and 1960. As in 1920, one of the major changes in the cultural climate derived from painting, when in 1948 the painters Emile Borduas and Jean-Paul Riopelle, along with the absurdist dramatist Claude Gauvreau, issued their *Refus Global*. Basically an attack on Duplessis's Quebec, their pamphlet was a claim for freedom from political and imaginative enclosure. But as freedom did not exist in the conventionally structured political world, the only way of claiming it was, the authors said, to utter a "collective refusal" of convention: to embrace abstraction, to embrace surrealism, to reject the possibility of "representation" in art or "meaning" in language (a position that would influence Paul-Marie Lapointe directly, and through him several contemporary poets and dramatists), and therefore to compose by means of "automatisme."

In 1953 another rebel against the status quo, Gaston Miron, established a new press, Editions de l'Héxagone. It was an important agency for making these revolutionary voices heard–publishing Lapointe, for instance, and (sporadically, for he long opted for silence rather than speech, in resistance to the linguistic status quo) Miron himself. Héxagone also became the center for a writer's group; it was there that poets would gather–Jean-Guy Pilon, Gilbert Langevin, Roland Giguère, Gilles Hénault, Fernand Ouellette. It was there that Juan Garcia would meet Miron and befriend Langevin, there that the revolutionary spirit of one generation was being handed on to another. In 1959 Duplessis died. When Jean Lesage took over as premier of Quebec in 1960, and won reelection in 1962 under the slogan "maîtres chez nous" (masters in our own house), the so-called Quiet Revolution was underway. In the decades to follow it would have a profound effect both on the political assumptions Canadians had of themselves and on the literary structures and strategies they chose to employ.

–W. H. New

Acknowledgments

This book was produced by Bruccoli Clark Layman, Inc. Karen L. Rood is senior editor for the *Dictionary of Literary Biography* series. Margaret A. Van Antwerp was the in-house editor.

Production coordinator is Kimberly Casey. Art supervisor is Cheryl Crombie. Copyediting supervisor is Joan M. Prince. Typesetting supervisor is Kathleen M. Flanagan. Michael D. Senecal is editorial associate. The production staff includes Rowena Betts, Charles Brower, Joseph Matthew Bruccoli, Patricia Coate, Mary Colborn, Mary S. Dye, Sarah A. Estes, Cynthia Hallman, Judith K. Ingle, Maria Ling, Warren McInnis, Kathy S. Merlette, Sheri Neal, Joycelyn R. Smith, and Virginia Smith. Jean W. Ross is permissions editor. Joseph Caldwell, photography editor, and Gabrielle Elliott did photographic copy work for the volume.

Walter W. Ross and Rhonda Marshall did the library research with the assistance of the staff at the Thomas Cooper Library of the University of South Carolina: Daniel Boice, Kathy Eckman, Gary Geer, Cathie Gottlieb, David L. Haggard, Jens Holley, Dennis Isbell, Jackie Kinder, Marcia Martin, Jean Rhyne, Beverley Steele, Ellen Tillett, Carole Tobin, and Virginia Weathers.

The editor expresses special thanks to Eric Thompson, Robin Van Heck, and Beverly Westbrook. Nicky Drumbolis of Letters, L. A. Wallrich of About Books, Richard Shuh and Linda Wooley of Alphabet Books, and Kenneth Landry of the *Dictionnaire des oeuvres littéraires du Québec* have provided valuable assistance in securing illustrative materials.

Canadian Writers, 1920-1959
First Series

Dictionary of Literary Biography

Ted Allan
(25 January 1916-   )

Terry Goldie
Memorial University of Newfoundland

BOOKS: *This Time a Better Earth* (London: Heinemann, 1939; New York: Morrow, 1939);

The Scalpel, the Sword: The Story of Dr. Norman Bethune, by Allan and Sydney Gordon (Toronto: McClelland & Stewart, 1952; Boston: Little, Brown, 1952; London: Hale, 1954; revised, Toronto: McClelland & Stewart, 1971; Boston: Little, Brown, 1971);

Quest for Pajaro, as Edward Maxwell (London: Heinemann, 1957);

Double Image, by Allan and Roger MacDougall (London: French, 1957);

Chu Chem: A Zen Buddhist-Hebrew Novel (Montreal: Editions Quebec, 1973);

My Sister's Keeper (Toronto & Buffalo: University of Toronto Press, 1976);

Willie the Squowse (Toronto: McClelland & Stewart, 1977; London: Cape, 1977; New York: Hastings House, 1978);

Love is a Long Shot (Toronto: McClelland & Stewart, 1984);

Lies My Father Told Me (Toronto: Playwrights Canada, 1984);

Don't You Know Anybody Else? (Toronto: McClelland & Stewart, 1985).

PLAY PRODUCTIONS: *The Money Makers,* Toronto, Jupiter Theatre, 1954; produced again as *The Ghost Writers,* London, England, London Arts Theatre, 1955;

Legend of Paradiso, London, England, Theatre Workshop, 1956;

Double Image, by Allan and Roger MacDougall, London, England, Savoy Theatre, 1957; pro-

Ted Allan (photograph by Sam Shaw)

duced again as *Gog and Magog,* Paris, Michodière Theatre, 1959;

The Secret of the World, London, England, Theatre Royale, 1962;

3

Chu Chem: A Zen Buddhist-Hebrew Musical, adapted by Allan from his novel, Philadelphia, Criterion Theatre, 1968;

I've Seen You Cut Lemons, London, England, Fortune Theatre, 5 December 1969; revised as *My Sister's Keeper,* Lennoxville, Quebec, Lennoxville Festival, 1974;

Love Streams, Los Angeles, Centre Stage, 1983;

The Third Day Comes, Los Angeles, Centre Stage, 1983;

Lies My Father Told Me, West Los Angeles, Westward Playhouse, 19 September 1983;

Willie the Squowse, Toronto, Young People's Theatre, December 1987.

MOTION PICTURES: *Out of Nowhere,* screenplay by Allan, Dublin Studios, 1966;

Lies My Father Told Me, screenplay by Allan, Pentacle VIII Productions/Pentimento Productions, 1975;

Lovestreams, screenplay by Allan, Cannon Films, 1983.

OTHER: "Lies My Father Told Me," in *Canadian Short Stories,* edited by Robert Weaver and Helen James (Toronto: Oxford University Press, 1952).

Although Ted Allan has been a successful writer of stories and of plays for all media, as well as a successful actor, he is best known for two of his less representative works. To the general public he is recognized as the author of the screenplay for *Lies My Father Told Me,* one of the few Canadian feature films which has been successful internationally, both commercially and critically. To many Canadians, to the Chinese, and to the Left of all countries, he is known for his collaborative biography of the Canadian socialist physician Norman Bethune.

Ted Allan was born Alan Herman, the son of Harry and Annie Elias Herman, in Montreal. His youth in the Jewish ghetto of Montreal, with vestiges of Eastern Europe surrounding him, was apparently a close approximation of that presented in *Lies My Father Told Me.* The socialist fervor of that time and place had a major effect on him, and Allan himself suggested such autobiographical connections when he played the important supporting role of the kindly Communist neighbor in the film. "Politics: Socialist. Religion: Humanist" reads the entry on him in *Contemporary Authors*–a perfect summation of the narrator in Allan's 1984 novel *Love is a Long Shot.*

Allan's first story was published in the radical Canadian magazine *New Frontier* in 1937, the year preceding his marriage to Kate Lenthier. He wrote his first article on Bethune for the same journal in the same year. He also interviewed Hemingway for the magazine. In 1939 he published his novel *This Time a Better Earth.* The terse style bears no small resemblance to that of Hemingway; for example, at one point the first-person narrator remarks on his past belief that there would always be time for himself and his generation: "But it hit me suddenly like a blow on the face that I could say that no longer. There was no more time . . . for me or for them."

The novel is apparently an autobiographical account of Allan's experience in the Spanish civil war and of his romance with a young woman who is killed in a car accident. Allan, like other North Americans, had gone to Spain "to fight against Fascism and for Freedom," as their slogan ran. In *This Time a Better Earth* he describes many of these idealists, among them a forty-year-old doctor who maintains the air of a bon vivant in the midst of death.

This character is presumably based on Bethune, about whom Allan and his coauthor Sydney Gordon comment in the foreword to their biography, *The Scalpel, the Sword* (1952): "one of us knew Bethune intimately and shared with him part of the agony of the Spanish war." The book itself suggests close knowledge of Bethune, but the sources of this information are never clarified. Allan and Gordon give the following justification: "In general, we have avoided using explanatory notes because in compiling our sources for statements, conversations and incidents, we found that our footnotes were so numerous as to constitute almost another book! Therefore, whenever a source is not given we would like the reader to know that all the conversations were either heard by one of us, described in Bethune's letters, or recalled by his intimates."

Such a disclaimer does not erase the fact that this omission seriously diminishes the value of the book as history. The purpose of the work is quite clearly expressed in the foreword to the 1971 revised edition: "We need to be reminded that there *are* men, heroic in stature and action, who bring hope and inspiration to the rest of us. Bethune was such a man." In the conclusion to this very romantic biography, Allan and Gordon look at Bethune's tomb in China and offer this summation: "For, in the memory of Bethune's

Cover for the revised version of Allan's 1969 play, I've Seen You Cut Lemons

Patricia Hamilton as Sarah in the 1974 Lennoxville production of My Sister's Keeper *(photograph by Paul Lindell)*

life, the great are reminded of the people from whom they draw their strength, and the people are reminded of the road that everyone can travel to greatness." Allan's screenplay on the life of Bethune is being made into a film, directed by Philip Borsos and starring Donald Sutherland.

Allan's background suggests obvious reasons why he should have been drawn to the famous Communist doctor from Canada, creator of the mobile transfusion service and hero in Spain and China. A subtler version of the heroic giant is the old grandfather, the rag peddler, in the original version of "Lies My Father Told Me," anthologized in *Canadian Short Stories* in 1952.

Between the appearance of the short story and its transformation into a feature film, Allan had a variety of experiences. In the 1940s, after working for the American propaganda office, he

wrote screenplays in Hollywood. In 1954 he went to England where he resided for nearly thirty years, achieving success as a writer and actor. In 1957 Allan and his wife, with whom he had two children (Julia, Norman Bethune), were divorced. In England he contributed, without credit, to Joan Littlewood's *Oh, What a Lovely War!*, produced in 1963, and wrote a number of plays, including *I've Seen You Cut Lemons*, directed in London in 1969 by Sean Connery and produced again in Canada, in Lennoxville, Quebec, in 1974, as *My Sister's Keeper*.

My Sister's Keeper, published two years after its Lennoxville performance, is not a novel play in style or subject, but the suggestions of incest and the constant tensions between the brother and sister who are its only characters make it good theater. Allan's versatility is suggested by

a novel by
Ted Allan
LOVE
is a
LONG SHOT

by the author of the award-winning screenplay
Lies My Father Told Me

Dust jacket for Allan's 1984 novel, winner of the Stephen Leacock Medal for Humour

the difference between *My Sister's Keeper* and another literary success of approximately the same period, his 1977 book, *Willie the Squowse*. This children's story about an acrobatic half-squirrel half-mouse won a prize for children's literature from the London *Times*.

Since his achievement with *Lies My Father Told Me,* which received an Academy Award nomination, Allan has been involved in the creation of a number of screenplays for people such as Ben Gazzara and John Cassavetes. Some of them seem to have died aborning and others have dragged on through innumerable delays, but Allan remains the confident "man who invented Ted Allan," as he was described by Kildare Dobbs in an insightful article published in *Maclean's* (February 1961). Allan said on arriving in London in the 1950s, "I have come to take George Bernard Shaw's place." He has not, but that will not stop him from pressing on. In recent years Allan has returned from Europe. He currently lives in Toronto.

At present his greatest success seems to be with the humorous reminiscence, a form which might perhaps be expected given his success with *Lies My Father Told Me* as story, film, and, most recently, play. (The stage version was produced in West Los Angeles in 1983 and published in 1984.) *Love is a Long Shot,* Allan's 1984 novel, extends this self-portrait through his teen-age years of socialist vision. With the same easy humor found in *Lies My Father Told Me* it explores the atmosphere defined in its last line: "God, what dreams we could dream in those wonderful days!" The novel was both a popular and critical success, winner of the Stephen Leacock Medal for Humour. The irony of such bourgeois Canadian applause and an award named for such a staunch imperialist as Leacock being given to a paean to a Communist youth would not be lost on Allan. In *Contemporary Authors* he states, "The quotes from the critics confirm a strong conviction of mine; the critics who praise my work are obviously extremely intelligent; the ones who attack my work are obviously stupid and insensitive."

Reference:

Kildare Dobbs, "The Man Who Invented Ted Allan," *Maclean's* (11 February 1961): 13, 33-35.

Patrick Anderson

(4 August 1915-17 March 1979)

Susan Gingell
University of Saskatchewan

BOOKS: *Poems* (N.p.: Privately printed, 1929);
On This Side Nothing (N.p.: Privately printed, 1932);
A Tent for April: Poems (Montreal: First Statement, 1945);
The White Centre (Toronto: Ryerson, 1946);
The Colour as Naked (Toronto: McClelland & Stewart, 1953);
Snake Wine: A Singapore Episode (London: Chatto & Windus, 1955);
Search Me, Autobiography–The Black Country, Canada and Spain (London: Chatto & Windus, 1957; New York: British Book Centre, 1958);
First Steps in Greece (London: Chatto & Windus, 1958);
Finding Out About the Athenians (London: Muller, 1961);
The Character Ball: Chapters of Autobiography (London: Chatto & Windus, 1963);
Dolphin Days: A Writer's Notebook of Mediterranean Pleasures (London: Gollancz, 1963; New York: Dutton, 1964);
The Smile of Apollo: A Literary Companion to Greek Travel (London: Chatto & Windus, 1964);
Over the Alps: Reflections on Travel and Travel Writing, with special reference to the Grand Tours of Boswell, Beckford and Byron (London: Hart-Davis, 1969);
Foxed!; or, Life in the Country (London: Chatto & Windus, 1972);
A Visiting Distance: Poems, New, Revised, and Selected (Ottawa: Borealis, 1976);
Return to Canada: Selected Poems (Toronto: McClelland & Stewart, 1977).

OTHER: *Eros: An Anthology of Friendship*, edited by Anderson and Alistair Sutherland (London: Blond, 1961); republished as *Eros: An Anthology of Male Friendship* (New York: Citadel Press, 1963).

PERIODICAL PUBLICATION: "A Poet Past and Future," *Canadian Literature*, 56 (Spring 1973): 7-21.

Patrick Anderson was an English expatriate journalist, travel writer, autobiographer, and poet who for some time wrote in and about Canada and became a major force in the shaping of Canadian poetry in the 1940s and 1950s. As the primary mover and a founding editor of the Montreal little magazine *Preview*, Anderson was at the center of a group concerned to assimilate the modernist influences of such poets as T. S. Eliot, W. H. Auden, Dylan Thomas, and C. Day Lewis and yet "make a Canadian voice." The cofounders of *Preview* remember him as a poet who was not happy unless he had spent three or four hours a day at his verse and whose professionalism shamed and encouraged them at the same time. As Bruce Ruddick recalls: "He was the conscience of our poetry, and the conscience of our working at poetry." Though his own style was not particularly influential, his very Englishness demanded from his Canadian contemporaries an answering attitude of professionalism as part of their anticolonial stance.

Born in Ashtead, Surrey, England, Anderson spent a largely unhappy village childhood. His parents separated when he was a boy, and Anderson, as he admitted in *Search Me* (1957), was "dangerously devoted" to his vivacious, strong-minded mother; his often confessional poems, such as "Dear Son," are at best thinly veiled accounts of his sexual feelings for her.

His descriptions of his school years reflect environments that were little, if any, more healthy, for he recalls, in *Dolphin Days* (1963), "the ugliness and fear of so much of the school-life I knew," and, in *Search Me*, a "'particularly sticky' adolescence." Yet by the time he was twelve, his writing talents had been recognized by his prep-school headmaster, and Anderson had adapted Bunyan's hymn "To Be a Pilgrim," turning it "into a personal manifesto: *to be a writer*." He earned a B.A. and an M.A. at Oxford where he was president of the Union, and in 1938 a Commonwealth Fellowship took him to New York City's Columbia University. In New York he met

Peggy Doernbach (who became his wife), and with her, "a hundred dollars, . . . and a fast, reconditioned Ford," he drove to Montreal in September 1940.

Supporting his wife and himself on the meager salary of a schoolmaster and private tutor, he quickly worked his way into the artistic life of the city, while his increasingly politically active wife drew them into Communist front activities. In 1942 he, along with F. R. Scott, Neufville Shaw, Bruce Ruddick, and Margaret Day (P. K. Page and A. M. Klein were to be drawn in later), founded *Preview*, a socially and politically committed literary organ whose idealistic purposes Anderson set out in a February 1943 editorial: "Our task is clear: not only to help in the winning of the war by our literary work . . . but also to supply something of the personal, the graceful and the heroic to the atmosphere of this half-empty Dominion." Anderson continued to be an important editor when *Preview* merged with John Sutherland's more consciously proletarian *First Statement* in 1946 to become *Northern Review*, though he resigned from the board in 1948 when Sutherland viciously attacked Robert Finch's *Poems* (1946).

But Sutherland's First Statement press had published Anderson's first Canadian chapbook, *A Tent for April* (1945). Two privately published collections of juvenilia, *Poems* (1929) and *On This Side Nothing* (1932), had appeared several years earlier in England. The poems of *A Tent for April* are characterized by a lush, often metaphysical imagery that Anderson himself has linked to a sublimated sexuality. In "Night Out," for example, the poet writes:

> Slid in the wet, glasses to grasp
> or stroke reflectively
> as possessed treasures in crystal houses,
> whose tight-rope rims flecked with foam
> summon the balled delicacy of the forefinger
> while grosser bottoms reassure with winks.

His Freudian interests, nurtured by his visits to Montreal's first psychoanalyst, influenced both the subject matter and imagery of these poems, and he grapples with his reactions to the Canadian environment in styles and forms learned from his British predecessors, particularly Auden, Thomas, and Stephen Spender.

Anderson's *The White Centre*, published in 1946, shows both stylistic and thematic continuity with the earlier volume. From a perspective of pained and disillusioned adulthood the speaker

Dust jacket for the 1963 edition of Anderson and Alistair Sutherland's anthology of prose and verse. The subject, according to Anderson's introduction, is "any friendship between men strong enough to deserve one of the more serious senses of the word 'love.' "

in these poems frequently looks back on the innocence and zest for life associated with the child, and similes and metaphors relating to childhood appear with compulsive regularity. Pictures of wartime Montreal figure large in the volume, and there are several self-conscious attempts to come to terms with what Canada is and what it means to be Canadian, "Poem on Canada" being the most notable of these. The idea of a vast and silent emptiness waiting to be possessed, a blankness waiting to have the human character inscribed on it predominates: "And the North was. With winter the snow came./Whole folios of it. Yet nothing written/except one thing, a bleak expectancy." The series of portraits of the shapers of Canadian history in the section subtitled "The Country Still Unpossessed" comprises the most memorable and frequently anthologized stanzas, perhaps because Anderson here abandons his uninspired free-verse form for an iambic pentameter line and frequently heightens his poetic effect with some well-placed rhymes, such as that of the couplet that rounds out the section on Louis Riel: "But they say his body made a great wound in the air/and God damn the English judge that put him there!"

In the postwar years Anderson returned to England several times, moving, in his own words from *Search Me,* "on the bohemian fringe of several literary circles." From 1948 to 1950 he was employed as an assistant professor at McGill University's Dawson College, but when his shaky marriage at last disintegrated, he made the decision to leave Canada and take up a lectureship at the University of Malaya. The poetic record of these years, *The Colour as Naked* (1953), reveals the observant man of the world in Anderson. The book opens with a Welsh seascape and poems of his British childhood and adolescence, moving through a number of convincing pictures of rural and urban Quebec life, touching in one poem on his Malaysian experience and looking back in another to impressions of New York. But in the closing pages he places "Leaving Canada" so that the book becomes a kind of farewell salute to the land that had been his home for a decade.

The impulse to celebrate life, most often that of nature, the child, or artist, is matched by a tendency to reveal the more tortured side of human existence or natural occurrence. Even landscapes that begin in green innocence are marked with gray reminders of the fallen world: "the blunt and puzzled rocks/litter the fields like bits of punishment." The reflection of an image-making power and a command of musical sounds and rhythms are the most distinguished qualities of this verse, qualities exemplified in the opening lines of "Song of Intense Cold":

> One night when the stars are exploding like nails
> comes Zero himself with his needle,
> an icicle full of the cold cocaine
> but as tall as the glittering steeple
> that pins us down in the town.

Anderson's weaknesses, however, are not far to seek. Chief among them are the profusion of run-on lines elaborating on successive images until the principal line of thought is obscured and the poet is luxuriating in a kind of decadent romanticism.

After Anderson left Canada, the self-confessed "incorrigible autobiographer," the travel writer, and the literary journalist overtook

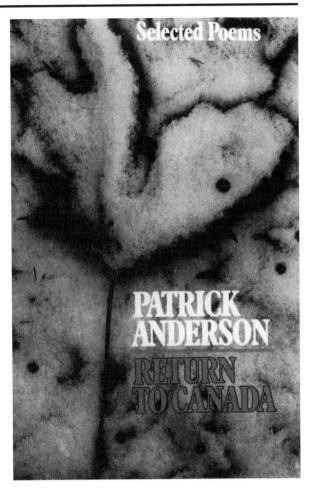

Cover for Anderson's last poetry collection. Part One, he explains in the preface, "contains either poems I particularly like or poems concerning areas of feeling important to me. . . . Part Two presents life in Montreal during the forties. . . . Part Three includes poems of my post-Montreal, exiled, ruralised, and now ageing self."

the poet. While also working as an English teacher he produced nine books of prose between 1955 and 1972. Extended attention is paid to his Canadian experience in three of these, *Snake Wine: A Singapore Episode* (1955), *Search Me, Autobiography–The Black Country, Canada and Spain* (1957), and *The Character Ball: Chapters of Autobiography* (1963). The genesis of some of his poems can be gleaned from these prose accounts, and seeing how a single period in his life is rendered in both prose and poetry (see, for example, "At Baie St. Paul" in *The Character Ball* and "Remembering Baie St. Paul" in the 1976 poetry collection, *A Visiting Distance*) gives the reader insight into how Anderson transmutes life into art. Eccentric character, exotic experience, and literary context are central to Anderson's concerns in the prose, and the overtly homosexual experience that was to become important in some of his later poems is also a focus. This interest found further manifestation in Anderson's editorship, with Alistair Sutherland, of *Eros: An Anthology of Friendship* (1961).

In his early fifties Anderson began again to write verse when, as he put it in *Return to Canada: Selected Poems* (1977), he "learned that there still were Canadians, both old and young, interested in my work." He did not, however, return to Canada until 1971. Then both reading tours and a visiting professorship at the University of Ottawa renewed his contacts with the Canadian artistic and academic worlds.

Two selections of his verse were published within a year of one another. Though there was a handful of new poems in each volume, the bulk of the verse was republished from earlier books and from his previously uncollected *Preview* pieces. Many of these poems were revised, though few radically; some were retitled or broken away from an original poem sequence, and much of the vague diction in the earlier versions was replaced by a more concrete, particularized, and clear-eyed description. Readers of the second volume, *Return to Canada*, should not be misled by the fact that dates of revision are not always given, for some of these poems underwent substantial rewriting.

In the poems of *A Visiting Distance* there is a reticent, even standoffish, rather than participatory perspective, and as Paul Denham pointed out in a December 1976 review for *CVII*, "Canada . . . is as exotic as Greece" in this self-consciously international book that has England as its home base, if one can speak of Anderson's having a sense of home at all. Whether in England or abroad, his position seems best defined by these lines from "Rink": "And I am master adult and alone,/inexpert, alien and responsible." His only intimacy is with himself, and the reader can tire of such manifestations of the compulsive autobiographer, since there is little ironic distance and virtually no sense of humor in the voice of the recurrent "I." Though less rhetorical than his earlier style, his manner in these poems is at times diffuse and precious; yet when Anderson does break away from his self-preoccupation, he is capable of creating portraits of great sensuousness. The voluptuous boy prostitute of "The Discipline of the Glass" is one such portrait: "If I choose to study, a book embossed with jewels/is given into my hands that my fingers may wander/

across onyx, jasper and ruby, stiff as the nipples/that flare on the slavegirls' breasts."

Return to Canada is the superior selection, republishing more of the best and fewer of the weaker early poems. The loosely defined "Part One" ("poems I particularly like or poems concerning areas of feeling important to me, or both") is notable for its variety of theme, idiom, and form, ranging from the spare, colloquial, but structured "Essex Lake" ("A lake is a simplification,/no problems with this one,/easy going, plain sailing,/a pure stain") to the imagistically striking "Drinker" with its more conventional diction ("he draws the long stalk of water up between his lips/and in his mouth there bursts its melting flower"). "Part Two" is composed of pictures of Montreal life during the 1940s. The revisions made to this particular set of poems are among the most notable improvements in terms of concreteness and convincing detail. The poems of "Part Three" are of Anderson's "post-Montreal, exiled, ruralised, and now ageing self," and all but two are previously uncollected or new. Free verse is the dominant form of these poems which are set chiefly in Essex, his home for the last years of his life. The closing poem of the book, however, finds Anderson once more dealing with Canadian experience and again exploiting the Freudian possibilities of the image of snow: "Between the sheets with my Lady of Canada/(whose bed is stupor of the immoderate snow)/I lay beside a ruthless virginity,/A boy again, dreaming the death of a hero."

Canadian poets and critics alike accord to Anderson a seminal role in establishing the modern idiom in Canada. John Sutherland, when he speaks in *Essays, Controversies and Poems* (1972) of "an achievement of more than Canadian value" and of the fact that Anderson's work "focuses much that is characteristic of modern poetry in Canada," perhaps summarizes best the stature of Anderson's accomplishments. He has won particularly enthusiastic praise from critical temperaments as diverse as those of Irving Layton and Northrop Frye, the latter placing Anderson in the pastoral tradition and finding in the best of his work "a beautifully controlled melody that does not try too hard for ingenuity either in sound or in meaning" (*The Bush Garden*, 1971). But in many ways Anderson has been his own best critic, at least of his early work. In "A Poet Past and Future" (*Canadian Literature*, Spring 1973), he admits to being "enthused over now one 'influence' and now another . . . often word-intoxicated," and in *Search Me* he refers to the way his images "broke up their poems like apples bursting through a paper bag." Wynne Francis, in *Canadian Literature* (Autumn 1962), has analyzed Anderson's fascination with and fear of Canada, pointing out that though he exploited aspects of Canada's physical environment, he "was not a nature poet. His Montreal mountain is a political symbol; snow is our chloroform and ice our state of social anaesthesia." Yet Anderson's years in Canada were obviously important to him as individual and as artist, and a whole generation of poets has testified to the strength of his impact on Canadian poetry.

References:

Wynne Francis, "Montreal Poets of the Forties," *Canadian Literature,* 14 (Autumn 1962): 21-34;

C. X. Ringrose, "Patrick Anderson and the Critics," *Canadian Literature,* 43 (Winter 1970): 10-23;

F. R. Scott and others, "Four of the Former *Preview* Editors: A Discussion," *Canadian Poetry,* 4 (Spring/Summer 1979): 93-119;

John Sutherland, "The Poetry of Patrick Anderson," *Northern Review,* 2 (April/May 1949): 8-20, 25-34.

Papers:

Anderson's papers are at the Public Archives, Ottawa, Ontario, and at McGill University Library, Montreal, Quebec.

Alfred Goldsworthy Bailey
(18 March 1905-   )

Malcolm Ross
Dalhousie University

BOOKS: *Songs of the Saguenay and Other Poems* (Quebec: Chronicle-Telegraph Publishing, 1927);

Tao (Toronto: Ryerson, 1930);

The Conflict of European and Eastern Algonkian Cultures, 1504-1700: A Study in Canadian Civilization (Saint John, New Brunswick: New Brunswick Museum, 1937; revised and enlarged edition, Toronto: University of Toronto Press, 1969);

Border River (Toronto: McClelland & Stewart, 1952);

Culture and Nationality: Essays (Toronto: McClelland & Stewart, 1972);

Thanks for a Drowned Island (Toronto: McClelland & Stewart, 1973);

Miramichi Lightning: The Collected Poems of Alfred Bailey (Fredericton: Fiddlehead, 1981).

OTHER: Frederick Williams-Taylor, *Messages to the University of New Brunswick,* edited by Bailey (Fredericton: University of New Brunswick, 1945);

Katherine F. C. MacNaughton, *The Development of the Theory and Practice of Education in New Brunswick, 1784-1900: A Study in Historical Background,* edited, with an introduction, by Bailey (Fredericton: University of New Brunswick, 1947);

The University of New Brunswick Memorial Volume, edited by Bailey (Fredericton: University of New Brunswick, 1950);

Catalogue of the Beaverbrook Art Gallery, edited by Bailey (Fredericton, 1959);

Literary History of Canada: Canadian Literature in English, edited by Carl F. Klinck, with the collaboration of Bailey and others, includes "Overture to Nationhood" (Chapter 4) by Bailey (Toronto: University of Toronto Press, 1965); republished as *Histoire Littéraire du Canada: Littérature canadienne de langue anglaise,* translated by Maurice Lebel (Quebec: Presses de l'Université Laval, 1970);

"Anthology of New Brunswick Poetry," selected by Bailey and Desmond Pacey, in *The Arts in New Brunswick,* edited by R. A. Tweedie, Fred Cogswell, and W. Stewart MacNutt (Fredericton: Brunswick Press, 1967), pp. 74-94;

Alfred Goldsworthy Bailey

The Letters of James and Ellen Robb: Portrait of a Fredericton Family in Early Victorian Times, edited by Bailey (Fredericton: Acadiensis, 1983).

PERIODICAL PUBLICATIONS: "The Significance of the Identity and Disappearance of the Laurentian Iroquois ... ," *Transactions of the Royal Society of Canada,* third series, 27 (1933), II: 97-108;
"The Indian Problem in Early Canada," *America Indigena,* 2 (July 1942): 35-39;
"The Basis and Persistence of Opposition to Confederation in New Brunswick," *Canadian Historical Review,* 23 (December 1942): 374-397;
"The Impact of Toynbee," *Queen's Quarterly,* 62 (Spring 1955): 100-110.

A poet of distinction in his own right, Alfred Goldsworthy Bailey has had a formative influence on a generation of younger poets, notably Elizabeth Brewster, Fred Cogswell, and Robert Gibbs. Of equal distinction has been his work as

historian, anthropologist, and university teacher and administrator.

Bailey, the son of Loring Woart and Ernestine Valiant Gale Bailey, was born in Quebec City but with family roots deep in the New Brunswick Loyalist tradition and in New England (he is a collateral descendant of Ralph Waldo Emerson). After receiving his B.A. (1927) from the University of New Brunswick, Bailey earned both an M.A. (1929) and a Ph.D. (1934) from the University of Toronto (with a year at the London School of Economics where he studied with Morris Ginsberg). On 8 September 1934 he married Jean Craig Hamilton. From 1935 to 1937 he served as assistant director and associate curator of the New Brunswick Museum, and in 1937 he joined the faculty of the University of New Brunswick where he established a separate department of history. He was made dean of arts in 1946 and academic vice president in 1965, retiring in 1970. Bailey was elected fellow of the Royal Society of Canada in 1951 and was appointed officer of the Order of Canada in 1978.

Bailey's progress as a poet from his early undergraduate volume *Songs of the Saguenay and Other Poems* (1927) to *Thanks for a Drowned Island* (1973) is a paradigm of the progress of Canadian poetry from nineteenth-century romanticism to a sophisticated and cosmopolitan art form. The early poems in *Tao* (1930), as well as those in *Songs of the Saguenay,* reflect Bailey's reading of Bliss Carman, Theodore Goodridge Roberts, and the Victorians. As he wrote in his "Literary Memories" (an unpublished manuscript on deposit at the University of New Brunswick's Harriet Irving Library), these early poems are mainly "scenic and atmospheric," often with "a vague and cosmic love interest."

It was in graduate school at Toronto that he encountered for the first time the thought of Oswald Spengler, Sir James Frazer, T. E. Hulme, and Karl Marx, along with the poetry of T. S. Eliot. One morning in 1931, when Roy Daniells (a fellow graduate student) read him Eliot's *The Waste Land,* he, as he put it in "Literary Memories," was seized by an excitement "such as I have never experienced before and have never experienced since. . . . The old symbols and intonations and meanings had become completely dead."

It was not long before this event that, in Montreal, a group of McGill students–A. J. M. Smith, F. R. Scott, and A. M. Klein, among others–had undergone a similar "conversion." In the late 1920s Smith was urging Canadian writers to lo-

Dust jacket for Bailey's 1952 collection that includes poems first published in such journals as Preview, Northern Review, Contemporary Review, *and* Fiddlehead

cate themselves in time as well as in space. The McGill poets had begun to explore the embattled mind of the city and the complex new idiom of Eliot and Ezra Pound. A. J. M. Smith was soon to speak of two traditions in Canadian writing–the "native" (preoccupied with landscape) and the "cosmopolitan" (urban, experimental, "modernist").

Bailey was one of the first to annihilate the distinction between the "native" and the "cosmopolitan." Although there are poems in *Border River* (1952), his first mature volume, which ape rather sedulously the manner and matter of Eliot, Bailey was discovering his own voice. "Native" subjects–the rivers and hills and shores of New Brunswick–are caught in startling new patterns which merge with images of the fatigue and the fury of the city. The historian's imagination is at work in many of these poems, recovering in vivid snapshots the Loyalist flight to Nova

Scotia, the early French settlement of Quebec, the dignity and the tragedy of the Algonkian Indian. In *Border River* and in later poems which appear in *Thanks for a Drowned Island*, Bailey, very conscious of his place in time, deals with a past made present and pressing on the future, a future in which time seems to break out of cycle into spiral, yearning toward the benedictions of hope.

Bailey is a difficult, even at times an obscure poet. In his "Literary Memories" he assures us that he does not "try to be difficult": "My mind leaps rapidly from one thought to another, sometimes omitting transitional ideas or images which not everyone may see as being implied. Symbolic meanings may be personal and not always shared with my readers.... Perhaps sometimes ... the reader should not focus his attention on the discrete images but instead try to catch the drift of meaning that plays over the poem as a whole.... I may try to make inchoate 'primordial' images having in sequence an emotional tone partly rendered by sound as well as by visual effects."

The poems in *Border River* and particularly the poems in *Thanks for a Drowned Island* show that Bailey, after his earlier discipleship to Eliot, had mastered Dylan Thomas, the dadaists, and the surrealists but was not mastered by them. With a vision shaped by his sense of time as much as by his sense of place, his mature poetry, whether it tells of the tramp steamers and oil slicks of the Bay of Fundy, the machine-bound creatures of the city, or the drift (and driftwood) of time itself, is proof of the truth of Bailey's deep belief that cultural colonialism is overcome not by putting up high walls but by pulling them all down.

The poet in Bailey is nourished by the historian, the anthropologist, and the critic. His pioneer study, *The Conflict of European and Eastern Algonkian Cultures, 1504-1700: A Study in Canadian Civilization* (1937), is generally regarded as a major contribution to anthropological method. In such poems as "Algonkian Burial" (collected in *Border River*) his scholarly knowledge has gone into the tissues of an imagination that transforms utterly what it has fed upon. In the collection of essays *Culture and Nationality* (1972) the key can be found to his awareness of the role of time in the Canadian culture. He gives here a penetrating analysis of the interplay of social and political forces in the emergence and falling away of "creative moments" in Canada's cultural history. As

Colour Chart.

Blue is to eye the balm of Mary.
Red tells a tale of pain and death.
There is no colour for the unhallowed breath
or for indescribable Faerie.

The ocean is to man the eye of nature.
It drafts the blue to edify the creature.
Red is exhaled by dragons in their season
and green glorifies the earth without reason.

The gold that gilds the goldenrod's petals
raises man's sense of worth to a higher power
than he is able to glean from other metals,
gleam as they may steadfastly from hour to hour.

Such colour is an act, blue is an act of grace.
Red   Red is a shiver as felt in a fever.
Gold remains the glory of the face
of earth, but green is the giver.

                              Alfred Bailey

Fair copy of a poem by Bailey collected in Thanks for a Drowned Island *(by permission of the author)*

the person most responsible for the founding of *Fiddlehead,* now the senior "little magazine" in Canada, Bailey has directly and indirectly given encouragement and provided an outlet for scores of the most promising young writers in Canada.

Reference:

M. T. Lane, "A Sense of the Medium: The Poetry of A. G. Bailey," *Canadian Poetry,* 19 (Fall-Winter 1986): 1-10.

Irene Baird
(9 April 1901-19 April 1981)

Catherine McLay
University of Calgary

BOOKS: *John* (Philadelphia & Toronto: Lippin-cott, 1937; London: Collins, 1937);
Waste Heritage (Toronto: Macmillan, 1939; New York: Random House, 1939);
He Rides the Sky (Toronto: Macmillan, 1941);
The North American Tradition (Toronto: Macmillan, 1941);
The Climate of Power (Toronto: Macmillan, 1971; London: Macmillan, 1971).

OTHER: "The Eskimo in Canada," in *The Canada Handbook* (Ottawa: Queen's Printer, 1967).

Cover for the 1973 paperback edition of Baird's novel about the gangs of unemployed men who gathered in Vancouver during the Depression

Irene Baird is an interesting and versatile writer, as her four very different novels testify. She is best known for her novel of social protest *Waste Heritage* (1939), which has been compared to John Steinbeck's *Of Mice and Men* and *The Grapes of Wrath* in subject matter, style, and tone. In the words of one commentator, Baird's 1939 novel is "a superb documentary–perceptive reporting from a dramatic era of history. It is also a work of art–an exciting, tightly-constructed novel."

Irene Todd Baird, daughter of Robert and Eva Todd, was born in 1901 in Carlisle, Cumberland County, England. She received her schooling there and in 1919 immigrated with her parents to Vancouver, British Columbia. Soon after she married Robert Baird and the couple settled in Vancouver, where their children, Robert and June, were born.

In Vancouver Baird began writing her first novel, *John,* which was published in 1937. It is a character study of John Dorey, son of an English businessman and a young Irish woman, who rejects a partnership in the family wool trade and chooses to live and die in obscurity on a coastal farm in British Columbia. The novel, with its elegiac account of John's simple life and brief romance, has been described as a pastoral idyll.

In 1937 the Bairds moved to Victoria, where Irene Baird experienced the Sit-Down of the Single Unemployed which she depicted movingly in *Waste Heritage.* In 1938 a thousand unemployed workers trekked to Victoria to protest the expulsion of some "sit-downers" from the Vancouver post office. Baird actually entered the buildings where the men were housed, accompanying her doctor (who was chief medical officer), and she has caught the tone of bitterness and frustration. The protagonist Matt Stroker is twenty-three, but he has never held a permanent job. Scarred by a fight several years ago in Regina, he is a tragic representative of young men who have no homes, no attachments, and no futures. His friend Eddy is simple; a head injury has affected his wits and his search for a pair of shoes leads to the violent and futile ending. The six weeks in Vancouver and Victoria, the Aschelon and Gath of the novel, lead to no better future for the men. Ironically, their fortunes can be improved only by a world war. The novel is an effective vehicle of social protest as readers share in the daily humiliations and suffering of men whose only crime is to want employment. The dialogue is terse and realistic and Baird has handled her male characters convincingly.

Reviews were highly favorable. The critic for the *Saturday Review of Literature* (16 December 1939) commented: "This is a black novel–black and bitter and compassionate and intensely sincere. . . . Baird writes with both fists and an angry will to be heard." Bruce Hutchison described the work in the *Victoria Daily Times* (30 December 1939) as "a piece of stark and odorous realism, . . . a social document of first-rate importance. . . . I think it is one of the best books that has come out of Canada in our time." But the onset of World War II diverted attention away from domestic problems and the sense of failure which they aroused. Although a French translation of Baird's novel entitled *Héritage Gaspillé* was published in 1946, the novel was out of print in English by 1942 and remained unavailable for thirty years.

In Victoria Baird wrote a third novel, *He Rides the Sky* (1941), as a tribute to the men of the RAF and RCAF. Based on actual letters from sons overseas which parents made available to her, it recounts the education of Pilot Sergeant Pete O'Halloran from his first letter aboard ship in March 1938 to his final one of 22 April 1940, the day before he is killed in action. In these two years Pete matures from an exuberant boy just out of school to a disciplined and courageous officer. While the book received very good reviews, and tributes by officials of the air force, sales were disappointing, and, like *Waste Heritage*, it soon went out of print.

In 1940 and 1941 Baird gave a series of radio addresses on aspects of the war and several of these were published by Macmillan in the pamphlet *The North American Tradition* (1941). Also in 1941 Baird began to write a column for the *Vancouver Sun*. The next year, in Vancouver, she joined the staff of the *Daily Province* but soon was offered a job at the National Film Board and

moved to Ottawa. During the next five years she traveled widely to show documentary films and to lecture on Canada's war work. She was Canadian representative of the National Film Board in Washington in 1944 and then in Mexico City. She returned to Ottawa in 1947 to join the Federal Department of Mines and Resources and then the Department of Northern Affairs and National Resources (which would become the Department of Indian Affairs and Northern Development). Apart from six months in 1951 as a United Nations consultant on information to Latin America, she served as senior information officer till 1962 and then as chief of Information Services, the first woman to head a federal information division. During these years she lectured on radio and television across Canada and the United States and traveled frequently to the Arctic. She also published poems, articles, and stories on the North in *Saturday Night, Beaver, North, Canadian Geographical Journal*, and the *UNESCO Courier*.

In 1967 Baird retired and settled in a flat in South Kensington, London. Here she completed her fourth novel, *The Climate of Power* (1971), based on her extensive government experience. It was also published in abridged form in the *Toronto Star Weekly* (May 1971). Set in Ottawa, the novel reflects what Baird described in a letter as "the shifting currents of policy and power" where men compete for "influence, prestige, high office." The protagonist George McKenna is an aging civil servant within months of retirement but determined to keep his position in the fictional Department of National Projects. George's conflict with his successor, the ambitious and unscrupulous Roy Wragge, leads to Roy's "accidental" death. McKenna is permanently crippled and his retirement with a young and unfaithful wife promises little happiness. The novel is uneven and at times melodramatic, yet it is absorbing and the descriptions of life in Nertserk and Glasgow Bay reveal Baird's deep understanding of the North.

In 1973 Baird returned to Victoria and settled there until her death in 1981. For *Waste Heritage* she has earned a central place in Canadian literature. In 1951 Professor E. C. McLean of Guelph remarked in a letter to Baird's publisher: "I do think our literature needed a book like *Waste Heritage* and we cannot afford to forget it." Because of encouragement from Dorothy Livesay and other writers and teachers, the novel was republished in paperback in 1973 and sold over

2,000 copies in the next six months. It is now a classic, a permanent record of one facet of Canadian life in those dark years.

Reference:

Michiel Horn, "Transient Men in the Depression," *Canadian Forum,* 54 (October 1974): 36-38.

Papers:

Manuscripts and correspondence pertaining to Baird's last three novels are in the Macmillan Collection at the McMaster University library.

Pierre Berton
(12 July 1920-)

Linda Shohet
Dawson College

BOOKS: *The Royal Family: The Story of the British Monarchy from Victoria to Elizabeth* (Toronto: McClelland & Stewart, 1954; New York: Knopf, 1954);

The Golden Trail: The Story of the Klondike Gold Rush (Toronto: Macmillan, 1954); republished as *Stampede For Gold: The Story of the Klondike* (New York: Knopf, 1955);

The Mysterious North (Toronto: McClelland & Stewart, 1956; New York: Knopf, 1956; London: Cassell, 1956);

Klondike: The Life and Death of the Last Great Gold Rush (Toronto: McClelland & Stewart, 1958); republished as *The Klondike Fever: The Life and Death of the Last Great Gold Rush* (New York: Knopf, 1959); republished under original title (London: Allen, 1960); revised and enlarged as *Klondike: The Last Great Gold Rush, 1896-1899* (Toronto: McClelland & Stewart, 1972);

Just Add Water and Stir (Toronto: McClelland & Stewart, 1959);

Adventures of a Columnist (Toronto: McClelland & Stewart, 1960);

The Secret World of Og (Toronto: McClelland & Stewart, 1961; Boston: Little, Brown, 1962);

The New City: A Prejudiced View of Toronto, photographs by Henry Rossier (Toronto: Macmillan, 1961);

Fast, Fast, Fast Relief (Toronto: McClelland & Stewart, 1962);

The Big Sell: An Introduction to the Black Arts of Door-to-Door Salesmanship & Other Techniques (To-

Pierre Berton

ronto: McClelland & Stewart, 1963; New York: Knopf, 1963);

The Comfortable Pew: A Critical Look at Christianity and the Religious Establishment in the New Age (Toronto: McClelland & Stewart, 1965; Philadelphia: Lippincott, 1965; London: Hodder & Stoughton, 1966);

My War With the Twentieth Century (Garden City: Doubleday, 1965);

Remember Yesterday (Toronto: Centennial Publishing, 1965);

The Cool, Crazy Committed World of the Sixties (Toronto: McClelland & Stewart, 1966); enlarged as *Voices from the Sixties* (Garden City: Doubleday, 1967);

The Centennial Food Guide, by Berton and Janet Berton (Toronto: Canadian Centennial Publishing, 1966); republished as *Pierre and Janet Berton's Canadian Food Guide* (Toronto: McClelland & Stewart, 1974);

The Smug Minority (Toronto: McClelland & Stewart, 1968; Garden City: Doubleday, 1969);

The National Dream: The Great Railway, 1881-1885 (Toronto: McClelland & Stewart, 1970);

The Last Spike: The Great Railway, 1881-1885 (Toronto: McClelland & Stewart, 1971);

Drifting Home (Toronto: McClelland & Stewart, 1973; New York: Knopf, 1974);

Hollywood's Canada: The Americanization of Our National Image (Toronto: McClelland & Stewart, 1975);

My Country: The Remarkable Past (Toronto: McClelland & Stewart, 1976);

The Dionne Years: A Thirties Melodrama (Toronto: McClelland & Stewart, 1977; New York: Norton, 1978);

The Wild Frontier (Toronto: McClelland & Stewart, 1978);

The Invasion of Canada, 1812-1813 (Toronto: McClelland & Stewart, 1980; Boston: Little, Brown, 1980);

Flames Across the Border: The Canadian-American Tragedy, 1813-1814 (Toronto: McClelland & Stewart, 1981; Boston: Little, Brown, 1981);

Why We Act Like Canadians: A Personal Exploration of Our National Character (Toronto: McClelland & Stewart, 1982);

The Klondike Quest: A Photographic Essay, 1897-1899 (Toronto: McClelland & Stewart, 1983);

The Promised Land: Settling the West, 1896-1914 (Toronto: McClelland & Stewart, 1984);

Vimy (Toronto: McClelland & Stewart, 1986);

Starting Out, volume 1: 1920-1947 (Toronto: McClelland & Stewart, 1987).

PLAY PRODUCTION: *Paradise Hill* (musical), book by Berton, Charlottetown, Charlottetown Festival, 3 July 1967.

MOTION PICTURE: *City of Gold*, story and commentary by Berton, National Film Board, 1957.

OTHER: *Great Canadians*, edited by Berton (Toronto: McClelland & Stewart, 1967);

Historic Headlines: A Century of Canadian News Dramas, edited by Berton (Toronto: McClelland & Stewart, 1967).

Pierre Berton has traveled far from his boyhood on the periphery of the Canadian frontier to the heart of establishment Toronto, where, as media guru and popular historian, he has been credited with "creating a new Canadian mythology." What strikes an observer initially is Berton's prodigious physical energy and creative virtuosity. Since publication of his first book in 1954, he has produced nearly one a year to become Canada's best-selling author; in addition he has written newspaper and magazine articles, radio, television, and film scripts, songs, musical revue sketches and librettos and has appeared regularly as panelist and host on television and radio. His seemingly boundless resources have occasioned countless jibes from reviewers. Margaret Atwood, reviewing Berton's 1977 book, *The Dionne Years: A Thirties Melodrama*, wittily suggested that Berton's fascination with the Canadian-born Dionne quintuplets was aroused by the unknown fact that he is a "set" of five Bertons, for as she explained: "Surely no one person could possibly do everything this 'Pierre Berton' is credited with doing, and he himself gives a hint of his true plurality when he says, 'It is obvious . . . that a work of this complexity is never the work of one man.' 'Pierre Berton,' as the evidence makes clear, is really a set of identical quintuplets whose mother wisely concealed their birth to keep them from becoming unwitting public fetishes, as the Dionnes did. (It didn't work, the Berton Quints became a public fetish anyway, though not unwittingly.)" But, like most reviewers of his many volumes of Canadian history, Atwood was forced to concede that Berton had put together "a compulsive read . . . meticulously researched, drawing on every conceivable source. . . ." These are qualities that readers have come to expect in Berton's books.

Berton shaking his plane loose from the snow during a trip to northern British Columbia described in The Mysterious North, *1956 (photograph by Art Jones)*

Berton's childhood and youth on the frontier stirred his imagination, his love for his country and the promise it held for the men and women who were drawn to the utmost tests of endurance exploring and expanding its boundaries. The heroic ventures of these pioneer explorers, set in relief against paeans to the Canadian landscape, became his favorite and recurrent subject. From his own father, Francis George Berton, who had abandoned a possible career at Queen's University to seek his pot of gold with the thousands rushing north in the first decades of the century, Berton inherited both a love of adventure and a clear grasp of economic reality. From his mother, Laura Beatrice Thompson Berton, author of *I Married the Klondike* (1954), came the literary heritage. His maternal grandfather, Phillips Thompson, had been the most famous journalist of his day in Ontario; his mother was an early member of the Canadian Authors' Association who never ceased her own writing even while she was living in the wilderness. She remembers her son writing stories at a young age, inventing tales on Sunday mornings to entertain his sister.

In 1941, after graduation with a B.A. from the University of British Columbia, Berton be-

came Canada's youngest city editor at the Vancouver *News-Herald,* where he remained for only one year before joining the Canadian army. After four years of service, he returned to work as feature writer for the Vancouver *Sun.* In 1946 he married Janet Walker (with whom he subsequently had seven children). In 1947 he moved east to Toronto as assistant editor at *Maclean's* magazine and rose to managing editor, a position he held until 1958. It was during this period that Berton began to produce his first books, feeling his way with a journalist's keen sense of public demand. His first volume, *The Royal Family: The Story of the British Monarchy from Victoria to Elizabeth* (1954), was published to answer the curiosity aroused by Elizabeth II's coronation two years earlier. After a novel for juvenile readers, Berton made his first major impact on the Canadian market, drawing on his childhood enthusiasm to write *The Mysterious North,* which garnered a 1956 Governor General's Award for nonfiction. For his next book, *Klondike: The Life and Death of the Last Great Gold Rush* (1958), the author won his second Governor General's Award. The volume enjoyed enormous sales for that time in Canada–10,000 copies–yet, in a 1978 interview with Jay Myers,

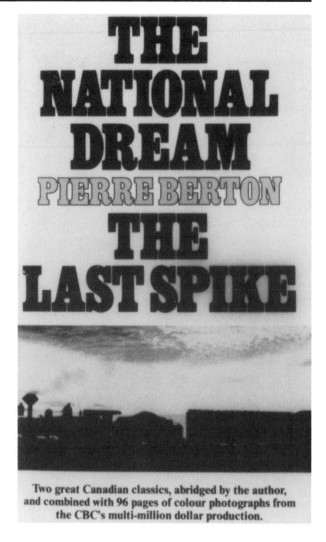

Berton in June 1973 during CBC television's filming of The National Dream, *based on his two-volume history of the Canadian Pacific Railway (photograph by Nick Morants, courtesy of the Canadian Pacific Railway)*

Cover for the 1974 abridged edition of Berton's railroad history

Berton said he felt audiences were not fully ready for popular history in the 1950s. He had seeded an interest and would wait for it to grow. A decade passed before he turned to writing history again.

Meanwhile he moved in 1958 to the *Toronto Star* as associate editor and columnist and turned his talents to some lighter fare–humor, collections of past columns–and to some serious commentary on North American mores. *Just Add Water and Stir* (1959), a collection of Berton's writings for the *Star,* won the Stephen Leacock Medal for Humour in 1960; journalistic acumen brought national newspaper awards for feature writing and staff correspondence in 1961. He at-

tacked the complacency of Canada's establishment drawing rebuttals from churchmen and politicians, but despite the self-righteous tone, his work sold well. *The Smug Minority* (1968), a pseudophilosophical dialogue between father and son on the past, present, and future of Western culture and society, was denounced as "shallow, superficial, insulting to the intelligence." Columnist Harry Bruce wrote that although Berton "wrote *The Smug Minority;* surely he doesn't have to be it, all by himself."

The 1967 centennial celebration of Confederation awakened a new national consciousness. By 1970 the audience for popular history had matured. Berton responded with a comprehensive

Dust jacket for Berton's history recounting the immigration of one million settlers to the prairie provinces at the turn of the twentieth century

two-volume history of the building of the Canadian Pacific Railway. *The National Dream* (1970) and *The Last Spike* (1971) were best-sellers. A television series brought the epic into virtually every Canadian home, and Berton was hailed as creator of a new Canadian mythology. According to his publisher Jack McClelland: Berton "brought an entirely new standard to the writing of Canadian history. He did his research extremely well. He presented his material in a readable and attractive narrative form, so successfully, that for the first time it became accessible to the great mass of the public in this country."

Although "Berton baiting" was almost a national sport by this time, newspaper and magazine reviews of the railway books were enthusiastic. One reviewer believed *The National Dream* should be required reading on every Canadian history course. . . . " Another felt it "should mark an important milestone in the attempt to breathe some life into our history." There were, however, some complaints. One commentator faulted Berton for an "abundance of clichés." Pro-

fessional historians expressed concern over "all the publicity hype" and offered more stringent criticism–valuable work by earlier historians had been overlooked, and there was a lack of critical perspective which resulted in a mere retelling of "the standard view of the C.P.R." There was clearly an unspoken rancor that "serious" historians were being overlooked while Berton was selling his product. Yet even historians admitted that the volumes contained "a wealth of anecdotal material," were well written, and had "struck a deeply responsive chord in Canada's reading public."

Berton accepts some of the academic criticism, acknowledging his debt to historian Donald Creighton, to whom he owed many of his interpretations. But Berton does not distinguish academic from popular history. "History is history. Good history is good history. I don't make any distinctions. If it's popular, it's something large numbers of people read. I would say my history is also scholarly. It's narrative history which is easier to read than expository history." He stresses character and setting. "History books should read as much like novels as possible." His volumes begin with a list of the "cast of characters," events are set against concrete physical backdrops, and much of the action evolves through dialogue.

Berton has moved from success to success since 1971, interspersing the histories with periodic returns to his earliest topics. *Drifting Home* (1973) is the journal of a nostalgic return to the Yukon, undertaken with his wife and children, following the trail left by his father and the gold prospectors. *Hollywood's Canada* (1975) provides a detailed account of 575 Hollywood films made from 1907 to 1960, set in Canada but hiding the Canadian national image "under a celluloid mountain of misconceptions."

The Dionne Years: A Thirties Melodrama (1977) sold over 50,000 hardcover copies. *Klondike* was reprinted in 1981 with 10,000 additional words that Berton had added in a 1972 revision.

At the beginning of the 1980s, Berton turned his attention further back in Canadian history to produce two volumes of history of the War of 1812. *The Invasion of Canada, 1812-1813* (1980) and *Flames Across the Border: The Canadian-American Tragedy, 1813-1814* (1981) won lavish praise and fired the public imagination as much as his railway books did. A Los Angeles reviewer called the second volume "a book to make historians raw with envy." Canadian man of letters

George Woodcock wrote: "The final test of good history writing is whether it changes our view of the past it deals with. I know I shall never again look on the War of 1812 as I did before I read Berton's two books. My view is now richer, deeper, and, I think, truer."

Berton's 1984 book completed the story of the opening of the Canadian West in the fifty years after Confederation. *The Promised Land: Settling the West, 1896-1914* tracks the immigration of more than one million settlers to the prairie provinces following the aggressive, bigoted policy of Clifford Sifton, Laurier's minister of interior at the turn of the twentieth century. And *Vimy* (1986) turns back to World War I to record one of the battles in which Canadian soldiers fought, a conflict that subsequently reinforced the growing Canadian nationalism of the postwar years.

Berton shows no sign of having completed his oeuvre. The immense amount of research for his books is handled by Berton and an assistant, with whom Berton shares a significant percentage of his profits. Berton insists on accuracy; material comes from original sources—archives, journals, diaries, newspaper files.

It is likely that he will be judged by posterity as Canada's first genuine media man, a man who knew how to manipulate every medium to transmit his message. The journalism will be of scant interest and the books of the 1960s will gather dust, but the volumes of history will be read as long as Canadians want to know more about their roots and to be entertained as they learn. Despite the critics' thrusts at his arrogance and lack of literary restraint, Pierre Berton has altered Canadians' perceptions of themselves, no small feat for any one man in a country as conservative as his.

Reference:

Jay Myers, "Interview with Pierre Berton," *Canadian Author and Bookman,* 54 (October 1978): 20-23.

Fred Bodsworth

(11 October 1918-   )

W. J. Keith
University of Toronto

BOOKS: *Last of the Curlews* (New York: Dodd, Mead, 1955; London: Museum Press, 1956; Toronto: McClelland & Stewart, 1963);

The Strange One (New York: Dodd, Mead, 1959; London: Longmans, 1960); republished as *The Mating Call* (New York: Pocket Books, 1961); republished under original title (Toronto: McClelland & Stewart, 1973);

The Atonement of Ashley Morden (New York: Dodd, Mead, 1964); republished as *Ashley Morden* (London: Longmans, 1965); republished under original title (Toronto: McClelland & Stewart, 1977);

The Sparrow's Fall (Garden City: Doubleday, 1967; London: Longmans, 1967; Scarborough, Ontario: New American Library, 1969);

The Pacific Coast (Toronto: Natural Science of Canada, 1970).

OTHER: "Wilderness Canada: Our Threatened Heritage," in *Wilderness Canada,* edited by Borden Spears (Toronto: Clarke, Irwin, 1970), pp. 17-29.

Charles Frederick Bodsworth is known to a wide range of magazine readers as a versatile and prolific journalist with a particular interest in wildlife. His permanent reputation, however, will depend upon his fiction, which invariably concerns itself with the relationship between human beings and their natural environment.

The son of Arthur John and Viola Williams Bodsworth, he was born at Port Burwell, Ontario (a small community on the northern shore of Lake Erie, southeast of London), where his father worked as a tinsmith. His teens coincided with the Depression, which prevented him from extending his formal education beyond high

Fred Bodsworth (photograph by Lois Mombourquette)

school. He worked for a time in the tobacco fields and on tugs on the lake, but in 1940 he obtained a job as reporter on a local newspaper, the *St. Thomas Times-Journal*. From there he moved in 1943 to the *Toronto Daily Star* and *Weekly Star*. A year later, he married Margaret Neville Banner; they have three children. From 1947 until 1955 he was an editor and regular writer for *Maclean's* magazine, during which period he contributed over seventy-five articles to that periodical alone.

During this period Bodsworth was also experimenting with short-length magazine fiction. One of these explored the plight of a possibly extinct bird, the Eskimo curlew, but to the author's annoyance the story got out of control and grew to a length that greatly limited its possible magazine market. Discouraged with it because he saw it only as a magazine story too long for most magazines to use, Bodsworth sent it to his agent in New York. The agent recognized its book potential and offered it to Dodd, Mead. *Last of the Curlews* (1955), Bodsworth's first novel, was the

result. It became a selection of several book clubs, went into a number of foreign translations, and on the strength of this success Bodsworth abandoned his career as a magazine journalist and became a free-lance writer, mainly of book-length fiction.

Last of the Curlews is a fictional account of what may have been the last male of the species, elaborated from a recorded sighting of a migrating pair in Texas in March 1945. Bodsworth follows the male's life as a solitary specimen waiting for a mate in the breeding grounds on the Arctic tundra, his migration via Newfoundland and Venezuela to Patagonia, his meeting with a female, and their return flight northward over the Andes to the Pacific and then across the Gulf of Mexico. At the very moment of mating, the female is shot on the Canadian prairies, and the male is left alone once more.

Superficially, Bodsworth's book follows in the tradition of the Canadian animal story associated with the names of Ernest Thompson Seton and Charles G. D. Roberts. But Bodsworth wrote in a period of greater scientific knowledge and interest. The emphasis in his work is not on exceptional individuals or on stories of unusual action and adventure. Bodsworth concentrates on life cycle, explaining so far as possible the bird's behavior as it follows its instinctive impulses to migrate, establish a territory, and reproduce its kind. In the novel man does not enter the story until the last chapter when a gun-happy farmer shoots the female, but all the chapters are interspersed with short sections, each entitled "The Gantlet," that give factual information about the record of man's lust to kill that brought the Eskimo curlew from abundance to near extinction between 1880 and 1910. *Last of the Curlews* combines narrative interest with scientific authority and expertise, and so sets the pattern for the rest of Bodsworth's work.

Since Bodsworth left *Maclean's* in 1955, he has worked as a free-lance writer, producing articles on subjects close to his interests and working for wildlife organizations and as a champion of wilderness conservation. He has regularly led ornithological tours and expeditions to various parts of the world, and he acted as president of the Federation of Ontario Naturalists from 1964 to 1967. He was awarded the Rothman's Merit Award for Literature in 1974.

In his second full-length fictional work, *The Strange One* (1959), a male barnacle goose from Barra in the Hebrides is blown off course by a hur-

FRED BODSWORTH was born in 1918 at Port Burwell, Ontario, a small fishing port on the north shore of Lake Erie. After completing the local village high school he worked on towing tugs, in tobacco fields, tried free-lance magazine writing, and finally wound up a cub reporter on the St. Thomas *Times-Journal*, a small city daily. Subsequently he worked several years as reporter and desk man on the *Toronto Daily Star* and *Toronto Star Weekly*. He is now a staff writer on *Maclean's Magazine*, Canada's widest read general-interest magazine, published at Toronto, Ontario.

He has been keenly interested in natural history, especially birds, since early childhood. He has also written many magazine articles on natural history topics, and during spare moments on newspaper and magazine assignments has observed and studied birds in all regions of Canada. Mr. Bodsworth is a director of the Federation of Ontario Naturalists and an active supporter of its conservation and nature education program.

Dust jacket for Bodsworth's novel about an Eskimo curlew who is possibly the last of his line

ricane, joins a flock of Canada geese in James Bay, and finds a mate of the related species. In this book, unlike *Last of the Curlews*, human beings come to the forefront. Rory Macdonald, also from Barra, takes a job researching goose migration in the Canadian North. There he meets Kanina, an Indian of the Swampy Cree who has been educated in white schools but is returning to her own community in the face of extreme racial prejudice. The relation between the man's fortunes and the bird's is obvious. The title derives from an Indian word applied to the unfamiliar goose, but it is also applicable to Rory and even more to Kanina, who has lost the skills that attach her to her own people but has not been accepted by the white world.

Together the two keep watch on the fugitive barnacle goose. As Rory tells Kanina, "the bond that develops between a pair of mated geese cannot be very different from what we call love." Forecastably, a romance develops between Rory and Kanina, and its course is governed by the behavior and fortunes of "the strange one." But just as the goose is pulled between two instinctive

urges, to return on migration to his own land and to stay with the flock from which he has gained a mate, so Rory is torn between the demands of his career and his loyalty to and love for Kanina. Judged by conventional novelistic criteria of realism and credibility, the work sounds highly contrived and artificial. But *The Strange One* makes no claim to being a conventional novel and should not be judged by such standards. Bodsworth has developed a literary form that he finds best suited to his aims: the moral fable. He is first and foremost a didactic writer, and he most often conveys his message by means of structural parallelism of the kind that is so evident here. Implicit in the form of the book is the intimate connection between the human and animal worlds and the need for awareness of the relationship between them.

The Atonement of Ashley Morden (1964) at first seems closer to standard novelistic preconceptions. The immediate emphasis is on human action. Ashley Morden, though he initially seems an alter ego of his creator (he goes on ornithological rambles and works in the Ontario tobacco fields), joins the Royal Canadian Air Force during World War II and becomes a bomb-aimer. During the devastating raids on Hamburg in 1943 he refuses to release his load of bombs, is court-martialed, convicted of cowardice, imprisoned, and dismissed in disgrace. His need for atonement, it should be stressed, results not from the act for which he was punished but from engaging in bombing raids in the first place. This atonement takes the form of working for peace rather than war. After the war, while he is a student, he becomes interested in bacteriology and later engages in research on an organism that causes a virulent tropical disease. As the result of an accident in his laboratory for which he is only marginally responsible, a lethal mutant is discovered, two persons die, and Morden is forced against his will into the Institute of Defense Sciences because his discovery is of crucial importance to germ warfare and the cold war. While he is experimenting on the effects of the bacteria on Arctic species, his plane containing infected mice makes a forced landing, and there is a chance of bacteriological disaster on a gigantic scale.

At this point the novel exhibits features of a science-fiction adventure story, but now the book takes an unexpected (and for some readers, doubtless, a disappointing) turn. Morden is rescued by another "strange one," a girl named Lilka Frahm who is living alone in the wilderness and seems like a cross between Rima in W. H. Hudson's *Green Mansions* (1904) and Miranda in Charles G. D. Roberts's *The Heart of the Ancient Wood* (1900). Here Bodsworth's structural parallelism appears once again. Lilka was living in Hamburg during the bombings (perhaps she owes her life to Morden's "crime"); later she survived Auschwitz. She has been brought up by her father (recently deceased) to live according to the dictates of nature and to avoid the company of men. She is able to show Morden the behavior of natural creatures in territorial disputes and contrast this with the wars of human beings who, in advancing beyond nature, have weakened the instinctive responses that guarantee the safety of the species. What began as a story of human action and conscience enlarges to involve the even broader questions of man's relation with the rest of the natural world and his obligations to the environment which he shares with other creatures. Morden's infected mice are more than counters in a story of science fiction and international politics; they become central symbols in an allegory of human responsibility and moral choice.

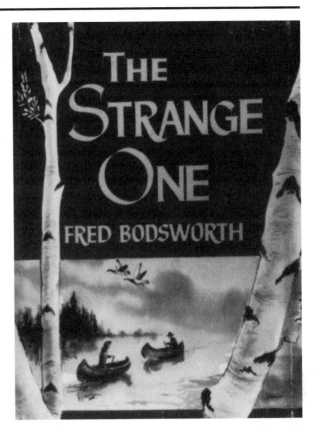

Dust jacket for Bodsworth's second full-length fictional work, in which the fortunes of a male barnacle goose and his mate run parallel to those of a human couple, Rory and Kanina

Bodsworth's last novel to date appeared in 1967. *The Sparrow's Fall*, which won the Doubleday Canadian Prize Novel Award, is simpler in structure but deals with similar moral themes. Ostensibly it is a story of endurance and survival in the Arctic. Jacob Atook, an Indian, is forced during an unusually hard winter to leave his pregnant wife, Niska, alone in her tent to go in search of caribou in the muskeg area. A dose of suspense and adventure is added when Jacob realizes that he is being tracked by Taka, an Indian who had hoped to marry Niska.

Bodsworth's main theme, however, lies elsewhere. Jacob and Niska are Christians and have been banished from the tribe for following Christian practices and being married secretly by the Christian missionary. Bodsworth suggests that the Christian emphasis on pity and forgiveness is psychologically at odds with the hunting instincts of the Indians. Jacob can proceed with the hunt only when he persuades himself that the *Manito* does *not* have pity on the fall of a sparrow—or of a caribou. And it is typical of Bodsworth's structural parallelism that the caribou Jacob is hunting proves to be a pregnant doe and so an equivalent in the natural world of his own wife. Jacob eventually triumphs over the wilderness and Taka by an intelligence that tips the balance over sheer strength and endurance, but Bodsworth leaves readers with the image of a man whose intellectual progress is gradually separating him, to his peril, from both the natural and human environments in which he finds himself. Far simpler in construction than *The Atonement of Ashley Morden,* the moral fable *The Sparrow's Fall* is a less explicit but no less probing examination of the choices human beings must make.

It is unfortunate that Bodsworth has produced no novel since *The Sparrow's Fall.* Not only was his fiction gaining in scope, but it was beginning to form an impressive oeuvre as well; each book, satisfying in itself, contributed to a larger pattern as a coherent unit within the context of his whole work. Bodsworth is an accomplished writer who brings to his work a viewpoint and a knowledge unusual in Canadian fiction. Few novelists can reproduce both the excitement of scientific research on the one hand and the instinctive responses of those who live close to the earth on the other. He is a skilled manipulator—and

transformer—of popular conventions, but, like most writers passionately concerned to inculcate a message, he is inclined to neglect the finer points of fictional technique. Action is sometimes summarized as baldly and unimaginatively as scientific information; his dialogue can be wooden, especially when intellectual argument is involved; and (as at the close of *The Atonement of Ashley Morden*) the didactic element can become too obtrusive. But Bodsworth has something of importance to say, and his blend of allegory and fiction, while currently unfashionable, is an appropriate way to say it. Not surprisingly, his books have proved more popular with general readers than with critics, but his significance in Canadian fiction is decidedly greater than his present reputation would suggest.

References:

Don Gutteridge, "Surviving the Fittest: Margaret Atwood and The Sparrow's Fall," *Journal of Canadian Studies,* 8 (August 1973): 59-64;
Joe Holliday, "Fred Bodsworth," *Canadian Author and Bookman,* 50 (Fall 1974): 12-13.

Louise Morey Bowman

(17 January 1882-28 September 1944)

Anne Cimon

BOOKS: *Moonlight and Common Day* (Toronto: Macmillan, 1922; London: Macmillan, 1923);
Dream Tapestries (Toronto: Macmillan, 1924; London: Macmillan, 1925);
Characters in Cadence (Toronto: Macmillan, 1938; London: Macmillan, 1938).

Louise Morey Bowman, a contemporary of Ezra Pound, H. D., and Amy Lowell, was one of a community of writers who ushered in the Modernist movement. She was early recognized in Canadian and American literary circles as a gifted practitioner of free verse. Her complex and individual vision wedded to an innovative style established Bowman as a pioneer of Canadian Modernism.

Bowman was born on 17 January 1882, in Sherbrooke, Quebec, at the time a predominantly English town in the Eastern Townships. Her father, Samuel Foote Morey, was the chief inspector for the Eastern Townships Bank. Her mother was the former Lily Louise Dyer. As befitted the daughter of a well-to-do family, Louise Morey was educated by private tutors, attended Dana Hall in Wellesley, Massachusetts, and traveled across Europe. In 1909 she married a Scotsman, Archibald Abercrombie Bowman, and moved to Toronto, where her husband worked as an electrical engineer for the Canadian Ingersoll Rand Company. It was in Toronto that Bowman published her first book of poetry, *Moonlight and Common Day* (1922), at the age of forty. Her poems had already appeared in various literary magazines, including the leading vehicle for the imagists, *Poetry* (Chicago), which published such major voices of the time as Ezra Pound, T. S. Eliot, Wallace Stevens, and Amy Lowell. *Poetry* publisher and editor Harriet Monroe praised Bowman's collection in a review headed "A Canadian Poet." She pointed out Bowman's modern and individual imagination, her simple and direct style, and recommended the book for its unusual unity and personality. Canadian reviewers were equally enthusiastic about the volume's modern tone. *Moon-*light *and Common Day* was dedicated to her mother, who died in 1897 when Bowman was fifteen. This early loss seems to have made the poet obsessively aware of the passage of time and of her own mortality. A child of the Victorian Age of Faith, Bowman expressed a blend of Christian and pagan feeling that was nondenominational. Her sacramental imagery of bread, wine, the colors crimson and gold, and her use of myth give a mystical intensity to Bowman's thematic exploration of love, death, beauty, and the relation between body and spirit. The search for a path, the "forgotten road" back to the imaginative world of the child, is another important theme in *Moonlight and Common Day*. In *Dream Tapestries*, Bowman's second collection of verse, the child, symbol of the innate wisdom and spontaneity of the spirit, reappears.

Dream Tapestries was published in 1924 with a dust jacket bearing appreciative remarks from Harriet Monroe and Amy Lowell. The collection won that year's Prix David from the Quebec government. One of the poems, "Oranges," a six-part meditation on the Puritan ethic set in a New England village, had won honorable mention in the competition for the 1922 Blindman Prize (South Carolina). The judge for this contest had been Amy Lowell, the "Empress of Imagism" herself. Lowell endorsed *Dream Tapestries* in a review published in *Poetry*, commenting on its authentic touch and richness of color and feeling. In this book Bowman continued to explore the birth and death cycle that fascinated her, though her technique proved bolder, more varied than in *Moonlight and Common Day*. Bowman experimented with the haiku, a Japanese form made popular by the imagists. One of the "Twelve Hokku on a Canadian Theme" included in *Dream Tapestries* demonstrates Bowman's ability to evoke in abbreviated lyric a typical Quebec scene of her time: "On city pavements/Two muffled, sombre nuns pace,/Behind laughing girls."

Canadian reviewers of this second volume were at times patronizing. One reviewer, in the *Canadian Forum*, took offense at a section entitled

"Songs of Women," remarking that the author was "too conscious of her sex." This section gave voice to different female personae such as the virgin, the whore, the witch, the childless woman. Bowman was never fearful of celebrating woman's power, and her vision of woman as creatrix, likening her to the ancient priestess who transcends societal roles, was a revisionary one in her time.

Bowman was an active member of the Canadian Authors' Association Montreal Branch, serving as president in 1937 and contributing often to their poetry yearbook. She shared a close friendship with another prominent member of the association, Frank Oliver Call. Call was a respected teacher at Bishop's College, a few miles outside of Sherbrooke. He had published a collection of verse, *Acanthus and Wild Grape* (1920), with a foreword endorsing the new vers libre technique. In the early 1980s an unpublished poem by Bowman was found in Call's personal library, a poem describing him and Bowman as kindred spirits. Their platonic relationship was based on a common love for poetry, gardening, painting, and music. Ralph Gustafson, who was a student of Call's and later won a Governor General's Award for *Fire on Stone: A Collection of Poetry* (1974), recalled being introduced to Bowman at a literary soirée. He remembers her as a "stately, generous, kindly lady" who showed interest in his work and was "exciting to a young poet on the threshold of being published himself." A studio photograph of Bowman, apparently taken for the dust jacket of *Moonlight and Common Day*, shows her to have been an attractive, strong-featured woman with a wistful air, dressed fashionably in black, fine strands of hair escaping from a narrow-brimmed hat.

In 1926, the year of her father's death, Bowman and her husband moved to Montreal, where they took up permanent residence. By this time Bowman's reputation was established internationally, her work published in Canadian, American, and British literary magazines. Her poems were included in such anthologies as *Our Canadian Literature: Representative Verse, English and French*, edited by Bliss Carman and Lorne Pierce (1922), and *New Harvesting 1918-1938*, edited by Ethel Hume Bennett (1938). Bowman also published numerous short stories, some of which were cited on the honor rolls of E. J. O'Brien's annual *Best American Short Stories*. Unfortunately, only one story, "Bitter Berry," which appeared in *The Canadian Mercury*, January 1929, remains in print. Its

gothic style compares to that of another contemporary writer, Edith Wharton, and shows Bowman to have had her own keen eye on society.

As a poet, Bowman felt kin to the romantics Keats, Shelley, and Wordsworth. Though she lived most of her adult life in cities, Bowman was primarily inspired by the memory of the picturesque landscape of her childhood. Hills, woods, orchards, and gardens are recurrent symbols for inner realities, the spiritual immanent in the material.

By the time her third book, *Characters in Cadence*, appeared in 1938, Bowman was fifty-six years old and a widow. In the fourteen years that had elapsed since publication of *Dream Tapestries*, her major themes had remained the passage of time and the nature of love, grounded in her own life experience. An epigraph taken from *A Letter to a Young Poet* (1932) by Virginia Woolf suggests that Bowman understood the poet's task to find relationship in apparent incompatibility and to create characters with poetic intensity. In *Characters in Cadence* Bowman demonstrates her ability to adopt a male persona, projecting herself into historical figures like George Washington and Oliver Cromwell. Her experimentation with "cadence," with line length, for a more musical verse showed her continued commitment to imagist techniques.

Bowman's obvious faith in the value of life alternated with a sense of existential dread that suffused her darkest poems. As a woman and a poet, she seemed aware of the limitations of her power in a patriarchal literary structure, and her poetry reflected a claustrophobia that recent feminist scholarship has shown numerous poets to share. "That is my story of moonlight–/no story at all, now say you?/but it all lies written/between the lines." This quotation from Bowman's first collection, *Moonlight and Common Day*, shows how she was early aware of her predicament as a woman poet and how she chose to tell the truth but tell it slant, to paraphrase Emily Dickinson. Bowman's idiosyncratic use of ellipsis marks at the end of lines also suggests that she left much unwritten. Her passionate, lyric voice often did not sit well with reviewers, who were condescending or dismissive of her vision. *Characters in Cadence* was scarcely, if at all, reviewed.

Bowman died on 28 September 1944 in Montreal. She was buried in her town of birth, Sherbrooke. Though her poetry continued to be anthologized for a few years after her death and she is mentioned in *The Oxford Companion to Cana-*

dian Literature (1983), her work now suffers neglect. Yet Bowman left an important legacy, a provocative vision of the sacredness of life, a powerful, honest exploration of woman's nature. Much of her work remains contemporary in message and technique.

Reference:

Avrum Malus, Diane Allard, and Maria Van Sundert, "Frank Oliver Call, Eastern Townships Poetry, and the Modernist Movement," *Canadian Literature*, 107 (Winter 1985): 61-68.

Charles Bruce

(11 May 1906-19 December 1971)

J. A. Wainwright
Dalhousie University

BOOKS: *Wild Apples* (Sackville, New Brunswick: Privately printed, 1927);

Tomorrow's Tide (Toronto: Macmillan, 1932);

Personal Note (Toronto: Ryerson, 1941);

Grey Ship Moving (Toronto: Ryerson/London: British Authors' Press, 1945);

The Flowing Summer (Toronto: Ryerson, 1947);

The Mulgrave Road (Toronto: Macmillan, 1951);

The Channel Shore (Toronto: Macmillan, 1954; New York: St. Martin's, 1955);

The Township of Time: A Chronicle (Toronto: Macmillan, 1959);

News and the Southams (Toronto: Macmillan, 1968);

The Mulgrave Road: Selected Poems (Porter's Lake, Nova Scotia: Pottersfield Press, 1985).

It is safe to say that in Canada Charles Bruce is considered a regional writer of some distinction. Bruce's artistic vision did focus on a fictional section of the Nova Scotia coast that he called the Channel Shore, a place that bears resemblance to the Chedabucto Bay region at the eastern end of the province where he grew up. In his best poetry Bruce wrote of life on the Shore and, in particular, of the dual current of land and sea within the people there. In his single novel and in his collection of linked short stories, Bruce created Shore families, gave them their own genealogies, and paid attention to the flow of time and to human experience within local history. Few writers in Canada have combined so convincingly the thematic territories of time and

place with a writing style that one perceptive critic has classified as "magic realism." Unfortunately, most other critics have ignored Bruce, and his literary reputation has lapsed since his death.

Charles Tory Bruce was born in Port Shoreham, Nova Scotia, the son of William Henry Bruce, a farmer-fisherman, and Sarah Tory Bruce, a former schoolteacher. On both sides he could trace his family roots in Nova Scotia back to the period immediately following the American Revolution, a fact that greatly influenced the subject matter and themes of his poetry and prose. As a boy, encouraged by an older sister, Bruce had poems and stories published in several local newspapers, including the Halifax *Evening Echo*. While studying for a liberal arts degree at Mount Allison University in Sackville, New Brunswick, he worked on the campus newspaper, *Argosy*, becoming editor in his senior year. His first collection of poems, *Wild Apples*, was privately published in 1927, the year of his graduation. (Mount Allison also awarded Bruce an honorary Litt.D. degree in 1952.) There are thirteen poems in this book, six of which are sonnets. Bruce was heavily influenced by the British Georgian poets and to some extent by the Confederation poet Bliss Carman; he wrote, for the most part, of beauty, love, and a generalized landscape of dream.

In 1927 Bruce joined the Halifax *Chronicle* and, after eight months, moved to the Canadian Press news agency in the same city. On 13 Decem-

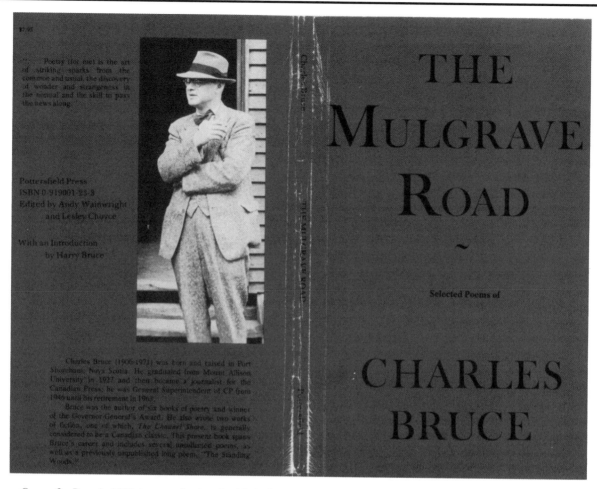

Covers for Bruce's 1985 poetry collection. Its title is the same as that of the 1951 volume which won Bruce a Governor General's Award.

ber 1929 he married Agnes King of Vancouver; they had four sons, of whom the third, Harry Bruce, also became an author (of *Nova Scotia,* 1975, and other chronicles of travel, cultural history, and social commentary). In 1933 Bruce was transferred to CP's head office in Toronto where he remained for thirty years. Macmillan of Canada published Bruce's second book of poems, *Tomorrow's Tide,* in 1932. A tension builds in this collection between form and subject matter. Although he wrote in a conventional manner, with fixed rhyme scheme and stress patterns, Bruce was more concerned with the physical landscape in which wind and water replace dream. The best poems draw directly on his Nova Scotia experience: the "Brief scraping as the weathered boats go down" and "The rugged stress of sea on stone."

In *Personal Note* (1941), published in pamphlet form, Bruce made his "statement of belief " about a world torn by World War II. As in his

later poems and prose, he insisted on "humankind's goodwill," a force that would overcome selfishness and "Systems." Unfortunately, the last part of this long narrative poem provides a rather sentimental defense of Britain's history and place in the modern world. There is no doubting the poet's integrity, but there is more propaganda here than poetry.

Bruce served as a war correspondent for Canadian Press in 1944-1945 and was missing in action for twenty-four hours after a bomber in which he was a passenger crash-landed in Belgium. His war experience was responsible for the long title poem of his next book, *Grey Ship Moving* (1945); here he tells of the troopship *Sappho* sailing from Halifax to England and of four Canadian lieutenants on board who meet and share memories and ambitions. But the essential aspect of this collection is that in it Bruce includes those poems he began to write in the late 1930s, poems in which he broke away from his tradi-

Cover for Bruce's only novel, in which he portrays three generations of a Nova Scotian family during the period 1919-1946

tional manner of writing verse. There is a long paean to the farmer-fishermen of Nova Scotia "who keep the salt in the blood," and it is evident in the shorter lyrics that the sea and earth of "lived experience" provide the inspiration and material that a poet needs.

Bruce was rising in the Canadian Press hierarchy. After the war he was promoted to general superintendent and became one of Canada's most respected newspapermen. Despite his job's daily grind he produced a substantial body of creative writing from 1946 to 1959, when he transformed his memories of the Chedabucto Bay area into his three finest books and into many poems and stories published in magazines and journals. He began to define his Channel Shore in earnest in *The Flowing Summer* (1947), a thirty-one-page narrative poem which relates the story of a young Toronto boy who returns to The Place, his father's boyhood home by the sea. Here his grandfather teaches him the rudiments

of fishing and haying, "the work that left your friendly mind alive / To men and women," and the depths of heritage and "patterned living."

The Mulgrave Road (1951) won Bruce the Governor General's Award for poetry. The lyrics here reveal the human factor in the territory of land and water, those people who are not "dry-footed" but who "Move in a sea of sense and waves of thought [that] / March to the shore of the mind." Those who leave the Shore discover later that region is the place at the heart of human experience. As Bruce puts it in his title poem, "And dust on the grass is dust on the grass / In Guysborough County or Port of Spain." But the most important theme has to do with people moving in the flow, "the skein of time." As one critic has said, "Bruce creates tangible images of time as if it were an object that could be grasped by the senses." The connection between past and present is emphasized throughout, the awareness of ancestors and heritage extolled.

Bruce's only novel, *The Channel Shore* (1954), contains much of his vision of his boyhood home (to which he returned many summers in his life), but his is an artistic vision that transforms and re-creates the facts of past and present. The plot is complex, covering three generations of Shore life from 1919 to 1946. A boy, Alan Marshall, grows up to learn that his father, Grant Marshall, adopted him at birth. Alan's blood father, Anse Gordon, is an unsavory character who returns to the Shore demanding loyalty that Alan finally rejects. In Alan's rejection one sees Bruce's emphasis on the family dependent not on blood ties but on experiential bonds of companionship and love; as well, the influence of individual experience is tempered by the heritage of community. Such a summary does not do justice to Bruce's evocation of his shorescape and its presence through time as a rock of ages. *The Channel Shore*, like Ernest Buckler's better-known work *The Mountain and the Valley* (1952), is one of few Canadian novels in which aspects of rural region are memorably present in a narrative with the universal theme of human kinship.

Bruce published stories about the Shore in many periodicals, ranging from *Maclean's* to *Dalhousie Review*. He included a number of them in a collection of linked short stories entitled *The Township of Time: A Chronicle* (1959). At the end of the book is a genealogical chart of Shore families whose evolution Bruce has followed from the latter part of the eighteenth century to 1950.

Charles Bruce retired from Canadian Press eight years before his death and wrote a book on the history of the Southam newspaper organization, *News and the Southams* (1968). He died in Toronto in 1971. His literary reputation now, as when he was alive, is based more on his poetry than on his prose; yet for twenty years (1959-1979) no article appeared in Canada on his verse. His prose fiction is not mentioned in Carl F. Klinck's *Literary History of Canada* (second edition, 1976). In the 1980s *The Channel Shore* and *The Township of Time* have been republished in the New Canadian Library, and a volume of selected poems by Bruce, entitled, like the 1951 collection, *The Mulgrave Road*, appeared in 1985. Certainly the audience that he once had will return, and, one hopes, critical attention to Bruce's work will not remain so limited.

References:

Richard C. Davis, "Tradition and the Individual Talent of Charles Bruce," *Dalhousie Review*, 59 (Autumn 1979): 443-451;

John Moss, *Patterns of Isolation* (Toronto: McClelland & Stewart, 1974), pp. 166-188;

J. A. Wainwright, "Days of Future Past: Time in the Fiction of Charles Bruce," *Studies in Canadian Literature*, 8, no. 2 (1983): 238-247;

Wainwright, *World Enough and Time: Charles Bruce, A Literary Biography* (Halifax: Formac, forthcoming, 1988).

Ernest Buckler
(19 July 1908-4 March 1984)

Gwendolyn Davies
Mount Allison University

BOOKS: *The Mountain and the Valley* (New York: Holt, 1952; Toronto: Clarke, Irwin, 1952);

The Cruelest Month (Toronto: McClelland & Stewart, 1963);

Ox Bells and Fireflies: A Memoir (New York: Knopf, 1968; Toronto: McClelland & Stewart, 1968);

Nova Scotia: Window on the Sea, photographs by Hans Weber (Toronto: McClelland & Stewart, 1973);

The Rebellion of Young David and Other Stories, edited by Robert Chambers (Toronto: McClelland & Stewart, 1975);

Whirligig: Selected Prose and Verse (Toronto: McClelland & Stewart, 1977).

From the publication of his first novel, *The Mountain and the Valley,* in 1952 until his death in 1984, Ernest Buckler occupied a unique position in the field of Canadian fiction. His richly textured prose style, sensitively developed protagonists, and vividly realized sense of place achieved a tone of intimacy and lyricism uncharacteristic of the work of many of his contemporaries. Now considered a classic of Canadian literature, *The Mountain and the Valley* is a poetical tour de force set in Buckler's native Annapolis Valley of Nova Scotia. Its depiction of a pastoral childhood world being eroded by contemporary urban values transcends regionalism and introduces a Buckler concern later developed in the pastoral idylls *Ox Bells and Fireflies* (1968) and *Nova Scotia: Window On the Sea* (1973).

Ernest Buckler, the son of Appleton Buckler (a farmer) and Mary Swift Buckler, was born of English and Loyalist stock in Dalhousie West, a small community approximately fifteen miles from the historic town of Annapolis Royal in Nova Scotia. His rootedness in this area is readily perceived in the detail of his fictional settings and in the knowledge of Valley history and genealogy which his central characters exhibit. By 1920 Buckler had completed his elementary and secondary schooling in this community and for the

Ernest Buckler (courtesy of McClelland and Stewart)

next decade worked to put himself through university. His summers during this period were spent in employment at Kent House in Greenwich, Connecticut, a vacation hotel Buckler once described as "delightfully conservative" and "muggy with monotony." However, Buckler enjoyed the people and the conversations he encountered at Kent House, and his experiences there may well have inspired him to use a summer hotel as a structural device in his second novel, *The Cruelest Month* (1963).

33

In 1929 Buckler graduated in mathematics from Dalhousie University and in 1930 received an M.A. in philosophy at the University of Toronto. He thrived on the intellectual environment of the university and wished to continue his education, but bad health and poor eyesight forced him to give up his academic ambitions. A five-year period spent in Toronto doing actuarial work for Manufacturer's Life Insurance Company also ended in ill health, and in 1936 Buckler returned to Nova Scotia's Annapolis Valley to take up a life of farming and writing at Centrelea, near his boyhood home.

With the exception of student pieces submitted to the *Dalhousie Gazette* and the *Trinity University Review,* Buckler had done little public writing by the time he returned to Nova Scotia in 1936. However, in 1937 he won a *Coronet* contest on "What is Coronet?" and in the same year came to the attention of Arnold Gingrich, the editor of *Esquire,* with a series of stimulating and "exegetical" letters on everything from the character of the magazine to the state of contemporary American writing. As Gingrich has noted in his autobiography, *Nothing But People* (1971), subscribers were soon writing "that they'd rather read what Buckler said about the issues than read the magazines themselves," and with this encouragement, Buckler eventually began to submit other material to *Esquire* and to other journals. Although still farming, he actively wrote for such magazines as *Maclean's, Saturday Night, Atlantic Advocate, Atlantic Monthly,* the *Family Herald,* and the *Star Weekly* from 1937 and 1964, and throughout that period he also submitted plays, stories, and talks to the Canadian Broadcasting Corporation.

However, even after *The Mountain and the Valley* was published in 1952, Buckler continued to describe himself as "a farmer who writes, not a writer who farms." His 1953 CBC broadcast "My First Novel" identified a complementary relationship between his two worlds, describing the way in which isolation and manual labor freed his mind of encumbrances so that images, phrases, and characters could take shape while "you're chopping, or hoeing, or whatever." "My thoughts are like mice," Buckler added in a characteristic domestic image; "When the mind is quiet, they seem to pop out of their holes and scutter about much more freely than when I'm in company." Thus, isolation was always to be an important criterion of writing for him. When writers congregate "in clutches, or coveys," he noted, "they dissipate with their tongues what they should be funnel-

ling through their pens.... Writers' shop talk isn't half as rewarding as people's, anyway." It is perhaps not surprising, then, that Buckler rarely ventured into the public limelight but preferred to live quietly among the Valley people who inhabited and inspired his literary world.

The Mountain and the Valley was more than six years in gestation, but the preoccupations, themes, and characters of the novel can be found in various disguises in the short stories of the 1940s. Such narratives as "The First Born Son" (*Esquire,* July 1941) and "The Clumsy One" (*Maclean's,* 1 August 1950) anticipated scenes in *The Mountain and the Valley* and introduced the insider-outsider conflict which brings a taut psychological edge to the novel. Like David Canaan, the central character in *The Mountain and the Valley,* the protagonists of these stories are often products of closely knit rural families in which the bonds of affection are expressed through physical gestures of kindness and homely scenes of domestic interaction. Buckler is a master at capturing magical moments in time, and his Christmas scenes, family excursions, and kitchen sequences often become catalysts for an individual's heightened recognition of the depth of love surrounding him. These moments of wordless communication are frequently presented through the eyes of a child and provide a lyrical balance to the toil and verbal inarticulacy which characterize much of Valley farm life in the stories and the novels. In the case of David Canaan of *The Mountain and the Valley,* the contrast is particularly dramatic. Physically and emotionally sustained by his love of the land and his family life, David is nonetheless an artist, a wordsmith who aspires to a world imaginatively and aesthetically richer than that of his Valley existence. Merely "different" when he is a child, he is perceptibly isolated when he is an adult, caught in a struggle between two forces without any visible resolution.

The strength of *The Mountain and the Valley* lies partly in Buckler's ability to evoke the interiority of David's world and partly in the rich prose style of the novel. Neither can be divorced from the other, for it is the intensity and richness of David's perceptions which give the prose its lush, lyric quality. His heightened boyhood responses to experience assume dizzying proportions as Buckler piles modifier upon modifier: "In that instant suddenly, ecstatically, burstingly, buoyantly, enclosingly, sharply, safely, stingingly, watchfully, batedly, mountingly, softly, ever so softly, it was Christmas Eve." This incremental style is particularly effective in capturing a sense of David's childhood ecstasy in moments of deeply felt time, an intensity of experience which becomes highly metaphorical as he moves toward adulthood and attempts to translate emotion and experience into art. As a writer, David tries to stretch language to its limits, groping for the right word combinations and colors to define the essence of sensation and to explain the way in which he perceives his environment: "Shape and colour reached out to him like voices. The black-green sweep of the spruces' lower limbs like an inhalation sustained immobile in the chest of the tree, . . . the yellow-green of the hemlock branches, twig-laced in a snow crystal pattern, like a breath outward, . . . the lemon-green murmurous-needled pine overturned by the wind, its ragged anchor of roots and earth like the shape of the thunder of its own falling. . . . And, beneath the trees, was the other, inch-boundaried, earth-clinging forest: the brown-green moss and the mayflower runners and botany-book topknots; the grey-green, antlered lichens."

With its accumulation of modifiers, symbols, verbal surprises, metaphors, and images, the style of *The Mountain and the Valley* often borders on obscurantism as well as on exuberance, but its complexity and abstractionism convincingly convey David's growing introspection, loneliness, and artistic frustration as he lives out his life on the family farm. Moreover, his inclination to present "The idea fronded suddenly like a million-capillaried chart of the bloodstream" is balanced by Buckler's use of a plain style to depict the thoughts and actions of the Valley folk who accept David as one of theirs but never succeed in understanding him. David can survive in this environment by adopting their language in moments of public interaction, but his true self lies in the trances, alter egos, fantasies, mirror images, and linguistic tours de force which Buckler creates as David's secret and increasingly satisfying world when family members are either dead or departed and he is left to run the farm for his grandmother.

While it is Buckler's elevation of language which does much to reveal the psychological complexity of his central character, it is also the author's control of time which brings an interesting dimension to the novel. The book opens and closes with a still point in time, the moment when the grandmother, Ellen (herself symbolic of time arrested because she has reverted to a kind of childhood), weaves remnants of family his-

tory into the rug she is making. It is characteristic of Buckler's rootedness in Nova Scotian society that he should introduce one of the province's oldest domestic crafts into the novel as a unifying device, for the prologue and the epilogue repeat the identical mat-making scene with Ellen. Between them Buckler weaves the chronicle of the Canaan family and of David's growth from the age of eleven until his death at thirty. Integrated into Ellen's rug are moments which have given emotional vibrancy to David's life, and symbolically, as he dies of a heart attack on the mountain at the end of the novel, the old lady places a piece of white lace–perhaps a fragment of her wedding dress–into the center of the rug to complete the cycle of Canaan family history which she has woven and recorded. As a partridge flutters from the foliage near David's body and soars over the mountain at the end, it signifies both the release and the irony of David's life within this cycle. Never successful in artistically conquering his mountain, he is at last physically and spiritually free of the Valley in death.

Buckler himself pointed out that *The Mountain and the Valley* is a novel of self-delusion, and underlying the lyricism and the delicacy of the book always lies the irony of David's belief that he will be the greatest writer in the world. His introspection defeats his ability to describe the Valley of his youth in narrative terms, and he dies as he has lived, in the hope that he will transcend his limitations. His illusion of literary success just moments before he dies is made doubly ironic by Buckler's recurring revelation of a world inside and outside the Valley grown indifferent to the rural and family values David wishes to recapture in his writing. Cars, railways, radios, and roads have destroyed the homogeneity of rural Nova Scotian life by the time of World War II and have left David with only his fantasies and his childhood memories to sustain him. Thus, the epiphanylike vision of success and happiness he experiences as he dies may temper the poignancy of the conclusion, but it also emphasizes the extent of both David's self-deception and Buckler's ironic vision.

There is virtually no plot in *The Mountain and the Valley*. Rather, the reader is drawn within the psychological complexities of David's experience from childhood to adulthood and, through that process, is also introduced to such Buckler preoccupations as the loss of rural (and childhood) innocence, the ascendance of urban (and adult) values, the destructiveness of time and death, and the alienation of the artist as he tries to reconcile these divergent forces. It is the artist who emerges as central to any resolution of Buckler's antithetical worlds, and in *The Mountain and the Valley*, as in Buckler's next work, *The Cruelest Month*, he is the figure who can interpret and wed different patterns in time. The Buckler artist, as Alan Young notes in his 1976 study of the author, "embodies the potential for the all-embracing vision which will resolve the antagonism between culture and nature that is inherent historically within the Canadian condition, and which will . . . unite past and present." Ultimately, he will "conquer, through art, the destructive forces of history itself."

Buckler's sensitive treatment of the artist-figure is one of the many features of *The Mountain and the Valley* which drew positive comments from critics when the book was published. The novel was reviewed favorably in the United States alongside Ernest Hemingway's *The Old Man and the Sea*, which appeared the same year. Seven thousand copies of the original hardcover edition of *The Mountain and the Valley* published by Henry Holt of New York were sold in the United States and one hundred and fifty thousand paperbacks appeared in the New American Library Edition. Sales, however, were not brisk in Canada, for only two hundred and fifty copies of the book were originally imported into Canada for publication under the Clarke, Irwin imprint. Subsequently, the New Canadian Library paperback edition appeared in 1961, and in recent years the novel has been added to high-school and university literature courses across the country. In spite of the reputation the book has developed, however, Buckler was known to remark somewhat wryly that "all the yachts you could build with your Canadian royalties you could sail in your bath tub." In the sales of *The Cruelest Month*, his second novel of the artist-figure, he was to be even more disappointed.

The Cruelest Month (1963) revolves around a group of talented but scarred individuals who twice in their adult lives congregate at a rural Nova Scotian guest house seeking purgation and wholeness. As Alan Young has pointed out in *Ernest Buckler*, it is no accident that the name of the hotel is Endlaw, an anagram of Henry David Thoreau's Walden, and that the rambling old house stands on the edge of a lake in a scene of unbroken wilderness and naturalness. To Buckler's character, Morse Halliday, a sophisticated and cynical American author who accidentally discovered

Endlaw through the *Saturday Review* classifieds, the inn and its neighboring area of Granfort are disembodied in time. The road to the house is lined by "Trees older than men. . . . Centuried spruces, lonelied by their own height," and nearby Granfort seems so ageless that "It washes you clean of whatever your chronic mood. This is the very soil where settlers from the old world first set foot on the New. You really feel it. An ancient rampart mounds graveyard-green from the horseshoe harbour." In this environment Morse is not the only one to renew his affiliation with natural man and the landscape. Endlaw becomes a rarefied green space in time for nearly all the characters, an environment that encourages them to move from glib statements on life in part one of the novel (1946) to serious reassessments of their spiritual purpose in part three (1951). By the time the group leaves the guest house in part four, there is a sense that at least several of them have achieved peace of mind and have been revitalized by their new insights.

In its organization *The Cruelest Month* moves from despair to purgation to renewal. This pattern is reinforced by a body of wasteland imagery that recalls the progression of T. S. Eliot's poem. As in *The Waste Land* (1922), modern man is shown to be in perilous condition at the beginning of the novel. Kate Fennison has sacrificed her youth in the service of her professorial father; Rex and Sheila Giorno have lost their mutual love and respect; Bruce Mansfield has abandoned a medical career because of the deaths of his wife and child; and Paul Creed has developed a heart condition which impedes the growth of both his writing and his love for Kate.

The bare bones of the narrative make it sound trite and sentimental. However, Buckler provides the reader with a long and analytical part three in which both art and love are discussed. In the exchanges which take place between the characters, love is shown to restrict the growth of an individual (hence the partial explanation of Buckler's original title "The Cells of Love") as well as strengthen his ability to carry on. However, in spite of the positive tone of the conclusion, it is not enough to offset the reader's uneasy suspicion that aridity may return to the artistic and emotional lives of the Endlaw group. The impression is reinforced by the fact that the novel ends in April, Eliot's "cruelest month." The rebirth of the land and the blooming of the lilacs should symbolize hope and regeneration. However, Paul gives not a lilac but a lilac root to

Dust jacket for Buckler's last book, a collection of verse, essays, and reminiscences that appeared in 1977

Kate, thereby signifying the transplanting of their love. In so doing, he drives both Kate and himself into liaisons which will temper their loneliness but which will violate the integrity each has represented in the novel. In addition, Buckler's introduction of a symbolic deer and a forest fire into the conclusion suggests purgation and rebirth, but the positive implications of both are undercut by the protagonists' compromises in part four. In a sense, the conclusion of *The Cruelest Month* is reminiscent of Buckler's vision of self-delusion at the end of the *The Mountain and the Valley*. The characters are able to restore themselves temporarily by taking respite in the pastoral green of Endlaw, but unlike the world of nature, they may lack the ability to sustain their process of regeneration and productiveness. In the words of the novel which Paul Creed destroys in the face of his approaching death, "People, shedding their leaves at the moment of leaving, never leaf out the same again; but a re-leafing tree is exactly the friend of last year."

The most persistent criticism leveled at *The Cruelest Month* was that it had a contrived plot, pedantic dialogue, and self-conscious language.

Many of these difficulties emanate from Buckler's attempt to develop the artist motif already treated in *The Mountain and the Valley*, for when he brings his characters together to discuss their philosophical or artistic directions, they have eloquent voices but very little flesh. Nonetheless, their views are important in revealing some of the pitfalls for the writer which Buckler himself clearly recognizes. Thus, it is significant that before he dies Paul Creed destroys the novel he has written so that no one can get to know him. Morse Halliday, in contrast, forsakes his usual cynicism for an uncharacteristic celebration of the spirit that unifies man. His thesis that people's "lighting" is the only "fibre in the world that's indestructible" sounds hauntingly like David Canaan's vision of love at the end of *The Mountain and the Valley*. In each case the writer's vision of literary transcendence is rather precariously based, and Buckler introduces a deflationary note at the end of the novel when Kate internalizes, "he will never get it right. . . . No writer ever gets it right." David Canaan died self-deluded in *The Mountain and the Valley*. At the conclusion of *The Cruelest Month*, Buckler seems to be suggesting that Morse Halliday and Paul Creed are as self-deceived and as isolated from society as their predecessor.

In Buckler's third book, *Ox Bells and Fireflies* (1968), he abandons the artist theme and a conventional narrative style to recall the world of rural Nova Scotia he had known as a boy. Subtitled *A Memoir,* the book is not only deeply personal but highly lyrical as well. However, Buckler, as he wrote in "My Third Book" (collected in Gregory Cook's *Ernest Buckler,* 1972), wanted it to be more than "just another wispily elegiac excursion into the 'happy valley' of childhood." For him the book was a record of a "way of life with all its distinctive customs, institutions, values, tasks, recreations, idioms of speech and behaviour, atmospheres, and textual variety." Thus, while it may seem to some to be merely a sentimental rendering of the past in its evocation of regional life, it in fact provides an imaginative insight into the cultural values and rural perspectives which once characterized Canada. As well, Buckler is too much of an ironist to ignore the thistles in his fields. Scenes in the book are caught in memory, but memory, like Buckler's boyhood world, contains a record of time's erosion. Inevitably, then, the lyricism of Buckler's account is punctuated by the narrator's record of the death, change, and perversity that marred even the golden years. The book opens on a note of physical death, and variations on this theme continue to recur and unify the memoir even as Buckler celebrates the ideal he once found in rural Nova Scotia.

The homogeneity of the life Buckler once knew is emphasized by the structure and shape he gives to *Ox Bells and Fireflies.* The work has fictional and dramatic scenes, but essentially it begins and ends with a child's impressions of his rural world. Between the beginning and ending points of the cycle, the story of the narrator's growth to perception is recorded in his own voice. As well, other viewpoints are introduced from time to time so that by the conclusion of the memoir, the reader feels that Buckler has woven into the narrative not only the fabric of his own life but also that of the people of Norstead. In a sense then, the boy stands for all humanity: "I'll call the village 'Norstead,' the boy 'I.' They stand for many. The time is youth, when time is young." At the very end, the "many" are no longer young, and their collective voice acts as a gloss on the mellowness of the narrator's memories as they sadly recall all that time and change have caused them to forfeit: "We no

longer see the things we used to see: Our own pulse in the lapping of the lake, our own snugness in the window pane. We see things we never used to see: the iron in the band of winter-cloud behind the factory chimney, the prison eyes in the dry blade of weaving sidewalk grass, the death mask of time in the rag of newspaper blowing down the gutter."

As in *The Mountain and the Valley,* Buckler's lyrical rhythmic language often tends to dominate *Ox Bells and Fireflies,* but the memoir is given a sense of unity and control by the consistent presence of the narrator and by the emerging character of Norstead itself. The kind of aesthetic and structural freedom which the "memoir" affords the author ("And there were songs the color of poppies . . . and roofs the sound of sleep . . . and thoughts the taste of swimming . . . and voices the touch of bread. . . . And fireflies and freedom . . .") was evidently appealing to Buckler, for even before *Ox Bells and Fireflies* reached the public he had again turned to a loosely organized, lyrical evocation of pastoral life as a subject. Although still unpublished, this work, *Christmas in Canada,* comprising a cantata composed by Keith Bissell to a text by Buckler, was performed for chorus, piano, and narrator in the 1967 Prince Edward Island Centennial celebrations and, in the view of Alan Young, it is inseparable in theme and technique from *Ox Bells and Fireflies* and from Buckler's next work, *Nova Scotia: Window on the Sea* (1973).

Christmas in Canada conjures up memories of Yuletide celebration and uses the activities of the season to illustrate the closeness, naturalness, and peacefulness of rural society. It reveals a society closely tied to family values, and, like Buckler's earlier works, reflects his background in the agriculturally rich Annapolis Valley of Nova Scotia. But if Nova Scotia is "rooted in the land," it is also "grounded in the sea." In recognition of this fact, Buckler turned to his province's other geographical feature in his 1973 work, *Nova Scotia: Window on the Sea.* Here amid a series of realistic visual images produced by German-born photographer Hans Weber, Buckler develops five impressionistic essays which attempt to capture and define the essence of his seabound province. Divided into sections entitled "Amethysts and Dragonflies," "Masts and Anchors," "Man and Snowman," "Faces and Universes," and "Counterfeit and Coin," *Nova Scotia* presents an interesting tension between the richness and lyricism of Buckler's prose style and the austerity and purity of Weber's photographs. Rather than clash, the two media seem to temper one another, with Buckler's romantic and simile-laden lines being given new definition by Weber's detailed photographs of grizzled faces and stark landscapes.

Although *Nova Scotia* seems in many respects to be a coffee-table book, its style and emphasis are consistent with other works in the Buckler canon. The author's preoccupation with urban blight, family unity, pastoral ideals, and the stimulation of the senses continues here as in earlier works, and here as well one finds the cumulative lists and phrases that build to a litany of praise as the writer excitedly contemplates the richness of his environment. At such moments the text seems to strain to dizzying heights, suggesting a mind delirious with the ecstasy of language and the provocation of the senses. Yet as the photographs function to ground Buckler's lyricism in experience, so too do the narrative sequences he introduces into such sections as "Man and Snowman" and "Faces and Universes." Typical of these is the episode in which an old man suffers a stroke. Robbed of speech and movement, he can no longer communicate in a conventional way. However, by exposing the reader to the family's comments on the old man and by taking the reader within the memory process of the invalid, Buckler is able to convey a sense of both the richness and the pain of the life he has lived. Humiliated by the failure of his body, he is nonetheless blessed by the brilliancy of his memory and the continuing excitement of his senses. As in the earlier works, time and death are unifying themes in "Man and Snowman," and as the old man lies dying, the grandchildren build a snowman in his image. It too will melt into time and nothingness, but in the concern and kinship of the youngsters, there is a revelation of an ongoing cycle of life and the endurance of familial bonds.

The balance between lyricism and realism is not always an easy one for Buckler to achieve and sustain, and there are moments in *Nova Scotia* when the author seems to lose control of his multiple and mellifluous images. Nevertheless, the book offers a powerful portrait of Nova Scotia as Buckler sees it, especially as a place where human lives evolve naturally in rhythm with the seasons, the sea, and the moods of the land. Buckler's Nova Scotia is certainly not one "of burgeoning Halifax and Canso oil refineries" nor of "seductive Tourist Bureau ads," noted William French in the Toronto *Globe and Mail* in 1973.

Rather, "it's a place of the mind, with spiritual qualities rooted in the land and the sea and the integrity of the family, where a man's wealth has nothing to do with his physical assets."

Buckler's preoccupation with the rural lifestyle of Nova Scotia and an individual's response to it received its last major treatment in *Nova Scotia: Window on the Sea*. His 1975 collection, *The Rebellion of Young David and Other Stories*, represents earlier work done in the *Esquire*, *Maclean's*, and *Atlantic Advocate* years of 1941 to 1959. Selected and arranged by Robert Chambers, the stories in this collection include such award-winning narratives as "The Quarrel" (*Maclean's* short story contest, 1948), straightforward in their narrative technique and nondramatic character. The publication of these stories in 1975 reinforced for Buckler's readers the themes of his major works and again illustrated the concern with the human spirit which underlies all his writing.

In 1977 *Whirligig: Selected Prose and Verse* appeared in Canada amid disappointed and even bewildered reviews by critics and admirers of Buckler's previous writing. Marking a complete departure from the lyrical and spiritual emphasis of the author's first five books, *Whirligig* is a collection of Ogden Nash-like verse, comic essays, and pseudoserious reminiscences. Often adopting the persona of a farmer-writer with a position-conscious wife, Buckler ranges over the world of Christmas-card-giving, rural partylines, boring visitors, and book publicity to bring a quality of unity to the otherwise diverse sketches. In an almost Leacockian way, the narrator is both inside and outside the community and therefore occupies a fitting position from which to comment on local follies as well as on his own.

On close examination, it is clear that the preoccupations of *Whirligig* are not always different from those of *The Mountain and the Valley* or *Ox Bells and Fireflies*. However, gone from the selections is the love affair with language which made Buckler's elegiac earlier works such exciting and breathtaking reading. A sense of humor and irony may have been the safety valves which kept the author balanced between despair and hope as he wrote the five other books, but Claude Bissell's suggestion in the introduction to *Whirligig* that this is a book about communalism, not individualism, does not offset the clichéd quality of its comic observations when measured against the sensitive imagery of Buckler's earlier writing. In many respects the worldly wise narrator of many of the *Whirligig* sketches reminds one of the glib

American author, Morse Halliday, in *The Cruelest Month*. There may be truth and even occasional sensitivity behind what each says, but there seems to be a spiritual shallowness in each that is never found in David Canaan of *The Mountain and the Valley* or the old farmer in *Nova Scotia*.

In his later years ill health affected Buckler's output, and as a result no book-length work appeared after *Whirligig*. Nonetheless, Buckler continues to enjoy a major literary reputation in Canada, a fact recognized in his lifetime by his being awarded honorary degrees, Canada Council Senior Arts fellowships, a Canadian Centennial Medal, the Order of Canada, the Stephen Leacock Medal for Humour, and various other literary honors. His novel *The Mountain and the Valley* still stands as his major achievement, but in all his works he succeeded in imaginatively translating his rural Nova Scotian environment and characters into universal terms. Ultimately, Buckler's style is the most lingering quality one carries away from a reading of his books. A master of fresh, imaginative similes; of dizzying crescendos of sensations and details; and of tender moments suspended in time, Buckler caught in his works the cultural texture of an entire society. In the words of William French, "Those of us who grew up in a world different from Buckler's Nova Scotia have to take it on faith that such a world did—and does—exist. But he makes it seem very real, which is the measure of his art."

Interview:

Donald Cameron, "Ernest Buckler: A Conversation with an Irritated Oyster," in his *Conversations with Canadian Novelists*, volume 1 (Toronto: Macmillan, 1973), pp. 3-11.

Bibliographies:

Michael Gnarowski, "Buckler, Ernest, 1908- ," in his *A Concise Bibliography of English-Canadian Literature* (Toronto: McClelland & Stewart, 1978);

John Orange, "Ernest Buckler: An Annotated Bibliography," in *The Annotated Bibliography of Canada's Major Authors*, edited by Robert Lecker and Jack David, volume 3 (Downsview, Ontario: ECW, 1981), pp. 8-56.

References:

Douglas Barbour, "David Canaan: The Failing Heart," *Studies in Canadian Literature*, 1 (Winter 1976): 64-75;

Claude Bissell, "Ernest Buckler: His Prose Reads Like Poetry," *Globe and Mail* (Toronto), 7 March 1984, p. 13;

Bissell, Introduction to Buckler's *The Mountain and the Valley*, New Canadian Library, no. 23 (Toronto: McClelland & Stewart, 1961), pp. vii-xii;

Bissell, Introduction to Buckler's *Whirligig: Selected Prose and Verse* (Toronto: McClelland & Stewart, 1977), pp. 7-9;

Robert Chambers, *Sinclair Ross and Ernest Buckler* (Toronto: Copp Clark, 1975);

Marilyn Chapman, "The Progress of David's Imagination," *Studies in Canadian Literature*, 3 (Summer 1978): 186-198;

Gregory M. Cook, ed., *Ernest Buckler* (Toronto: McGraw-Hill Ryerson, 1972);

Gwendolyn Davies, "Ernest Redmond Buckler (1908-1984)," *Canadian Literature*, 103 (Winter 1984): 187-189;

L. M. Doerksen, "*The Mountain and the Valley*: An Evaluation," *World Literature Written in English*, 19 (Spring 1980): 45-56;

D. J. Dooley, *The Moral Vision in the Canadian Novel* (Toronto: Clarke, Irwin, 1979);

Dooley, "Style and Communication in *The Mountain and the Valley*," *Dalhousie Review*, 57 (Winter 1977-1978): 671-683;

Margery Fee, "Ernest Buckler's 'The Mountain and the Valley' and 'That Dangerous Supplement . . . ,'" *Ariel*, 19 (January 1988): 71-80;

William French, "In Buckler Country, Neighbour is a Holy Word," *Globe and Mail* (Toronto), 2 June 1973, p. 36;

Arnold Gingrich, *Nothing But People: The Early Days at Esquire* (New York: Crown, 1971);

J. M. Kertzer, "The Past Recaptured," *Canadian Literature*, 65 (Summer 1975): 74-85;

Bruce MacDonald, "Word-Shapes, Time and the Theme of Isolation in *The Mountain and the Valley*," *Studies in Canadian Literature*, 1 (Summer 1976): 194-209;

John Moss, *Patterns of Isolation in English-Canadian Fiction* (Toronto: McClelland & Stewart, 1974);

Moss, *Sex and Violence in the Canadian Novel: The Ancestral Present* (Toronto: McClelland & Stewart, 1977);

Gerald Noonan, "Egoism and Style in *The Mountain and the Valley*," in *Atlantic Provinces Literature Colloquium Papers* (Halifax, Nova Scotia: Atlantic Canada Institute, 1977), pp. 68-78;

Laurence Ricou, "David Canaan and Buckler's Style in *The Mountain and the Valley*," *Dalhousie Review*, 57 (Winter 1977-1978): 684-696;

Eileen Sarkar, *"The Mountain and the Valley:* The Infinite Language of Human Relations," *Revue de l'Université d'Ottawa*, 44 (July-September 1974): 354-361;

Andrew Seaman, "Fiction in Atlantic Canada," *Canadian Literature*, 68-69 (Spring-Summer 1976): 26-39;

D. O. Spettigue, "The Way It Was," *Canadian Literature*, 32 (Spring 1967): 40-56;

Warren Tallman, "Wolf in the Snow," *Canadian Literature*, 5 (1960): 7-20; 6 (1960): 41-48;

A. M. Westwater, "Teufelsdrockh is alive and doing well in Nova Scotia: Carlylean Strains in *The Mountain and the Valley*," *Dalhousie Review*, 56 (Summer 1976): 291-298;

Alan Young, *Ernest Buckler* (Toronto: McClelland & Stewart, 1976);

Young, "The Genesis of Ernest Buckler's *The Mountain and the Valley*," *Journal of Canadian Fiction*, no. 16 (1976): 89-96;

Young, Introduction to Buckler's *The Cruelest Month*, New Canadian Library, no. 139 (Toronto: McClelland & Stewart, 1977), pp. vii-xiii;

Young, Introduction to Buckler's *Ox Bells and Fireflies*, New Canadian Library, no. 99 (Toronto: McClelland & Stewart, 1974), pp. xi-xvi;

Young, "A Note on Douglas Barbour's 'David Canaan: The Failing Heart,'" *Studies in Canadian Literature*, 1 (Summer 1976): 244-246;

Young, "The Pastoral Vision of Ernest Buckler in *The Mountain and the Valley*," *Dalhousie Review*, 53 (1976): 219-226.

Papers:
The Ernest Buckler Manuscript Collection, Thomas Fisher Rare Book Library, University of Toronto, contains the main body of Buckler's manuscripts and correspondence. The Ernest Buckler Collection, Public Archives of Nova Scotia, Halifax, Nova Scotia, has correspondence, manuscripts, personal books, journals, reviews, audio tapes, and newspaper clippings given to the archives after Buckler's death in 1984; the collection is closed until 2014 except with permission of the donor. The Archibald MacMechan Papers, Dalhousie University Archives, includes Buckler's correspondence with MacMechan in the 1920s and 1930s.

Morley Callaghan
(22 February 1903-   )

William Dunn

BOOKS: *Strange Fugitive* (New York: Scribners, 1928; Edmonton: Hurtig, 1970);

A Native Argosy (New York: Scribners, 1929; Toronto: Macmillan, 1929);

It's Never Over (New York: Scribners, 1930; Toronto: Macmillan, 1930);

No Man's Meat (Paris: Edward W. Titus, At the Sign of the Black Manikin, 1931);

A Broken Journey (New York: Scribners, 1932; Toronto: Macmillan, 1932);

Such Is My Beloved (New York & London: Scribners, 1934; Toronto: Macmillan, 1934);

They Shall Inherit the Earth (New York: Random House, 1935; Toronto: Macmillan, 1935; London: Chatto & Windus, 1936);

Now That April's Here and Other Stories (New York: Random House, 1936; Toronto: Macmillan, 1936);

More Joy in Heaven (New York: Random House, 1937; Toronto: Macmillan, 1937);

Luke Baldwin's Vow (Philadelphia: Winston, 1948; Toronto: Winston, 1948);

The Varsity Story (Toronto: Macmillan, 1948);

The Loved and the Lost (New York: Macmillan, 1951; Toronto: Macmillan, 1951; London: MacGibbon & Kee, 1961);

Morley Callaghan's Stories (1 volume, Toronto: Macmillan, 1959; 2 volumes, London: MacGibbon & Kee, 1962, 1964);

The Many Colored Coat (New York: Coward-McCann, 1960; Toronto: Macmillan, 1960; London: MacGibbon & Kee, 1963);

A Passion in Rome (New York: Coward-McCann, 1961; Toronto: Macmillan, 1961; London: MacGibbon & Kee, 1964);

That Summer in Paris: Memories of Tangled Friendships with Hemingway, Fitzgerald and Some Others (New York: Coward-McCann, 1963; Toronto: Macmillan, 1963; London: MacGibbon & Kee, 1963);

An Autumn Penitent (Toronto: Macmillan, 1973);

Winter, photographs by John de Visser (Toronto: McClelland & Stewart, 1974; New York: New York Graphic Society, 1974);

Morley Callaghan, early 1960s (photograph by Barry Callaghan)

A Fine and Private Place (New York: Mason & Charter, 1975; Toronto: Macmillan, 1975);

Close to the Sun Again (Toronto: Macmillan, 1977; New York: St. Martin's Press, 1977);

No Man's Meat & The Enchanted Pimp (Toronto: Macmillan, 1978);

A Time for Judas (Toronto: Macmillan, 1983; New York: St. Martin's Press, 1984);

Our Lady of the Snows (Toronto: Macmillan, 1985; New York: St. Martin's Press, 1986);

The Lost and Found Stories of Morley Callaghan (Toronto: Lester & Orpen Dennys/Exile, 1985);
The Man with the Coat (Toronto: Exile, 1987).

PLAY PRODUCTIONS: *To Tell the Truth,* Toronto, New Play Society at the Royal Alexandra Theatre, 7 February 1949;
Going Home, Toronto, New Play Society at Royal Ontario Museum Theatre, 24 March 1950.

OTHER: "Author's Commentary," in *Sixteen by Twelve: Short Stories by Canadian Writers,* edited by John Metcalf (Toronto: Ryerson, 1970), pp. 19-21.

PERIODICAL PUBLICATIONS: "The Plight of Canadian Fiction," *University of Toronto Quarterly,* 7 (January 1938): 152-161;
"An Ocean Away," *Times Literary Supplement,* 4 (June 1964): 493;
Tribute to Robert Weaver, in "Bob Weaver Has Lots of Friends," *Performing Arts in Canada,* 10 (Fall 1973): 15;
"James T. Farrell: A Tribute," *Twentieth Century Literature,* 22 (February 1976): 26-27.

Novelist and short-story writer Morley Callaghan, in the view of many, is Canada's most distinguished writer. He is unquestionably the first to have established a major international reputation, which he started building in the late 1920s in the little magazines of Paris and the slick monthlies of New York where his first short stories appeared. A brief participant in the Lost Generation scene in Paris during the late 1920s, Callaghan returned home to Toronto where he has remained, writing long after his famous contemporaries had died or ceased to be productive.

Writing in a direct, unadorned language from a nonjudgmental point of view, Callaghan has often dealt with the struggle of flawed but noble individuals to make it in a hostile or indifferent world. Although some critics have likened his approach to Hemingway's, Brandon Conron, in his 1966 *Morley Callaghan,* notes this difference: "Moral rather than physical courage is his [Callaghan's] concern." He is an author who has steadfastly gone his own independent way, leaving others to contend with the passing literary fads.

Publisher Thomas McCormack, whose St. Martin's Press brought out three Callaghan novels in recent years, conceded in a 1978 interview that Callaghan may suffer for not being plugged into the latest vogue. "But he is part of the spinal literature of the 20th century that people will remember. There is that feeling in reading Callaghan of being in the real vintage wine."

Edward Morley Callaghan was born in Toronto 22 February 1903, the second of two sons of Thomas and Mary Dewan Callaghan, Roman Catholics of Irish descent. He was named after John Morley, biographer of Edmund Burke. Callaghan was raised in a middle-class home where there was much music and discussion of literature. While attending Riverdale Collegiate, the young Callaghan had his first writing published, a feature article that appeared in the *Star Weekly.* He received twelve dollars for it.

Callaghan enrolled at St. Michael's College, University of Toronto, where he continued to write nonfiction and began experimenting with fiction. He was influenced by American and European writers. "At the time, I was also reading wildly," he recalled in *That Summer in Paris* (1963). "I read Dostoyevski, Joseph Conrad, Sinclair Lewis, Flaubert; *The Dial, The Adelphi,* and the old *Smart Set,* edited by H. L. Mencken and George Jean Nathan; Katherine Mansfield, D. H. Lawrence—everything."

In 1923 he joined the staff of the *Toronto Star.* He got the job by offering to work the first week free. "If I'm any good, keep me on," a confident Callaghan said to a crusty old editor. By the end of the week, Callaghan was given a weekly salary of twenty dollars. He worked as a reporter during summer vacation and three afternoons a week during the school year for the next four years.

He met Ernest Hemingway at the *Toronto Star.* Hemingway, who had been a European correspondent for the *Star,* was back briefly in Toronto writing from the newsroom. The two reporters became friends and often would go to the *Star* library to chat and exchange the short stories they wrote in their spare time. During one of their meetings, Hemingway, Callaghan recalls, told him: "You're a real writer. You write big-time stuff. All you have to do is keep on writing." Hemingway, who was Callaghan's senior by three and a half years, offered to circulate his short stories in Europe when Hemingway returned there.

After graduating from St. Michael's in 1925 with a bachelor of arts degree, Callaghan enrolled in Osgoode Hall Law School in Toronto. While he did graduate from law school three years later and was admitted to the bar,

Callaghan never practiced law, having decided to make a career of writing. "When I finished up my last year, I had a book out already. The natural thing was I figured I was going to be a very big writer," Callaghan once said.

His first short story, "A Girl With Ambition," appeared in the Paris magazine *This Quarter* in 1926. Other early stories soon appeared in *transition* and the *Exile*. These stories brought Callaghan to the attention of F. Scott Fitzgerald, who alerted his editor, Maxwell Perkins of Scribners in New York. At Perkins's invitation, Callaghan came to New York in the winter of 1928 to meet the famous editor. There were no hints of what was to come. Perkins took the nervous and hopeful Torontonian out to lunch. The conversation, by Callaghan's report in *That Summer in Paris*, was rambling and innocuous.

On the way back to Scribners after lunch, the conversation abruptly changed. "Almost as if it had slipped his mind, Perkins said Scribners would publish my novel, and then in the following season they would also like to do a book of short stories." Perkins also scheduled two Callaghan stories for publication in *Scribner's* magazine. The stories appeared in the July 1928 issue. The cover of that issue bore a yellow band that read: "New Fiction Star–Morley Callaghan." Inside the magazine it was noted, "It will be remembered that on the other occasion when we presented two stories in the same number the writer was Ernest Hemingway." That was the first of many times that Callaghan's work would be linked with Hemingway's.

Scribners published Callaghan's first novel, *Strange Fugitive* (1928), a few months later. The book offers a portrayal of Toronto during its years of Prohibition and underworld violence. The main character is bootlegger Harry Trotter, who is caught up in the underworld and his own conflicting emotions. His lust for power and recognition takes him further into the world of crime and eventually destroys him. Callaghan explores the dreariness of the underworld and the price one must pay for the trip through it. The characters are so average, so common, suggesting that anyone could find himself in their situations.

At times melodramatic, with the emotional depth of the main character not fully developed, *Strange Fugitive* remains an ambitious first book, rich in background and plotting, although the dialogue is often forced. Critic and author R. P. Blackmur, in *Hound and Horn* (1929), found the book to be in the "Chicago-Paris-Hemingway measure of hard-boiled realism" and concluded that it "fell short." Cleveland B. Chase, writing in the *New York Times*, judged the novel to be a "distinguished first novel. . . . What he has done he has done well." The book brought its author to the attention of many, especially in the United States, where he received his earliest support.

A Native Argosy, Callaghan's first collection of short stories, was published in 1929. Most of the stories, which were culled from the little magazines and some mass-circulation periodicals, clearly demonstrated Callaghan's superior ability with the short-story format. Many of the locales of the stories are Canadian but the themes are not. Instead the writer deals in universals and themes common to North America, something Callaghan has continued to do, refusing to become a generically Canadian writer.

With two books to his credit, Callaghan married his college sweetheart, Loretto Florence Dee, on 16 April 1929. The couple sailed to Paris for their honeymoon. The trip allowed Callaghan the opportunity to look up his old *Toronto Star* pal Hemingway and to meet Fitzgerald, who had brought him together with Scribners. Callaghan and his wife stayed in Paris seven months. But the trip was to have a lasting and unfortunate influence on Callaghan.

The two former *Star* reporters spent several afternoons in Paris, boxing in the basement of the American Club. Hemingway fancied himself a skilled boxer. Callaghan was, having been a member of the University of Toronto boxing team. During one sparring match in which Fitzgerald served as timekeeper, Callaghan, who stood 5' 8", managed to drop his bigger opponent. Callaghan recalled the incident in his 1963 memoir, *That Summer in Paris*. "Stepping in, I beat him to the punch. The thing must have been just right. I caught him on the jaw; spinning around he went down, sprawled out on his back." By Callaghan's account, Hemingway wasn't hurt, except for his pride. Fitzgerald, for his part, alibied for Hemingway's fall, saying he had mistakenly let the round go on for four minutes, unfairly tiring Hemingway.

The experience strained the friendship between Callaghan and Hemingway. And perhaps worse, it fixed Callaghan in the minds of many as a peripheral character in the Lost Generation saga. In many books on that era and in much that has been written on Callaghan since then, the incident is dredged up; yet often Callaghan's qualities as a writer are dealt with superficially,

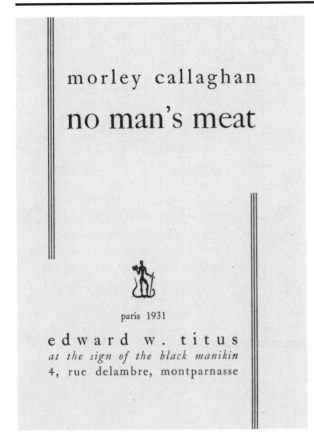

Title page for Callaghan's early novella about a love triangle formed by a man, his wife, and their lesbian friend

or overlooked. Tiring of the Paris scene, Callaghan returned home in the fall of 1929.

Before leaving Paris, Callaghan completed a novella, *No Man's Meat* (1931), and started a novel, *It's Never Over* (1930), which he completed in Toronto. *It's Never Over* deals with the execution of Fred Thompson for murdering a policeman in a speakeasy and the impact the execution has on three friends. The book's title suggests the main themes of the story: the influence of the past on the present and the powerful drive to cling to the past. Although Thompson is dead, his sister Isabelle refuses to accept this fact and go on with her own life. She hounds those who were close to her brother in a confused attempt to somehow keep his memory alive and make sense of his death. Her obsession leads her to ruin the life of Thompson's best friend, John, and to drive him apart from his lover, Lillian.

The repeated confrontations at one point tempt John to kill Isabelle but ultimately they prove cathartic. Isabelle's obsession has exposed and weakened Thompson's friends. But their true feelings and relations are liberated in the process, creating a fragile peace and finally the chance to look to the future. Isabelle's motivation is not sufficiently explained. The dialogue is often wooden and inappropriate for the story's drama. Yet the characters are believable–if bland–and the drama is achieved against a realistic backdrop of Toronto in the 1920s.

F. Scott Fitzgerald was critical of the book in a letter to a friend: "If you think Callaghan hasn't completely blown himself up with this deathhouse masterpiece, just wait and see the pieces fall." But American critic Edmund Wilson, an early supporter of Callaghan, advised him to ignore Fitzgerald's remarks, as Callaghan reported in the 1972 edition of *It's Never Over*. "Scott would know how good a book that was," said Wilson, who believed Fitzgerald's criticism was a result of the fallout from the Paris boxing incident.

Although it would be years before Callaghan returned to Europe, his work continued to appear there. The 1931 novella *No Man's Meat* was published in a signed edition of 525 copies in Paris by Edward W. Titus's Black Manikin press. A daring and unusual book for its time, *No Man's Meat* follows the evolution of a love triangle between a husband and wife and their lesbian friend. Rich in symbolism and irony, *No Man's Meat* contrasts with the author's earlier novels. It is set in the tranquil Canadian lake country, not in the turbulent city, and the characters are more sophisticated than those of the earlier novels.

Bert Beddoes and his wife, Teresa, are a progressive couple who have "gone beyond all undisciplined impulses and had achieved a contented peacefulness." That peacefulness is disrupted and so is Beddoes by the visit of Jean. The self-confident Beddoes longs for Jean and eventually seduces her. But the tables are turned as Beddoes's wife leaves him not because of the seduction but because she too is in love with Jean. Because of the subject matter and the book's limited edition, it drew very little attention for decades.

The 1930s proved a productive period for Callaghan, who saw five novels, a collection of short stories, and the novella published. He also wrote two plays during that decade. The author was hitting his stride and refining his own distinctive style. "Writing had to do with the right relationship between the words and thing or person being described," Callaghan once said. "The words should be as transparent as glass."

A Broken Journey, published in 1932, is a novel of missed opportunities and failed dreams and people's inability to adjust to reality. Peter Gould and his beautiful and impulsive fiancée, Marion, appear to be a happy, secure couple. Yet they are driven apart by Marion's mother, a disappointed woman who pursues Peter to rekindle her own passions. Having lost his fiancée, Peter drifts into a destructive affair with someone new. Subsequent attempts by Marion and Peter to recapture their earlier happiness fail. The author introduces the element of religion into the story in the character of Father Vincent Sullivan, a timid priest whose good intentions and convenient theology cannot help Peter or Marion.

Callaghan, whose own liberal Catholicism was to him simply a fact of life, nevertheless explores religious themes and the Catholic Church more fully in subsequent novels. *Such Is My Beloved,* published in 1934, is a book rich in religious imagery. Father Dowling, "the most eager young priest at the Cathedral," has set out to help and reform two prostitutes, but finds that he is abandoned by his church and parishioners who oppose his efforts, fearing a scandal. The priest's life is the life of Christ as it might be lived in modern times in an urban setting. The action of the book takes place between February and Easter. Like Christ, Father Dowling rises above his own suffering and finds "a peace within him."

Reviews of *Such Is My Beloved* were generally favorable. Critic and author Mary Colum, writing in *Forum and Century* (April 1934), found Callaghan's portrayal of Dowling "drawn with such subtlety and insight that it is powerfully convincing to readers." While faulting him for a style that was "too often queerly pedestrian," Colum nevertheless judged Callaghan a profound and sensitive writer. *Such Is My Beloved* was the last book by Callaghan to be published by Scribners. The parting was amicable.

Random House brought out Callaghan's next novel, *They Shall Inherit the Earth,* which appeared in 1935. Callaghan, still exploring biblical themes in this work, borrowed from the stories of Cain and Abel and the prodigal son. Andrew Aikenhead cajoles his estranged son, Michael, into rejoining the family for a week at the lake to resolve past differences. The reunion fails and ends in tragedy as Dave, the son of Aikenhead's second wife, drowns. What is not known is that Michael contributed to his stepbrother's death by harassing Dave with an oar while he swam and then ignoring Dave's cries for help as he drowned.

Michael's brutality was triggered by resentment of Dave for being the favorite son.

Michael does nothing to correct the assumption of many that his father was somehow responsible for the drowning. It is only at the end that Michael privately admits his guilt to his father. The admission leads to a reconciliation between the two. In a selfless attempt to protect this delicate relationship and his son, Aikenhead sacrifices his own good name by refusing to make public Michael's responsibility for the drowning.

The book is one of Callaghan's longest works. The narrative wanders at times. Despite the length, there is insufficient exploration of Michael's overriding bitterness toward his father. In *O Canada: An American's Notes on Canadian Culture* (1964) Edmund Wilson faulted the novel on that score yet conceded that it was a "rather interesting book, which deals with Canadian life in a somewhat more various way than the author's previous novels."

While writing his novels, Callaghan continued to turn out a steady stream of short stories during much of the 1930s. Thirty-five were gathered together in the 1936 collection titled *Now That April's Here and Other Stories.* Whereas the earlier short story collection contained many pieces that first appeared in the little magazines, this one comprises mostly stories from the slicks: the *New Yorker, Atlantic Monthly, Esquire, Harper's Bazaar,* and others.

A critic for the *New York Times* once said of Callaghan: "If there's a better short-story writer in the world, we don't know where he is." Further tribute to Callaghan's talents as a short-story writer is the fact that he had pieces in fourteen of Edward O'Brien's twenty-six annual anthologies, *The Best Short Stories.* As Brandon Conron notes, Callaghan's short stories follow a "recognizable formula. They are all self-contained anecdotes. Their opening is usually a declarative statement that sets the stage for a drama that most frequently is psychological and involves little action. A problem is posed and, by description, dialogue, and internal monologue, the story moves with easy economy through a climax to an ending which may not resolve the dilemma but invariably leaves it haunting the reader's mind."

Ever the observant reporter, Callaghan often got ideas for his short stories and novels from events happening around him. That was the case with his 1937 novel, *More Joy in Heaven,* which was loosely based on the colorful life of bank robber Red Ryan. After a priest and others in high places secured Ryan's release from a Canadian jail, he vowed he was going straight. Overnight Ryan became a celebrity in Toronto society. His reform ended abruptly one night, however, when he was shot dead in a liquor store holdup.

Callaghan's fictional account of this strange case concerns what went wrong with Kip Caley and the society that would not let him live, except as a curiosity. The novel portrays a prodigal son who painfully discovers that he cannot go home again and live peacefully in an insensitive and contradictory society. As always, in this novel Callaghan writes plainly and directly. There is much religious imagery and also repeated images of imprisonment and freedom. The story is as much a sociological study as it is a novel. While it has been criticized for its melodrama, especially in its ending which has the repentant and misunderstood Caley dying in a burst of bullets, the fiction is mirroring fact.

After publication of *More Joy in Heaven*, Callaghan unexpectedly entered what for him was a dry spell. Although he was involved in other projects, he wrote little fiction from 1938 to 1947. Callaghan has called this "the dark period of my life." The author traced his initial lack of productivity to a numbness triggered by the spreading war in Europe.

His sabbatical from novel and short-story writing was helped along by a flirtation with the theater. In 1938 he was asked by New York Theatre Guild producer Lawrence Langner to write a stage play from his 1935 novel, *They Shall Inherit the Earth*. He did. The result was "Turn Again Home." He wrote a second play that year, "Just Ask for George." Both plays were optioned for Broadway. But neither was produced because of a lack of financial backing and the unavailability of key actors. They were finally staged, under the titles *Going Home* and *To Tell the Truth*, a decade later in Toronto.

In 1940 Callaghan became a regular contributor to *New World*, writing monthly commentaries for the Canadian magazine for the next eight years. He spent the summer of 1942 aboard a Royal Canadian Navy ship, gathering material for a propaganda film for the National Film Board. The film was eventually produced, but Callaghan had dropped out of the project because of artistic and conceptual disagreements.

Looking for new challenges, he joined the on-air staff of the CBC radio program *Things To Come* in 1943. The program, later renamed *The Citizen's Forum*, was on the air until 1947. An offer

Dust jacket for Callaghan's novel set in Montreal, winner of a 1951 Governor General's Award

from Hollywood to become a screenwriter came in 1944. Callaghan turned it down. When asked why, years later, Callaghan shrugged: "It was not a big money deal–$250 a week. I was not at all convinced I would do well in Hollywood. This business of writing commercially is a tricky business."

In 1947 Callaghan joined the panel of the CBC radio quiz show *Beat the Champs*. That show and *The Citizen's Forum* earned Callaghan a mass audience, many of whom were unfamiliar with his novels and stories. It was not until a few years after the war that Callaghan truly returned to his writing. He started in 1947 by turning out short stories and the next year began a new novel, *The Loved and the Lost*, which was finally published in 1951.

Two minor works were published in 1948, *Luke Baldwin's Vow*, a juvenile novel expanded from a *Saturday Evening Post* story, and *The Varsity Story*, a fictionalized account of life at the University of Toronto. The latter was commissioned by the university for a fund-raising campaign.

In the early 1950s Callaghan continued his radio appearances as a regular on the CBC show *Now I Ask You* and began appearing on television as a panelist on the show *Fighting Words*. The moderator of the program was the influential theater critic Nathan Cohen; other panelists included poet Earle Birney, lawyer Frank Turpane, and Ottawa Mayor Charlotte Whilton. One of the benefits of Callaghan's radio and television work was the travel it afforded to other Canadian cities, where Callaghan constantly looked for material for his fiction. He found it in Montreal, then as now, Canada's most exotic and wide-open city. He used the French city as the backdrop for *The Loved and the Lost*. The book explores the then explosive topic of relations between whites and blacks. It is one of Callaghan's best and strongest books.

Peggy Sanderson, an attractive white woman concerned with the plight of blacks, seeks to befriend and help them. To that end, she spends much time in the black clubs and neighborhoods of Montreal, arousing the ire of Montreal's white establishment and the suspicions of blacks. Her journey into the black world strains her relationship with Professor Jim McAlpine, an urbane intellectual whose liberal values are found to be sorely wanting. Peggy's simple decency and humanity provoke such hatred that she is eventually murdered.

With this book Callaghan effectively explores the weaknesses of the human soul and the gap between intentions and actions and what is and should be. It is a perceptive exploration of race relations, years ahead of its time. The book, which Edmund Wilson called "remarkable," sold over 500,000 copies in paperback alone. It was adapted as a musical for Broadway but was not produced because of lack of financing.

The Loved and the Lost won Canada's Governor General's Award for fiction in 1951, the first of several major awards Callaghan was to receive. Four years later Callaghan won the $5,000 fiction prize of *Maclean's* magazine (16 April 1955) for the novella "The Man With the Coat," which appeared in the magazine on 16 April 1955, and which was published in book form in 1987 by Exile Press, a Toronto firm run by Callaghan's son, the writer Barry Callaghan.

Although he had a lifelong commitment to fiction, Callaghan maintained a friendly if distant relationship with Toronto's newspapers, taking on special assignments over the years. He went to Rome in 1958 on a special assignment for the *To-ronto Star Weekly* magazine to cover the death of Pope Pius XII and the election of his successor, Pope John XXIII.

Callaghan's third collection of short stories was published in 1959 under the title *Morley Callaghan's Stories*. Forty-four of the stories come from his early collections. Another twelve, written from 1936 to 1953, appear for the first time in book form. In the introduction to the collection, the author wrote: "I can see that I have been concerned with the problems of many kinds of people but I have neglected those of the very, very rich. I have a story that begins, 'Once upon a time there were two millionaires,' but I haven't finished it yet."

Callaghan, in fact, never put the wealthy in his novels. However, in his 1960 novel, *The Many Colored Coat,* which was adapted from the novella "The Man With the Coat," he focuses on the world of the high-level executive. Harry Lane, Callaghan's protagonist, is a successful, young public-relations officer for a Montreal distillery. A man on the corporate fast track, Lane rises quickly. He innocently becomes involved in a shady oil scheme. When it fails, others look for a scapegoat and find it in Lane. An honorable if naive man, Lane sets out to prove his innocence. But no one will listen. He becomes a sorry figure around Montreal, constantly wearing a tailor-made suit from his better days. The suit is the symbol of his former power and the truth that others refuse to see. Like the biblical Joseph of the many-colored coat, Lane is wrongly accused and persecuted yet forgives his accusers.

While biblical themes abound, the novel tells a secular story of the duplicity of corporate life and modern values. The scenes of the power establishment and boardroom politics are insightful. This book, like so many of Callaghan's, divided the critics, including those in his own country. In a letter to Callaghan Canadian novelist Hugh MacLennan contended *The Many Colored Coat* "is over most people's heads, and possibly mine, also. . . . To me this is a deeply disturbing, rather wonderful and hard-to-comprehend novel." George Woodcock, editor of the quarterly *Canadian Literature,* complained in the summer 1964 issue that the novel was too long and that it hovers "uneasily between sharpness of caricature and the flabbiness of sentimental pseudo-realism." Edmund Wilson examined the response of critics and the public to Callaghan's novels in "Morley Callaghan of Toronto," a 1960 profile in the *New Yorker*. He concluded that the

Dust jacket for the first American edition of Callaghan's 1961 novel that draws on his coverage of Pius XII's death for the Toronto Star Weekly *magazine*

endings of Callaghan's books are possibly "too bleak for the ordinary reader, who may already have been disconcerted by beginning what seems to be an ordinary novel." Wilson further wonders "whether the primary reason for the current underestimation of Morley Callaghan may not be simply a general incapacity–apparently shared by his compatriots–for believing that a writer whose works may be mentioned without absurdity in association with Chekhov's and Turgenev's can possibly be functioning in Toronto." Coincidentally, the Royal Society of Canada awarded Callaghan the Lorne Pierce Medal for Literature the same year that Wilson's piece appeared. The society gave Callaghan the prize not for a single work but for "a body of work which will endure."

Since 1952 Callaghan had been living in a handsome house in the exclusive Rosedale neighborhood of Toronto. There he settled easily into a quiet existence, writing most days in a second-floor study and receiving the occasional literary visitor in his comfortable first-floor library. Callaghan has described his home in Toronto as his "monastery," a place of solitude, admittedly far removed from the excitement and connec-

tions of the literary nerve center in New York City. Yet he has found Toronto a "really true world," free of distractions, a place where he has had the peace to pursue his own creativity.

The year 1961 saw publication of *A Passion in Rome*, a novel that draws on his 1958 coverage of Pope Pius XII's death. Sam Raymond, a tough and experienced photographer in Rome to cover the election of a new pope, falls in love with a beautiful but troubled American expatriate, singer Carla Caneli. Sam sets out to rehabilitate the alcoholic woman. To salvage Carla's life would be, for Raymond, to create the masterpiece he never painted as a failed artist. He does succeed in rehabilitating her life and career. But that success ends their love affair as a strong and confident Carla leaves to resume her vocation. Devastated at first, Raymond eventually realizes it as his own artistic triumph. "No matter how I feel," he says, "she still gives me a tremendous pride in life."

The book elicited an immediate, sharp response from the critics. Columbia University professor Robert Gorham Davis, writing in the *New York Times Book Review* of 15 October 1961, dismissed the characters as "insensitive, vulgar, and above all unconvincing." Davis finds "very disturbing . . . the involvement of the dead Pope's image with Sam's erotic designs on Carla." Yet a *Newsweek* critic said the book was "gripping and inspiring; original and powerful," and British novelist and critic Anthony Ward noted *A Passion in Rome* was "a distinguished book and it requires and merits very careful reading."

Mixed reviews weren't the only problem Callaghan had to face in the early 1960s. There was also the ghost of Ernest Hemingway. Hemingway's suicide caused many writers to rediscover the fact that Callaghan had been an early friend of his. The burgeoning Hemingway industry revived interest in Callaghan. Editors and reporters began calling Callaghan for his memories of the early days with Hemingway. Callaghan, with good reason, eventually tired of it all, especially the reporters' rehashing of the unfortunate boxing match.

Callaghan decided to set the record straight with his 1963 book, *That Summer in Paris: Memories of Tangled Friendships with Hemingway, Fitzgerald and Some Others*. The book presents an insider's view of Paris in 1929. While Callaghan does recall many light and interesting moments, his overall view is not flattering. He remembers the pettiness, jealousies, and competitiveness of many in Paris then. The best part of the memoir deals with Callaghan's relationships with Hemingway and Fitzgerald and the sparring match that brought them together for an afternoon and drove them apart for a lifetime. The three begin to emerge not simply as friends but as proud stars on the same team, Scribners, all of them competing for the literary championship. "The irony of events kept tormenting me. I had gone to Paris, confident that I would find there a deepening friendship with Ernest, and a fine warm intimacy with Scott. I had found some strange tangled relationships between Scott and Ernest, but there had been a lot of admiration and respect, too. Out of my hopeful eager journey had come all this shameful petty rancor and wounded vanity, and suspicion."

The book may have settled matters on what transpired in Paris in 1929 but it fed the debate among critics over Callaghan's merits as a writer. Norman Mailer wrote, in his *Cannibals and Christians*, 1966, of *That Summer in Paris:* "It is not a good book. It is in fact a modest bad dull book which contains a superb short story about Hemingway, Fitzgerald, and Callaghan." William Saroyan

said of the book: "Times change, the world changes, and that had been a time, and a world. And those were writers, and one of them, Morley Callaghan, writing easily, has kept the whole thing real in all of its youth and sorrow."

By the time *That Summer in Paris* was published most of the participants of that summer were years dead. Callaghan had become the last of the Lost Generation. A few years later he became embroiled in a revealing flap in his native country. The Canadian government (belatedly, in the opinion of many) recognized their native son with plans to make him an Officer of the Order of Canada in 1967. He surprised everyone by rejecting the honor because it was as "Officer," which was one step below the Order's Companion level of recognition that had been awarded to some other writers. Callaghan viewed the Order of Canada medal as a slight. "If they want to toss medals in my direction, make sure they're the good ones." Two "good medals," or at least tangible honors, did come his way: the $15,000 Molson Prize and the $50,000 Royal Bank Award. Both were presented in 1970 in recognition of Callaghan's contribution to literature.

Despite the resulting financial security and his advanced years, Callaghan felt compelled to keep up a steady writing pace. In 1974 *Winter* was published. It is a minor book, a collection of photos of Canadian winters taken by John de Visser with a short accompanying text by Callaghan.

Callaghan's curious but interesting novel, *A Fine and Private Place*, appeared the following year. This work is Callaghan's rebuttal to his critics and his declaration of literary principles. The book is a roman à clef with Callaghan appearing in the disguise of the main character, novelist Eugene Shore.

Shore lives and writes quietly in Toronto. An Edmund Wilson-type character, Starkey Kunitz, stirs up a hornet's nest in literary circles with his lavish praise for Shore's talents. Al Delaney, an insecure young academic, is aroused by the controversy and decides to write the definitive biography of Shore as the fastest way to make his own mark in the literary world. Delaney becomes obsessed with Shore, alternately respecting and resenting the man, his success, and his work. Delaney's obsession blinds him to the meaning of Shore's writing. When Shore dies suddenly, Delaney and others are left to try to discover the truth about the man and his work.

Callaghan in the late 1970s (photograph by William Dunn)

Delaney finally does understand Shore's work in which the establishment is often portrayed as immoral and the supposed outlaws of that society are, in fact, criminal-saints. A revealing passage in the book comes just before Shore's death. He says: " 'Al wonders why I haven't reached for a headline by stabbing my wife in the belly, why I haven't put on big alcoholic scenes in bars. Right, Al? Wrestled lions in Africa?' He snorted with contempt. 'For what? To be loved here as a big public personality? What would it make me?' " Lisa responds to Shore: " 'The town whore I suppose.' "

While the book is not without self-indulgence, the underlying story of a literary man's hold on the lives and minds of others is a solid one. Brandon Conron called *A Fine and Private Place* "an absorbing tale . . . an unashamed defense of his narrative technique, a scathing and often hilarious rebuke to academically hidebound critics."

While Callaghan's short stories have not been in the major slick magazines for many years, his work began turning up during the

1970s in *Exile,* a small Canadian literary quarterly. *Exile* became Callaghan's laboratory, running excerpts from his works-in-progress. One such work-in-progress became the novel *Close to the Sun Again,* published in 1977. In this work, Ira Groome, an outwardly successful man, discovers at the height of his career that his lifelong pursuit of power and wealth has left him burned out. After a drunken car accident, Groome clings to life in a hospital. His dazed mind flashes back thirty years and unlocks the hidden cause of his unhappiness–the loss of a mysterious woman whom he had loved.

The book, one of Callaghan's shorter novels, is taut and sparely written. Callaghan said of the book, "I think the writing is awful good. I am proud of it." Lapsing into the jargon of the boxing ring, he added: "I've got to lick them with this new book–those guys out there." "Them," of course, were the critics. Unfortunately the book was published in the United States during a newspaper strike in New York and thus valuable exposure was lost, adversely affecting U.S. sales. In Canada, however, critic George Woodcock, who

Born in Toronto in 1903, Morley Callaghan is a graduate of the University of Toronto and of Osgoode Hall. He was called to the bar in 1928 but never practised; his part-time work as a cub reporter on the *Toronto Star* alongside Ernest Hemingway had infected him with the ambition to be a full-time writer, and his short stories were being sold to prominent magazines. Although he has travelled widely, and lived for some time in Paris during the golden years of Hemingway and Fitzgerald (recalled in *That Summer in Paris*), Callaghan has spent most of his life in Toronto, quietly producing a stream of novels which have gained him admiration around the world and a nomination for the Nobel Prize in Literature.

A Fine and Private Place is his seventeenth published work. His outstanding contribution to Canadian literature has been recognized by a number of honours, including the Governor General's Award and the Canada Council Medal. Callaghan is married and has two sons.

ISBN 0-7705-1277-1

Dust jacket for Callaghan's roman à clef in which he appears as the novelist Eugene Shore

had panned previous books by Callaghan, described this one as "the best writing Callaghan had done in forty years." The Toronto *Globe and Mail* named it "the best Canadian novel" of the year.

Callaghan saw a slightly revised version of his underground novella, *No Man's Meat,* published in 1978 in a trade edition. Macmillan of Canada published the story along with a new novella titled *The Enchanted Pimp.* The new story covers some familiar Callaghan ground with new twists. A pimp, hiding behind a veneer of respectability, seeks to salvage yet exploit a noble prostitute who is struggling in a corrupt world. The two stories were not published in the United States.

In his later years, Callaghan seems to have stepped up his pace, at least his rate of publications. His novel *A Time for Judas* appeared in Canada in 1983 and the following year in the United States. It is a daring and most intriguing book, proof that Callaghan has not lost his special touch and talent. The book tells a dramatic new version of the story of Christ's crucifixion and resurrection. The fictional vehicle for this audacious re-creation of Christ's final days is the narrator's

discovery of a manuscript from the period written by Philo of Crete, the scribe to Pontius Pilate. The manuscript is discovered by a modern archaeologist, setting the stage for what follows: Callaghan's engaging and provocative rewriting of biblical history. For the most part, reviews were positive. The critic for the *New Yorker* said of the book: "Mr. Callaghan's writing is clear and cool. . . . His account of the arrest of Jesus the Galilean, . . . the trial, and the crucifixion and its aftermath is as vivid as a story never told before. And its essence is bold and darkly persuasive."

In 1984, after fifty-five years of marriage, Callaghan's wife, Loretto, died. The author stayed on, alone, in the Toronto house that they had shared. Two grown sons, Barry and Michael, and their families live in the area.

Within the space of several months, Callaghan saw two more books published in his native Canada and in the United States, where he had made it big so many years ago. *Our Lady of the Snows,* a full-length novel that is a reworked and greatly expanded version of the novella *The Enchanted Pimp,* appeared in Canada in 1985 and in the United States in early 1986. Also, in 1985, the Canadian publishing house of Lester &

Orpen Dennys, in conjunction with Exile Editions, brought out a short-story collection titled *The Lost and Found Stories of Morley Callaghan*. The collection includes twenty-six short stories never published in book form before. The stories, however, are among Callaghan's best, having appeared from 1930 to the 1950s in such magazines as *Esquire*, the *New Yorker, Harper's Bazaar,* and the *Yale Review,* among others. The collection was put together by Barry Callaghan, a university literature professor, in tribute to his father. "Since I've got two books out in a year's time, I don't know if I should speed up or sit back for a while," joked Callaghan in early 1986.

But, not one to sit back and take things easy, Morley Callaghan started in on yet another book. It is not the memoirs that friends and publishers urged him to write. "Many people have asked me to go on with my memoir. I can't bear to write it. I would somehow feel that it means I was through as a writer." Instead, Callaghan is immersed in a new work of fiction. "You always hope, if I do get this right, it will be the one that throws light on what you've done before," he observed. "This will make it all clear."

Callaghan continues to write. And his books continue to sell steadily, not only the more recent ones but the reprints of his earliest works as well. The late novelist James T. Farrell observed in a 1973 *Publishers Weekly* interview that of all the writers in their generation: "I think now that he [Callaghan] may be the best writer of the lot."

Interview:

Donald Cameron, "Morley Callaghan: There are Gurus in the Woodwork," in his *Conversations with Canadian Novelists, Part Two* (Toronto: Macmillan, 1973).

Biographies:

Victor Hoar, *Morley Callaghan* (Toronto: Copp Clark, 1969);

Patricia Morley, *Morley Callaghan* (Toronto: McClelland & Stewart, 1978).

References:

Walter Allen, *The Short Story in English* (Oxford: Clarendon, 1981);

Donald R. Bartlett, "Callaghan's 'Troubled (and Troubling)' Heroines," *University of Windsor Review*, 16 (Fall-Winter 1981): 60-72;

E. L. Boback, "Seeking 'Direct, Honest, Realism': The Canadian Novel of the 1920s," *Cana-*

dian Literature, 89 (Summer 1981): 84, 97, 99, 100;

Matthew J. Bruccoli, "Interview with Allen Tate," in *Fitzgerald/Hemingway Annual 1974*, edited by Bruccoli and C. E. Frazer Clark, Jr. (Englewood, Col.: Microcard, 1975), p. 104;

Brandon Conron, *Morley Callaghan* (New York: Twayne, 1966);

Conron, "Morley Callaghan as a Short Story Writer," *Journal of Commonwealth Literature*, 3 (July 1967): 58-75;

Conron, ed., *Morley Callaghan, Critical Views on Canadian Writers* (Toronto: McGraw-Hill Ryerson, 1975);

Wilf Cude, "Morley Callaghan's Practical Monsters: Downhill from Where and When?," in *Modern Times: A Critical Anthology*, edited by John Moss (Toronto: NC, 1982), pp. 69-78;

Hallvard Dahlie, "Destructive Innocence in the Novel of Morley Callaghan," *Journal of Canadian Fiction*, 1 (Summer 1972): 39-42;

D. J. Dooley, "The Leopard and the Church: The Ambiguities of Morley Callaghan," in his *Moral Vision in the Canadian Novel* (Toronto: Clarke, Irwin, 1979), pp. 61-77;

John Glassco, *Memoirs of Montparnasse* (Toronto: Oxford University Press, 1970), pp. 88-91, 97-102, 221;

Journal of Canadian Studies, special issue on Callaghan, edited by Ralph Heintzmann, 15 (Spring 1980);

Judith Kendle, "Callaghan and the Church," *Canadian Literature*, 80 (Spring 1979): 13-22;

Kendle, "Callaghan as Columnist, 1940-48," *Canadian Literature*, 82 (Autumn 1979): 6-20;

Kendle, "Spiritual Tiredness and Dryness of the Imagination: Social Criticism in the Novels of Morley Callaghan," *Journal of Canadian Fiction*, 16 (1976): 115-130;

Margaret Lawrence, "Morley Callaghan," *Saturday Night*, 14 July 1928, pp. 8, 11;

Tom Marshall, "Tragic Ambivalence: The Novels of Morley Callaghan," *University of Windsor Review*, 12 (Fall-Winter 1976): 33-48;

Robin Mathews, "Morley Callaghan and the New Colonialism: The Supreme Individual in Traditionless Society," *Studies in Canadian Literature*, 3 (Winter 1978): 78-92;

Robert L. McDougall, "The Dodo and the Cruising Auk: Class in Canadian Literature," *Canadian Literature*, 18 (Autumn 1963): 11, 13-14, 17;

John J. O'Connor, "Fraternal Twins: The Impact of Jacques Maritain on Callaghan and

Charbonneau," *Mosaic,* 14 (Spring 1981): 145-163;

John Orange, "Lines of Ascent: Hugh Hood's Place in Canadian Fiction," *Essays on Canadian Writing,* 13-14 (Winter-Spring 1978-1979): 119, 120, 123-126, 127;

David Staines, ed., *The Callaghan Symposium* (Ottawa: University of Ottawa Press, 1981);

Fraser Sutherland, *The Style of Innocence: A Study of Hemingway and Callaghan* (Toronto: Clarke, Irwin, 1972);

William Walsh, "Morley Callaghan," in his *A Manifold Voice: Studies in Commonwealth Literature* (New York: Barnes & Noble, 1970), pp. 185-212;

F. W. Watt, "Morley Callaghan as Thinker," *Dalhousie Review,* 39 (Autumn 1959): 305-313;

Edmund Wilson, "Morley Callaghan of Toronto," *New Yorker,* 36 (26 November 1960): 224-237;

George Woodcock, "Callaghan's Toronto: The Persona of a City," *Journal of Canadian Studies,* 7 (August 1972): 21-24.

Papers:

Individual items of Callaghan's papers appear in archival collections at York University Library, Downsview, Ontario; The University of Toronto Library; Concordia University Library, Montreal (Radio Drama Collections); Queen's University Library, Kingston, Ontario (Lorne Pierce Papers); McMaster University Library, Hamilton (Macmillan Papers); the Metropolitan Toronto Library; and the Public Archives of Canada, Ottawa.

Emily Carr

(13 December 1871–2 March 1945)

George Woodcock

SELECTED BOOKS: *Klee Wyck* (Toronto & New York: Oxford University Press, 1941);

The Book of Small (Toronto: Oxford University Press, 1942; London & New York: Oxford University Press, 1943);

The House of All Sorts (Toronto & London: Oxford University Press, 1944);

Growing Pains: The Autobiography of Emily Carr (Toronto: Oxford University Press, 1946);

The Heart of a Peacock, edited by Ira Dilworth (Toronto: Oxford University Press, 1953);

Pause: A Sketch Book, edited by Dilworth (Toronto: Clarke, Irwin, 1953);

Hundreds and Thousands: The Journals of Emily Carr (Toronto & Vancouver: Clarke, Irwin, 1966).

Everything important came late in Emily Carr's life. Now she is recognized as one of the most vital modern Canadian painters, and her memoirs and diaries hold a high place among Canadian autobiographical writings. Yet she did not have her first major exhibition of paintings until she was fifty-six, after being ignored through the decades of hard work in which she formed her style. And she did not publish her first book until she was seventy. Indeed, she had only started writing a few years before then, when her health made it impossible for her to paint with such vigor as she had done in the past, and she needed a new channel through which her creative energies could flow. But when she did begin, she wrote immediately with the kind of ease that usually comes from years of practice, and she applied to her new art all the clarity of observation and vividness of presentation she had developed in her painting. But she added also a sense of comedy that finds little scope for expression in her visual art, and a sharp perception of the frailties of human beings and the virtues of animals, whom–as she looked out of the heart of her irremediable loneliness–she preferred.

Emily Carr was born in 1871, into an English family that had settled in Victoria. Her father, Richard Carr, was a merchant who had come via the California goldfields and acquired a

Emily Carr, 1904 (private collection)

where she went in 1899 and worked and studied for five years, and in France, where she went in 1910 and stayed a year.

Much more important in ultimate consequence was the visit she made in 1898 to the Indian villages of the ocean shore of northern Vancouver Island. Here she did her first sketches of the Coast Indians and their vanishing totemic art and tried to capture on whatever surface was available—paper, cardboard, or canvas—the feeling of the dense primeval forests of the Pacific coast. She had found her inspiring ambience and her inexhaustible subject. Apart from technique, the academies of Europe and North America had little to teach her, for what she saw in British Columbia, in its landscapes and ways of life, was a very personal vision, and she had to find her own way to express it.

She was not moving artistically in what, for Edwardian western Canada, was a popular direction, and by the time she returned from France to Victoria in 1911 at the age of forty, it was evident that she could not earn a living by painting. She turned her home into a boardinghouse and supplemented her living in other ways, such as breeding sheepdogs and making ceramic objects for sale to the tourists. All this interfered with her painting, and for the next fifteen years the only times she could devote herself wholeheartedly to art were the summers she spent working among the Indians of the Queen Charlotte Islands and the northern rivers, the Skeena and the Nass. But it was in these brief interludes that she finally found herself as a painter, developing her own striking color spectrum and mastering the strange alterations of shadow and light that characterize the coastal world. Perhaps to an aesthetic purist the content of her paintings, their haunting evocation of the loneliness and pathos of the Indian villages with their decaying poles, would seem of secondary interest, but to Carr it was of prime importance. If she was not a literary painter in the sense of trying to create stories on canvas, there was always a strong poetic element in her work, at once reminiscent and elegiac, and this element in her pictorial art later found another way of expression in her writing.

Not until 1927 did Carr begin to receive the recognition she deserved and, indeed, expected. Marius Barbeau had drawn the attention of National Gallery officials to her work, and in that year the first major exhibition of her work was held in Ottawa. Not only did it bring the beginnings of public recognition, but, perhaps more im-

house on the half-rural verge of Beacon Hill Park. Victoria was then a tiny city which the gold rushes of the 1850s and 1860s had changed from the fur-trading post of earlier decades, but it was still a remote place on an ultimate frontier. British Columbia had joined Canada only a few months before Carr's birth, and Victoria was still the destination for many parties of Indians from the northern coast of British Columbia.

As Carr grew into adolescence, she developed patterns of frustration in her life that remained with her to the end. Her mother—also Emily Carr—died when Carr was twelve and her father when she was fourteen. She grew into young womanhood under the tutelage of a strait-laced elder sister who did not sympathize with her developing passion for art. In 1891, however, having won her guardian's sympathy, she was able to leave home and take up studies at the California School of Design in San Francisco. She remained there for more than three years, but the experience had remarkably little evident effect on her later development as a painter, and the same applies to subsequent periods in England,

Carr in her studio, October 1933 (photograph by H. U. Knight, courtesy of the Victoria City Archives)

portant for Carr, it also introduced her to artists who saw with eyes like hers. The Group of Seven (Franklin Carmichael, Lawren Harris, A. Y. Jackson, Franz H. Johnston, Arthur Lismer, J. E. H. MacDonald, and F. Horsman Varley) took her to their collective heart. Harris became a close friend who encouraged her to continue in the way of painting she had chosen. In the eyes of her Victoria neighbors she was still an eccentric aging woman who went shopping with a perambulator whose passengers were cats, dogs, and her favorite monkey. But she had moved personally as well as pictorially into the mainstream of modern Canadian painting, and it was during the decade after the National Gallery Exhibition that she painted the great interpretations of the coastal forest which are now regarded as her finest work.

The year 1937–the end of the great decade of painting–represented the major shift in the direction of Carr's creativity. She found she was suffering from heart disease. She had to give up her summer trips to the Indian villages. Though she did not entirely abandon her painting, she had to paint less. But the urge to create was as demanding as ever, and when she could not paint all day, she turned to writing.

Carr was not an intellectual, and her major passions–those that really possessed her–were visual. Nothing she ever wrote could even begin to rival in incandescent intensity such paintings of the magic decade as *Stumps and Sky* (probably 1934) or *Scorned as Timber, Beloved of the Sky* (1935). But she did present, among her various books, an unusual exercise in autobiography which is not only the account of a rather lonely, frustrated, yet in the end triumphant life, but also an exemplary narrative of the maturing of artistic creativity.

The first of the autobiographical books, *Klee Wyck* (the title of which Carr assures us means "Laughing One"), was published in 1941 and won that year's Governor General's Award for nonfiction. It establishes the basis of her artistic life by describing in its first sketch the crucial 1898 trip to Ucluelet which introduced her to the Indian villages of the coast. Other chapters deal with her later visits to the Queen Charlottes and the northern rivers and her encounters with the reserve-rotted Indians around Vancouver and Victoria. *Klee Wyck* is a gentle and appealing book, true to facts and details so that the Indian way of living is never idealized, yet the Indians them-

Page from Carr's sketch book included in Pause, *her record of the period she spent in an English sanatorium in 1903 and 1904 (by permission of Ira Dilworth from a sketch book in his possession)*

Carr seated in front of her painting Sunshine and Tumult
*(photograph by Harold Mortimer Lamb, courtesy of the
Vancouver Art Gallery)*

selves are described entirely without patronage as self-sufficient people living differently from white men. One feels that these are the only human beings whom Carr is willing to regard as equal to her beloved animals. Perhaps the Indians are not such victims as they first appear, for they have an extraordinary ability to live within the white man's world according to rhythms that are archaic and their own.

The Book of Small (1942), which followed *Klee Wyck*, is about Carr's childhood in Victoria. Like *Klee Wyck*, it is less a narrative than a series of vignettes, but the mosaic technique does build up a vivid picture of life in a small colonial capital more than a century ago, and it projects the personality of an observant, imaginative child, who already has an inclination to loneness and to viewing the world with a critical and ironic eye. There are, as in all her books, times when whimsy takes arbitrary control, and other points at which the language loses its customary simplicity and becomes a gushing flow, but such occasions are not frequent, and in general one is

impressed by the originality of Carr's insights and the freshness of her writing.

In *The House of All Sorts* (1944) Carr moves forward to the period after 1911 when she was forced to earn her living as a boardinghouse keeper and dog breeder. As the title suggests, her experience was a mixed one which brought her into the company of people pleasant and unpleasant. The episodic form which Carr once again uses is admirably adapted to the series of character sketches and accounts of strange happenings that form the meat of the book. There is a prevalent impression that the author, in telling her tales, is making the best of a bad job and getting a return in the way of material for a satiric commentary on mankind out of what must have been an intensely frustrating period in her life.

Growing Pains (1946) is the most substantial of Carr's memoirs. An autobiography, taking us up to her seventies, it was completed shortly before her death and published posthumously. It follows the chronological pattern of a life, but the individual scenes are still important, so that what one has in the end is a series of significant episodes linked by a narrative whose real theme is Carr's development into the special kind of painter she became. It is written with vigor and a good deal of humor, directed as much against herself as against the other figures who variously arouse her affection or her somewhat malicious amusement.

Two lesser books were edited for publication by Ira Dilworth after Carr's death, both of them appearing in 1953. *The Heart of a Peacock* consists of stories and sketches, mostly about animals the author has known, and *Pause: A Sketch Book* is an account, illustrated with drawings by Carr, of the period she spent in an English sanatorium between 1903 and 1904.

Extremely valuable to those interested in the way painters develop and the thoughts they have about their work at the time of creation is another posthumously published book, *Hundreds and Thousands: The Journals of Emily Carr* (1966). One feels remarkably near to the painter at work as one reads passages such as the following, which is quite typical of the journals: "I woke up this morning with 'unity of movement' in a picture strong in my mind. I believe Van Gogh had that idea. I did not realise he had striven for that till quite recently so I did not come by the idea through him. It seems to me that clears up a lot. I see it very strongly out on the beach and cliffs. I felt it in the woods but did not quite realise what I was feeling. Now it seems to me the first thing to seize in your layout is the direction of your main movement, the sweep of the whole thing as a unit. One must be very careful about the transition of one curve of direction into the next, vary the length of the wave of space but *keep it going*, a pathway for the eye and the mind to travel through and into the thought. For long I have been trying to get these movements of the parts. Now I see there is only one movement. It sways and ripples. It may be slow or fast, but it is only one movement sweeping out into space but always keeping going–rocks, sea, sky, one continuous movement." The abundance of such passages makes *Hundreds and Thousands*, though the least consciously planned of Carr's writings, perhaps the best.

Taken in general, Emily Carr's writings not only have a great human interest in tracing the development of an original creative talent against much discouragement, but they also show a remarkable power of visualization and thus, with notable success, transfer one of the attributes of painting to prose.

References:

Paula Blanchard, *The Life of Emily Carr* (Seattle: University of Washington Press, 1987);

Ruth Gowers, *Emily Carr* (Leamington Spa, England & New York: Berg, 1987);

Eva-Marie Kröller, "Literary Versions of Emily Carr," *Canadian Literature*, 109 (Summer 1986): 87-98;

Doris Shadbolt, *The Art of Emily Carr* (Vancouver: Douglas & McIntyre / Toronto: Clarke, Irwin, 1979);

Maria Tippett, *Emily Carr: A Biography* (Toronto: Macmillan, 1979);

Janet Warner, "Emily Carr's Tennyson," *Canadian Literature*, 113-114 (Summer-Fall 1987): 114-126.

Papers:

Many of Carr's papers are at the Public Archives of British Columbia.

Robert Charbonneau

(3 February 1911-26 June 1967)

Valerie Raoul
University of British Columbia

BOOKS: *Ils posséderont la terre* (Montreal: Editions de l'Arbre, 1941);

Connaissance du personnage (Montreal: Editions de l'Arbre, 1944);

Fontile (Montreal: Editions de l'Arbre, 1945);

Petits Poèmes retrouvés (Montreal: Editions de l'Arbre, 1945);

La France et nous (Montreal: Editions de l'Arbre, 1947);

Les Désirs et les jours (Montreal: Editions de l'Arbre, 1948);

Aucune Créature (Montreal: Beauchemin, 1961);

Chronique de l'âge amer (Montreal: Editions du Sablier, 1967);

Romanciers canadiens (Quebec: Presses de l'Université Laval, 1972).

RADIO: *Précieuse Elisabeth*, Radio-Canada, 16 June 1949;

Fontile, Radio-Canada, 8 July 1951;

Les Désirs et les jours, Radio-Canada, 21 October 1951.

OTHER: "Aucun Chemin n'est sûr," in *Cahiers de l'Académie Canadienne-Française*, no. 4, *Contes et Nouvelles* (Montreal, 1959), pp. 19-37.

PERIODICAL PUBLICATIONS: "François Mauriac," *Relève*, 4 (September 1934): 64-75;

"Vers d'été," *Nouvelle Relève*, 4 (September 1945): 326-333; 4 (November 1945): 384-389;

"Aspects du roman," *Nouvelle Relève*, 4 (March 1946): 763-770; 5 (May 1946): 40-45; 5 (June 1946): 165-169;

"Précieuse Elisabeth," *Ecrits du Canada Français*, no. 57 (1986).

Robert Charbonneau (photograph by Georges Beullac, courtesy of Kenneth Landry)

Robert Charbonneau's main contribution to the development of the novel in Quebec lies in his portrayal of inner conflict in the characters he creates. He was also one of the first writers in Quebec to theorize on the techniques of novel writing. His importance on the Montreal literary scene in the 1930s and 1940s extends beyond his creative writing to include his involvement with the literary review *La Relève*, his activities in the worlds of journalism, publishing, and broadcasting, and his controversial defense of the autonomy of Quebec literature.

Robert Charbonneau was born to Joseph-Arthur and Alma Robert Charbonneau in Montreal. He spent his early childhood in Farnham, in the Eastern Townships, but returned to Montreal for his education. He studied at the Ecole Saint-Stanislas, the Collège Sainte-Marie, and the Université de Montréal, obtaining a diploma in journalism in 1934. During the summers, in spite of fragile health, he worked for the Canadian Pacific, laying railroad tracks. His father and later his brothers were employed by the C. P. Telegraph Company, and his consciousness of this modest, nonintellectual background became an important component of his novels.

Before finishing high school Charbonneau had already become active in Jeune Canada, a nationalist youth movement which envisaged an independent state of Quebec where the French language and the Catholic religion would flourish. His first radio broadcasts were made in 1933 and 1934 on behalf of this organization. In 1934, with his friend Paul Beaulieu, he founded *La Relève*, which they described as a "review of literature, art and philosophy" whose aim was to provide a forum for the younger admirers of the French-Canadian nationalist Lionel Groulx (1878-1967). Charbonneau's fervor enabled him in 1934, at the height of the Depression, to obtain a position with *La Patrie*, where he rapidly progressed from translating telegrams to interviewing distinguished visitors such as André Malraux and Jacques Maritain. In 1937 he left Montreal for a year to work for *Le Droit* in Ottawa. On his return he became assistant news editor at *Le Canada*, where he remained until 1942.

By 1940 the initial antisocialist attitude of *La Relève* had evolved into support for an antibourgeois form of Christian democracy. The title was modified to *La Nouvelle Relève*, and more space was devoted to literature and international concerns. At this time Charbonneau founded the publishing company Editions de l'Arbre with Claude Hurtubise, who replaced Beaulieu at *La Nouvelle Relève* in 1943.

In 1941 Charbonneau published his first novel, *Ils posséderont la terre*, which won the Prix David, and in the following year he became editor of a bilingual review, *Shel-Dite*. *La Nouvelle Relève* adopted a policy of support for contemporary French-Canadian writers, reflected particularly in a special number on the death of Hector de Saint-Denys Garneau, a contributor and old friend of Charbonneau, and in an important essay by Charbonneau in 1946, "Aspects du roman." Editions de l'Arbre published Roger Lemelin, Yves Thériault, Anne Hébert, and Berthelot Brunet's *Histoire de la littérature canadienne-française;* during the war they produced works by exiles from Europe and reeditions of French authors. Charbonneau, exempt from military service on medical grounds, became official adviser to the Canadian government on matters of publication (1944-1945) and a founding member of the Académie Canadienne-

Française (1944); at this time he also corresponded with French aviator and writer Antoine de Saint-Exupéry. In 1944 he married Madeleine Brisset, with whom he subsequently had three children, and published *Connaissance du personnage*, a collection of essays on the novel and novel writing that had originally appeared in *La Relève*.

The following year his second novel, *Fontile*, was published, and in 1946 it was awarded the Prix Duvernay by the Saint-Jean-Baptiste Society, whose president later confessed that he would not have allowed Charbonneau to win the prize had he known that the author supported the civil liberties movement. In 1945 Charbonneau also published a collection of poems, *Petits Poèmes retrouvés*, and became president of the Société des Editeurs Canadiens. The year 1946 saw the beginning of his dispute with several prominent French writers and publishers, notably Georges Duhamel and Louis Aragon. The initial cause was the publication in Canada of works by writers such as Charles Maurras who were blacklisted in France as collaborators with the Germans during World War II. Charbonneau defended the right to publish what they had written before the war, regardless of their current political position. The quarrel developed into a broader discussion of the degree of independence from French literature to which the writers of Quebec should aspire. Charbonneau resumed the arguments in a collection of essays, *La France et nous*, published in 1947. With the end of the war, Quebec publishers lost their right to publish French authors and, with it, their main source of income. In 1948 both Editions de l'Arbre and *La Nouvelle Relève* were forced to close down. Ironically, Charbonneau was admitted at this time to the prestigious French Académie Ronsard. His third novel, *Les Désirs et les jours* (1948), was one of the last published by Editions de l'Arbre.

Charbonneau became assistant news editor at *La Presse* (1949-1950) and wrote his first radio play, *Précieuse Elisabeth*, a detective story broadcast by Radio-Canada in 1949. In 1950 he was appointed assistant director of *La Semaine à Radio-Canada*, where he worked with Robert Elie, whom he succeeded as director in 1953. In 1951 radio adaptations of his second and third novels were aired. In 1952 and 1953 he broadcast a series of eighteen lectures on French-Canadian novelists, published posthumously as *Romanciers canadiens* in 1972. In 1955 he assumed responsibility for the script service of Radio-Canada. He remained in this post until 1965, when the service

Caricature by Robert La Palme showing Charbonneau and French philosopher Jacques Maritain in conversation as Saint Thomas Aquinas looks on

was cut back and he became a consultant. It was Charbonneau who encouraged Roger Lemelin to adapt *Les Plouffe* (1948) for television. He wrote one *nouvelle,* "Aucun Chemin n'est sûr," published in *Cahiers de l'Académie Canadienne-Française* (1959), and two other novels (*Aucune Créature,* 1961, and *Chronique de l'âge amer,* 1967) before his untimely death at Saint-Jovite in 1967, from a heart attack. In 1965 he was awarded the Pierre Chauveau Medal by the Canadian Royal Society.

Although Charbonneau wrote five novels over a period of fifteen years, it is his first that has received the most critical attention. *Ils posséderont la terre* was written shortly after the sudden deaths of two of the author's friends, and the long prologue attains an intensity of feeling new to the Quebec novel. In the prologue André Laroudan reviews his past as his friend Edward Wilding is about to enter a monastery. In the first chapter it is Edward's point of view, on his return a year later, which is conveyed by means of the *style indirect libre.* From the second chapter on, as the conflict between working-class and bourgeois backgrounds develops and the two friends become rivals in love, the novel deteriorates into psychological analysis by an intrusive author. At the end Edward leaves Quebec for the West with the mysterious Lyône, while André remains behind with Edward's exemplary cousin, Dorothée.

The title refers to Jérôme and Fernand, two "meek" victims who die young but "inherit the earth" through faith in God.

Fontile, the imaginary town where the action of *Ils posséderont la terre* is set, gives its name to Charbonneau's second novel, which focuses on the personality problems of Julien Pollender, another young hero whose loyalties are divided–between books and business, poetry and politics, religion and his love for Armande Aquinault–and who dies, melodramatically, a sacrifice to his self-absorption and pride. Julien suffers from the same inability to love or communicate as André and Edward, and the same atmosphere of stifling family relationships and sexual repression prevails. In Charbonneau's third novel, *Les Désirs et les jours,* Auguste Prieur is a young man who, in spite of apparent success, suffers from the limitations imposed by being a French-Canadian in 1930s Quebec, with its corrupt political system and hypocritical moral values.

Aucune Créature is the only one of Charbonneau's novels in which the central character is middle-aged, as was the author in 1960. Georges Hautecroix is a writer, conscious that his dream of producing a work to inspire the nation will never be fulfilled. He is prepared to abandon his family and career for Sylvie, but returns to the fold when she is killed by a former lover.

Literature and religion are reinstated as the central values in his life.

Charbonneau's last novel, the semi-autobiographical *Chronique de l'âge amer,* deals with a group rather than an individual crisis. In the first part Charbonneau recounts the origins of *La Relève:* the anonymous narrator is the founder of a nationalist journal, *La Revue.* The political and social scene in Quebec in 1934 and 1935 is resurrected with interesting sidelights on various prominent political figures, especially Paul Gouin. The second part traces the divergent paths of the various members of the group.

In *Connaissance du personnage* Charbonneau proclaimed that the novelist should repress any moralizing, ideological tendencies. This stand was new in French-Canadian literature. Although the importance accorded to religion, literature, and politics in his novels contributes to a distinct ideological atmosphere, the moral issues are depicted in fictional situations, to be solved by the characters rather than commented on by the author. Although he does not always succeed in imparting life to his characters and has been compared to François Mauriac in his control over them, Charbonneau paved the way for subsequent novelists in Quebec, such as André Langevin and André Giroux, who have continued the tradition of psychological novels which he helped to instigate.

In 1986 a special issue of *Ecrits du Canada Français* was devoted to Charbonneau. Entitled *Robert Charbonneau parmi nous* and presented by Paul Beaulieu, it includes articles by Willie Chevalier and Gilles Archambault on Charbonneau the man, and by Jean-Louis Gagnon, Gilles Marcotte, Jean-Charles Falardeau, Jacques Allard, and Roger Duhamel on Charbonneau the writer. Added to these are a previously unpublished one-act play, "Précieuse Elisabeth," and a selection of letters and documents. This collective tribute to Charbonneau is evidence that he is still considered important, and provides a useful point of departure for further studies of his work.

References:
Paul Beaulieu, ed., *Robert Charbonneau parmi nous,* special issue of *Ecrits du Canada Français,* no. 57 (1986);

Madeleine Ducrocq-Poirier, *Robert Charbonneau* (Montreal: Fides, 1973);

Madeleine-Blanche Ellis, *Robert Charbonneau et la création romanesque* (Montreal: Editions du Lévrier, 1948);

Jean-Charles Falardeau, "La Génération de *la Relève*" and "Robert Charbonneau et le rêve de l'adolescent," in his *Notre Société et son roman* (Montreal: HMH, 1967), pp. 101-121 and pp. 135-180;

M.-G. Hesse, "Le Thème de la jeunesse chez Robert Charbonneau," *L'Action Nationale,* 62 (March 1973): 584-600;

Patrick Imbert, "Relectures: *Ils posséderont la terre* de Robert Charbonneau ou la problématique existentielle," *Lettres Québécoises,* 30 (Summer 1983): 55-56;

Romain Légaré, "L'Œuvre romanesque de Robert Charbonneau," *Action Nationale,* 32 (November 1948): 209-223;

Gilles Marcotte, *Une Littérature qui se fait* (Montreal: HMH, 1962), pp. 43-45;

Allan McAndrew, "A Canadian Disciple of François Mauriac, Robert Charbonneau," *University of Toronto Quarterly,* 16 (October 1946): 42-50;

John O'Connor, "Fraternal Twins: The Impact of Jacques Maritain on Callaghan and Charbonneau," *Mosaic,* 14 (Spring 1981): 145-163;

Réjean Robidoux and André Renaud, *Le Roman canadien-français du vingtième siècle* (Ottawa: Ottawa University Press, 1966), pp. 115-125.

Philip Child

(19 January 1898-6 February 1978)

Dennis Duffy
University of Toronto

SELECTED BOOKS: *The Village of Souls* (London: Butterworth, 1933; Toronto: Ryerson, 1948);

God's Sparrows (London: Butterworth, 1937; Toronto: McClelland & Stewart, 1978);

Blow Wind, Come Wrack, as John Wentworth (London: Jarrolds, 1945);

Day of Wrath (Toronto: Ryerson, 1945);

Mr. Ames Against Time (Toronto: Ryerson, 1949);

The Victorian House and Other Poems (Toronto: Ryerson, 1951);

The Wood of the Nightingale (Toronto: Ryerson, 1965).

Philip Child's poetry and fiction will be remembered primarily on the basis of two works, his historical novel, *The Village of Souls* (1933), and his autobiographical poem, *The Victorian House* (collected with other verse in 1951). These works, as well as his others, come from a preoccupation with the facts of pain and loss, which grants to his works a quality of emotional richness that compensates for their often pedestrian form.

Born in Hamilton, Ontario, in the Victorian house he was to write about, Child came from a comfortable background. His father, William Addison Child, a leading figure in the steel industry, came from New England, while his mother, Elizabeth Helen Harvey Child, was of Anglo-Canadian ancestry. Scenes from his childhood appear in *The Victorian House* and in his novel of his World War I experiences, *God's Sparrows* (1937).

In 1915 he entered Trinity College, University of Toronto. In 1917 he enlisted in the army and was sent to the western front as an artillery subaltern in World War I. The horrors of the war remained with him for the rest of his life, providing material not only for *God's Sparrows* but for his last, long poem, *The Wood of the Nightingale* (1965), as well.

He returned to Trinity College in 1919 and graduated in 1921, when he was among the first to win the Moss Scholarship, the University of

Philip Child

Toronto's most prestigious undergraduate award. His Harvard M.A. in 1923 was preceded by an affiliated B.A. at Christ's College, Cambridge. Married to Gertrude Potts in 1923 (the union resulted in two children), he filled the post of lecturer in English at Trinity (1923-1926). In 1928 he took a doctorate at Harvard, while also working in New York as a journalist and settlement worker. He taught at the University of British Columbia in 1928, then returned to tutoring and writing at Harvard. He moved back to his native

Hamilton before the publication of *The Village of Souls* in 1933.

By far the finest of his works, *The Village of Souls* is not an autobiographical work, as so many first novels are. Instead, it is an engrossing, haunting account of a voyageur's life in New France as he attempts to choose between two women in his life. Since these two women represent two different environments (Lys the world of France, Anne, the Indian, the New World), the novel embodies in Jornay's struggle the enduring theme in Canadian fiction: the accommodation of newcomers to the new environment.

Based largely on documents such as the *Jesuit Relations,* the historical background remains firmly in the rear as the reader observes a split, tormented, violent man unable to choose between the two realities he longs to embrace. Ultimately Jornay's role is a passive one, since the choice is made for him. Lys dies nursing inhabitants of an up-country Indian village ravaged by smallpox, itself a grim parody of the Indian village of souls believed to exist in the afterlife. Following Lys's appearance to him during a moment when he is lost, delirious, and near death in a blizzard, Jornay is reunited with Anne and the two of them proceed further into the *pays d'en haut* as the novel concludes. In addition to its concern with a perennial Canadian theme, the novel's chief interest lies in the manner in which it blends an unobtrusive sense of historical accuracy into its central preoccupation with psychic splitting and the fantastic. The historical and the mythical merge in a single dreamlike–or nightmarish–texture.

Child won some praise for this work, as for his subsequent books; in most cases those who were enthusiastic approved of the moral stance the novels took–against war in *God's Sparrows,* against Nazi Germany in *Day of Wrath* (1945), and against the pressures of urban blight (both environmental and psychological) in *Mr. Ames Against Time* (1949). Some critics dismissed his didactic bent, but nonetheless admired his idealism; of these, Desmond Pacey, writing in *Literary History of Canada* (1965), is characteristic: "Child is a Christian humanist who believes . . . that every individual is supremely important in the eyes of God; his novels are rich in compassion and in a sense of the necessity of human brotherhood and love."

The year 1937 saw the publication of *God's Sparrows* (published by McClelland and Stewart in 1978 as a New Canadian Library paperback), a

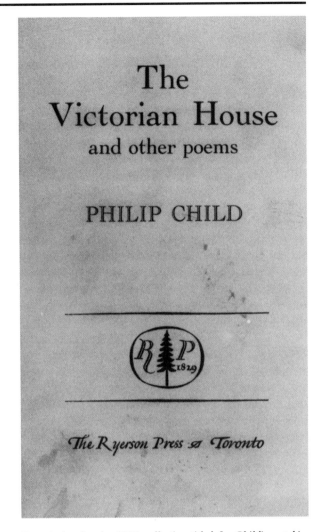

Dust jacket for the 1951 collection titled for Child's autobiographical poem about English-Canadian upper-class life

work combining the family saga with the Great War novel. Its hero, Daniel, is another of Child's split heroes, torn between the Roundhead culture of his father and the Cavalier one of his mother. A dreamy, idealistic young man, he survives the war after seeing his every illusion shattered. Significantly, his cousin Quentin, a tougher minded alter ego to Daniel, dies and appears to him in a vision. The novel stops rather than concludes, with the hero's near-dead body exhumed from a pile of corpses. It is as if the war experience proved so powerful that the author was unable to impose upon it a satisfactory literary form–a task he accomplished with some success in his final poem, *The Wood of the Nightingale.* The narrative there, dealing with figures beheld at a greater distance, produces a more satisfying aesthetic experience, one with all the neatness of fable.

Child returned to Trinity in 1942, the year of his appointment as Chancellor's Professor of English. Involved in producing a history of the college, he became a well-known institution there. Many recall his emotion-charged readings aloud in class and his familiar habit of lighting a pipe while answering students' questions, the eyes of the class members fixed firmly on the match as its flame advanced toward his fingers. Especially to newcomers on staff, Child was an unfailing source of good humor, encouragement, and wisdom.

During the World War II years he produced the thriller *Blow Wind, Come Wrack* (1945) under the pseudonym of John Wentworth (Hamilton is the seat of Wentworth County) and the fabular *Day of Wrath* (1945), set in wartime Germany. *Mr. Ames Against Time* (1949), winner of the Ryerson Fiction Award and a Governor General's Award, adapts the thriller form to the story of a father's sacrifice of his health and life to redeem a straying son framed for a murder.

The Victorian House, once a standard text for the Ontario Grade XIII English examination, describes the speaker's memory-packed survey of his family home as he shows it to an obtuse real-estate agent. The poem captures an era of English-Canadian upper-class life, mingling domestic and social rituals into a pattern of leisurely appreciation of the best of both British and U.S. culture. Unselfconsciously "colonial" in its outlook, that Canadian culture's deep conservatism is expressed in the speaker's resolve to repair the house and continue to live in it.

The house itself is an embodiment of familial values, a place of continuity. Hence, houses in the Anglo-Protestant subculture of Canada (and especially of Loyalist Ontario) where Mazo de la Roche's "Jalna" offers another example come to represent a great, good, accommodating place with room for all kinds of temperaments. Child's fiction and poetry draw amply upon this sensibility; the house is both setting and resonant image. There are two main expressions of the experience and aspirations that underlie it. *The Village of Souls,* for example, tells of the process of accommodating to the new environment, of making an Ontario home in what had once been wilderness; *The Victorian House* tells of the need to maintain social structures, for their comfort and for their strength. In these two reactions to place we can see the degree to which Child drew on—and also continued to declare—the Upper-Canadian dream of a peaceful and well-ordered world.

References:

Dennis Duffy, *Gardens, Covenants, Exiles: Loyalism in the Literature of Upper Canada/Ontario* (Toronto: University of Toronto Press, 1982);

Duffy, "Memory   Pain. The Haunted World of Philip Child's Fiction," *Canadian Literature,* 84 (Spring 1980): 41-56;

Douglas Jones, *Butterfly on Rock: A Study of Themes and Images in Canadian Literature* (Toronto: University of Toronto Press, 1970), pp. 45-47;

William H. Magee, "Philip Child: A Re-Appraisal," *Canadian Literature,* 24 (Spring 1965): 28-36.

Papers:

Child's papers are at the National Library of Canada, Ottawa.

Adrienne Choquette

(2 July 1915-13 October 1973)

Alexandre L. Amprimoz
Brock University

BOOKS: *La Coupe vide* (Montreal: Fernand Pilon, 1948);

La Nuit ne dort pas (Quebec: Institut Littéraire du Québec, 1954; enlarged edition, Notre-Dame-des-Laurentides, Quebec: Presses Laurentiennes, 1979);

Laure Clouet (Quebec: Institut Littéraire du Québec, 1961);

Je m'appelle Pax (Notre-Dame-des-Laurentides, Quebec: Presses Laurentiennes, 1974);

Le Temps des villages (Notre-Dame-des-Laurentides, Quebec: Presses Laurentiennes, 1975).

OTHER: *Confidences d'écrivains canadiens-français*, edited by Choquette (Trois-Rivières, Quebec: Editions du Bien Publique, 1939).

For many years the urban novel of French Canada has generally been set against the background of Montreal. Among the rare novels dedicated to the charm of Quebec City, Adrienne Choquette's *Laure Clouet* (1961) is, if not the best, certainly one of the most refined attempts to represent the nostalgia of old French-Canadian traditions. Yet this, too, is a generalization. Choquette reached past nostalgia, and while the title character of *Laure Clouet* seems restricted by convention (the house, the church, the river, the Plains of Abraham), this novel, like her other works, asks also that its apparent simplicities be read as illusions.

Adrienne Choquette was born to Henri Choquette, a physician, and his wife, Rose-Albertine Amyot Choquette, at Shawinigan Falls, Quebec. Orphaned at an early age, she studied at the Ursuline school in Trois-Rivières (1924-1931) before becoming a civil servant and, later, a journalist. Her first book, *Confidences d'écrivains canadiens-français*, was a collection of interviews with French-Canadian writers published in 1939, two years after Choquette had accepted a position with the Trois-Rivières radio station CHLN.

Adrienne Choquette, late 1940s (courtesy of Kenneth Landry)

Her second book, a novel, *La Coupe vide*, appeared in 1948. It is the story of a femme fatale and her effect on the lives of four teenagers captivated by her mysterious sensuality. A not-too-realistic first novel dealing with a daring subject, *La Coupe vide* was not a success. It found few enthusiastic readers in Church-dominated Quebec.

In 1954, under the title *La Nuit ne dort pas*, Choquette published a collection of stories in a more realistic vein. The book, generally received with more favor than *La Coupe vide*, won the Prix David, the highest award sponsored by the Quebec Ministry of Cultural Affairs.

In 1961 Choquette became a major literary figure in Quebec. The publication of *Laure Clouet* brought her long-awaited recognition and the Prix du Grand Jury des Lettres. Choquette's short novel is the story of a *vie manquée;* her Laure Clouet comes across as a more educated, more intelligent, and wealthier Félicité–the protagonist of Gustave Flaubert's *Un Coeur simple* (1877).

Laure is a forty-four-year-old spinster who begins to discover the simple pleasures of life only after her mother's death. Normal activities, such as having the kitchen repainted, become real joys because they represent consequences of the protagonist's own decisions, not those of her mother, who was a good but authoritarian woman.

Roger Duhamel, a noted Quebec critic, has written that *Laure Clouet* is "un des récits les plus achevés de la littérature québécoise" (one of the most accomplished stories of Quebecois literature). More recent readings of *Laure Clouet* have not gone much beyond the general praise accorded the novel when it first appeared. But the most striking aspect of Choquette's work is that it is traditional only in content. The sociological references create an illusion of satisfaction with the past; the simplicities of style suggest conventional solutions to Laure's circumstances. In an early review in the *University of Toronto Quarterly,* Duhamel hinted at the tensions between representation and formal implication: "En apparence, rien n'est changé, et cependant, par d'obscurs cheminements, l'âme de Laure est transformée. Un incident minime suffira à lui en faire prendre conscience. A-t-on assez mesuré les embûches d'un récit aussi lisse, où les seuls mouvements se situent au palier du coeur? Tout l'art d'Adrienne Choquette est là, fait de discrétion, de finesse, d'intuition. Elle multiplie les formules heureuses avec un naturel qui fait oublier qu'elles puissent être concertées. Sans s'écarter de son thème central, la romancière trace de Québec, en touches légères, une fresque moqueuse et amusée. Elle donne libre cours à sa verve pour nous promener à travers la galerie des ancêtres Clouet.... Un personnage en émerge, inoubliable, portant en lui les conditions de la durée. Un milieu social y est inscrit, qui est décrit sans concession à l'imagerie d'Epinal ni à la charge véhémente. Tout est mesuré et le ton est toujours juste. La perfection formelle de cette longue nouvelle la fera triompher du temps par la vertu du style" (In appearance, nothing has changed, and, nevertheless, by obscure processes, Laure's soul is transformed. A minimal incident suffices

to make her aware. Has one fully estimated the traps of a narrative so polished that the only movements take place on the level of the heart? All of Adrienne Choquette's art is there, made of discretion, subtlety, intuition. She multiplies the happy formulas so naturally that one forgets that they can be connected. Without deviating from her central theme, the novelist sketches, with light touches, a mocking and amusing fresco of Quebec. She gives free rein to her verve to walk us through the gallery of Clouet ancestors.... One character emerges, unforgettable, carrying in her the conditions of a long life. A social milieu is inscribed there, which is described without concession to the imagery of Epinal nor to violent caricature. All is measured and the tone is always true. The formal perfection of this long *nouvelle* will make it triumph over time by virtue of its style).

Later comments by Suzanne Paradis and others have intensified our understanding of the way form and structure shape meaning in Choquette's work, and reshape the way we understand what she has written. In some ways, one incident in *Laure Clouet* serves as a structural paradigm for what is going on. Laure inherits her house (or the shapes of her history), but rather than simply leave it alone, she contemplates opening it up to a young couple. She seeks first the advice of her parish priest and that of Madame Bois, one of her mother's old friends. The cryptic character of the advice they give her–as vocally silent, contradictory, and hard to read as is the "message" of the past or of any inheritance from good-but-authoritarian parents– affects the way a reader reads the novel. It is dangerous, the ambiguity suggests, to accept the "message" (or the novel) as a simple, socially "realistic," referential text; what is really going on is happening between the message given and the message received–in the deceptively quiet silences of Laure's own choices. In some sense, therefore, the novel is undermining the very genre it is impersonating–undermining the illusions of social realism–which is not without social implications and also calls attention to the potential independence of literary form.

Choquette died on 13 October 1973. The following year her first posthumously published book appeared: *Je m'appelle Pax.* Pax is a contented dog reflecting on his happy condition. This text for children contains an introduction by the noted Quebec writer Robert Choquette, a cousin of the author. In 1975 *Laure Clouet* and *La*

Nuit ne dort pas were published in one volume by Fides. In his introduction to the book, Romain Légaré affirms that Choquette had: "un réel talent littéraire, une profonde sensibilité, de solides dons psychologiques, l'originalité du style et de l'inspiration" (a real literary talent, a deep sensibility, a solid gift for psychology, originality in style and inspiration).

The same year another book by Choquette was published by the Presses Laurentiennes: *Le Temps des villages*. In her introduction to this collection of sixteen related stories, Quebec writer Suzanne Paradis sums up the importance of this book and defines the perspective of Choquette's entire work: "On lira avec émotion et admiration *Le Temps des villages,* non pas par nostalgie d'une époque révolue, mais parce qu'il illustre avec une exemplaire simplicité les dons de l'écrivain sa maîtrise, son lumineux accès aux voies, sinon fermées du moins obscures, de l'âme et du coeur humain" (It is with emotion and admiration that one will read *Le Temps des villages,* not because it evokes a gone era, but because it illustrates with exemplary simplicity the talent of the writer, her craftsmanship, her luminous access to the ways, if not closed, nevertheless obscure, of the soul and of the human heart).

This statement seems particularly wise when one realizes that *Le Temps des villages,* while occasionally comic, is not at heart nostalgic. Violent acts occur in these stories. The violence contrasts so acutely with the peaceful life of a Quebec village–the (conventional) background against which the stories are set–that the theme of solitude, central in Choquette's work, is amplified by the revelation of more intense forms of suffering.

In 1978 Paradis published *Adrienne Choquette lue par Suzanne Paradis,* the first book-length study of Choquette. This volume contains a penetrating and enthusiastic essay that runs over 140 pages as well as new, unpublished material by Choquette: eleven poems and two unfinished manuscripts. Also in 1978 the third edition of *La Coupe vide* appeared. A collection of reviews follows the text and gives the reader an idea of the mixed reception the book received in 1948. In 1979 an enlarged edition of *La Nuit ne dort pas* appeared, including two previously unpublished stories: "Sortilège" and "Le Rendez-vous." (Choquette had published about three dozen stories between 1933 and 1965 in such journals as *Le Devoir, La Famille,* and *Amérique-Française,* some of which remain uncollected.)

In spite of her literary range–her attempts to work in long as well as short forms, her stylistic breaks from strict traditional formalism–Adrienne Choquette is remembered primarily as the author of one book, *Laure Clouet.* Perhaps the reasons for this are sociological as much as they are stylistic. While some recent critics–Paradis, Marineau–have been redirecting scholarly attention to the texts, and to instructive ways to read the texts, the general impression of Choquette is that she was one of the last writers of a bygone era. By this view *Laure Clouet* becomes a social perhaps more than an aesthetic document: a witness not so much to the particular life of a woman as to the more general, restricted character of life in the last years before the Quiet Revolution transformed ideology and politics as well as literature in modern Quebec.

References:
Alvine Bélisle, "Je m'appelle Pax," *Livres et Auteurs Québécois* (1974): 254-257;

Théophile Bertrand, "Turlupinage à 'votre auteur préféré,' " *Lectures,* 5 (April 1949): 449-454;

Gilles De LaFontaine, "L'Imaginaire dans les contes et récits," introduction to *Contes et récits de la Mauricie,* edited by De LaFontaine and G. Rousseau (Trois-Rivières, Quebec: Editions Cédoleq, 1982), pp. 11-30;

Line Marineau and De LaFontaine, *Adrienne Choquette: Nouvelliste de l'émancipation* (Charlesbourg, Quebec: Presses Laurentiennes, 1984);

Jean Ménard, *La Vie littéraire au Canada français* (Ottawa: Editions de l'Université d'Ottawa, 1971), pp. 220-222;

Suzanne Paradis, *Adrienne Choquette lue par Suzanne Paradis: Une Analyse de l'oeuvre littéraire d'Adrienne Choquette* (Notre-Dame-des-Laurentides, Quebec: Presses Laurentiennes, 1978);

Gabrielle Poulin, *Romans du pays* (Montreal: Bellarmin, 1980), pp. 326-331.

Robert Choquette
(22 April 1905-   )

Michael Greenstein
Université de Sherbrooke

BOOKS: *A travers les vents* (Montreal: Edouard Ga-
rand, 1925; revised and enlarged edition,
Montreal: Louis Carrier, 1927);
La Pension Leblanc (Montreal & New York: Louis
Carrier/Editions du Mercure, 1927);
Metropolitan Museum (Montreal: Herald Press,
1931);
Poésies nouvelles (Montreal: Albert Lévesque,
1933);
Le Fabuliste La Fontaine à Montréal (Montreal: Edi-
tions du Zodiaque, 1935);
Le Curé de Village: Scènes de la vie canadienne (Mon-
treal: Granger, 1936);
Les Velder (Montreal: Bernard Valiquette, 1941;
New York: Brentano's, 1941);
Suite marine: Poème en douze chants (Montreal: Socie-
té d'Edition et de Librairie Paul Péladeau,
1953);
Œuvres poétiques, 2 volumes (Montreal: Fides,
1956; revised and enlarged, 1967);
Elise Velder (Montreal & Paris: Fides, 1958);
Poèmes choisis (Montreal: Fides, 1970);
Sous le règne d'Augusta (Montreal: Leméac, 1974);
Le Sorcier d'Anticosti et autres légendes canadiennes
(Montreal: Fides, 1975);
Moi, Petrouchka (Montreal: Stanké, 1980);
*Le Choix de Robert Choquette dans l'œuvre de Robert
Choquette* (Notre-Dame-des-Laurentides, Que-
bec: Presses Laurentiennes, 1981).

MOTION PICTURES: *Santé et bonheur*, screenplay by Choquette, O.N.F., 1939;
Le Curé de village, screenplay by Choquette, Quebec Productions, 1949;
De pére en fils, screenplay by Choquette, O.N.F.,
1951.

TELEVISION: *Il était une fois*, adapted by Francis
Croisset, CBC, 14 March 1954;
Le Timide, CBFT, 2 June 1954;
Chez les Latour, CBFT, 7 June 1954;
Le Lampe, CBFT, 26 September 1954;
Portraits d'ancêtres, CBFT, 14 November 1954;

Robert Choquette (photograph by Kèro)

"Fiançailles à Noël," CBFT, *Fantasies canadiennes*,
26 December 1954;
Élisabeth, CBFT, 22 September 1955-13 October
1955;
Née pour un p'tit pain, CBFT, 20 October 1955-10
November 1955;
Il était une robe, CBFT, 17 November 1955-8 De-
cember 1955;
Le Billet doux, CBFT, 15 December 1955-5 Janu-
ary 1956;
La Nuit du carrefour, adapted by Choquette from
Georges Simenon's novel, CBFT, 12 Janu-
ary 1956-2 February 1956;
Le Fils du bedeau, CBFT, 9 February 1956-1
March 1956;

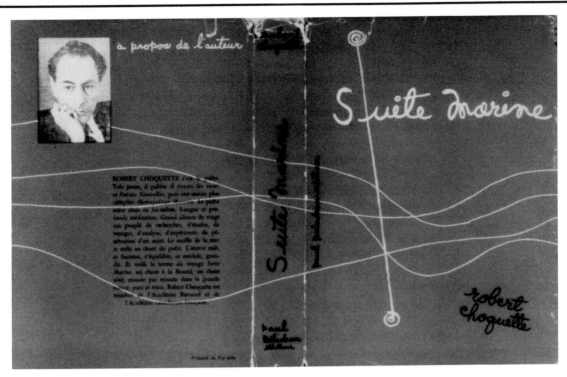

*Dust jacket for Choquette's 1953 volume, winner of the Prix de Poésie de l'Académie Française, the Prix David, and the Prix
Edgar Poe*

Monsieur Gallet, décédé, adapted by Choquette from Georges Simenon's novel, CBFT, 8 March 1956-29 March 1956;

Assurance-vie ou Le Bénéficiare, CBFT, 27 July 1956;

L'Étrangleur, CBFT, 5 October 1956-26 October 1956;

De fil en aiguille, CBFT, 2 November 1956-23 November 1956;

La Chase à pépère, CBFT, 30 November 1956-21 December 1956;

Les Vacances de Monsieur Maigret, adapted by Choquette from Georges Simenon's novel, CBFT, 28 December 1956-18 January 1957;

Brigitte, CBFT, 25 January 1957-15 February 1957;

Un beau Brummel, CBFT, 22 February 1957-15 March 1957;

Le Voyage à Rome, CBFT, 22 March 1957-12 April 1957;

Élise Velder, CBFT, 26 April 1957-17 May 1957;

Un homme à la fenêtre, CBFT, 24 May 1957-14 June 1957;

Un roman-savon, CBFT, 21 June 1957-12 July 1957;

Tu lis trop, Anatole, CBFT, 7 September 1958;

Mme Velder et Papineau chez les Gédéon Plouffe, CBFT, 28 December 1958;

Le Démon de midi et demi, CBFT, 16 August 1959;

Un cas de paresthénie, CBFT, 4 October 1959;

La Pension Velder, CBFT, 9 October 1957-16 July 1961;

Maigret et la grande perche, adapted by Choquette from Georges Simenon's novel, CBFT, 15 April 1962;

Sous le règne d'Augusta, CBFT, 7 February 1963;

Ta nuit est ma lumière, 6 September 1970;

Drôle de couple, ou Du tac au tac, CBFT, 13 March 1973;

À chacun sa leçon, CBFT, 5 May 1973;

Quinze ans plus tard, CBFT, 12 September 1976.

RADIO: *Le Curé de village,* CKAC, 5 January 1935-June 1938;

La Pension Velder, CBF, 3 October 1938-4 September 1942;

Métropole, CBF, 4 October 1943-29 June 1956.

Robert Choquette has received many literary awards for his poetry, yet he is equally recognized for his novels, his radio and television dramas, and his diplomatic career as the first Canadian consul-general in Bordeaux and Canadian ambassador to Argentina, Uruguay, and Paraguay. Born in Manchester, New Hampshire, on 22 April 1905 to Canadian parents, Joseph-

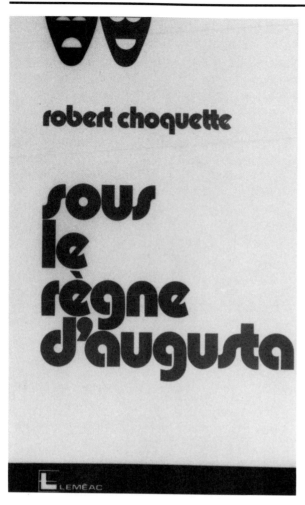

Cover for the published version of Choquette's four-act play first broadcast on Montreal's CBFT television in February 1963

Alfred and Ariane Payette Choquette, Robert-Guy Choquette remained in the United States until his ninth year. He has made light of this double nationality and dual personality by claiming that at border crossings he would show his certificate of baptism to American customs officials while to Canadians he offered the next episodes of his *radio-romans*, or radio-novels. The family moved to Lewiston, Maine, where Choquette's father, a physician, set up his practice, while summer vacations were spent at the coast, a setting which influenced the poem *Suite marine* (1953). With the death of Mme Choquette in 1913, the maternal grandparents took charge of the children in Montreal until Dr. Choquette was able to join them.

At Montreal's *collège* Notre-Dame Choquette learned piano and took singing lessons in addition to his regular studies, and at the *collège* Saint-Laurent from 1917 to 1921 he pursued classical studies and acted in the school's theatrical troupe. From 1921 to 1926 he continued his studies at Loyola College, where, in addition to the poetry of Musset, Lamartine, and Hugo, he was exposed to Keats, Shelley, and Wordsworth. This romantic influence may be seen in his early poetry which he began writing at this time. In 1925 he published his first volume of poetry, *A travers les vents,* which won the Prix David the following year.

After graduating from Loyola with a B.A., Choquette left Montreal for eight months on an automobile trip through the United States to Los Angeles and back. The voyage provided the young writer with a transcontinental vision and openness to future travel. On his return to Montreal he published *La Pension Leblanc* (1927), a novel of manners set in a summer resort in Quebec, and he worked as a journalist for the Montreal *Gazette* before becoming literary editor of the *Revue Moderne.* During this period he was also secretary and vice president of the Canadian Authors' Association as well as secretary and librarian of the Montreal Ecole des Beaux Arts. Choquette's second volume of poetry, *Metropolitan Museum,* appeared in 1931 and won the Prix David the following year.

Whereas his first collection consists of a variety of shorter lyrical poems, this epic of urban life is one long poem, a fresco of civilization, written in response to a visit made to the Metropolitan Museum of Art in New York City. Choquette evokes the past preserved in this stone temple through a series of voices from previous civilizations–prehistoric, Egyptian, Chaldean, Assyrian, Greek, Roman, and early Christian. In the second part of the poem the poet leaves the museum and turns to the future, speculating on science, doubt, and fear. *Poésies nouvelles* (1933) continues focusing on twentieth-century America, using such contemporary images as railways, boats, submarine cables, airplanes, and the telegraph. Using the image of a transcontinental train ride, the poet celebrates the Canadian geographic reality by means of a series of cinematic juxtapositions.

Choquette's connection to radio, television, and film was more than occasional. He began writing for radio in 1932. His first *radio-roman, Le Curé de village* (The Village Priest), appeared in print in 1936, with a regionalist subject appropriate to predominantly rural Quebec society. The radio series *La Pension Velder,* which served as the basis for his 1941 novel, *Les Velder,* depicted urban life in a Montreal boardinghouse. The connection to television was even more frequent. Choquette developed sixteen *télétheâtres* and wrote scripts for seventeen series programs, all broadcast on CBFT between 1954 and 1973. Also, *La Pension Velder* and *Quinze ans plus tard* became *téléromans* in 1961 and 1976. Choquette recast *Le Curé de village* as a film in 1949 and wrote screenplays for two other motion pictures.

In September 1942 Choquette and his wife, the former Marguerite Canac-Marquis, whom he married in 1937 (the couple later had two children), left Montreal for Smith College, Northampton, Massachusetts. They spent the next year there, where Choquette, as author in residence, lectured on Canada and on writing for radio. At Smith he also added a few thousand lines to the manuscript for his next major volume of poetry, *Suite marine,* which was published twenty-two years after *Metropolitan Museum.* These 6,000 lines of alexandrine verse divided into a dozen cantos have an epic quality. In the prologue to *Suite marine* the poet, a "nouveau Tristan," surveys the sea with his companion, Iseut. The rhythm of the sea represents all of nature that inspires the poet, while Iseut represents immortal beauty. For this poem Choquette won the Prix de Poésie de l'Académie Française, his third Prix David, and

the Prix Edgar Poe. In 1956 all of Choquette's poems were collected in two volumes under the title *Œuvres poétiques.*

Choquette's third novel, *Elise Velder,* which appeared in 1958, was developed as a new version of the radio sketches he had used for *Les Velder.* By 1961 he lessened his activities in radio and television; he spent time in Paris and traveled to Greece and Italy. In 1963 in Ottawa he became an official of the Canadian Centennial Commission, and in 1964 he was named Canadian consul-general at Bordeaux. In 1968 he continued his diplomatic career as Canadian ambassador to Argentina, Uruguay, and Paraguay but returned to Canada in 1970 to devote more time to writing. From 1971 to 1973 he served as director-general of Information Canada in Quebec. He received an honorary doctorate from the Université de Sherbrooke in 1972.

References:
Carlo Fonda, "Le Privilège de vivre: Réflexions sur Robert Choquette," *Canadian Literature,* 37 (Summer 1968): 28-39;

Renée Legris, *Robert Choquette* (Montreal: Fides, 1973);

Legris, *Robert Choquette: Romancier et dramaturge de la radio-télévision* (Montreal: Fides, 1977).

Catherine Anthony Clark

(5 May 1892-24 February 1977)

J. Kieran Kealy
University of British Columbia

BOOKS: *The Golden Pine Cone* (Toronto: Macmillan, 1950);
The Sun Horse (Toronto: Macmillan, 1951);
The One-Winged Dragon (Toronto: Macmillan, 1955);
The Silver Man (Toronto: Macmillan, 1958; London: Macmillan, 1959);
The Diamond Feather; or, The Door in the Mountain: A Magic Tale for Children (Toronto: Macmillan, 1962; London: Macmillan, 1962);
The Man with Yellow Eyes (Toronto: Macmillan, 1963; London: Macmillan, 1963; New York: St. Martin's Press, 1964);
The Hunter and the Medicine Man (Toronto: Macmillan, 1966).

Born in London, England, to Edgar and Catherine Smith, Catherine Anthony Smith immigrated to Canada in 1914 where, five years later, she married Leonard Clark and settled on a ranch in the mountainous Kootenay region of British Columbia. Here, for some thirty-two years, she juggled her responsibilities as a wife and mother of two children with her career as a writer. In 1950, at the age of fifty-eight, she published her first book, *The Golden Pine Cone,* an enchanting narrative which may well be Canada's first true fantasy, for it is dominated not by European goblins and elves but by the Ice Witch and the Pearl Folk, figures traditionally associated with the mythology of the Northwest Coast Indians whose lore permeates the British Columbia wilderness so familiar to Clark. Moreover, Clark does not make the traditional distinction between the real and the fantastic; both exist simultaneously in her novels, just as they do in the Indian legends from which her stories are drawn.

The Golden Pine Cone tells the story of two children, Bren and Lucy, who leave the security of their parents' log cabin for the world beyond, that quasi-supernatural place which Clark calls the "Inner World." Here they rescue their magical dog and return a mysterious pine cone to its proper owner, the Indian Tekontra. Fittingly, in this world, as in Indian lore, there is no absolute good or evil, and thus the story ends not with the defeat of the villain, Nasookin, but with his reacceptance of his social responsibilities.

Clark's next fantasy, *The Sun Horse* (1951), is her most widely acclaimed, winning the Canadian Library Association's Book of the Year for Children Award in 1952. In it two young children, Mark and Giselle, through the intervention of one of Clark's most memorable creations, the Flame-Lighter Woman, rescue Giselle's father, who became lost while searching for the legendary Sun Horse. This rescue, accomplished only after an extremely treacherous climb to the nest of the demonic Thunderbird, gives evidence of Clark's consistent affirmation of the active person, the "doer" who has the courage to accept his social responsibilities.

The One-Winged Dragon (1955), Clark's third fantasy, is her least successful, probably because it tries to assimilate far too many disparate cultures. As a result, the one-winged dragon who transports Michael and Jenni to the Inner World seems totally out of place in the wild North. The story once again is of a rescue, in this case of the enigmatic Kwong Hu's daughter. As in most of Clark's books, however, the text's primary purpose is to describe the maturation of the two protagonists, who must not only defeat the villainous Flower-Witch but also their own fear and insecurity. Not surprisingly, the tale ends when the children are joyfully reunited with the "outer-world" families, finally realizing the true worth of such familial relationships.

The Silver Man (1958) continues this emphasis on the growth of the protagonist, focusing on Clark's most fully developed protagonist, Gilbert Steyne, an orphan who is desperately trying to adjust to a foster home where he feels unwanted and unloved. His journey to the Inner World begins when, while gazing into a magical crystal, he is suddenly and miraculously transported, in dreamlike fashion, to another world. Once there, however, Gilbert finds the same environment

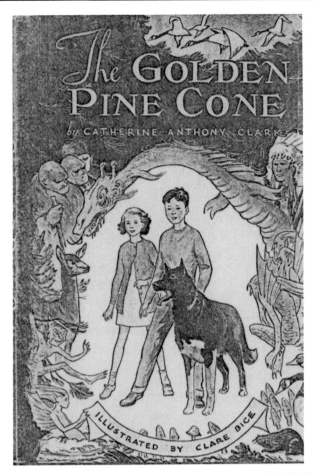

Dust jacket and illustration from Clark's first fantasy

and, in fact, the same problems which faced Clark's earlier heroes. Specifically, he must help a young Indian girl, Kawitha, in her attempts to save her brother Kunshat, the enchanted Silver Man. As in other works, however, this quest is complemented by Gilbert's development into a truly selfless human being, a journey which ends when he consciously chooses to abandon the happiness he has found in this world to save his beloved Kawitha's brother. But his sacrifice is not without reward, for he is now able to return to his world confident both of his own identity and of his ability to fit into his adopted family.

In *The Diamond Feather* (1962) Clark's emphasis changes somewhat, for she focuses far less on her two protagonists, Jon and Firelei, than she does on the most prominent figure they find in the Inner World: a bitter prospector whose lust for gold causes him to leave his family and, with them, all sense of dignity. Fittingly called the Frozen Man, the prospector symbolizes the selfishness that Clark attacks in all of her fantasies. Through the love of the children, however, the prospector is finally able to face his grief and be reunited with his lost family in the world beyond death.

In *The Hunter and the Medicine Man* (1966) Clark's de-emphasis of the youthful protagonists, in this case Richard and Anne Gale, continues. The true hero, in fact, is the enigmatic Hunter, brother of the Indian chief whose rescue is the object of the quest that unifies the story. Initially disillusioned by man and his universal selfishness, the Hunter is finally convinced by the children that he must return to his tribe and help save his imprisoned brother. Though the rescue is successful, the Hunter dies, finally finding the peace he had always sought. The adventure over, the children ride home over the mountain upon which the adventure first began, reminding the reader for one final time just how near Clark's fantasy world is.

Catherine Anthony Clark died at the age of eighty-four in Victoria, British Columbia. Though she published only seven books in her career (the six considered here and a traditional boy's adventure story, *The Man with Yellow Eyes* [1963], for the Buckskin Book series), her importance should not be underestimated. In a country with no real tradition of fantasy, she created six fantasies. And, though her plots may occasionally seem somewhat formulaic and her characters a bit predictable, one cannot help but applaud the tenacity of her belief that people could learn to be selfless and, in doing so, could create a true community. The ideal, she firmly believed, simply lay hidden somewhere in the real world, just beyond the mountains.

Critical response to Clark, though sparse, has been quite favorable. Joan Selby and Gwyneth Evans, in particular, praise her success in creating a genuinely Canadian mythology which synthesizes Indian legend, fairy tale, and folk lofe within the framework of the beloved British Columbia landscape that inspired her fantasies. Though largely unread today, particularly by the children for whom her stories were created, Clark nonetheless retains her role as one of Canada's first and most successful children's fantasists.

References:

Gwyneth Evans, " 'Nothing Odd *Ever* Happens Here': Landscape in Canadian Fantasy," *Canadian Children's Literature*, nos. 15-16 (1980): 22-25;

J. Kieran Kealy, "The Flame-Lighter Woman," *Canadian Literature*, 78 (Autumn 1978): 32-42;

Joan Selby, "Catherine Anthony Clark: Myth-Maker," *British Columbia Library Quarterly*, 24 (January 1961): 26-31;

Selby, "The Creation of Fantasy: the Fiction of Catherine Anthony Clark," *Canadian Literature*, 11 (Winter 1962): 39-45.

John Coulter

(12 February 1888-1 December 1980)

Geraldine Anthony
Mount Saint Vincent University

BOOKS: *The House in the Quiet Glen and the Family Portrait* (Toronto: Macmillan, 1937);
Radio Drama Is Not Theatre, by Coulter and Ivor Lewis (Toronto: Macmillan, 1937);
Transit Through Fire (Toronto: Macmillan, 1942);
Churchill (Toronto: Ryerson, 1944);
Deirdre of the Sorrows (Toronto: Macmillan, 1944); republished as *Deirdre* (Toronto: Macmillan, 1965);
Turf Smoke (Toronto: Ryerson, 1945); republished as *Turf Smoke on Manhattan* (Dublin: Talbot, 1949);
The Blossoming Thorn (Toronto: Ryerson, 1946);
Riel (Toronto: Ryerson, 1962);
The Trial of Louis Riel (Ottawa: Oberon, 1968);
The Drums Are Out (Chicago: De Paul University Press, 1971);
François Bigot (Toronto: Hounslow, 1978);
Prelude to a Marriage: Letters and Diaries of John Coulter and Olive Clare Primrose (Ottawa: Oberon, 1979);
In My Day (Toronto: Hounslow, 1980).

PLAY PRODUCTIONS: *Father Brady's New Pig*, Toronto, Arts and Letters Club Theatre, 1937;
The House in the Quiet Glen, Toronto, Hart House Theatre, 1937;
The Family Portrait, Toronto, Hart House Theatre, 1938;
Holy Manhattan, Toronto, Arts and Letters Club Theatre, 1940;
Mr. Churchill of England, Toronto, Arts and Letters Club Theatre, 1942;
Transit Through Fire, University of Toronto, Convocation Hall, 1943;
Oblomov, Toronto, Arts and Letters Club Theatre, 6 March 1946;
The Drums Are Out, Dublin, Abbey Theatre, 12 July 1948;
Riel, Toronto, Royal Ontario Museum Theatre, 25 February 1950;
Sleep, My Pretty One, London, St. James Theatre, March 1954;

John Coulter (photograph by Mario Geo, Toronto)

A Capful of Pennies, Toronto, Central Library Theatre, 22 March 1967;
The Crime of Louis Riel, London, Ontario, Dominion Drama Festival, 5 April 1967;
The Trial of Louis Riel, Regina, Saskatchewan, Saskatchewan House, 14 June 1967.

TELEVISION: *Come Back to Erin*, CBC, 1955;
Transit Through Fire, CBC, 1955;
Riel, GM Presents, CBC, 23 April 1961;
Mr. Oblomov, Playdate, CBC, 1 November 1962;
The Drums Are Out, FM Theatre, CBC, 4 May 1969.

RADIO: *Sally's Chance*, BBC (Belfast), 1925;

A Tale of Old Quebec, BBC (London), 1935; CBC, 1935;

The Family Portrait, BBC (Belfast), 1935; produced again as *Stars of Brickfield Street*, CBC, 1938;

Pigs, CBC, 1940; produced again as *Clogherbann Fair*, BBC (Belfast), 1948;

Quebec in 1670, The Living History Series, CBS, 1940;

This Is My Country, CBC, 1941;

This Great Experiment, CBC, 1942;

The Trial of Joseph Howe, CBC, 4 February 1942;

Transit Through Fire, CBC, 8 March 1942;

Mr. Churchill of England, CBC, 1943;

Deirdre, Tuesday Night, CBC, 20 April 1946;

Oblomov, BBC (London), 1946; *Wednesday Night*, CBC, 19 November 1961;

The Drums Are Out, Wednesday Night, CBC, 11 July 1950;

While I Live, CBC, 1951;

Riel, Wednesday Night, CBC, 4 April 1951;

A Capful of Pennies, CBC, 1967;

The Crime of Louis Riel, Tuesday Night, CBC, 10 December 1968;

The Red Hand of Ulster, CBC, 9 February 1974.

PERIODICAL PUBLICATIONS:

FICTION

"The Agitator," *Ulster Review*, 1 (October 1924): 108-109;

"The Catholics Walk," *Living Age*, 323 (22 November 1924): 433-435;

"In the Dormitory," *Ulster Review*, 2 (December 1925): 324-326;

"Boy at a Prayer Meeting," *Adelphi*, 3 (May 1926): 808-815;

"The Novice," *Adelphi*, 2 (September 1928): 57-58;

"Dinner Hour at the Mill," *New Adelphi*, 10 (September 1935): 373-374;

"Down Our Street," *Ireland's Saturday Night* (16 April 1936).

NONFICTION

"On the Art of the Playwright," *Curtain Call*, 9 (January 1938): 7;

"The Canadian Theatre and the Irish Exemplar," *Theatre Arts Monthly*, 22 (July 1938): 503-509;

"Why Sabotage the Theatre?," *Canadian Review of Music and Art*, 1 (May 1942): 5, 6, 18;

"Toward a Canadian Theatre," *Canadian Review of Music and Art*, 4 (August-September 1945): 17-20;

"Time for Dusting Off the Drama Festival," *Saturday Night*, 62 (22 March 1947): 22;

"A Festival Adjudicator Should Wear Two Masks," *Saturday Night*, 62 (26 April 1947): 18-19;

"Words for Music: Confessions of a Librettist," *Theatre Arts*, 31 (September 1947): 32-34;

"Lament for Healey Wilian," *Monthly Letter of the Arts and Letters Club* (19 February 1968).

The "Dean of Canadian playwrights," John Coulter, was an Ulsterman from Belfast, forty-eight years old when he arrived in Canada in 1936, literally in pursuit of a young writer, Olive Clare Primrose, with whom he had fallen in love in London. They were married in Toronto on 4 July 1936, and, instead of bringing his bride back to London as he had intended, Coulter remained with "Babs" permanently in Toronto. Already a committed dramatist, Coulter brought to Canada the rare talent for perfection of style in playwriting. He also brought the farsightedness of the mature supporter of the arts to a culturally underdeveloped country, and he plunged immediately into needed organization, cofounding the Canadian Conference of the Arts and supporting, with others, the formation of the Canada Council and the Stratford Shakespeare Festival. Through radio, the press, and finally television, Coulter was persistent in his appeal to young Canadians to produce Canadian drama.

John Coulter was born of Protestant parents, Francis and Annie Clements Coulter, in Belfast, Northern Ireland, and he grew up in "no man's land" between the Roman Catholic Falls Road and the Protestant Shankhill Road, watching the rioters' violence, frequently beaten by both sides, but imbued with his parents' generous, unbiased view of mankind. Educated at the Belfast School of Art and Technology and at Manchester University, Coulter was employed as resident master of Wesley College, Dublin, in 1914, where the Abbey Theatre became his habitat and William Butler Yeats his idol. One evening Coulter visited Yeats and his wife in their home on Stephen's Green. Coulter was hypnotized by Yeats's voice and mystique, but even more impressed by Yeats's business acumen. Inspired by Yeats, Coulter returned to Belfast in 1919 to begin a fundraising campaign to build a theater for the Ulster Players. But in 1920 conflict between Catholics and Protestants flared up again, and Coulter fled to England. There he wrote radio plays and other feature programs for the BBC, while at the same time working as managing editor of John Middleton Murry's journal, *New Adelphi*.

THE HOUSE
IN THE
QUIET GLEN
A COMEDY

by
JOHN COULTER
Author of
"The Family Portrait"

Dust jacket for the first paperback edition of the stage play based on Coulter's radio drama Sally's Chance *(courtesy of the John Coulter Archive, Mills Memorial Library, McMaster University)*

Of all the literary pieces produced by Coulter in those years from 1920 to 1936, perhaps the most significant (because they highlight his two later trends in drama) were the radio plays *A Tale of Old Quebec* and *The Family Portrait*. *The Family Portrait*, a stage comedy originally entitled "The Folks in Brickfield Street," was rewritten for radio and produced by BBC radio in Belfast in 1935, published by Macmillan in 1937, and chosen in 1938 by BBC as one of its twelve best radio plays in fifteen years of broadcasting. It was also produced by CBC radio, Toronto, in 1938 under the title *Stars of Brickfield Street*, and under its original title as a stage play at Hart House Theatre, Toronto, in 1938. In 1948 it was produced by the Group Theatre in Belfast and had a long, successful run. It was also produced by Lennox Robinson as an Abbey Theatre School

production at the Abbey Theatre, Dublin. In 1956 it was revised for television by Rita Greer Allen under the title *The Sponger*, and produced on 6 March 1956 on CBC-TV *GM Theatre*. *A Tale of Old Quebec* was his first Canadian historical and romantic verse drama; *The Family Portrait* was one of his realistic dramatizations of Ulster life. *A Tale of Old Quebec* was commissioned by BBC radio for shortwave transmission to Canada as England's salute to the Quebec tercentenary in 1930. With the rock as archetypal image of Quebec, it poetically records Jacques Cartier's explorations, French Catholic missionaries' work among the Indians, England's ships of war, General James Wolfe's victory over General Louis Joseph de Montcalm, and the final merging of New France with English Canada.

The Family Portrait dramatizes a Belfast family's unsuccessful attempt to stifle the artistic impulses of their playwright son. Alec's play eventually succeeds in London, and overnight he becomes a star, to the chagrin of his working-class family who belatedly claim to have supported his talent all along. *The Family Portrait* highlights Coulter's gift for realistic dialogue, sharply revealing the idiosyncrasies of his characters and providing ground for a subtle criticism of Belfast's lower middle class: their lack of appreciation for the arts, their puritanical Protestantism, their materialistic values, and their ignorance of social movements.

It was at John Middleton Murry's office at the *New Adelphi* in London that Coulter first met Olive Clare Primrose, the daughter of Dr. Primrose, head of the Medical School at the University of Toronto. Coulter said it was love at first sight. Their marriage was postponed for fear of hurting their respective companions. Primrose had been living with a woman friend in London. Coulter explores this relationship in the unproduced play "One Weekend in Spring" (1943). Originally entitled "Sketch for a Portrait," the longer version, "One Weekend in Spring," sensitively explores this relationship between two women, one of whom obviously has latent lesbian tendencies. This was possibly the woman with whom Primrose had been living in London. Coulter had been living for many years with his close friend, the Irish artist James Sleator. When at last Coulter revealed his intentions of marrying Primrose, it was with disastrous effects. Sleator could not accept what he termed "disloyalty," and he and Coulter parted bitter enemies, never to be reconciled. All this is recorded in Coulter's play "Portrait of a Painter" (1980) which has not yet been pro-

Coulter in the early 1930s (courtesy of the John Coulter Archive, Mills Memorial Library, McMaster University)

duced. "Portrait of a Painter" was written at Geraldine Anthony's request and remains unpublished and unproduced in the Coulter Archive at McMaster University, Hamilton, Ontario. It is Coulter's attempt, in the last year of his life, to portray his and Sleator's relationship, in which, for Sleator, an undercurrent of latent homosexual tendencies was apparent and came to an emotional climax when Coulter revealed his intention to marry Primrose. Coulter's marriage was, nevertheless, a richly happy and rewarding union. His wife was his colleague and confidante, listening to his plans for plays, making suggestions, correcting manuscripts. She put his career before her own, and when their two daughters were born (Primrose in 1938 and Clare in 1942), Babs Coulter took over the care of household and family so that her husband could give his full time to writing.

Coulter's plays may be divided into three categories: the Irish plays of which he is a master, the Canadian historical dramas, and those plays neither Irish nor Canadian which delineate the human spirit in conflict with itself. Of the Irish plays, one of his first successful attempts was *Sally's Chance* (1925), produced by Tyrone Guthrie on BBC radio in Belfast. During Coulter's first year in Canada, he adapted it for the stage, retitled it *The House in the Quiet Glen*, and produced it at the 1937 Dominion Drama Festival, where it won all but one of the awards, breaking every Festival record as a prizewinning play. Its colorful characterization, racy dialogue, and authentic atmosphere reveal a folk drama similar in form to Lady Gregory's farces but differing widely in its Ulster dour tone and idiom. The simple plot revolves around young Sally, whose parents arrange her marriage to the rich, old widower Robert Dogherty. But Sally is already in love with Dogherty's son, Hughie, a fearfully timid lad. It is Sally who confronts the old man and her parents, and wins. A fresh and spontaneous approach combined with convincing Ulster dialogue account for this play's success. It was followed closely by another Irish play, his first actually written in Canada, in 1937, *Father Brady's*

New Pig (subsequently retitled, first *Pigs* and then *Clogherbann Fair*), for which Coulter won another award at the 1940 Dominion Drama Festival. Under the title *Father Brady's New Pig*, it was first produced as a stage play by the Arts and Letters Club Theatre in Toronto, then revised for radio as *Pigs* and produced on CBC radio in 1940, and presented again as the original stage play, *Father Brady's New Pig*, at the 1940 Dominion Drama Festival, there winning an award. Eventually it was retitled *Clogherbann Fair* in a longer radio version for BBC radio in Belfast, Ireland, in 1948, and again produced there on 15 December 1954 on the *Wednesday Matinee Program*.

A two-year interlude (1938-1940) in New York City with his wife and family gave Coulter an opportunity to improve his radio-playwriting techniques at CBS-WABC in a series of American history plays, *The Living History Series*. While in New York he also wrote a sentimental Irish-American stage play, "Holy Manhattan," later adapted as the novella *Turf Smoke* (1945).

During the World War II years Coulter wrote the play *Mr. Churchill of England*, which became the basis of his later biography *Churchill* (1944). He used a living-newspaper technique in a series of vignettes, weaving description, dialogue, symbolism, and excerpts from Churchill's speeches into a unified whole. Under the title *Mr. Churchill of England* it was first produced as a stage play by the Arts and Letters Club Theatre in Toronto in 1942, receiving favorable reviews. In 1943 it was revised for radio and produced by CBC in Toronto.

It was also during this period that Coulter became interested in writing librettos for new Canadian radio operas. With Healey Willan as composer, Coulter wrote the librettos for two original radio operas: *Transit Through Fire*, produced on CBC radio, 8 March 1942, on young Canadians facing the burden of war in their quest for life's meaning; and *Deirdre,* produced by CBC radio's *Tuesday Night* program, 20 April 1946, using the ancient Irish legend in a new and sensitive approach. Commissioned by CBC radio, they were both extraordinarily successful. *Transit Through Fire* was called by critics Canada's first opera of professional caliber and the authentic voice of Canada. Critics noted in both operas Coulter's powerful and poetic librettos which they said could stand alone and be produced independently as poetic dramas.

The year 1946 was a fruitful one for Coulter. In addition to production of the opera

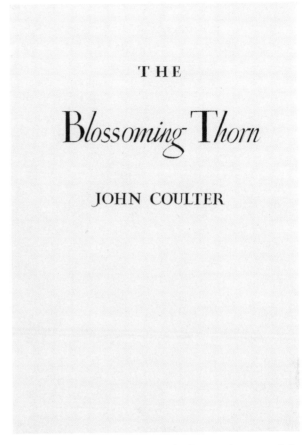

T H E

Blossoming Thorn

JOHN COULTER

Dust jacket for Coulter's only book of poetry (courtesy of the John Coulter Archive, Mills Memorial Library, McMaster University)

Deirdre, the play *Oblomov* was written and staged, and Coulter's one book of poetry, *The Blossoming Thorn*, appeared. It was also a year of introspection for Coulter, brought on by the death of his close friend and father-in-law, Dr. Primrose, the deaths of other family members, and by his wife's sudden illness with polio. Coulter adapted Ivan Goncharov's 1858 novel *Oblomov* into a stage play, a radio play, and a television drama. As a stage play, *Oblomov* was produced at the Arts and Letters Club Theatre, 6-9 March 1946. It was produced by the Group Theatre, Belfast, in 1959, and again at the Arts and Letters Club Theatre in 1959. It was also produced at the Talbot Theatre, University of Western Ontario, summer 1967. The radio adaptation was given its premiere performance by the BBC under Val Gielgud and Donald McWhinney in 1946, and in 1954 it was widely produced on radio in countries in Europe, Asia, Africa, and Australia. It was presented in Toronto on CBC radio's *Wednesday Night* program on 19 November 1961. Coulter revised it for television as *Mr. Oblomov*, and it

From the manuscript for Coulter's play Riel *(courtesy of the John Coulter Archive, Mills Memorial Library, McMaster University)*

was produced on CBC-TV's *Playdate* on 1 November 1962. It has been translated into more than a dozen languages, including Arabic and Urdu. This play brought Coulter international recognition but not Canadian acclaim. Canadians failed to empathize with the "superfluous man," the antiactivist who withdraws from a decadent civilization, feeling that no contribution of his could redeem it. Goncharov emphasized the psychological lethargy and the sociological factors in Russian society contributing to his hero's disintegration; Coulter examined the philosophical and comical aspects. Coulter's plot revolves around the calculated attempts of friends to bring Oblomov back to their so-called sane way of living. Produced on radio, television, and stage, *Oblomov* reached every continent in the world.

The Blossoming Thorn is romantic in style and derivative of Yeats. It sings of the sorrows of the exiled man, of the bereavement of those who have lost their loved ones, of the seasonal changes that accompany and revitalize one's moods.

In the years that followed Coulter drew upon his personal knowledge of controversy and rebellion in Ireland to produce fictional and historical heroes in several plays; the most outstanding were *The Drums Are Out* and *God's Ulsterman*. *The Drums Are Out* had its world premiere at the Abbey Theatre, Dublin, on 12 July 1948, playing to full houses for five weeks, although scheduled for only one week. Originally written in 1947 for the Dominion Drama Festival, that festival refused to stage it for reasons that they termed "production difficulties"; later, Canadian producers admitted their objections to the theme. Finally in 1950 it was produced at the Dominion Drama Festival, winning for Coulter the Sir Barry Jackson Trophy for the best play. Coulter revised it for CBC radio; it was presented on the *Wednesday Night* program on 11 July 1950, and on the CBC *Radio Showcase* on 7 August 1967 and 4 May 1969. Coulter then revised it for television, and it was produced on CBC-TV, Toronto, *FM Theatre*, on 4 May and 7 August 1969.

In *The Drums Are Out* the IRA theme is of so controversial a nature that, as noted above, Canada at first refused to produce it. *The Drums Are Out* deals with a 1920s Belfast family sharply divided by political and religious issues. Protestant Sergeant Sheridan is faced with either turning in the Catholic IRA leader who is in love with his daughter and has taken refuge in his home or giving up his career. He chooses the latter course.

Dust jacket for the first of Coulter's three plays about Canadian insurgent Louis Riel

The IRA members are treated as romantic heroes in this play. *God's Ulsterman* is a two-play sequence for stage: *Dark Days of Ancient Hate* and *The Red Hand of Ulster*. The first is merely a preface to the second, which was revised for radio and produced on CBC radio, Toronto, on 9 February 1974. In *God's Ulsterman*, written while on a year's vacation in Ireland in 1971, Coulter sees the new IRA as a group of violent, vindictive men. Yet in both plays the prophetic theme is the same—that there are absolute antinomies in religion and politics, conflicts and contradictions so fixed and final that they cannot naturally be resolved.

In 1950 Coulter searched for a Canadian hero who might have been pivotal in a dangerous revolutionary crisis, and he discovered Louis Riel. It was Coulter who brought this forgotten man to life again and revealed to Canadians Riel's dimensions as a national hero. Before Coulter's play, only the Métis, that downtrodden French-Indian minority group in Manitoba, revered Riel as a prophet; after Coulter's play, Canadians saw him for the first time as a victimized leader, the Father of Manitoba, and the symbol of the Indian, French, and English elements that constitute Canada's heritage. In studying Riel's history, Coulter discovered passion and violence similar to those of Northern Ireland's history. The same hostilities existed in Canada in 1869—between French and English, Catholics and Orangemen, Irish and Scottish, Métis and Canadian. Coulter's finished play *Riel* developed eventually into a trilogy: *Riel, The Crime of Louis Riel,* and *The Trial of Louis Riel. Riel* premiered in a small theater in Toronto's Royal Ontario Museum on 25 February 1950, but never received the major production it deserved until 13 January 1975, when it was produced at the National Arts Centre, Ottawa. Coulter revised it for radio, and it was performed on CBC radio's *Wednesday Night* program on 4 April and 9 May 1951. He later revised it for television, and it was produced by CBC-TV *GM Presents* on 23 and 30 April 1961, in Canada. It has since been televised in Great Britain, the United States, and several European countries.

The Crime of Louis Riel was a shortened version of *Riel* presented at the Dominion Drama Festival in London, Ontario, on 5 April 1967 and awarded the regional prize for the best Canadian play. It was revised for CBC radio's *Tuesday Night* program and presented on 10 December 1968.

The Trial of Louis Riel, a documentary of the actual trial, was commissioned by the Regina, Saskatchewan, Chamber of Commerce for the Centennial Year and was produced on 14 June 1967 in the ballroom of Saskatchewan House in a mock-up of the original courthouse, using the audience as spectators at the trial. It has since become an annual tourist attraction each summer in Regina. The action in Coulter's play *Riel* takes place in the Northwest Territories in 1869 as the land is being taken unjustly away from the Métis and sold by the Hudson Bay Company to Canada. Riel leads his people in rebellion, rightfully claiming Manitoba for his Métis people under the British flag. Riel is defeated and retreats to Montana. In part two of the play he returns in 1885 in answer to the pleas from the Métis, leads another rebellion, is defeated, unjustly tried for treason, and hanged. Canadian government and Church leaders are revealed as conspirators, allowing Riel to be hanged in order to gain Manitoba

Title page for the volume Coulter began after his wife's sudden death

as a province for Canada. In form the play closely resembles works of Bertolt Brecht's epic theater with its characters as symbols, its elevated language, its documentary techniques, its distancing from the audience, and its rapid succession of scenes producing a composite picture. *Riel* constituted the peak of Coulter's dramatic career in Canada.

Another play centering on a historical hero is *A Capful of Pennies. A Capful of Pennies* premiered at the Central Library Theatre, Toronto, on 22 March 1967. It was also revised for CBC radio that same year. *A Capful of Pennies* depicts incidents in the volatile life of the actor Edmond Kean. *François Bigot and The Fall of Quebec* is yet another play on a rebel. *François Bigot and The Fall of Quebec,* later entitled simply *François Bigot* and published by the Hounslow Press, Toronto, in 1978, has not, as yet, been produced. This play offers an ironic historical reconstruction of eighteenth-century Quebec and its fall because of the dishonest machinations of Bigot, intendant of New France from 1748 to 1759. Both Kean and Bigot are dramatized as violent megalomaniacs, rebellious and harmful to those over whom they have control. These plays reveal Coulter's double interest: in megalomaniacs and in the trial as subjects for dramatic tension.

The sudden death of his wife, after their return from Ireland in 1971, temporarily brought to a halt Coulter's play-writing career. All the enthusiasm and excitement of his creative activities seemed to die with her. For the first time in forty years, Coulter had to face life alone. He took refuge in a task that became a labor of love–the editing of his wife's journals and diaries in a poignant and romantic volume, *Prelude to a Marriage* (1979). He also began the writing of his memoirs, recalling the events and theater personalities of nearly a century in the rich and memorable book *In My Day* (1980). In addition he wrote a few one-act plays, as yet unproduced, which may be found in the Coulter Archive.

Coulter wrote steadily to the day of his death, editing early plays for publication, answering letters, attempting new short plays. He died suddenly on 1 December 1980, as he was looking through some manuscripts. He was approaching his ninety-third year. Canada's oldest and most revered playwright had spent forty-four years writing and encouraging the production of Canadian drama and had followed its growth closely from the early days of radio plays to its contemporary period. His personal career in theater was a constant, bitter struggle to get his plays produced and to keep Canadian drama alive. In a letter dated 22 February 1980, he mentioned his writing as being "of some interest, or even some help, to the unfortunates who must write in years to come." Public recognition of his work came late in his life but it came, through radio and television interviews and through the press. Coulter's role in transforming what he called "the bleak wilderness of the arts in Canada in those years into the blossoming artistic life of Canada today" has been publicly acknowledged. John Coulter succeeded beyond his expectations.

References:

Geraldine Anthony, *John Coulter* (Boston: Twayne, 1976);

Anthony, ed., *Stage Voices* (Garden City & Toronto: Doubleday, 1978), pp. 1-26;

Nathan Cohen, "Louis Riel Just Will Not Die," *Toronto Daily Star*, 24 November 1966, p. 40.

Papers:

The John Coulter Archive, containing all Coulter's manuscripts, is located at Mills Memorial Library, McMaster University, Hamilton, Ontario.

Alan Crawley

(23 August 1887-28 July 1975)

W. H. New
University of British Columbia

WORK: *Contemporary Verse: A Canadian Quarterly*, edited by Crawley, nos. 1-39 (September 1941-Fall/Winter 1952).

In their memoirs, writers such as Dorothy Livesay, P. K. Page, Ethel Wilson, and George Robertson have remembered Alan Crawley for his speech, his bearing, his features, and especially his energy and his sensitivity. Eloquent, aquiline, hawklike, Spanish-looking: such are their adjectives. His voice showed traces of private-school accent, yet he disparaged the imitation Britishness that many Canadians of his generation identified with class. A champion of the Canadian voice, and of its relevance to literary modernism, he was, as editor of *Contemporary Verse,* one of the leading forces that reshaped Canadian poetry in the 1940s. Despite his physical blindness, he had insight–"the blind eyes still seeming alive as they looked downward at a book," remembered Dorothy Livesay–and a generous enthusiasm for the new poets of his time.

Born on 23 August 1887 in his maternal grandparents' home in Cobourg, Ontario, he was the third child (the first two having died in infancy) of Charles James Crawley and his wife, Maude Buck Crawley. Charles Crawley was a bank clerk who had left Gloucestershire in 1875 for New York, and then homesteaded in Holland, Manitoba. He had met his wife near Holland when she was visiting her sister, who had married an Englishman there. After their marriage the Crawleys moved to England, but did not settle, and came back to Canada (on an inheritance, following Charles's father's death) in time for Alan's birth, returning shortly to Manitoba, where Charles Crawley opened a private bank. A second son, Jack, was born six years later (he died in World War I). Given an upper-class country gentleman's upbringing in the 1890s, Alan Crawley was sent off to board at St. John's College School, Winnipeg, at the age of eight. Never robust, he enjoyed both books and the outdoors, and spent some free time climbing in the Rock-

Alan Crawley at eighty-four on the dust jacket for Joan McCullagh's history of Contemporary Verse. *This history shows how, under Crawley's editorship from 1941 to 1952, "the magazine charted the establishment of modernism in Canadian poetry."*

ies. But he did not go on to university. Instead, he articled with a Winnipeg law firm (Machray, Sharpe) in 1905, and was admitted to the bar in 1911. And it was the law that indirectly led him to literature. Weak eyesight prevented him from being accepted for military service in 1914, but legal business took him to London. There he met Harold Monro, who had established the influential Poetry Bookshop in 1915, and they began an extended correspondence.

In Winnipeg in 1915 Crawley had married Jean Horn, the daughter of a well-to-do business-man involved in the Grain Exchange, and to-gether with a friend, H. A. V. Green, the Crawleys organized an amateur theatrical group, the Community Players of Winnipeg, which per-formed in the city in their own theater for the next decade. Meanwhile Alan Crawley continued with corporation law, and his legal career might have gone ahead uninterruptedly were it not for the changing social climate in Winnipeg and for changes in Crawley's health.

In 1918 Crawley and two colleagues severed their connection with Machray, Sharpe (which be-came an investment firm) and set up their own legal practice. But in 1932 Winnipeg (which had been the site of a major, violent strike in 1919 and was a continuing center of conflict between the social establishment and the politically active working class) was rocked by a financial scandal. John Machray (of Crawley's former law firm, the son of an Anglican archbishop and now the chan-cellor and treasurer of the University of Mani-toba) became involved in an embezzlement scheme. An Anglican himself, but now disen-chanted with many of the publicly declared val-ues of Establishment figures, Crawley left the church. His involvement in the law also ended a year later, for while he was spending the summer near Kenora, Ontario, Crawley's eyesight deterio-rated completely, the result of a viral infection called chorditis.

In 1934 the Crawleys moved to Victoria, Brit-ish Columbia, with their two sons, David and Mi-chael, and at this point Crawley's literary career began in earnest. He learned braille; he adapted to the new dependency; blindness (he later averred) "made me much more tolerant and more sociable." The love of poetry, moreover, con-tinued, and his wife read aloud to him, at first so that he would be able to learn some poetry by heart. But he became involved in a wider literary circle when in 1935 he attended a lecture on Amer-ican poetry. Insisting that modern British writers were as good as Americans, he drew attention to himself, and a local poet named Doris Ferne in-vited him to meet other Canadian writers—particularly Floris Clark McLaren and Anne Marriott—so that he could find out what was hap-pening in his own country. He moved to Caulfeild (in the municipality of West Vancouver) in 1936, and by 1937 he had met the poet

Dorothy Livesay, who was living in nearby North Vancouver. In 1939 the two of them worked on some poetry readings for broadcast on a Vancou-ver radio station. The sound of poetry particu-larly preoccupied Crawley (he was not convinced that writers—Earle Birney and E. J. Pratt, he specified—made the best readers of their own works). So involved had he become in West Coast literary circles by 1941, giving readings and pub-lic lectures, that when a group of writers (Livesay and McLaren among them) raised the idea of start-ing a new, modernist little magazine, they asked Crawley to edit it. He accepted (and Floris Clark McLaren, still living in Victoria, became business manager); the first issue of *Contemporary Verse: A Canadian Quarterly* appeared later that year.

At this date the voices of modernism were rel-atively few in Canada, and primarily centered in Montreal. The *McGill Fortnightly Review* had run from 1925 to 1927, the *Canadian Mercury* from 1928 to 1929. The *Canadian Poetry Magazine*, the mouthpiece of the generally traditional Canadian Authors' Association, had begun in 1936, and the more socially reformist magazine of political commentary, *Canadian Forum*, continued to flour-ish. In some senses more radical was the socialist journal *New Frontier*, which ran from 1936 to 1937. But most poets were still writing in conven-tional modes. Crawley wanted the 1940s to be a decade of poetic renaissance. Eclectic in his taste—he prized lyric and dramatic verse most (and liked narrative least)—he sought to avoid espous-ing particular causes in poetry. When the left-leaning *Preview* and *First Statement* began (in Montreal) in 1942, both committed to the social function of poetry, Crawley issued a liberal mani-festo of his own: "The aims of CONTEMPO-RARY VERSE are simple and direct and seem worthy and worthwhile. These aims are to entice and stimulate the writing and reading of poetry and to provide means for its publication free from restraint of politics, prejudices and placa-tions, and to keep open its pages to poetry that is sincere in theme and treatment and technique."

Each issue of *Contemporary Verse* was four-teen pages long, lithographed, and shaped by Crawley's sense of quality. He dismissed both senti-mentalism and obscurity, and wrote "A poem isn't a picture. It's a statement of an idea. . . . Make your language like your speech. Be brief, clear-cut." Constantly he was writing to poets—to encourage them to contribute, to offer advice or support, or to suggest revisions to those who had submitted work for publication. Jean Crawley read the letters and poems submitted, several times, until Alan learned them by heart, and she often typed replies; Alan sometimes put the poems into braille if he wanted to return to them later. Crawley's correspondence constitutes a small history of changes in English-Canadian poetic styles in the 1940s. They are analyzed in Joan McCullagh's history, *Alan Crawley and "Contemporary Verse"* (1976).

The first issue of the magazine contained work by Earle Birney, Doris Ferne, A. J. M. Smith, Anne Marriott, Leo Kennedy, Dorothy Livesay, Floris Clark McLaren, and P. K. Page. In postwar years many new names were added to this list of contributors. Crawley was the first to publish James Reaney (in issue 18), Jay Macpherson (in issue 27), and Daryl Hine (in issue 37); he printed early work by Wilfred Watson, Margaret Avison, Phyllis Webb, Marya Fiamengo, Elizabeth Brewster, and also poems by Malcolm Lowry, Anne Wilkinson, Ralph Gustafson, A. M. Klein, Frank Scott, Louis Dudek, Roy Daniells, L. A. MacKay, Alfred Goldsworthy Bailey, Raymond Souster, George Woodcock, and Irving Layton. The magazine is a running record of the major poets of the decade. Many of the poems of P. K. Page's *The Metal and the Flower* (1954) appeared first in *Contemporary Verse*. Thirty years later, when Dorothy Livesay founded a new journal, she paid Crawley a tribute by naming her new magazine after the old one: *CV/II*. Crawley's journal outlived both *Preview* and *First Statement*, and poets remember the editor–and his encouragement and criticism–with open affection.

The first issue had spelled out Crawley's hopes: "Conviction was added to my belief that beauty and truth is not all-told; that there are many writers of our own times who can speak to us in words and images and forms that interest and appeal; and that, for most of us, their writings are too hard to come by. A small group of readers and writers, sharing these feelings, send out this first issue of CONTEMPORARY VERSE: A CANADIAN QUARTERLY, in high hope that it and succeeding numbers may play a worthy part in the building of Canadian literature." But inevitably the literary scene continued to change. One sign of such alteration of the climate involved the appearance of new magazines in eastern Canada. Impatient with *Northern Review* (John Sutherland's journal, assembled from the amalgamation of *Preview* and *First Statement*), Raymond Souster had begun *Contact* in Toronto in 1951; he espoused the influence of American

writing–especially that of Cid Corman, Robert Creeley, and Charles Olson. The center of Canadian verse had changed. Fewer manuscripts were submitted to *Contemporary Verse,* and Crawley was increasingly distrustful of his own editorial judgment. With issue number 39, in 1952, the magazine folded.

Alan and Jean Crawley moved shortly thereafter to the Okanagan Valley, near Penticton, British Columbia, to live with their son Michael; soon after, all three returned to Vancouver Island, to live at Cordova Bay, near Victoria. Jean Crawley died there in 1971; Alan Crawley died four years later, just a few weeks short of his eighty-eighth birthday. He became a footnote in many histories of modern Canadian writing, but his influence was much more personal and much more powerful than such scarce mention suggests. The words of the late critic Lionel Stevenson, in a 1970 letter to Joan McCullagh, provide a more measured epitaph: "I hoped that a new venture in Canadian poetry, such as this one, would show a fresh and native talent that was not dominated by alien models as earlier Canadian poets had been in their day. Instead, I found the fashionable tones and moods of Eliot-Auden, which I was beginning to find tedious in English and American periodicals. . . . As the subsequent issues came out, I soon changed my opinion as to the magazine's merits, and with the advantage of hindsight I realize that the first number marked the debut of a periodical that was of outstanding significance in modern Canadian poetry."

References:

Wynne Francis, "Literary Underground: Little Magazines in Canada," *Canadian Literature,* 34 (Autumn 1967): 63-70;

Joan McCullagh, *Alan Crawley and "Contemporary Verse"* (Vancouver: University of British Columbia Press, 1976);

Floris Clark McLaren, "Contemporary Verse: A Canadian Quarterly," *Tamarack Review,* 3 (Spring 1957): 55-63;

George Robertson, "Alan Crawley and Contemporary Verse," *Canadian Literature,* 41 (Summer 1969): 89-96;

Ethel Wilson, "Of Alan Crawley," *Canadian Literature,* 19 (Winter 1964): 33-42.

Papers:

Crawley's correspondence is at Queen's University, Kingston, Ontario, and at the University of Toronto.

Roy Daniells

(6 April 1902-13 April 1979)

George Woodcock

BOOKS: *Deeper into the Forest* (Toronto: Mc-
Clelland & Stewart, 1948);

The Chequered Shade (Toronto: McClelland & Stewart, 1963);

Milton, Mannerism and Baroque (Toronto: University of Toronto Press, 1963);

Alexander Mackenzie and the North West (London:
Faber & Faber, 1969; New York: Barnes &
Noble, 1969);

John Milton: Introductions, by Daniells and others,
edited by John Broadbeat (Cambridge: Cambridge University Press, 1973).

OTHER: Thomas Traherne, *A Serious and Patheti-
cal Contemplation of the Mercies of God, in Several Most Devout and Sublime Thanksgivings for
the Same*, edited by Daniells (Toronto: University of Toronto Press, 1941).

For Roy Daniells, scholarship was his vocation and poetry his avocation. For, even though
he will probably be remembered in the long run
for his own two books of verse, it was another
poet–Milton–who most engaged his attention.

Daniells was a lifelong and natural academic
in the best sense. Born in London, England, to
James and Constance Daniells, he came to Canada as a child and grew up in Victoria. This was
a Plymouth Brethren household, and, as he recounts in a posthumously published autobiographical essay, "Plymouth Brother" (*Canadian Literature*, Autumn 1981), it took him almost a lifetime to reject the constraints of his early training.
He was educated at the Universities of British Columbia (B.A., 1930) and Toronto (M.A., 1931;
Ph.D., 1936) and taught first at Victoria College
in Toronto (1934-1937) and then at the University of Manitoba, where he was head of the Department of English from 1937 to 1946. In 1948 he
married Laurenda Francis (with whom he subsequently had two daughters) and began his tenure
as head of the English department at the University of British Columbia, a position he held until
1965, when he became University Professor.
Laurenda Daniells subsequently became archivist

Dust jacket for Daniells's first book of verse

of the University of British Columbia, a position
she still held in 1987. Roy Daniells's dedication
to the academic life was shown not only by his
deep involvement in university affairs but also by
his activity in the Royal Society of Canada, of
which he was president in 1970-1971. During his
lifetime he received many honors, including the
Lorne Pierce Medal (1970) and honorary degrees
from Queen's and McMaster Universities and the
Universities of Toronto, New Brunswick, Windsor, and British Columbia. He was named Companion of the Order of Canada in 1972.

There was nothing of the pedant in Daniells, as the breadth of his interest and the variety of his writings show. He explored Milton's Italian affiliations in *Milton, Mannerism and Baroque* (1963). He made an excursion into Canadian history with *Alexander Mackenzie and the North West* (1969). He wrote critical essays on seventeenth-century poets–including an early re-evaluation of Thomas Traherne–and on Canadian writing in the nineteenth and twentieth centuries; these have not been collected. He was one of the associate editors of the *Literary History of Canada* (1965).

Daniells's breadth of interest is reflected in the contradictions that are more apparent than real within his poems. He seems at first a traditionalist (he admitted his debt to Milton and Marvell), but soon one discovers that, just as his thought roves over whole Canadas of speculation, so his verse–using tried forms–achieves the idiosyncratic rhyme and diction that mark truly religious poets and notably those of the seventeenth century who so influenced him.

Daniells's history of publication as a poet ranged from the 1940s to the 1960s, but he belonged to no school and cannot be seen as typical of any period. His output was small and slowly produced–*Deeper into the Forest* (1948) published when he was forty-six and *The Chequered Shade* (1963) when he was sixty-one; in his last years he did not publish the verse he continued to write. Most of his poems were sonnets, and he adapted the form to his own uses with a virtuosity rare among modern poets. But in *Deeper into the Forest* he included one memorable long poem in quatrains, "Farewell to Winnipeg," in which the folk hero Louis Riel becomes the center of a complex meditation on the threatened world in modern times.

Daniells's best sonnets were those in his second book, *The Chequered Shade*. The way of speaking is contemporary; the human condition is seen within the traditional frame but through the eyes of modern man. In many of the poems, based on texts from the Psalms and the New Testament,

Dust jacket for Daniells's 1963 poetry collection, which includes numerous sonnets based on texts from the Psalms and the New Testament

the agony that marks man's relationship with what is not himself–whether God or Nature–is celebrated, often with humor, always with curiously reverent irreverence. The notions of immortality that inspire a sonnet such as "Advice 2"–about an old man dying–have a stubborn unorthodoxy which reminds one that Daniells started life as a Plymouth Brother.

> What the old, wise indomitable man
> Gave you, retain and foster till it flower
> Deep in your heart; then pass the hard
>   seed on
> To germinate in others its pure power.
> When the old councillor must veer to sea,
> O do not grieve. He goes. And you are he.

Robertson Davies

(28 August 1913-   )

Diana Brydon
University of British Columbia

BOOKS: *Shakespeare's Boy Actors* (London: Dent, 1939; New York: Salloch, 1941);

Shakespeare for Young Players: A Junior Course (Toronto: Clarke, Irwin, 1942);

The Diary of Samuel Marchbanks (Toronto: Clarke, Irwin, 1947; revised, 1966);

Overlaid: A Comedy (Toronto: French, 1948);

Eros at Breakfast and Other Plays (Toronto: Clarke, Irwin, 1949);

Fortune, My Foe (Toronto: Clarke, Irwin, 1949);

The Table Talk of Samuel Marchbanks (Toronto: Clarke, Irwin, 1949; London: Chatto & Windus, 1951);

At My Heart's Core (Toronto: Clarke, Irwin, 1950);

Tempest-Tost (Toronto: Clarke, Irwin, 1951; New York: Rinehart, 1952; London: Chatto & Windus, 1952);

A Masque of Aesop (Toronto: Clarke, Irwin, 1952);

A Jig for the Gypsy (Toronto: Clarke, Irwin, 1954);

Renown at Stratford: A Record of the Shakespearian Festival in Canada 1953, by Davies and Tyrone Guthrie (Toronto: Clarke, Irwin, 1954);

Twice Have the Trumpets Sounded: A Record of the Stratford Shakespearian Festival in Canada 1954, by Davies and Guthrie (Toronto: Clarke, Irwin, 1954);

Leaven of Malice (Toronto: Clarke, Irwin, 1954; New York: Scribners, 1955; London: Chatto & Windus, 1955);

Thrice the Brinded Cat Hath Mew'd: A Record of the Stratford Shakespearian Festival in Canada 1955, by Davies, Guthrie, Boyd Neel, and Tanya Moiseiwitsch (Toronto: Clarke, Irwin, 1955);

A Mixture of Frailties (Toronto: Macmillan, 1958; New York: Scribners, 1958; London: Weidenfeld & Nicholson, 1958);

A Voice from the Attic (Toronto: McClelland & Stewart, 1960; New York: Knopf, 1960); republished as *The Personal Art: Reading to Good Purpose* (London: Secker & Warburg, 1961);

A Masque of Mr. Punch (Toronto: Oxford University Press, 1963);

Robertson Davies

Marchbanks' Almanack (Toronto: McClelland & Stewart, 1967);

Four Favourite Plays (Toronto: Clarke, Irwin, 1968);

Fifth Business (Toronto: Macmillan, 1970; New York: Viking, 1970; London: Macmillan, 1971);

Stephen Leacock (Toronto: McClelland & Stewart, 1970);

Hunting Stuart and Other Plays, edited by Brian Parker (Toronto: New Press, 1972);

91

The Manticore (Toronto: Macmillan, 1972; New York: Viking, 1972; London: Macmillan, 1973);

Question Time (Toronto: Macmillan, 1975);

The Revels History of Drama in English, Volume VI: 1750-1880, by Davies, Michael Booth, Richard Southern, Frederick Marker, and Lisa-Lone Marker (London: Methuen, 1975);

World of Wonders (Toronto: Macmillan, 1975; New York: Viking, 1976; London: W. H. Allen, 1977);

One Half of Robertson Davies: Provocative Pronouncements on a Wide Range of Topics (Toronto: Macmillan, 1977; New York: Viking, 1978);

The Enthusiasms of Robertson Davies, edited by Judith Skelton Grant (Toronto: McClelland & Stewart, 1979);

The Rebel Angels (Toronto: Macmillan, 1981; New York: Viking, 1982; London: Lane, 1982);

Robertson Davies: The Well-Tempered Critic: One Man's View of Theatre and Letters in Canada, edited by Grant (Toronto: McClelland & Stewart, 1981);

Brothers in the Black Art (Richmond, British Columbia: Alcuin Chapbook, no. 1, 1981);

High Spirits (Markham, Ontario: Penguin, 1982; New York: Viking, 1983);

The Mirror of Nature (Toronto: University of Toronto Press, 1983);

What's Bred in the Bone (Toronto: Macmillan, 1985; New York: Viking, 1985);

The Papers of Samuel Marchbanks (Toronto: Irwin, 1985; New York: Viking, 1986).

PLAY PRODUCTIONS: *Overlaid,* Ottawa, Ottawa Drama League, 1947;

Eros at Breakfast, Ottawa, Ottawa Drama League, 1948;

The Voice of the People, Montreal, Montreal Repertory Theatre, 1948;

At the Gates of the Righteous, Peterborough, Ontario, Peterborough Little Theatre, 1948;

Hope Deferred, Montreal, Montreal Repertory Theatre, 19 March 1948;

Fortune, My Foe, Kingston, Ontario, International Players, August 1948;

At My Heart's Core, Peterborough, Ontario, Peterborough Little Theatre, 28 August 1950;

King Phoenix, Toronto, North Toronto Theatre Guild, 1950;

A Masque of Aesop, Toronto, Upper Canada College, 2 May 1952;

A Jig for the Gypsy, Toronto, Crest Theatre, September 1954;

Hunting Stuart, Toronto, Crest Theatre, 22 November 1955;

Love and Libel, adapted by Davies from his novel *Leaven of Malice,* Toronto, Royal Alexandra Theatre, 2 November 1960; New York, Martin Beck Theatre, 6 December 1960; produced again as *Leaven of Malice,* Toronto, Hart House Theatre, 11 October 1973;

A Masque of Mr. Punch, Toronto, Upper Canada College, 29 November 1962;

Question Time, Toronto, St. Lawrence Centre, 25 February 1975;

Pontiac and the Green Man, Toronto, Macmillan Theatre, University of Toronto, 26 October 1977.

TELEVISION: *Fortune, My Foe,* CBC, 7 May 1953;

Overlaid, First Person, CBC, 14 December 1960;

Brothers in the Black Art, CBC, 17 January 1974.

OTHER: "The Theatre," in *The Arts as Communication,* edited by D. C. Williams (Toronto: University of Toronto Press, 1962), pp. 17-32;

"Epilogue," "Ontario," and "Prologue," in *Centennial Play,* by Davies, Arthur Murphy, Yves Thériault, W. O. Mitchell, and Eric Nicol (Ottawa: Centennial Commission, 1967);

Feast of Stephen: An Anthology of Some of the Less Familiar Writings of Stephen Leacock, edited, with an introduction, by Davies (Toronto: McClelland & Stewart, 1970);

"The Deptford Trilogy in Retrospect," in *Studies in Robertson Davies' Deptford Trilogy,* edited by Robert G. Lawrence and Samuel L. Macey (Victoria: University of Victoria, 1980), pp. 7-12;

"Fifty Years of Theatre in Canada," in *The Arts in Canada: The Last Fifty Years,* edited by W. J. Keith and B.-Z. Shek (Toronto: University of Toronto Press, 1980), pp. 69-80.

PERIODICAL PUBLICATIONS: "The Double Life of Robertson Davies," as Samuel Marchbanks, *Liberty* (April 1954): 18-19, 53-58;

"A Dialogue: The State of Theatre in Canada," *Canadian Theatre Review,* 5 (Winter 1975): 16-36;

"A Return to Rhetoric: The Brockington Lecture," *Queen's Quarterly,* 87 (Summer 1980): 183-197;

"Leaven of Malice: A Theatrical Extravaganza," *Canadian Drama,* 7, no. 2 (1981): 117-190;

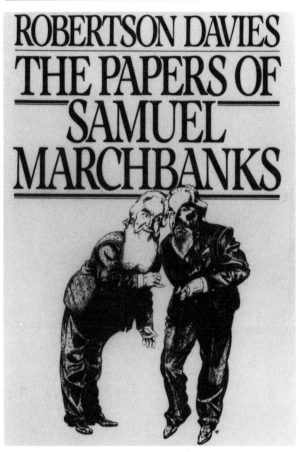

Dust jacket for the first American edition of the 1985 volume that includes The Diary of Samuel Marchbanks, The Table Talk of Samuel Marchbanks, *and material drawn from* Marchbanks' Almanack

"A Rake at Reading," *Mosaic,* 14 (Spring 1981): 1-20.

With the publication of the Deptford trilogy, Robertson Davies attained an international reputation as one of Canada's foremost men of letters. Perhaps his controversial public personality as a newspaper editor, columnist, and reviewer, and from 1961 until 1981 as Master of Massey College at the University of Toronto, combined with his striking personal appearance–Davies is six feet tall, with a flowing white beard and a fondness for academic gowns–has contributed as much as his novels and plays to the reputation he now enjoys. Certainly, as Davies himself said of Ben Jonson, a dramatist whose work he admires, he is one of those writers whose personal character is inextricably involved with his work. Davies has always valued wholeness, and his own work makes a satisfying whole. His output has been extremely varied: drama, journalism, criticism, novels, speeches, even a Royal Commission Report

have all flowed from his pen. But his work is held together by an individual vision which continues to mature and evolve without changing its essential nature. Although Canadians have been slow to accept Davies's vision as a reflection of their own experience, he has succeeded in capturing the popular imagination and in impressing the literary establishment with his entertaining blend of wit and high seriousness.

Davies was born in the village of Thamesville, Ontario, on 28 August 1913, the youngest of three sons of newspaper publisher and Liberal senator William Rupert Davies and his wife, Florence Sheppard McKay Davies. When Davies was five, the family moved to another small town, Renfrew, in the Ottawa Valley, and from there to the city of Kingston when Davies was twelve. These movements define the geographical heart of Davies's fictional worlds: his best work is rooted in a thorough knowledge of that region of Ontario which lies between Kingston and Toronto. Although he lived in Kingston, from 1928 to 1932 he attended Upper Canada College in Toronto (Colborne College of *Fifth Business, The Manticore,* and *What's Bred in the Bone*). Here his interest in music was encouraged, he was active in school dramatics, and he edited the school paper in his final year.

Because he was, in his own words, a "Lopsided Boy," capable of learning anything that interested him "in record time" but hopeless in mathematics, he did not qualify for entrance to the university. Instead, arrangements were made for Davies to attend Queen's University in Kingston as a special student, not working toward a degree. After three successful years at Queen's, where he read widely and was active in the Drama Guild, he went on to Balliol College, Oxford. Here he involved himself once more in student theater and obtained his B.Litt. in 1938 for a thesis he published the following year, entitled *Shakespeare's Boy Actors.* Already in this early work Davies displays that assured and formal style which stamps everything he has done and which Robert Cluett, after a computer analysis of Davies's prose, has labeled "the Tory Mode" (*Journal of Canadian Studies,* 1977). Here, too, emerge a love of the theater and an interest in the actor's perspective on drama, two concerns which have preoccupied Davies throughout his career.

His parents' enthusiasm for the stage had stimulated his interest very early in life: he remembers his first appearance in public at the age of three in an opera called *Queen Esther,* and as a schoolboy he kept lengthy diaries recording his responses to the many performances he saw. It is not surprising, therefore, that after graduation, Davies joined the Old Vic Company, working from December 1938 to December 1939 at various jobs, as assistant stage manager, research assistant, teacher of theater history, and bit actor. With the outbreak of war, the company was disbanded, and Davies was rejected for military service. He married Brenda Matthews, the Australian-born stage manager of the Old Vic, on 2 February 1940. After a honeymoon in Wales, they returned to Canada, where Davies became literary editor of *Saturday Night,* then a weekly review of politics, finance, and the arts. The first of his three daughters was born that December. Two years later he became editor of the Peterborough *Examiner.* He was to hold this post for the next twenty years.

For Davies, recording and commenting on his experiences is as much a part of life as living them. Since his youth he has kept diaries, notebooks, and scrapbooks, in which he jots down ideas or assembles information and on which he may draw for his writing. Davies has always combined writing with other work. For twenty-eight years he was a journalist; for twenty he was a university professor. (He retired in June 1981.) He has sat on committees and boards; he has had the ordinary experiences of a dedicated family man. All of this he considers necessary to his life as a writer. In "The Conscience of the Writer" (collected in *One Half of Robertson Davies,* 1977) he explains: "My kind of writer–I can speak for no other–needs other work and a routine to keep him sane." Later he likens the life of a writer to a long self-analysis. Davies's lifelong interest in psychology is well documented. As a young man, he read Freud's collected works "from end to end." After forty, dissatisfied with "Freud's reductive train of thought," he turned to the collected works of C. G. Jung. Jung, he feels, is better suited to the older mind and to a country like Canada, which he believes is both "fuzzier" and "more humane" than the United States. In "What May Canada Expect from her Writers?" (*One Half of Robertson Davies*) he argues that "the literature of a country is in many ways like the dreams of a man. . . . Canada does dream, but it pays very little heed to its dreams." Believing that what the stage mocks is what society fears, Davies sets out to make us take heed. His preface to *Question Time* (1975) can be taken as a summary of all his work: this play, he writes, "is about the relation-

ship of the Canadian people to their soil, and about the relationship of man to his soul. We neglect both at our peril." This neglect, the drama of the unlived life, is as recurrent a theme as the spiritual journey toward understanding, and it too may occur at a national as well as an individual level. In a much-quoted statement from *The Enthusiasms of Robertson Davies* (1979) Davies explains to Peter C. Newman: "A lot of people complain that my novels aren't about Canada. I think they are, because I see Canada as a country torn between a very northern, rather extraordinary, mystical spirit which it fears and its desire to present itself to the world as a Scotch banker. This makes for tension. Tension is the very stuff of art." These thematic tensions are reflected in Davies's style, in the tensions between satire and romance and between realism and melodrama that sometimes seem to mar his plays while contributing to the richness of his novels. They are also the source of his comedy.

In 1943 Davies began a weekly column under the title "The Diary of Samuel Marchbanks," which ran under various titles in the Peterborough *Examiner* and several other Canadian newspapers until 1953. Selections from these columns were collected in *The Diary of Samuel Marchbanks* (1947), which was revised and updated in 1966, in *The Table Talk of Samuel Marchbanks* (1949), and in *Marchbanks' Almanack* (1967). Marchbanks is Davies's alter ego or double, his shadow self. Although they share a birth date and are alike in physical appearance, they differ in temperament. Davies, posing as Marchbanks, writes in "The Double Life of Robertson Davies" (1954) that Davies is married; Marchbanks is a bachelor. "He is fawningly courteous; I am forthright. He is mangled by self-doubt and self-criticism; I am untouched by these ridiculous ailments. He has a conscience as big as a grand piano; I have no more sense of obligation than a tomcat. He makes excuses for everybody and tries to be charitable; I know a boob or a phony when I see one and I see a great many. He is inclined to be moderate in pretty nearly everything; I regard moderation as a sign of physical or intellectual weakness. He is just about everything which I detest; I am everything which he fears and seeks to avoid." Marchbanks admits to making life difficult for Davies. People tend to confuse the two of them, taking the fictional Marchbanks's testy comments for Davies's own opinions. This kind of tongue-in-cheek reversal of what is normally expected characterizes the

CANADIAN
FICTION MAGAZINE

John Reeves' Literary Portraits

Davies on the cover of the 1980 special issue of Canadian
Fiction Magazine

humor of the Marchbanks books. Marchbanks is a useful persona, providing distance while satisfying Davies's sense of fun. The trilogy of Marchbanks commentary as a whole is Davies's first step from journalism toward fiction.

In keeping with his contrary nature, Marchbanks begins his diary with a "Warning to the Reader" which is the direct opposite of those often found preceding works of fiction. This warning begins: "This is not a work of fiction, but of history—a record of the daily life of a Canadian during one of the early years of the Atomic Age. All the people mentioned in it are real; all the incidents described are actual happenings." The diary runs from New Year's Day to the last day of the year and is divided into four sections according to the seasons. Marchbanks's crotchety personality and his unending battles with his furnace throughout most of the year and with his garden in the few short months of summer provide a minimum line of continuity. The chief delight of this

book and of its sequels is in the outrageous pronouncements and clever satire which arise from Marchbanks's contemplation of the simplest events of everyday life. His targets are many, but the folly of politics and the deadening puritanism of Canadian society are chief among them.

The Table Talk of Samuel Marchbanks, designed to prove that the art of conversation still flourishes, is organized around the eating of a "simple seven course dinner" in an attempt to call up the atmosphere of the dinner table. The book does not really succeed—the impression it makes is of a haphazard series of observations and anecdotes. Marchbanks's character continues to hold it together, but it is not a book to read in one sitting.

Marchbanks' Almanack has a tighter structure and a clearer focus, following up Davies's lifelong interest in astrology. Each of the twelve sections corresponding to the signs of the zodiac are divided into sections devoted to Character Description, Enchantment-of-the-Month, Health Hints, Meditations at Random, Letters from Wizard Marchbanks's files, Excerpts from his Notebook, and Apothegms from his conversation. Several interlocking stories emerge through the letters. Most entertaining are the details of Marchbanks's lawsuit with his troublesome neighbor Dandiprat and the endless entanglements with the bureaucracy as recorded in the letters from that ubiquitous civil servant Haubergeon Hydra.

During the years Davies was creating the persona of Marchbanks as a sharp-tongued critic of Canadian folly, he was also writing and directing plays. In the absence of a professional theater in Canada, he involved himself with the amateur stage. In 1947 Davies and his wife were active in organizing and directing the Peterborough Little Theatre. In 1946 Davies's one-act *Overlaid* won a prize offered by the Ottawa Drama League, and it was produced in 1947. *Overlaid*, a naturalistic comedy set in a farm kitchen in rural Canada, is probably Davies's most popular one-act play. An unexpected windfall of money brings the conflict between Pop and his forty-year-old daughter Ethel to a head. Pop's longing for the wider world of romance and culture finds some satisfaction in the Sunday broadcasts from the Metropolitan Opera. Ethel values respectability, duty, and renunciation; she longs above all for a granite headstone that will mark her grave in the cemetery. Pop's generosity of spirit causes him to be temporarily "overlaid" by Ethel's belief in her own rightness, and he grants her wish. Pop's vitality and outrageousness, however, remain effective counters to the intellectual and spiritual deprivations which dominate the world.

Another one-act play, *Eros at Breakfast*, followed in 1948. Winner of the Gratien Gélinas Prize for the best Canadian play at the Dominion Drama Festival that year, it is a fantasy set in the solar plexus of a young man falling in love. Davies took the idea of presenting the various organs of the body as competing individuals within a complex bureaucracy from the didactic skits presented in school health lessons. Despite its slightly pretentious use of Greek names for the various characters, the drama plays well. Two of Davies's recurrent preoccupations are dramatized here in an entertaining fashion. The puritanism of Canadians is satirized through Aristophantes' behavior and pronouncements: "A Canadian's Intelligence is not an instrument of fun, Crito; it is a curb upon his baser instincts." And the comic conflicts between the various representatives of Thought and Feeling within Mr. P. S. are used to demonstrate how important it is to give each its due.

The Voice of the People (also written in 1948), a domestic comedy based on a fictional letter to the editor, is less successful. Davies patronizes his lower-class characters and allows his didacticism to override his comedy. *At the Gates of the Righteous* (1948) is weak for similar reasons. With *Hope Deferred* (1948) Davies is on surer ground. Based on Bishop Laval's banning of Governor Frontenac's plans to produce Molière's *Tartuffe* in Quebec in 1693, this play raises the questions: "Must art come last? Can real goodness and greatness come without it?" It ends with the talented Indian girl Chimène, who has been educated in France, leaving her native land for France once more. Canada seems doomed to remain a colony: from exporting furs she has moved to exporting talent.

The bitterness of *Hope Deferred* is accorded a more extended exploration in Davies's first full-length play, *Fortune, My Foe*, also produced in 1948. Davies wrote this work hurriedly because his friend Arthur Sutherland had asked for a Canadian play to be presented at his summer theater in Kingston. At the beginning of the play Nicholas, a young academic, contemplates leaving Canada for a more successful career in the United States. Professor Rowlands, his older colleague, complains: "This raw, frost-bitten country has worn me out, and its raw, frost-bitten people have numbed my heart." Yet by the end of the

play Rowlands has been revitalized, and Nicholas has decided to remain. A puppet production of Don Quixote staged by a European immigrant effects this transformation. Even in a climate as inhospitable to art as Canada's, art can work its magic. The ending of *Hope Deferred* is reversed in *Fortune, My Foe* by Nicholas's insistence, which is also Davies's, that "if we all run away it will never be any better.... [F]or some of us there is no choice: let Canada do what she will with us, we must stay."

Davies tells a story about Canada's treatment of her artists: when an experimental theater in Norway wanted to present *Fortune, My Foe*, winner of the Gratien Gélinas Prize at the 1949 Dominion Drama Festival, they appealed to the Canadian consulate for help in creating a convincing Canadian background, only to be told that the consulate "did not consider the play suitable for foreign audiences, as it presented an unfavourable picture of Canada." Davies challenged this utilitarian conception of the role of art in society in everything he did. As a result of his efforts, this kind of incident is less likely to happen today.

In 1950 Davies wrote and directed another three-act play with a similar theme, *At My Heart's Core*. Like *Fortune, My Foe*, it presents a number of characters who are disturbed and changed by the arrival of a stranger in their midst. The time is 1837, during the rebellion led by William Lyon MacKenzie in Upper Canada. Although the main characters have the names of real historical personages–Susanna Moodie, Catharine Parr Traill, and Frances Stewart–the action is fictional. These three women are tempted to various forms of dissatisfaction with their isolation in the backwoods of Canada. Their sufferings are complex and convincing, but the play is not entirely successful, partly because their tempter, the mysterious Cantwell, lacks convincing motivation for his actions. Davies intended the play to be acted in the style of the period, with a "judicious dash of exaggeration." Such a production might make the quest for motivation superfluous. The problem is typical of Davies's dramatic style, however: ideas take precedence over character development.

Davies had told Graham McInnes in 1947 that if he failed to get his plays produced in England by the time he was forty, he would turn to novels. In 1951 he published his first novel, *Tempest-Tost*, set in the fictional town of Salterton (based on Kingston, Ontario). Constructed about a little theater production of Shakespeare's *Tem-*

Dust jacket for the first American edition of volume three in Davies's Deptford trilogy

pest, the novel reveals the parallels and disjunctions between the lives of Shakespeare's characters and its own, while satirizing some small-town prejudices and conveying information about the theater. Although ideas still predominate over character development, the novel form allows Davies's humor and his didacticism wider scope.

Three young men are in love with the rich and attractive Griselda Webster, but none are equal to her. She recognizes that Roger Tasset, a "planner of twenty shabby seductions," cannot share her belief (also Davies's) that "chastity is having the body in the soul's keeping," a lesson Monica Gall must also learn in *A Mixture of Frailties* (1958) and that Maria Theotoky reasserts in *The Rebel Angels* (1981).

Griselda's most ludicrous suitor is Hector Mackilwraith, a repressed forty-year-old schoolteacher who learns through his confused feelings for Griselda that his elevation of reason above

emotion has denied him self-knowledge and made him act the fool. The novel's title and its epigraph from *Macbeth* refer to his mental and spiritual turmoil. Mackilwraith can be seen as an earlier version of Dunstan Ramsay, the narrator of Davies's most successful novel, *Fifth Business* (1970). Although their characters and their dilemmas are similar, Mackilwraith is viewed as a comical figure; he is seen from the outside by an omniscient, ascerbic, and didactic narrator, whereas Ramsay is allowed his dignity because he tells his own story. The shift in point of view–from the outside to the inside–and in focus–from the entire town to a single representative character– reveals the development of Davies's imagination from the real but limited achievement of the Salterton trilogy to the uneven greatness of the Deptford trilogy.

Davies seems to think in threes. The story of Griselda's third unsuccessful suitor, Solly Bridgetower, is taken up in the two novels which follow *Tempest-Tost*. Solly's subservience to his tyrannical mother causes Griselda to scorn him in *Tempest-Tost*, is challenged by his growing love for Pearl Vambrace in *Leaven of Malice* (published in 1954 and winner of that year's Leacock Medal for Humour), and finally is defeated in *A Mixture of Frailties*.

A false engagement notice, maliciously entered in the Salterton *Evening Bellman* to embarrass its editor along with Solly and Pearl, first brings the couple together, providing *Leaven of Malice* with its plot: the solving of the mystery of who entered it and why. Davies himself loves practical jokes. But the moralist in him distinguishes between jokes begun in a spirit of fun or used with satiric intent and jokes begun out of envy or designed to injure. Humphrey Cobbler, the high-spirited English organist, one of the most attractive figures in the trilogy, embodies Davies's love of a good joke, while Bevill Higgin, the shabby elocutionist, embodies the poisonous desire to harm. Cobbler is serious without being solemn. Like Davies, he demolishes pretensions, especially those of the second-rate, the stingy, and the self-important. He plays the fool, but his is the voice of wisdom. It is no accident that his ally is Dean Knapp, who delivers a sermon on malice in the denouement, where what was falsely announced at the beginning of the novel is genuinely announced at the end: Solly and Pearl, who changes her name to Veronica, are engaged.

The comic movement from the false to the true becomes a movement from death to new life

Dust jackets (first American editions) for Davies's trilogy-in-progress. Volume one deals with a group of people drawn together by the death of the wealthy and eccentric Francis Cornish; volume two treats Cornish's mysterious life. Davies has recently completed volume three.

in *A Mixture of Frailties,* which begins with Solly's mother's death and ends with his son's birth. The comic pattern is complicated here by a double story. Mrs. Bridgetower's will requires the formation of a trust fund to pay for the education abroad of a young Salterton woman until Veronica should give birth to a son. Solly and Veronica's efforts to thus dissolve the fund parallel the story of Monica Gall's education as a singer. As in all Davies's writing, the theme of education and of a psychological growth toward wholeness is linked with biting satire of Canadians at home and abroad. But Davies first achieves here what eludes him in the plays of this period and later–a satisfying balance between the conflicting demands of realism and melodrama.

During the years he worked on the Salterton trilogy, Davies served as a governor on the Board of Directors of the Stratford Shakespeare Festival, which he helped found, and he

wrote three books in collaboration with others (*Renown at Stratford,* 1954; *Twice Have the Trumpets Sounded,* 1954; and *Thrice the Brinded Cat Hath Mew'd,* 1955) commemorating its first three years. In 1951 his contribution to the Royal Commission on National Development in the Arts, Letters and Sciences was published in the form of a dialogue between two characters named Lovewit and Trueman (*Canadian Theatre Review,* 1975). A three-act play, *A Jig for the Gypsy,* produced in 1954 in Toronto and London, is competent in its treatment of familiar Davies ideas, but its Welsh setting removes it from the immediate attention of Canadians in search of a national literature. *A Masque of Aesop* (1952) and *A Masque of Mr. Punch* (1963), both of which Davies wrote for the students of Upper Canada College to perform, are also of peripheral interest.

After working as visiting professor at Trinity College from 1961 to 1962, Davies (appointed

Master of Massey College in 1961) moved in 1963 to the Master's Lodge at Massey College, a new graduate institution at the University of Toronto established as a gift from the Massey Foundation. Named Edgar Stone Lecturer in Dramatic Literature in 1964, he established the Graduate Centre for the Study of Drama with Clifford Leech. In 1961 he won the Lorne Pierce Medal from the Royal Society of Canada. In 1967 he was elected a fellow of the Society, and in 1972 he became a companion of the Order of Canada.

Until his retirement in 1981, Davies combined his duties as a professor with his career as a writer, never abandoning the theater entirely, but directing most of his energies toward his fiction. In 1960 he had adapted *Leaven of Malice* for the stage. Produced in Toronto in 1960 under the title *Love and Libel* and directed by Tyrone Guthrie, it went on to Detroit, Boston, and New York, where it failed on Broadway, partly because of the revisions Davies was forced to make to suit an American audience. Its successful revival in a somewhat different form in 1975 during the Shaw Festival at Niagara-on-the-Lake proves once again that "Canadian taste is not New York taste." Because drama is so dependent on nationality and a living tradition, it is less exportable than fiction. Davies has written much about the theater as a house of dreams. His experience as an undergraduate in England and his failure on Broadway reinforced his belief that literary excellence is determined as much by interest in the subject matter as by intrinsic merit. Englishmen and Americans were not interested in the dreams of the Canadian people. Davies set himself the task of presenting these dreams, and thereby explaining his nation to the world.

He told Donald Cameron in an interview collected in *Conversations with Canadian Novelists* (1973) that in *Fifth Business* he was "trying to record the bizarre and passionate life of the Canadian people." The novel takes the form of a letter addressed to his headmaster, and more fundamentally, his God, by the retired schoolmaster Dunstan Ramsay, in which he provides a justification for his life, outlining the complex drama behind his seemingly bland exterior. The plot is circular: a stone in a snowball thrown at Dunstan by his friend Boy when they are children initiates the action: that same stone discovered in Boy's mouth after his mysterious death concludes it. Although Davies began the book as an exploration of guilt, it became an investigation of responsibil-

ity and of the repercussions of a single action. In response to the popularity of *Fifth Business*–it stayed on the Canadian best-seller lists for forty-one weeks and was on the *New York Times* list–Davies wrote two sequels. *The Manticore* (1972; winner of a Governor General's Award in 1973) deals with the effects of Boy's action, inasmuch as it symbolizes his entire way of life, on his son David, as revealed through the process of Jungian analysis after his father's death. *World of Wonders* (1975) portrays the many dimensions of its impact on Paul Dempster, whose premature birth it had inadvertently caused.

Although this trilogy has given rise to a great deal of ingenious academic criticism, inspired in part by Davies's love of esoteric lore, Davies asserts that its story is "plain enough": "a happening which is only in part an accident sets in motion a train of incidents that strongly influence the lives of three men, and each man's personality determines the way in which he accepts what comes to him. To one it brings revelation; to another disillusionment and death; to the third wealth, fame and revenge." Each of the three undergoes a symbolic death and rebirth symbolized by the taking of a new name. The prudent, repressed, yet questing Dunstable takes the name of a saint, Dunstan. The superficial, materialistic Percy Boyd takes a name (his childhood nickname Boy) which epitomizes his inability to grow up. Paul Dempster, when he becomes an egotistical magician, becomes Magnus Eisengrim, a magus who has come to terms with his wolfish shadow.

In telling each of their stories, Davies is concerned with the manipulation of point of view and with everyone's need to be the hero of his own romance. Davies works hard to individualize his main characters, while demonstrating the ways in which their lives may be seen to conform to Jungian archetypes. But patterns which are totally convincing in *Fifth Business,* where the narrator himself is a historian and hagiographer, appear contrived in the two later books. David Staunton and Eisengrim sound too much like Ramsay to compel belief in their separateness from their creator.

Nonetheless, the trilogy remains compelling reading. Like the magician Eisengrim's entertainments, it satisfies the reader's need for wonder without insulting his intelligence. Although some of the fun of the earlier Salterton books has disappeared, it has been replaced by what Dr. Von Haller of *The Manticore* calls "the comedy company of the psyche," with its power to reveal the spiritual truths underlying appearances and to bring the seeker after truth to wisdom. The richness of observed detail, the evocation of mystery and romance, and the ambitious attempt to synthesize documentary and myth form the Deptford trilogy's chief strengths. They redeem the occasionally heavy-handed didacticism that has threatened Davies's work throughout his career.

In Davies's fictional world there are only two kinds of people: those who are for life and those who are against it. Life is seen as a perpetual struggle between these two groups, and between these two principles within the individual soul. The novel form enables Davies to explore these conflicts with subtlety. The drama does not. The plays of this period, although still promising, appear overly schematic and unconvincing, while the novels show an increased range of emotional maturity. *Fifth Business* captured the imagination of the nation, and its powerful harnessing of the contradictions within the Canadian psyche seems likely to endure the test of time. Davies's prejudices tend to loom larger in the compressed form of the stage play. The snobbery and misogyny of *Hunting Stuart* (produced in 1955), for example, recur in *The Rebel Angels*, the first novel of a new trilogy, but in the novel these are tempered by other preoccupations—with the distinction between wisdom and knowledge, with the importance of tradition, and with the role of the university in society. Narrated alternately by Maria Theotoky, a graduate student, and by Simon Darcourt, one of her professors, *The Rebel Angels* provides stories of intrigue and romance while exploring the disorderly depths beneath the apparently smooth surface of a modern university. Its real interest, however, seems to lie in arcane knowledge for its own sake. Maria and Simon are not individualized. Their voices sound the same.

Whereas characters and their quests for a Jungian-inspired individuation dominate the Deptford trilogy, characters recede before ideas in what may come to be seen as the Cornish family trilogy. The Deptford characters undergo remarkable transformations. The characters in the following two novels, *The Rebel Angels* and *What's Bred in the Bone* (1985), true to the proverb of the latter title, remain unchanged, their natures determined by cultural and biological breeding. The fatalism of these most recent novels may reflect their nature, in part at least, as romans à clef, or it may reflect an effort on Davies's part, as Patri-

cia Monk suggests, to move beyond a Jungian framework in his investigations into the relations between body and soul (somatotyping).

For much of his career, Davies has seemed an old-fashioned artist, writing against the grain of his times. Davies has not changed, but fashion has. In *What's Bred in the Bone* Davies's conservatism, his didactic self-consciousness, and his patriarchal values seem comfortably attuned to the mood of his time. Francis Cornish's death had begun the action of *The Rebel Angels;* his life, told by the Angel of biography, the Lesser Zadkiel, and the Daimon Maimas, his Guardian Angel, provides the story of *What's Bred in the Bone*, which was short-listed for the 1986 Booker Prize and given the 1986 Canadian Author's Association Literary Award for best fiction and the Medal of Honor for Literature by New York's National Arts Club in 1987. Francis seems meant to be a representative Canadian, which his lover Ruth defines, apparently with authorial endorsement, as "a psychological mess." Unlike the characters of the Salterton and Deptford trilogies, Francis never sorts himself out. That task is left for later generations—for Simon Darcourt, who is writing Cornish's biography, and for Maria, Simon's muse.

Despite the increased acclaim these new novels have brought him, Davies's critical reputation still rides on *Fifth Business. The Rebel Angels* and *What's Bred in the Bone* await a third completing volume before final assessment will be possible. Published in the years that elapsed between the two novels, *High Spirits* (1982) is a collection of amusing, playful ghost stories written over eighteen years to celebrate Gaudy Night, the annual Christmas party at Massey College; the stories are entertaining sports designed to be spoken for the amusement of an occasion.

The Table Talk of Samuel Marchbanks includes the assertion that "No man's newspaper writings should be saved and produced in evidence against him." Neither Marchbanks nor Davies need have worried. Davies's journalism, while uneven in interest, has aged remarkably well. The 1985 republication of much of the Marchbanks trilogy in a single volume—*The Papers of Samuel Marchbanks*—with footnotes and annotations by the author in a spoof of scholarly activity, attests to the continuing popularity of this persona. Besides the three Marchbanks books, three other collections of Davies's writings have appeared. *A Voice from the Attic*, composed at the invitation of Alfred Knopf and first published in 1960, is the most coherently organized. Conceived as a call to the "clerisy," Davies's term for "people who like to read books," this is a book about reading which asserts the need for traditional values. The title, taken from a poem by Patrick Anderson, refers to Davies's Canadian perspective; he is speaking to the world from "America's attic." *One Half of Robertson Davies*, composed of pieces that were written to be spoken, is understandably less substantial although it remains a fascinating volume for what it reveals about Davies's personality and interests. The four Larkin-Stuart Lectures, delivered at Trinity College in 1976 and essential reading for any student of Davies's work because of their masterly analysis of his recurrent preoccupations with evil and insanity and their handling in fiction, are included here. The three Alexander Lectures, delivered at University College, University of Toronto, in 1982 and printed in *The Mirror of Nature* (1983), develop Davies's lifelong interest in melodrama. These published talks are, in his words, "an extended plea for imaginative sympathy toward the theatre of the nineteenth century." *The Enthusiasms of Robertson Davies* (1979) and *Robertson Davies: The Well-Tempered Critic* (1981) round out the picture of Davies as an influential critic of Canadian culture and shaper of Canadian opinion, roles which have not received the attention accorded Davies the author and playwright yet which are important for understanding the man and his place in Canadian cultural history.

No final assessment of Davies's achievement can be made until his work is completed. He continues to win new acclaim. Over the course of his career he has received honorary degrees from approximately twenty universities in the United States and Canada. Like Dunstan Ramsay, he finds old age congenial. Whatever new heights his artistry may reach, however, his place in Canadian letters and his contribution to world literature are assured. Davies is that rare author, a man whose books are genuinely popular with a large audience while continuing to appeal to the critical establishment. Elegantly written, Davies's novels are entertaining without sacrificing seriousness and substantial without sacrificing fun. They conform to the vision of wholeness that has sustained his writing throughout his long career. Davies's fiction offers his readers an illusion of control. The author leads his readers through the ceremonies of unveiling the follies and discerning the mysteries of existence from the safety of an assured position within the order the text main-

tains. Davies's commitment to order, while recognizing the fascinating power of all that threatens it, enables his readers to trust his authority and so feel confirmed in their own human dignity as spectators at the sports the novels expose. High moral seriousness and wicked comedy have seldom met more harmoniously.

Interviews:

Donald Cameron, "Robertson Davies: The Bizarre and Passionate Life of the Canadian People," in his *Conversations with Canadian Novelists*, volume 1 (Toronto: Macmillan, 1973), pp. 30-48;

Renée Hetherington and Gabriel Kampf, "*Acta* interviews Robertson Davies," *Acta Victoriana*, 97, no. 2 (1973): 69-87;

Geraldine Anthony, "Robertson Davies," in her *Stage Voices: Twelve Canadian Playwrights Talk About Their Lives and Work* (Toronto: Doubleday, 1978), pp. 55-84;

Alan Twigg, "Robertson Davies: World of Wonders," in his *For Openers: Conversations with 24 Canadian Writers* (Madiera Park, British Columbia: Harbour, 1981), pp. 31-44;

"Robertson Davies in Conversation with Michael Hulse," *Journal of Commonwealth Literature*, 22, no. 1 (1987): 119-135.

Bibliography:

John Ryrie, "Robertson Davies, An Annotated Bibliography," in *The Annotated Bibliography of Canada's Major Authors*, volume 3, edited by Robert Lecker and Jack David (Downsview, Ontario: ECW, 1981), pp. 57-280.

References:

Peter Baltensperger, "Battles with the Trolls," *Canadian Literature*, 71 (Winter 1967): 59-67;

Nancy Bjerring, "Deep in the Old Man's Puzzle," *Canadian Literature*, 62 (Autumn 1974): 49-60;

Elspeth Buitenhuis, *Robertson Davies* (Toronto: Forum House, 1972);

Canadian Drama, special issue: *Robertson Davies: Dramatist*, 7, no. 2 (1981);

Robert Cluett, "Robertson Davies: The Tory Mode," *Journal of Canadian Studies*, 12 (February 1977): 41-46;

Wilfred Cude, "The College Occasion as Rabelaisian Feast: Academe's Dark Side in *The Rebel Angels*," *Studies in Canadian Literature*, 7, no. 2 (1982): 184-199;

Cude, "Miracle and Art in *Fifth Business*," *Journal of Canadian Studies*, 9 (November 1974): 3-16;

Paul Davey, "The Structure of Davies' Deptford Trilogy," *Essays on Canadian Writing*, 9 (Winter 1977-1978): 123-133;

Anthony B. Dawson, "Davies, his Critics, and the Canadian Canon," *Canadian Literature*, 92 (Spring 1982): 154-159;

Theo and Eileen Dombrowski, "Every Man's Judgement: Robertson Davies' Courtroom," *Studies in Canadian Literature*, 3 (Winter 1978): 47-61;

D. J. Dooley, "Baptizing the Devil: *Fifth Business*," in his *Moral Vision in the Canadian Novel* (Toronto: Irwin, 1978), pp. 109-122;

Robert Fulford, "Divine Comedies," *Saturday Night*, 100 (October 1985): 5, 6, 8, 10;

Carole Gerson, "Dunstan Ramsay's Personal Mythology," *Essays on Canadian Writing*, 6 (Spring 1977): 100-108;

Barbara Godard, "Robertson Davies' Dialogic Imagination," *Essays on Canadian Writing*, 34 (Spring 1987): 64-80;

Godard, "World of Wonders: Robertson Davies' Carnival," *Essays on Canadian Writing*, 30 (Winter 1984-1985): 239-286;

Judith Skelton Grant, *Robertson Davies* (Toronto: McClelland & Stewart, 1978);

Helen Hoy, "Poetry in the Dunghill: The Romance of the Ordinary in Robertson Davies' Fiction," *Ariel*, 10 (July 1979): 69-98;

Journal of Canadian Studies, special issue on Davies, 12 (February 1977);

Patricia Köster, "'Promptings Stronger' than 'Strict Prohibitions': New Forms of Natural Religion in the Novels of Robertson Davies," *Canadian Literature*, 111 (Winter 1986): 68-82;

Robert G. Lawrence and Samuel L. Macey, eds., *Studies in Robertson Davies' Deptford Trilogy* (Victoria: University of Victoria, 1980);

Marco P. LoVerso, "Dialectic, Morality, and the Deptford Trilogy," *Studies in Canadian Literature*, 12, no. 1 (1987): 69-89;

Hugo McPherson, "The Mask of Satire: Character and Symbolic Pattern in Robertson Davies' Fiction," *Canadian Literature*, 4 (Spring 1960): 18-30;

John Mills, "Robertson Davies," in *Canadian Writers and Their Works*, edited by Robert Lecker, Jack David, and Ellen Quigley (Toronto: ECW, 1985), pp. 19-78;

David M. Monaghan, "Metaphor and Confusion," *Canadian Literature*, 67 (Winter 1976): 64-73;

Patricia Monk, *The Smaller Infinity: The Jungian Self in the Novels of Robertson Davies* (Toronto: University of Toronto Press, 1982);

Monk, "Somatotyping, Scatomancy, and Sophia: The Relation of Body and Soul in the Novels of Robertson Davies," *English Studies in Canada*, 12, no. 1 (1986): 79-100;

Patricia Morley, *Robertson Davies* (Toronto: Gage, 1977);

John Moss, "The Double Vision of Robertson Davies or, The Deptford Rapes," in his *Sex and Violence in the Canadian Novel: The Ancestral Present* (Toronto: McClelland & Stewart, 1977), pp. 107-122;

Ivan Owen, "The Salterton Novels," *Tamarack Review*, 9 (Autumn 1958): 56-63;

Michael Peterman, *Robertson Davies* (Boston: Twayne, 1986);

Gordon Roper, "Robertson Davies' *Fifth Business* and 'That Old Fantastical Duke of Dark Corners,' C. G. Jung," *Journal of Canadian Fiction*, 1, no. 1 (1972): 33-39;

Moses Steinberg, "Don Quixote and the Puppets: Theme and Structure in Robertson Davies' Drama," *Canadian Literature*, 7 (Winter 1961): 45-53;

Susan Stone-Blackburn, *Robertson Davies: Playwright* (Vancouver: University of British Columbia Press, 1985);

Ronald Sutherland, "The Relevance of Robertson Davies," in his *The New Hero: Essays in Comparative Quebec/Canadian Literature* (Toronto: Macmillan, 1977), pp. 73-83;

Ellen Warwick, "The Transformation of Robertson Davies," *Journal of Canadian Fiction*, 3, no. 3 (1974): 45-51;

David Wyatt, "Davies and the Middle of the Journey," in his *Prodigal Sons: A Study in Authorship and Authority* (Baltimore & London: Johns Hopkins University Press, 1980), pp. 129-149.

William Arthur Deacon
(6 April 1890-5 August 1977)

Clara Thomas
York University

BOOKS: *Pens and Pirates* (Toronto: Ryerson, 1923);

Peter McArthur (Toronto: Ryerson, 1923);

Poteen: A Pot-pourri of Canadian Essays (Ottawa: Graphic, 1926);

The Four Jameses (Ottawa: Graphic, 1927; revised edition, Toronto: Ryerson, 1953);

My Vision of Canada (Toronto: Ontario Publishing, 1933).

OTHER: "Literature in Canada–in its Centenary Year," in *Yearbook of the Arts in Canada,* edited by Bertram Brooker (Toronto: Macmillan, 1929), pp. 23-31;

Open House, edited by Deacon and Wilfred Reeves (Ottawa: Graphic, 1931);

"What a Canadian Has Done for Canada," in *Our Sense of Identity,* edited by Malcolm Ross (Toronto: Ryerson, 1954), pp. 209-216.

PERIODICAL PUBLICATION: "The Reviewer," *Canadian Author and Bookman,* 38 (Fall 1959): 4-7.

William Arthur Deacon

William Arthur Deacon is best remembered as, for four decades, Canada's leading literary journalist. From 1922 to 1928 he was literary editor of Toronto's *Saturday Night,* a prestigious weekly with a national readership, from 1928 to 1936 of the *Mail and Empire* and from 1936 to 1960 of the *Globe and Mail,* both leading daily newspapers based in Toronto. He was proud to claim the distinction of being the first full-time literary journalist in Canada; when he died his central and dynamic place in the development of Canadian literature was acknowledged by William French, his successor at the *Globe and Mail,* who headed his obituary with the words, "He made a structure for Canadian literature."

Deacon was born in Pembroke, Ontario, in 1890 to Sarah Annie Davies and William Henry Deacon. His lawyer father died when he was a baby, and he and his mother moved to Stanstead, Quebec, to live with her parents, retired from the Methodist ministry, and her sister, whose husband was principal of Stanstead College, a Methodist coeducational boarding school. Deacon attended the college for both his primary and secondary schooling. In 1907 he entered Victoria College in Toronto. He left in 1909 without finishing his degree and for a few years drifted in and out of a variety of occasional jobs. In 1911 he married Gladys Coon of Weston, Ontario, and shortly thereafter began training in law, moving to Winnipeg where he was sponsored by his uncle, Thomas Russ Deacon, and articling in the office of Frank Simpson in Dauphin, Manitoba.

Meanwhile he had become a committed member of the Theosophical Society, the religious philosophical organization that had been founded in 1875 by Mme Helena Petrovna Blavatsky and that came to its peak of popularity between 1900 and 1925. He had also become a dedicated writer, convinced that the law was not for him and that it was his opportunity and mission to promote the cause of Canadian literature and the fortunes of its writers. He and his wife had divorced, and with his second wife, Sally Townsend Syme Deacon, henceforth his staunch partner in life and literature, he moved to Toronto and, by happy chance, to the position as literary editor of *Saturday Night*. He and Sally Deacon had three children, William, Deirdre, and Mary.

He was ambitious to become a first-class essayist, and, to that end, he wrote for both American and Canadian periodicals and newspapers, publishing reviews and articles in the *New York Times* and the *New York Post* literary supplements, in the *Saturday Review* and the *American Mercury*, as well as in the *Manitoba Free Press*, the *Canadian Magazine*, and many other publications. Two collections of his essays were published in the 1920s: *Pens and Pirates* (1923) and *Poteen: A Pot-pourri of Canadian Essays* (1926). Many of these essays show a real facility for occasional pieces, often humorous, on a very wide range of topics; some of them, "The Bogey of Annexation," for instance, first written for H. L. Mencken of the *American Mercury*, advance cogent, forceful, and deeply felt arguments; the essays he wrote for *Poteen* on the current state of Canadian literature and criticism are important literary-historical documents; and one of them, "What a Canadian Has Done For Canada," is a minor satirical classic in Canadian literature. This last, based on Arthur Stringer's novel *Empty Hands* (1924), satirizes with hilarious effect the misinformation about survival in the Canadian wilderness purveyed in Stringer's work.

Deacon's *Peter McArthur* (1923) was written for Lorne Pierce's Makers of Canadian Literature series and adheres to its part-biography, part-collection format. McArthur was a congenial subject: Deacon had known him personally in his last years, although by then McArthur had largely ceased writing the nostalgic sketches of rural life that had won him an international reputation. The work for which Deacon is best remembered, however, is *The Four Jameses* (1927), an account of four of Canada's most eccentric poets, James Gay, James Gillis, James McIntyre, and James MacRae. The book began as a joke on

Sally Townsend Syme, who became Deacon's second wife in the early 1920s

these four men, all of whom took their work very seriously, as well as a pointed satire on pretentious literary criticism, but Deacon came to love and respect the seriousness of his subjects' intentions. By the time he had finished, the work was more tribute than joke, but nonetheless funny. The status of *The Four Jameses* as a small classic of Canadian humor is attested by its continued popularity; a revised edition appeared in 1953 and was republished in 1974.

Deacon's final book, *My Vision of Canada* (1933), was inspired by his theosophical sense of Canada's destiny and given urgency by the tensions and anxieties aroused by the Depression and by the fear of a drift toward war that Deacon shared with many others. The book is nationalistic in its every argument and prescriptive in its tone, urging that Canada should hasten to break her ties to Britain and stand ready, with confidence, to fulfill the glorious future that Deacon saw as her appointed role among nations. It is a cranky book, often hectic in tone, but as the only utopian, visionary work to emerge from Canada in the 1930s, it remains an interesting document.

Dust jacket for Deacon's first essay collection

Deacon had been a charter member of the Winnipeg Branch of the Canadian Authors' Association, founded in 1921. In the 1930s he was president of the influential Toronto Branch, and from 1946 to 1948 he was national president. He was one of the small group of men who agitated for, and succeeded in establishing, the Canadian Writers' Foundation and the Governor General's Awards, and from 1944 to 1949 he was chairman of the board for these awards. He also organized the establishment of the Stephen Leacock Medal for Humour, and for many years he chaired its annual presentation dinner.

Perhaps Deacon is most gratefully remembered by the scores of writers with whom he corresponded and whose work he tirelessly encouraged. Letter writing was his avocation, writers were his favorite correspondents, and the craft of writing was his constant enthusiasm. After his retirement four publishers approached him to write his memoirs; he contracted with Doubleday to write two volumes, a history of Canadian literature and an anecdotal, personalized collection of memoirs. Because of Sally Deacon's ill health and then his own, he was unable to finish either volume. William Arthur Deacon suffered a long, sad decline in health; when he died in 1977 William French's memorial article in the *Globe and Mail* (9 August 1977) was his best and truest epitaph. It concludes thus: "When Deacon retired as literary editor in 1960, the publishing industry organized a banquet in his honor. Speaker after speaker praised him prompting him, when it came his turn to reply, to react with dismay. 'Surely the capable and honest critic would not be tendered a banquet,' he said. 'He would be hated and reviled–possibly stoned. Wherein have I failed?'" That failure, of course, was his success.

Biography:

Clara Thomas and John Lennox, *William Arthur Deacon: A Canadian Literary Life* (Toronto: University of Toronto Press, 1982).

Papers:

The William Arthur Deacon Manuscript Collection is at the Thomas Fisher Rare Book Library, University of Toronto. Michèle Lacombe, John Lennox, and Clara Thomas have prepared a computerized index to this collection (Deakdex, Scott Library, York University).

Mazo de la Roche
(15 January 1879-12 July 1961)

D. M. Daymond
University of Guelph

BOOKS: *Explorers of the Dawn* (New York: Knopf, 1922; London: Cassell, 1924);

Possession (New York: Macmillan, 1923; London: Macmillan, 1923; Toronto: Macmillan, 1923);

Low Life: A Comedy in One Act (Toronto: Macmillan, 1925);

Delight (New York: Macmillan, 1926; Toronto: Macmillan, 1926);

Come True (Toronto: Macmillan, 1927);

Jalna (Boston: Little, Brown, 1927; London: Hodder & Stoughton, 1927; Toronto: Macmillan, 1927);

Low Life and Other Plays (Boston: Little, Brown, 1929; Toronto: Macmillan, 1929);

The Return of the Emigrant (Boston: Little, Brown, 1929);

Whiteoaks of Jalna (Boston: Little, Brown, 1929; Toronto: Macmillan, 1929); republished as *Whiteoaks* (London: Macmillan, 1929);

Portrait of a Dog (Boston: Little, Brown, 1930; London: Macmillan, 1930; Toronto: Macmillan, 1930);

Finch's Fortune (Boston: Little, Brown, 1931; London: Macmillan, 1931; Toronto: Macmillan, 1931);

Lark Ascending (Boston: Little, Brown, 1932; London: Macmillan, 1932; Toronto: Macmillan, 1932);

The Thunder of New Wings (Boston: Little, Brown, 1932);

The Master of Jalna (Boston: Little, Brown, 1933; London: Macmillan, 1933; Toronto: Macmillan, 1933);

Beside a Norman Tower (Boston: Little, Brown, 1934; London: Macmillan, 1934; Toronto: Macmillan, 1934);

Young Renny (Boston: Little, Brown, 1935; London: Macmillan, 1935; Toronto: Macmillan, 1935);

Whiteoaks: A Play (Boston: Little, Brown, 1936; London: Macmillan, 1936);

Whiteoak Harvest (Boston: Little, Brown, 1936; London: Macmillan, 1936);

The Very House (Boston: Little, Brown, 1937; London: Macmillan, 1937);

Growth of a Man (Boston: Little, Brown, 1938; London: Macmillan, 1938; Toronto: Macmillan, 1938);

The Sacred Bullock and Other Stories of Animals (Boston: Little, Brown, 1939; London: Macmillan, 1939; Toronto: Macmillan, 1939);

Whiteoak Heritage (Boston: Little, Brown, 1940; London: Macmillan, 1940; Toronto: Macmillan, 1940);

Wakefield's Course (Boston: Little, Brown, 1941; London: Macmillan, 1942; Toronto: Macmillan, 1942);

The Two Saplings (London: Macmillan, 1942);

Quebec: Historic Seaport (Garden City: Doubleday, Doran, 1944; London: Macmillan, 1946);

The Building of Jalna (Boston: Little, Brown, 1944; Toronto: Macmillan, 1944; London: Macmillan, 1945);

Return to Jalna (Boston: Little, Brown, 1946; Toronto: Macmillan, 1946; London: Macmillan, 1948);

Mary Wakefield (Boston: Little, Brown, 1949; London: Macmillan, 1949; Toronto: Macmillan, 1949);

Renny's Daughter (Boston: Little, Brown, 1951; London: Macmillan, 1951; Toronto: Macmillan, 1951);

A Boy in the House (London: Macmillan, 1952);

A Boy in the House and Other Stories (Boston: Little, Brown, 1952; London: Macmillan, 1952);

Whiteoak Brothers: Jalna 1923 (Boston: Little, Brown, 1953; London: Macmillan, 1954; Toronto: Macmillan, 1953);

Variable Winds at Jalna (Boston: Little, Brown, 1954; London: Macmillan, 1954; Toronto: Macmillan, 1954);

The Song of Lambert (London: Macmillan, 1955; Toronto: Macmillan, 1955; Boston: Little, Brown, 1956);

Ringing the Changes: An Autobiography (Boston: Little, Brown, 1957; London: Macmillan, 1957; Toronto: Macmillan, 1957);

Mazo de la Roche, 1923

Bill and Coo (London: Macmillan, 1958; Toronto: Macmillan, 1958; Boston: Little, Brown, 1959);

Centenary at Jalna (Boston: Little, Brown, 1958; London: Macmillan, 1958; Toronto: Macmillan, 1958);

Morning at Jalna (Boston: Little, Brown, 1960; London: Macmillan, 1960; Toronto: Macmillan, 1960);

Selected Stories of Mazo de la Roche, edited, with an introduction, by Douglas Daymond (Ottawa: University of Ottawa Press, 1979).

PLAY PRODUCTIONS: *Low Life,* Toronto, Trinity Memorial Hall, 14 May 1925;

Come True, Toronto, Hart House Theatre, 16 May 1927;

The Return of the Emigrant, Toronto, Hart House Theatre, 12 March 1928;

Whiteoaks, by de la Roche and Nancy Price, London, Little Theatre in the Adelphi, 13 April 1936;

The Mistress of Jalna, Bromley, Kent, U.K., New Theatre, 12 November 1951.

OTHER: George F. Nelson, ed., *Northern Lights: A New Collection of Distinguished Writing by Ca-*

nadian Authors, introduction by de la Roche (New York: Doubleday, 1960).

PERIODICAL PUBLICATIONS:
FICTION
"The Thief of St. Loo," *Munsey's Magazine,* 28 (October 1902): 182-187;

"The Years at the Spring," *Metropolitan,* 35 (May 1911): 141-152;

"Portrait of a Wife," *Canadian Nation,* 1 (February 1928): 13-17;

"She Went Abroad," *Bystander,* 31 (2 April 1930): 24-29, 40;

"Dummy Love," *Harper's Bazaar,* 67 (April 1932): 86-87, 105-106;

"Baby Girl," *London Mercury,* 26 (October 1932): 498-507;

"Love in the Highlands," *Harper's Bazaar,* 68 (August 1933): 30-31, 88, 94;

"Come Fly With Me," *Atlantic Monthly,* 173 (March 1944): 97-100;

"Spring Song," *Canadian Home Journal,* 40 (April 1944): 5-6, 22-24.

NONFICTION
"The Past Quarter Century," by de la Roche, Stephen Leacock, and Morley Callaghan, *Maclean's* (March 1936): 36, 38;

"My First Book," *Canadian Author and Bookman*,
    28 (Spring 1952): 3-4;
" 'I Still Remember. . . ,' " *Maclean's*, 70 (April
    1957): 15-17, 80, 82, 84-90.

Mazo de la Roche was among Canada's
most popular and prolific writers in the first half
of the twentieth century. Although the extent
and variety of her contribution to Canadian literature have not been widely acknowledged in contemporary criticism, she achieved international
recognition and admiration for a substantial
body of work, including twenty-three novels,
more than fifty short stories, a history, three biographical works, and numerous plays and tales
for children. During her lifetime, the chronicles
of the Whiteoak family of Jalna, one of the most
successful family chronicles in Canadian literature, sold more than eleven million copies in one
hundred and ninety-three English editions and
ninety-two foreign editions. Her admirers included writers, publishers, producers, and enthusiastic readers from more than a dozen countries.
One of the most widely read writers in Canadian
literary history, de la Roche has retained a place
in the popular market, and many of her books remain in print. Like Laura Salverson, Martha
Ostenso, Robert Stead, Frederick Philip Grove,
and Morley Callaghan, she contributed to the
gradual shift toward realism that characterized
the Canadian novel in the early decades of the
twentieth century, and at a time when Canadian
fiction was dominated by historical novels and sentimental stories of village and rural life, she frequently challenged codes of conduct associated
with Victorian morality and tempered the pleasant world of escape with realism.

A sensitive and imaginative writer with an ap-
titude for transforming personal experience into
art and creating vital characters, lively dialogue,
and dramatic incident, de la Roche characteristically offers a mixture of realism and romance, sentimentalism, and melodrama. Frequently she
combines realistic settings with characters who expand into symbolic or psychological archetypes.
The combination of these elements in her most
successful novels exploits the impact of realism
and the suggestive power of romance and
strengthens the presentation of her most recurrent concerns—instinct, repression, freedom, and
tradition. Strongly attracted to unrestrained individuals who challenge barren respectability and
conventional codes of conduct in search of
greater freedom and fulfillment, de la Roche

also dramatizes the destructive effects of uncon-
trolled individualism and the need for continuity
and tradition. As responses to the disruptive and
violent conflicts created by these excesses and oppositions, de la Roche emphasizes man's capacity
for selflessness, endurance, and love.

Mazo de la Roche was born 15 January
1879 and died 12 July 1961. The only child of a
salesman, William Roche, and his wife, Alberta
Lundy Roche, a carpenter, de la Roche adopted
the French prefix to her family name as a child.
After spending several years in Newmarket, a village twenty miles north of Toronto, her family
moved to Toronto where Caroline Clement, de la
Roche's cousin, came to live with them. Clement
became de la Roche's trusted and close companion, and for seventy years they were seldom separated. Soon after her arrival, Clement was
initiated into the world of her cousin's "Play." According to de la Roche's autobiography, this private world began as a dream and later became
the basis for characters and events in her fiction.
In 1931 de la Roche and Clement took the unusual step of adopting two orphaned children of
friends they had met while traveling in Italy in
1929.

From 1885 until 1910 de la Roche lived in
Toronto where she attended the Ontario School
of Art for a time and studied under George
Agnew Reid, the president of the Ontario Society
of Artists. Then, in 1910, her family settled at
Rochedale, a fruit and stock farm west of Toronto on the shore of Lake Ontario. They remained there until 1915 when William Roche's
death prompted a return to Toronto. There, confronted by increasingly serious financial difficulties, de la Roche, whose writing career had
begun in 1902 with the publication of a short
story in *Munsey's Magazine*, committed herself to
a career in writing. By 1927, when she was
awarded the *Atlantic Monthly* prize for fiction and
achieved widespread recognition with *Jalna*, she
had published a variety of works, including several plays, a collection of linked short stories entitled *Explorers of the Dawn* (1922), and two novels:
Possession (1923), an account of the hardships and
romantic attachments of a novice farmer in a setting similar to Rochedale; and *Delight* (1926), a
comic and often erotic novel depicting the experiences of a beautiful immigrant girl in a small Ontario town during the early 1900s.

Delight was written while de la Roche was stay-
ing at her summer cottage on the edge of a large
estate near Clarkson, Ontario, and this setting pro-

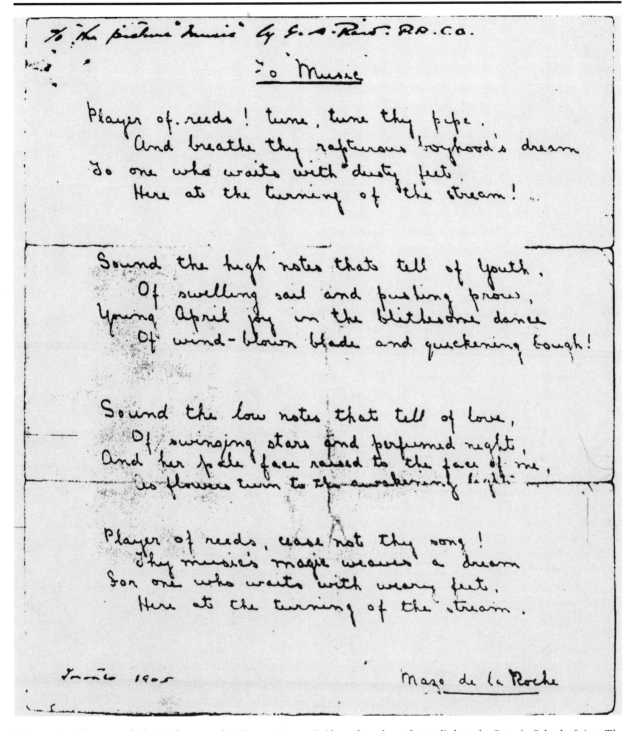

Manuscript of a poem de la Roche wrote for George Agnew Reid, under whom she studied at the Ontario School of Art. The poem is now in the Reid Scrapbook at the Art Gallery of Toronto.

vided the model for Jalna, the home of the Whiteoak family whose history de la Roche developed in sixteen novels which appeared from 1927 to 1960. In general, the chronicle of the Whiteoaks is coherent and consistent in its framework, chronology, characterization, and themes.

After *Jalna*, nine novels carry the Whiteoak history forward until 1954, while the remaining six move back in time to examine events in the history of the family. The three novels which followed *Jalna* proceed in a direct chronological fashion through events culminating in the death of Adeline Whiteoak, the family matriarch (*Whiteoaks of Jalna*, 1929), the inheritance of Adeline's fortune by her grandson Finch (*Finch's Fortune*, 1931), and the family's financial difficulties during the early years of the Depression (*The Master of Jalna*, 1933). With one exception, the following twelve in the series, published from 1935 to 1960, alternate between tracing the history of the Whiteoak family before *Jalna* (1851-1924) and narrating the events which follow *The Master of Jalna.* The six novels which return to the past do so in no clearly organized pattern. The initial three, *Young Renny* (1935), *Whiteoak Heritage* (1940), and *The Building of Jalna* (1944), develop the past of the family, but *Mary Wakefield* (1949) and *Whiteoak Brothers: Jalna 1923* (1953) move forward to describe events just prior to those dealt with in *Jalna,* and *Morning at Jalna* (1960), although written last, deals with one of the earliest periods in the history of the Whiteoak family.

The Whiteoak novels suffer from repetition, formulaic plotting, sentimentality, and illogical resolution of emotional situations; the extent of the Whiteoak history, however, and the gradual expansion of that history without sacrificing unity and continuity, the humor, irony, and sympathy with which de la Roche manages a large cast of characters, the wealth of fine descriptions of nature, the sharp definition of scene and background, and the consistent expression of concern for the decline of an era and the erosion of its values are considerable achievements. As in all of de la Roche's work, the central and unifying themes of the Whiteoak chronicles are individual freedom and tradition, and the Jalna books clearly reveal her desire for stability without repression and independence without disorder and disintegration.

The imaginative history of the Whiteoaks records de la Roche's skeptical reaction to the modern world and her nostalgia for an earlier existence, perhaps partly idealized, as childhood recollections often are. Her sense of loss as well as her doubt are not simply a result of her recognition that the English influence was being weakened in Canada, though she clearly experienced this attenuation as a loss; she found too much in the emerging world which was destructive of a way of living and an attitude toward life which she cherished, perhaps not only as an idealized memory but also as a dream fostered by the constricting circumstances of her own childhood. In defiance of change, de la Roche clung tenaciously to a past in which memory and fantasy

De la Roche with her cousin and companion, Caroline Clement, 1934

were interchangeable and created for herself and the multitudes who have read and continue to read her fiction, worlds appearing more free, more vital, and more stable than the present one.

The Whiteoaks are distinguished by their capacity for embracing the contradictory values which fascinated de la Roche all her life. In their capacity for embracing contradictory values, the Whiteoaks mirror the personal and artistic choices of their creator, and Jalna emerges as a symbol not only of the divided nature of Canadian culture but also of the creative potential stemming from the tension between individualism and tradition.

In 1929 de la Roche traveled abroad for the first time. Following the success of *Jalna* she became a celebrity, honored in Canada and abroad, and until 1938, when rumors of war and ill health forced her to return to Toronto, she made her home in England. Throughout these years she devoted a considerable proportion of her time to traveling and to raising her two adopted children. While writing the Whiteoak novels, she also published a variety of other works, including two children's books, *The Song of Lambert* (1955) and *Bill and Coo* (1958); a history, *Quebec: Historic Seaport* (1944); an autobiography, *Ringing the Changes* (1957); two adaptations of the Whiteoak novels for the theater, *Whiteoaks* (produced and published in 1936) and *The Mistress of Jalna* (produced in 1951); two collections of short stories, *The Sacred Bullock and Other Stories of Animals* (1939) and *A Boy in the House and Other Stories* (1952); and four novels: *Lark Ascending* (1932), a romance set in Italy; *The Thunder of New Wings* (1932), about the self-destructive struggles of a large English family; *Growth of a Man* (1938), a bildungsroman tracing its hero's progress from an impoverished childhood to successful maturity; and *The Two Saplings* (1942), a novel exploiting the romance formula of two children exchanged at birth. Although most of this writing was overshadowed by the Whiteoak novels, several of these works are of more than passing interest and provide evidence that de la Roche's imaginative focus did not become restricted to the world of the Whiteoak family.

De la Roche's earliest novels were ignored or, because of their realistic themes and numerous sexually suggestive scenes, dismissed as offensive by large segments of the Canadian public. From the time of her first novel, however, she was associated with the movement toward greater realism in Canadian fiction, and in the years that followed *Jalna*, she was frequently identified as a leader in the evolution of the Canadian novel. By the late 1930s, however, critics began to complain of the repetitious quality of the Jalna series and its atmosphere of romantic unreality. Since that time de la Roche has frequently been dismissed as a popular writer of domestic romances without depth, sophistication, or serious themes. More recent criticism, however, while acknowledging the limitations of de la Roche's fiction, has focused on the mixture of elements from the novel and the romance in her work, examined her fiction in the context of the regional idyll, and related the Jalna novels to the Loyalist myth in Upper Canada.

Although Mazo de la Roche's work does not rank among the most important Canadian fiction, her achievement and her contribution to Canadian literature are considerable. At a time when Canadian writing was dominated by historical fiction and sentimental stories of village and rural life, she challenged prevailing fashions with novels such as *Possession* and *Delight*, and despite

Mazo de la Roche in 1957, at the age of seventy-eight (photograph by Paul Rockett)

the many romantic elements in her work she added to the development of realism in the Canadian novel. Although her first book was not published until she was more than forty years of age, she produced a substantial and varied number of works, many of which offer useful insights into a part of the social history of rural Ontario. In addition she gave imaginative expression to several of the tensions that sociologists, literary critics, and historians have come to regard as central to an understanding of Canadian culture.

Biographies:
Ronald Hambleton, *Mazo de la Roche of Jalna* (Toronto: General Publishing, 1966);

Hambleton, *The Secret of Jalna* (Toronto: General Publishing, 1972).

References:
Edward Killoran Brown, "The Whiteoaks Saga," *Canadian Forum*, 12 (October 1931): 23;

D. M. Daymond, "Lark Ascending," *Canadian Literature*, 89 (Summer 1981): 172-178;

Daymond, "Mazo de la Roche's Forgotten Novel," *Journal of Canadian Fiction*, 3, no. 2 (1974): 55-59;

Daymond, "Nature, Culture and Love: Mazo de la Roche's *Explorer of the Dawn* and *The Thunder of New Wings*," *Studies in Canadian Literature*, 1 (Summer 1976): 158-169;

Daymond, "*Possession:* Realism in Mazo de la Roche's First Novel," *Journal of Canadian Fiction*, 4, no. 3 (1975): 87-94;

Daymond, "Whiteoak Chronicles: A Reassessment," *Canadian Literature*, 66 (Autumn 1975): 48-62;

Joan Doig, "Mazo de la Roche's *Delight:* An Unexpected Source," *Studies in Canadian Literature*, 5 (Fall 1980): 305-315;

Dennis Duffy, "The Foundations of Jalna," in his *Gardens, Covenants, Exiles: Loyalism in the Literature of Upper Canada/Ontario* (Toronto: University of Toronto Press, 1982), pp. 76-91;

Hugh Eayrs, "Bookman Profiles: Mazo de la Roche," *Canadian Bookman*, 20 (October-November 1938): 17-22;

Pelham Edgar, "The Cult of Primitivism," in *Yearbook of the Arts in Canada 1928/1929*, edited by Tertram Brooker (Toronto: Macmillan, 1929), pp. 39-42;

Jo-Ann Fellows, "The 'British Connection' in the Jalna Novels of Mazo de la Roche: The Loyalist Myth Revisited," *Dalhousie Review*, 56 (Summer 1976): 283-290;

George Hendrick, *Mazo de la Roche* (New York: Twayne, 1970);

Michelle Le Normand, "Mazo de la Roche," *Lectures*, 8 (October 1951): 113-117;

Dorothy Livesay, "Getting It Straight," *Impulse*, 2 (1973): 29-35;

Livesay, "The Making of Jalna: A Reminiscence," *Canadian Literature*, 23 (Winter 1965): 25-30;

Livesay, "Mazo de la Roche 1879-1961," in *The Clear Spirit*, edited by Mary Quayle Innis (Toronto: University of Toronto Press, 1966), pp. 242-259;

Livesay, "Remembering Mazo," in *Selected Stories of Mazo de la Roche*, edited by Daymond (Ottawa: University of Ottawa, 1979), pp. 11-13;

Jocelyn Moore, "Mazo de la Roche," *Canadian Forum*, 12 (July 1932): 380-381;

Sterling North, *The Writings of Mazo de la Roche* (Boston: Little, Brown, 1938);

Desmond Pacey, Introduction to de la Roche's *Delight* (Toronto: McClelland & Stewart, 1961), pp. vii-x;

B. K. Sandwell, "The Work of Mazo de la Roche," *Saturday Night*, 68 (November 1952): 7;

J. G. Snell, "The United States at Jalna," *Canadian Literature*, 66 (Autumn 1975): 31-40;

Edward Weeks, "Mazo de la Roche," in his *In Friendly Candor* (Boston: Little, Brown, 1959), pp. 84-97.

Papers:
The major collection of de la Roche's correspondence and manuscripts is at the University of Toronto Library. Additional materials are housed at the Public Archives, Ottawa; at Queen's University Library, Kingston, Ontario; and at the University of British Columbia Library, Vancouver.

Alfred DesRochers
(5 October 1901-12 October 1978)

Richard Giguère
Université de Sherbrooke

BOOKS: *L'Offrande aux vierges folles* (Sherbrooke: Privately printed, 1928);

A l'ombre de l'Orford (Sherbrooke: Privately printed, 1929);

Paragraphes (Montreal: Librairie d'Action Canadienne-Française, 1931);

A l'ombre de l'Orford suivi du Cycle du village (Montreal: Fides, 1948);

Le Retour de Titus (Ottawa: Editions de l'Université d'Ottawa, 1963);

Elégies pour l'épouse en-allée (Montreal: Parti Pris, 1967);

Œuvres poétiques, 2 volumes, edited by Romain Légaré (Montreal: Fides, 1977).

OTHER: [Témoignages...], in *La Poésie canadienne-française*, edited by Paul Wyczynski, Bernard Julien, Jean Ménard, and Rejéan Robidaux (Montreal: Fides, 1969), pp. 395-398.

PERIODICAL PUBLICATIONS: "L'Avenir de la poésie en Canada francais," *Idées*, 4 (July 1936): 1-10; 4 (August 1936): 108-126;

"La Poésie au Canada français," *Culture*, 3 (January 1942): 155-160;

"Bornoyages," *Carnets Viatoriens*, 17 (January 1952): 20-27;

"Louis Dantin et la 'génération perdue,'" *Les Carnets Viatoriens*, 17 (October 1952): 120-127;

"Notes sur la poésie moderne," *Liberté*, 6 (November-December 1964): 413-420.

Alfred DesRochers, 1960s (courtesy of Kenneth Landry)

Alfred DesRochers is one of the most important Quebec writers of the period between the two world wars. Today he is better known as a poet than as a journalist or literary critic, although his poetic activity extended over more than forty years, from 1922 to 1967, and includes some eight thousand verses which appeared either in the collections published during his lifetime or in newspapers and magazines of the 1930s and 1940s. His critical works comprise the first-rate volume of "interviews littéraires," *Paragraphes*, published in 1931, along with numerous essays, articles of criticism, and reviews which have not been collected in book form. To this must be added lectures, forewords, and prefaces to a number of books, plus a voluminous correspondence with several writers of the 1930s and 1940s–Robert Choquette, Émile Coderre, Louis Dantin, Claude-Henri Grignon, Germaine Guèvremont, Rina Lasnier, and Clément Marchand. DesRochers left a half-dozen unfinished series of poems and other unpublished verse which were brought together by Romain Légaré in the two-

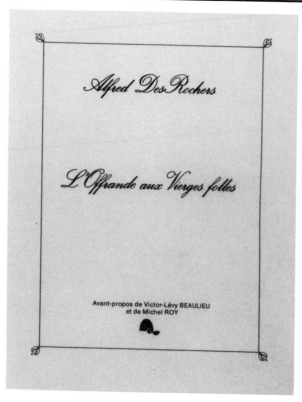

Cover for the 1974 edition of DesRochers's first book, which appeared as a privately printed limited edition in 1928

volume *Œuvres poétiques* of 1977.

Born to Honorius DesRochers, a farmer, and his wife, Zéphirine Marcotte DesRochers, at Saint-Elie d'Orford, near Sherbrooke (160 kilometers east of Montreal), Alfred DesRochers was inspired by this picturesque corner of the Eastern Townships and by the adventurous lives of the coureurs de bois, which his forebears had led in that locality. For a while he attended a *collège*, but after the death of his father he was obliged, while still in his teens, to work at various small jobs–delivery boy, clerk in a hardware store, bushworker, apprentice in a foundry–before marrying Rose-Alma Brault, in 1925, with whom he subsequently had six children. That same year he began to work at the Sherbrooke newspaper *La Tribune.* There it was that he met several young writers, Jovette-Alice Bernier and Eva Senécal, among others, founded the Société des Ecrivains de l'Est, and became the leading spirit of a literary movement which flourished toward the end of the 1920s and the beginning of the 1930s. The concerns of this Sherbrooke group went beyond the region of the Eastern Townships, and DesRochers was soon organizing get-togethers which drew writers from Montreal, Trois-

Rivières, Quebec, and even New England.

It was on the occasion of one of these meetings, in 1929, that DesRochers invited Louis Dantin (Eugène Seers) to come to Sherbrooke. Although Dantin was living in Boston, he was the dean of French-Canadian criticism at the time, and his meeting with DesRochers resulted in a friendship that would last until Dantin's death in 1945. DesRochers's first books were two poetry collections, *L'Offrande aux vierges folles* (1928) and *A l'ombre de l'Orford* (1929), both published at his own expense. The second book, in particular, was an important one for DesRochers. It was republished in 1930 by Montreal's dynamic Librairie d'Action Canadienne-Française, which assured him a new readership; highly acclaimed by Montreal critics, it was awarded three prizes for literature, including the prestigious Prix David (1932).

Criticism is unanimous in saying that the first two collections of DesRochers's works clearly set themselves apart from the rest of his poetry. These collections are the best organized and most balanced, particularly *A l'ombre de l'Orford,* which contains thirty-three poems: dedicatory verses; the celebrated poem of introduction, "Je suis un fils déchu"; the two-part "Cycle des bois et des champs" ("La Naissance de la chanson" and "À l'ombre de l'Orford," each composed of fourteen sonnets); and a section comprising three long poems among which is the imposing "Hymne au vent du Nord." They also demonstrate DesRochers's versatility in handling a variety of themes. The poet could be at the same time the troubadour of a delicate love and the realistic observer of the labors of farm and lumber camp; he could sing of the North and of freedom, of adventure, and of wide open spaces while also revealing himself as a poet of small places, of inner states, and of the human heart. The subjects of his poems embrace the superhuman exploits of the explorers, of the coureurs de bois and lumberjacks, along with traditional village crafts and the jobs of workers in the textile mills. DesRochers was equally at home in celebrating the north wind in an epic hymn as he was in composing sonnets or rondeaux to praise the joys of the heart and of the flesh. Good Parnassian that he was, he emphasized form, varied his tone, played with sound, and exploited the riches of vocabulary; his language was sometimes elaborate, as in his use of literary French, sometimes homely, as in his use of the spoken language, anglicisms, or swear words.

DesRochers shortly before his death in 1978 (photograph by Kèro)

During World War II DesRochers served as a private in the Canadian army, and for a while he held a position in Ottawa as translator in Parliament; after the cessation of hostilities he returned to *La Tribune* in Sherbrooke, only to leave this paper for good in 1950. Following a two-year stay at Claire-Vallée, he settled in Montreal, where he worked as a translator for Canadian Press (1953-1956); then he took semiretirement. With the exception of the poems and articles that appeared in newspapers and magazines and the 1948 republication of *A l'ombre de l'Orford* in an edition which also included *Cycle du village* and the poem "Ma Patrie," DesRochers's literary activities were fairly reduced during the 1940s and 1950s.

As a matter of fact, his last new book of entirely new material published before 1963 was *Paragraphes,* which appeared in 1931. This work of criticism brought together thirteen articles, some new and others which had been previously published, and was arranged in the form of imaginary interviews with books–not authors–by critics and poets of the 1930s and especially by women like Jovette-Alice Bernier, Alice Lemieux, Simone Routier, and Eva Senécal. In this book, as in other articles which appeared in periodicals, DesRochers showed himself to be a critic with a new and accurate assessment of Quebec writers both present and past, as well as a theorist, a keen defender of traditional poetry and versification.

During the 1960s DesRochers resumed publishing books of poetry: *Le Retour de Titus* (1963), a series of fifty "stances royales" inspired by the love of the Roman emperor Titus and Berenice; and *Elégies pour l'épouse en-allée* (1967), a series of forty-nine elegiac sonnets composed following the death of his wife in 1964. But these poems, as in the case of the unfinished thematic series, "Échos de chansons mortes," "Nous irons jouer dans l'île, roman lyrique," "Le Retour de l'enfant prodigue," which appeared again in "Choix de poésies éparses" (*Œuvres poétiques,* volume two), are of less importance in comparison with DesRochers's first collections.

Toward the end of his life Alfred Des-Rochers was awarded prizes and distinctions which crowned his work and established his position as one of the major writers in Quebec literature during the interwar period. He received the Prix Duvernay in 1964, was given an honorary doctorate by the Université de Sherbrooke in 1976, and in 1978 was made a Companion of the Order of Canada, one of the highest distinctions which can be awarded to a Canadian citizen.

References:

Joseph Bonenfant, Janine Boynard-Frot, Richard Giguère, and Antoine Sirois, *À l'ombre de Des-Rochers: Le Mouvement littéraire des Cantons de l'Est* (Sherbrooke: La Tribune/Presses de l'Université de Sherbrooke, 1985);

Roger Chamberland, *A l'ombre de l'Orford/Alfred DesRochers: Chronologie, bibliographie, et jugements Critiques* (Montreal: Fides, 1979);

Louis Dantin, "Le Mouvement littéraire des Cantons de l'Est," *La Tribune* (Sherbrooke), 29 November 1930;

Richard Giguère, "Alfred DesRochers, Œuvres poétiques I et II," *Livres et Auteurs Québécois 1977* (1978): 115-118;

Gustave Lamarche, "Duel avec Alfred Des-Rochers," *Carnets Viatoriens*, no. 3 (1942): 195-202;

Séraphin Marion, "Alfred DesRochers, réaliste et poète," *Revue Dominicaine* (November 1930): 611-630;

Jacques Pelletier, "Alfred DesRochers, critique," *Voix et Images du Pays*, no. 7 (1973): 121-136;

Jack Warwick, "Alfred DesRochers, Reluctant Regionalist," *Queen's Quarterly*, 71 (Winter 1965): 566-582.

Léo-Paul Desrosiers

(11 April 1896-20 April 1967)

Ivor A. Arnold
University of Western Ontario

BOOKS: *Ames et paysages* (Montreal: Editions du Devoir, 1922);

Nord-Sud (Montreal: Editions du Devoir, 1931);

Le Livre des mystères (Montreal: Editions du Devoir, 1936);

L'Accalmie. Lord Durham au Canada (Montreal: Editions du Devoir, 1937);

Les Engagés du Grand Portage (Paris: Gallimard, 1938; Montreal: Fides, 1946); translated by Christina van Oordt as *The Making of Nicolas Montour* (Montreal: Harvest House, 1978);

Commencements (Montreal: Editions de l'Action Canadienne-Française, 1939);

Les Opiniâtres (Montreal: Imprimerie Populaire, 1941; New York: Brentano's, 1941);

Sources (Montreal: Imprimerie Populaire, 1942);

Iroquoisie (Montreal: Études de l'Institut d'Histoire de l'Amérique Française, 1947);

L'Ampoule d'or (Paris: Gallimard, 1951; Montreal: Fides, 1957);

Les Dialogues de Marthe et de Marie (Montreal: Fides, 1957);

Vous qui passez (Montreal: Fides, 1958);

Les Angoisses et les tourments (Montreal: Fides, 1959);

Rafales sur les cimes (Montreal: Fides, 1960);

Dans le nid d'aiglons, la colombe. Vie de Jeanne Le Ber, la recluse (Montreal: Fides, 1963);

Paul de Chomedey, sieur de Maisonneuve (Montreal: Fides, 1967).

Léo-Paul Desrosiers (courtesy of Archives Nationales du Québec, Montreal)

Léo-Paul Desrosiers was born in Berthier-en-Haut, Quebec, son of Louis and Marie Olivier Desrosiers, and the youngest of the boys in a traditionally large Quebec family numbering fourteen. His childhood was spent happily in a house dating back to 1798 that had known three generations of hardworking, plain-living farmers. His parents were simple, loyal Quebeckers, and while it was his mother who developed his taste for works of imagination, it was Louis Desrosiers who awakened his love for history and story-telling. Many family tales eventually found their way into his novels and short stories.

His formal education, too, was true to the tradition for the sons of well-to-do Quebeckers of the times. He attended the Séminaire de Joliette where he showed no vocation for the priesthood but read literature voraciously, while at the same time displaying his already independent cast of mind, as he seems to have graduated in spite of the formal lessons he mostly neglected. From 1916 to 1919 he was a student at the Université de Montréal. Again he went his own educational way, emulating many of his literary compatriots by studying law with no intention to practice it. Too retiring a person to engage in the fray of the world of the barrister, he prepared himself for future writing by devouring the historical offerings of the Municipal Library of the City of Montreal, and in the process became a fervent admirer of the separatist patriot, the *abbé* Lionel-Adolphe Groulx.

After an unsuccessful foray into the world of business following graduation (in the wake of one of his forebears, he opened a collection agency in the city of Quebec), he turned to journalism, with a job on the much respected nationalistic daily *Le Devoir,* for which he worked as Ottawa Parliamentary correspondent from 1920 to 1928. While enjoying the work, he found the day-to-day pressures drained his energies and left him little time for his literary endeavors, in which he was being encouraged by his wife: the 1922 publication of his first work, *Ames et paysages,* a volume of anecdotal tales drawn for the most part from childhood memories, coincided with his marriage to Marie-Antoinette Tardif, better known under her pen name of Michelle Le Normand.

His appointment in 1928 to the post of French editor of the *Proceedings and Orders of the House of Commons* (Ottawa), while a demanding one, left him less extenuated at the end of a working day and afforded more ample vacation time, mostly spent in his much-loved Gaspé, so that he was able to work more regularly at his first full-length novel, *Nord-Sud,* published in 1931. The novel records the exodus in the 1840s of young Quebeckers in stagnant economic times, as the main character Vincent Douaire leaves behind his love and his homeland to seek an uncertain future in the 1849 California gold rush. It is significant to note that Vincent was Desrosiers's paternal grandfather's name and that of four other paternal forebears who in fact left for California, one indeed returned with a fortune.

In 1936 he produced a second collection of short stories, *Le Livre des mystères,* in which he displayed a growing talent for accomplished psychological studies, especially of young women who seem undeserving victims of an inimical Providence (the heroine of "L'Une d'elles" seems to foreshadow the heroine of the later full-length psychological novel *L'Ampoule d'or*). While working on a new full-length historical novel, Desrosiers kept up with his nonfictional historical studies. In 1937 he produced *L'Accalmie,* a portrait of Lord Durham, an important figure in Ca-

nadian history who is largely regarded by Quebeckers as a villain in the drama of their survival as a minority, and, in 1939, *Commencements,* an early study of the role of the Iroquois Indians in French-Canadian history appeared.

The year 1938 saw the fruition of years of work lavished on what critics consider his best-written novel, *Les Engagés du Grand Portage* (translated into English in 1978 as *The Making of Nicolas Montour*). The plot revolves around the rivalries and individual ambitions within a special fur brigade of the North West Company, the now defunct competitor of the Company of Adventurers Trading into Hudson's Bay. Here Desrosiers showed that he had become capable of constructing a more tightly knit plot than is evident in *Nord-Sud,* while also displaying a considerable skill in creating a sense of the epic grandeur of the rugged backdrop to the hardships of these early voyageurs.

In 1941 Desrosiers finally left the House of Commons to accept an appointment to the position of chief librarian of Montreal's municipal library, which he no doubt hoped would allow him to devote himself more fulfillingly to writing and research. He may himself have become aware of the need to sacrifice the quality of these to the incessant deadlines of his Ottawa job, for it is clear that the two other novels he was able to complete by the time he made this career change do not live up to the promise of *Les Engagés du Grand Portage.* Devoted to depicting the survival instincts of his compatriots, they tend to be pedestrian in style and are disappointing.

Les Opiniâtres (1941) tells of the trials of daily life in New France under the constant threat of marauding Indians, and *Sources* (1942) projects the same sense of innate tenacity into the contemporary scene as an urban heroine exchanges the life of the modern city for the never-ending struggle to wrest a living from a recalcitrant land. Her strength is drawn from her roots.

In contrast, his psychological novel *L'Ampoule d'or* (1951) is a moving poetic study of the sufferings brought on to all appearances by the cruel fate of circumstance, in the shape of a father who understandably intervenes in an illicit affair between a young Gaspé girl, Julienne, and her married lover, Silvère. Julienne resigns herself to finding consolation in the traditions of her religious faith.

All three novels, however, are able to evoke in the reader a sense of Desrosiers's belief in the ordinary Quebecker's innate strength in the face of adversity, at times seemingly turning the latter into a near-mythic antagonist.

Such deep metaphysical concerns emerged even more strongly in Desrosiers's last major fictional work, a trilogy entitled *Vous qui passez* (*Vous qui passez*, 1958; *Les Angoisses et les tourments*, 1959; *Rafales sur les cimes*, 1960). This overly long and verbose study narrates with much didacticism the trials in the modern world of a Quebec engineer, Romain Heurfils, and his wife, at odds with materialism and the downgrading of faith. It never had the impact its author felt it deserved.

Desrosiers also published *Iroquoisie* (1947), a historical study of the role of Amerindians in general, and of the Iroquois in particular, in the fate of New France, as well as lengthy biographies of three notable figures in the religious and political life of Quebec: *Les Dialogues de Marthe et de Marie*, 1957 (about Marguerite de Bourgeoys), *Dans le nid d'aiglons, la colombe*, 1963 (on Jeanne Le Ber), and *Paul de Chomedey, sieur de Maisonneuve*, 1967. In addition he authored in his lifetime many articles of both a critical and political nature and wrote prefaces for several important publications.

A shy and essentially solitary figure in spite of a serene marriage, Desrosiers never quite reached the literary heights to which he aspired. He achieved national recognition, however, as winner of the Prix de la Province de Québec for his *Les Engagés du Grand Portage*, the Prix Duvernay for *L'Ampoule d'or*, and in 1963 the Lorne Pierce Medal for his work as a whole. In 1944 he was elected to the Royal Society of Canada. He was a founding member in that same year of the Académie Canadienne-Française, a member of the historical Société des Dix, and, before his retirement in 1953, principal of Montreal's School of Library Science. He died 20 April 1967 after a brief illness, leaving two sons, Louis and Claude, and predeceased by his wife in 1964.

References:

Michelle Gélinas, *Léo-Paul Desrosiers ou le récit ambigu* (Montreal: Presses de l'Université de Montréal, 1973);
Julia Richer, *Léo-Paul Desrosiers* (Ottawa: Fides, 1966).

Papers:

The original typescript of *Les Engagés du Grand Portage* is at the Municipal Library in Montreal.

Selwyn Dewdney

(22 October 1909-18 November 1979)

James Reaney
University of Western Ontario

SELECTED BOOKS: *Wind Without Rain* (Toronto: Copp Clark, 1946);

The Map That Grew (Toronto: Oxford University Press, 1960);

Indian Rock Paintings of the Great Lakes, by Dewdney and Kenneth E. Kidd (Toronto: University of Toronto Press, 1962; revised and enlarged, 1967);

They Shared to Survive: The Native Peoples of Canada (Toronto: Macmillan, 1975);

The Sacred Scrolls of the Southern Ojibway (Toronto & Buffalo: University of Toronto Press, 1975);

Relevés et travaux récents sur l'art rupestre amérindien, by Dewdney and Gilles Tassé (Montreal: Laboratoire d'archéologie de l'Université du Quebec, 1977);

Christopher Breton (Toronto: McClelland & Stewart, 1979).

OTHER: Norval Morriseau, *Legends of My People, the Great Ojibway*, edited, with an introduction, by Dewdney (Toronto: Ryerson, 1965).

Selwyn Hanington Dewdney is, probably, more widely known as an authority on aboriginal Canadian art and culture than he is as a novelist. But although his reputation may endure longer with such definitive works as *Indian Rock Paintings of the Great Lakes* (a 1962 collaboration with Kenneth E. Kidd) and *The Sacred Scrolls of the Southern Ojibway* (1975), it is to the novels that students of Canadian culture will have to turn not only to explain the drives behind the Indian research but also to map that stage in Canadian cultural history when, for the first time, those of European descent began to depict the way the native people had of looking at the world. Dewdney is a pivotal character in any study of how the cultural gap between the two cultures began to be bridged. His semi-autobiographical novels are the best key to a man who played so many roles: painter, psychiatric art therapist, illustrator and writer of children's books, muralist, teacher, artist's midwife, master canoeist, and general creative focus.

Dewdney was born in Prince Albert, Saskatchewan, to English-Canadian parents, Alfred Daniel and Alice Ashwood Hanington Dewdney. His father, an Anglican minister, eventually became the bishop of Keewatin, at the time (1922) an enormous diocese sweeping up from Lake of the Woods into the Arctic. With his father in 1928 Dewdney made a 3,800-mile journey to Ojibway, Cree, and Eskimo missions, which obviously left an indelible mark on this son of the parsonage who eventually took leave of his father's church but never for one day forgot the people and the landscapes to which this journey introduced him. Eight hundred miles of this journey were traveled by canoe with nineteen-year-old Dewdney paddling bow.

Christopher Breton (1979), finished the year before he died, charts in fictional form most of the high points of Dewdney's later life. Through his hero, Christopher Breton, Dewdney conveys his deep love for the Lake of the Woods area in whose capital, Kenora, he attended high school after the family moved there in 1922 from Prince Albert. Like his hero, Dewdney eventually came south to Toronto for further education; both he and Breton attended art school, but unlike his hero he also attained a B.A. from the University of Toronto, a high-school teaching certificate, and the experience of teaching two years at the high school in Owen Sound, all this by 1936, after which his life can be followed further by consulting his first novel, *Wind Without Rain* (1946). Like Christopher Breton, though, Dewdney could never stay continuously in southern Ontario. When he first laid eyes on it in 1928 he was shocked by its rocklessness and its genteel, elmy English landscape. His true love was the Pre-Cambrian Shield and both his curriculum vitae and his novels show a pendulum movement in which college winters at Toronto were balanced with summers either as a student missionary to Ojibway or surveying in Kapuskasing or ex-

Selwyn Dewdney (courtesy of Irene Dewdney)

periencing some other cleansing northern expedition. These North-South swings stopped only with Dewdney's death; in the novels they provide a value system in which the South is corrupt but the Shield is always waiting with its healing purity and native wisdom.

Married to Irene Donner in 1936 (they eventually had four children, including the poet Christopher Dewdney and the science and science fiction writer Alexander Keewatin Dewdney), Dewdney became a teacher at Sir Adam Beck Collegiate in London, Ontario, little dreaming that ten years later he would resign in protest against the unfair demotion of a fellow teacher and then write a scathing satire based on those years and their events called *Wind Without Rain.* His ten years as a teacher in London gave him an experience of materialism, banality, and futility of such peculiar strength that *Wind Without Rain* almost reads like one of his Indian books; the natives of London become a strange WASP tribe whose sa-

cred scrolls and secret pictographs Dewdney has deciphered. The reader, of course, may not realize that this novel is indeed about the capital of southwestern Ontario, for Dewdney has skillfully amalgamated an Owen Sound cityscape with his London sufferings; this means that a hunk of Pre-Cambrian rock in the harbor can be used for symbolic purposes despite the fact that London, Ontario, knows nothing about the Shield or a harbor in more ways than one.

As Dewdney himself came to London in 1936, the hero of *Wind Without Rain* comes to West Kirby, an ultra-Puritan small-big town where he has been hired as an instructor at the local collegiate. What he has really been hired to do is almost lose his soul in the struggle between two opposing forces. On the side of the corrupt South, reared by the shores of Lake Erie, we have the principal, J. C. Bilbeau, minotaur of the corridors, arch-manipulator of power, introducer of slick American anti-intellectualism, two-way radios in every classroom: " 'Do not,' he paused solemnly for emphasis, 'jeopardize that career by absorbing ideas, let alone expressing them, which are not in accordance with those accepted by society.' "

On the side of the Shield we have Angus Macdonald, captain of summer surveying camps where the hero, John Westley, learned to be a man; liberal, idealist, and doomed to be hounded to his death by Bilbeau, who frames him with a charge of teaching atheism in the classroom. Actually, according to the author, it was his publisher, Copp Clark, who hounded Macdonald; Dewdney originally had thought to end the story in a low realistic key with John Westley leaving the futile collegiate rat pit for carpentry: "Now on a job like this when you go home at night you can *see* what you've done." But the publisher thought it would be more exciting to have Angus Macdonald fall from a cliff. With either ending, the same point is made: Canadians live in a magnificent northern country but very few of them can live up to it. A stupid system puts men like Bilbeau in control of all the power, and those who know what the land is saying are stifled in the general senseless futility: "West Kirby is full of big ideas, little men and old women.... The old women are the school principals, church elders, bank managers and city council."

Read with a sense of liberation by many young people at the time, this novel did not, as it should have, lead to a half dozen more. Defended by Toronto reviewers (William Arthur Deacon and Barker Fairley), it was compared to the Bobbsey Twins sagas and denounced in Vancouver as having set back the Canadian novel for a hundred years. Despite the controversy, the Canadian public was not responsive enough; given the way they appear in the novel, one can hardly imagine them being stirred by anything. However, the book kept up an underground reputation, treasured for its hilarious descriptions of various kinds of fleshy businessmen. In 1974 McClelland and Stewart, Toronto, gave it new life in paperback to a much changed and more receptive audience.

After leaving Sir Adam Beck Collegiate, Dewdney in effect free-lanced for the rest of his life. This meant doing everything from making plaster plaques to conducting art therapy at the local mental hospital to carrying out the research for his books on Amerindian culture. If he had remained a high-school teacher he might have led an easier life. His new life meant meeting such people as Carl Atwood, University of Toronto zoology professor and father of author Margaret Atwood, through the Quetico Foundation in connection with his research into Indian pictographs; meant becoming the cultural godfather of London, Ontario, with his mentorship of such artists as Jack Chambers, Greg Curnoe, and Norval Morriseau; meant that instead of teaching schoolchildren geography and art, he taught artists, and he taught a wide audience his Pre-Cambrian vision. Although he wrote only one more novel, he became the sort of person who appears in other writers' novels.

Christopher Breton starts out in the Lake of the Woods country not far away from a place that very much resembles Kenora. The hero visits a mission church whose graveyard has been half-flooded by rising lake levels (there is a new dam). The waters have not only desecrated the graves of this mysterious church but also released something dangerous from the past. The hero's father is an Anglican minister who represents in his bleak repressiveness all the emptiness Dewdney sees in WASP culture. Christopher Breton and his brother go to art school in the South; their love-hate relationship drives Breton to near madness and back to the northern wilderness where he leads the life of wandering canoeist-painter. All the false values represented by J. C. Bilbeau in *Wind Without Rain* appear again, but they are muted by the northern landscape, the northern viewpoint, and the Nishinahbi Indians: "There was the dream they had shared with him of a scholar's community in the bush, so designed that it would include the technical resources of the city ... without the alienation of abstract surroundings of glass and cement and hordes of human insects fluttering like moths around the neon light. When Joan had speculated that such a community might be wedded to a Nishinahbi one in what she called a 'social symbiosis,' Chris had protested, 'Now you are dreaming.' But Joan had only smiled a quiet confidence and a gentle 'Maybe not.' "

Christopher Breton's eventual union with a Nishinahbi woman is, of course, tragically dogged by his father's presence. White culture is seen as destroying itself even on the very brink of liberation. Still, the "maybe not" is obviously a hope that, if it is not quite supported by the novel, is indeed supported by this novelist's whole creative life.

Once in a lecture at the University of Western Ontario, Dewdney showed a slide of a sha-

Dust jacket for Dewdney's children's book, published in 1960

man's eagle nest. The notion behind this huge nest made out of stones is that the shaman would sleep in it at night and be visited by a vision of a great totemic eagle. Completely missing the point, a student said: "Isn't the nest too big for an eagle? How can a bird nest on such hard stones?" After responding, Dewdney went on to say that the Ojibway viewed reality in exactly the opposite way to that of the literal-minded student. To the Ojibway, dream and symbol were objective realities; material affairs were wraithlike and insubstantial. That the citizens of London, Ontario, do not and may never share this Ojibway belief is what Dewdney's two novels and his whole life are all about.

How did he become a figure written about by other novelists? Readers of Margaret Atwood's *Surfacing* (1972) may remember that the heroine's father is drowned while studying pictographs in northern Ontario. Dewdney's fiction shows Canadian society just beginning to grapple with what is implied in the traditions of its northernness, its sharing the Pre-Cambrian Shield with an older culture. Now other, younger novelists, such as Atwood, carry on this literary father's treatment of such "social symbiosis."

Papers:
The Selwyn Dewdney Collection, which is a private research collection of over 7,000 items, including manuscripts (some unpublished), diaries, correspondence, slides, artwork, annotated monographs, pictograph reproductions, and historical photographs, is presently held by the Royal Ontario Museum in Toronto.

George Elliott

(4 July 1923-   )

David Jackel
University of Alberta

BOOKS: *The Kissing Man* (Toronto: Macmillan, 1962);

God's Big Acre: Life in 401 Country (Toronto: Methuen, 1986).

OTHER: "Four Little Words," in *76: New Canadian Stories*, edited by Joan Harcourt and John Metcalf (Ottawa: Oberon, 1976), pp. 53-62;

"The Bittersweet Man," *New Quarterly*, 5 (Spring 1985): 37-46;

"Side Trip," in *Magic Realism and Canadian Literature: Essays and Stories*, edited by Peter Hinchcliffe and Ed Jewinski (Waterloo: University of Waterloo/Wilfrid Laurier University, 1986), pp. 77-82;

"Hutchinson's Lock," *New Quarterly*, 5 (Winter 1986): 7-15.

George Elliott's *The Kissing Man* (1962) has gradually acquired for its author a firmly established reputation as one of the important chroniclers of small-town life in Ontario and a secure place in the tradition of fictional treatments of this subject that begins in the nineteenth century with Sara Jeannette Duncan's *The Imperialist* (1904), receives classic expression in Stephen Leacock's *Sunshine Sketches of a Little Town* (1912), and has continued with Alice Munro's *Dance of the Happy Shades* (1968) and *Lives of Girls and Women* (1971).

Elliott was born in London, in southwestern Ontario. As a young man he worked for a time in radio and as a journalist before beginning a successful career as an advertising executive. Elliott's work has had no direct connection with his fiction, but the area of Ontario in which he was born and raised provided him with the settings and themes for *The Kissing Man.*

The book is a collection of eleven short stories, linked by recurring scenes and characters, with a single setting—a small Ontario town and the farming country around it. The town is unnamed, enabling Elliott to deal with the spirit of

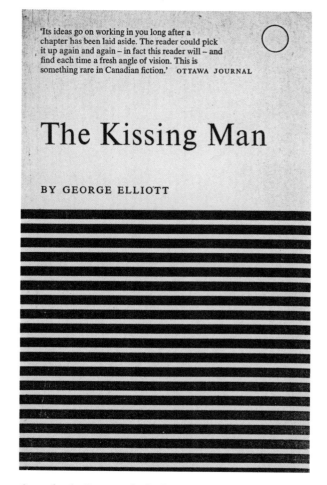

'Its ideas go on working in you long after a chapter has been laid aside. The reader could pick it up again and again – in fact this reader will – and find each time a fresh angle of vision. This is something rare in Canadian fiction.' OTTAWA JOURNAL

The Kissing Man

BY GEORGE ELLIOTT

Cover for the first paperback edition of Elliott's 1962 story collection set in a small Ontario town and surrounding farming country

a region rather than the mere particulars of life in a specific locality. And his treatment of time, in individual stories and in the collection as a whole, allows Elliott to place the spirit of his region in the wider context of enduring human concerns; only one specific year, 1918, is mentioned, and the stories move backward and forward from this date, portraying the relationships among three generations of characters.

The individual stories exhibit a striking combination of the ordinary and the fantastic. The physical qualities of the region and the characters are evoked by a limited but telling selection of precise details. At the same time the actions of the characters and the events of the stories move the reader's attention away from realism toward symbolism and myth. For example, the central figure of the title story is a mysterious stranger who appears in the town's general store on three different days to kiss three lonely women. His action is not, however, one of consolation or comfort; the three women derive from it a fuller, but not reassuring, awareness of the state of their lives, and Froody, the young woman working in the store who witnesses these events, is pushed toward a chilling perception of what maturation and later life can bring.

In "The Commonplace" Froody's sexual awakening is symbolized by the ritualistic dance she performs in the woods with Bertram Sunbird, the oldest boy in a strange and gypsylike family that appears in the town one spring and vanishes with the coming of winter. Honey Salkald, the boy who witnesses this scene (and is a witness and participant in several of the stories), is, like Froody in "The Kissing Man," bewildered and then disturbed by his first encounter with one of the mysteries of life.

Honey Salkald appears in the book's final story, "The Way Back," but is here only a minor character. The central figure is Dan, whose father has broken the ritual of life in the town by allowing the birth of his son to take place without the presence of "the grinder man"—the mysterious, and seemingly timeless, figure who is summoned to stand outside the house whenever a child is born. Dan grows up as an outcast as a result, and it is not until he becomes an adult that he recognizes that "the grinder man" is a necessary symbol of the sustaining tradition provided by the acts of love and memory that link one generation with another and also unify the community.

The importance of sustaining traditions, and the dangers of disregarding tradition and dividing the community, are Elliott's main themes in *The Kissing Man*, apparent throughout the stories themselves and stressed by the book's epigraph, taken from T. S. Eliot's *Notes Towards the Definition of Culture* (1948): "But when I speak of the family, I have in mind a bond which embraces . . . a piety towards the dead, however obscure, and a solicitude for the unborn, however

remote." The emphasis on ritualized action in the stories suggests another connection with Eliot.

Elliott has avoided making comments on his work; as Dennis Duffy puts it in an article for *Canadian Literature* (Winter 1975), he is "cagey in public converse." Duffy has, however, reported some of Elliott's remarks: " 'nostalgia' means going home, but *with pain;* it is a feeling we seek refuge in because the pain nostalgia brings is preferable to the anguish of the present; if themes and passions in various of the stories in the collection remain unresolved, it is because nothing in life is ever resolved." The world as presented in *The Kissing Man* is, then, not sentimentalized and idyllic. The sustaining traditions are there, but so are the perennial problems of the human condition.

Commentators on Elliott's work are numerous; those who have commented have done so favorably, even while noting that his style is occasionally awkward, that the blending of reality and fantasy is not successful in all of the stories, and that the created symbols are in some cases too contrived. Nevertheless, as Duffy states, Elliott's best stories are likely to find a permanent place in Canadian literature. At their best, they become "metaphors for grace, for man's refusal to slog along in an impoverished existence, whatever pain it may cause him to take larger views and gaze upon a world that may not even have room for him."

When *The Kissing Man* appeared in 1962 Robert Harlow, writing for *Canadian Literature*, expressed his hope that the collection would be the "beginning of a literary career" that could win for Elliott status comparable to that of John Updike or J. D. Salinger. Such has not, unfortunately, been the case, although his output has increased in the 1980s. Since 1962 Elliott has published only a few short stories, among them "Four Little Words" (1976), a skillful treatment of the isolating qualities of urban life which lacks the firm sense of place and the compassionate insight evident in the best stories of *The Kissing Man*.

In 1986 Elliott's book *God's Big Acre: Life in 401 Country* appeared to favorable reviews. Profusely illustrated with the photographs of John Reeves, *God's Big Acre* is a commentary on life along Ontario's Highway 401. Elliott spends most of his time with the farmers of 401 country, who have modernized and yet have resisted the automated attitudes that might have accompanied such modernization. He also visits roadside attractions—wholesale outlets, a cookie factory— and talks to the truckers who make their living from the highway. He is firmly in admiration of the society Highway 401 has spawned. People there are independent and spirited, and difficult to categorize, like the best of Elliott's graceful fictional characters.

References:

Frank Davey, *From There to Here: A Guide to English-Canadian Literature Since 1960* (Erin, Ontario: Press Porcépic, 1974), pp. 97-98;

Dennis Duffy, "George Elliott: *The Kissing Man*," *Canadian Literature*, 63 (Winter 1975): 52-63;

Clara Thomas, "New England Romanticism and Canadian Fiction," *Journal of Canadian Fiction*, 2 (Fall 1973): 80-86.

Northrop Frye

(14 July 1912-   )

Robert D. Denham
Modern Language Association

See also the Frye entry in *DLB 67, Modern American Critics Since 1955.*

BOOKS: *Fearful Symmetry: A Study of William Blake* (Princeton: Princeton University Press, 1947);

Anatomy of Criticism: Four Essays (Princeton: Princeton University Press, 1957);

Culture and the National Will (Ottawa: Carleton University for the Institute for Canadian Studies, 1957);

By Liberal Things (Toronto: Clarke, Irwin, 1959);

The Changing Pace of Canadian Education (Montreal: Sir George Williams University, 1963);

The Educated Imagination (Toronto: Canadian Broadcasting Corporation, 1963; Bloomington: Indiana University Press, 1964);

Fables of Identity: Studies in Poetic Mythology (New York: Harcourt, Brace & World, 1963);

T. S. Eliot (Edinburgh: Oliver & Boyd, 1963; New York: Grove, 1963; revised edition, Edinburgh: Oliver & Boyd, 1968; New York: Capricorn, 1972);

The Well-Tempered Critic (Bloomington: Indiana University Press, 1963);

A Natural Perspective: The Development of Shakespearean Comedy and Romance (New York: Columbia University Press, 1965);

The Return of Eden: Five Essays on Milton's Epics (Toronto: University of Toronto Press, 1965); republished as *Five Essays on Milton's Epics* (London: Routledge & Kegan Paul, 1966);

Fools of Time: Studies in Shakespearean Tragedy (Toronto: University of Toronto Press, 1967);

The Modern Century (Toronto: Oxford University Press, 1967; London & New York: Oxford University Press, 1969);

A Study of English Romanticism (New York: Random House, 1968; Brighton: Harvester Press, 1983);

Silence in the Sea (St. John's, Newfoundland: Memorial University of Newfoundland, 1969);

The Stubborn Structure: Essays on Criticism and Society (Ithaca: Cornell University Press, 1970; London: Methuen, 1970);

The Bush Garden: Essays on the Canadian Imagination (Toronto: Anansi, 1971);

The Critical Path: An Essay on the Social Context of Literary Criticism (Bloomington: Indiana University Press, 1971; Brighton: Harvester Press, 1983);

On Teaching Literature (New York: Harcourt Brace Jovanovich, 1972);

The Secular Scripture: A Study of the Structure of Romance (Cambridge: Harvard University Press, 1976);

Spiritus Mundi: Essays on Literature, Myth, and Society (Bloomington: Indiana University Press, 1976);

Northrop Frye (photograph by Brian Willer/Maclean's)

Northrop Frye on Culture and Literature: A Collection of Review Essays, edited by Robert D. Denham (Chicago: University of Chicago Press, 1978);

Creation and Recreation (Toronto & Buffalo: University of Toronto Press, 1980);

Criticism as Education (New York: School of Library Service, Columbia University, 1980);

The Great Code: The Bible and Literature (New York: Harcourt Brace Jovanovich, 1982; Lon-

don: Routledge & Kegan Paul, 1982; Toronto: Academic Press, 1982);

Divisions on a Ground: Essays on Canadian Culture, edited by James Polk (Toronto: Anansi, 1982);

The Myth of Deliverance: Reflections on Shakespeare's Problem Comedies (Toronto: University of Toronto Press, 1983; Brighton: Harvester Press, 1983);

The Harper Handbook to Literature, by Frye, Sheridan Baker, and George W. Perkins (New York: Harper & Row, 1985);

Northrop Frye on Shakespeare, edited by Robert Sandler (Markham, Ontario: Fitzhenry & Whiteside/New Haven: Yale University Press, 1986).

OTHER: "The Argument of Comedy," in *English Institute Essays: 1948,* edited by D. A. Robertson, Jr. (New York: Columbia University Press, 1949), pp. 58-73;

"The Church: Its Relation to Society," in *The Living Church,* edited by Harold Vaughan (Toronto: United Church Publishing House, 1949), pp. 152-172;

"Blake's Treatment of the Archetype," in *English Institute Essays: 1950,* edited by Alan S. Downer (New York: Columbia University Press, 1951), pp. 170-196;

John Milton, *Paradise Lost and Selected Poetry and Prose,* edited, with an introduction, by Frye (New York: Holt, Rinehart & Winston, 1951);

"Trends in Modern Culture," in *The Heritage of Western Culture: Essays on the Origin and Development of Modern Culture,* edited by Randolph C. Chalmers (Toronto: Ryerson Press, 1952), pp. 102-117;

Pelham Edgar, *Across My Path,* edited, with an introduction, by Frye (Toronto: Ryerson Press, 1952);

William Blake, *Selected Poetry and Prose of William Blake,* edited, with an introduction, by Frye (New York: Random House, 1953);

"Oswald Spengler," in *Architects of Modern Thought,* first series (Toronto: Canadian Broadcasting Corporation, 1955), pp. 83-90;

Charles Trick Currelly, *I Brought the Ages Home,* edited, with an introduction, by Frye (Toronto: Ryerson Press, 1956);

Sound and Poetry: English Institute Essays, 1956, edited, with an introduction and a preface, by Frye (New York: Columbia University Press, 1957);

"Notes for a Commentary on *Milton*," in *The Divine Vision: Studies in the Poetry and Art of William Blake*, edited by Vivian de Sola Pinto (London: Gollancz, 1957), pp. 99-137;

E. J. Pratt, *The Collected Poems of E. J. Pratt*, second edition, edited, with an introduction and a preface, by Frye (Toronto: Macmillan, 1958);

"Poetry," in *The Arts in Canada: A Stocktaking at Mid-Century*, edited by Malcolm Ross (Toronto: Macmillan, 1958), pp. 84-90;

William Shakespeare, *The Tempest*, edited, with an introduction, by Frye (Baltimore: Penguin, 1959; revised, 1970);

"Religion and Modern Poetry," in *Challenge and Response: Modern Ideas and Religion*, edited by Chalmers and John A. Irving (Toronto: Ryerson Press, 1959), pp. 23-36;

Peter F. Fisher, *The Valley of Vision: Blake as Prophet and Revolutionary*, edited, with an introduction, by Frye (Toronto: University of Toronto Press, 1961);

"The Critical Discipline," in *Canadian Universities Today: Symposium Presented to the Royal Society of Canada in 1960*, edited by George Stanley and Guy Sylvestre (Toronto: University of Toronto Press, 1961), pp. 30-37;

Design for Learning: Reports Submitted to the Joint Committee of the Toronto Board of Education and the University of Toronto, edited, with an introduction, by Frye (Toronto: University of Toronto Press, 1962);

"Shakespeare's Experimental Comedy" and "The Tragedies of Nature and Fortune," in *Stratford Papers on Shakespeare*, edited by B. W. Jackson (Toronto: Gage, 1962), pp. 2-14, 38-55;

"The Developing Imagination," in *Learning in Language and Literature* (Cambridge: Harvard University Press, 1963), pp. 31-58;

"Literary Criticism," in *The Aims and Methods of Scholarship in Modern Languages and Literatures*, edited by James Thorpe (New York: Modern Language Association, 1963), pp. 57-69;

Romanticism Reconsidered: Selected Papers of the English Institute, edited, with a foreword, by Frye (New York: Columbia University Press, 1963);

"Allegory" and "Verse and Prose," in *Princeton Encyclopedia of Poetry and Poetics*, edited by Alex Preminger (Princeton: Princeton University Press, 1965), pp. 12-15, 885-890;

"Nature and Nothing," in *Essays on Shakespeare*, edited by G. W. Chapman (Princeton: Princeton University Press, 1965), pp. 35-58;

"The Structure and Spirit of Comedy," in *Stratford Papers on Shakespeare, 1964*, edited by Jackson (Toronto: Gage, 1965), pp. 1-9;

"William Blake," in *English Romantic Poets and Essayists: A Review of Research and Criticism*, edited by Carolyn W. Houtchens and Lawrence H. Houtchens (New York: Modern Language Association, 1966), pp. 1-31;

"Reflections in a Mirror," in *Northrop Frye in Modern Criticism*, edited by Murray Krieger (New York: Columbia University Press, 1966), pp. 133-146;

Blake: A Collection of Critical Essays, edited, with an introduction, by Frye (Englewood Cliffs, N.J.: Prentice-Hall, 1966);

"The Keys to the Gates," in *Some British Romantics: A Collection of Essays*, edited by Frye, James V. Logan, and John E. Jordan (Columbus: Ohio State University Press, 1966), pp. 3-40;

"William Blake," in *Encyclopedia of Philosophy*, edited by Paul Edwards (New York: Macmillan, 1967), pp. 319-320;

"Literature and Myth," in *Relations of Literary Study; Essays on Interdisciplinary Study*, edited by Thorpe (New York: Modern Language Association, 1967), pp. 22-54;

"John Keats," in *Encyclopedia Americana* (New York: Americana Corporation, 1968), XVI: 328-331;

"Research and Graduate Education in the Humanities," in *Journal of the Proceedings and Addresses of the Twentieth Annual Conference of the Association of Graduate Schools in the Association of American Universities*, edited by W. Gordon Whaley (Austin: University of Texas Press, 1968), pp. 37-43;

Shakespeare Series, volumes 1 and 2, edited, with an introduction, by Frye (Toronto & London: Macmillan, 1968; New York: Odyssey Press, 1968);

"America: True or False?," in *Notes for a Native Land: A New Encounter with Canada*, edited by Andy Wainwright (Ottawa: Oberon Press, 1969), pp. 52-55;

"Sign and Significance," in *Claremont Reading Conference: Thirty-Third Yearbook*, edited by Malcolm P. Douglass (Claremont, Cal.: Claremont Graduate School, 1969), pp. 1-8;

"The University and Personal Life: Student Anarchism and the Educational Contract," in

Higher Education: Demand and Response, edited by W. R. Niblett (San Francisco: Jossey-Bass, 1970), pp. 35-51;

"Myth and Poetry," in *The Concise Encyclopedia of English and American Poets and Poetry,* edited by Stephen Spender and Donald Hall (London: Hutchinson, 1970), pp. 187-190;

Literature: The Uses of the Imagination, 12 volumes, edited by Frye and others (New York: Harcourt Brace Jovanovich, 1972-1973);

"History and Myth in the Bible," in *The Literature of Fact: Selected Papers from the English Institute,* edited by Angus Fletcher (New York: Columbia University Press, 1976), pp. 1-19;

"Summation," in *Symposium on Television Violence/ Colloque sur la violence à la télévision* (Ottawa: Canadian Radio-television and Telecommunications Commission, 1976), pp. 206-215;

"Haunted by Lack of Ghosts: Some Patterns in the Imagery of Canadian Poetry," in *The Canadian Imagination: Dimensions of a Literary Culture,* edited by David Staines (Cambridge: Harvard University Press, 1977), pp. 22-45;

The Practical Imagination: Stories, Poems, Plays, edited by Frye, Sheridan Baker, and George Perkins (New York: Harper & Row, 1980);

"Criticism and Environment," in *Adjoining Cultures as Reflected in Literature and Language,* edited by John X. Evans and Peter Horwath (Tempe: Arizona State University, 1983), pp. 9-21;

"The Authority of Learning," in *The Empire Club of Canada: Addresses 1983-1984* (Toronto: Empire Club Foundation, 1984), pp. 196-206;

"Vision and Cosmos," in *Biblical Patterns in Modern Literature,* edited by David H. Hirsch and Nehama Aschkenasy (Chico, Cal.: Scholars Press, 1985), pp. 5-17;

"Approaching the Lyric," in *Lyric Poetry: Beyond New Criticism,* edited by Chaviva Hošek and Patricia Parker (Ithaca: Cornell University Press, 1985), pp. 31-37;

"The Survival of Eros in Poetry," in *Romanticism and Contemporary Criticism,* edited by Morris Eaves and Michael Fischer (Ithaca: Cornell University Press, 1986), pp. 15-29.

PERIODICAL PUBLICATIONS: "Wyndham Lewis: Anti-Spenglerian," *Canadian Forum,* 16 (June 1936): 21-22;

"Music and the Savage Breast," *Canadian Forum,* 18 (April 1938): 451-453;

"The Great Charlie," *Canadian Forum,* 21 (August 1941): 148-150;

"Music in Poetry," *University of Toronto Quarterly,* 11 (January 1942): 167-179;

"The Anatomy in Prose Fiction," *Manitoba Arts Review,* 3 (Spring 1942): 35-47;

"The Nature of Satire," *University of Toronto Quarterly,* 14 (October 1944): 75-89;

"A Liberal Education," *Canadian Forum,* 25 (September 1945): 134-135; (October 1945): 162-164;

"Blake on Trial Again," review of *William Blake: The Politics of Vision* by Mark Schorer and *The Portable Blake* edited by Alfred Kazin, *Poetry,* 69 (January 1947): 223-228;

"Education and the Humanities," *United Church Observer,* 9 (1 August 1947): 5, 25;

"The Eternal Tramp," *Here and Now,* 1 (December 1947): 8-11;

"The Pursuit of Form," *Canadian Art,* 6 (Christmas 1948): 54-57;

"The Function of Criticism at the Present Time," *University of Toronto Quarterly,* 19 (October 1949): 1-16;

"The Four Forms of Prose Fiction," *Hudson Review,* 2 (Winter 1950): 582-595;

"Levels of Meaning in Literature," *Kenyon Review,* 12 (Spring 1950): 246-262;

"Poetry and Design in William Blake," *Journal of Aesthetics and Art Criticism,* 10 (September 1951): 35-42;

"A Conspectus of Dramatic Genres," *Kenyon Review,* 13 (Autumn 1951): 543-562;

"The Analogy of Democracy," *Bias,* 1 (February 1952): 2-6;

"Comic Myth in Shakespeare," *Transactions of the Royal Society of Canada,* third series, 46 (June 1952): 47-58;

"Three Meanings of Symbolism," *Yale French Studies,* no. 9 (1952): 11-19;

"Characterization in Shakespearean Comedy," *Shakespeare Quarterly,* 4 (July 1953): 271-277;

"Towards a Theory of Cultural History," *University of Toronto Quarterly,* 22 (July 1953): 325-341;

"The Language of Poetry," *Explorations: Studies in Culture and Communication,* no. 4 (February 1955): 80-90;

"English Canadian Literature, 1929-1954," *Books Abroad,* 29 (Summer 1955): 270-274;

"The Transferability of Literary Concepts," *Association of the Princeton Graduate Alumni,* 30-31 (December 1955): 54-60;

"La poesía anglo-canadiense," translated by Jaime Rest, *Sur*, no. 240 (May-June 1956): 30-39;

"Blake's Introduction to Experience," *Huntington Library Quarterly*, 21 (November 1957): 57-67;

"The Study of English in Canada," *Dalhousie Review*, 38 (Spring 1958): 1-7;

"Literature as Possession," *Kenyon Alumni Bulletin* (January-March 1960): 5-9;

"Academy without Walls," *Canadian Art*, 18 (September-October 1961): 296-298;

"Haliburton: Mask and Ego," *Alphabet*, 5 (December 1962): 58-63;

"Ned Pratt: The Personal Legend," *Canadian Literature*, no. 21 (Summer 1964): 6-9;

"The Social Importance of Literature," *Educational Courier*, 39 (November-December 1968): 19-23;

"The University and the Heroic Vision," *Wascana Review*, 3 (1968): 83-87;

"Mythos and Logos," *Yearbook of Comparative Literature*, 18 (1969): 5-18;

"Rear View Crystal Ball," *Canadian Forum*, 50 (April-May 1970): 54-55;

"Literature and the Law," *Law Society of Upper Canada Gazette*, 4 (June 1970): 70-77;

"Education and the Rejection of Reality," *University of Toronto Graduate*, 3 (June 1971): 49-55;

"The Quality of Life in the Seventies," *University of Toronto Graduate*, 3 (June 1971): 38-48;

"Universities and the Deluge of Cant," *University of Waterloo Gazette*, 12 (14 June 1972): 2;

"The Responsibilities of the Critic," *Modern Language Notes*, 91 (October 1976): 797-813;

"Literature, History and Language," *Bulletin of the Midwest Modern Language Association*, 12 (Fall 1979): 1-7;

"The Meaning of Recreation: Humanism in Society," *Iowa Review*, 11 (Winter 1980): 1-9;

"*Il Cortegiano*," *Quaderni d'italianistica*, 1 (1980): 1-14;

"The Bridge of Language," *Science*, 212 (10 April 1981): 127-132;

"The Double Mirror," *Bulletin of the American Academy of Arts and Sciences*, 35 (December 1981): 32-41;

"The Beginning of the Word," *Indirections*, 6 (Winter 1981): 4-14;

"The Meeting of Past and Future in William Morris," *Studies in Romanticism*, 21 (Fall 1982): 303-318;

"Literature as Critique of Pure Reason," *Descant*, 14 (Spring 1983): 7-21;

"Literary and Linguistic Scholarship in a Postliterate World," *PMLA*, 99 (October 1984): 990-995;

"Myth as the Matrix of Literature," *Georgia Review*, 38 (Fall 1984): 465-476;

"The World as Music and Idea in Wagner's *Parsifal*," *Carleton Germanic Papers*, 12 (1984): 37-49;

"La letteratura e la arti figurative," *Lettera Italiane*, 3 (1985): 285-298;

"Lacan et la parole dans sa plénitude," *Ornicar? Revue du Champ Freudien*, 33 (April-June 1985): 11-14;

"The Expanding World of Metaphor," *Journal of the American Academy of Religion*, 53 (December 1985): 585-598.

Northrop Frye is one of the few twentieth-century critics in North America with an international reputation. Harold Bloom refers to Frye as "the foremost living student of Western literature," adding that he is "certainly the largest and most crucial literary critic in the English language" since Walter Pater and Oscar Wilde. Lawrence Lipking and A. Walton Litz see Frye as one of the four major critics of this century, placing him in the company of T. S. Eliot, Ezra Pound, and I. A. Richards. "More than any other modern critic," says Lipking, "he stands at the center of critical activity."

In his own country Frye's reputation is also considerable. In 1982 the Canadian weekly, *Maclean's*, devoted its cover story to his work, and *The Great Code* (1982) remained for a number of months on the Canadian best-seller list. A public figure in Canada, Frye has frequently been summoned from the quiet confines of Victoria College (Toronto) to perform public duties, such as serving on the Canadian Radio-television and Telecommunications Commission, to address the annual meetings of bar associations, psychiatrists, publishers, educators, and scientists, and to speak at public colloquia of all sorts. He received the Royal Bank Award in 1978, a prize given to those "whose outstanding achievement is of such importance that it is contributing to human welfare and the common good"; was awarded the Canada Council Medal in 1978; received the Pierre Chauveau Medal from the Royal Society of Canada in 1970; was elected companion of the Order of Canada in 1972; and won a Governor General's Award in 1987. Many of Frye's three dozen honorary degrees have come from Canadian universities. One of the reasons that Frye is an intellectual hero at home is that, for all of his attention to the European literary tradition, he has at the same time always managed to keep his eyes fastened on things Canadian—not just upon his country's art and literature but upon its entire national consciousness and sense of identity.

While influential (he has had a direct influence on writers such as Jay Macpherson, D. G. Jones, and Margaret Atwood), his mythopoeic comments on Canadian writing have not been uniformly accepted. Works such as *The Bush Garden* (1971)—which collects his rhetorically effective "Conclusion" to the first edition of *The Literary History of Canada*—together with *The Modern Century* (1967) and *Divisions on a Ground* (1982), have been among the clearest expositions of his theories about Canadian literature and cultural origin. Several of his phrases—especially "the bush garden" and "the garrison mentality," and the challenge of the question "Where is here?"—have become critical watchwords in Canada. Yet Frye has also been challenged for the perceived limits of his criticism: its Protestant, Eurocentric, Ontario-based precepts, and the politics of its desire for design.

Frye's international reputation rests largely on the grand design of literary theory developed in *Anatomy of Criticism* (1957), on his studies of Blake, Shakespeare, and the Bible, and on the large body of social and practical criticism he has written since the mid 1930s. A 1979 study revealed that among the most frequently cited writers in the arts and humanities Frye ranked only behind Marx, Aristotle, Shakespeare, Lenin, Plato, Freud, and Barthes. This survey of more than 900,000 citations in articles and books that were published during 1978 and 1979 revealed, moreover, that *Anatomy of Criticism* was the most frequently cited work in the arts and humanities written by a twentieth-century author.

Frye was born and spent the first five years of his life in Sherbrooke, Quebec. After World War I, his father, Herman Edward Frye, a hardware salesman, moved the family to Moncton, New Brunswick, where his mother, Catharine Maud Howard Frye, the daughter of a Methodist minister, tutored him at home until the fourth grade. Frye completed his secondary schooling in Moncton, graduating from Aberdeen High School in 1928. After enrolling for a brief period in a business course, he made his way to Toronto, where in 1929 he entered Victoria College at the University of Toronto. The most influential teachers during Frye's undergraduate years were E. J.

Dust jacket for Frye's first book. "I suppose," he once remarked, "I have learned everything I know from Blake in one way or another."

Pratt, one of Canada's distinguished poets; Pelham Edgar, who introduced Frye to Blake; and J. D. Robins, whose interest in primitive and popular literary forms undoubtedly contributed to Frye's lifelong interest in archetypes.

Frye placed first in the Honour Course in Philosophy and English all four years at Victoria College, graduated in 1933, studied theology at Emmanuel College (University of Toronto), and spent the summer of 1934 as a circuit-riding student preacher in a remote outpost of the United Church near Shaunavon in southwestern Saskatchewan. But he had no real inclination toward the parish ministry, reporting that at Emmanuel College he "spent more time doing English literature than theology," the latter of which for him "was largely Frazer's *Golden Bough*." After graduating from Emmanuel in 1936, he went to Merton College, Oxford, on a fellowship; returned to Victoria College the following year as a lecturer in English literature; married Helen Kemp, a classmate; went back to Merton College in 1938 to complete his studies; and in 1939 came home again to Victoria, where he has spent his entire academic career. He moved quickly through the academic ranks, from assistant professor in 1942 to full professor in 1948. Frye became chair of the English department in 1952, principal of the college in 1959, University Professor in 1967, and chancellor of Victoria University in 1979.

From the time he first began to publish essays and reviews on music, art, film, and opera as a student at Emmanuel College, Frye has been a prolific writer. Fifty-five years after his first published essay, his bibliography contains, in addition to the more than forty books he has written and edited, more than 500 articles, reviews, monographs, lectures, contributions to books, and interviews, and scores of unpublished lectures.

The basis of Frye's fundamental convictions about literature are rooted in the poetic vision of William Blake, the writer to whom he devoted his first book, *Fearful Symmetry* (1947). This study is widely recognized as one of the most important contributions to the understanding of Blake's poetry, especially his prophetic works. The book examines generally the relation between the mythology Blake created and the Western literary tradition. Blake is best understood, according to Frye, when his work is seen as a unified mythology in which the supreme figure of the artist plays a central role. Frye argues, against those who see Blake's vision as private, mystical, or deranged, that Blake's poetry is typical, that he belongs squarely in the tradition of English literature, and that he should be read in imaginative, rather than simply historical, terms. Seeing Blake in these terms illustrates "the doctrine that all symbolism in all art and religion is mutually intelligible among all men, and that there is such a thing as the iconography of the imagination." Throughout the book Frye charts the "grammar" of this iconography–the way Blake represents his symbolic vision, which is at once individual and conventional. He treats the relation of Blake to Spenser and Milton and especially to the Bible, ranging freely over Blake's entire work yet giving particular attention to the prophecies. He concludes that the archetypal approach can be applied not just to Blake but to the reading of other poets as well. One of the reasons that *Fearful Symmetry* helped to revolutionize Blake studies is that Frye derived his principles for reading Blake from Blake himself. Remarking on this in the preface to a 1962 republication of *Fearful Symmetry,* Frye says, "the somewhat unusual form and structure of my commentary was

derived from my absorption in the larger critical theory implicit in Blake's view of art. Whatever importance the book may have, beyond its merits as a guide to Blake, it owes to its connection to the critical theories that I have ever since been trying to teach, both in Blake's name and my own." In another context, Frye remarks, "I suppose I have learned everything I know from Blake in one way or another."

Frye's vision of literature is a continuous one, and it forms a large pattern like those encyclopedic works that have captured his own imagination. "With some people," he says, "continuity takes a revolutionary and metaphoric direction. . . . With me, continuity has taken a more gradual direction . . . because the principles . . . formulated [early] are still working as heuristic assumptions, and they are the only ones available to me." These principles receive their fullest expression in *Anatomy of Criticism.* Standing back from that work, as Frye urges us to do in the presence of a novel or poem, we discover an aesthetic that is fundamentally romantic, a method that systematically relates literature to other literature, a set of highly schematic principles for organizing knowledge about literature, and a dialectical vision that seeks to hold in tension the opposing thrusts of both literature and criticism. The bold purpose of *Anatomy of Criticism* is to develop a comprehensive system of critical principles and terms, derived from literature itself, for understanding literature. Frye has always maintained that schematic structures–dialectical and hierarchical and cyclical models–are an inescapable part of literary criticism because literature itself is schematic, and nothing is more obvious in *Anatomy of Criticism* than the intricately detailed and ingenious way that Frye categorizes the literary structures and conventions that make up his theories of modes, symbols, myths, and genres.

In the first essay of the *Anatomy of Criticism* ("Historical Criticism"), Frye uses the hero's power of action to distinguish five primary modes of literature (mythical, romantic, high mimetic, low mimetic, and ironic). For each of the modes, Frye identifies the characteristics of its fictional forms (both comic and tragic) and its thematic forms (both encyclopedic and episodic). The analysis of these twenty modal categories illustrates that, although there are two poles to literature (the mimetic and the mythical), the structural principles of narrative remain constant. The theory of modes is also a general theory of literary history. Frye argues that literature has moved historically from myth, which has no concern for plausibility, toward realism and accurate description. But the low-mimetic and ironic modes of the nineteenth and twentieth centuries are "plausible adaptations" of fictional conventions that are rooted in the earliest myths. Frye refers to the tendency of fictions to move gradually toward verisimilitude as "displacement," meaning that narrative structure is always a conventional form of an earlier story.

In the second essay ("Ethical Criticism") Frye distinguishes the phases of symbolism or the contexts within which we interpret literature. Using an expanded version of the four medieval levels of meaning, he illustrates how each phase of symbolism (literal, descriptive, formal, mythical, and anagogic) has its own kind of symbol and has a different conception of narrative (*mythos*) and meaning (*dianoia*); and he shows the relation between each phase and a particular form of both art and criticism.

Frye is interested primarily in the last two phases of symbolism (the archetypal and the anagogic) because they go beyond the explication of poetic texture at the literal level, the documentary criticism of the descriptive level, and the interpretative commentary of the formal level. By emphasizing the generic relationship of poems to other poems, archetypal criticism embraces the social function of poetry. Beyond this, it views the symbol as a natural object with a human meaning, and so it is also "a part of the total imitation of nature that we call civilization." From this perspective, poetry becomes a product of a vision of the goals of human work. The archetypal critic, according to Frye, is tempted to see art as an ethical instrument, just as in the descriptive phase he or she is tempted to see truth as the external goal of art, and in the literal and formal phases, beauty. But because none of these external standards can ultimately determine the value of literature for Frye, he moves beyond the archetypal phase and the goals of civilization, where art is not an end in itself, "to culture, where it is disinterested and liberal and stands on its own feet." This is the anagogic or mythopoeic phase, and in this phase, according to Frye, we have the feeling that we have been drawn to the center of the order of words where the symbol is a monad, reflecting the entire poetic universe. The experience of literature at the anagogic level is similar to what Blake means by apocalypse, and Frye's account of anagogy in the second essay is the clear-

est expression in *Anatomy of Criticism* of his deeply romantic sensibility.

Archetypal patterns are most clearly discernible in myth, according to Frye, because mythical stories present a world of pure, abstract literary design. The third essay of *Anatomy of Criticism*, "Archetypal Criticism," develops this thesis in detail. Here Frye provides an elaborate taxonomy of the structure of archetypal imagery, classifying it from the perspective of both meaning (*dianoia*) and narrative (*mythos*). The diagrammatic framework of the theory of myths, especially Frye's treatment of the basic narrative patterns (romance, comedy, tragedy, and irony), is the fullest and most elaborately conceived section of *Anatomy of Criticism*.

Finally, the fourth essay of *Anatomy of Criticism*, "Rhetorical Criticism," develops a theory of genres. The principles that underlie still another of Frye's intricately constructed taxonomies are the radical of presentation (the original or ideal way that a literary work is presented), the predominant rhythm, and the mimetic form of the four primary genres–drama, *epos*, fiction, and lyric. The radical of presentation is the basis for differentiating the four genres from each other, and the rhythm and form are used to identify the literary species within the larger generic types.

A brief summary of topics does little justice to *Anatomy of Criticism*, a book that ranges, with stylistic elegance and wit, over the entire Western literary tradition. *Anatomy of Criticism* is frequently regarded as the most significant and influential piece of Anglo-American critical theory of the past fifty years. It was largely on the basis of this book that the English Institute devoted one of its 1965 sessions to Frye's influence as a critic. In his introduction to the published proceedings, Murray Krieger observed that Frye "has had an influence–indeed an absolute hold–on a generation of developing literary critics greater and more exclusive than that of any one theorist in recent critical history." Frye's work was also the subject of a major international symposium at the University of Rome, Italy, in May 1987.

Frye speaks in the preface to *Anatomy of Criticism* of the need for a volume of "practical criticism, a sort of morphology of symbolism," to complement the "pure critical theory" of that book, and in the decades that followed he did produce a large body of practical criticism. *Fables of Identity* (1963), a collection of essays, examines, among other things, the work of Spenser, Shakespeare, Milton, Blake, Byron, Yeats, Dickinson,

Joyce, and Stevens. Frye has written four books on Shakespeare, one on Milton, still another on Eliot. His other volumes of selected essays–*The Stubborn Structure* (1970), *Spiritus Mundi* (1976), and *Northrop Frye on Culture and Literature* (1978)–contain dozens of examples of practical criticism, as does his selection of essays and reviews on Canadian writers and artists, *The Bush Garden* (1971). His *A Study of English Romanticism* (1968) has separate chapters devoted to Shelley, Keats, and Beddoes. The list of such studies, many of them uncollected, is lengthy.

More often than not Frye's practical criticism is directed not toward detailed commentary on individual works but toward a writer's entire canon. "The great merit of explicatory criticism," he says, "was that it accepted poetic language and form as the basis of poetic meaning. . . . At the same time it deprived itself of the great strength of documentary criticism: the sense of context." It thus tended to slight the larger structural principles and conventions that connect literary works with each other. Frye's typical approach, then, is to place individual poems, plays, and novels within the context of a writer's complete work and to relate them by way of generic and archetypal principles to the literary tradition–what he calls "the total order of words." Frye's contextualism, using the word in both senses just described, is like Eliot's belief that literature from the time of Homer has had a simultaneous existence and forms a simultaneous order. But he goes beyond Eliot in attempting to identify the conventions that permit the poet to create works of literature out of earlier ones.

One continues to be reminded throughout all of Frye's work of his romantic sensibility and his predisposition to the forms of romance. He refers to Coleridge's division of literary critics into either Iliad or Odyssey types, meaning that their interests lean either toward tragedy, realism, and irony, on the one hand, or toward comedy and romance, on the other; and in *A Natural Perspective* (1965) he says of himself: "I have always been temperamentally an Odyssean critic." This helps to explain the prominence in Frye's literary universe of Blake, Spenser, Milton, the later Shakespeare, Shelley, Keats, Coleridge, William Morris, and Wallace Stevens. Frye locates such writers in the "central tradition of mythopoeic poetry," the primary tendencies of which, he says, are romantic, revolutionary, and Protestant. He sees Romanticism as one of the most important revolutions in the history of culture, representing a profound

change in poetic imagery and an equally profound change in the traditional idea of four levels of reality, that "topocosm" against which the images are portrayed. The significance Frye attaches to Romanticism as a revolutionary cultural movement, as well as his preference for comic and romantic forms, most fully treated in *The Secular Scripture* (1976), goes a long way toward explaining the selection of writers whose works he has treated in some detail.

Since the early 1970s Frye has devoted much of his writing to broadly cultural subjects, even though such subjects were anticipated by or implicit in his earlier work. *The Educated Imagination* (1963) and *The Well-Tempered Critic* (1963), for example, point to the ultimate relationship between literature and social meaning. But the past twenty years have seen Frye self-consciously turn his attention to the social function of both literature and criticism. *The Modern Century* and the essays in parts one of *The Stubborn Structure* and *Spiritus Mundi* focus on the social, moral, and philosophical aspects of the products of culture.

The widest ranging of Frye's essays in cultural criticism is *The Critical Path* (1971), a book that exemplifies the centrifugal direction that Frye believes criticism must ultimately take. His approach in this book is implicit in his claim that the process of interpreting the social myths of culture is "very similar to criticism in literature" and that "different forms of critical interpretation cannot be sharply separated, whether they are applied to the plays of Shakespeare, the manuscripts of the Bible, the American Constitution, or the oral tradition of an aboriginal tribe." The main assumption on which the book is based, then, is that while the literary critic is not qualified to handle all the "technical contexts" of culture, he or she is especially prepared to interpret the cultural phenomena that form the social environment of literature. "The modern critic," Frye says, "is a student of mythology, and his total subject of study embraces not merely literature, but the areas of concern which the mythical language of construction and belief enters and informs. These areas constitute the mythological subjects, and they include large parts of religion, philosophy, political theory, and the social sciences."

Frye examines a wide range of such subjects in *The Critical Path:* the difference between oral and writing cultures, Renaissance humanism, the critical theories of Sidney and Shelley, Marxism and democracy, the idea of progress, advertising and propaganda, social contract theories and con-

Frye in the classroom (photograph by Brian Willer/Maclean's)

ceptions of utopia, contemporary youth culture, McLuhanism, theories of education, and so on. What holds these diverse topics together is the framework of Frye's discussion. Whatever the issue, he sets it against the background of what he sees as the two opposing myths of Western culture: the conservative myth of concern, which values coherence, continuity, and social commitment, and the liberal myth of freedom, which values detachment, tolerance, and respect for the individual. Out of the tension between freedom and concern, Frye says, "glimpses of the third order of experience emerge, a world that may not exist but completes existence, the world of the definitive experience that poetry urges us to have but which we never quite get. If such a world existed, no individual could live in it. . . . If we could live in it, of course, criticism would cease, and the distinction between literature and life would disappear, because life itself would be the continuous incarnation of the creative word." The doctrine of the imagination being proposed in this oracular rhetoric takes us back to *Anatomy of Criticism*, for the twin values Frye holds in tension in that book are a centrifugal ethical and social criticism forever extended outward toward the myth of concern, and a detached, disinterested centripetal criticism of literary structure and convention. But they also take us forward to *The Great Code: The Bible and Literature*.

The Bible has been a part of Frye's imaginative universe from the beginning. He experienced the Bible in his early years as a natural aspect of growing up in the evangelical tradition. But it was not until he began teaching that he realized the impossibility of understanding the Western literary tradition without a thorough grounding in the Bible. Although Frye has devoted a great deal of his time in the 1980s to setting down his ideas on the Bible and literature, the relations between the two have been a lifelong interest. *Fearful Symmetry* and *Anatomy of Criticism* are strewn with sentences and paragraphs about the Bible that embody many of the fundamental principles upon which *The Great Code* is based: the cyclic vision of the Bible, its literal meaning, its position as the definitive mythical, archetypal, and typological structure of narrative and imagery in the Western heritage.

Although subtitled "The Bible and Literature," *The Great Code* is not about the ways that the Western literary tradition has been directly influenced by the Bible. It is rather about the literary characteristics of the Bible itself: its language, myths, metaphors, typological structure, imagery, and rhetoric. Throughout, Frye's treatment of the poetic character of the biblical text is fundamentally antihistorical and antimimetic. He also maintains that theology and the traditions of biblical hermeneutics do not contribute much to his fundamental aim. Still, the main contours of a theology manifest themselves throughout the book: a theology of immanence rooted firmly in nineteenth-century doctrines of creation, on the one hand, and apocalypse, on the other–a romantic theology that seeks to democratize the kerygma. The primary characteristic of all of Frye's criticism is its continuity. If we step back from *The Great Code*, we realize that its language, method, assumptions, and central ideas are grounded in the study of William Blake that Frye began in the 1930s.

Interviews:

Tim Traynor, Jerry Wadsworth, and Pete Miller, "Northrop Frye and Literature," *Gazette* (University of Western Ontario), 12 March 1963, p. 6;

Gregory Baum, "The Voice in the Crowd," *Media I* (Toronto: CBC Publications, 1966), pp. 12-18;

Bob Bossin, "An Interview," *Random* (January 1969): 18-22;

Bruce Mickleburgh, "The Only Genuine Revolution," *Monday Morning* (February 1969): 20-26;

Mickleburgh, "Educating the Imagination," *Monday Morning* (March 1969): 22-28;

John Ayre, "Into the Wilderness: An Interview on Religion with Northrop Frye," *Acta Victoriana*, 94 (February 1970): 39-50;

Johan Aitken, "There Is Really No Such Thing as Methodology," *Orbit 1*, 1 (February 1970): 4-7;

Justin Kaplan, "A Conversation with Northrop Frye, Literary Critic," *Harvard Magazine*, 77 (July-August 1975): 52-56;

Philip Chester, "A Conversation with Northrop Frye: Education, Religion, Old Age," *Varsity*, 22 October 1976, pp. 14-15;

Hugh Oliver, "A Literate Person is First and Foremost an Articulate Person," *Interchange*, 7, no. 4 (1976-1977): 32-38;

Bruce Reynolds, "Eminent Victorians: The Frye Interview," *Strand*, 1 March 1978, pp. 5-11;

John Plaskett, "Interview," *Vic Report*, 7 (Winter 1978-1979): 3-6;

Elizabeth and Gregory Cowan, David Stewart, and Richard Costa, "Frye's Literary Theory in the Classroom," *CEA Critic*, 42 (January 1980): 32-42;

Bryant Fillion, "Literature, Language, and Learning: Purposes and Importance of Literature in Education," *Language Arts*, 57 (April 1980): 199-206;

Robert Fulford, "From Nationalism to Regionalism: The Maturing of Canadian Culture," in *Aurora: New Canadian Writing in 1980*, edited by Morris Wolfe (Toronto: Doubleday, 1980), pp. 5-15;

D. G. Bastian, "Fearful Symmetry: Northrop Frye on Victoria, the Bible, and the Canadian Way," *Vic Report*, 9 (Summer 1981): 9-12;

John Cargill and Angela Esterhammer, "*Acta* Interview: Northrop Frye," *Acta Victoriana*, 106 (Fall 1981): 58-70;

Deborah Shackleton, "Canadian Energy: Dialogues on Creativity: Northrop Frye," *Descant*, 12, nos. 32-33 (1981): 216-226;

Andrew Kaufman, "Northrop Frye on Literature and Religion," *Newspaper* (University of Toronto), 27 October 1982, p. 5;

Imre Salusinszky, "An Interview with Northrop Frye," *Scripsi* (University of Melbourne), 2, no. 4 (1984): 220-226;

Deanne Bogdan, "Moncton, Mentors, and Memories: Reflections with Northrop Frye," *Studies in Canadian Literature*, 11 (Fall 1986): 246-269.

Bibliographies:

Robert D. Denham, *Northrop Frye: An Enumerative Bibliography* (Metuchen, N.J.: Scarecrow Press, 1974);

Denham, *Northrop Frye: An Annotated Bibliography of Primary and Secondary Sources* (Toronto: University of Toronto Press, 1988).

Biography:

John Ayre, *Northrop Frye: A Critical Biography* (Don Mills, Ontario: General Publishing, forthcoming 1988).

References:

Iqbal Ahmad, "Imagination and Image in Frye's Criticism," *English Quarterly*, 3 (Summer 1970): 15-24;

Johan L. Aitken, "Northrop Frye and Educational Theory: Some Implications for Teaching," *Teacher Education*, 10 (April 1977): 50-59;

Charles Altieri, "Northrop Frye and the Problem of Spiritual Authority," *PMLA*, 87 (October 1972): 964-975;

Altieri, "Some Uses of Frye's Literary Theory," *CEA Critic*, 42 (January 1980): 10-19;

Margaret Atwood, "Northrop Frye Observed," in her *Second Words: Selected Critical Prose* (Toronto: Anansi, 1982), pp. 398-406;

John Ayre, "The Mythological Universe of Northrop Frye," *Saturday Night*, 88 (May 1973): 19-24;

Bruce Bashford, "Literary History in Northrop Frye's *Anatomy of Criticism*," *Connecticut Review*, 8 (October 1974): 48-55;

Walter Jackson Bate, "Northrop Frye," in *Criticism: The Major Texts*, edited by Bate, revised and enlarged edition (New York: Harcourt Brace Jovanovich, 1970), pp. 597-601, 609, 615-617;

Ronald Bates, *Northrop Frye* (Toronto: McClelland & Stewart, 1971);

Catherine Belsey, "Northrop Frye," in her *Critical Practice* (London: Methuen, 1980), pp. 21-29;

Ralph Berry, "Shakespearean Comedy and Northrop Frye," *Essays in Criticism*, 22 (January 1972): 33-40;

Don H. Bialostosky, "Literary 'Romanticism and Modernism' in Robert Langbaum's *The Poetry of Experience* and Northrop Frye's *Anatomy of Criticism*," *Cahiers roumains d'études littéraires*, 1 (1982): 110-117;

Frank W. Bliss and Earl R. MacCormac, "Two Poles of Metaphor: Frye and Beardsley," *Journal of Aesthetic Education*, 11 (January 1977): 33-49;

Deanne Bogdan, "Northrop Frye and the Defence of Literature," *English Studies in Canada*, 8 (June 1982): 203-214;

John Casey, "A 'Science' of Criticism: Northrop Frye," in his *The Language of Criticism* (London: Methuen, 1966), pp. 140-151;

Richard Conville, "Northrop Frye and Speech Criticism," *Quarterly Journal of Speech*, 56 (December 1970): 417-425;

David Cook, *Northrop Frye: A Vision of the New World* (New York: St. Martin's, 1985);

Eleanor Cook and others, eds., *Centre and Labyrinth: Essays in Honour of Northrop Frye* (Toronto: University of Toronto Press, 1983);

Peter M. Cummings, "Northrop Frye and the Necessary Hybrid: Criticism as Aesthetic Humanism," in *The Quest for Imagination: Essays in Twentieth-Century Aesthetic Criticism*, edited by O. B. Hardison, Jr. (Cleveland: Press of Case Western Reserve University, 1971), pp. 255-276;

Mark Czarnecki, "The Gospel According to Frye," *Maclean's*, 95 (5 April 1982): 40-44;

Frank Davey, "Northrop Frye," in his *From There to Here* (Erin, Ontario: Press Porcepic, 1974), pp. 106-112;

Robert D. Denham, "An Anatomy of Frye's Influence," *American Review of Canadian Studies*, 14 (Spring 1984): 1-19;

Denham, "Common Cause: Notes on Frye's View of Education," *CEA Critic*, 42 (November 1979): 23-28;

Denham, "Frye and the Social Context of Criticism," *South Atlantic Bulletin*, 39 (November 1974): 63-72;

Denham, "Frye's Theory of Symbols," *Canadian Literature*, 66 (Autumn 1975): 63-79;

Denham, Introduction to *Northrop Frye on Culture and Literature*, edited by Denham (Chicago: University of Chicago Press, 1978), pp. 1-64;

Denham, *Northrop Frye and Critical Method* (University Park: Pennsylvania State University Press, 1978);

Denham, "Northrop Frye and Rhetorical Criticism," *Xavier University Studies*, 11 (Spring 1972): 1-11;

Denham, "Science, Criticism, and Frye's Metaphysical Universe," *South Carolina Review*, 7 (April 1975): 3-18;

Michael Dolzani, "The Infernal Method: Northrop Frye and Contemporary Criticism," in *Centre and Labyrinth*, edited by Cook and others, pp. 59-68;

Jan Ulrik Dyrkjøb, *Northrop Fryes litteraturteori* (Copenhagen: Berlingske Verlag, 1979);

Herbert Feder, "Northrop Frye's Aestheticism and Moral Development," *Interchange*, 11, no. 1 (1980-1981): 76-90;

John A. Fekete, "Northrop Frye: A Critical Theory of Capitulation," in his *The Critical Twilight: Explorations of Ideology in Anglo-American Literary Theory from Eliot to McLuhan* (London: Routledge & Kegan Paul, 1977), pp. 107-131;

William O. Fennell, "Theology and Frye: Some Implications of *The Great Code*," *Toronto Journal of Theology*, 1 (Spring 1985): 113-121;

Richard Finholt, "Northrop Frye's Theory of Countervailing Tendencies: A New Look at the Mode and Myth Essays," *Genre*, 13 (Summer 1980): 203-257;

Michael Fischer, "The Imagination as a Sanction of Value: Northrop Frye and the Uses of Literature," *Centennial Review*, 21 (Spring 1977): 105-117;

Angus Fletcher, "Northrop Frye: The Critical Passion," *Critical Inquiry*, 1 (June 1975): 741-756;

John Fraser, "Mr. Frye and Evaluation," *Cambridge Quarterly*, 2 (Spring 1967): 97-116;

Rosalind Gabin, "Northrop Frye: Modern Utopian," *Classical and Modern Literature*, 3, no. 3 (1983): 151-164;

Alexander Globe, "Apocalypse Now: Frye's Vision of the Bible," *Canadian Literature*, 97 (Summer 1983): 182-191;

Leon Golden, "Aristotle, Frye, and the Theory of Tragedy," *Comparative Literature*, 27 (Winter 1975): 47-58;

Rudolf B. Gottfried, "Our New Poet: Archetypal Criticism and *The Faerie Queene*," *PMLA*, 83 (October 1968): 1362-1377;

Wayne Grady, "The Educated Imagination of Northrop Frye," *Saturday Night*, 96 (October 1981): 19-24, 26, 28;

Gerald Graff, "Northrop Frye and the Visionary Imagination," in his *Poetic Statement and Critical Dogma* (Evanston: Northwestern University Press, 1970), pp. 73-78;

Alan Grob, "The Uses of Northrop Frye: 'Sunday Morning' and the Romantic Topocosm," *Studies in Romanticism*, 22 (Winter 1983): 587-615;

Marshall Grossman, "The Vicissitudes of the Subject in Frye's *Anatomy of Criticism*," *Texas Studies in Language and Literature*, 24 (Fall 1982): 313-327;

A. C. Hamilton, "Northrop Frye: The Visionary Critic," *CEA Critic*, 42 (November 1979): 2-6;

V. G. Hanes, "Northrop Frye's Theory of Literature and Marxism," *Horizons: The Marxist Quarterly*, 24 (Winter 1968): 62-78;

Geoffrey Hartman, "The Sacred Jungle 3: Frye, Burke, and Some Conclusions," in his *Criticism in the Wilderness* (New Haven: Yale University Press, 1980), pp. 86-114;

Paul Hernadi, "Northrop Frye," in his *Beyond Genre: New Directions in Literary Classification* (Ithaca: Cornell University Press, 1972), pp. 131-151;

John Holloway, "The Critical Zodiac of Northrop Frye," in his *Colours of Clarity* (London: Routledge & Kegan Paul, 1964), pp. 153-160;

Graham Hough, "Myth and Archetype II," in his *An Essay on Criticism* (New York: Norton, 1966), pp. 148-156;

Ben Howard, "Fancy, Imagination, and Northrop Frye," *Thoth*, 9 (Winter 1968): 25-36;

Fred Inglis, "Professor Northrop Frye and the Academic Study of Literature," *Centennial Review*, 9 (Summer 1965): 319-331;

David Jackel, "Northrop Frye and the Continentalist Tradition," *Dalhousie Review*, 56 (Summer 1976): 221-239;

Frederic Jameson, *The Political Unconscious* (Ithaca: Cornell University Press, 1981), pp. 68-75;

W. T. Jewkes, "Mental Flight: Northrop Frye and the Teaching of Literature," *Journal of General Education*, 27 (Winter 1976): 281-298;

Jewkes, "Structure, Relevance, and the Teaching of Literature," *CEA Critic*, 42 (November 1979): 37-43;

George Johnston, "Northrop Frye: Some Recollections and Observations," *CEA Critic*, 42 (January 1980): 21-25;

D. G. Jones, "Myth, Frye, and Canadian Writers," *Canadian Literature*, 55 (Winter 1973): 7-22;

Toshihiko Kawasaki, "The Ruby and the Planetarium: The Formalism of Northrop Frye," *Eigo bungaku sekai*, 9 (December 1974): 2-6;

W. J. K[eith], Introduction to "Northrop Frye and the Bible: A Review Symposium," *University of Toronto Quarterly*, 52 (Winter 1982-1983): 127;

Pauline Kogan, *Northrop Frye: The High Priest of Clerical Obscurantism* (Montreal: Progressive Books and Periodicals, 1969);

Barbara D. Korpan, "Literary Evolution as Style: The 'Intrinsic Historicity' of Northrop Frye and Juri Tynianov," *Pacific Coast Philology*, 2 (April 1967): 47-52;

Richard Kostelanetz, "The Literature Professors' Literature Professor," *Michigan Quarterly Review*, 17 (Fall 1978): 425-442;

Murray Krieger, "The Critical Legacy of Matthew Arnold; or, The Strange Brotherhood of T. S. Eliot, I. A. Richards, and Northrop Frye," *Southern Review*, 5 (April 1969): 457-474;

Krieger, ed., *Northrop Frye in Modern Criticism* (New York: Columbia University Press, 1966);

Richard Kuhns, "Professor Frye's Criticism," *Journal of Philosophy*, 56 (10 September 1959): 745-755;

F. H. Langman, "Anatomizing Northrop Frye," *British Journal of Aesthetics*, 18 (Spring 1978): 104-119;

Alvin A. Lee, "Old English Poetry, Mediaeval Exegesis and Modern Criticism," *Studies in the Literary Imagination*, 8 (Spring 1975): 47-73;

Frank Lentricchia, "The Historicity of Frye's *Anatomy*," *Salmagundi*, 40 (Winter 1978): 97-121;

Gerald Lindrop, "Generating the Universe through Analogy," *PN Review,* 3 (1977): 41-45;

Lawrence I. Lipking, "Northrop Frye: Introduction," in *Modern Literary Criticism, 1900-1970,* edited by Lipking and A. Walton Litz (New York: Atheneum, 1970), pp. 180-188;

Louis Mackey, "Anatomical Curiosities: Northrop Frye's Theory of Criticism," *Texas Studies in Language and Literature,* 23 (Fall 1981): 442-469;

Eli W. Mandel, "Toward a Theory of Cultural Revolution: The Criticism of Northrop Frye," *Canadian Literature,* 1 (Summer 1959): 58-67;

Frank McConnell, "Northrop Frye and *Anatomy of Criticism,*" *Sewanee Review,* 92 (Fall 1984): 622-629;

R. D. McDonald, "Frye's *Modern Century* Reconsidered," *Studies in Canadian Literature,* 4 (Winter 1979): 95-108;

George McFadden, "Twentieth-Century Theorists: Mauron, Cornford, Frye," in his *Discovering the Comic* (Princeton: Princeton University Press, 1982), pp. 165-173;

Robert Merrill, "The Generic Approach in Recent Criticism of Shakespeare's Comedies and Romances," *Texas Studies in Language and Literature,* 20 (Fall 1978): 474-487;

Hugo Meynell, "Northrop Frye's Idea of a Science of Criticism," *British Journal of Aesthetics,* 21 (Spring 1981): 118-129;

Robert Mugerauer, "The Form of Northrop Frye's Literary Universe: An Expanding Circle," *Mosaic,* 12 (1979): 135-147;

Kenji Nakamura, "Northrop Frye: Criticism as Knowledge," *Bulletin* (College of General Education, Osaka University), 18 (March 1970): 81-103;

Daniel T. O'Hara, "Against Nature: On Northrop Frye and Critical Romance," in his *The Romance of Interpretation: Visionary Criticism from Pater to de Man* (New York: Columbia University Press, 1985), pp. 147-204;

S. M. Pandeya, "Theory of Style: A Note on the Ideas of T. S. Eliot, Northrop Frye and Mammata," in *Essays and Studies: Festschrift in Honour of Prof. K. Viswanatham,* edited by G. V. L. N. Sarma (Machilipatnam, India: Triveni Publishers, 1977), pp. 95-101;

Bruce W. Powe, "Fear of Fryeing: Northrop Frye and the Theory of Myth Criticism," *Antigonish Review,* 49 (Spring 1982): 123-144;

Powe, "McLuhan and Frye, Either/Or," in his *A Climate Charged* (Oakville, Ontario: Mosaic Press, 1984), pp. 55-58;

Suresh Raval, "Criticism as Science: Richards and Frye," in his *Metacriticism* (Athens: University of Georgia Press, 1981), pp. 144-152;

Wayne A. Rebhorn, "After Frye: A Review-Article on the Interpretation of Shakespearean Comedy and Romance," *Texas Studies in Language and Literature,* 21 (Winter 1979): 553-582;

Donald R. Riccomini, "Northrop Frye and Structuralism: Identity and Difference," *University of Toronto Quarterly,* 49 (Fall 1979): 33-47;

Paul Ricoeur, "*Anatomy of Criticism* or the Order of Paradigms," in *Centre and Labyrinth,* edited by Cook and others, pp. 1-13;

P. J. M. Robertson, "Northrop Frye and Evaluation," *Queen's Quarterly,* 90 (Spring 1983): 151-156;

Leo Rockas, "The Structure of Frye's *Anatomy,*" *College English,* 28 (April 1967): 501-507;

Julián Rodríguez, "Preliminary Notes to Northrop Frye's Theory Concerning the Relationship of Myth to Literature," *Revista Canaria de Estudios Ingleses,* 9 (November 1984): 123-128;

William Rueckert, "Literary Criticism and History: The Endless Dialectic," *New Literary History,* 6 (Spring 1975): 491-512;

James Schroeter, "The Unseen Center: A Critique of Northrop Frye," *College English,* 33 (February 1972): 543-557;

Warren Shibles, "Northrop Frye on Metaphor," in his *An Analysis of Metaphor in Light of W. M. Urban's Theories* (The Hague: Mouton, 1971), pp. 145-150;

Jon Slan, "Writing in Canada: Innis, McLuhan, and Frye: Frontiers of Canadian Criticism," *Canadian Dimension,* 8 (August 1972): 43-46;

Glenna Davis Sloan, *The Child as Critic: Teaching Literature in the Elementary School,* revised edition (New York: Teachers College Press, Columbia University, 1984);

Francis Sparshott, "Frye in Place," *Canadian Literature,* 83 (Winter 1979): 143-155;

Philip Stevick, "Novel and Anatomy: Notes Toward an Amplification of Frye," *Criticism,* 10 (Spring 1968): 153-165;

Rosemary Sullivan, "Northrop Frye: Canadian Mythographer," *Journal of Commonwealth Literature,* 18, no. 1 (1983): 1-13;

W. John Teunissen, "The *Anatomy of Criticism* as a Parody of Science," *Southern Humanities Review,* 14 (Winter 1980): 31-42;

Clara Thomas, "Towards Freedom: The Work of Northrop Frye," *CEA Critic,* 42 (November 1979): 7-11;

Memye Tucker, "Northrop Frye: The Uses of Criticism," *CEA Critic,* 42 (November 1979): 12-17;

Andrew Von Hendy, "A Poetics for Demogorgon: Northrop Frye and Contemporary Criticism," *Criticism,* 8 (Fall 1966): 318-335;

Evan Watkins, "Criticism and Method: Hirsch, Frye, Barthes," *Soundings,* 57 (Summer 1975): 257-280;

Grant Webster, "The Missionary Criticism of Northrop Frye," *Southern Review* (Australia), 2, no. 2 (1966): 164-169;

David White, "Northrop Frye: Value and System," *Criticism,* 15 (Summer 1973): 189-211;

Donald Wiebe, "The 'Centripetal Theology' of *The Great Code," Toronto Journal of Theology,* 1 (Spring 1985): 122-127.

Papers:
Many of Frye's papers are at the E. J. Pratt Library of Victoria University, University of Toronto.

Hugh Garner
(22 February 1913-30 June 1979)

J. M. Zezulka
University of Western Ontario

BOOKS: *Storm Below* (Toronto: Collins, 1949);

Cabbagetown (Toronto: Collins, 1950; revised, Toronto: Ryerson, 1968);

Waste No Tears, as Jarvis Warwick (Toronto: Export, 1950);

Present Reckoning (Toronto: Collins, 1951);

The Yellow Sweater, and Other Stories (Toronto: Collins, 1952);

The Silence on the Shore (Toronto: McClelland & Stewart, 1962);

Hugh Garner's Best Stories (Toronto: Ryerson, 1963);

Author! Author! (Toronto: Ryerson, 1964);

Men and Women (Toronto: Ryerson, 1966);

The Sin Sniper (Richmond Hill, Ontario: Simon & Schuster, 1970);

A Nice Place to Visit (Toronto: Ryerson, 1970);

Violation of the Virgins and Other Stories (Toronto & New York: McGraw-Hill Ryerson, 1971);

Three Women (Toronto: Simon & Pierre, 1973);

One Damn Thing After Another (Toronto & New York: McGraw-Hill Ryerson, 1973);

Death in Don Mills (Toronto & New York: McGraw-Hill Ryerson, 1975);

The Intruders (Toronto & New York: McGraw-Hill Ryerson, 1976);

The Legs of the Lame, and Other Stories (Ottawa: Borealis, 1976);

Murder Has Your Number (Toronto & New York: McGraw-Hill Ryerson, 1978).

PLAY PRODUCTION: *A Trip for Mrs. Taylor,* Brockville, Ontario, Brockville Theatre Guild, 4 November 1966.

OTHER: Alice Munro, *Dance of the Happy Shades,* foreword by Garner (Toronto: Ryerson, 1968).

Hugh Garner was a maverick in his life and in his fiction. His vision, in his novels and in the short stories which are his most memorable work, was formed by his multifarious experiences during the Depression, the Spanish civil war, North Atlantic convoy duty, and by his sympathy for what he called the bottom half of humanity.

Garner's name will always be associated with Toronto's Cabbagetown, where he attended school before quitting at the age of sixteen. He

Hugh Garner

was born to Matthew and Annie Fozard Garner in Batley, Yorkshire, England, and came to Toronto with his parents when he was six. Shortly thereafter, Matthew Garner deserted the family, and there can be little doubt that Hugh Garner's sympathy for the working-class poor had its origin in the effect of this desertion on his mother. It also accounts for the fierce independence that was characteristic of the man. Garner rode the rails in Canada and the United States during the Depression until 1937, when he enlisted in the Abraham Lincoln Brigade and joined the Loyalist cause in Spain. After he was discharged from the Royal Canadian Navy in 1945, he turned to writing as a career. He had married Marie Alice Gallant in 1941, and to finance a writing career frequently interrupted by bouts of drunkenness, he turned to journalism and to hack writing, publishing 439 articles and essays in his lifetime, in addition to his output of 17 books, including short-story collections, a volume of one-act plays, and novels.

Storm Below (1949), Garner's first book, is based on his World War II experiences on North Atlantic escort duty. The plot involves an Ordinary Seaman on his first tour of duty, who dies of a fractured skull sustained in a fall aboard the

corvette H. M. S. *Riverford*. The novel's real interest lies in Garner's handling of the crew's superstitious reactions to the presence of a dead body aboard ship and in his exploration of their private thoughts and lives. Garner's sociological interest in his characters has led some critics to associate his work with the tradition of the naturalistic novel.

The sociological approach of his first novel is handled more surely in *Cabbagetown* (1950), which takes its title from a Depression-era slum situated in east-central Toronto and tells the stories of several families trying to cope with the effects of the Depression. The novel's ostensible focus is on the career of Ken Tilling, a semi-autobiographical figure, from his graduation from technical school in 1929 until his enlistment in the international brigades in 1937. Garner's noteworthy achievement is his depiction of the characters associated with Ken, delineated with an eye for the minutiae of the social and economic conditions in which they live and of the urban geography by which most of them feel imprisoned. Although *Cabbagetown* quickly became a bestseller, Garner was not satisfied with it. It had been truncated before being published, its language pared of much of its "impropriety"–hence when the book was republished in 1968 Garner first refashioned it, the better to reflect the language of the people he wished to represent. *Cabbagetown* was followed by *Waste No Tears* (1950), written under the pseudonym Jarvis Warwick in just ten days, and *Present Reckoning* (1951), an equally hastily written story about the postwar readjustments of an artillery sergeant. Beyond occasional flashes of wit, neither novel has much to recommend it; if anything, their appearance suggests that, as was often the case, the Garners were in financial difficulties.

The year 1952 saw publication of *The Yellow Sweater, and Other Stories*, his first story collection. "The Conversion of Willie Heaps," about a young boy's nearly fatal encounter with a deranged fundamentalist, shared the *Northern Review* prize in 1951 and was included in *Best American Short Stories* for 1952. Three other stories also made the anthology's honor roll that year. Apart from *Storm Below*, Garner's only explorations of nonurban subjects and themes, many of them inspired by his travels during the Depression, are found in his short stories. His shrewdly sensitive observations into character have no better expression than in these stories.

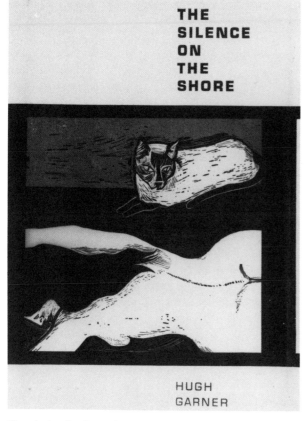

Dust jacket for Garner's 1962 novel about the tenants of a dilapidated Toronto boardinghouse

Dust jacket for Garner's account of his life, beginning with his birth in England and his family's move to Toronto's Cabbagetown, "the largest Anglo-Saxon slum in North America"

In the following decade Garner wrote only the occasional story. Most of his energy in these years was devoted to magazine journalism, principally with *Saturday Night* and with *Liberty,* which he edited for a year. In 1959 a Senior Arts Fellowship from the Canada Council enabled him to divert some of his energies from journalism, and he composed the first draft of *The Silence on the Shore* (1962), his most complex work. The didacticism and sentimentality evident in his earlier works are less obtrusive in this novel, the story of the interrelationships and private lives of the tenants of a dilapidated boardinghouse. As in *Cabbagetown* Garner's strength reveals itself in his penetration into the private hells of his protagonists. Although some of his characters are grotesques, Garner's general avoidance of symbolism prevents them from becoming universal types; rather, they are simply representatives of an urban substratum where life is always an uphill grind.

Major recognition came to Garner in 1964, when he received the Governor General's Award

for Fiction for *Hugh Garner's Best Stories* (1963), a collection of twenty-four stories, including twelve from his first collection. In the years following this success Garner's creative energy seemed to wane. *Author! Author!* (1964), a collection of humorous essays, was not well received; nor was *Men and Women* (1966), a collection of short stories, or *Three Women* (1973), a trilogy of one-act plays. His detective novels, *The Sin Sniper* (1970), *A Nice Place to Visit* (1970), and *Death in Don Mills* (1975), lack depth but sold well. With the exception of his autobiography, *One Damn Thing After Another* (1973), the only significant new work of this late period is *The Intruders* (1976).

In *The Intruders* Garner returns to Cabbagetown to examine the impact that forty years of change have had on the neighborhood. The focus is on the disillusioned suburbanites who have infiltrated Cabbagetown in search of community involvement. What these middle-class professional families discover, however, is that class consciousness is difficult to overcome. In the end they relinquish the neighborhood to those who have always been there, the punks and the drunks and the working poor. Garner's lifelong concern for the people of this neighborhood was suitably commemorated in 1982 with the dedication of a housing development, the Hugh Garner Co-operative.

Although Garner avoided pretension as assiduously as he shunned literary coteries or fashions, he loved telling stories, and he had tremendous respect for his craft. He championed the cause of the down-and-out and was, above all, a gifted short-story writer. His stories continue to be anthologized in Canada and abroad.

References:

Allan Anderson, "An Interview with Hugh Gar-

ner," *Tamarack Review*, 52 (Third Quarter 1969);

Doug Fetherling, *Hugh Garner* (Toronto: Forum House, 1972);

John G. Moss, "A Conversation with Hugh Garner," *Journal of Canadian Fiction*, 1 (Spring 1972);

Paul Stuewe, *Hugh Garner and His Works* (Toronto: ECW, 1984).

Papers:

Douglas Library, Queen's University, has collected notes by Garner, press clippings, first editions, manuscripts, and correspondence.

John Glassco

(19 December 1909-29 January 1981)

George Woodcock

BOOKS: *Contes en crinoline*, as Jean de Saint-Luc (Paris: Gaucher, 1929);

The Deficit Made Flesh (Toronto: McClelland & Stewart, 1958);

Under the Hill; or, The Story of Venus and Tannhauser, by Glassco and Aubrey Beardsley (Paris: Olympia Press, 1959; London: New English Library, 1966; New York: Grove Press, 1967);

The English Governess, as Miles Underwood (Paris: Olympia Press, 1960); republished under Glassco's name as *Harriet Marwood, Governess* (Don Mills, Ontario: General Publishing, 1976);

A Point of Sky (Toronto: Oxford University Press, 1964);

Squire Hardman, as George Coleman (N.p.: Passtime Press, 1966);

Memoirs of Montparnasse (Toronto & New York: Oxford University Press, 1970);

The Temple of Pedastry, as Hideki Okada (North Hollywood, Cal.: Hanover House, 1970);

Selected Poems (Toronto: Oxford University Press, 1971);

Fetish Girl, as Sylvia Bayer (New York: Venus Library, 1972);

Montreal (Montreal: DC Books, 1973);

The Fatal Woman: Three Tales (Toronto: Anansi, 1974).

OTHER: *The Journal of Saint-Denys-Garneau*, translated by Glassco (Toronto: McClelland & Stewart, 1962);

English Poetry in Quebec, proceedings of the Foster Poetry Conference, 12-14 October 1963, edited by Glassco (Montreal: McGill University Press, 1965);

Louis Joseph Quesnel, *Selected Poems and Songs After the Manuscripts in the Lande Collection*, translated by Glassco (Montreal: Lawrence M. Lande Foundation, McLennan Library, McGill University, 1970);

The Poetry of French Canada in Translation, edited, with an introduction, by Glassco, includes translations by Glassco (Toronto: Oxford University Press, 1970);

The Complete Poems of Saint-Denys-Garneau, translated by Glassco (Ottawa: Oberon, 1975);

John Glassco (photograph by Gaby, Montreal)

Monique Bosco, *Lot's Wife*, translated, with an introduction, by Glassco (Toronto: McClelland & Stewart, 1975);

Leopold von Sacher-Masoch, *Venus in Furs*, translated by Glassco (Burnaby, British Columbia: Blackfish Press, 1977);

Jean-Yves Soucy, *Creatures of the Chase*, translated by Glassco (Toronto: McClelland & Stewart, 1979);

Jean-Charles Harvey, *Fear's Folly*, translated by Glassco, edited by John O'Connor (Ottawa: Carleton University Press, 1982).

PERIODICAL PUBLICATIONS: "The Opaque Medium: Remarks on the Translation of Poetry with a Special Reference to French-Canadian Verse," *Meta* (March 1969): 27-30;

"The Art of Pornography," *Edge*, 9 (Summer 1969): 101-113.

John Glassco has produced a small number of usually short books, written with considerable gaps over a period stretching from the 1920s to his final writings during the 1970s. His first publication, a surrealist poem called "Conan's Fig," appeared in *transition* in 1928; his last was a translation of Jean-Charles Harvey's *Les Demicivilisés* (1934) which appeared in 1982. But, sparse and intermittent though his creation may have been, everything he did had a virtuosity that earned him the respect of Canadian writers of all generations. With skill and versatility he touched on many fields; as he himself once remarked, he was "as much a novelist, anthologist, translator and pornographer" as a poet. He was also a fine memoirist.

Glassco first became known to Canadian readers as a poet, author of *The Deficit Made Flesh*, which appeared in 1958, and *A Point of Sky*, published in 1964. His prose works, mostly written before the verse, were either unpublished until the 1970s–*Memoirs of Montparnasse* (1970) and *The Fatal Woman* (1974)–or had appeared pseudonymously–the early *Contes en crinoline* (1929) by "Jean de Saint-Luc" and such later exercises in mannered pornography as *The English Governess* (1960) by "Miles Underwood" and *Fetish Girl* (1972) by "Sylvia Bayer."

Glassco, the son of Archibald P. S. Glassco, a bursar, and Beatrice Rawlings Glassco, was born in Montreal in 1909. He received the patrician education his well-to-do father thought essential at Selwyn House School, Bishop's College School, and Lower Canada College. He went to McGill University in 1925 but left in 1928 without graduating. In spite of his father's disapproval, he preferred to complete his education in Paris, which was still an artistic *ville lumière*, especially for English-speaking expatriates. He stayed in France for three years, until he contracted tuberculosis and was forced to return to Canada. Partly in France, but mostly in the hospital awaiting a critical operation, he wrote his account of this interlude, *Memoirs of Montparnasse*, which many critics believe the best work of Canadian autobiography.

Appearing more than forty years after its first chapters were written (though, as Thomas Tausky demonstrates in his *Canadian Poetry* article of 1983, Glassco substantially edited the work before its reappearance), *Memoirs of Montparnasse* was a strange projection out of time, rather like the long-delayed publication by Robert Bridges of the poems of Gerard Manley Hopkins, except that in Glassco's case the discoverer who revealed the long-concealed work was the author, looking with astonishment at his past self. "This young

Robert McAlmon, John Glassco, and Graeme Taylor in Nice, 1929

counters that decorate *Memoirs of Montparnasse*—encounters with George Moore and James Joyce and Ernest Hemingway ("his eyes were curiously small, shrewd and reticent, like a politician's"), with Gertrude Stein ("a rhomboidal woman") and Ford Madox Ford and André Breton and a score of others as celebrated—are described not only with a real visual evocativeness but also with a twist to the visual that opens windows for deeper looks into characters. And all is recorded with a glittering freshness which gives the book a sense of complete contemporaneity with the scene and the time and the people it invokes.

In 1935, having survived his crucial operation, Glassco retired to the rural obscurity of Foster, in the Eastern Townships of Quebec, and immersed himself in the local life, even serving as mayor of Foster from 1952 to 1954. Meanwhile as a writer he was developing a self probably few of his neighbors suspected. He tells us that about the time he moved to Foster, "I came under the renewed influence of Huysmans, Pater, Villiers, Barbey d'Aurevilly and others of the so-called Decadents, and decided to write books utterly divorced from reality, stories where nothing happened."

The result was a curious division in Glassco's work. With most writers prose tends toward realism and verse is likely to be the vehicle of fantasy. Glassco's poems are largely concerned with the simple actualities of rural life, and it has always been his prose that, with the exception of *Memoirs of Montparnasse*, has been lodged in the private world and written consciously "after" the nineteenth-century Decadents. A direct link between Glassco and the Decadents is offered in *Under the Hill; or, The Story of Venus and Tannhauser* (1959), his brilliant completion of Aubrey Beardsley's unfinished erotic romance with the same title, in which, as Frank Davey remarked in *From There to Here* (1974), Glassco succeeds "in forging from emotionally-charged and thoroughly fleshly phenomena a cold, impersonal sculpture of graceful metaphor and geometric dehumanizing image."

Dehumanization—the transformation of character through pain—is the theme of Glassco's one novel, the pseudonymously published *English Governess*, which appeared in 1976 under his own name as *Harriet Marwood, Governess*. In a clever and even graceful parody of a well-made Victorian novel, the subjection of young Richard Lovel by whip and cane to the will of the already dehumanized Harriet is ingeniously developed, so that

man is no longer myself; I hardly recognize him."

Whether because of the precocity of his talent or the peculiar intensity of the life he and others lived in that place and time, Glassco wrote a remarkably appealing account of what it was to be young in the magical Paris of the late Third Republic.

It was not merely a setting of inexpensive romance that Paris gave to Glassco and many others. It was the sense of a living literary world and the opportunity to meet—gathered as they have never been gathered since—so many of the great writers and grandiose literary failures of the early twentieth century. One could adapt Oscar Wilde's famous remark about Frank Harris and say that John Glassco met all the major figures of the time—once. But once can be enough if the eye is sharp and the memory clear, and the en-

Dust jacket for the 1976 edition of Glassco's parody of a Victorian pornographic novel

just as the form of the novel becomes a criticism of ordinary sentimental fiction, so the content is a satire on ordinary respectable manners.

The Fatal Woman, Glassco's other important work of fiction, consists of three long stories that depart deliberately in the direction of fantastic improbability from the plausible verisimilitudes of *The English Governess*. The first, "The Black Helmet," is linked to that novel since memories of sadistic acts performed by a departed Miss Marwood haunt the thoughts of the fantasizing onanist, Mairobert. A pair of sinister siblings, distantly reminiscent of Jean Cocteau's enfants terribles, descend on Mairobert in his decaying and debt-ridden house. The female sibling, Miss Delarachet, traumatically ravishes and transforms him. It is, Glassco rather curiously explains, "a retelling of the Endymion myth." The origin in Greek myth of the second tale, "The Fulfilled Destiny of Electra," is obvious in the tale's action as well as its title, even though it is set in a tourist-oriented Canadian village and two realistically portrayed policemen serve as the mechanical destroyers of the male victim.

The third tale, "Lust in Action," which Glassco describes as a specimen of the "satirical and ribald," has a special interest as an example of a theme rare in Canada, the inverted utopia. Women have taken over the earth and have subdued men, who are castrated at twenty but enjoy a grace period until then, although, any lapse into overt sexuality brings punishment and, in bad cases, early cutting. The story centers on a rebellion in a prison for boys. Two of the more recalcitrant inmates take two wardresses hostage under the threat of exposing themselves and showing obscene papers. One of them even ravishes an ancient lesbian guard, but they are finally caught by troopers armed with lassos and carried off for knacking. The satire has topical targets; it belongs in its final form to a period when jail riots and militant feminism are familiar phenomena. Glassco is in fact taking us to the level at which fantasies escape from privacy and have public consequences, which is always disastrous, as historically under fascism and nazism.

As a poet Glassco stands in the classic tradition, and his combination of the elegiac and bucolic modes links him with the Augustans rather than with the Decadents. Such a stance owes much to his familiarity with the poetry of France and also that of Quebec; and his excellent translations of the poems of Hector de Saint-Denys-Garneau (*The Complete Poems of Saint-Denys-Garneau*, 1975) and other Quebec writers should be considered a part of his poetic oeuvre, for he had achieved the rare feat of writing English poetry while translating from the French.

His own poems are largely concerned with his experience of rural life in the Eastern Townships ("no way of living but a mode of life" as he has described it). He is writing about a used-up land, and his poems are full of the images of abandoned farmhouses and decaying roads. In such poems reflections on the human condition are never far removed from descriptions of the countryside.

In "Luce's Notch" the poet returns after fifteen years over a pass in the hills where in the past "the road became a pathway, lost its face / In hummocks, boulders, chattering streams and then / Died in a thin flat meadow fenced with stones[.]" Now it is impossible to get this far, even with a vehicle, but the poet climbs there, stands alone

seeing how in this height
That leans over the green gulf of Bolton
Glen,

With the interinvolved valleys locked in the
   haze
Of still midsummer, how in this dizzy
   height
Robin and swallow still fight against the
   wind
Blown from the mountain whose thin
   meadows run
Rippling into the sky—stand here again
Beside the wreck of Aaron Luce's barn,
Fronting the valley after fifteen years,
Seeing nothing I did not see that day,
Feeling only the same despair before things
Still alien, still mysterious, still removed.

And from the scene that does not fundamentally
change, the poet's thoughts turn to himself, who
does.

I see only
Beauty continues, and so do not I.
I have become an ageing eye through
   which
A young man looks again and trembles,
   lost
To his own present—and he had no past—
For all his future is what I have become,
A man on a mountain after fifteen years,
A man implicit in that careless heart
Even then when all his idle study was
To drive about the hills in search of
   strangeness.

In such poems Glassco shows the sensitivity
toward the natural world that so strangely bal-
ances the deliberate artificiality of his fiction, and
he combines a true joy in beauty with a sense of
the pathetic in human existence, so that one
often has a feeling of luxuriant melancholia
rather than common pessimism. "Luce's Notch,"
with its muted reflective tone, shows Glassco's ability to catch the right note—Wordsworthian here
more than Augustan—for the setting and the subject. He is, indeed, a master of echoes, of parody
and pastiche, in the best of senses, which is what
makes him such an accomplished translator.

By no means are all of Glassco's poems
rural, though the bucolic verses reflect his daily
life and are strikingly numerous. But there are
the other poems that move into the mythology of
literature and of history, "The Death of Don
Quixote" and "Brummel at Calais," for example;
and these skillfully evoke different and appropriate modes. "The Death of Don Quixote" is somewhat Browningesque, and "Brummel at Calais" is

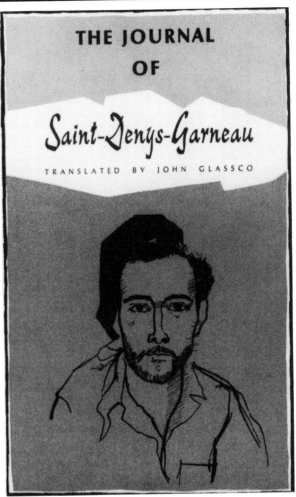

Dust jacket for the first English translation of the Montreal
poet Saint-Denys-Garneau's journal covering the years
1935-1939

written in a kind of shadowed Regency style.
Such poems are elegiac in tone, yet, like true elegies, they are not in the last record pessimistic.
An ironic triumph is allowed to those who fall, so
that even in describing the pathos of Brummel's
end the poet thus addresses us:

For see, even now in the long implacable
   twilight,
The triumph of his veritable art,
An art of being, nothing but being, the
   grace
Of perfect self-assertion based on nothing,
As in our vanity's cause against the void
He strikes his elegant blow, the solemn re-
   port of those
Who have done nothing and will never die.

This is the assertion of the sufficiency of dan-
dyism in the sense Baudelaire gave to the word,

147

and the philosophy of the nineteenth-century dandy (whether Brummel, Baudelaire, or Wilde) was undoubtedly an important element in the attitudes that inspired John Glassco's writings–prose and verse alike.

References:

David Cobb, "Elegant Pornographer," *Canadian Magazine* (21 February 1976): 8-11;

Frank Davey, "John Glassco," in his *From Here to There* (Erin, Ontario: Press Porcépic, 1974), pp. 122-125;

Kildare Dobbs, "The Great Glassco: Memoirs of a Gentleman of Pleasure," *Maclean's* (August 1975): 48, 50, 52;

Leon Edel, Introduction to Glassco's *Memoirs of Montparnasse* (Toronto: Oxford University Press, 1970), pp. vii-xi;

Edel, "John Glassco (1909-1981) and His Erotic Muse," *Canadian Literature*, 93 (Summer 1982): 108-117;

John Lauber, "Liberty and the Pursuit of Pleasure: John Glassco's Quest," *Canadian Literature*, 90 (Autumn 1981): 61-72;

Robert McAlmon, *Being Geniuses Together 1920-1930. Revised and with Supplementary Chapters by Kay Boyle* (New York: Doubleday, 1968), pp. 265-266, 307, 332-333, 340, 355-356;

Kathy Mezei, "Like the Wind Made Visible," *Canadian Literature*, 71 (Winter 1976): 83-87;

W. H. New, "John Glassco," in *Contemporary Novelists*, edited by James Vinson, second edition (New York: St. Mark's, 1976), pp. 524-526;

Morse Peckham, *Art and Pornography: An Experiment in Explanation* (New York: Basic, 1969), pp. 42, 218;

Fraser Sutherland, *John Glassco: An Essay and Bibliography* (Toronto: ECW, 1984);

Thomas E. Tausky, "*Memoirs of Montparnasse:* A Reflection of Myself," *Canadian Poetry*, 13 (Fall/Winter 1983): 59-84.

Papers:
Glassco's papers are at the Public Archives of Canada in Ottawa and at McLennan Library, McGill University, Montreal.

Claude-Henri Grignon

(8 July 1894-3 April 1976)

Kenneth Landry
Université Laval

BOOKS: *Le Secret de Lindbergh* (Montreal: Editions de la Porte d'Or, 1928);

Ombres et clameurs. Regards sur la littérature canadienne (Montreal: Albert Lévesque, 1933);

Un Homme et son péché (Montreal: Editions du Totem, 1933); translated by Yves Brunelle as *The Woman and the Miser* (Montreal: Harvest House, 1978);

Le Déserteur et autres récits de la terre (Montreal: Editions du Vieux Chêne, 1934);

Précisions sur "Un Homme et son péché" (Montreal: Editions du Vieux Chêne, 1936).

MOTION PICTURES: *Un Homme et son péché,* screenplay by Grignon, Quebec Productions Corporation, 1948;

Séraphin Poudrier, screenplay by Grignon, Quebec Productions Corporation, 1949.

TELEVISION: *Les Belles Histoires des pays d'en haut,* Radio-Canada, 1956-1970.

RADIO: *Les Belles Histoires des pays d'en haut,* CBF (Montreal), 1939-1962; CKVL (Montreal), 1963-1965.

PERIODICAL PUBLICATION: *Les Pamphlets de Valdombre,* 1-5 (December 1936-June 1943).

Novelist, journalist, writer of short stories, literary critic, and pamphleteer, Claude-Henri Grignon was one of Canada's most prolific scriptwriters for radio and television. An energetic and versatile individual, he ventured beyond the literary and cultural spheres, serving a ten-year term as mayor of his native village of Sainte-Adèle. Nonetheless, his main interests lay in writing and publishing. Always blunt in his writing, Grignon made no apologies for his strong likes and dislikes. Once, when he was asked to describe himself in the course of an interview, he confided: "I am thin-skinned and passionate, a peasant, self-taught, a man of the earth earthy, a dreamer, a ro-

mantic, an indomitable individualist, a poet, a devout Catholic. . . . I have chosen to become a writer in order to be free and to assert myself."

Born in the small community of Sainte-Adèle, in the Laurentian mountain region north of Montreal, Eugène–Henry (his real name) was the youngest son of a country doctor and veterinarian, Wilfrid Grignon, and an Acadian mother, Eugénie Baker Grignon. After grade school and a brief stint at the Collège Saint-Laurent in Montreal (1909-1910), he returned home, whereupon his father hired private tutors in an effort to complete his son's classical education. The young Grignon then spent a year and a half at the Institut Agricole d'Oka, learning the rudiments of agriculture, but he much preferred reading on his own. It was at this time that he "discovered" the French classical authors, the romantics, the Parnassians and the symbolists. In his memoirs, he recalls that this period, one of intense curiosity and intellectual discovery, was one of the happiest of his life.

When his father died in 1915, Grignon remained in Montreal, finding work first as a penny-a-liner for various newspapers, then as a customs official, and, finally, as a civil servant. In 1916 he married Thérèse Lambert, who remained his life-long companion. The same year, he embarked on a career as a journalist, starting at *L'Avenir du Nord* in Saint-Jerôme under the pseudonym of Claude Bâcle. Subsequently, he adopted the name of Claude-Henri. He worked for a series of newspapers with nationalistic and liberal leanings, *La Minerve* (1920), *Le Nationaliste* (1921-1922), and *Le Matin* (1923-1924). In the meantime, he associated with other young writers, attended meetings (1920-1926) of the waning Ecole Littéraire de Montréal, and even published a long article (1925) on the controversial French Catholic writer, Léon Bloy (1846-1917). He continued to submit articles, usually under pen names, to various periodicals, including *La Revue populaire* (1931-1934), the monthly *Bulletin des Agriculteurs* (1941-1970, under the name of le

Grignon's pseudonymous inscription to Jean-Charles Harvey in Ombres et clameurs *(Bibliothèque de l'Université Laval, photograph courtesy of Kenneth Landry)*

Père Bougonneux, or The Old Grouch), and numerous politically oriented newspapers under the direction of his friend and mentor, Olivar Asselin: *Le Canada* (1931), *L'Ordre* (1934-1935), and *La Renaissance* (1935).

For a short time he worked as a publicist, secretary to Iréné Vautrin, liberal member of the National Assembly, and minister in charge of the provincial Département de la Colonisation. In 1936, when the Union Nationale party came to power under Maurice Duplessis, Grignon promptly lost his appointment. Having returned to Sainte-Adèle for good, he was responsible for the literary section of the newspaper *En Avant* (1937-1939) while at the same time single-handedly publishing a review which contributed

greatly to his notoriety as a pamphleteer and a skilled polemicist: *Les Pamphlets de Valdombre* (1936-1943). His two main targets, provincial politics (under Premier Maurice Duplessis) and literature (both French and French-Canadian), afforded him an ideal opportunity to vindicate his staunchly traditional beliefs as a Roman Catholic and as a defender of the rights of rural Quebeckers, whom he called "la paysannerie." Not since the satirical writings of Arthur Buies (*La Lanterne*, 1868-1869), Jules Fournier (*L'Action*, 1911-1916), or Victor Barbeau (*Les Cahiers de Turc*, 1921-1927) had there been a lampoonist and *enfant terrible* of such singular purpose. Grignon inevitably made scores of enemies as he anathematized his detractors with his truculent

Woodcuts by Maurice Gaudreau for the 1935 edition of Grignon's Un Homme et son péché *(courtesy of Kenneth Landry)*

prose in the style of the irrepressible Léon Bloy. In 1938 he may have been one of the first to coin the term *joual* to designate Quebecois slang. For almost seven years he wrote, printed, financed, and even distributed his monthly *Pamphlets*. In the final three years, the issues appeared at irregular intervals as other projects took up more and more of his time.

As he became better known in literary circles, Grignon also began publishing his works in book form: in 1928, a topical background novel, *Le Secret de Lindbergh;* in 1933, a selection of his literary criticism, *Ombres et clameurs,* which reflects a candid attitude toward his fellow writers; and in 1934, a series of short stories dealing with the French-Canadian "paysan," *Le Déserteur et autres récits de la terre.* During this period, when the Depression was at its peak, he also published a rustic novel that has since become a classic in Quebec literature: *Un Homme et son péché* (1933). The protagonist, Séraphin Poudrier, a miserly misanthrope, easily ranks with the likes of George Eliot's Silas Marner, Balzac's Père Grandet, or Molière's Harpagon as the universal embodiment of avarice. The novel, which chronicles the main character's obsessive stinginess, was an unqualified commercial success (several editions and 120,000 copies sold by 1985). In 1935 the author was awarded the Prix David, the highest literary

award in Quebec. An English translation appeared in print in 1978: *The Woman and the Miser.* For unknown reasons another translation, by Frances Ebbs-Canavan, titled "A Man and his Sin: Romance," found in the author's personal papers in 1976, remains unpublished.

The serialized version of the novel for radio (1939-1962) and television (1956-1970), under the title *Les Belles Histoires des pays d'en haut,* captured public attention for more than thirty years. Generations of listeners and viewers saw what was less a portrait of avarice than a fresco depicting the way of life of the early settlers in the Laurentian mountains at the turn of the century. The series resembles Balzac's *Comédie humaine* in the vastness of its panorama and remains one of the few successful attempts at portraying rural themes in French Canada in a realistic rather than in an idealized manner. The popular hour-long weekly television series ended at the author's request. Having written over 55,000 pages of text, Claude-Henri Grignon retired from scriptwriting to draft his memoirs. He was working on a biography of Olivar Asselin at the time of his death.

References:

Conrad Bernier, "Le Rêve d'enfance de Grignon: Écrire pour rester libre," *La Presse,* 10 April 1976;

Cahier d'histoire des pays d'en haut, special issue on Grignon, no. 20 (December 1983);

George Maloof, "Claude-Henri Grignon: Esquisse biographique," *Modern Language Studies*, 6 (Fall 1976);

France Ouellet, *Répertoire numérique du fonds*

Claude-Henri Grignon (Montreal: Bibliothèque Nationale du Québec, 1985);

Janet M. Paterson, "L'Univers de Séraphin Poudrier," *Journal of Canadian Fiction*, no. 19 (1977): 106-111.

Lionel Groulx
(13 January 1878-23 May 1967)

Phyllis M. Senese
University of Victoria

SELECTED BOOKS: *L'Education de la volonté en vue du devoir social* (Montreal: A.C.J.C., 1906);

Une Croisade d'adolescents (Quebec: L'Action Sociale, 1912);

Les Rapaillages (vieilles choses, vieilles gens) (Montreal: Le Devoir, 1916);

La Confédération canadienne (Montreal: Le Devoir, 1918);

La Naissance d'une race (Montreal: Bibliothèque de l'Action Française, 1919);

Chez nos ancêtres (Montreal: Bibliothèque de l'Action Française, 1920);

Lendemains de conquête (Montreal: Bibliothèque de l'Action Française, 1920);

Vers l'émancipation (Montreal: Bibliothèque de l'Action Française, 1921);

L'Appel de la race, as Alonié de Lestres (Montreal: Bibliothèque de l'Action Française, 1922); translated by J. S Wood as *The Iron Wedge* (Ottawa: Carleton Library, 1986);

Notre maître, le passé, (first series, Montreal: Bibliothèque de l'Action Française, 1924; second and third series, Montreal: Granger, 1936, 1944);

Dix ans d'Action française (Montreal: Bibliothèque de l'Action Française, 1926);

L'Enseignement français au Canada, 2 volumes (volume 1, Montreal: Albert Lévesque, 1931; volume 2, Montreal: Granger, 1933);

Au Cap Blomidon, as Alonié de Lestres (Montreal: La Devoir, 1932);

Le Français au Canada (Paris: Libraire Delagrave, 1932);

Lionel Groulx in 1913 (courtesy of Kenneth Landry)

Orientations (Montreal: Editions du Zodiaque, 1935);

Directives (Montreal: Editions du Zodiaque, 1937);

Histoire du Canada français depuis la découverte, 4 volumes (Montreal: L'Action Nationale, 1950-1952);

Pour bâtir (Montreal: L'Action Nationale, 1953);

Rencontres avec Dieu (Montreal: Fides, 1956);

Une Femme de génie au Canada: La Bienheureuse Mère d'Youville (Montreal: Comité des Fondateurs de l'Eglise Canadienne, 1957);

Notre Grande Aventure: L'Empire français en Amérique du Nord (1535-1760) (Montreal: Fides, 1958);

Dollard est-il un mythe? (Montreal: Fides, 1960);

Le Canada français missionaire (Montreal: Fides, 1962);

Chemins de l'avenir (Montreal: Fides, 1964);

La Découverte du Canada: Jacques Cartier (Montreal: Fides, 1966);

Constantes de vie (Montreal: Fides, 1967);

Roland-Michel Barrin de La Galissonière, 1693-1756 (Quebec: Presses de l'Université Laval, 1970); translated by John Flinn (Toronto: University of Toronto Press, 1970);

Mes Mémoires, 4 volumes (Montreal: Fides, 1970-1974);

Abbé Groulx: Variations on a Nationalist Theme, translations by Joanne L'Heureux and Susan Mann Trofimenkoff, edited by Trofimenkoff (Vancouver: Copp Clark, 1973);

Lionel Groulx, Journal 1895-1911 (Montreal: Presses de l'Université de Montreal, 1984).

By the time of his death in May 1967 *Abbé* Lionel Groulx had enjoyed a reputation as the leading exponent of French-Canadian nationalism for nearly half a century. In his native province of Quebec his passing was marked by a state funeral and an official day of mourning. In subsequent years his memory has been honored by the naming of schools, streets, halls, and even a subway station after him. During his life he was awarded honorary degrees in letters and law from the Université de Montréal, Université d'Ottawa, and Memorial University, the Tyrrel Medal of the Royal Society of Canada, special recognition from the Canadian Historical Association, as well as innumerable awards from nationalist, historical, and literary groups in Quebec and France. Admirers and critics alike agreed that Groulx had profoundly altered the way in which the Quebecois saw themselves, their province, and their future. He did not invent Quebec nationalism, but in synthesizing existing currents of thought, he gave his countrymen a new, vigorous life. Groulx was not merely an intellec-

tual. He was directly involved in a broad range of initiatives to galvanize popular opinion, ranging from publishing in almost every available outlet, to organizing pilgrimages to historic sites, to speaking and teaching throughout Quebec, Ontario, Manitoba, in New England and in France, and regularly appearing on radio, then television, broadcasts. His life was dedicated to his work and little else. Unrelenting activity was the hallmark of his life, and he labored to the day of his death. In spite of his outstanding and long career as history professor, editor, essayist, poet, and novelist, Groulx was largely unknown outside his own province. Except for academic circles, English-speaking Canadians have encountered him or his work rarely.

Nothing in Groulx's family background suggested the acclaim and controversy that were to mark his life. He was born in rural Vaudreuil, Quebec, on 13 January 1878, the fourth child of Léon Groulx (1837-1878) and Philomène Salomée Pilon Groulx (1849-1943). A month after Groulx's birth, his father died in a smallpox epidemic. Lionel Groulx and his brother Albert were the only children of the marriage to survive a subsequent diphtheria epidemic. In early 1879 Mme Groulx married William (Guillaume) Emond (1854-1924), a farmer from Vaudreuil. Groulx wrote often and warmly about the happy, hardworking family that grew out of his mother's second marriage. Despite, or perhaps because of, the modest circumstances of his childhood, Groulx developed an unbreakable religious faith and a tenacious love of the land of his province, both of which were evident in virtually everything he wrote. Whether he was writing about constitutional issues, assessing the impact of industrialization and urbanization on traditional values, or recounting nostalgic reminiscences, an intense attachment to place, to Quebec, animated it all.

As a student Groulx tried expressing his commitment to "Dieu et Patrie" in poetry. Several of these early poems were originally published before World War I, and a number of them can be found in *Lionel Groulx, Journal 1895-1911* (1984). "Paysage d'hiver et paysage d'âme" and "La Moelle des lions" both appeared under the pseudonym Lionel Montal in *Le Semeur* in 1910 and 1911. "La Leçon des érables" was first published in 1913 but had its widest circulation as part of the collection of short stories about Groulx's childhood, *Les Rapaillages (vieilles choses, vieilles gens)* (1916). These stories, which were largely autobio-

Cover, with woodcut by Maurice Gaudreau, for the 1935 edition of Groulx's collection of stories based on his childhood (courtesy of Kenneth Landry)

graphical in nature, were designed to evoke the past of Quebec, to pay tribute to the sturdy virtues of a simpler time when a love of the land and an unembarrassed devotion to religious values were supposedly common. The short stories and poetry draw on the nineteenth-century literary tradition in Quebec of pastoral purity and piety. While Groulx would not return to these two literary forms after 1915, they represent early examples of the emotional attachment he felt to the place that was home and the values that Catholicism represented for him. These particular poems and stories had a long life in *Les Rapaillages*, which would eventually go through nine editions of over 300,000 copies.

From 1884 to 1899 Groulx was educated at the parish school in Vaudreuil, the Séminaire de Ste-Thérèse-de-Blainville (now a provincial *collège* named for Groulx), and the Grand Séminaire de Montréal, although poor health was to cut short his early ecclesiastical training. The generosity of friends enabled him to undertake advanced studies in philosophy, theology, and literature in

Rome, Paris, and Fribourg from 1906 to 1909. With the exception of these years, from 1899 to 1915 he taught almost every academic subject and served as spiritual adviser to several student groups at the Collège de Valleyfield. Having been ordained a priest in 1903, Groulx embarked on a pastoral career not as a parish priest: he was first and foremost a teacher, at Valleyfield and then a professor of Canadian history at the Université Laval de Montréal (which became the Université de Montréal in 1920) from 1915 to his retirement in 1949. All of Groulx's teaching and writing flowed from his unshakable conviction that Quebec's very survival as a distinct society was threatened in direct proportion to the decline of Catholicism as the animating force of life in the province. He witnessed the effects of secularism on Catholicism in Italy and France and spent his life calling for a rejuvenation of Catholic fervor in Quebec, particularly among the young who, as adults, would be responsible for national survival. Over time Groulx's views on *la nation canadienne-française* would prove to be more durable than his call for Catholic revival. Nevertheless, the Catholic Church recognized his contributions to the spiritual life of his province by naming him an honorary canon of the diocese of Montreal in 1943. A great number of Groulx's spiritual writings have survived in pamphlet form, and a large portion of his historical writing deals with aspects of Church history in Quebec, missionary endeavors, and spiritual biographies. Most of Groulx's historical writings originated in his lectures at Valleyfield and particularly at the Université de Montréal. With only summer vacations and occasional leaves from his teaching responsibilities available for research in the archives at Quebec City, Montreal, Ottawa, and elsewhere, archives that were only just beginning to be organized professionally, Groulx's self-taught historical scholarship steadily matured, culminating in the publication of his master work, the four-volume *Histoire du Canada français depuis la découverte* (1950-1952). Even in retirement he produced many more historical studies, among them *Une Femme de génie au Canada: La Bienheureuse Mère d'Youville* (1957), *Dollard est-il un mythe?* (1960), *La Découverte du Canada: Jacques Cartier* (1966), and the posthumously published *Roland-Michel Barrin de La Galissonière, 1693-1756* (1970).

Parallel with his teaching career, Groulx had an equally impressive life as a nationalist propagandist. Prior to moving to Montreal in 1915, he had already come to the attention of the foremost nationalist of the day, Henri Bourassa, by participating in the founding of the nationalist youth organization Association Catholique de la Jeunesse Canadienne-Française and through his letters to Bourassa published in *Le Devoir* calling for drastically improved teaching of national history in Quebec's schools. Once in Montreal Groulx moved in the Bourassa orbit and in 1917 joined the *Ligue des Droits du Français,* becoming the single most prolific contributor to the Ligue's controversial journal *L'Action Française* from 1917 to 1928, as well as its editor from 1920 to 1928. As editor he made *L'Action Française* the focal point of nationalism in Quebec in the 1920s. He provided the inspiration and intellectual authority and endorsed *L'Action Nationale,* the successor to *L'Action Française,* founded in 1933 and still appearing monthly. In the last twenty years of his life, ostensibly in retirement, Groulx most effectively combined his love of history and his faith in the national destiny of Quebec by founding in late 1946 the *Institut d'Histoire de l'Amérique Française,* editing its *Revue* and continuing to publish and lecture on nationalist themes at a scarcely slowed pace. His last major project was the completion of his four-volume *Mes Mémoires* which appeared from 1970 to 1974.

Groulx dedicated his lengthy career to the twin objectives of fostering self-confidence and self-respect among the Quebecois by promoting faith in his rallying cry, *maîtres chez nous* (masters in our own house), while at the same time striving to create in Quebec a modern industrial society animated by social Catholicism. For Groulx nationalism was an attitude so firmly fixed in the history of Quebec that it required no reasoned demonstration from first principles. The characteristics of common origins, language, history, and religion that united the Quebecois as a people were readily apparent. In his early years survival of *la nation canadienne-française* was not absolutely certain. He grew up as relations between English and French in Canada went into serious decline in the years after Confederation as a consequence of the hanging of Louis Riel and the revival of British imperialism that pushed Canada into the Boer War and World War I. For Groulx, the nation did not require defining; it demanded salvation.

When he considered the condition of Quebec, Groulx grasped almost instinctively the extent to which his nation was facing the possibility of extinction. By the end of the nineteenth century industrialization and the shift from rural to urban living had dramatically altered the character of Quebec society. Control of the economy was in the hands of an English-speaking minority while the exploited working class was overwhelmingly French. English was the language of business and increasingly of the work place. The province's politicians catered to business interests with few tangible benefits accruing to the majority of people. In cataloguing the destructive influences of modern economic forces in Quebec, Groulx was convinced that there did exist a remedy. The Quebecois, he argued, were responsible for the sorry state in which they found themselves; they had lost control of their material condition and had become indifferent toward their religion. Until they accepted responsibility nothing would change. He believed that Confederation represented a contract between English and French, and that within Quebec the Quebecois should, and must, be masters of their own economic and political destiny to allow the development of a society that reflected the character of the nation. Catholicism was the paramount national characteristic. In a truly French Quebec, Catholic social values, not secular materialism, would inspire a society that was economically and politically modern and progressive. As a providential people, the Quebecois had a duty to create a thriving Catholic society in North America, an example of an alternative to the excesses of socialism and liberal capitalism. Simply put, a revitalized nation would serve as a filter, screening out the evils of modern civilization and thereby allowing Catholic social teachings to shape a model, modern society. Groulx always believed that history demonstrated the validity of his views by revealing the design of providence in the province's past. The French language, the expression of the soul of the nation, bound past, present, and future in a seamless whole. Groulx recognized that what to him was self-evident was something the Quebecois needed to be taught to believe. Self-confidence could only be restored through a rigorously national *and* Catholic system of education. National renewal was valid only in the service of Catholic rebirth. Just how to achieve the marriage of a Catholic social vision and economic modernization was something Groulx was not able, or prepared, to detail despite the relentless secularization of Quebec during his lifetime.

To a high degree the intensity and confusion evident in Groulx's blending of nationalism

Groulx's commentary "Comment j'écris" (How I Write), an unpublished essay included in Hommage à Lionel Groulx, *edited by Maurice Filion (1978)*

and Catholicism resulted from his stay in Europe from 1906 to 1909. He witnessed firsthand the violent attacks on religion in Catholic Italy and France, enhancing his perceptions of modern civilization as the agent of a destructive secularism. It never occurred to him that it might be too late to build an industrial society in Quebec free of secular influences. At the same time he simply could not comprehend that nationalism was itself a secular religion and that for twentieth-century Catholics the ideology of nationalism could be as dangerous as socialism or communism. For him nationalism was the tool by which Quebec was to be saved from secularism, not made its victim.

Two particularly striking examples of Groulx's approach, and of the contradictions inherent in it, are the only novels he wrote, both under the pseudonym Alonié de Lestres, *L'Appel de la race* (1922) and *Au Cap Blomidon* (1932). They have appeared in numerous editions as well as in comic-book form and as comic-strip panels in *Le Devoir* in the 1930s. Of the two, *L'Appel de la race* (translated in 1986, using Groulx's original title, as *The Iron Wedge*) is the more controversial and better known. It crystallizes more vividly than any other work the deficiencies of Groulx's constant indiscriminate intermingling of Catholicism, language, history, and nationalist rhetoric.

The central argument of *L'Appel de la race* is that a loss of one's native language, separation from one's native soil, voluntary or otherwise, is nothing less than a renunciation of nationality, of identity. French-Canadians who turned to speaking English invited personal and national destruction. The process was simple: a new language introduced alien values and ideals which in their turn undermined and destroyed the family. Once family life was in disarray the end of the nation was not far behind. The novel is a disturbing tale of a French-Canadian, Jules de Lantagnac, who in his youth abandons his origins for life among the English-speaking elite of Montreal and Ottawa where he marries an English-Canadian who has converted to Catholicism for his sake. In due course four children, with English names, complete the Lantagnac household. Suddenly, at the age of forty-three, Jules is gripped by a profound malaise realising that he has lost his French-Canadian heritage and his children have never known it. Following a pilgrimage to his ancestral home in the Quebec countryside, he is determined to reverse the situation. The tensions generated by his quest for a French cultural and linguistic revival in his home, in direct contrast to

his wife's English background, are played against the backdrop of his newfound parliamentary career in support of Franco-Ontarians in their battle against the attempt to eliminate French-language education in their province. His struggle, both personal and political, splits the family: his wife and two children leave; two remain to join his crusade for "their people." The plot only thinly disguises Groulx's presence in the novel. Jules's family history and ancestral home are direct transpositions of Groulx's own. Through Jules come all Groulx's favorite ideas about *la nation*, culture, language, history, the urgent need for a revival of French-Canadian self-esteem, and, above all else, the redemptive power of Catholicism.

On the most transparent level the novel symbolizes the disastrous "mixed marriage" of French and English in the Canadian Confederation, which by 1922 appeared quite precarious and its survival in doubt. In this sense the novel merely reflects Groulx's distaste for Confederation, his certainty of its imminent, inevitable collapse, and the consequent need to establish a coherent separate French-Canadian identity–an early evocation of Quebec separatism. On a much deeper level *L'Appel de la race* exposes the confusion of Groulx's thinking. In staging the tragedy of the Lantagnac household, Groulx uses Catholicism as a divisive force in the family rather than one of unity. To be Catholic is to be French. Add nationalism to this prescription for French exclusivity and Groulx's arguments immediately transgress papal injunctions against the dangers of injudiciously blending the faith and the essentially secular forces of nationalism. In the novel, and in everything he wrote and believed, Groulx never understood, or admitted, the extent to which nationalism exhibited a tendency to become a religion in its own right, destroying in its wake the spiritual values Groulx so keenly professed.

The only other novel Groulx wrote, *Au Cap Blomidon*, was far less didactic and controversial but no less popular. It is the story of the young descendant of an Acadian family, Jean Bérubé, who struggles to recapture the land lost by his family at the time of the Acadian deportations in 1755. Living in Quebec, Bérubé is drawn on a pilgrimage to his ancestral homeland, not unlike Jules de Lantagnac, where he labors, suffers, and ultimately prays for a miracle to restore to him his inheritance. In the end he succeeds. As is the case in *L'Appel de la race*, *Au Cap Blomidon* thinly dis-

Groulx in later life (photograph by Antoine Désilets)

guises Groulx's experiences and emotions, once again wrapping nationalist expectations in a cloak of religious fervor. In both novels a nationalist hero loyal to the memory of his ancestors, drawn by a mystical tie to the land and aided by divine inspiration and intervention, prevails over all evils and odds against the English. *Au Cap Blomidon* was little more than a platform on which Groulx could display his concerns about national survival, pride, and integrity. It also allowed him to expound at length on the virtue of struggle to achieve national strength and self-reliance.

This call to struggle for national renewal always carried with it the most contentious element of Groulx's thinking–Quebec separatism. Quebec as the homeland of French-Canadians constituted for them *la patrie, la nation.* Its very existence, its language, its culture, its history and, above all, its religion set the province apart from the rest of Canadian and North American society. Groulx could never decide whether this separateness, embodied in the unique character of Quebec, was to be merely psychological and spiritual or whether

it demanded immediate political, economic, and geographic expression in a separate, independent Quebec. Whenever he concluded that independence was a desired goal for Quebec, he always emphasized the need to prepare for this eventuality but had no substantive, specific program to offer through which to achieve it.

Through the long years of his writing career, Groulx changed few of his opinions and developed only nuances in style and approach. Consequently, the enormous body of his life's work has a continuity and repetitiousness that in no way detracts from Groulx's importance as a writer. His views have passed in and out of popularity since the early years of the century. As nationalism rises and falls in importance in the life of Quebec, so too does Groulx's audience. Anyone who attempts to understand Quebec and the Quebecois in the years before 1967 must come to terms with Groulx and the body of his writing.

Lionel Groulx's injunction to be *maîtres chez nous* fell on fertile ground in Quebec throughout the decades of his labors. Several generations of nationalists had been taught by him to revere and struggle for *la nation canadienne-française.* Teachers, clergy, politicians, journalists, labor leaders, and students had all come under his spell. His influence as the historian of Quebec was not challenged until the late 1950s when former students began to question his interpretations of the past and prescriptions for the future. In his way he had made separatism, as a political option, respectable. In the 1920s when he had first entertained the possibility of an independent Quebec, Confederation seemed on the verge of collapse. While it had limped along through depression and another world war, Groulx always had doubts about the future of Canada, especially since English-speaking Canadians did not see Confederation as a contract between two peoples or nations. Without acknowledgment of that duality, Canada was no more certain of survival after the 1920s than he had then believed it to be. As the government of Quebec in the 1960s began to gain greater control over key sectors of the province, the influence of Groulx's arguments was clearly evident, although Groulx was distressed by much of what occurred. The impressive gains in nationalist terms were offset by the steady decline of Catholicism as the system of values guiding society, particularly in education. In Groulx's view it was not enough for the Quebecois to control the material dimensions of their destiny: in turning from Catholicism they were abandoning their destiny as a providential people.

References:

M. Filion, ed., *Hommage à Lionel Groulx* (Montreal: Leméac, 1978);

G. Frégault, *Lionel Groulx tel qu'en lui-même* (Montreal: Leméac, 1978);

J.-P. Gaboury, *Le Nationalisme de Lionel Groulx: Aspects idéologiques* (Ottawa: Editions de l'Université d'Ottawa, 1970);

G. E. Giguère, *Lionel Groulx biographie* (Montreal: Bellarmin, 1978);

Lionel Groulx: 100e anniversaire de sa naissance 1878-1978, special issue of *Revue d'Histoire de l'Amérique Française,* 32 (December 1978);

Lionel Groulx, ptre (13 janvier 1878 - 23 mai 1967): L'Homme; L'Oeuvre, special issue of *L'Action Nationale,* 57 (June 1968);

J. Rémillard and M. Dionne, *L'Oeuvre de chanoine Lionel Groulx: Témoignages, Bio-bibliographie* (Montreal: Academie Canadienne-Française, 1964).

Papers:

Groulx's papers comprise one of the major sources of Quebec history in the twentieth century. Thousands of letters, sent and received by Groulx, manuscripts of published and unpublished works, sermon notes, drafts for proposed texts, and his personal library have been preserved at the Fondation Lionel-Groulx. Under the direction of Mme Juliette Rémillard, this private archive, 261 avenue Bloomfield, Outremont, Quebec, is open to all researchers.

Germaine Guèvremont
(16 April 1893-21 August 1968)

Michael Benazon
Champlain College-Lennoxville

BOOKS: *En pleine terre* (Montreal: Editions Paysana, 1942; enlarged, Montreal: Paysana, 1946);

Le Survenant (Montreal: Beauchemin, 1945); translated in *The Outlander* (1950); definitive French language edition (Montreal & Paris: Fides, 1974);

Marie-Didace (Montreal: Beauchemin, 1947; revised, 1948); translated in *The Outlander* (1950);

The Outlander, translated by Eric Sutton (New York: Whittlesey House, 1950; Toronto: McGraw-Hill, 1950)—comprises *Le Survenant* and *Marie-Didace;* Sutton's translation republished as *Monk's Reach* (London: Evans, 1950).

TELEVISION: *Une Grosse nouvelle*, Radio-Canada, 23 June 1954-13 October 1954;

Le Survenant, Au Chenal du Moine, and *Marie-Didace,* Radio-Canada, 2 November 1954-30 June 1960;

L'Adieu aux îles, Radio-Canada, 3 June 1968 and 9 September 1968.

RADIO: *Le Survenant* and *Marie-Didace,* Radio-Canada, 15 and 22 July 1951;

Le Survenant, Radio-Canada, 31 August 1953-6 May 1955.

PERIODICAL PUBLICATIONS: "Le Plomb dans l'aile," *Cahiers de l'Académie Canadienne-Française,* 4 (1959): 69-75;

"La Maison de ma tante," *Nouveau Journal* (7 October 1961);

"A l'eau douce," *Châtelaine,* 8 (April 1967): 34-35, 74, 76, 78, 80, 82;

"Le Premier Miel: Un Chapitre inédit de Germaine Guèvremont," *Le Devoir,* 31 October 1967, p. 21.

Germaine Guèvremont has been acclaimed for her lyrical and naturalistic treatment of the *habitants* who lived amid the islands and inlets of

Germaine Guèvremont (photograph by Gaby, Montreal)

the St. Lawrence River near Sorel, Quebec. By some critics she is regarded as the last of the older generation of Quebec novelists who took a nostalgic view of rural existence. Yet Guèvremont was keenly aware that the old way of life was in decay, an awareness she conveyed through her use of an underlying irony and through her creation of the figure of the disruptive stranger, a boisterous symbol of the new attitudes that sought entry into the closed world of Quebec village life. Coincidentally in 1945, as Guèvremont was publishing *Le Survenant,* one of the last in the tradition of the novels of the soil, another Quebec writer, Gabrielle Roy, produced *Bonheur d'occasion,* one of the first of the new urban novels, which was to mark the beginning of a distinct change in Quebec literary tastes.

Germaine Guèvremont was born Marianne Germaine Grignon in Saint-Jérôme, Quebec, into a well-established middle-class family. Her lawyer father, Joseph-Jérôme Grignon, spent much of his leisure time writing articles and poetry. Her mother, Valentine Labelle Grignon, was a committed and (for her time) emancipated painter, with an eye for the beauties of nature. Germaine Grignon's cousin Claude-Henri Grignon, a well-known Quebec novelist, encouraged her at critical moments in her literary career. She had been provided with a standard convent education at Sainte-Scholastique and then at Saint-Jérôme and Lachine. When she was eighteen her parents took the unusual step of sending her for a year to Loretto Abbey in Toronto to study English and piano. On her return in 1912 she worked as court stenographer and secretary in the local *Palais de Justice.* The same year she published her first article.

Germaine Grignon married Hyacinthe Guèvremont 24 May 1916, and for the next four years the couple lived in Ottawa. At the end of that period they moved to her husband's native town of Sorel, where they participated in the running of a family business. Following the death of one of her children in 1926, Mme Guèvremont fell into a depression from which she was revived by the initiative of her brother-in-law, who persuaded her to take up journalism. She reported for the English-language *Gazette* and for the French *Courrier de Sorel* until the collapse of her husband's business led, in 1935, to their removal to Montreal. Although Germaine Guèvremont had not been fully happy in Sorel, her fifteen-year sojourn in the region provided her with the images, character types, language, and situations that she later transmuted into literature. Her husband and his family served as models for the Beauchemins who are featured in each of her three books. She frequently accompanied her husband on his hunting and fishing expeditions in the river channels near Sorel, and it is largely from such excursions that she acquired her familiarity with the natural phenomena of the region.

In Montreal Guèvremont was, of necessity, the principal breadwinner of the family. For a time she was again employed as a court stenographer and secretary. From 1938 to 1945 she contributed over forty articles, interviews, and tales to *Paysana,* a monthly magazine about rural life. In 1942 she collected a number of these sketches for publication under the title *En pleine terre.*

This book, though it contains several charming tales, lacks unity. The first and largest section, "Paysanneries" (Rural Sketches), deals with the joys and sorrows of the Beauchemins, a family of farmers who live on the banks of the St. Lawrence River. The second section, "Contes," consists of three (four in the enlarged edition of 1946) tales set in the same region but unrelated to the Beauchemins. Though the stories are often amusing and sometimes moving, they have no great depth of insight, and the condescending tone makes it difficult for the modern reader to identify with the characters or to note any particular significance in their lives. Guèvremont does reveal, however, an ability to create a country setting and to establish a mood in a series of short descriptive passages. Concerned, at first, by the apparent lack of critical interest in the book, Guèvremont solicited a review from the poet Alfred DesRochers; she need not have worried, however, for the critical notices were generally favorable.

On DesRochers's advice, Guèvremont set out almost immediately to develop the setting, characters, motifs, and images of *En pleine terre* into the more ambitious format of a novel. Published at her own expense early in 1945 by Beauchemin of Montreal, *Le Survenant* at first received mixed reviews. It did, however, win the Prix Duvernay and Quebec's Prix David. A second edition was published in Paris in 1946, and the novel was awarded the Prix Sully-Olivier de Serres.

Le Survenant may be regarded as the first of a projected three-part chronicle of the Beauchemin family. It is set a little later than *En pleine terre,* during the years immediately preceding World War I. Didace Beauchemin, the dynastically minded head of the family, is now attempting to adjust to life as a widower. His son, Amable, is ill-adapted to the responsibility and labors expected of the eldest son in a farmer's family, and Amable's wife, Alphonsine, is equally ill-suited to her role of farmer's spouse.

The novel comprises a series of related episodes dominated by the presence of the *survenant,* the mysterious stranger, or outlander, who arrives suddenly one night on the Beauchemin farm. In the course of a year he unintentionally brings about profound changes in the lives of his hosts and their neighbors. The charm-

Postage stamp celebrating Guèvremont's 1945 "novel of the soil"

ing *survenant* is linked to some of the underlying myths in French-Canadian literary culture. There is an element in him of the coureur de bois, the restless, adventurous, free-spirited wanderer associated with the journeys of exploration in old Quebec. Because he is also associated with modern attitudes held in the outside world, the *survenant* may be taken as a symbol of the change that in the mid 1940s was about to sweep away the traditional values and way of life of Quebec rural society.

Guèvremont's naturalistic technique and slightly ironic style reveal none of the condescension that tarnishes *En pleine terre*. The attention to detail and the accuracy of her metaphors bring to fruition the promise inherent in her earlier work. Like Louis Hémon's *Maria Chapdelaine* (1916) and Ringuet's *Trente Arpents* (1938), *Le Survenant* is an acknowledged Quebec classic, though it lacks the thematic depth and intensity of these earlier novels of the soil.

In 1947 Guèvremont published *Marie-Didace,* a short sequel to *Le Survenant,* a winding-

down of the history of the Beauchemins begun in *En pleine terre.* His hopes for a male heir to the Beauchemin farm dashed by the death of Amable, old Didace takes comfort in the birth of his granddaughter and insists she be given his name. *Marie-Didace* chronicles the deaths of Didace and his second wife and Alphonsine's decline into self-pity and mental illness. As in *Le Survenant,* the author's final position is ambivalent: the Beauchemins with their strengths and virtues will disappear. The community, however, rallies to support the survivors: the capable but lonely Angélina Desmarais will mother the parentless child, and the parish will manage the family property so that it may eventually pass on to Marie-Didace. Despite individual misfortune and calamity, the community remains strong. Though the *survenant* never returns, Angélina is vouchsafed a final vision: on a scrap of newspaper she reads that he apparently died a hero's death in World War I. Ironically Angélina resolves to conduct herself as his widow, cherishing forever the memory of the man who abandoned her. The publication of *Marie-Didace* was followed by nearly unanimous acclaim from the critics.

Guèvremont apparently had in mind a third volume to complete the trilogy she began with *Le Survenant*. Unfortunately only one chapter of the projected novel ever appeared–"Le Plomb dans l'aile"–published in *Cahiers de l'Académie Canadienne-Française* in 1959. From 1947 to the end of her life, Guèvremont busied herself in writing and editing radio, television, and film scripts based on her stories and novels. In 1966 she began work on her memoirs. Although she appears to have completed the first volume, entitled "Le Premier Miel," she published only two extracts from it in 1967, one in *Châtelaine* and one in *Le Devoir*. The manuscript and other papers are still in the possession of the Guèvremont family.

In her native Quebec, Guèvremont has had a modest critical reception. During the 1950s she was well known to the public through the television dramatization of her novels, for which she wrote the scripts. In recent years, however, the mood has changed. French-Canadian readers prefer fiction that more closely mirrors the realities of the age over nostalgic writing that describes, however effectively, a world they have sought to put behind them. In 1951 Eric Sutton's translation of *Le Survenant* and *Marie-Didace* in one volume, entitled *The Outlander*, won the Governor-General's Award for fiction for Guèvremont. Despite the 1978 paperback republication of this translation, Guèvremont is not familiar to English-Canadians, who tend to read Quebec literature in order to gain insight into the current social issues of the region.

The best of Guèvremont's work is suffused with a gentle lyrical quality that is the product of a keen observation of natural phenomena and of a familiarity with country life. Through her use of French-Canadian expressions, she provides her characters with a strong flavor of authenticity. At the same time an underlying comic irony prevents excessive nostalgia or sentiment. Her fiction does not introduce the high drama found in some regional writers who also deal with a lost rural world. The work of Guèvremont has there-

fore had a limited appeal to readers outside her native region. Yet there is every reason to suppose that she will continue to hold the attention and respect of students of literature who appreciate her contribution to a major cultural myth.

Interviews:

William Arthur Deacon, Interview with Guèvremont, *Globe and Mail*, 13 April 1946, p. 9;

Louis Pelletier-Dlamini, "Germaine Guèvremont: Rencontre avec l'auteur du *Survenant*," *Châtelaine*, 8 (April 1967): 31-33, 84, 86, 88;

Alice Parizeau, "Germaine Guèvremont, écrivain du Québec," *La Presse*, 3 February 1968, pp. 12-15.

References:

Renée Cimon, "Germaine Guèvremont," *Dossiers de documentation sur la littérature canadienne-française* (Montreal: Fìdes, 1969);

Raymond Douville, "La Tragédie du Chenal du Moine," *Cahiers des Dix*, 35 (1970): 55-67;

Jean-Pierre Duquette, *Germaine Guèvremont: Une Route, une maison* (Montreal: Presses de l'Université de Montréal, 1973);

Rita Leclerc, *Germaine Guèvremont* (Montreal & Paris: Fides, 1963);

Anthony Mollica, Introduction to Guèvremont's *The Outlander*, translated by Eric Sutton (Toronto: McClelland & Stewart, 1978), pp. v-xv;

Suzanne Paradis, "Germaine Guèvremont et le vertige des îles," *Cahiers de l'Académie Canadienne-Française*, 14 (1972): 33-43;

Jean-Paul Pinsonneault, "Germaine Guèvremont, peintre de l'âme paysanne et poète terrien," *Lectures*, 10 (November 1953): 97-107;

Jeanette Urbas, *From "Thirty Acres" to Modern Times* (Toronto: McGraw-Hill Ryerson, 1976), pp. 25-31;

André Vanasse, "La Rupture définitive. La Notion d'étranger dans la littérature canadienne-française," *L'Action Nationale*, 55 (March 1966): 606-611;

Heinz Weinman, "Nomade et Sédentaire," *Critère*, 10 (January 1974): 11-18.

Charles Yale Harrison

(16 June 1898-17 March 1954)

Neil Besner
University of Winnipeg

BOOKS: *Next Please! The Story of Greco and Carillo* (New York: International Labor Defense, 1927);

Generals Die in Bed (London: Douglas, 1930; New York: Morrow, 1930);

A Child Is Born (New York: Cape & Smith, 1931);

Clarence Darrow (New York: Cape & Smith, 1931);

There Are Victories (New York: Covici-Friede, 1933);

Housing Becomes a National Issue (New York: New York City Housing Authority, 1937);

Housing Confronts Congress (New York: New York City Housing Authority, 1937);

A Housing Tale of Two Cities, London and New York (New York: New York City Housing Authority, 1937);

What Price Subsidy! (New York: New York City Housing Authority, 1937);

Meet Me on the Barricades (New York: Scribners, 1938);

Nobody's Fool (New York: Holt, 1948);

Thank God for My Heart Attack (New York: Holt, 1949).

OTHER: *Eight Reasons for Public Housing,* edited by Harrison (New York: New York City Housing Authority, 1937).

In the course of his varied careers in Canada and the United States as a journalist, theater manager, real-estate salesman, public-relations consultant, radio commentator, and housing expert, Charles Yale Harrison wrote fiction, biography, autobiography, and several pamphlets on public housing–the first of their kind. But it was his shattering experience as a soldier in a Canadian regiment in World War I that inspired his major achievement, the novel *Generals Die in Bed* (1930). Compared in the 1930s with fictional and autobiographical classics of World War I literature such as Erich Maria Remarque's *All Quiet on the Western Front* (1929), Ernest Hemingway's *A Farewell to Arms* (1929), Robert Graves's *Good-Bye to All That* (1929), and Siegfried Sassoon's *Mem-*

oirs of an Infantry Officer (1930), *Generals Die in Bed* can be read as a forerunner of the most celebrated contemporary Canadian novel to deal with World War I, Timothy Findley's *The Wars* (1977).

Harrison was born in Philadelphia to Lewis and Sophia Frumer Harrison. He left school in grade four–because of an argument with a teacher, the oft-repeated story goes, over *The Merchant of Venice.* At sixteen Harrison was in Montreal and working for the *Montreal Star,* a job he left to enlist in the Royal Montreal Regiment. He served as a machine gunner in France and Belgium, was wounded in the foot on 8 August 1918, during the major battle at Amiens, and was shipped back to Montreal. In 1920 he married Emily Courtier, with whom he subsequently had one son, Yale Peter. *Generals Die in Bed,* Harrison's first full-length book, was published in 1930 and dedicated to "the bewildered youths–British, Australian, Canadian and German–who were killed in that wood a few miles beyond Amiens on August 8, 1918."

Harrison's novel was first published in England, and then in America by a publisher who had at first rejected it. Robert F. Nielsen, who wrote a 1971 master's thesis on Canadian fiction about World War I, comments in his introduction to the 1975 republication (by Potlatch) of Harrison's novel on the possibility of its influence on Remarque's *All Quiet on the Western Front:* "As early as 1928 portions of the manuscript had appeared in several magazines, including German publications, which leads one to wonder if Remarque had read them and was influenced while creating *All Quiet on the Western Front.* There are striking similarities between the two books, notably the scenes in which the central characters have horrendous experiences of killing enemy soldiers at close range, and the discussions amongst the soldiers about why they are fighting the war."

Conjecture about Harrison's influence on Remarque aside, it is clear that *Generals Die in Bed* was generally well received, not only in the West, on both sides of the Atlantic, in German, French, Czechoslovakian, and Spanish translations, but also in Russian and Chinese. Ford Madox Ford's comments, quoted in Nielsen's introduction, provide insight into the novel's international reception: "I think this is a hell of a good book. It is a plain unvarnished account of things without any literary frills–it ought to be a good antidote for all the gush of ain't it awful literature which romanticizes the war in a subtle sort of way. *Generals Die in Bed* has a sort of flat-footed straightness about it that gets down the torture of the front line about as accurately as one can ever get it, I think."

Harrison's first-person narrator takes the reader on a hellishly vivid journey beginning with the regiment's departure from Bonaventure Station in Montreal–in a scene which should be read against other fictional accounts of Canadian departures for war, such as Hugh MacLennan's in *Two Solitudes* (1945) or Findley's in *The Wars*–and directly to the trenches and battlefields in Belgium and France. The most remarkable aspect of Harrison's style–what one reviewer described as his "short, stabbing sentences"–immerses the reader in the soldiers' viscerally immediate, present-tense, and yet eerily depersonalized experience. Arranged in twelve brief episodic chapters, the novel counterpoints the phantasmagorical intensity of bombardments and hand-to-hand combat with the soldiers' brief interludes of rest away from the front lines. The mind-numbing brutality of the war renders the soldiers amoral, fear-haunted specters who discover that their real enemies are not the Germans, but "the lice, some of our officers and Death."

All of the eighteen-year-old narrator's companions are killed–by snipers, shellbursts, or flamethrowers–and in the most gripping scene in the novel, he is decorated for bayoneting a German soldier and taking the soldier's brother and another German as prisoners. The scene typifies the novel's unremitting focus on what the men in the trenches on both sides experience as the unnatural, arbitrary, and unmotivated killing they toil at under the command of their officers, who inhabit another sphere, utterly removed from the men. And in the culminating chapter, ironically entitled "Vengeance," the regiment slaughters hundreds of unarmed German troops at the behest of a general who has lied to them about the recent German torpedoing of an Allied hospital ship which had actually been carrying munitions along with wounded soldiers. In its style and its stance *Generals Die in Bed* is one of the bleakest of the antiwar novels to appear in the 1930s in any language.

Returning to Montreal from Amiens, Harrison worked at various jobs there before moving to New York, where his chief occupations were as a housing expert and public-relations consultant. In 1931, the year his wife died, Harrison wrote the first book-length biography of the lawyer, *Clarence Darrow*. In 1932 he wed Edna Margolin. This second marriage ended in divorce; his third, to Eva Shapiro, began in May 1940. Harrison was the first in the United States to write about public low-rent housing in a series of pamphlets, all published in 1937–*Housing Becomes a National Issue; Housing Confronts Congress; A Housing Tale of Two Cities, London and New York;* and *What Price Subsidy!* His other novels include *A Child Is Born* (1931), *There Are Victories* (1933), *Meet Me on the Barricades* (1938), and *Nobody's Fool* (1948); none of these is as powerful as *Generals Die in Bed*. Harrison's last book, an autobiographical work entitled *Thank God for My Heart Attack*, appeared in 1949, and he died of heart disease five years later.

That Harrison is only remembered today for one novel does not diminish the significance of his contribution to Canadian and to world literature. *Generals Die in Bed* speaks to postwar readers in an idiom all too familiarly fragmented, the most compelling creation of a distressingly contemporary imagination.

References:

Robert F. Nielsen, "A Barely Perceptible Limp: The First World War in Canadian Fiction," M.A. thesis, University of Guelph, 1971;

Nielsen, Introduction to Harrison's *Generals Die in Bed* (Hamilton, Ontario: Potlatch, 1975).

Anne Hébert

(1 August 1916-   )

Lorraine Weir
University of British Columbia

BOOKS: *Les Songes en équilibre* (Montreal: Editions de l'Arbre, 1942);
Le Torrent (Montreal: Beauchemin, 1950; enlarged, Montreal: HMH, 1963); translated by Gwendolyn Moore as *The Torrent* (Montreal: Harvest House, 1973);
Le Tombeau des rois (Quebec: Institut Littéraire du Quebec, 1953); translated by Peter Miller in *The Tomb of the Kings,* bilingual edition (Toronto: Contact, 1967);
Les Chambres de bois (Paris: Seuil, 1958); translated by Kathy Mezei as *The Silent Rooms* (Don Mills, Ontario: Musson, 1974);
Poèmes (Paris: Seuil, 1960); translated by Alan Brown as *Poems* (Don Mills, Ontario: Musson, 1975);
Le Temps sauvage, La Mercière assassinée, Les Invités au procès (Montreal: HMH, 1967);
Dialogue sur la traduction à propos du "Tombeau des rois," by Hébert and Frank Scott (Montreal: HMH, 1970);
Kamouraska (Paris: Seuil, 1970); translated by Norman Shapiro (Don Mills, Ontario: Musson, 1973; New York: Crown, 1973);
Les Enfants du Sabbat (Paris: Seuil, 1975); translated by Carol Dunlop Hébert as *Children of the Black Sabbath* (Don Mills, Ontario: Musson, 1977; New York: Crown, 1977);
Héloïse (Paris: Seuil, 1980); translated by Sheila Fischman (Toronto: Stoddart, 1982);
Les Fous de Bassan (Paris: Seuil, 1982); translated by Fischman as *In the Shadow of the Wind* (Toronto: Stoddart, 1983).

PLAY PRODUCTION: *Le Temps sauvage,* Quebec, Théâtre du Nouveau Monde at the Palais Montcalm, 8 October 1966.

MOTION PICTURES: *Les Indes parmi nous,* screenplay by Hébert, National Film Board, 1954;
La Canne à pêche, screenplay by Hébert, National Film Board, 1959;
Saint-Denys Garneau, screenplay by Hébert, National Film Board, 1960.

Anne Hébert, early 1950s (courtesy of Kenneth Landry)

RADIO: *Les Invités au procès, Le Théâtre du grand prix,* Radio-Canada, 20 July 1952;
Trois de Québec, by Hébert and others, Radio-Canada, 1953.

One of Canada's major twentieth-century writers, Anne Hébert has followed a markedly original path in her work. The author of two of the masterpieces of modern Canadian writing, the cycle of poems entitled *Le Tombeau des rois* (first published in 1953; translated into English, 1967) and the novel *Kamouraska* (1970; translated, 1973), Hébert has perhaps more than any other modern Quebec writer analyzed the profound impact of the Jansenist cosmology upon a cross section of human types representing its most thoroughly bound victims. Through her exploration of the classic themes of guilt, evil, violence, exile, and the anguish of isolation, she has created a fully unified oeuvre which is both brilliantly executed and profound in its understanding of the psychology of pain and entrapment.

Anne Hébert was born in Saint-Catherine de Fossambault, a village near Quebec City, on 1 August 1916. Raised in a literary household, Hébert received her early education at home from a private tutor and from her father, the poet and literary critic Maurice Hébert. She has said that from her father she both acquired her knowledge of grammar and syntax and received her first encouragement as a poet. Later she attended the Collège Notre-Dame-de-Bellevue and the Collège Mérici in Quebec and was drawn to the literary circle of her cousin, the poet Hector de Saint-Denys Garneau. This group included such major contributors to Quebec culture as Jean Le Moyne, Robert Elie, Claude Hurtubise, Robert Charbonneau, and André Laurendeau. From this period of late adolescence dates Hébert's interest in the theater and her earliest involvement in it, putting on plays in the church hall at Saint-Catherine with Saint-Denys Garneau and Jean Le Moyne. At this time she also read widely in the avant-garde literature of France, particularly the writings of Jules Supervielle, René Char, and Paul Éluard. The poems later collected as *Les Songes en équilibre* (1942) were published from 1939 on in such journals as *La Relève, Les Gants du Ciel, Cité Libre,* and *Esprit.*

Although many of the themes and images of her later works are to be found in Hébert's first volume, *Les Songes en équilibre* is radically different in several significant respects from the great cycle *Le Tombeau des rois* and the meditations of *Mystère de la Parole,* both of which formed part of Hébert's 1960 volume, *Poèmes* (translated, 1975). On the whole the volume is diffuse, employing much lyric repetition in the romantic mode. Whereas the evolved symbol system presented in *Le Tombeau des rois* is concise, at times convoluted to the point that some critics have thought it hermetic, in Hébert's initial experiments the persona of the inquiring innocent is often adopted not only to support the lyrical openness of the verse but also to render statements of faith expressive of a conservative Catholic girlhood. A sacramental theology which becomes progressively more demythologized in *Mystère de la Parole* is here

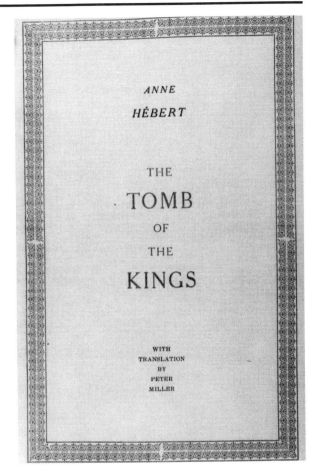

Cover for the bilingual edition of Hébert's poem cycle
Le Tombeau des rois

presented translucently in a poem like "Communion":

Je suis le pain du bon Dieu,
A mon tour je Lui donne à communier,
Il me reçoit;
Et, après l'action de grâce,
Comme les petits enfants
Il fait ses demandes,
Sans parler,
Simplement
Parce que je suis là,
Dans son coeur
Et qu'Il me reçoit.

(I am God's bread; in my twin I give Him communion. He receives me and after the act of grace, like little children, He makes His demands, without speaking, simply, because I am there, in his heart, and He receives me.)

Perhaps the most striking aspect of this, and other, early poems is the paradigmatic stance of the speaker. Here she is passive, the action of the poem consisting in God's reception of her rather than her partaking of communion. Though, of course, she does act, stress is laid not upon her own initiative and its consequences but rather upon the mystical transaction of "grace" which results in her willing submission to God's unspoken "demands." In turn, this homage is emblematized in the figure of the divine heart wherein the speaker is received. Initially figured as the bread which is about to undergo ritual transubstantiation, she becomes implicitly both that which is consumed and that which is transformed and received. This is, of course, a familiar conceit of devotional verse. What is particularly interesting, however, is the transformation of this theme in Hébert's second volume of poems, *Le Tombeau des rois*. In this volume the speaker experiences a profound mutilation of self which is both violent and passive. Thus in "La Fille maigre" the speaker is obsessed with the polishing of her bones in preparation for the time when "Un jour je saisirai mon amant / Pour m'en faire un reliquaire d'argent. // Je me pendrai / A la place de son coeur absent" (One day I will seize my lover to make of him a silver reliquary. I'll hang myself in the place of his absent heart). Whereas the figures of "Communion" signify submission to a transformation process through the experience of the sacred, in "La Fille maigre" transformation centers on death for both lover and speaker.

In "En guise de fête," the next poem in *Le Tombeau des rois*, a cryptic rationale for this process is provided. Echoed again and again in Hébert's fiction, this poem, perhaps more than any other single component of her system, provides an understanding of the shape of the whole:

Le monde est en ordre
Les morts dessous
Les vivants dessus.

Les morts me visitent
Le monde est en ordre
Les morts dessous
Les vivants dessus.

Les morts m'ennuient
Les vivants me tuent.

(The world is in order. The dead below, the living above. The dead visit me. The world is in order. The dead below, the liv-

ing above. The dead annoy me, the living kill me.)

Between *dessus* (above) and *dessous* (below), there is in French only one letter. On that letter hangs our expectation of order in life, and equally our knowledge of chaos, disorder, evil, death, suffering. The poems comprising *Le Tombeau des rois* depict a world in which choice–whether of order or of chaos–is not available. Rather, the poet witnesses to the triumph of Jansenism, the occlusion of body from mind, and the shifting guises of death which are its fruit.

By the time of *Mystère de la Parole*, however, the faith of such a poem as "Communion" has been transformed into aesthetic statement: "je crois à la vertu de la poésie, je crois au salut qui vient de toute parole juste, vécue et exprimée. Je crois à la solitude rompue comme du pain par la poésie" (I believe in the virtue of poetry, I believe in the salvation that comes from every right word, lived and expressed. I believe in solitude broken like bread by poetry). This is in part a reflection of Hébert's movement away from the practice of Catholicism during this period, a movement associated with the sudden death of her sister, Marie, at the age of thirty. It may be argued, however, that the major shift in Hébert's work is not from a Catholic to a non-Catholic view of the world but rather from a Jansenist to a Gnostic one. The Gnostic vision of the function and necessity of evil, the incursions of order into the ground of chaos, the revelation of truth in an inverted world, has increasingly characterized Hébert's work from *Le Torrent* (1950) to *Héloïse* (a 1980 partial return to the stark oppositions of *Le Tombeau des rois*) to *Les Fous de Bassan* (1982).

Les Songes en équilibre was awarded the Prix David in 1943, the year after its publication. In the same year the tragic death of Hébert's cousin, Saint-Denys Garneau, occurred, and for some time thereafter Hébert worked in seclusion on the novellas and stories which were published in 1950 as *Le Torrent*. Because of her stark depiction of the repressive effects of Jansenist Catholicism, Hébert not only had difficulty finding a publisher, finally paying for publication out of her own pocket, but also experienced difficulty at the hands of the critics. Whereas some readers responded to the appearance of *Héloïse* (which was translated into English in 1982) with dismay, believing the novel's Parisian setting to be indicative of a turning away from Quebec and a lessening of Hébert's status as a Quebecois writer, in the

Dust jacket for the first English translation of Hébert's Les Chambres de bois, *winner of the Prix de la Province de Québec and the Prix France-Canada*

early 1980s some worried that such stories as "Le Torrent" were altogether too revealing of a side of Quebec life which should be kept hidden.

"Le Torrent" is the story of François Perrault, son of a brutal and brutalized woman, Claudine, who takes revenge on the world for her own sorrows by psychic mutilation of her child. When François refuses to return to school and conform to his mother's dream of his becoming a priest, she strikes him on the head with her keys. There is tragic irony in the deafness which ensues, for François is both locked ever more deeply into his inner world and freed from the threat of the seminary. "Dispossessed of the world," he experiences the direct violence of his own feelings at last, contrives his mother's violent death, and lives in isolation and fear, detached from the external world. Some time later, possessed by desire, François is moved to find human companionship. He encounters a tramp selling trinkets by the roadside and tries to communicate his wish to buy the tramp's female compan-

ion. Enough money is put down and the woman, whom he calls Amica, departs with him. But loss of his solitude is for François loss of shelter and of security, and when at last Amica robs him and escapes, François discovers that he has lost everything. He longs only for death in the violent waters of the torrent. "What do I have left to renounce?," he asks, and concludes that he has only himself.

Between 1945 and 1954 Hébert became involved in theater, radio, and film. She collaborated in the presentation of *Trois de Québec* on Radio-Canada in 1953 and in the same year joined the National Film Board staff, becoming in August 1954 a writer of screenplays, a position which she held again in 1959 and 1960. During this period she wrote screenplays for three films, *Les Indes parmi nous* (1954), *La Canne à pêche* (1959), and *Saint-Denys Garneau* (1960). The middle years of the decade were spent in Paris as a result of an award from the Royal Society of Canada (made on 21 May 1954) which enabled Hébert to devote herself exclusively to writing.

Hébert's play *Les Invités au procès* was broadcast on 20 July 1952 in the Radio-Canada series *Le Théâtre du grand prix*. A verse drama written for radio, this play was not published until 1967 when it appeared together with the television drama *La Mercière assassinée* and the more widely known *Le Temps sauvage* (first performed by the Théâtre du Nouveau Monde at the Palais Montcalm in Quebec on 8 October 1966). Of the three plays the last seems the most central within Hébert's oeuvre, working as it does with the themes of "Le Torrent" and of her first novel, *Les Chambres de bois* (1958; translated as *The Silent Rooms*, 1974). Like Claudine Perrault, Agnès Joncas and her family live in isolation, her four daughters and one son existing in a state of more or less latent rebellion against their domineering mother. As we discover later in the play, Agnès is–like Claudine–making reparation, though not for her own sin but for that of her deceased sister, Nathalie, whom Agnès had brought up after the death of their parents. When Nathalie becomes pregnant by Agnès's fiancé and leaves her, Agnès is resolved to flee the occasions of sin and bring up her own children untouched by the world. But, like Catherine, the young heroine of *Les Chambres de bois*, Agnès is powerless to prevent the incursions of chaos, and her world is broken at last. After Nathalie's death her daughter Isabelle comes to live with Agnès and falls in love with Sébastien, Agnès's son. Their departure together signals the end of Agnès's dream of a pure world for her children. Even the seclusion of a house on an isolated mountain cannot preserve them. Her dream of perfect motherhood shattered, Agnès is left with her own corrosive bitterness and little else.

Although Catherine of *Les Chambres de bois* seems to fare rather better, we may be less optimistic if Hébert's first novel is seen as the complement of *Héloïse*. Both novels are concerned with voyages into the underworld. In the first case it is the strange, incestuous world of Michel and Lia, brother and sister who share a barren, tormented solitude. In the second case it is the underground world of the vampire Héloïse who lures young Bernard away from his fiancée Christine and succeeds in destroying them both. Like Catherine, Christine makes desperate attempts to restore normalcy as she sees Bernard turning away from her, but the familiar routines of cooking and cleaning cannot repress the upsurge of evil. As in Hébert's poem "En guise de fête" (its crucial lines repeated as the epigraph to *Héloïse*), the

worlds of above and below are semantically discrete yet metaphysically interpenetrant. The violence of love gives access to both the ecstatic and the demonic. Catherine of *Les Chambres de bois* is, however, more fortunate than Christine for she is able to escape to the seaside where she meets and falls in love with Bruno and at last frees herself from Michel and the enclosed world of their apartment. In *Héloïse*, in contrast, no escape is permitted. Christine is raped and murdered, Bernard is seduced into the underworld of Héloïse and her demonic master, Xavier Bottereau, and the eruption of violence into the world is complete.

After its publication in Paris in 1958, *Les Chambres de bois* was awarded the Prix de la Province de Québec as well as the Prix France-Canada; Hébert also won the Prix Duvernay for this novel and for her work as a whole. Hébert returned home to Quebec from her first three-year period in Paris but throughout the 1960s alternated between Paris and Montreal. She was repeatedly honored for her work during this decade. In June 1960 she was elected to the Royal Society of Canada, and in 1961 she received the Governor General's Award for poetry (for *Poèmes*, the 1960 volume uniting a slightly revised and regrouped version of the poems first published in 1953 as *Le Tombeau des rois* and *Mystère de la Parole*, with Hébert's important essay, "Poésie, solitude rompue," bridging the two works). In 1961-1962 Hébert was honored by the Canada Council with a bursary. In 1967 she received the Molson Prize from the same organization and in 1969 her first honorary doctorate, from the University of Toronto; others followed, from the Université de Québec à Montréal (1979) and from McGill University (1980).

This was the period of the composition of *Kamouraska*, four years in the writing, published in Paris by Seuil in 1970. Considered by many to be Hébert's finest novel, winner of the Prix des Libraires de France in 1971, and certainly one of the masterpieces of contemporary Quebec writing, *Kamouraska* is another in Hébert's series of investigations into the psychology of Jansenist Quebec. A complex novel, this narrative moves in and out of the memories of Madame Jérôme Rolland as she attends her husband on his deathbed. Based on the historical events surrounding the murder in 1839 of Achille Taché, Seigneur de Kamouraska, Hébert's novel explores through intricately structured flashbacks the brief married life of Elisabeth d'Aulnières, wife of Antoine

Hébert, mid 1980s (photograph by Kèro)

Tassy (Hébert's version of Taché), who conspires with her lover, Doctor George Nelson, in the murder of her brutal husband. Thus does George Nelson discover death and evil and, as Elisabeth says, "a corner of the known world gives way and falls to pieces." But as he flees across the border to the United States, Nelson attracts the attention of others. Blood is everywhere: on his sleigh, encrusted upon the horse's reins, in his fur rugs, on his hands and clothes. Though he escapes into anonymity and recrimination, Elisabeth does not. After standing trial and enduring a brief prison sentence, she is left to live a life of boredom and propriety. Her real prison sentence is her next marriage, to Jérôme Rolland. Securely ensconced in a large house, surrounded by children and servants, she epitomizes the schism between the reality of the body–of bloodshed, violence, sexuality, passionate love–and the claustrophobic life of the respectable woman in nineteenth-century Quebec. Like the persona of many of the poems in *Le Tombeau des rois*, she views herself in mirrors, sits before windows, etches her name in the glass with her ring, becomes glass, but still burns with the anguish of her imprisonment, her abandonment by George Nelson, and with the desperate conflation of rage and powerlessness which is her fate.

Made into a brilliant film by Claude Jutra in 1963, *Kamouraska* has, more than any of her other works, made Hébert known to an English-speaking audience. But the isolation of this novel from the body of Hébert's work as a whole has perhaps cast it in a curious light for some readers, making it both more of a historical novel and more of an oddity than it is if it is seen within the context of the oeuvre. A brief comparison with Hébert's next novel, *Les Enfants du Sabbat* (1975; translated as *Children of the Black Sabbath*, 1977), may make this clearer.

Like *Kamouraska*, *Les Enfants du Sabbat* is concerned with the violent interface between two worlds which seem at first to be utterly incompatible but prove in the end to be simply opposite sides of the same coin. Just as for Catherine (of *Les Chambres de bois*) and Christine (of *Héloïse*) to fall in love is to fall into violence and death, so for Elisabeth d'Aulnières (*Kamouraska*) and Sister Julie of the Trinity (*Les Enfants du Sabbat*) to assume the mask of propriety is to encounter evil and bloodshed. Whereas in *Kamouraska* Hébert selects the imagistic repertoire of a particular historical incident set within a violently dualistic milieu, in *Les Enfants du Sabbat* she works within the systems of witchcraft and orthodox religion in order to open them into each other. It is a facet of the

Dust jacket for the first English translation of Les Fous de Bassan, *winner of France's Prix Fémina for 1982*

distinction made earlier between *dessus* and *dessous* in "En guise de fête."

A young nun of the Sisters of the Precious Blood, Sister Julie is the daughter of two witches who filled her with knowledge of the rites of the black sabbath, the mysteries of the other side of the world. Set in another isolated, mountaintop world like that of *Le Temps sauvage, Les Enfants du Sabbat* draws together the rituals of orthodox Catholicism, the routines of convent life and superstition, with the more explicitly violent and debauched rituals of witchcraft. Yet, as always when Hébert deals with the subject matter of traditional Catholicism, her intent far transcends social commentary or critique. Sister Julie must work back through the mysteries of her childhood, turning the convent world upside down in the process, in order to reclaim her life and finally escape from the prison of a self bound into one system *or* the other. Her task is one of synthesis for, as Hébert has said, "La vie n'était pas donnée de soi. Il fallait presque faire un acte de sacrilége pour s'en emparer" (Life wasn't given to one. It was almost necessary to commit an act of sacrilege to take possession of it). Sister Julie accomplishes what is virtually unthinkable for Elisabeth d'Aulnières-Rolland: she frees herself for the experience of a future.

"La prose, c'est une autre forme poétique" (Prose is another poetic form), Hébert has said; perhaps nowhere in her fiction is this more evident than in *Les Fous de Bassan,* which received the Prix Fémina for 1982. Here the drowned voices and skeletal women of *Le Tombeau des rois* encounter their mutilated, claustrophobic lives in the context of Griffin Creek, a village strongly suggestive of the Gaspé region of Quebec with its descendants of Loyalist settlers of centuries ago. Borrowing both thematically and stylistically from William Faulkner's *The Sound and the Fury* (1929), Hébert's narrative is a circular one, slipping from present-tense interior monologue in both first and, intradiegetically, third persons for the narrative of the Reverend Nicholas Jones, autumn 1982, to a chapter of letters dated summer 1936, from young Stevens Brown to Michael Hotchkiss. Between that chapter and the concluding one–the last letter from Stevens to Hotchkiss in autumn 1982–is played out the central drama of the novel, Stevens's murder of his cousins Nora and Olivia Atkins. In three chapters a series of monologues is cut and spliced together, ranging from the idiot Percival Brown's narrative with its overtones of Faulkner's Benjy to the narratives of the two young girls whose moods, filled with sexual desire, fear, and longing for the sea, dominate life in Griffin Creek.

Feared, anticipated, and in a sense enjoyed, death comes as a climax, a moment of triumph, in this novel filled with violence. As Olivia says at the end of her undated narrative: "Having acquired the right to inhabit the ocean's depth, its darkness, having paid my weight in flesh and bones to the fierce luminous fish, a drop of night in the night, neither moon nor sun can reach me now." Olivia's triumph marks the power of violence to transform the world, a power which is known most intimately by Hébert's female characters who are themselves most fully transformed by its enactment. As Hébert has said of violence, "C'est certainement une volonté de ne pas accepter le monde tel qu'il est, tel qu'on l'a fait. Vouloir le refaire, c'est un geste violent . . ." (It is certainly a will not to accept the world as it is, as one has made it. To wish to remake it is a violent gesture . . .). For Hébert the gothic tradition in fiction has provided a vehicle for exploration of the resources and penalties of strategies of violence within a traditional, patriarchal society.

One of the great writers of modern Quebec, Anne Hébert has created a complex and tightly unified system which transcends particularized settings or milieux for the exploration of the profoundest forces at work in human life. Her refusal to be bound by the concerns of the moment, whether of political or literary fashion, has produced an oeuvre of stylistic diversity and experimentation as well as of thematic daring and moral courage. It constitutes a challenge which has not yet been fully taken up by Quebec critics and a work hardly begun by those in English-speaking Canada.

Interviews:

Michelle Lasnier, "Anne Hébert, la magicienne," *Châtelaine* (April 1963): 28;

Jean-Paul Kauffman, "De Paris, elle réinvente le Québec," *La Presse,* 12 December 1970;

Gisèle Tremblay, "*Kamouraska* ou la fureur de vivre," *Le Devoir,* 12 June 1971, p. 13;

Donald Smith, "Anne Hébert et les eaux troubles de l'imaginaire," *Lettres Québécoises,* 20 (Winter 1980-1981): 65-73;

André Vanasse, "*L'Ecriture et l'ambivalence,* entrevue avec Anne Hébert," *Voix et Images,* 7 (Spring 1982): 441-448.

Bibliography:
Janet Paterson, "Bibliographie d'Anne Hébert," *Voix et Images,* 7 (Spring 1982): 505-510.

References:
Georges Amyot, "Anne Hébert et la renaissance," *Ecrits du Canada Français,* 20 (1965): 233-253;

Ulric Aylwin, "Au pays de la fille maigre: *Les Chambres de bois* d'Anne Hébert," *Cahiers de Sainte-Marie,* 4 (April 1967): 37-50;

Aylwin, "Vers une lecture de l'œuvre d'Anne Hébert," *Barre du Jour,* 2 (Summer 1966): 2-11;

Gerard Béssette, "La Dislocation dans la poésie d'Anne Hébert," *Revue de l'Université d'Ottawa,* 36 (January-March 1966): 50-60;

E. D. Blodgett, "Prisms and Arcs: Structures in Hébert and Munro," in *Figures in a Ground,* edited by Diane Bessai and David Jackel (Saskatchewan: Modern Press, 1978), pp. 99-121;

Denis Bouchard, *Une Lecture d'Anne Hébert* (Montreal: Cahiers du Québec/Hurtubise HMH, 1977);

Marie Couillard, "*Les Enfants du Sabbat* d'Anne Hébert: Un Récit de subversion fantastique," *Incidences IV,* no. 2-3 (May-December 1980): 77-83;

Josette Féral, "Clôture du moi, clôture du texte dans l'œuvre d'Anne Hébert," *Voix et Images,* 1 (December 1975): 241-264;

Gilles Houde, "Les Symboles et la structure mythique du *Torrent,*" *Barre du Jour,* 16 (October-December 1968): 22-46; 21 (September-October 1969): 22-68;

D. G. Jones, "Myth, Frye and Canadian Writers," *Canadian Literature,* 55 (Winter 1973): 7-22;

Eva-Marie Kröller, "La Lampe dans la fenêtre: The Visualization of Québec Fiction," *Canadian Literature,* 88 (Spring 1981): 74-82;

René Lacôte, *Anne Hébert* (Paris: Seghers, 1969);

Hubert Larocque, "Anne Hébert, *Poèmes*: Index, concordance et fréquences," thesis, Université de l'Ottawa, 1973;

Sylvie Leblond, "Le Drame de Kamouraska d'après les documents l'époque," *Cahiers des Dix,* 37 (1972): 239-273;

Albert Le Grand, "Anne Hébert et l'exil au royaume," *Etudes Françaises,* 4 (February 1968): 3-29;

Pierre-Hervé Lemieux, *Entre Songe et parole—Structure du "Tombeau des rois" d'Anne Hébert*

(Ottawa: Editions de l'Université d'Ottawa, 1978);

Jean-Louis Major, *Anne Hébert et le miracle de la parole* (Montreal: Presses de l'Université de Montréal, 1976);

Gilles Marcotte, "Solitude de la poésie," in his *Le Temps des poètes* (Montreal: HMH, 1969), pp. 35-63;

Marcotte, "*Le Tombeau des rois* d'Anne Hébert," in his *Une littérature qui se fait* (Montreal: HMH, 1962), pp. 272-283;

Kathy Mezei, "Anne Hébert: A Pattern Repeated," *Canadian Literature*, 72 (Spring 1977): 29-40;

Pierre Pagé, *Anne Hébert* (Montreal: Fides, 1965);

Suzanne Paradis, *Femme fictive, femme réelle* (Quebec: Garneau, 1966);

Gabrielle Pascal, "Soumission et révolte dans les romans d'Anne Hébert," *Incidences IV*, no. 2-3 (May-December 1980): 59-75;

Patricia Purcell, "The Agonizing Solitude: The Poetry of Anne Hébert," *Canadian Literature*, 10 (Autumn 1961): 51-61;

Guy Robert, *La Poétique du songe* (Montreal: A.G.E.U.M., 1962);

Réjean Robidoux and André Renard, *Le Roman canadien-français du 20e siècle* (Ottawa: Editions de l'Université d'Ottawa, 1966);

Lucille Roy, *Entre la lumière et l'ombre: l'univers poétique d'Anne Hébert* (Sherbrooke, Quebec: Editions Naaman, 1984);

Delbert W. Russell, *Anne Hébert* (Boston: Twayne, 1983);

F. R. Scott, *St.-Denys Garneau and Anne Hébert*, revised edition (Vancouver: Klanak, 1978);

Patricia Smart, "La Poésie d'Anne Hebert: une perspective féminine," *Revue de l'Université d'Ottawa*, 50 (January-March 1980): 62-68;

Serge A. Thériault, *La Quête d'équilibre dans l'oeuvre romanesque d'Anne Hébert* (Hull, Quebec: Editions Asticou, 1980);

Adrien Thério, "La Maison de la belle et du prince ou l'enfer dans l'oeuvre romanesque d'Anne Hébert," *Livres et Auteurs Québécois* (1971): 274-284;

Lorraine Weir, " 'Fauna of Mirrors': The Poetry of Hébert and Atwood," *Ariel*, 10 (July 1979): 99-113;

Paul Wyczynski, "L'Univers poétique d'Anne Hébert," in his *Poésie et symbole* (Montreal: Déom, 1965).

François Hertel
(Rodolphe Dubé)

(31 May 1905-4 October 1985)

Richard Giguère
Université de Sherbrooke

BOOKS: *Les Voix de mon rêve* (Montreal: Albert Lévesque, 1934);

Leur Inquiétude (Montreal: Albert Lévesque, 1936);

L'Enseignement des Belles-Lettres (Montreal: Aux Ateliers de l'Entr'aide, 1939);

Le Beau Risque (Montreal: Bernard Valiquette/ Editions de l'Action Canadienne-Française, 1939);

Mondes chimeriques (Montreal: Bernard Valiquette, 1940);

Axe et parallaxes (Montreal: Editions Variétés, 1941);

Pour un ordre personnaliste (Montreal: Editions de l'Arbre, 1942);

Strophes et catastrophes (Montreal: Editions de l'Arbre, 1943);

Anatole Laplante, curieux homme (Montreal: Editions de l'Arbre, 1944);

Nous ferons l'avenir (Montreal: Fides, 1945);

Cosmos (Montreal: Serge Brousseau, 1945);

Journal d'Anatole Laplante (Montreal: Serge Brousseau, 1947);

Quatorze (Paris: René Debresse, 1948);

Six Femmes, un homme (Paris: Editions de l'Ermite, 1949);

Jeux de mer et de soleil (Paris: Editions de l'Ermitage, 1951);

Mes Naufrages (Paris: Editions de l'Ermite, 1951);

Un Canadien errant (Paris: Editions de l'Ermite, 1953);

Claudine et les écueils, suivi de La Folle (Paris: Editions de l'Ermite, 1954);

Afrique (Paris: Nouvelles Editions de l'Ermite, 1955);

Jérémie et Barabbas (Paris: Editions de la Diaspora Française, 1959);

O Canada, mon pays, mes amours (Paris: Editions de la Diaspora Française, 1959);

Journal philosophique et littéraire (Paris: Editions de la Diaspora Française, 1961);

François Hertel (photograph by Harcourt, Paris; courtesy of Kenneth Landry)

Poèmes européens (Paris: Editions de la Diaspora Française, 1962);

Du séparatisme québécois (Paris: Editions de la Diaspora Française, 1963);

Méditations philosophiques, 1952-1962 (Paris: Editions de la Diaspora Française, 1964);

Anthologie 1934-1964 (Paris: Editions de la Diaspora Française, 1964);

La Morte (Paris: Editions de la Diaspora Française, 1965);

175

Poèmes perdus et retrouvés, anciens et nouveaux
(Paris: Editions de la Diaspora Française,
1966);

Vers une sagesse (Paris: Editions de la Diaspora
Française, 1966);

Louis Préfontaine, apostat (Montreal: Editions du
Jour, 1967);

Cent Ans d'injustice? Un Beau Rêve: Le Canada
(Montreal: Editions du Jour, 1967);

Poèmes d'hier et d'aujourd'hui, 1927-1967 (Paris: Editions de la Diaspora Française, 1967);

Du métalangage (Paris: Editions de la Diaspora
Française, 1968);

*Divagations sur le langage, suivies de quelques
discours aux sourds* (Paris: Editions de la Diaspora Française, 1969);

Tout en faisant le tour du monde (Paris: Editions de
la Diaspora Française, 1971);

Souvenirs, historiettes, réflexions (Paris: Editions de
la Diaspora Française, 1972);

Nouvelles Souvenirs, nouvelles réflexions (Paris: Editions de la Diaspora Française, 1973);

Mystère cosmique et condition humaine (Montreal: La
Presse, 1975);

*Souvenirs et impressions du premier âge, du troisième
âge* (Montreal: Stanké, 1976).

PERIODICAL PUBLICATIONS: "La Littérature
canadienne-française (son rôle dans une
éducation nationale)," *Action Nationale*, 5
(May 1935): 277-289;

"L'Avenir de notre littérature," *Action Nationale*,
16 (October 1937): 128-143;

"Petit Traité du vrai, en soi et au dehors," *Action
Universitaire* (January 1942): 25-26;

"Contemplation et dilettantisme," *Nouvelle Relève*
(April 1942): 391-403;

"Les Évolutions de la mentalité au Canada
français," *Cité libre*, 1 (February 1951):
40-52;

"De Villon à Saint-John Perse," *Cahiers de l'Académie Canadienne-Française*, no. 11 (1967):
16-28.

The active career of François Hertel, poet,
novelist, essayist, storyteller, philosopher, moralist, aesthete, and literary critic, spanned a period
of some fifty years. It is especially as a poet, essayist, and philosopher that Hertel searched for
truth without ever finding it, first through his religious "vocation" and later through his teaching
and writing. A raiser of consciousness, a humanist in the broad sense of the term, a writer full of

spirit and often of rancor, he stirred up intense reactions in the Quebec of the "great darkness."

Hertel, who signed all of his books with this
pseudonym, was born Rodolphe Dubé in 1905
in Rivière-Ouelle, a village 120 kilometers
downriver from Quebec City. The son of Joseph
and Alice Lévesque Dubé, he studied at the
Collège de Sainte-Anne-de-la-Pocatière and at
the Séminaire de Trois-Rivières; when he was
twenty he joined the Jesuits at the Scolasticat de
l'Immaculée Conception in Montreal, where he
embarked on a lengthy course of studies. He
began to write verse, and in 1932 submitted a
few poems to a contest under the pseudonym of
François Hertel, the name of a soldier and hero
(1642-1722) from French-Canadian history, and
had his first poems published. After taking his *li-
cence* in philosophy and theology, he was ordained a priest in 1938, subsequently finishing
his doctorate and teaching his favorite subjects—
literature, history, and philosophy—at the *collèges*
of Jean-de-Brébeuf, Sainte-Marie, and André
Grasset in Montreal. Later he taught at the
Collège des Jésuites in Sudbury, a city in northern Ontario, where he founded a newspaper,
L'Ami du Peuple. In 1943 he became a secular
priest and contributed to various Montreal periodicals, and in 1946-1947 was the director of
Amérique Française, one of the most highly regarded literary and cultural reviews of postwar
Quebec.

Hertel's private life and teaching career
reached a turning point when, shaken by a religious crisis in 1946, the former Jesuit obtained
permission for a gradual return to lay life. Students in the *collèges*, in whom he had aroused a
lively admiration, considered him their master;
he was simultaneously a learned man and a mentor, a critic of authority, a scathing iconoclast, an
advocate of risk and daring, a spirit in continual
ferment. This admiration did not extend to a certain elite, who considered him a danger to the
state. Feeling suffocated by religious orthodoxy,
cultural stagnation, and the social and political
conservatism then prevalent in Quebec, Hertel
left Montreal for Paris in 1947, and in 1949 he
began a life of exile in France. In Paris he was
the director of an art review, *Rythmes et Couleurs*,
and of a publishing house, La Diaspora
Française, through which he published most of
his works. During the 1950s, 1960s, and 1970s
Hertel continued writing and publishing, giving
courses and lectures throughout France and at
the same time contributing to periodicals in Que-

bec. From time to time he made conspicuous forays back to his native land.

Hertel's literary output has been prolific: some forty published books, to say nothing of lectures, articles, and book reviews which appeared in newspapers and magazines, prefaces, and letters. In one of his last essays, Hertel suggested that his work be divided into six parts: the dogmatic period (before 1947), the period of doubt (around 1947), the period of the roving Canadian (the 1950s), the period of justification (the 1950s and the beginning of the 1960s), the period of theories of language (from 1964), and the period of return (the 1970s).

Emphasis must first of all be laid on the writings of Hertel as a philosopher and essayist, a dozen books in which he developed the principal ideas of his vision of the world. Although Hertel the philosopher is in evidence throughout these works, there are only a few important books in which he took a stand when confronted with the great tendencies of his day–the atheistic existentialism of Jean-Paul Sartre, the Christian existentialism of Gabriel Marcel, the personalism of Emmanuel Mounier. For Hertel philosophy implied a spirit of research, the very opposite of attachment to any one system, and this spirit involved the rejection of St. Thomas Aquinas and of Aristotelianism as well as of any kind of dogmatism. In a 1967 article in *Livres et Auteurs Canadiens* Jean Tétreau clearly traced the evolution of the master's thought and all that Hertel owed to the great philosophers, from Descartes, Pascal, Hegel, Kant, Spinoza, and Maine de Biran to those of the present day. All things considered, Hertel sought an original explanation of the universe, of matter, of mind, and of time, all of which was viewed as "le seul en soi possible." For him there was only a "constantly moving and ascending reality, the eternal dynamism of the indefectible cosmos."

Theology may seem like only an accessory to Hertel's work as a philosopher, but it constitutes nonetheless the epistemological basis of his work. Even after the crisis of 1946, the central figure of God is omnipresent, as much in Hertel's poetry and novels as in his essays and treatises. In a 1976 article in *Voix et Images* Gilles Thérien explained that from the *Journal d'Anatole Laplante* (1947) to *Mystère cosmique et condition humaine* (1975) the apostate rubs out and progressively effaces any trace of God, but the concept of God remains. The new truth of the "smiling nihilist" is but the underside, that part of his first credo to which he has given a relative meaning. The philosopher continues to believe in a kind of superior wisdom in man, in the Symbol with a capital S, in the Cosmos with a capital C.

Hertel the essayist was interested in the social order and politics as much as he was in aesthetics or in the philosophy of language, and he never hesitated to become involved in the discussions of the hour. As an anticapitalist he defended, in his *Pour un ordre personnaliste* (1942), a social corporatism and a personalism anchored in the reality of 1940s Quebec. In his inquiries into the restlessness of the youth of the 1930s, which he discussed in *Leur Inquiétude* (1936), he followed Jacques Maritain and Nicholas Berdiaeff in denouncing the tyranny of the machine, the death of the individual, and the myth of rationalism, and took a stand on the problems of the Great Depression, of bilingualism, of Laurentian regionalism, and of the economic inferiority of Quebec. From the 1930s Hertel declared himself in favor of a Laurentian State independent of the rest of the Dominion of Canada, a position based on the nationalist ideology of Canon Lionel-Adolphe Groulx's conception of the history and destiny of Quebec. This does not mean that Hertel accepted Quebec society as it was–quite the contrary, as is evident from his virulent poem "Au pays du Québec" written in 1939–and he continued to defend his position in *Nous ferons l'avenir* (1945), *Du séparatisme québécois* (1963), and *Cent Ans d'injustice?* (1967).

In his essays on language–*Du métalangage* (1968) and *Divagations sur le langage* (1969)–Hertel the aesthete philosophizes on a kind of ontology of representation, the "méta" of *métalangage* being that which stands at the top of the scale of values. The hierarchy of spiritual values is taken up even at this level–at the bottom lies poor objective language, while symbolic language stands at the top. The signifiers or the acoustic images (*signifiants*) tend toward an ultimate, mysterious, ineffable concept or "thing meant" (*signifié*), which is called the Cosmos. Hertel never freed himself of a spiritualistic vision of the world and of an essentially humanistic culture as represented by the Bible, the Greek and Roman traditions, the French classics, and the works of world-renowned poets.

It is owing especially to his poetry that Hertel's work is included in anthologies of Quebec literature. In forty years he produced a dozen collections, more than half of which appeared between 1937 and 1951. These poems are bittersweet, lyrical, ironic, vindictive, and at times choleric; sometimes they are descriptive, sometimes philosophical, but always speculative. Hertel included some one hundred titles in *Poèmes d'hier et d'aujourd'hui, 1927-1967* (1967), "a definitive selection . . . of those poetic writings of mine which most deserve to be appreciated."

This volume comprises meditative and romantic selections from the first collections as well as religious poems of the 1940s, metrical verses of *Les Voix de mon rêve* (1934), as well as free verse, psalmlike verses reminiscent of Paul Claudel, and lyrical prose of *Axe et parallaxes* (1941) and *Strophes et catastrophes* (1943). These poems must be read in the context of the spiritual preoccupations that characterize Quebec poetry written during the World War II years, as evidenced in the works of Rina Lasnier, Roger Brien, and Gustave Lamarche. But while certain poets–Alain Grandbois and Simone Routier, for example–were coming home from Europe and others (the Automatistes and later the members of the Hexagone group) were tending to root themselves more deeply in Quebec, toward the end of the decade Hertel took the road to exile. His poetry went into exile, too, so to speak. It became either philosophical, but often garrulous, too intellectual, too closely reasoned, or religious and metaphysical, imitating Claudel's verse but with dubious results. Still, there are some important poems dating from this period, such as "Ballade sur mon âme," "Au pays du Québec," and "Prose pour un jeune poète."

The 1950s and 1960s marked Hertel's return to classical verse and to the more intimate voice of the 1930s, but in a language more under control and stripped of an excess of lyrical effusiveness. From the five collections which appeared from 1951 to 1967, all anthologies of Quebec poetry include poems from *Mes Naufrages* (1951; "Le Gai Naufrage," "Le Chant de l'exilé"), the most personal and agonizing of Hertel's books of verse.

As a novelist and storyteller Hertel has been forgotten. There is no doubt that in his fictional works meditation and dialogue are more important than polished structures; although the characters are rich and varied, in the last analysis Hertel is more of a moralist and philosopher than a fiction writer. It is nonetheless true that *Le Beau Risque* (1939), *Anatole Laplante, curieux homme* (1944), and *Journal d'Anatole Laplante* are biting satires on the intellectual milieu of the time. They are books which take a stand, very often in

Cover, with illustration by Alfred Pellan, for one of Hertel's satires of Quebecois intellectual life (courtesy of Kenneth Landry)

a peremptory manner, and consequently they fostered lively partisanship and attracted sympathizers, but they also created enemies for Hertel. The collections *Six Femmes, un homme* (1949) and *Jérémie et Barabbas* (1959) reveal that Hertel's technique as a storyteller surpasses his ability as a novelist.

The autobiographical narrative, reportage, and play writing are lesser genres to which Hertel devoted himself more or less successfully in *Un Canadien errant* (1953), *Afrique* (1955), and *La Morte* (1965), respectively. The recollections, anecdotes, and reflections–*Souvenirs, historiettes, réflexions* (1972), *Nouvelles Souvenirs, nouvelles réflexions* (1973), and *Souvenirs et impressions du premier âge, du troisième âge* (1976)–of the 1970s shed light on the history of Quebec society during the 1930s and 1940s.

In his 1975 book *De l'Ordre et de l'Aventure* Jacques Blais reminds his readers that certain of Hertel's books were well received in their day by such friends and followers as Jean-Charles Falardeau, Gabriel Lussier, and Gustave Lamarche. The poet Alfred DesRochers wrote in 1943 that the author of *Strophes et catastrophes* "possesses one of the keenest and most fertile minds of his generation" and that his works demonstrate "a perpetual and ever-changing crisis in his thinking." But this unpredictable and unmethodical temperament was also capable of disturbing minds unaccustomed to such a character. From 1937 to 1946 Hertel was the target, as were others, of several attacks in the newspaper *Le Jour*, whose editor, Jean-Charles Harvey, saw in him "a brilliant but superficial mind"; Sébastien Melmoch spoke of "our national swaggerer," while Pierre Gélinas nicknamed him "Father Manifeste Montretout," who made himself "the apostle of his own person and of his vanity."

During the 1950s the critic Jean Ethier-Blais remained one of the few admirers of Hertel in Quebec and rose to his defense in his series of articles on the French-Canadian exiles Marcel Dugas, Paul-Émile Borduas, and Hertel. But the eulogy of the master by one of his former disciples is too extravagant to be convincing. Beginning in the middle of the 1960s, handbooks on "French literature in Quebec" by Pierre de Grandpré and his collaborators commented extensively on Hertel's writings, but studies in the 1960s, 1970s, and 1980s by Jean Tétreau, Robert Giroux, and Gilles Thérien, dealing with aspects of Hertel's work as poet or essayist, are more comprehensive and better documented.

Despite the fact that Hertel was a prolific writer, and one whose works are relevant to the Quebecois tradition, the former Jesuit who lived in exile in France for more than thirty years is today known only to historians of Quebec literature and to those friends or former pupils of Hertel who are still living. An ironic twist is that today's college and university students, members of the social group for whom he was a mentor during the 1930s and 1940s, are not aware of his name.

References:

Jacques Blais, "Le Lyrisme religieux et François Hertel," in his *De l'Ordre et de l'Aventure, La Poésie au Québec, 1934-1944* (Quebec: Presses de l'Université Laval, 1975), pp. 231, 239-252;

Jean Ethier-Blais, "François Hertel: Le Train sifflera deux fois," in his *Signets II* (Montreal: Cercle du Livre de France, 1967), pp. 159-174;

Ethier-Blais, "Introduction à la poésie de François Hertel," *Action Nationale*, 29 (March 1947): 332-346;

Robert Giroux, "François Hertel: Le Surhomme noyé," *Présence Francophone*, no. 6 (1973): 29-43;

Jean Tétreau, "François Hertel: Une Pensée, un style, un art de vivre," *Livres et Auteurs Canadiens, 1966* (Montreal: Jumonville, 1967), pp. 204-208;

Tétreau, *Hertel: L'Homme et l'oeuvre* (Montreal: Pierre Tisseyre, 1986);

Gilles Thérien, "François Hertel, curieux homme," *Voix et Images*, 2 (September 1976): 47-59.

Paul Hiebert

(17 July 1892-6 September 1987)

Louis K. MacKendrick
University of Windsor

BOOKS: *Sarah Binks* (Toronto: Oxford University Press, 1947; London: Oxford University Press, 1947);

Tower in Siloam (Toronto: McClelland & Stewart, 1966);

Willows Revisited (Toronto: McClelland & Stewart, 1967);

Doubting Castle: A Spiritual Autobiography (Winnipeg: Queenston, 1976);

For the Birds (Winnipeg: Peguis, 1980);

Not as the Scribes (Winnipeg: Queenston, 1984).

PERIODICAL PUBLICATIONS: "The Comic Spirit at Forty Below Zero," *Mosaic*, 3 (Spring 1970): 58-68;

"Avenues of Research Suggested by the Fletchers Castoria Box," *Canadian Literature*, 100 (Spring 1984): 139-146.

Paul Gerhardt Hiebert is considered one of Canada's outstanding humorists largely on the strength of one masterful book, *Sarah Binks* (1947). His mock-biography of "the Sweet Songstress of Saskatchewan" stands as a touchstone in Canadian letters for other exercises in the genre, a model of literary burlesque that reflects the essential generosity, geniality, and wry self-examination of the national humor.

Hiebert was born in Pilot Mound, Manitoba, of Russian Mennonite-cum-Methodist immigrants, John and Maria Penner Hiebert. He grew up in small prairie towns with such varied employment as farm worker, cub reporter, and teacher. He received a B.A. in philosophy from the University of Manitoba (1916) and an M.A. in Gothic and Teutonic philology from the University of Toronto (1917). He graduated with an M.Sc. in physics and chemistry from McGill University in 1921, where he also earned a Ph.D. in Chemistry (1924), winning a Governor General's Medal for science. Thereafter, Hiebert, who married Dorothea Cunningham in 1926, was professor of chemistry at the University of Manitoba until his retirement to Carman, Manitoba, in 1953. In

1948 he was the second recipient of the Stephen Leacock Medal for Humour for *Sarah Binks*, and he was president of the Canadian Authors' Association in 1948-1949.

While he continued until late in life to write humorous sketches, he turned increasingly to writing serious meditations on the life of the spirit. These serious commentaries attracted less attention than the works of "Binksiana," but despite his retreat from the public eye following retirement, Hiebert (and Sarah) continued to attract a coterie of enthusiasts. *Sarah Binks* had inspired a CBC radio adaptation in 1948, shortly after the book's publication, and a musical stage version in 1968. Sarah re-emerged in 1981 when actor Eric Donkin mounted a one-man stage adaptation of some of the book's scenes, a performance which traveled throughout Canada: it was called "The Wonderful World of Sarah Binks, Sweet Songstress of Saskatchewan." Donkin assumed the identity of "Rosalind Drool," one of the handfuls of ostensible Binks biographers whose books precede the "authoritative" *Sarah Binks;* Ms. Drool provided both an inimitable (self-serving) version of Sarah's life and an indescribable, intentionally overwrought reading of Sarah's verse. One or two further satiric essays followed–most notably "Avenues of Research Suggested by the Fletchers Castoria Box," which appeared in the *Canadian Literature* anniversary issue of 1984; this essay plays once again with academia, bemusedly reflecting on the academic possibilities in so-called newly discovered Binksiana, as a reaction to the actual academic interest then being generated in the work of Hiebert. This was one of his last publications; he died in Winnipeg on 6 September 1987.

Sarah Binks is a burlesque of literary biography and a satire of literary critics and criticism, contrasting a fervent hagiographic manner with a subject of low degree. It is not clear if Hiebert had particular targets in mind. One of the earliest Binks poems appears, with no indication that it is to be read as a parody, in an issue of the *Canadian Poetry Magazine*, the outlet of the Canadian

Dust jacket for Hiebert's sequel to Sarah Binks

Authors' Association. But by the time the book appeared–it is cast both as anthology and biography, using the verse to interpret the life and vice versa–it was clear that Hiebert's targets included provincialism, presumptiveness, sentimentality, academic enthusiasm (too often clouded by local pride), academic method (too often cluttered by attention to minutiae at the expense of common sense), and the "simple" failure to distinguish between "good" and "bad" writing. That Sarah wrote "good" bad verse perhaps explains why some readers initially thought Sarah was a real Saskatchewan poet. That Hiebert should have relied for humorous effect on numerous stereotypes of region, gender, and ethnicity–and that he should himself have presumed to be able to distinguish aesthetic values–perhaps also explains why the book has not enjoyed uniform appeal. Sometimes it cuts close to reality. In its day it was one of several signs of resistance to critical and literary romanticism. Throughout the book, moreover, tone is of paramount importance.

Hiebert (and his persona-biographer) follow

a timeworn biographical format. He records the poet's rural childhood, takes account of her neighbors (including one Matilda Schwantzhacker, the "least cross-eyed of the thirteen Schwantzhacker sisters"), seeks influences on Sarah's work and finds them in a hired man and a pet and a climactic trip to Regina with a traveling salesman, after which her work is divided into the pre-Regina and post-Regina periods (or, as the text has it, the "P.R. and P.R. periods respectively"). Hiebert's ironies cut in several directions. There follows Sarah's "Dark Hour," in turn followed by "Recognition and Success," for she wins a horse thermometer as a poetry prize for a contest run by *Horsebreeder's Gazette*. The prize proves her downfall, for she dies an early death, at age twenty-three, when she bites through the thermometer and succumbs to mercury poisoning. What sustains the comedy is the disparity between such events and the tonal seriousness with which the biographer treats them. Throughout he seeks significance; he includes an authoritative "Index of

Cover for the 1980 collection Hiebert describes in the preface as "chicken feed"–"the odds and ends of writing that clutter up the place, those bits and pieces which accumulate much like leftovers in a refrigerator after a series of meals"

Poems," provides footnotes (often, true to type, pettishly disparaging the slanted attention of other Binksian scholars, including the fulsome Rosalind Drool), and cites literary, geological, and agricultural sources as proof of his conclusions. But the conclusions are circuitous and sententious ("All geology is founded on a rock"), exposing the degree to which much biographical and critical interpretation relies on cliché. The biographer also "proves" his points by repeatedly quoting from Sarah's verse.

The verse is one of Hiebert's greatest comic achievements. Much of it is occasional, a way of constituting an argumentum ad hominem, so that the "Grizzlykick Symphony" hyperbolically celebrates Matilda Schwantzhacker's liaison with a young man, and "Hi, Sooky, Ho, Sooky" is a mock pig call. Hiebert's sense of the momentum of banality is exquisite; rhetorically, the rhymes

leave their best ironic deflation to the end. A stanza from "How Prone is Man" is characteristic:

> Anon to quit his downy bed,
> And greet the morn with drooping mush,
> To scan with cross-eyed gleam in the head,
> The babbling birdlet on the bush.

Paradoxically, the cleverness sometimes almost lifts these rhymes to the legitimately lyric, as in "Spreading Time" or the last (again deflationary) stanza of "The Farmer and the Farmer's Wife":

> And when at night the chores are done,
> And hand in hand they sit and beam,
> He helps himself to applejack,
> And she to Paris Green.

This last is the kind of poem, the biographer avers, that shows Sarah's development beyond her early verse. The "unsureness" of the early "The Genius," the biographer affirms, shows up in lines such as these:

> . . . in my little book,
>   I write verses,
> Sometimes they don't rhyme–
>   Curses!

In "The Parson's Patch," he laconically goes on, "her rhyming of 'visible' with 'contemplation' is not in the best traditions of Saskatchewan literature." Nor are her translations from the German, we are told, always as faithful as they might have been, as when she translates "Die Lorelei" as "The Laurel's egg"–"instead of 'Laura's eye.'" And although her "translation of the river Rhein as the river 'Clean' is masterful," the biographer hastily adds, she sometimes "loses, if not the actual content, at least some of the spirit of the original." This sense of authorial understatement further guides the biographer when he comes to weigh Sarah's ostensibly greatest work, *Up From the Magma*. Daunted by it, he at least measures it–it is a cubic foot of verse–but deferentially he leaves interpretation open: it is "still the unopened treasure house of Saskatchewan's literature." And so, despite the comedic cleverness of so much of the doggerel, the reader's interest turns to the burlesque of the biographical form.

The authorial persona, who is fond of such terms as "genius," "flawless gems," and "classical lyric," is often self-congratulatory, as well as given to making stale observations on the poetic nature. Hiebert's exposure of inflated metaphor is unsparing; the biographer is a romantic and blinkered enthusiast whose proneness to hyperbole is a particular delight. All the clichés of critical sentimentality are present in the biographer's rhapsodic approach, and his language alone is one of Hiebert's substantial comic achievements: "Already in this moment of Sarah's greatest triumph Death had marked that shining mark for its own soon aim and the daisies were burgeoning restlessly, nay, impatiently in the sod."

Willows Revisited (1967) is a sequel to *Sarah Binks*, a book designed to parody the numerous national and local centennials that Canada was undergoing in that decade. Ostensibly a study and "history" of Saskatchewan's fictitious School of Seven–a not-so-sly dig at the real-life Group of Seven who had claimed since the 1920s to be Canada's national school of painting–the book examines the work of the seven poets who gather to celebrate the province's semicentennial and the quarter centennial of Sarah Binks's passing. All are unstinting in their praise for Sarah, each of them professes a particular literary creed that differs from hers, and each gives way to none of the others in ambition or ego. Hence Hiebert's seven literary-biographical portraits are engagingly high spirited, and though the book never won the affectionate following that *Sarah Binks* did, it nonetheless contains some brilliant parodic sections, including the transcript of the school's attempt to devise a new and acceptable national anthem. Many sacred Canadian oxen are gored here, including regionalism, anti-Americanism, and multiculturalism, but the results are finally uneven. The School, characterized by its use of bovine symbolism and the quality of "innerness," includes John Swivel ("the Great Dean of Saskatchewan letters"), a former tombstone salesman whose verse is preoccupied with life's vanity; Bessie Udderton, the buoyant poet who faces the total reality of food; Professor Balaam Bedfellow, a "bird-poet" and primitivist who contradictorily writes tortured verse; and Osiris Jones-Jones, Saskatchewan's laureate and impartial civil servant. None of these individual characters is as sharply drawn as Sarah, nor is the satire as focused, nor the doggerel as clever.

While occasional subsequent essays demonstrate Hiebert's unwearied satiric spirit, the same caveat, unevenness, applies to his late collection of radio and television talks, poems, essays (Hiebert refers to them as "chicken feed") entitled *For the Birds* (1980). Many of these pieces are

nostalgic. Some are Binksian, such as "The Snearth in Saskatchewan Literature" and several ludicrous items on academic activities and personnel at St. Midget's College. Some–"Flections and Reflections on Literature and Ham," for example–are autobiographical. Perhaps the best works in the collection are "Out Where the West Begins," which parodies a Western, and "Diet and Doctrine," on fowl suppers in prairie parishes. "What Makes People Laugh?" is a bemused reflection on the way science and academia analyze humor but still miss essential points. A radio talk, this reflection ends seriously: "Laughter, the psychiatrists tell us, is an escape. It is an escape from an obsession with ourselves."

Such a sentiment also underlies Hiebert's other writings, a trio of books about the place of human beings in the universe. *Tower in Siloam* (1966), *Doubting Castle* (1976), and *Not as the Scribes* (1984) are the personal testament of Hiebert the scientist addressing himself to God, persuasively reconciling the spiritual with his professional disciplines. *Tower in Siloam* argues for "a single underlying reality" in the universe, a purposive rather than a deterministic creation whose direction has been toward the evolution of human personality. *Doubting Castle* is, in Hiebert's words, admittedly "an altogether fundamentalist book in its insistence upon the belief in God." Hiebert's attention to autobiographical topics in "Frontier Religion" and "College Days" leads to his discussions entitled "The Religious Implications of Science" and "Divine Justice"; he also treats issues of evil, truth, will, and faith. In this book the author harmonizes characteristically his personal systems of religion, philosophy, and science with warmth and unapologetic commitment. In *Not as the Scribes* Hiebert continues his fundamental emphasis on a loving, not a regulatory, deity, and on Christian goodwill, again reflecting his own human generosity toward matters of belief.

Yet Hiebert is best known for *Sarah Binks*; it remains a profusion of unremitting satiric and comic pleasures. The book has assumed the status of a classic in Canadian humor, for its unwithered wit rises above slapstick and banal jokery, and it has the rare virtue of constant contemporaneity.

References:
Bob Haverluck, " 'Can Any Good Thing Come From Nazareth?': Comedy in the Prairie Hin-

terland," *Journal of Canadian Studies*, 18 (Summer 1983): 27-41;

Gerald A. Noonan, "Incongruity and Nostalgia in Sarah Binks," *Studies in Canadian Literature*, 3 (Summer 1978): 264-273;

Henry P. Schreiber, "A Chemist Among the Literati," *Chemistry in Canada*, 1 (December 1949): 19-22;

Reynold Siemens, "Reactions to Sarah," *Canadian Literature*, 75 (Winter 1977): 111-115;

Siemens, "Sarah Binks in Retrospect: A Conversation with Paul Hiebert," *Journal of Canadian Fiction*, 19 (1977): 65-76;

A. L. Wheeler, "Up From the Magma and Back Again with Paul Hiebert," *Manitoba Arts Review*, 6 (Spring 1948): 3-14;

Lloyd Wheeler, Introduction to Hiebert's *Sarah Binks* (Toronto: McClelland & Stewart, 1964), pp. vii-xiii.

Papers:
Paul Hiebert's papers are at the University of Saskatchewan in Saskatoon.

Grace Irwin
(14 July 1907-   )

Barbara Pell
Trinity Western University

BOOKS: *Least of All Saints* (Toronto: McClelland & Stewart, 1952; Grand Rapids: Eerdmans, 1957; London: Paternoster Press, 1960);

Andrew Connington (Toronto: McClelland & Stewart, 1954; Grand Rapids: Eerdmans, 1958; London: Paternoster Press, 1960);

In Little Place (Toronto: Ryerson, 1959; Grand Rapids: Eerdmans, 1959);

Servant of Slaves (Toronto: McClelland & Stewart, 1961; Grand Rapids: Eerdmans, 1961; London & Edinburgh: Oliphants, 1963);

Contend with Horses (Grand Rapids: Eerdmans, 1968; Toronto: McClelland & Stewart, 1969);

The Seventh Earl (Toronto: McClelland & Stewart, 1976; Grand Rapids: Eerdmans, 1976);

Three Lives in Mine (Toronto: Irwin, 1986).

OTHER: B. L. Kurth and M. McManns, eds., *Little Songs for Little People*, includes contributions by Irwin (Toronto: Oxford University Press, 1942);

H. Harold Kent, *An Architect Preaches*, edited by Irwin (London: Independent Press, 1957);

Kent, *The House of Christmas*, edited by Irwin (Grand Rapids: Eerdmans, 1964);

Kent, *Job Our Contemporary*, edited by Irwin (Grand Rapids: Eerdmans, 1967);

Grace Irwin (photograph by Peter Redman)

Kent, *The Unveiling of Jesus Christ: A Companion to the Apocalypse,* edited by Irwin (Toronto: Welch, 1978).

For most of the past thirty-five years Grace Irwin has combined a full-time professional life as teacher and pastor with the steady production of Christian novels and biographies. She combines deep conviction with common sense and competent writing. While not in the mainstream of Canadian literature, she has been a popular writer among evangelicals.

Irwin was born in Toronto, the youngest of five children of John and Martha Fortune Irwin. Her father was a Methodist lay preacher, an immigrant from Northern Ireland who became a member of the Toronto Morality Department. His forced demotion (over the issue of theater policing) led to straitened circumstances for the family, and his sense of failure precipitated his death at age sixty-five when Irwin was ten. Despite her youth, Irwin was deeply influenced by her affection and respect for her father. She has suggested that this attachment has contributed to her unmarried state; it has certainly been reflected in her books. She gives as her lifelong guide his creed: "It's not a question of going to Hell or not going to Hell. What we have to do is to find out what is right for us and do it no matter what the rest of the world does." He was a widower when he married Martha Fortune, a schoolteacher ten years his junior; she was a strong, intelligent, and resourceful woman who provided for her family after her husband's death and lived with her younger daughter until her own death in 1954.

Irwin grew up in an affectionate family; her closest siblings were her sister Irene (later Mrs. W. H. Clarke) and her youngest brother John. He was a forestry engineer who later (with his brother-in-law) founded the distinguished Canadian publishing company Clarke, Irwin (and later his own company, The Book Society of Canada, now Irwin Publishing), of which Grace Irwin is a director. She was educated at Howard School and Parkdale Collegiate Institute in Toronto, and took her B.A. with honors in classics at Victoria College, University of Toronto (1929), a College of Education specialist certificate (1930), and an M.A. in Greek at the University of Toronto (1932). Irwin was a charismatic teacher of Latin, Greek, English, and ancient history at Humberside Collegiate Institute, Toronto, from 1931 to 1969, and the head of the classics department

for the last twenty-seven of those years. From 1952 to 1956 she also served on the University of Toronto senate.

After her retirement Irwin became a "lecturer-at-large," and, in 1974, copastor of her church, Emmanuel (Christian Congregational); she was ordained in 1979 and has been the pastor there since 1980. One of the most important influences in her life was the original pastor of this church, H. Harold Kent, a gifted preacher, principled but unpolitical, who had been hounded out of his former church. Irwin was, in her words, "from 1940 till his death in 1972 . . . an admirer, supporter, promoter, frequent car-driver, member of his then congregation, charter member and deacon of his new congregation, editor of his books of sermons, friend."

Irwin spent two months at the British School of Archaeology in Athens in 1959, and several periods researching her biographies in London, England, in 1958-1959, 1969, and 1971. But, for the most part, her life has been (in her words) "spectacularly unspectacular." She has lived all her life in Toronto (for the past sixty-seven years at the same address), spending her summers since 1926, apart from travel, at her cottage on Loon Echo Island, Haliburton. She "attended one public school, one high school, one university" and spent her teaching career in one school. The church which she now pastors she helped to found in 1953. It is against this extraordinary (for contemporary times) background of stability and security that Irwin has highlighted her fictional dramas of the change and confusion of modern values in religion, education, and society. At times, consequently, she sounds like "a voice crying in the wilderness."

Least of All Saints (1952) is the best, and best known, of Irwin's four novels, possibly because of the literary distancing between the author and her protagonist, an objectivity which she did not maintain in her later novels. It is the story of Andrew Connington, a cynical agnostic who enters the ministry in order to exercise his considerable intellectual and rhetorical gifts. Successful and admired in a prestigious church on the strength of his deception, he nevertheless is challenged by several spiritual crises and the influence of his devout fiancée and finally comes to genuine faith. The hero's intellectual tensions, the love story, and his final conversion are convincing and unsentimental. Irwin also vividly re-creates the setting of Toronto in the 1920s. The novel, published fifteen years after its inception and after many pub-

Dust jacket for Irwin's 1954 novel about a minister in conflict with the members of his wealthy congregation

lishers' rejections, made Irwin an instant "best-seller" and popular lecturer.

The sequel, *Andrew Connington* (1954), which Irwin wrote over five summer vacations, depicts the converted evangelical in conflict now with the worldly, nominal Christians of his wealthy congregation. His dismissal from his church and his temporary estrangement from his wife are redeemed in their final reconciliation, his strengthened faith, and a new ministry in a poor interdenominational "mission" on the outskirts of Toronto. The church politics are realistic, but the treatment of the hero has become more romantic.

Fourteen years later Irwin concluded the Connington trilogy in *Contend with Horses* (1968). The minister, twenty-four years after part two and six years after his wife's tragic death, is coping with a number of problems: a rebellious son who wants to marry a Roman Catholic; a supportive and stable church which is, however, neither prosperous nor prestigious; an attractive, wealthy widow who is in love with him (but settles for editing his books of sermons); and a corrupt lawyer who contrives the death of an elderly client and who is miraculously killed by a heart attack. The

Christian themes are again presented clearly, intelligently, and with deep conviction, although the narrative is rather fragmented. But the romantic apotheosis of the hero, modeled in the last two books on H. Harold Kent, weakens the objective realism of the fiction.

The same problem characterizes *In Little Place* (1959), ostensibly a "novel-documentary," but really a barely disguised autobiography of Irwin's life as a devout Christian, a contented spinster, and a committed classics teacher—all outmoded by the radical changes in modern society and education, the loss of, in Irwin's phrase, "the once familiar Christian and classic values." Irwin gives a powerful, courageous, and articulate defense of an unfashionable position, but as fiction, the novel sinks beneath the weight of righteous didacticism.

Irwin's talents find their natural genre in her "biographical novel" of John Newton, *Servant of Slaves*. Praised as "the best historical novel" of 1961 by the *University of Toronto Quarterly* "Letters in Canada" review, it is a well-researched and dramatized composite of the many lives of Newton: sailor, womanizer, freethinker, slave trader, convert, theologian, hymn-writer, and husband.

July 18, 1955. 11 a.m.

The President's guests had gradually but inevitably gravitated towards the point of interest. A few couples still stayed *along* the main *gallery* or in one of the Chinese galleries at the *floor* end. A Half a *dozen intimates chatted with* Dr. Ransom and his *party* family chatted cordially with half a dozen intimates *at* the top of the shallow steps where they had *stood* formed the "receiving line". Not far away some others, late diners or constitutionally ascetic, displayed no interest in food. *But for almost a hundred* the table *in the central of the sunk beneath the square* *forelights* But it was ten-thirty, the smell of steamy coffee *filled* the air and *from* the first ring of groups decently *separated* like the *innermost* ripple *from* a stone *thrown* in water, almost a hundred people *shifted* *irregularly* concentric around the *great long spread* table, *not* beneath the square *softly* skylight.

Deliberately detached and trying not to draw attention by her detachment, Aran *Wang* stood watching them. She looked as though she *was trying to* find a particular *if* had come up the steps and slightly away from the throng in order to search for some particular person, *as though* meantime she was *happily* would be *looking* for her; as

Silence

First page of the manuscript for Irwin's "novel-documentary" In Little Place *(by permission of the author)*

The plot (especially the account of his youthful exploits at sea) is fascinating and suspenseful; the characterization psychologically realistic; the eighteenth-century English background carefully documented; the whole book (in the words of the *UTQ* writer) "conscientious, honest, and decent." If *The Seventh Earl* (1976), another "dramatized biography," is not quite as successful in condensing the eighty-four years of the life of the Earl of Shaftesbury into dramatized vignettes, part of the problem lies in the intransigence and complexity of the material—political intrigue and socioeconomic reform in nineteenth-century England. Shaftesbury is an idealized hero, but the conditions he tried to reform are portrayed in all their sordid reality.

In *Three Lives in Mine* (1986) Irwin writes a "protest" against the "feminist" hostility toward "the Male Fact." She intertwines her autobiography with the lives of the three men who most influenced her: her father, her brother, and her friend H. Harold Kent. Their biographies are, at times, tedious, didactic, and characterized by the Irwin style, with a diction and convoluted sentence structure indebted to the classics teacher. But the book is enlivened by the voice of this remarkable woman—resolutely unfashionable and opinionated, occasionally naive ("The tag of religious novelist surprised me."), but joyfully independent and optimistic and gratefully committed to her faith.

Watson Kirkconnell
(16 May 1895-26 February 1977)

W. H. New
University of British Columbia

SELECTED BOOKS: *Kapuskasing: An Historical Sketch* (Kingston, Ontario: Jackson Press, 1921);

Victoria County Centennial History (Lindsay, Ontario: Watchman-Warder Press, 1921); revised, with the assistance of Frankie L. MacArthur, as *County of Victoria Centennial History* (Lindsay, Ontario: Victoria County Council, 1967);

International Aspects of Unemployment (London: Allen & Unwin, 1923; New York: Holt, 1923);

The European Heritage: A Synopsis of European Literary Achievement (London: Dent, 1930);

The Tide of Life and Other Poems (Ottawa: Ariston, 1930);

The Eternal Quest (Winnipeg: Columbia Press, 1934);

A Canadian Headmaster: A Brief Biography of Thomas Allison Kirkconnell, 1862-1934 (Toronto: Clarke, Irwin, 1935);

Golden Jubilee of Wesley College (Winnipeg: Columbia Press, 1938);

Canada, Europe, and Hitler (Toronto: Oxford University Press, 1939);

Titus the Toad (London & Toronto: Oxford University Press, 1939);

The Flying Bull and Other Tales (Toronto: Oxford University Press, 1940);

The Ukrainian Canadians and the War (Toronto: Oxford University Press, 1940);

Canadians All: A Primer of Canadian National Unity (Ottawa: Director of Public Information, 1941; revised, 1941);

Twilight of Liberty (Toronto: Oxford University Press, 1941);

Our Ukrainian Loyalists (Ukrainian Canadian Committee) (Winnipeg: Ukrainian Canadian Committee, 1943);

Seven Pillars of Freedom (Toronto: Oxford University Press, 1944; revised edition, Toronto: Burns & MacEachern, 1952);

The Humanities in Canada, by Kirkconnell and Arthur S. P. Woodhouse (Ottawa: Humanities Research Council of Canada, 1947);

Kirkconnell at Oxford University, early 1920s (courtesy of the Acadia University Library)

The Celestial Cycle: The Theme of Paradise Lost in World Literature, with Translations of the Major Analogues (Toronto: University of Toronto Press, 1952; New York: Gordon Press, 1967);

Canadian Toponymy and The Cultural Stratification of Canada (Winnipeg: Ukrainian Free Academy of Sciences, 1954);

The Kirkconnell Pedigree: A Genealogical Sketch of the Family from the Earliest Times (Wolfville, Nova Scotia: Privately printed, 1954); 22 annual supplements printed (1954-1976);

The Mod at Grand Pre: A Nova Scotia Light Opera in Two Acts (Wolfville, Nova Scotia: Privately printed, 1955);

The Baptists of Canada: A Pocket-book History (Toronto: Historical Committee of the Baptist Federation of Canada, 1958);

Sixteen Decades of Parsonages (Wolfville, Nova Scotia: Printed by Davidson Brothers, 1964);

That Invincible Samson: The Theme of Samson Agonistes in World Literature, With Translations of the Major Analogues (Toronto: University of Toronto Press, 1964);

Centennial Tales and Selected Poems (Toronto: University of Toronto Press for Acadia University, 1965);

A Slice of Canada: Memoirs (Toronto: University of Toronto Press for Acadia University, 1967);

The Fifth Quarter-Century: Acadia University, 1938-1963 (Wolfville, Nova Scotia: Governors of Acadia University, 1968);

Scottish Place Names in Canada (Winnipeg: Canadian Institute of Onomastic Sciences and the Ukrainian Free Academy of Sciences, 1970);

Place Names in Kings County, Nova Scotia (Wolfville, Nova Scotia, 1971);

Awake the Courteous Echo: The Themes and Prosody of Comus, Lycidas, and Paradise Regained in World Literature, with Translations of the Major Analogues (Toronto: University of Toronto Press, 1973);

Climbing the Green Tree and Some Other Branches (Wolfville, Nova Scotia: Privately printed, 1976);

The Flavour of Nova Scotia (Windsor, Nova Scotia: Lancelot Press, 1976);

Medieval Mosaic: A Genealogical Supplement to "Climbing the Green Tree" (Wolfville, Nova Scotia: Privately printed, 1976).

OTHER: *Manitoba Poetry Chapbook, 1933*, edited by Kirkconnell (Winnipeg: Israelite Press for the Canadian Authors' Association, Manitoba Branch, 1933);

The Acadia Record, 1938-1953, fourth edition, revised and enlarged by Kirkconnell (Wolfville, Nova Scotia: Acadia University, 1953);

Elihu Woodworth, *The Diary of Deacon Elihu Woodworth, 1835-1836*, transcribed by Frederick Irving Woodworth, edited by Kirkconnell (Wolfville, Nova Scotia: Wolfville Historical Society, 1972);

Cecil Francis Lloyd, *Rest, Perturbèd Spirit: The Life of Cecil Francis Lloyd, 1884-1938, Presented in a Cento of Excerpts from His Letters*, edited by Kirkconnell (Windsor, Nova Scotia: Lancelot Press, 1974).

TRANSLATIONS: *European Elegies: One Hundred Poems Chosen and Translated from European Literature in Fifty Languages* (Ottawa: Graphic, 1928);

North American Book of Icelandic Verse (New York: Carrier & Isles, 1930);

The Magyar Muse: An Anthology of Hungarian Poet-
    ry, 1400-1932 (Winnipeg: Kanadai Magyar
    Ujsag Press, 1933);
Canadian Overtones: An Anthology of Canadian Po-
    etry Written Originally in Icelandic, Swedish,
    Norwegian, Hungarian, Italian, Greek and
    Ukrainian (Winnipeg: Columbia Press,
    1935);
A Golden Treasury of Polish Lyrics (Winnipeg: Pol-
    ish Press, 1936);
Janos Arany, *The Death of King Buda: A Hungar-*
    ian Epic Poem, translated by Kirkconnell and
    Lulu Putnik Payerle (Cleveland: Benjamin
    Franklin Bibliophile Society, 1936);
Seraphin Marion, ed., *The Quebec Tradition: An An-*
    thology of French-Canadian Prose and Verse
    (Montreal: Editions Lumen, 1946);
A Little Treasury of Hungarian Verse (Washington:
    American Hungarian Federation, 1947);
Adam Mickiewicz, *Pan Tadeusz; or, The Last Foray*
    in Lithuania (Toronto: University of Toronto
    Press for the Millennium of Christian Po-
    land Celebration Committee, 1962; New
    York: Polish Institute of Arts and Sciences
    in America, 1962);
The Ukrainian Poets, 1189-1962, translated by
    Kirkconnell and C. H. Andrusychen (To-
    ronto: University of Toronto Press for the
    Ukrainian Canadian Committee, 1963);
Mécs László, *The Slaves Sing: Selected Poems*
    (DePere, Wisconsin: St. Norbert Abbey
    Press, 1964);
Taras Shevchenko, *Poetical Works: The Kobzar,* trans-
    lated by Kirkconnell and Andrusychen (To-
    ronto: University of Toronto Press for the
    Ukrainian Canadian Committee, 1964);
László, *I Graft Roses on Eglantines,* translated by
    Kirkconnell and Raymond J. Conrad, edited
    by Elek Horvath (Toronto: Printed by
    Weller, 1968);
The Hungarian Helicon, 1950-1976 (Wolfville,
    Nova Scotia: Acadia University, 1986).

The position Watson Kirkconnell occupies
in Canadian literary history is especially subject
to changes in political attitude. A conservative in
the left-leaning 1930s, he was often attacked
then, and for a decade or so after, for his political utterances. At the same time he was a sin-
gularly successful academic and cultural administrator who was widely praised for his erudition,
wit, and understanding; many of the administrative systems he set up are still functioning in
the 1980s, affecting research and publication in

Canada far beyond the borders of the campuses
with which he was affiliated. Kirkconnell resisted
more trends than political ones. Multilingual in
dominantly unilingual environments, he was also
a rhyming poet in an age of free verse, a member of the Canadian Authors' Association (from
1922 on) in years when many leading writers
(such as F. R. Scott) dismissed it for literary
boosterism, and a committed Christian at a time
when religion was losing its influence on many
other people's lives. It is neither as poet nor as
critic and politician that he is most honored a decade after his death, however, but as anthologist
and translator. In these efforts he was little short
of revolutionary, for the task he effectively set himself in the early 1920s was to change the way Canadians thought about who they were.

Watson Kirkconnell was born 16 May 1895
in Port Hope, Ontario, the third of five children
born to the headmaster of Port Hope High
School, Thomas Allison Kirkconnell (d. 1934),
and his wife, Bertha Watson Kirkconnell
(1867-1957), a teacher. The family was of Scots
background. Watson Kirkconnell's great-grand-
father, Walter Kirkconnell, had emigrated from
Iona to Argenteuil County in Quebec in 1819.
As Kirkconnell's early biography of his father (*A
Canadian Headmaster,* 1935) and his late work on
genealogy–*The Kirkconnell Pedigree* (1954) and
Climbing the Green Tree and Some Other Branches
(1976)–show, he was keen to honor origins and
to trace ancestral connections further still. J. R.
C. Perkin–whose *Morning in His Heart* (1986) is
the standard source for biographical information
(a bibliography in this book, compiled by James
B. Snelson, lists some 1,800 publications by or concerning Kirkconnell)–notes that Kirkconnell's maternal line may have been descended from St.
Margaret, an eleventh-century queen of Scotland,
who may in turn have been descended from St.
Stephen (978-1038), a king of Hungary. Such a
family story may well have motivated Kirkconnell's early interest in Hungary; in any event
Hungary was to influence one important dimension of his professional career.

Frail, he did not attend school till he turned
seven, but he soon gained on lost time, and
found a special facility for languages. The family
moved to Lindsay, Ontario, where he attended
high school, acquiring a basic understanding of
French, German, Latin, and Greek, graduating
in 1913. That fall he went directly on to Queen's
University in Kingston, taking Honours Classics
(he won the medals for both Latin and Greek),

and was already intent on postgraduate studies in comparative literature. By 1916 he had earned his M.A. The onset of World War I had, however, altered the sequence of educational events. He had military training as early as 1912 and was in the Queen's reserve during 1915-1916. After a brief stint on the staff of Royal Military College, he anticipated going overseas with the 253rd Battalion of the Canadian Expeditionary Force, but he was found medically unfit and so instead served in Canada, putting his facility with modern languages to work, from 1916 to 1919, as a captain with the Department of Internment Operations.

In 1919 he contemplated embarking on a career in music; although a series of flu epidemics put a stop to those aspirations, he remained active in musical circles, both as choirmaster and librettist. (He wrote *The Mod at Grand Pre,* first published in 1955 and, with music by Edwin A. Collins, performed at Wolfville, Nova Scotia, in March 1956.) In 1920 a career in journalism beckoned. But in 1921 an I. O. D. E. Fellowship enabled him to attend Lincoln College, Oxford, for a year. He was active in Oxford Union debates; he continued to develop his interests in Balkan Europe; and he further expanded his expertise, for he specialized in economics, and his thesis for his B.Litt., *International Aspects of Unemployment,* was published in 1923, two years after his degree was awarded.

Returning to Canada, he was appointed to Wesley (later United) College in Winnipeg; a one-year position as an English instructor turned into an eighteen-year stay (he became a full professor in 1933, was active in community affairs, and for the last seven years served as head of the department of classics). All this while he kept learning more languages. In some sense studying languages was both therapy and escape. He had married Isabel Peel in 1924, but a year later she died giving birth to twin boys, Thomas and James. Kirkconnell withdrew. For the next five years (until he married Hope Kitchener, a native of Lindsay, in 1930), Isabel's mother looked after the children, and Kirkconnell lived in a men's residence at the college. As an extended tribute to Isabel, he began to translate elegies from some fifty languages, offering the resulting manuscript to Allen and Unwin (who had published his book on unemployment). They rejected it, doubting the ability of anyone to comprehend fifty languages. In response, Kirkconnell submitted his translations to various English academic authorities in Slavonic, Romance, and other language groups. All praised the quality. But no one would publish Kirkconnell's translations until Graphic Press of Ottawa issued the book in 1928 as *European Elegies.* It attracted wide applause, though it made little money; Graphic shortly afterward went bankrupt. But verse translation had now become a main occupation for Kirkconnell.

By 1967 he had translated some 4,000 pages; in 1986 there appeared posthumously his *Hungarian Helicon,* a collection of verse translations from Hungarian, done over four decades, involving everything from elegies to epics and from medieval religious lyrics to contemporary political manifestos–a total of 1,148 pages in manuscript. Kirkconnell also wrote conventional verse (*The Tide of Life and Other Poems,* 1930; *The Eternal Quest,* 1934); children's fiction (*Titus the Toad,* 1939); a biography of his father and critical accounts of both European and Canadian literary achievements (*The European Heritage,* 1930); and the annual reviews of new "publications in other languages" for the *University of Toronto Quarterly,* covering the years 1935-1965. Books of verse translations from Icelandic, Hungarian, Polish, Lithuanian, French, and Ukrainian followed from 1930 to 1977. And in 1935 appeared *Canadian Overtones,* an anthology of poems written in Canada in seven "unofficial" Canadian languages: Icelandic, Swedish, Norwegian, Hungarian, Italian, Greek, and Ukrainian. This project no doubt derived from his sensitivity, in Winnipeg, to the real multilingual character of prairie life. It was also a major first foray into the notion of Canadian "multiculturalism," an idea which would not markedly influence government policy, critical norms, or publication schedules for another forty years. Kirkconnell recognized early that "Canadian Literature" included writings in more languages than simply English and French.

As the 1930s progressed, Kirkconnell also became more and more involved in political and religious declarations and controversies. Again these were substantially shaped by his knowledge of languages. In 1938 he toured Europe, lecturing at Debrecen University in Hungary on Hungarian literature (the university later awarded him an honorary degree). Subsequent speeches and publications such as *Canada, Europe, and Hitler* (1939) vociferously protested Nazi expansionist policies; *Canadians All* (a 1941 government pamphlet on national unity) and *The Ukrainian Canadians and the War* (1940) championed the cause of patriotism and interethnic understanding. In 1940 Kirk-

Cover for Kirkconnell's controversial exposé of communism in Canada, published in 1944

connell assisted in the founding of the federal government's Nationalities Branch (later the Canadian Citizenship Bureau), though he turned down an invitation to head it. Many of his speeches (for example, to the Canadian and Empire clubs) and articles in such journals as *Saturday Night* went into separate offprint forms for wider distribution. *Twilight of Liberty* (1941), however, and *Seven Pillars of Freedom* (1944)–the latter alluding transparently to Lawrence of Arabia and attempting to expose the presence of communism in Canada–fiercely attacked communism as a threat as great as the Nazi regime. For this position he was attacked, both in print and in cartoon.

The reverse side of Kirkconnell's anticommunism was his ongoing (though by no means doctrinaire) commitment to the Baptist Church. Indeed, in his various roles within the church (moderator of the Red River Association of Baptist Churches in 1937; president of the Baptist Union of Western Canada, 1938-1940; member

of various conventions) he sought to resolve doctrinal disputes and to reconcile opposing factions. One of his signal accomplishments was the establishment of a single national denominational body for the church, the Baptist Federation of Canada (the term *union* being rejected on political grounds), in 1944. Another example of his skills at organizing large amounts of information and at using this information for diplomatic change was the work he did for the Royal Society of Canada, to which he had been elected in 1936. Resisting a government proposal in 1942–that all university faculties of arts, commerce, education, and law be closed for the duration of the war–Kirkconnell led a campaign that not only reversed the proposal but also led to the establishment in 1943 of the Humanities Research Council (which in 1977 changed its name to the Canadian Federation for the Humanities). Funding for research in the humanities was arranged following the report that Kirkconnell and Arthur S. P. Woodhouse prepared in 1947, a survey entitled *The Humanities in Canada* (1947).

There were connections between church and education. In 1940 Kirkconnell left Winnipeg to become head of the English department at McMaster University in Hamilton, Ontario (then a Baptist school), and in 1948 he was appointed the ninth president of another Baptist institution, Acadia University in Wolfville, Nova Scotia, a position he occupied until he retired in 1964. But Kirkconnell's resistance to restrictive theological positions regarding education showed in his enthusiasm for the creative writing program at McMaster and in his opposition, in 1965, to an attempt on the part of the United Baptist Convention to insist that all Acadia professors hold strict Baptist doctrinal belief. Such resistance also perhaps shows in Kirkconnell's own verse, which (while conventional in form) is frequently comic, with the occasional risqué innuendo, as in the connected series he called *The Flying Bull and Other Tales* (1940). In this work several characters gather in a prairie location and tell each other stories during a storm. "The Lawyer's Tale of the Abandoned Farmhouse," from the collection, rushes forward in swift satiric Skeltonics and tells a tale of twin boys and hell-motivated ghostly coincidences:

"My name is Beynon-Jones," he said.
"I have a lost twin-brother, Jim.
So like myself, from heel to head,
That none can tell me quite from him.

Back home in Devonshire as youths,
Black rivalry in love estranged us.
Through ten grey years of lies and truths,
In that, at least, Time has not changed us.
I wed my blue-eyed Susan, Sir,
But Jim one night, as I had feared
Impersonated me with her
As husband, and then disappeared,
Taking my honour and my cash
To distant lands in one fell smash."

Centennial Tales and Selected Poems followed in 1965, sponsored by Acadia University. The university has repeatedly honored Kirkconnell: with an honorary degree (in 1964, one of thirteen he received altogether, in addition to knighthoods from Poland and Iceland), a festschrift entitled *The Undoing of Babel* (1975) edited by J. R. C. Perkin (Acadia's president), the Perkin-Snelson biobibliography, the editing of Kirkconnell's papers (held at Acadia and Queen's), and the naming of a library room after him.

After moving to Nova Scotia Kirkconnell continued to be active in administration and publication. Twice resisting appeals to run for political office, he involved himself with community hospital boards and operettas as well as with the financially troubled university. He published a trio of critical works on Milton and Miltonic analogues in world literatures (*The Celestial Cycle*, 1952; *That Invincible Samson*, 1964; *Awake the Courteous Echo*, 1973) and a tribute to his friend, the poet Cecil Francis Lloyd (1884-1938), *Rest, Perturbèd Spirit* (1974). He continued to publish hymns and wry poems, which alike express his love of order. He produced a book of memoirs entitled *A Slice of Canada* (1967), more translations, and various pamphlets on place names and local sites. A heart attack in 1964 scarcely slowed him down, and after his retirement, from 1966 to 1968, he stayed on in administration as interim head of the English department at Acadia, and he lived out his retirement in Wolfville. He left numerous essays, children's tales, libretti, anthologies, and other projects unpublished when he died on 26 February 1977. His poetry is slight, his criticism marked by its time, his dramatic work the expression of a man whose facility with language led him to entertain others. Literary historians note him now for his appreciation of the multilingual literary character of Canada and for his administrative adeptness in helping to preserve the humanities against political attack.

References:

J. R. C. Perkin, *Morning in His Heart: The Life and Writings of Watson Kirkconnell* (Wolfville, Nova Scotia: Lancelot Press for Acadia University Library, 1986)–includes a bibliography of writings by and about Kirkconnell prepared by James B. Snelson;

Perkin, ed., *The Undoing of Babel: Watson Kirkconnell, The Man and His Work* (Toronto: McClelland & Stewart, 1975).

Papers:

Kirkconnell's papers are at the Acadia University Library and at the Douglas Library, Queen's University.

A. M. Klein

(14 February 1909-20 August 1972)

M. W. Steinberg
University of British Columbia

BOOKS: *Hath Not a Jew ...* (New York: Behrman's Jewish Book House, 1940);

The Hitleriad (New York: New Directions, 1944);

Poems (Philadelphia: Jewish Publication Society of America, 1944);

Poems of French Canada (Montreal: Canadian Jewish Congress, 1947);

Seven Poems (Montreal: Canadian Jewish Congress, 1948);

Huit Poèmes Canadiens (en anglais) (Montreal: Canadian Jewish Congress, 1948);

The Rocking Chair and Other Poems (Toronto: Ryerson, 1948);

The Second Scroll (New York: Knopf, 1951; Toronto: McClelland & Stewart, 1951);

The Collected Poems of A. M. Klein, edited, with an introduction, by Miriam Waddington (Toronto: McGraw-Hill Ryerson, 1974);

Beyond Sambation: Selected Essays and Editorials 1928-1955, edited by M. W. Steinberg and Usher Caplan (Toronto: University of Toronto Press, 1982);

A. M. Klein: Short Stories, edited by Steinberg (Toronto: University of Toronto Press, 1983);

A. M. Klein: Literary Essays and Reviews, edited by Steinberg and Caplan (Toronto: University of Toronto Press, 1987).

PLAY PRODUCTION: *Conscience,* adapted by Klein from Pedro Bloch's play *The Hands of Euridice,* New York, Booth Theatre, 15 May 1952.

A. M. Klein (photograph by the Garcia Studio)

Abraham Moses Klein, born of immigrant parents, Colman and Yetta Morantz Klein, in 1909, was brought up in Montreal and, except for the year 1937-1938 spent practicing law in Rouyn, Quebec, lived his life there. His formative years were spent in the self-contained Jewish community of the Montreal ghetto centering around St. Lawrence Boulevard. Aside from the workplace–the factory or the small shop–the synagogue and the home were the centers of activity. The pattern of life within this community was uniquely Jewish. The religious holidays, both festive and solemn, were key events in the annual cycle of seasons, and the code of religious observances, in varying degrees practiced, was the norm of accepted behavior. The community developed its own institutions, which allowed a high degree of social and cultural self-sufficiency. For the most part, except in business, it had few links with the non-Jewish segments of the population in Montreal, and virtually no links with the rest of Quebec or the rest of Canada. Its ties were with similar Jewish communities in other Canadian or American cities and with family members who remained behind in eastern European towns and villages. News from overseas, by letter or courtesy of some newly arrived immigrant, was sporadic and often tragic; almost every household received reports of pogroms and poverty, of increasing prohibitions and threats. Klein's imagination was shaped by this pattern of life and these accounts, and from his early experiences, in large measure, stemmed both his continuing commitment to Jewish causes and needs and a strong current of insecurity, personal and communal.

Klein's responses were shaped also by his home and by his learning. In his poem "Autobiographical" (*The Collected Poems of A. M. Klein*, 1974) Klein fondly describes the ghetto environment of his childhood:

> My mother, blessing candles, Sabbath-flamed,
> Queenly in her Warsovian perruque;
> My father pickabacking me to bed
> To tell tall tales about the Baal Shem Tov—
> Letting me curl his beard.

Klein's was a religious home, one in which precept found daily expression through ceremony and the observance of the Torah laws that defined traditional Jewish life. Though Klein later in life questioned some aspects of orthodoxy and departed from some practices, he was never able or willing to break the strong ties that bound him to the Judaism of his parents. The tension in many of Klein's poems derives from this ambivalence in his attitude toward faith and the traditional practices that express it. Quite apart from matters of faith, these practices, carefully observed in childhood and youth and sympathetically recalled during his later life, helped root him in his Jewish culture and folkways. His awareness of his place in a continuing tradition enabled him to achieve even in his most personal poems a transcendence of self and an enlargement of the meaning and significance of his experience. This awareness is made clear in "Psalm XXXVI–A Psalm Touching Genealogy" in *Poems* (1944):

> Not sole was I born, but entire genesis:
> For to the fathers that begat me, this
> Body is residence. Corpuscular,
> They dwell in my veins, they eavesdrop at my ear,
> They circle, as with Torahs, round my skull,
> In exit and in entrance all day pull
> The latches of my heart, descend, and rise—
> And there look generations through my eyes.

The bond to his people was reinforced by his studies. On completing his elementary Jewish education at the Talmud Torah, he studied for several years with private tutors, whom he mentions affectionately in several poems and stories. As an adolescent his commitment to Judaism was so strong that he considered going to a yeshiva for rabbinic training. Instead, however, he embarked upon a secular career. After graduating from Baron Byng High School, a silver medalist, he entered McGill University in the fall of 1926. He graduated with his B.A. in 1930 and proceeded to take his law degree at the University of Montreal in 1933.

The main thrust of Klein's life at this time, determined by his beginnings and by the pressure of the social environment which tended to confine Jews to Jewish associations, was toward Jewish concerns. While at McGill he became a leading figure in Canadian Young Judaea, the Zionist youth movement. In 1928 he became editor of its national periodical, the *Judaean*, and a year later was appointed educational director of Young Judaea, a position which he held until June 1932. These activities marked the beginning of his career as a journalist and, in a broad sense, a popular educator. He editorialized and commented on events pertaining to the Jewish scene in the *Judaean* and later, for a brief period, in the *Canadian Zionist*. From the early 1930s on he contributed articles and reviews to the *Canadian Jewish Chronicle*, and he prepared outlines for study groups in Young Judaea on such topics as the history of the Jews in Poland and the treatment of the Jew in English literature.

Much of his early creative writing reflects his interests and increasing involvement. In many poems and in nearly all his early short stories Klein turned to Jewish themes, historical and contemporary, to Jewish legend, fable, and folklore for his inspiration and material. In doing so he was no doubt motivated primarily by his own deepening interest and the writer's felt need to draw from his own learning and direct experience. But he was also writing for a specifically Jewish audience, adult and juvenile, who constituted the readership of the periodicals with which he was associated. Thus many of his early published poems and nearly all his early short stories appeared first in the *Judaean*. In part at least, he wrote with the conscious intent to stimulate his own people's interest in a literature about themselves.

To regard Klein in this early period as a Jewish poet writing only on Jewish subjects is, however, an oversimplification, but a fairly common one, prompted perhaps by the fact that most of his best-known early poems, such as "Greeting on This Day" and "Out of the Pulver and the Polished Lens," derive from his Jewish background as well as by the fact that his first published volume of poetry, *Hath Not a Jew . . .* (1940), presents exclusively poems from the world of Jewish experience. In a letter to A. J. M. Smith in 1943 Klein expressed his annoyance with the tendency to apply a limiting label to his work. An examination of his poetry, published and unpublished, written during his university years (his most prolific period), shows that he wrote at least as many poems on subjects not specifically Jewish—love, the seasons and landscapes, the social milieu, and so on—as on Jewish themes. In 1932 Klein assembled most of his completed poems into two collections, "Gestures Hebraic" and "Poems," neither of which has been published. The former contains his "Jewish" poems, and the latter, with some notable exceptions, such as "The Diary of Abraham Segal, Poet" and "The Soirée of Velvel Kleinburger," includes poems not specifically Jewish in content. A third unpublished collection, "Poems," assembled in 1934, consists chiefly of his children's verse drawn largely from Jewish legend, folklore, and animal fables. Poems from this collection had been published, for the most part, in the *Judaean.*

Klein's Zionist and Jewish activity was by no means an exclusive concern in the late 1920s and early 1930s. During these university years his love of language and literature found new outlets. He became active in the debating union and quickly won fame as an eloquent and incisive speaker, witty and rhetorical. His debating partner was his close friend David Lewis, who later became national secretary and then leader of the CCF (Co-operative Commonwealth Federation), the socialist-labor party of Canada. Klein also contributed articles to the *McGill Daily,* and he founded a university literary magazine, the *McGilliad.* He was fortunate in that his years at McGill coincided with the development of an exciting literary movement spearheaded by A. J. M. Smith and F. R. Scott and actively supported by Leon Edel and Leo Kennedy, among others. The group challenged the rather staid conventionally romantic poetry of the period. Klein quickly became associated with them, and his own poetry was affected. Klein's early verse had been mark-

edly influenced by Keats in its sensuous language and in its imagery. While this influence remained because it was well suited to Klein's temperament and taste, Klein, like the other poets in the McGill movement, responded to the metaphysical qualities of John Donne and to the modernist verse of W. B. Yeats and T. S. Eliot. His association with the McGill group continued through the 1930s, and he was well represented in the first major anthology that reflected the new poetry, *New Provinces: Poems by Several Authors* (1936).

Klein's interest in Zionism intensified after he finished his formal schooling. As the Zionist movement gained momentum in the 1930s and as the spread of fascism and anti-Semitism became an ever more threatening menace, his involvement in matters Jewish increased. He served for a short while as associate director of the Zionist Organization of Canada in 1936 and as editor of the *Canadian Zionist* in 1936 and 1937. During these years and after, he often toured towns in Ontario and Quebec and on occasion visited communities in other parts of Canada lecturing and organizing on behalf of Zionism. This concern found expression in his poetry and fiction and in hundreds of articles and editorials, published chiefly in the *Canadian Jewish Chronicle.*

In many respects the mid 1930s were difficult years for Klein. Upon graduating from law school, he started to practice law in association with Samuel Chait, a friend from Young Judaean days, but a year later he entered partnership with Max Garmaise, a former fellow student at law school with whom he maintained a lifelong friendship. In the short story "Whom God Hath Joined," written during this period, Klein describes his boredom and sense of futility in trying to establish a law practice in Montreal during the Depression years. After his father's death in 1934 Klein took on the financial burden of his family and added to his responsibility when he married his childhood sweetheart, Bessie Kozlov, in 1935.

These personal factors and the growth of fascism and virulent anti-Semitism at home and abroad, and the inequities present in society and made more manifest during the Depression, resulted in a shift in emphasis in Klein's writing. Although in his earlier poetry Klein was at times critical of contemporary society, his writing at this time was more sharply and consistently concerned with social issues, as evidenced by his poem "Blueprint for a Monument of War" and in his poetic sequences "Of Daumiers, A Portfolio," "Of Castles in Spain," and "Barricade Smith: His Speeches," all published in 1937 and 1938 (and later included in *The Collected Poems of A. M. Klein*). The disheartening, chaotic aspect of the social order is also reflected in two of the short stories written at that time, "Friends, Romans, Hungrymen" and "Beggars I Have Known" (collected, with many others, in *A. M. Klein: Short Stories*, 1983). After two years of relatively unsuccessful effort to establish a law practice in Montreal, Klein persuaded Garmaise to open a branch in Rouyn, Quebec, in 1936. A year later Klein relocated in Rouyn, but he stayed for only a year. In part because of his mother's importuning and in part because he missed the social and intellectual stimulation of Montreal, he returned, rejoining the law firm of Samuel Chait.

Immediately upon his return to Montreal in November 1938, Klein assumed the editorship of the *Canadian Jewish Chronicle*, the leading Anglo-Jewish weekly in Canada. He gladly accepted the challenge and the opportunity, and for the next seventeen years his was an important voice in the Jewish community. His responsibilities as editor prompted him to write weekly editorials and commentaries on current events and issues, on personalities prominent in the news, and on aspects of contemporary Jewish life, religious and cultural, viewed historically. He contributed also poems, stories, translations from Hebrew and Yiddish literature, book reviews, and articles on literature and related subjects.

Although many of Klein's editorials were written in haste and often out of a sense of duty to organizations and institutions in the community, they cannot, with few exceptions, be regarded as hackwork. These prose pieces, written regularly week after week, constitute, in effect, an intellectual and to some extent literary history of A. M. Klein. Many of his articles and editorials are, not surprisingly, ephemeral, but many transcend the occasions that prompted them. All, however, record the history of the period from 1930 to 1955: the Great Depression, the rise of Nazism, the Holocaust, World War II, and the reestablishment of a Jewish state in Israel.

Klein saw one of his major functions as editor to be a popular educator. He believed that he had the responsibility to inform the non-Jewish world of the Jewish condition–its achievements and its plight–but even more important, to convey to the young Jewish North American-born generation some knowledge of their cultural heritage. In the *Canadian Jewish Chronicle* he pub-

Dust jacket for the first American edition of Klein's only novel, set in Canada, Italy, Morocco, and Israel

lished his own translations of classical Hebrew and Yiddish works, drew constantly on the Bible and rabbinic commentaries to establish or illustrate argument, and wrote articles on contemporary Jewish leaders–poets, scholars, and statesmen. Many of his editorials were, in effect, brief sermons as he expatiated on the historical background and contemporary relevance of Jewish holidays or urged support for Zionist causes or Jewish philanthropic agencies, Hebrew schools, and other public institutions.

The second major responsibility that Klein undertook as editor was to help shape the responses of his people to the significant events of the time, particularly Zionism and anti-Semitism, and to counter as forcefully as possible through his editorials attacks on the lives and aspirations of his fellow Jews. The journalist, according to Klein, had to do more than report on the world's activities: his reporting had to be informed by a sensitive conscience which operated within a framework of beliefs and values. He decried the attitude of pseudoimpartiality or "spectatorial and olympian aloofness" from the realities of struggle because no one had the right to be neutral on moral questions.

Although the effectiveness of Klein's journalism was at times diminished by his fondness for unusual diction, for archaic and foreign terms, erudite and even esoteric allusion, for the most part he was an eloquent spokesman for his people and champion of their causes. Logical and dispassionate, he could argue coolly, building a careful case and appealing to reason, but he was at least equally effective in responding to opponents by means of wit, satire, and invective. The most frequently recurring tone in his prose, however, was that of morality, sincerity, and passionate conviction—the preacher or prophet teaching, warning, and scolding his readers and defying his people's enemies. Klein's journalism is a body of prose writing which occupies a place alongside his poetry and fiction as a contribution to Canadian letters. It provides, in addition, a record, virtually daily for almost two decades, of Klein's responses to the concerns that preoccupied him. As such, it is valuable for an understanding of him and his creative writings.

Shortly after becoming editor of the *Canadian Jewish Chronicle,* Klein took on another role. Beginning in 1939 a close association developed between him and Samuel Bronfman, the strong-willed and philanthropic founder of a distillery empire, who had just been elected president of the Canadian Jewish Congress and who became an increasingly powerful figure in the Canadian-Jewish community in the decades that followed. Klein became Bronfman's speech writer and adviser on matters Judaic. It is difficult to estimate what influence, if any, Klein's connection with Bronfman had on the policies of the Canadian Jewish Congress or on Klein's other activities, but the relationship developed into a warm and respectful one. Subsequently Klein was appointed, on a part-time basis, to the public relations staff of Seagram's, and he was kept on its payroll even after his illness totally incapacitated him.

Despite his many involvements in the 1940s, Klein allowed himself to be persuaded, probably by his old friend and debating partner at McGill, David Lewis, to enter politics and stand for election as a CCF candidate. He accepted the nomination in 1944 to oppose the Communist incumbent, Fred Rose, in the riding of Montreal Cartier. Klein's discontent with social conditions and his interest in change were evidenced throughout the 1930s directly and by implication in many

poems and short stories, particularly his poems prompted by the Depression and the Spanish civil war. He considered himself a liberal socialist and was outspoken in his opposition to fascism and to totalitarian communism. Party politics had been a marginal consideration in his life, and it was with divided feelings, as entries in his diary record, that he accepted the invitation to stand for the 1945 election. Before the campaign got well under way, however, Klein withdrew. A subsequent entry into politics had a different outcome. In 1949 Klein accepted the CCF nomination for the Montreal Cartier riding, opposing the incumbent Liberal M.P., Maurice Hartt. He campaigned vigorously but was badly defeated, a rejection by a largely Jewish electorate that embittered Klein, who undoubtedly felt that his services to the community deserved better recompense.

Between these two political campaigns in the 1940s Klein engaged in yet another activity: teaching. Partly at the urging of Bronfman and partly because, as he indicated in a letter to a friend, Meyer Weisgal, he felt an attraction to the academic life, he accepted a post in the English department at McGill University in 1945. He taught there for three years, successfully, after which he gave up his lectureship and returned to his law practice and other engagements.

Despite his many nonliterary pursuits in the 1940s, Klein found time to continue with his creative writing, both poetry and fiction, and he participated in the literary movements that centered in Montreal. Although Klein published individual poems in a variety of journals and literary magazines from the late 1920s on, his first volume of poetry, *Hath Not a Jew . . . ,* appeared in 1940 under the imprint of Behrman's Jewish Book House, New York. Klein had to turn again to American publishers for his next two volumes, *The Hitleriad* and *Poems,* in 1944. Apart from three pamphlets published by the Canadian Jewish Congress in Montreal, *Poems of French Canada* (1947), *Seven Poems* (1948), and *Huit Poèmes canadiens (en anglais)* (1948), Klein did not find a Canadian publisher until 1948 when *The Rocking Chair and Other Poems* was published by the Ryerson Press in Toronto.

Nearly all the poems in *Hath Not a Jew . . .* were written in the late 1920s and early 1930s and assembled in Klein's three unpublished collections of verse, "Gestures Hebraic," "Poems" of 1932, and "Poems" of 1934. In *Hath Not a Jew . . .* Klein deliberately chose from his works only poems dealing with Jewish subjects, a fact that reflects his increasing preoccupation with the Jewish situation in an increasingly hostile world. His poems range through history, past and current, presenting dramatic incidents in the Holy Land and of the Diaspora such as the massacre at Hebron and the pogroms in Europe; some movingly describe famed characters such as Reb Levi Yitschok, Spinoza, and the Baal Shem Tov; and others present with wit and warmth such recognizable character types as the cantor, scholar, matchmaker, and junk dealer. His irony at times suggests a critical awareness of shortcomings, as in the poems "Landlord" and "Preacher," but, on the whole, the tone is genial and tolerant. In general Klein creates for his people a dignified counterportrait to the degrading stereotyped image circulated by anti-Semites.

The theme of Zionism runs through many poems, reflecting Klein's passionate commitment to the reestablishment of a Jewish homeland. For Klein, the concept of a national homeland was more than a political idea and more than the result of a desire for a haven for oppressed Jews. His reach for Zion was primarily the religious yearning for the old home, the fabled city, and the holy land, and for the renewal of the covenant. Zion had an imaginative reality for him and expressed an imaginative and spiritual need, in some measure akin to his continuing yearning for the warm, safe world of his childhood. The central motif in *Hath Not a Jew* . . . , however, is anti-Semitism, a topic given terrible immediacy in the 1930s by the Nazis. Klein gives this subject perspective in "Sonnet in Time of Affliction" and "Design for Mediaeval Tapestry," for example, by referring directly or through image and allusion to instances of anti-Semitism in biblical and postbiblical times and in various regions. In "Childe Harold's Pilgrimage" he depicts the callous indifference of the Western world to the brutal, genocidal policies of the pro-Nazi regimes, while in many other poems he examines the wide range of Jewish responses to this recurring tragedy, from pious or passive acquiescence to active resistance.

The seriousness with which he treats the themes of anti-Semitism and Zionism is counterbalanced to some extent by his witty portraits of recognizable Jewish character types but even more by his sequences of poems based on legend, folklore, and fable. These poems reveal another aspect of Klein–his capacity to respond in a simple, childlike way to a world of magic and mys-

tery. This world, often comic, presented in an aura of whimsy and wonder, has at times, as it does in many fairy tales and animal fables, a fearsome, menacing underside, an aspect that is very much a part of a child's world, real or imagined. In all his work Klein's outlook, essentially romantic, frequently optimistic, is rarely free from this nightmarish element.

Poems (1944) continues Klein's two central themes, anti-Semitism and Zionism. In his poem "In Re Solomon Warshawer" Klein outlines movingly the historic process of persecution culminating in the ultimate confrontation with the German dictator, and in "Ballad of the Thwarted Axe" and "Ballad of the Days of the Messiah" he depicts even more graphically the violence engendered by Nazi anti-Semites. The long allegorical romance in Spenserian stanzas, "Yehuda Halevi: His Pilgrimage," about the attempted return to Zion by the medieval poet-scholar, reveals clearly Klein's own deep longing. The major portion of *Poems*, however, is composed of a series of thirty-six psalms, most of which were written in the early 1940s. Like the biblical psalms upon which these are in many ways modeled, they are, by and large, prayers of thanksgiving, of praise and supplication. In the main they are personal poems, reflecting the poet's own aspirations and uncertainties, his fear of sickness or failure, his religious doubts, and his striving for faith. Klein included in this series a sequence of nuptial poems, written a decade earlier, well before his own marriage, but probably in anticipation of it. They are tender, finely wrought descriptions of the ritual stages followed on a wedding day. The blending in these poems of the sensuous and solemn creates a quality of holy delight in which physical and spiritual pleasures are inseparable.

The concern for Zion and the outcry against the evil of anti-Semitism are also present in Klein's psalms, but these themes are subordinated. The poet frequently contrasts, directly and by implication, a depraved and violently destructive world with his vision, like the biblical psalmist's, of a world of peace. The juxtaposition of pastoral imagery of green pastures and still waters with the imagery of bombing planes and concentrations camps–of the Messianic dream with the Nazi reality–creates a powerful effect.

In *The Hitleriad* (1944) Klein addresses himself specifically to the Nazi situation. In this simple and direct satire Klein catalogues the Nazis and their crimes. Although there is some clumsiness in this poem and the occasional flat joke or bathetic line, on the whole it is a skilled and powerful piece of satire. The wit is sharp, the rhetoric commanding, and the insults and invective imaginative. But despite the wit and the explosive force of Klein's wrath in this poem, *The Hitleriad* does not fully succeed. The horror of the Holocaust and the evil of its perpetrators cannot be conveyed through the conventions of satire, no matter how great nor how sincere the poet's indignation and rage.

Klein's poetic activities in the 1940s were not limited to the writing of his own poems. In a letter to Leo Kennedy in 1945 he commented on the literary renaissance occurring in Montreal which, he said, reminded him of the late 1920s, the time of the McGill movement. Klein in the early 1940s, perhaps through his friendship with F. R. Scott, became linked with a group of writers known as the *Preview* poets. Though never active in this group, in which Patrick Anderson and P. K. Page, among others, were central figures, he contributed to their journal and allowed his name to appear on the masthead in 1944. Although Klein was quite rightly identified with the *Preview* poets, he was also "persona grata" to a second group, the *First Statement* poets, that centered on John Sutherland, Louis Dudek, and Irving Layton. Dudek and Layton, in particular, had a high regard for Klein and for his poetry, though they were not uncritical of some aspects of his verse. Both the *Preview* and *First Statement* groups believed that they contributed to Klein's development as a poet, influencing him to turn away from what seemed an undue preoccupation with Jewish themes and a tendency toward sentimentalism–a view that probably does have limited validity. In addition to the stimulation of these poetry groups, however, other factors affected Klein's poetry in the 1940s. The war was drawing to a close; with the defeat of Nazi Germany, the threat of fascism receded. In addition the pronounced surge of Canadian nationalism which manifested itself during the war years and continued after heightened the national consciousness of writers. For Klein and many of his contemporaries the Canadian scene, especially the urban social scene, became the center of attention as they tried to come to grips with the realities of Canadian society in an attempt to discover a Canadian identity and perhaps to help shape it.

The Rocking Chair and Other Poems (1948) reflects this change; the poems in this collection express Klein's response to persons, things, and places, to issues Canadian and, more particularly, French-Canadian. In "The Provinces" Klein, with vivid, homely imagery describing landscape and vocation, characterizes the varied Canadian regions; the familial analogy he uses conveys the sense of unity and the yearning for it experienced by Canadians. In poems such as "Pawnshop," "Commercial Bank," and "Filling Station" he describes familiar businesses in commonplace Canadian settings. In other poems, for example "The Snowshoers" and "The Sugaring," he writes about scenes and activities more specifically Quebecois. Much more frequently, however, his attention is focused on the city of Montreal, his "spiritual mother," and his response is more intensely personal, as in the poem "Montreal": "You are part of me, O all your quartiers–/. . ./ You are locale of infancy, milieu/Vital of institutes that formed my fate."

In all that he describes, whether through symbol, allusion, or precise minute detail, Klein is essentially romantic, revealing the capacity to perceive freshly the wonder of things. These poems reflect the attitude that Klein demonstrated early in his career when he wrote in the *McGill Daily* (10 December 1927) that "one need not tour to the four corners of the world to be filled with a spirit of strangeness–the street corner will suffice. . . . there the red-letter box stands, a confessional holier than any other." Every event, he went on to say, even water gushing from a tap, is a miracle. His romantic interest in Quebec, and more particularly Montreal, extends to its people. Klein presents to his reader a broad cross section of French-Canadians, ranging from ordinary folk with simple faith and large families to industrial and financial barons, from rowdy students and sedate scholars to gangsters and demagogic politicians, and from pompous functionaries to humbly devout and devoted sisters of mercy.

In these portraits of people Klein is also basically a romantic. Although he does not blink away faults or excuse them, and his comments are often ironical and at times strongly satirical, the general impression that these portraits leave, as was the case with the earlier Jewish portraits in *Hath Not a Jew . . .* , is one of tolerance and genial acceptance. Even for the popular Montreal mayor Camillien Houde, seen as a country uncle with sunflower seeds in his pocket and at the same time as a dangerous demagogue, there is admiration and respect. All of Klein's subjects come into a comprehensive embrace almost Chaucerian in breadth and delight.

As in his earlier Jewish poems, in his French-Canadian poems Klein drew on his own experience, his firsthand knowledge of the *canadiens* and their culture. His warm, empathic attitude to this community stemmed largely from his recognition of affinities with his own background–a clinging to accustomed ways, to one's own language and religion, and to a sense of unique peoplehood. A. J. M. Smith, in a 1946 article in *Les Gants du Ciel,* summed up this response. "Dans l'entité patriarchale, traditionelle et ecclésiastique qu'est le Canada français, Klein a trouvé un univers que sa sensibilité juive lui permet de comprendre et d'aimer" (In the patriarchal, traditional and ecclesiastic entity that is French Canada, Klein found a universe that his Jewish sensibility permitted him to understand and love).

The rocking chair of the title poem, which symbolizes movement without progress, also conveys a quality of domestic tranquillity, and the spinning wheel transformed in terms of contemporary reality into the grinding wheel of industry recalls also the pace and quality of an earlier life. The clinging to the past may have prevented the mid-twentieth-century *canadien* from playing his full role in Canadian society, but Klein, with a strong sense of his own people's heritage, is not unsympathetic to this nostalgic insistence on the old virtues and inherited values. While his portrait of the cripples crawling on their knees up the ninety-nine stairs to the shrine of St. Joseph is an ironic presentation of naive faith as viewed by a detached rationalist onlooker, Klein at the same time admires and even envies these simple people who know "the surgery's in the heart." Klein's response to the French-Canadian scene is, then, somewhat ambivalent, but the tilt in favor of a warm empathy is marked.

Klein's sympathy with French Canada was probably deepened by his awareness that it, like his own Jewish community, was a minority society constantly on the defensive, striving to preserve its cultural identity, its language and religion from the encroachments of larger outside forces. Klein, as a liberal humanist, also defended, chiefly in his journalism, the rights of other minority groups: Negroes in South Africa and on specific occasions in southwestern Ontario; the Japanese on the Pacific coast; Jehovah's Witnesses in Quebec; and the Canadian Indian. His poem "Indian Reservation: Caughnawaga" is a moving account of the Indian's plight.

Although Klein's personal views and feelings find expression in *The Rocking Chair and Other Poems,* he is more detached, objective, than in his earlier "Jewish" poems. His ability to maintain greater psychic distance may have resulted in a less declamatory tone and reduced his tendency toward sentimentality, but it also diminished the passion and force generated by the expression of the innermost convictions and concerns of the poet. Something of this deeply personal involvement breaks through in a number of selections in *The Rocking Chair and Other Poems.* The sense of loveliness produced by the scenes from Mount Royal or the joy experienced in the sights and activities on the Montreal streets are inseparable from the poet's memories of his childhood and youth. Perhaps the clearest, profoundest personal statement is to be found in the concluding poem, "Portrait of the Poet as Landscape." The theme of the neglected artist and the effect on him of an indifferent or corrupting society is a moving general indictment.

Klein's fiction, like his poetry, was an important part of his activity during his university years in the late 1920s and early 1930s. From 1929 to 1933 he published fourteen short stories, nearly all in Jewish publications. The subject matter, like that of many of his poems of this period, centers on Jewish holidays and ceremonies, such as the Sabbath, Chanukah, Passover, and involves animals and demons, mystical visitants, and a wide range of characters familiar to the Jewish scene–the scribe or scholar, the *shlimazl* or community functionary. The tone of these stories is comparable to that of the early poems–a blending of wit and whimsy, of sentimentality and wry humor; a respect for simple human dignity; and an acceptance of the weaknesses that seem, perhaps fortunately, an inevitable component in the human comedy.

With these stories Klein followed the tradition of the great Jewish short-story writers, such as I. L. Peretz, Chaim Nachman Bialik, Sholom Aleichem, and S. J. Agnon. Klein might have been influenced in the kind of story he wrote at this time by the fact that he was then educational director of Canadian Young Judaea and editor of the *Judaean,* in which most of these early stories appeared. He wrote with a specific readership in mind and with a specific purpose: to heighten his readers' sense of their separate Jewish identity, their awareness of their cultural heritage and of their current circumstances. He did not write, however, as an apologist or educator; pri-

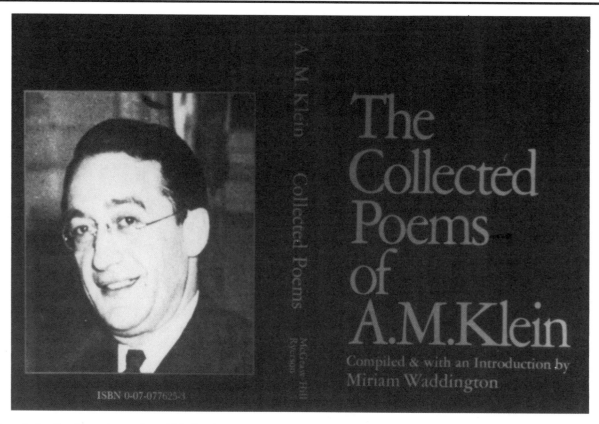

Dust jacket for the posthumously published volume compiled by Miriam Waddington to "present an overall chronological picture"
of Klein's work as a poet

marily he was a storyteller who entertained and commented on the human situation.

The mid 1930s saw a shift in emphasis in Klein's short stories. His widening range of activities, both in literary circles and in the legal profession, brought him in touch with a larger world of experience, one reflected in the unpublished stories "Whom God Hath Joined" and "Portrait of an Executioner." The Great Depression, the problem of increasing financial responsibility after the death of his father, the growing threat of fascism, and the intensifying Nazi menace are reflected in "Friends, Romans, Hungrymen," "Beggars I Have Known" and the anti-Nazi satire "Blood and Iron."

In the mid 1940s, after a lapse of a few years, Klein turned again to the short-story genre. His dark view of the world provoked by the Depression and Nazism was worsened by the horror of the Holocaust and his perception of the cynical and immoral indifference of the democratic world. In three stories written between 1943 and 1945, "Detective Story," "We Who Are About To Be Born," and "One More Utopia," Klein expresses a very negative attitude toward

life. While there is a glimmer of hope at the end of "One More Utopia," there seems an expression of total despair in the other two.

Toward the end of the 1940s and into the 1950s Klein's stories reflected more of the current political concerns. Postwar global political maneuverings, perhaps his own involvement in political campaigning, and the nascent cold war affected his short fiction. "And It Shall Come to Pass" (1948), a story about the atomic bomb and world annihilation, and "A Fable" (1952), a satiric animal fable about quarrelsome politicians who cannot subordinate their selfish interests to the common good even to save themselves, reveal Klein's doubts about man's ability to govern rationally and perhaps even to survive. Also political are two of Klein's best short stories, written in this late period, "Letter From Afar" and "The Bells of Sobor Spasitula," in which he presents themes that he had used in his editorials for the *Canadian Jewish Chronicle*–Soviet purges and Soviet censorship of the arts in an attempt to create a culturally monolithic society.

Klein's interest in prose-fiction writing in the 1940s was not limited to the short story. He planned a major historical novel on the Golem legend, a topic that fascinated him, and he collected extensive material for it. In the Klein Papers at the Public Archives in Ottawa, there are copious notes on this subject and two complete chapters that probably belong to this work. There are also several stories, "The Inverted Tree," "Hapaxlegomenon," "Stranger and Afraid," and "Adloyada," unfortunately incomplete, which Klein may well have intended to develop as novels. He did complete a novel in 1946 or 1947 entitled originally "Comes the Revolution," later renamed "That Walks Like a Man." The story was based on the revelations by Igor Gouzenko, a Soviet embassy cipher clerk in Ottawa, of an extensive Soviet spy network operating in Canada and the United States. Klein, who had a keen interest in detective stories and was familiar with some of the persons and places mentioned in the testimony before the Royal Commission that investigated the charges, wrote the spy thriller in the hope that it would bring him fame and fortune. Though the novel moves quickly and creates suspense, it is not distinguished, and after sending it off to many publishers without success, he abandoned it.

Klein's only published novel, *The Second Scroll,* appeared in 1951. Two years earlier Klein had been sent by the Canadian Jewish Congress to report on the newly established state of Israel, the displaced persons camps in Europe, and the Jewish communities in North Africa. Upon his return he was sent on a lecture tour across Canada to speak about conditions in the places he visited and to win support for the policy of "the ingathering of the exiles." He also published in the fall of 1949, in the *Canadian Jewish Chronicle,* a serialized account of his journey, which became, in some respects, the blueprint of his novel, *The Second Scroll.* This highly poetic narrative, through a series of interlocking symbols, conveys Klein's interpretation of Jewish history past and present, with its underlying premise of the special relationship of God, the Jewish people, and the land of Israel–an eternal covenant. In this sense, contemporary events–the sufferings in Nazi extermination camps and the miraculous restoration of a people to their own homeland–parallel earlier enslavement in Egypt and exodus to the Holy Land, as recorded in the first scroll.

On the basis of the relatively simple plot structure of a Canadian journalist's search for a long-lost uncle who survived the Holocaust and made his way through Europe and North Africa

to Israel, Klein raises a series of questions, metaphysical and ethical: the relationship between good and evil; God's role and man's responsibility in determining human destiny, a question involving the role of man's reason and his will, their limits, and the place of faith. Klein, through the action and the pattern of symbols that give meaning to it, attempts to reconcile these concepts and in the course of the narrative develops the drama of man, perplexed by the tragic twists of history, losing God but compelled to find Him again. The national theme–the rebuilding of the Jewish homeland in Israel after an exile of 2,000 years–is inseparable from the religious theme, for it provides evidence of the miraculous sustaining of the covenant, and the redemption clearly suggests the fulfillment of the Messianic promise. This happy outcome renews the optimism essential to the religious view of good and evil as having their places in a divine order and plan.

Another literary activity, almost an obsessive engagement, in the late 1940s and early 1950s was Klein's work on James Joyce's *Ulysses.* "What I am engaged on," Klein wrote to Leon Edel on 22 January 1948, "is a line-by-line, or rather page by page, commentary on *Ulysses,* tracking down all the allusions, indicating in the abstruser stream-of-consciousness paragraphs the mental associations and sequence, explicating text, and relating the parts to the whole, etc. etc." Unfortunately, this work was never completed, but three articles were published and widely acclaimed by Joyce scholars: "The Oxen of the Sun" (*Here and Now,* January 1949); "The Black Panther: A Study in Technique" (*Accent,* Spring 1950); and "A Shout in the Street" (*New Directions in Prose and Poetry,* no. 13, 1951).

At this time also Klein returned to an earlier interest briefly expressed in the 1930s, the writing of drama. In 1936 he completed a short three-act comedy in verse based on the antics of Hershel Ostropoler, a legendary folk hero who lived by his wits and whose jests and exploits were the subject of many Yiddish tales. Klein published the text of the play, entitled simply *Hershel of Ostropol,* in the *Canadian Jewish Chronicle* in 1939. He returned to this character in the 1950s with his one-act musical comedy "Worse Visitors We Shouldn't Have." His brief attempt to get this play produced in New York failed. He attempted two other plays, a serious drama entitled "The Icepick," based on the assassination of Leon Trotsky in Mexico, and a musical comedy, "O Canada," but he did not get very far with the writing of either. Klein seems to have invested much more of himself in another work intended for the stage, translating and adapting *The Hands of Euridice*, a work by a Brazilian Jew, Pedro Bloch. Klein was intrigued by what he considered the psychological complexity and subtleties of this tragedy, and he regarded his role in shaping the final form of the play, retitled *Conscience*, more as that of coauthor than translator. The play, which was experimental, a staged dramatic monologue, was performed in 1952 in New York by the well-known Yiddish actor Maurice Schwartz. To Klein's deep disappointment, it failed dismally, and scheduled performances in New York and other cities were canceled.

In the 1950s, until he suffered a nervous breakdown in mid decade, Klein continued as editor of the *Canadian Jewish Chronicle*, and he lectured frequently to Jewish audiences in Canada and the United States on the Holocaust and on the newly emergent state of Israel, and occasionally he addressed groups on English writers, specifically James Joyce and Gerard Manley Hopkins. His breakdown, when it occurred, came as a shock. Yet, in retrospect, one can discern that the notes of frustration and fear which are found scattered in his earlier writing were becoming more strongly expressed with the passing years, and his sense of failure was becoming more pronounced. Although he had always been esteemed by those writers whose opinions he respected–E. J. Pratt, A. J. M. Smith, F. R. Scott, Irving Layton, and Louis Dudek, and the critics W. E. Collin, Leon Edel, E. K. Brown, Northrop Frye, and Desmond Pacey, to mention but a few– he felt neglected by the general reading public and by the Jewish community. After a short period spent in a hospital in late summer 1954, he attempted to return to his normal routine, but by the end of 1956 he withdrew from most of his activities and from virtually all contact with friends and family. Klein, who was delighted in 1949 when he received the Governor General's Award for Poetry for *The Rocking Chair and Other Poems*, responded faintly in 1957 when he was honored by the Royal Society of Canada with the Lorne Pierce Medal. His deep depression lasted until his death on 20 August 1972.

Since his death, Klein has continued to attract critical attention. His work has been widely anthologized, internationally, and many critics currently regard him as the single most important English-language Canadian writer of the

first half of the twentieth century. A major editorial project is under way in the 1980s, under the general directorship of Zailig Pollock, bringing all of Klein's published and significant unpublished work into print; volumes of his essays and editorials and his short stories appeared in 1982 and 1983; and a collection of his literary essays and reviews appeared in 1987. The last of these is divided into three sections, the first concerning such subjects as the *Zohar* and the poet J. I. Segal, the second recording Klein's enthusiasms for Kafka and others, and the third gathering his several commentaries on Joyce. Edited volumes of poetry and various unpublished manuscripts are still to come.

Klein's achievement through his writings is many-faceted. Steeped in the culture and traditions of his people, he gave effective expression in poems, stories and essays, to his sense of their rich historic past, biblical and postbiblical, and to their present situation as a minority group–their sufferings and insecurity, and their celebrations and aspirations. His writings also express a sympathetic understanding of French-Canadian life and an appreciation of its values and did so at a time when in a divided Canada the non-French-speaking majority ignored or misunderstood this culture, or treated it with condescension. His ability to relate as well as finely distinguish between differing cultural and religious concepts is seen clearly in his novel *The Second Scroll*, perhaps his greatest single literary achievement. In terms of the poetic language, the wealth of allusions, the interlaced levels of meaning presented largely through an intricate use of symbolism, this novel is a uniquely rich and profound work.

Klein's learning and passionate convictions, his humor and wit, playful, ironic, and satiric, and his ability to fuse thought and passion, frequently suffused with lyric beauty, impart to his writings a depth and sophistication which, together with the broad appeal of a sentimental yearning for the past, for the childlike and fanciful, and for the simple virtues, ensure him an eminent place on the Canadian literary roster. His contribution to the literary scene goes beyond his own writings. His role in the community of writers, the Montreal Group in the 1930s and the *Preview* and *First Statement* groups in the 1940s, helped to stimulate poetic activity and widen its scope of subject and style.

In addition to his poetry, novels, and short stories, Klein wrote book reviews, much literary criticism, and translations from Hebrew and Yiddish literature. His work as a journalist, however, deserves special mention. He put to the service of the causes he defended or espoused all the powers of rhetoric, the incisive logical quality of mind, the force of passion that informed all his commitments. As editor of the *Canadian Jewish Chronicle* from 1938 to 1955 he was a spokesman for the Jewish community, which was living through the traumatic days of Hitler, World War II, and the painful but exhilarating rebirth of the Jewish state of Israel. Through his many activities and achievements Klein, though he may not have appreciated the fact in his time, undoubtedly made a deep and lasting impression on his generation, one that will continue as long as his works are read.

Bibliographies:

David Rome, *Jews in Canadian Literature: A Bibliography* (Montreal: Canadian Jewish Congress and Jewish Public Library, 1962);

Usher Caplan, "A. M. Klein: A Bibliography and Index to Manuscripts," in *The A. M. Klein Symposium*, edited by Seymour Mayne (Ottawa: University of Ottawa Press, 1975).

References:

D. M. R. Bentley, "Nightmare Ordered," *Essays on Canadian Writing*, 28 (Spring 1984): 1-45;

M. I. Broad, "Art & the Artist: Klein's Unpublished Novella," *Journal of Canadian Fiction*, no. 30 (1980): 114-131;

Richard Cavell, "Nth Adam: Dante in Klein's *The Second Scroll*," *Canadian Literature*, 106 (Autumn 1985): 45-53;

W. E. Collin, "The Spirit's Palestine," in his *The White Savannahs* (Toronto: Macmillan, 1936), pp. 207-231;

Louis Dudek, "A. M. Klein," *Canadian Forum*, 30 (April 1950): 10-12;

Leon Edel, "Abraham M. Klein," *Canadian Forum*, 12 (May 1932): 300-302;

G. K. Fischer, *In Search of Jerusalem: Religion and Ethics in the Writings of A. M. Klein* (Montreal: McGill-Queen's University Press, 1975);

E. S. Fisher, "A. M. Klein: Portrait of the Poet as Jew," *Canadian Literature*, 79 (Winter 1978): 121-127;

N. Golfman, "Semantics and Semitics," *University of Toronto Quarterly*, 51 (Winter 1981-1982): 175-191;

M. Greenstein, "History in *The Second Scroll*," *Canadian Literature*, 76 (Spring 1978): 37-46;

Journal of Canadian Studies, special Klein issue, 19 (Summer 1984);

Dorothy Livesay, "The Polished Lens: Poetic Techniques of Pratt and Klein," *Canadian Literature*, 25 (Summer 1965): 33-42;

Tom Marshall, ed., *A. M. Klein* (Toronto: Ryerson, 1970);

Seymour Mayne, ed., *The A. M. Klein Symposium* (Ottawa: University of Ottawa Press, 1975);

Ira Nadel, "The Absent Prophet in Canadian Jewish Fiction," *English Quarterly*, 5 (Spring 1972): 83-92;

Desmond Pacey, "A. M. Klein," in his *Ten Canadian Poets* (Toronto: Ryerson, 1958), pp. 254-292;

Z. Pollock, "Sunflower Seeds: Klein's Hero and Demagogue," *Canadian Literature*, 82 (Autumn 1979): 48-58;

K. C. Russell, "Blasphemies of A. M. Klein," *Canadian Literature*, 72 (Spring 1977): 59-66;

A. J. M. Smith, "Abraham Moses Klein," *Les Gants du Ciel*, 11 (Spring 1946): 67-81;

M. W. Steinberg, "A. M. Klein as Journalist," *Canadian Literature*, 82 (Autumn 1979): 21-30;

Steinberg, "The Conscience of Art: A. M. Klein on Poets and Poetry," in *A Political Art: Essays and Images in Honor of George Woodcock*, edited by W. H. New (Vancouver: University of British Columbia Press, 1978), pp. 82-94;

Steinberg, "Poet of a Living Past," *Canadian Literature*, 25 (Summer 1965): 5-20;

Steinberg, "A Twentieth Century Pentateuch," *Canadian Literature*, 2 (Autumn 1959): 37-46;

Miriam Waddington, *A. M. Klein* (Toronto: Copp Clark, 1970);

L. Weir, "Portrait of the Poet as a Joyce Scholar: An Approach to A. M. Klein," *Canadian Literature*, 76 (Spring 1978): 47-55;

Milton Wilson, "Klein's Drowned Poet," *Canadian Literature*, 6 (Autumn 1960): 5-17.

Papers:

The major collection of Klein's papers—notebooks, diaries, letters—is at the Public Archives of Canada in Ottawa. The collection includes an unpublished novel, "That Walks Like a Man."

Raymond Knister

(27 May 1899-29 August 1932)

Lee Briscoe Thompson
University of Vermont

BOOKS: *White Narcissus* (Toronto: Macmillan, 1929; New York: Harcourt, Brace, 1929; London: Cape, 1929);

My Star Predominant (Toronto: Ryerson, 1934; London: Melrose, 1934);

Collected Poems, edited, with a memoir, by Dorothy Livesay (Toronto: Ryerson, 1949);

Selected Stories of Raymond Knister, edited, with an introduction, by Michael Gnarowski (Ottawa: University of Ottawa Press, 1972);

Raymond Knister: Poems, Stories and Essays, edited by David Arnason (Montreal: Bellrock Press, 1975);

The First Day of Spring: Stories and Other Prose, edited, with an introduction, by Peter Stevens (Toronto: University of Toronto Press, 1976).

OTHER: *Canadian Short Stories*, edited, with an introduction, by Knister (Toronto: Macmillan, 1928).

PERIODICAL PUBLICATIONS: "The Canadian Short Story," *Canadian Bookman*, 5 (August 1923): 203-204;

"A Poet in Arms For Poetry," *Canadian Magazine*, 68 (October 1927): 28, 38-39;

"The Poetry of Archibald Lampman," *Dalhousie Review*, 7 (October 1927): 348-361;

Youth Goes West: A Play in One Act, Poet Lore, 39, no. 4 (1928): 582-585.

Raymond Knister with his daughter, Imogen, in 1932

Poet, fiction writer, critic, anthologist, and journalist, Raymond Knister was in Canadian writing of the 1920s and early 1930s an active and important force for imagism, for spare prose, and for themes of rural and everyday life. Knister published in all genres in Canada, the United States, and Britain. His death at age thirty-three meant he had little time to establish his popular and scholarly reputation, but in recent years that reputation has been secured, assuring him permanent status both as a skilled writer and as one of the initiators of modernism in Canadian letters.

Born on a farm near Comber in North Essex County, Ontario, John Raymond Knister grew up in close contact with the rural environment that would directly inform his fiction, his poetry, and his literary philosophies. His family, of German and Scottish extraction, stressed hard work and achievement, and young Knister's life revolved around schooling, chores, and the Methodist Church. Somewhat isolated, with only his sister Marjorie for a playmate and an increasingly severe habit of stuttering, Knister turned to the companionship of books and the satisfactions of his own writing. Even after his high-school education was complete and the Knisters moved from a corn-and-oats operation to fruit farming near Blenheim in Kent County, the boy continued to devote his free time to the written word, reading widely in British, American, and European literature, submitting poetry manuscripts to publishers in North America and overseas.

In 1919 the Knisters allowed Raymond to register at Victoria College, but pneumonia and pleurisy cut short his studies. His enforced return to the rural life was unexpectedly instructive. Wrote Knister of this period: "When I got back to the farm and recovered my health, by dint of working fourteen to sixteen hours in the field until autumn, I began to change my views about writing. There was something about the life that I lived, and all the other farm people round me, something that had to be expressed, though I didn't know just how." Decided upon the short story and resolved that "One must be objective," Knister produced "The One Thing" and "was not surprised, though rather gratified" to have it published by the well-regarded Iowan journal, the *Midland*. Farm stories and poems "with the eye on the object" began to flow from his pen and make appearances in important little magazines, including the prestigious Chicago journal *Poetry* and the avant-garde Parisian periodical *This Quarter*. Such articles of the 1920s as "The Canadian Short Story" (*Canadian Bookman*, August 1923) and "The Poetry of Archibald Lampman" (*Dalhousie Review*, October 1927) show Knister as an informed and perceptive critic, active in the nationalist/literary concerns of that decade and in experimentation with such modernist developments as realism and imagism.

Knister spent much of 1922 and 1923, when he was not engaged in private literary projects, as a reviewer for the Windsor *Border Cities Star* and the *Detroit Free Press*. A meeting with *Midland* publisher J. T. Frederick led to part of one year's service as editor of that midwestern journal to which he had already contributed many pieces. There followed a stint of taxi-driving in Chicago and continued reviewing for both the *Chicago Evening Post* and *Poetry*.

Returning in late 1924 to Ontario, first to a farm and then to Toronto, Knister started to make frequent contributions to the *Star Weekly* in the form of light sketches of rural life in mythical Corncob Corners. These homey vignettes were the bread-and-butter side of the increasing domi-

Drawing of Knister by his wife, Myrtle Gamble Knister, used on the title page for the 1975 collection Raymond Knister: Poems, Stories and Essays

nance of fiction in Knister's writing. He finished two still-unpublished novels, "Group Portrait" (later revised and retitled "Soil in Smoke") and "Turning Loam" (previously known as "Back Concessions," "Easy Going," and "The Happy Family"). Shortly after, he began to write *White Narcissus*, the novel which was published in 1929 in Canada, the United States, and Great Britain. *White Narcissus* contrasts human romanticism and nature's realism, as a successful writer, Richard, tries to persuade his hometown sweetheart, Ada, to choose him over her parents. Critics assessed the book as interesting and competent, perhaps flawed in plotting and characterization but effectively realistic in its descriptions of rural Ontario, lyrical in style, and unmistakably Canadian.

One of the assets of city life for Knister was its literary opportunities, and he made the acquaintance of such writers as Morley Callaghan, Mazo de la Roche, Merrill Denison, and Charles G. D. Roberts. A correspondence began with A. J. M. Smith, poet and editor of the *McGill Fortnightly Review*, on the subject of a projected (but never realized) literary journal, to be called "Revisions." By the late 1920s a respected figure in eastern Canadian literary circles; called upon to lecture at the University of Toronto on the poetry of D. C. Scott; a reviewer for *Saturday Night*, the *New Outlook*, and the *Canadian Magazine*; a prolific and distinguished fiction writer, regularly accorded one to three stars in Edward O'Brien's *Best Short Stories* volumes for 1925 through 1931, Knister was a logical choice as anthologist of the first *Canadian Short Stories* collection (1928). Critics proclaimed the anthology "excellent" and valuable in both selection and introduction.

Knister, meanwhile, did not altogether neglect poetry, for he assembled a selection of his verse under the title *Windfalls for Cider*, which was accepted for publication by Lorne Pierce of Ryerson. The foreword to that unlucky volume, dated 26 November 1926, was a succinct challenge to the entrenched romanticism of current Canadian letters and a declaration of Knister's aesthetic:

> Birds and flowers and dreams are real as sweating men and swilling pigs. But the feeling about them is not always so real any more when it gets into words. Because of that, it would be good just to place them before the reader, just let the reader picture them with utmost economy and clearness, and be moved by little things and great. Let him snivel, or be uncaring, or make his own poems from undeniable glimpses of the world.
>
> It would be good for the flowers and birds and dreams, and good for us. We would love them better, and be more respectful. And we might feel differently about many other common things if we saw them clearly enough. In the end we in Canada here might have the courage of our experience and speak according to it only. And when we trust surely, see directly enough, life, ourselves, we may have our own Falstaffs and Shropshire Lads and Anna Kareninas.

Knister's photograph on the title page for Essays on Canadian Writing, *Fall-Winter 1979-1980*

Because of financial setbacks the appearance of *Windfalls for Cider* was delayed until the 1949 publication of Dorothy Livesay's edition of Knister's *Collected Poems*. If Livesay's controversial memoir has since been challenged, the caliber of many of those Knister poems has not. Particularly admired have been "The Hawk," "Boy Remembers in the Fields," "Lake Harvest," "A Row of Stalls," and "The Plowman." All move the reader by their descriptions of nature, man, and mood so sharply etched that a surreal echo is achieved. The metrics are a fluid free verse, seemingly effortless yet disciplined into that effect of inevitability by a skilled poet's ear for the ways of plain human speech.

Drama, too, had a small place in the Knister canon. In 1922 he dramatized a short story he had written the previous year, "The Loading," and declared his models to be Strindberg and Chekhov, his intention to capture the monotony of or-

dinary life. Some six years later, under the title *Youth Goes West*, the play was published in an important American magazine, *Poet Lore*. The pattern had not yet ceased of foreign rather than Canadian publishers being the first to take a chance on Knister.

In Knister's private life, a brief engagement in 1926 to an Iowan woman, Marion Font, ended (according to one account) when she insisted he stop writing. A fair gauge of his emotional recovery may be his marriage in Toronto a year later to Myrtle Gamble. A daughter, Imogen, was born in June of 1930, after the couple's move to Port Dover. The responsibilities of marriage and then parenthood reinforced Knister's determination to achieve financial security through his writing; he soon was known as a prodigious writer capable of producing as many as 6,000 words a day, of an article or story per week, and of indefatigable revision.

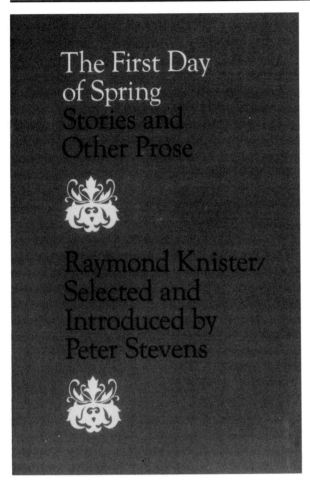

Cover for the collection that represents "an important rediscovery of one of Canada's best writers of the 1920s"

Years of struggle appeared to have paid off when, in 1931, Knister was awarded first prize in the Graphic Publishers' annual novel contest for *My Star Predominant*, a fictional rendering of the life of John Keats. While the award did bring Knister some acclaim, Graphic succumbed to bankruptcy before either full payment of the promised $2,500 or publication of the novel. Indeed, the book did not appear until 1934, two years after Knister's death, and inevitably prompted comparisons of its subject with the star-crossed destiny of the author.

Undaunted by the failure of the prize money to materialize in 1931, Knister went ahead with his plan to familiarize himself with another region of Canada by moving to Montreal. That year in Quebec, although perhaps the most economically severe for the Knisters, was sweetened by literary and personal relationships with other struggling writers such as Leo Kennedy, Frederick Philip Grove, Dorothy Livesay, A. M.

Klein, and F. R. Scott. Faced, as they all were, with the difficulty of publishing in the Great Depression, and eager to show the new directions of young Canadian poets, Knister and Kennedy began to collaborate upon an anthology of modern Canadian verse. Only in 1936, under the title of *New Provinces*, did the anthology appear—and without Knister's name or selections from his work.

For the first six months of 1932 Knister settled his family in Ste. Anne de Bellevue and produced a good half-dozen stories. During that final summer, the Knisters were helped by his former teacher and longtime supporter, critic Pelham Edgar, to find accommodations in Port Hope. Knister's intention was to commute from there to Toronto, having accepted Lorne Pierce's offer of a permanent position with the Ryerson Press, as well as a free-lance consultation on the prose choices for a planned Canadian anthology. At a time of renewed opportunities and high reputation, Knister drowned tragically on the last day of a short family vacation at Stoney Point, Lake St. Clair. While subsequent critical treatments of Knister's life and writings have been colored by lingering questions about the possibility of depression and suicide, most recent commentators have been inclined to argue against this theory and to assert Knister's firm confidence in his writing and his future.

Although critical commentary since his death has tended to focus on a budding talent untimely lost, one does well to take note of the remarkable amount Knister was able to accomplish in only a decade. He published the first anthology of Canadian short stories, with a valuable introduction; two novels (with two more drafted and one outlined); a play; at least thirty-two poems and fifty short stories (many later widely republished); some fifty-seven articles and reviews under his own name, apart from numerous unsigned or pseudonymous pieces for American newspapers; and seminal discussions of his nation's and his time's literature. Posthumously published editions of his verse and prose have renewed interest in this early imagist writer, this incisive poet of spoken language and captor of sensory experience. Both in poetry and in fiction, his sharp, simple images and clear, strong, rhythmic language are remarkably powerful. Among his creative and critical writings one may find a truly Canadian modernist fighting, as were his cosmopolitan contemporaries, to move Canadian letters out of romantic Victorian complacencies but choosing a route quite different from his associates' complicated (to some, neocolonial) metaphysical and mythopoeic pursuits. To see clearly enough and to write of it clearly enough: these were Knister's highest goals and in them he was often successful.

Bibliographies:

Marcus Waddington, "Raymond Knister, A Bibliographical Note," *Journal of Canadian Fiction*, 4, no. 2 (1975): 175-192;

Margery Fee and Ruth Cawker, eds., *Canadian Fiction: An Annotated Bibliography* (Toronto: PMA, 1976), p. 63;

A. Burke, "Raymond Knister: An Annotated Checklist," *Essays On Canadian Writing*, 16 (Fall-Winter 1979-1980): 20-61.

References:

David Arnason, Preface to *Raymond Knister: Poems, Stories and Essays*, edited by Arnason (Montreal: Bellrock Press, 1975), pp. 7-10;

Imogen Givens, "Death by Drowning," *Books in Canada*, 16 (August/September 1987): 38;

Givens, "Raymond Knister–Man or Myth?," *Essays on Canadian Writing*, 16 (Fall-Winter 1979-1980): 5-19;

Leo Kennedy, "A Poet's Memoirs," *CV/II*, 2 (May 1976): 23-24;

Kennedy, "Raymond Knister," *Canadian Forum*, 12 (September 1932): 459-461;

Dorothy Livesay, "Death by Drowning," *Books in Canada*, 16 (April 1987): 15-16;

Livesay, "Raymond Knister: A Memoir," in *Collected Poems of Raymond Knister*, edited by Livesay (Toronto: Ryerson, 1949), pp. xi-xii;

Don Precosky, "Ever With Discontent. Some Comments on Raymond Knister and His Poetry," *CV/II*, 4 (Spring 1980): 3-9;

Peter Stevens, "The Old Futility of Art: Knister's Poetry," *Canadian Literature*, 23 (Winter 1965): 45-52;

Milton Wilson, "Klein's Drowned Poet: Canadian Variations on an Old Theme," *Canadian Literature*, 6 (Autumn 1960): 5-17.

Papers:

Knister's papers are at Victoria College Library, Toronto, and Queen's University Archives, Kingston, Ontario.

Albert Laberge

(18 February 1871-4 April 1960)

B.-Z. Shek
University of Toronto

BOOKS: *La Scouine* (Montreal: Privately printed, 1918); translated by Conrad Dion as *Bitter Bread* (Montreal: Harvest House, 1977);

Quand chantait la cigale (Montreal: Privately printed, 1936);

Visages de la vie et la mort (Montreal: Privately printed, 1936);

Peintres et écrivains d'hier et d'aujourd'hui (Montreal: Privately printed, 1938);

La Fin du voyage (Montreal: Privately printed, 1942);

Scènes de chaque jour (Montreal: Privately printed, 1942);

Journalistes, écrivains et artistes (Montreal: Privately printed, 1945);

Charles de Belle, peintre-poète (Montreal: Privately printed, 1949);

Le Destin des hommes (Montreal: Privately printed, 1950);

Fin de roman (Montreal: Privately printed, 1951);

Images de la vie (Montreal: Privately printed, 1952);

Le Dernier Souper (Montreal: Privately printed, 1953);

Propos sur nos écrivains (Montreal: Privately printed, 1954);

Hymnes à la terre (Montreal: Privately printed, 1955);

Anthologie d'Albert Laberge, edited by Gérard Bessette (Montreal: Cercle du Livre de France, 1963).

Photograph of Albert Laberge by Emile Maupas reproduced on the endpapers for Peintres et écrivains d'hier et d'aujourd'hui, *1938 (courtesy of Kenneth Landry)*

Albert Laberge was a pioneer of naturalism and realism in French-Canadian fiction, modes that developed late in Quebec because of the powerful conservative influences of clerical and lay ideologues. Together with his friend Rodolphe Girard's *Marie Calumet* (1904), Laberge's novel, *La Scouine*, published privately in an edition of sixty copies in 1918 (translated as *Bitter Bread*, 1977), launched a short-lived foray against the idealized *roman de la fidélité* which presented the Quebec countryside as a haven of tranquillity and spiritual Catholic values. With a few notable excep-

tions (especially Ringuet's *Trente Arpents*, 1938), the Quebec novel eschewed realism until World War II, and it was not until the late 1950s and the 1960s that a neonaturalist trend reappeared, some four decades after *La Scouine*, in works by Gérard Bessette, Marie-Claire Blais, and Roch Carrier.

Laberge was born to farmers, Pierre and Joséphine Boursier Laberge, in Beauharnois, south of Montreal, one of nine children. His pri-

211

mary and secondary schooling took place in the area of his birthplace. In 1888 he began his *cours classique* at the well-known Jesuit institution, the Collège Sainte-Marie in Montreal, from which he was expelled four years later for having been caught reading "dangerous" fiction.

Thanks to a doctor uncle, Laberge began to read French romantic and symbolist poets and then Balzac and Zola. In 1891 he became familiar with the works of Guy de Maupassant, who had a strong effect on him. The next year he became linked to leading figures of the Ecole de Montréal, a modernist literary group, which he would leave soon afterward, probably for personal reasons. Laberge began to publish short stories in Montreal periodicals in 1895. By the end of his life he had published fourteen volumes (all at his own expense in small private editions), of which nine were short-story collections. The rest were sketches and biographies of Quebec journalists, writers, and artists. These had their source in his career as a journalist with the Montreal daily *La Presse*, where for twenty-three years he was art critic and for thirty-six years, sports editor.

Laberge wrote his major work, the novel *La Scouine*, over a period of twenty-two years, from 1895 to 1917. He reestablished ties with the Ecole de Montréal paradoxically during that group's regionalist phase. In 1909 he read before the Ecole an excerpt from *La Scouine*, chapters of which began to appear in various Montreal periodicals. That same year his twentieth chapter, which describes a sexual encounter between Charlot Deschamps, a member of the novel's central family, and a drunk and mud-stained Irishwoman, appeared in *La Semaine*. The archbishop of Montreal, Msgr Paul Bruchési, condemned this text as "[de] l'ignoble pornographie" and added: "Il faut couper le mal dans sa racine" (One must nip evil in the bud). For seven years Laberge remained silent, before again offering excerpts from *La Scouine* to a number of journals. He took even greater care in publishing several chapters from a novel he would never complete, "Lamento," by using the pen name Adrien Clamer. This work was centered on a sexually obsessed female character.

La Scouine finally appeared in its entirety in 1918. Its dedication, seemingly ironic, given Laberge's anticlericalism and his novel's demythification of traditional rural values, reads: "A mon cher frère Alfred qui, près des grands peupliers verts, pointus comme des clochers d'église, laboure et ensemence de ses mains le champ paternel, je dédie ces pages ... " (To my dear brother Alfred who, near the great green poplars, pointed like church belfreys, labors and sows with his hands our father's field, I dedicate these pages ...).

The novel has been described as a series of tableaux of rural life in the Beauharnois area, from 1853 until about the end of the century, loosely tied together by the tribulations of the Deschamps family, and the evolution of the life of one of the two twin daughters, Paulima, nicknamed La Scouine because of her malodorous bedwetting into adolescence. The story can be divided into four parts: from Paulima's birth to her sixteenth birthday; from her sister Caroline's marriage until the fateful fall of brother Charlot from the roof of a house he was building for a bride he would never have; the gradual breakdown of the Deschamps family through greed and violence; and the death of the father, Urgèle, and the mother Mâço's move, with Paulima and Charlot, to a house next to the cemetery in her native village. The entire work is syncopated by an unvaried refrain, symbolizing the bitter bread of the Deschampses' evening meal and entire existence: "le pain du souper ... lourd comme du sable, au goût sur et amer" (the supper bread ... heavy like sand, with the sour and bitter taste) and which will be marked with a knife, ironically, in the sign of the cross. Gilles Dorion, in his essay *La Scouine* for the *Dictionnaire des œuvres littéraires du Québec* (volume 2, 1980), has summed up generally well the novel's basic pessimism and fatalism and shabby portrait of human behavior: "Selon ce roman, aucun amour, aucune tendresse n'existe entre les êtres. Les rapports humains baignent dans l'égoïsme le plus asséchant.... La misère et la mort sont le lot commun" (According to this novel, no love, no tenderness exists among the characters. Human relations are steeped in the most draining egoism.... Misery and death are the common lot). One could add that a key naturalist trait of the work is its general assimilation of humans and animals, with stress on man's lower, purely biological behavior.

Critics Gérard Bessette, Jacques Brunet, Paul Wyczynski, and others have gone even further, interpreting Laberge's novel as one that is totally impassive, clinical, bereft of any ideological insights or explanations. This view can be contested by pointing to the sharper focus put on the class divisions in the countryside than was the

Cover for a later edition of the 1963 collection comprising six extracts from Laberge's novel La Scouine *and twelve short stories*

case before *La Scouine*; to Laberge's wail about "les éternels exploités de la glèbe" (the eternal exploited ones of the land); to his admiration of some of the minor characters, especially the female teachers and other women and the old beggar; to his clear sympathy for the francophones who are prevented from voting and beaten and humiliated by anglophone Tories, and for those cheated by the merchant Linche, whose name seems to be a veiled version of the Irish *Lynch*. All of these touches, however, do not take away from the somber, crushing tonality of the novel. And Gabrielle Pascal is convincing when she states in *Le Défi d'Albert Laberge* (1976) that the anticlerical, antitraditionalist Laberge seems to come full circle and join his adversaries (no doubt unwit-

tingly) by his profound pessimism about earthly life and his puritanical, guilt-ridden treatment of sexuality.

Critical evaluation of the novel's style and structure ranges from near-total deprecation to exaggerated praise for an alleged total fusion of form and content. Most critics have questioned the choice of the title, since other characters are equal in importance to Paulima. One could argue, though, that her misanthropy, cruelty, perversity, and arrested infantilism are symbolic of the harsh universe created by Laberge.

In any case Albert Laberge is an important writer who was neglected by official literary history in Quebec until the 1960s. During the Quiet Revolution, in a period when traditional ideologies were sharply questioned, his work was republished and given its rightful place, in spite of its inadequacies and rough-hewn character. Gérard Bessette's *Anthologie d'Albert Laberge* appeared in 1963, followed by a facsimile edition of *La Scouine* in 1968 (Réédition-Quebec) and another published by L'Actuelle in 1972. The first critical edition, edited by Paul Wyczynski and including his long introduction and copious notes, appeared in 1986. A ballet entitled *La Scouine* was created in Montreal by Les Grands Ballets Canadiens in 1977, choreographed by Fernard Nault.

References:

Gérard Bessette, Preface to *Anthologie d'Albert Laberge*, edited by Bessette (Montreal: Cercle du Livre de France, 1963), pp. vii-xxxiii;

Jacques Brunet, *Albert Laberge, sa vie et son œuvre* (Ottawa: Editions de l'Université d'Ottawa, 1969);

Gabrielle Pascal, *Le Défi d'Albert Laberge* (Montreal: Editions Aquila, 1976);

B.-Z. Shek, *Social Realism in the French-Canadian Novel* (Montreal: Harvest House, 1977), pp. 52-54;

Thuong Vuong-Riddick, "Une Relecture de *La Scouine*," *Voix et Images*, 3 (September 1977): 116-126.

Papers:

Laberge's papers are at the University of Ottawa and at Université Laval, Quebec City.

Dorothy Livesay

(12 October 1909-   )

Lee Briscoe Thompson
University of Vermont

BOOKS: *Green Pitcher* (Toronto: Macmillan, 1928);

Signpost (Toronto: Macmillan, 1932);

Day and Night (Boston: Humphries, 1944; Toronto: Ryerson, 1944);

Poems for People (Toronto: Ryerson, 1947);

Call My People Home (Toronto: Ryerson, 1950);

New Poems, edited by Jay Macpherson (Toronto: Emblem Books, 1955);

Selected Poems of Dorothy Livesay (Toronto: Ryerson, 1957);

The Colour of God's Face (Vancouver: Unitarian Service Committee, 1964);

The Unquiet Bed (Toronto: Ryerson, 1967);

The Documentaries (Toronto: Ryerson, 1968);

Plainsongs (Fredericton: Fiddlehead, 1969; revised and enlarged, 1971);

Collected Poems: The Two Seasons (Toronto: McGraw-Hill Ryerson, 1972);

A Winnipeg Childhood (Winnipeg: Peguis, 1973); republished as *Beginnings: A Winnipeg Childhood* (Toronto: New Press, 1975);

Nine Poems of Farewell, 1972-1973 (Windsor, Ontario: Black Moss, 1973);

Ice Age (Erin, Ontario: Press Porcépic, 1975);

The Woman I Am: Best Loved Poems from One of Canada's Best Loved Poets (Erin, Ontario: Press Porcépic, 1977);

Right Hand Left Hand, edited by David Arnason and Kim Todd (Erin, Ontario: Press Porcépic, 1977);

The Raw Edges: Voices From Our Time (Winnipeg: Turnstone, 1981);

The Phases of Love (Toronto: Coach House Press, 1983);

Feeling The Worlds (Fredericton: Fiddlehead, 1984);

Beyond War: The Poetry (Vancouver: Privately printed, 1985);

Selected Poems: The Self-Completing Tree (Victoria & Toronto: Press Porcépic, 1986).

OTHER: *Collected Poems of Raymond Knister,* edited, with a memoir, by Livesay (Toronto: Ryerson, 1949);

"Mazo de la Roche," in *The Clear Spirit,* edited by Mary Quayle Innes (Toronto: University of Toronto Press, 1966), pp. 242-259;

"The Documentary Poem: A Canadian Genre," in *Contexts of Canadian Criticism: A Collection of Critical Essays,* edited by Eli Mandel (Chicago: University of Chicago Press, 1971; revised edition, Toronto: University of Toronto Press, 1977), pp. 267-281;

40 Women Poets of Canada, edited by Livesay and Seymour Mayne (Montreal: Ingluvin, 1971);

"A Writer in the Depression," in *Essays in B.C. Political Economy,* edited by Paul Knox and Philip Reznick (Vancouver: New Star, 1974);

Joan McCullagh, *Alan Crawley and "Contemporary Verse,"* foreword by Livesay (Vancouver: University of British Columbia, 1976);

Woman's Eye: 12 B.C. Poets, edited, with a foreword, by Livesay (Vancouver: Air, 1978);

Christina van der Mark, *In Due Season,* introduction by Livesay (Vancouver: New Star Press, 1979), pp. i-iii;

Selected Stories of Mazo de la Roche, edited by Douglas Daymond, memoir by Livesay (Ottawa: University of Ottawa Press, 1979), pp. 11-13;

Down Singing Centuries; Folk Literature of the Ukraine, translated by Florence Randal Livesay, compiled and edited by Dorothy Livesay and Louisa Loeb (Winnipeg: Hyperion, 1981).

PERIODICAL PUBLICATIONS: "This Canadian Poetry," *Canadian Forum* (April 1944): 20-21;

"The Poetry of Anne Marriott," *Educational Record* (Quebec), 65 (April-June 1949): 87-90;

"The Polished Lens: Poetic Techniques of Pratt and Klein," *Canadian Literature,* 25 (Summer 1965): 33-42;

"The Sculpture of Poetry: On Louis Dudek," *Canadian Literature,* 30 (Autumn 1966): 26-35;

Dorothy Livesay (photograph by Janosz Meissner)

"Search for a Style: The Poetry of Milton Acorn," *Canadian Literature*, 40 (Spring 1969): 33-42;

"Song and Dance," *Canadian Literature*, 41 (Summer 1969): 40-48;

"Getting It Straight," *Impulse*, 2, nos. 3-4 (1973): 29-35;

"Tennyson's Daughter or Wilderness Child? The Factual and Literary Background of Isabella Valancy Crawford," *Journal of Canadian Fiction*, 2 (Summer 1973): 161-167;

"The Hunters Twain," *Canadian Literature*, 55 (Winter 1973): 75-98;

"Carr and Livesay," *Canadian Literature*, 84 (Spring 1980): 144-147;

"The Woman Writer and the Idea of Progress," *Canadian Forum*, 62 (November 1982): 18-19, 35.

Dorothy Kathleen Livesay may be evaluated as one of Canada's foremost modern writers by several criteria. First there is abundance: twenty-two published volumes of verse or prose; three edited books; nearly five hundred poems in periodicals and anthologies; approaching one

hundred fifty articles, reviews, and open letters; two dozen short stories and vignettes; approximately eighty journalistic pieces; five plays; five poetry broadsides; four librettos or texts for interpretive dance; and new work, particularly her memoirs, in preparation. Then there is versatility: poetry, fiction, essay, literary criticism, journalism, anthologizing, founding/editing of several periodicals. Third is recognition–two Governor General's awards for poetry (1944, 1947); the Order of Canada (1987); the Governor General's "Persons" Award (1984); the Lorne Pierce Medal of the Royal Society of Canada (1947) for a significant contribution to Canadian literature; the President's Medal from the University of Western Ontario for poetry (1954); honorary degrees from the University of Waterloo (1974), Athabaska (1983), McGill (1985), and Simon Fraser (1987) universities; fellow of St. John's College, University of Manitoba (1976), and Trinity College, University of Toronto (1987); a Canada Council Fellowship (1958-1959) and a Senior Arts Grant (1977); visits as the guest of foreign governments and universities; a half-century of predominantly praising reviews; accolades from fellow poets and general readers; spotlighting on Canadian radio, in numerous interviews, on various audio recordings, and as the subject of a Toronto film *The Woman I Am.* The breadth of her impact has been undernoticed until comparatively recently, but it has come to be recognized at last as vast, born of active participation in nearly six decades of Canadian literary development and a refusal to identify herself with any single school or confining category.

Livesay has often described herself as growing up "in a garden," in the sense that both of her parents were writers, voracious readers, nurturers of Livesay's literary interests, providers of a fertile garden for their daughter. J. F. B. and Florence Randal Livesay, who met as journalists at the *Winnipeg Telegram* and married in 1908, would go on to make their marks in Canadian culture: the father as manager of the Canadian Press, essayist, and war historian; the mother as poet, novelist, and translator of Ukrainian literature. Born in Winnipeg into middle-class circumstances, Livesay and her younger sister, Sophie, were encouraged artistically from childhood. The texture of those prairie years would be captured in poetry and in the collection of short fiction entitled *A Winnipeg Childhood* (1973).

When, about 1920, the family shifted to Toronto and also acquired property at Clarkson, Livesay became acquainted with new aspects of the Canadian landscape: the lushness of Ontario, the brilliance of its autumns, and the conservative traditions and ceremonies of the Eastern establishment. Livesay attended first a private girls' school, Glen Mawr, and then a four-year honors course in modern languages at the University of Toronto. A bespectacled "bluestocking," she and her best friend, Eugenia "Jim" Watts, at first took little interest in the opposite sex but enormous interest in such writers as Emily Dickinson, Katherine Mansfield, D. H. Lawrence, and, later Bernard Shaw, Walt Whitman, Virginia Woolf, and Emma Goldman. The sophistication of even her earliest juvenilia may be attributed in part to the enriching influence in the Livesay household of everything from *Poetry* (Chicago) to the verse of Siegfried Sassoon. Throughout her youth Livesay's parents supported her educational ambitions and discreetly promoted publication of her adolescent writings.

In 1928, encouraged by two poetry awards, Livesay published with Macmillan of Canada a slim sixteen-paged volume of poetry, *Green*

Pitcher. For the work of a university sophomore, the book was remarkably well received, reviewed in such as the *Times Literary Supplement* and by such as Charles Bruce and Raymond Knister. Critics noted at once her skill with free as well as traditional verse forms; the musicality of her lines; a lyrical love of nature; and the recurrence of images of wind and rain, of flowers, of sun and night. Clarity of image and control of strong emotion impressed several commentators enough to predict great things for the young poet.

After a "junior year abroad" at Aix-en-Provence, soaking up French culture and attempting to record it all in a few articles for the *Toronto Star* and in a still unpublished novel, Livesay returned to her senior year at Toronto. There she had her first encounter, via a colorful professor named Otto Van der Sprenkel, with theoretical Marxism. Graduating with a degree in French and Italian in 1931, Livesay was sent to Paris to do a *thèse d'études supérieures* at the Sorbonne. In a Canadian circle which included future historian Stanley Ryerson and James critic Leon Edel, Livesay acquired some familiarity with Marx, Engels, and the left-wing French novelist Henri Barbusse. Of more impact, however, was her witnessing of police brutality, workers' parades, and civil disobedience. In the meantime, a tempestuous love affair prompted poems that would wait forty years to be published. Livesay dutifully completed an excellent study of the influence of the French symbolists and English metaphysicals on contemporary British poets such as the Sitwells, Aldous Huxley, T. S. Eliot. In the process she found herself increasingly alienated from the elitism and obscurantism of poets like Eliot as well as the sort of imagist poetry she had practiced as an undergraduate. By her return in 1932 to Canada and her first realization of the Great Depression, social concerns ruled her thinking.

Livesay's father was hoping she would try journalism, the teaching of languages, or diplomacy; certain critics and writer friends like Raymond Knister urged her to perfect her lyric poetry. To the newly radicalized young poet, these suggestions were anachronistic. Indeed she had that very reaction to the book of her own poetry that appeared months after her return once again to Toronto. *Signpost* (1932), nearly four times the length of *Green Pitcher,* was divided into "Sober Songs," "Pastorals," and "Variations." Critics delighted in the succinctness of language, sure hand with an image, lyrical beauty, modernist experimentation with form, and absence of senti-

was little reality in it, at the time.......I felt perfectly at ease, and could talk without feeling the discomfort of professional mockery. Bliss advises me to get my degree, even if it is a grind — perhaps because it is one. Talked to him about his Sappho, and Hérédia... Remember his half-senility, his "softness", above all, his hat. Oh, these artistic creatures, who are afraid of newspaperwomen & yet do their best to catch the public eye! Charles G. D. is more careful, nay, exceedingly careful of his appearance: he realizes that in the long run elegance is more attractive aux dames.

Page from Livesay's journal, 1928, describing a dinner with Bliss Carman and Charles G. D. Roberts (by permission of the author)

mental mush. To Livesay, however, it was no longer appropriate to be writing, no matter how evocatively, of rural Ontario scenes or the agonies of a private love. One reviewer who agreed with her put it this way: "Dorothy Livesay's poetry is poetry of herself, her own mind, and is still romantic in that sense. It has not enough contact with life."

Determined to take concrete action and see how the lower classes lived, Livesay enrolled in a social-work course which called for a first year of study in Toronto and a second year of apprenticeship in an agency. Assignment to the Family Service Bureau in Montreal provided a rapid lesson in poverty and repression. Livesay turned abruptly away from Georgian and imagist poetry and began to write proletarian verse, agit prop drama, and Marxist leaflets. Artifacts of her activism in the Young Communist League, the Progressive Arts Club, and the League Against War and Fascism, as well as samples of the literature produced in the service of those causes, have been collected in Livesay's 1977 retrospective of the 1930s, *Right Hand Left Hand*.

Critical assessment of Livesay's writing of this period has tended to be cool and dismissive, arguing that she deliberately and disastrously sacrificed her lyrical gifts and innate subtlety to what she regarded as a higher cause—proletarian literature and social revolution. Certainly, such poems as "Pink Ballad" have little more than enthusiasm and sincerity to commend them, but Livesay was feeling her way toward a new style of expression that would culminate splendidly in such pieces as her famous industrial poem "Day and Night" or the anguished and triumphant "Lorca." And the mass chants for labor halls, albeit crude, were obviously rhythmic, in accord with her lifelong principle that music underlies all poetry.

In the fall of 1934 social work took Livesay to Englewood, New Jersey, as caseworker for families on relief. While dismayed by her first encounter of racial prejudice against blacks, Livesay was positively stimulated by the diversity of her friendships, the countercultural experience of being Marxist and "color-blind," and the cultural energies of Franklin D. Roosevelt's New Deal. In New Jersey bookshops she discovered exciting new literary models in Britain's C. Day Lewis, Stephen Spender, and W. H. Auden—poets who managed to fuse revolutionary vision with lyricism and passion. At last she could see a way to reconcile the personal and the public/political; the way was

open to the dramatic jazz rhythms of the 1944 collection, *Day and Night*.

Illness, possibly a nervous breakdown, forced Livesay to return to Clarkson in 1935. Months spent recuperating in bed allowed her time to write of American steel mills, discrimination, and other social realities. E. J. Pratt accepted "Day and Night" for his first issue of *Canadian Poetry Magazine* (1936), declaring it "one of the best things I have ever seen you do." *New Frontier*, a leftist monthly, not only published her poetry, fiction, and reviews but also invited her to become western editor. Selling *New Frontier* subscriptions, speaking about modern poetry, writing articles about the places she visited, and learning about such aspects of Canadian labor history as the On to Ottawa Trek, the Regina Riots, and company towns such as Corbin, Livesay in 1936 moved westward toward Vancouver and a new phase—geographical, literary, and private—of her life.

In Vancouver Livesay quickly landed a family welfare job, which meshed nicely with her social activism and left-wing companionship. In August 1937 she married Duncan Macnair, a Scot of similar political and literary interests, who was also selling *New Frontier*. A writers' group they formed convinced the city to let them convert an old bath house on English Bay into the West End Community Centre. Domestic, political, and cultural activities cut to a trickle the number of poems and articles Livesay was able to complete and publish in this period. The birth of a son, Peter, and a daughter, Marcia, increased for a time the difficulties of full concentration on creative writing. In addition Livesay became an editor of Alan Crawley's journal, *Contemporary Verse*, which kept her in touch with a lively West Coast group of writers but was added responsibility. All of these commitments provided valuable material and instruction for a volume of poetry that would win Livesay one of her country's highest literary awards.

When *Day and Night* appeared in 1944, all but the most conservative Canadian critics greeted it with high praise. The collection of verse from 1934 to 1943 was arranged chronologically, from the most urgent of social indictments through personal and pastoral poems to a concluding portrait of the unexpected vitality World War II had given a shipyard town. The majority of reviewers lauded the intense expression, innovative driving rhythms, and overt bitterness of the social commentaries as much as or more than the lyrics of nature and the personal themes. Particularly appreciated was Livesay's clarity throughout: the crystalline imagery, the refreshing intelligibility, the precise control of sound, and the purity of tone. "Lorca," "The Child Looks Out," "The Outrider," "The Fallow Mind," "Prelude for Spring," "West Coast," and the title poem were repeatedly cited at the time and have been often published since. And nobody was much surprised at *Day and Night* carrying off the 1944 Governor General's Award for poetry.

After the war the *Toronto Star* sent Livesay to Europe for three months to report on conditions in Britain, Germany, and France. She sent some thirty articles back to Canada, tackling everything from the United Kingdom's shortage of milk to perceptions of UNESCO–Livesay's customary micro/macrocosmic range. Despite the fact that this was her most concentrated journalistic period, Livesay managed to draft a lengthy verse drama about Métis hero Louis Riel, eventually revised and published as "Prophet of the New World" in *Collected Poems: The Two Seasons* (1972).

More remarkably, Livesay wrote and brought together the poems for a second Governor General's Award-winner: *Poems for People* (1947). She divided the volume in three: "Poems of Childhood," "Poems for People," and "Poems as Pictures." The first section demonstrates, more freely than before, her celebration of sound; the second speaks with great sensitivity of war and its aftermath; the third sketches vivid vignettes from British Columbia to Wales. Once again there is the richly restrained diction, the energy and sensitivity, and the humanitarianism. More than ever before, Livesay shows her ability to see wholly through the eyes of others–the child's, the war veteran's.

In 1947 Livesay was awarded the Lorne Pierce Gold Medal of the Royal Society of Canada "in recognition of work of outstanding distinction throughout the years." The accompanying citation by W. O. Raymond applies as accurately to her subsequent writing as it did to the work then honored: "Whether she deals with Nature or Man, her art is never static or merely photographic. Professor E. K. Brown has written that her special power is energy, fiery and [some]-times smoky energy. Her individual quality is revealed in the dash and originality of her poetic imagery. Sharpness of outline, vivid colouring, impressionistic flashes of lyricism, are characteristics of her work. Yet her intuitive flair does not run into romantic extravagance, but is disciplined by

Livesay, circa 1928 (courtesy of the author)

careful and conscientious artistry. Her poetry is aesthetically as well as ethically sincere; and the dedication of her imaginative gifts to popular causes does not impair that beauty of pattern and rhythm which is one of the most attractive qualities of her verse."

From her childhood tended by Ukrainian girls on the cultural patchwork quilt of the prairies, through her ethnically diverse friendships in university, abroad, and in social work, Livesay has always been drawn to those different from herself and her WASP origins. That factor, combined with her instinct to defend underdogs (immigrants, blacks, native peoples, workers, veterans, women), made almost inevitable her writing next of a poetic exposé of injustices to Canada's Japanese in World War II. Encouraged by Malcolm Lowry and others, inspired by the nisei (literally, second-generation) student who boarded with her one winter, Livesay conceived of *Call My People Home* (1950) as a documentary poem to be read on radio. A restrained and balanced plea for reconciliation and brotherhood, the poem chronicles from multiple angles the evacuation and internment of Japanese fisher families from the Pacific coast. Reviews were mixed. The control, irony, imagery, and compassion were admired; some criticism was directed specifically to the more prosaic narrative parts and, more generally, to the problems of cadence in poetry especially created for radio. If the critics were uneasy with her innovation, not so her audiences. The poem was performed, when partly complete, on CBC in Vancouver; repeated in Montreal; printed in full in *Contemporary Verse;* and then republished in Ryerson Chapbook form, together with ten shorter poems full of sun and fire, trees and darkness. There have been several CBC repetitions since then, and another reprinting in Livesay's 1968 *The Documentaries.* The title poem of *Call My People Home* continues to be a frequent request at college and high-school readings.

During the early years of the 1950s Livesay put considerable effort into trying to break in a big way into fiction. Encouraged by interest expressed in a story entitled "The Glass House" (*Northern Review,* 1950; republished in Martha Foley's *The Best American Short Stories,* 1951), she made numerous fiction submissions to magazines but rarely was successful. Having been taught by her father to honor fiction above verse, Livesay has always seemed ruefully puzzled by the insistence of the majority of her readers that poetry is her major gift, her prose a minor talent in comparison.

Correspondence of this period shows Livesay increasingly restive under family obligations and eager to establish a more satisfying career, preferably in teaching. A short stint leading a creative-writing class at the University of British Columbia Extension Department was followed by an appointment in 1953 as director of the Young Adult Department of YMCA Vancouver. While she set up adult-education classes and such popular programs as Housewife's Holiday, she also continued to find time for verse. In 1955 Jay Macpherson edited a small chapbook of ten selections, *New Poems,* considered by some to be Livesay's best work to that point. "Bartok and the Geranium," an exciting and ambiguous juxtaposition of perfectly sustained images, is certainly one of the poems by Livesay most often anthologized and requested at readings. Another, perhaps even more popular, is "Lament," a moving poem about her father's death, recognized by the University of Western Ontario's President's Medal the previous year.

From 1956 to 1958 Livesay wrestled with the teaching of difficult adolescents and left with relief when a bursary for overseas study in educational methods became available. Her son Peter was planning to work a year with a land survey crew before starting university, and his sister Marcia had won a scholarship to a progressive school in Colorado. Leaving her husband at home, Livesay eagerly set off in the autumn of 1958 for studies at the Institute of Education, University of London. Nobody could have guessed that Duncan Macnair would collapse and die less than six months later.

Livesay has been candid about the cycles of grief, relief, and guilt that came with widowhood. Poems from this period, published largely in periodicals and later in the "Poems from Exile" section of *Collected Poems,* are sharp with images of death, mortality, dismemberment, counterpointed by a bright excitement about the new freedom open to the poet no longer bound by family responsibilities. With a strong sense of putting a gray, largely frustrating decade behind her, Livesay headed for Paris and a research position with UNESCO. In 1960 she accepted a UNESCO teaching post in Northern Rhodesia.

The African experience, of three years' duration, had an enormous impact upon Livesay. She immediately achieved a rapport with her black, adult students that contrasted strikingly with the condescension of her British colleagues toward their classes. After years of focus primarily upon the personal, her eyes were once again turned to the larger scene: the transition from tribal to industrial, from Northern Rhodesia to the new nation of Zambia–a gigantic, complex, and vital proceeding. As well, Livesay threw herself into her exploration of the texture, color, and taste of life in an alien world, characteristically scorning any ethnocentrism that would dismiss Zambian culture as inferior to or less attractive than the European or North American. Her letters, essays, and diaries from this period are rich with detailed description, anecdote, humanistic concern, and a rejoicing both in the warmth of her social contact and in the exhilaration of attending a country's birth.

Most important from a literary viewpoint was the way Africa brought Livesay into contact with song and dance. In an essay on the subject Livesay tells of students jitterbugging in the common room and of their delight when she participated. "And so Africa set me dancing again!" Lyricism had been part of her thought and work from the earliest years. She was daughter to a translator of Ukrainian songs, attended as a youngster by Slavic girls who sang as they worked. Anglicanism in childhood and adolescence had introduced her to the Psalms, the Song of Songs, and the aural pleasures of the liturgy. Whitman, free verse, and the ancient dance of sex were all part of her young adult pursuit of uninhibited rhythm. Even through the most radicalized and prosaic period her assaults on industrial madness had been repeatedly cast in assembly-line rhythms. In personal poetry of the 1940s and 1950s, natural rhythms did not abate. However, an increasing sense of stricture and confinement weighted her feet, saddened her song. It was a predictable condition in one who was mother of two; wife to an authoritarian older man; a working woman beset by financial and professional anxieties; a Western Canadian female writer in a national culture dominated by an Eastern male elite; and a citizen of a nation with a self-image of reserve and caution. Autonomous at last in the bright light of the "dark continent," she gave free rein to a sensuous appreciation of Africa's colors, sounds, and movements. The section "To Speak With Tongues" in *Collected Poems* and the 1964 publication of *The Colour of God's Face* (republished in the *Unquiet Bed*, 1967, and in *Collected Poems* as the "Zambia" sequence) demonstrate this new emphasis: the beating of drums, the drumming of rain, the circles of sun and moon, dance and ritual, life and love.

Returning to Canada in 1963, Livesay suffered severe doubts. The country seemed dull, grey, crass; few fully appreciated her African writings or had much interest in events beyond their frontiers; out of the public eye for so long, she felt shy about her poetic abilities, uncertain where she would fit in with such new poetry as the Black Mountain movement. Gradually put at ease by attending outdoor readings, teaching creative writing at the University of British Columbia, and coming to know the major faces and trends on the Canadian literary scene, Livesay found herself perfectly in tune with many elements of the 1960s. The hippie celebration of love, peace, and self-expression; the interest in artifacts of native peoples and natural lifestyles; and the experiments in expansion of consciousness and of language were all intensely compatible with the new openness to life that she felt and wished to embody in her art.

Small surprise that she should at this juncture fall in love with a much younger man with whom she discovered over the next five years the fullness possible in man-woman relationships. The impact on her writing was direct: *The Unquiet Bed*. Fresh, frank, spare, an expression of utter vulnerability and honesty, this book abandons structured meter and conventional rhyme almost entirely but stays taut and close to the bone, never sloppy or vague. It flows and ebbs, shouts and whispers, is altogether (as many noticed) a book to be read aloud. The treatment of sex and love is beautiful, with no blinking from pain, ecstasy, contradiction, or weakness, eager for communication whatever the personal price. The title poem anticipates feminist themes and gives illustration to Livesay's many decades of expressing a woman's perspectives. The last of the four lean stanzas warns simply:

> The woman I am
> is not what you see
> move over love
> make room for me

Reviewers of *The Unquiet Bed* praised its wit, maturity, candor, and wisdom, announcing that Livesay had outstripped the work of younger poets in sensitivity, erotic intensity, and directness.

On the heels of this triumph Livesay published *The Documentaries*, six poems reflecting Canadian historical events: "Ontario Story," "The Outrider," "Day and Night," "West Coast," "Call My People Home," and "Roots." Her intent was primarily to inform young Canadians about their past and the similarities between the concerns of the 1960s and those of the 1930s and 1940s. Critics, although approving, were contradictory in their reasons: some thought the poems excellent but only incidentally appealing as history; others considered them weak as art but perceptive as social documents. It must be said that Livesay has always and with some justification resented certain reviewers' dismissal of her political and public writing as less worthy than her apolitical material and makes no apology for that or any other phase of her writing. That some still consider the social impulse an immature stage in her development, however, is clear from such incidents as the wry treatment of the 1930s in the 1980 film about Livesay, *The Woman I Am*.

Yet another product of this poet's reemergence in Canada was *Plainsongs*, published in 1969 and again in expanded form in 1971. The collection's blend of objective description, pacifist and socially aware verse, and poems both passionate and specifically erotic was considered equal in quality and of a piece with the accomplishment of *The Unquiet Bed.*

Back in 1957 Desmond Pacey had edited and introduced a volume entitled *Selected Poems of Dorothy Livesay,* covering 1926 through 1956. While much of his analysis is valid today, Pacey wisely made plain that it was "impossible to predict just what turn" Livesay's poetry would take, that her track record of "constantly experimenting and growing in skill and power" guaranteed new directions. How true that was is seen at a glance in *Collected Poems: The Two Seasons* of 1972. No better commentary on this collection has been written than Livesay's own foreword, which explains in part:

> These poems . . . create an autobiography: a psychic if not a literal autobiography. All the people I have known intimately, loving or hating, are here. They have acted as catalysts. But there seems to be another source of poetry, quite outside one's conscious experience. I am not sure about its origin, internal or external. What happens is that one is "taken over" by other voices. . . . Does that account for the variety of styles one comes up with? Even within the space of one year I may write formally or informally; in a structured, almost classical style, or in a free arrangement of associations. Whatever the cause, always, I believe, I hear music behind the rhythm of the words. And always one or more of these symbols occur: the seasons; day and night; sun, wind and snow; the garden with its flowers and birds; the house, the door, the bed. Especially do I note the dichotomy that exists here between town and country— that pull between community and private identity that is characteristic of being a woman; and characteristic, for that matter, of life "north," life in Canada. Perhaps we are a country more feminine than we like to admit, because the unifying, regenerative principle is a passion with us. We make a synthesis of those two seasons, innocence and experience.

> Because publishing poetry in Canada during the thirties, forties and fifties was nothing like what it became in the sixties—a bonanza!—my books that surfaced had layers of poems beneath them which were forced to remain submarine. For this reason I have arranged the unpublished poems as if they were in books of their own, with individual titles (I delight in "naming" and in finding titles).

The book demonstrated what the readers of her poetry had known for several decades: that Livesay is one of Canada's best modern poets, and one who deserves an international audience.

The *Collected Poems* was no sign that Livesay was ending her career nor was *Nine Poems of Farewell, 1972-1973* (1973). In 1975 Livesay produced *Ice Age,* a book of verses which draws on the accumulated past but zeroes in on the feminine psyche and on aging, often in combination. Grandmother, old lady, elderly artist, underestimated silverhead, experienced explorer, sage individual contemplating extinctions personal and global—the facets glitter separately, then overlap. As one critic noted, in this work Livesay was still taking chances, the mark of a classy—no, a *great* poet. Free verse and street slang, contemporaneous references, vulgar humor, confessions, tenderness and defiance, irony and unabashed loneliness show Livesay unconcerned with promoting any late-life image of the impeccably wise senior bard. Tough, compassionate, straightforward yet subtle, offering warm hope simultaneously with a chilling glimpse of apocalypse, personal and ever political, Livesay's *Ice Age* testifies not to any glacial retreat but rather to her continuing profound balance of innocence and experience.

Wanting to reach new readers, in 1977 Livesay authorized the publication of the paperback *The Woman I Am: Best Loved Poems from One of Canada's Best Loved Poets,* providing a comprehensive selection of poems from 1926 to 1977. In accord with her oft-voiced complaint that anthologists kept passing over her recent work for such old favorites as "The Three Emilys," "Green Rain," and "Bartok and the Geranium," she allowed only thirty-three selections to be taken from her first eleven volumes; thirty-nine poems dated from her more recent work, several seeing print for the first time. The newest verses typically tackle mistreatment of native peoples and of children, Canadian disunity, abuse of the media, the case of a recently murdered poet. Increasingly prosaic, rather like "found" conversational poems, many of these selections reinforced Livesay's pronouncements that she wishes in her final years to concentrate upon prose.

Indeed, in the midst of her poetry, Livesay had already returned to her first literary love. In 1973 she drew together short stories which had been in the making since at least the 1950s and

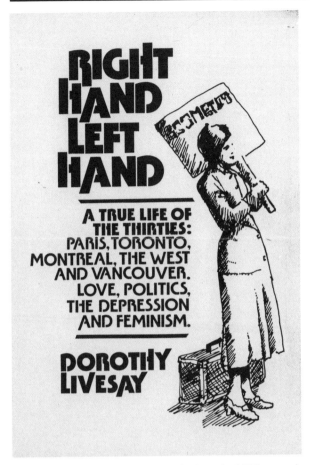

Cover for the paperback edition of Livesay's 1930s memoir that includes poems, letters, stories, plays, and diary entries

possibly the 1920s. Entitled *A Winnipeg Childhood* for the first, 1973 edition (*Beginnings* prefixed to the title of the 1975 edition), the stories followed a lightly disguised Dorothy ("Elizabeth") through her early years in Winnipeg, before the family's move to Ontario. The rendering of a child's universe is startlingly authentic, her prairie world vividly real. The descriptive simplicity, a surreal dwelling upon the commonplace, the strong empathy of the stories, and a lucid, fluid, rhythmic prose all charmed reviewers. Only a few saw no connection with her poetry and felt she should stick to verse.

In a format now widely imitated, Livesay in 1977 published *Right Hand Left Hand*, subtitled somewhat awkwardly *A True Life of the Thirties: Paris, Toronto, Montreal, the West and Vancouver. Love, Politics, the Depression and Feminism.* A remarkable account of the 1930s from a highly individual and intelligent point of view, the book is a collage of poems, letters, stories, plays, diary entries, photographs, clippings, theater programs,

and articles, all linked by explanatory authorial notes. Livesay resisted the natural temptation to trim and delete, to clean up and remove foolishness. Ever one to let the portrait stand with all its warts, Livesay has often alarmed family and friends by her insistence on telling things the way they were, undoctored. Her attitude seems to have no part of exhibitionism, no matter how much Livesay admits to an artist's ego. Rather it appears to derive from a passionate commitment to truth and an irrepressible optimism that directness, candor, and veracity are always preferable. The artist is not there to prettify but to document in the most sensitive way he or she can. Thus in *Right Hand Left Hand* Livesay terms herself "duped" by communism and prints some of her pretentious juvenile letters. Generously, she includes important work of other Canadians of that era, in the same impulse that has so often moved her to promote the works of others (Raymond Knister, Milton Acorn, Pat Lowther, Isabella Valancy Crawford, Anne Marriott, among them).

Readers applauded her benevolence and dedication, the integrity of the collage, and the fascinating testimony both of a time of national trauma and of a developing talent. Feminists, the young, political and intellectual historians, nostalgists, social scientists, the literati, veterans of the period–all mined *Right Hand Left Hand* for what most interested them. A few, however, complained of a randomness, partialness, or unevenness in the overall effect, failing to see any deliberate artistic purpose in the format.

In overview, the years 1965 to 1985 were almost crushingly busy professionally for Livesay. Shuttling from one end of Canada to the other, with countless speaking engagements at local libraries and prestigious universities, Livesay threw her energies into teaching and writer-in-residenceships in British Columbia, Alberta, Manitoba, Ontario, and New Brunswick. In Winnipeg she founded, subsidized, and edited a journal dedicated to poetry and its criticism, named *CV/II* in remembrance of Alan Crawley's *Contemporary Verse* of the 1940s. She has produced two anthologies of Canadian women's writing: *40 Women Poets of Canada*, a collaboration with Seymour Mayne, in 1971, and *Woman's Eye: 12 B.C. Poets* in 1978. She has been active in a vast range of organizations united only by the larger links of humanism, social concern, and a caring about knowledge–the Committee for an Independent Canada, the League of Canadian Poets, the Association of Canadian University Teachers of English, World Federalists, Amnesty International, the Unitarian Church, and so forth. A list of her correspondents over these years reads like a *Who's Who* of Canadian letters, politics, and history, but she has also devoted much time to counseling unknown writers, journalists, and graduate students, and to encouragement of fledgling periodicals. Add to this numerous literary articles; reviews; concerned letters to members of Parliament, the Canadian Broadcasting Corporation, and dozens of other authorities; and feisty theoretical disputes with fellow writers. Nor can the student of Livesay—or Canadiana—ignore her prodigious personal correspondence, which has not slackened in volume or liveliness from the 1920s to the present. Housed at the Universities of Manitoba and Alberta and at Queen's University, its range, depth, and even sheer bulk attest to her centrality in modern Canadian culture.

Now "retired" to Galiano Island and Victoria, British Columbia, Livesay continues to keep abreast of national and international events, give readings, write articles, and prod the young out of complacency and inertia. She is also at work on a book about her parents and the 1920s. Livesay has helped perpetuate the literary memory of her mother, Florence Randal Livesay, assisting in the preparation of a doctoral thesis on her mother, coediting a book of Florence Livesay's Ukrainian translations, and facilitating the publication of her early diaries written during the Boer War. Livesay would like as well to do justice to her own African years, to write more short stories, to continue expanding her knowledge of the poets of other nations, and to lend continuing support to women artists in Canada. The impressive diversity of her interests, the unabated candor of her observations, and the sparkling clarity of her sensibilities are evident in the sampling of poetry, essays, and other items assembled in the *Room of One's Own* special double issue on Livesay (volume 5, 1979). Plagued though she has been over the years by arthritis, gout, lung cancer, and other health problems, Livesay continues to be intellectually and artistically vital, still dispensing the advice that is at the center of her art:

> Give credence to the heart!
> Those who proceed
> by logic and good sense
> are withered at the start—
> never achieve
> old age's innocence[.]

Interviews:

Helen Mintz and Barbara Coward, "The Woman I Am . . . ," *Grape* (9-22 May 1973): 10, 21; republished as "Being a Writer in The Thirties: An Interview with Dorothy Livesay," *This Magazine*, 7 (January 1974): 19-21;

Bernice Lever, "An Interview with Dorothy Livesay, *Canadian Forum*, 55 (September 1975): 45-52;

Doug Beardsley and Rosemary Sullivan, "An Interview with Dorothy Livesay," *Canadian Poetry: Studies, Documents, Reviews*, 3 (Fall-Winter 1978): 87-97;

Jørn Carlsen, "Dorothy Livesay: Interview," *Kunapipi*, 1 (Summer 1979): 130-134;

Marsha Barber, "An Interview with Dorothy Livesay," *Room of One's Own*, 5, nos. 1-2 (1979): 13-34;

Joyce Marshall, "Dorothy Livesay: A Bluestocking Remembers," *Branching Out*, 7, no. 1 (1980): 18-21;

Alan Twigg, "Matrona," in his *For Openers: Conversations with 24 Canadian Writers* (Madiera Park, British Columbia: Harbour, 1981), pp. 129-137;

Heather Robertson, "Dorothy Livesay at 73–The Unquiet Thoughts of a Romantic Feminist," *Quill & Quire*, 49 (March 1983): 4, 6;

Bruce Meyer and Brian O'Riordan, "Dorothy Livesay: Unabashed Romantic," in their *In Their Words: Interviews with Fourteen Canadian Writers* (Toronto: Anansi, 1984), pp. 72-84.

Bibliography:

Alan Ricketts, "Dorothy Livesay: An Annotated Bibliography," in *The Annotated Bibliography of Canada's Major Authors*, edited by Robert Lecker and Jack David, volume 4 (Downsview, Ontario: ECW, 1983), pp. 129-203.

References:

Dawn Aspinall, Charles Lillard, Anne Marriott, and Pat Lowther, "Book Reviews," *Prism International*, 13 (Summer 1973): 137-141;

Anne Blott, "Room of One's Own: The Dorothy Livesay Issue," *Fiddlehead*, 127 (Fall 1980): 85-90;

E. K. Brown, *On Canadian Poetry* (Toronto: Ryerson, 1943), pp. 70, 83-94;

W. E. Collin, "My New Found Land," in his *The White Savannahs* (Toronto: Macmillan, 1936), pp. 147-173;

Alan Crawley, "Dorothy Livesay—An Intimate Biography," *Educational Record*, 61 (July-September 1945): 169-173; republished in *Leading Canadian Poets*, edited by W. P. Percival (Toronto: Ryerson, 1948), pp. 117-124;

Debbie Foulks, "Livesay's Two Seasons of Love," *Canadian Literature*, 74 (Autumn 1977): 63-73;

Jean Gibbs, "Dorothy Livesay and the Transcendentalist Tradition," *Humanities Association Bulletin*, 21 (Spring 1970): 24-39;

Phil Hall, "The Self-Completing Poet," *Canadian Forum*, 67 (August/September 1987): 37-39;

Patrick Lane, "The *Collected Poems* of Dorothy Livesay," *Blackfish*, 4-5 (Winter-Spring 1972-1973);

D. Leland, "Dorothy Livesay: Poet of Nature," *Dalhousie Review*, 51 (Autumn 1971): 404-412;

B. Mitchell, " 'How Silence Sings' in the Poetry of Dorothy Livesay," *Dalhousie Review*, 54 (Autumn 1974): 510-528;

Patricia Morley, "Learning and Loving During the Lost Years," *Atlantis*, 3, no. 2, pt. 1 (Spring 1978): 145-150;

Room of One's Own, special issue on Livesay, edited by Margo Dunn, Janice Pentland-Smith, Gayla Reid, Helene Rosenthal, Gail van Varseveld, Eleanor Wachtel, and Jean Wilson, 5, nos. 1-2 (1979);

Robin Skelton, "Livesay's Two Seasons," *Canadian Literature*, 58 (Autumn 1973): 77-82;

Peter Stevens, "Dorothy Livesay: The Love Poetry," *Canadian Literature*, 47 (Winter 1971): 26-43; republished in *Poets and Critics*, edited by George Woodcock (Toronto: Oxford University Press, 1974), pp. 33-52;

Stevens, "Out of the Silence and Across the Distance," *Queen's Quarterly*, 78 (Winter 1971): 579-591;

Kent Thompson, "Reviews," *Fiddlehead*, 73 (Summer 1967): 79-83;

Lee Briscoe Thompson, *Dorothy Livesay* (Boston: G. K. Hall, 1987);

Lorraine Vernon, "Livesay's Coming of Age," *Lakehead University Review*, 6 (Fall-Winter 1973): 246-250;

S. Zimmerman, "Livesay's Houses," *Canadian Literature*, 61 (Summer 1974): 32-45.

Papers:

The Department of Archives and Special Collections, Elizabeth Dafoe Library, University of Manitoba, Winnipeg, Manitoba, has manuscripts, galleys, correspondence, diaries, clippings, photographs, memorabilia, and a guide published in 1986 entitled *The Papers of Dorothy Livesay: A Research Tool;* the Bruce Peel Special Collections Library, University of Alberta, Edmonton, Alberta, holds poetry manuscripts and typescripts, two exercise books, and business correspondence with Ryerson Press; and the Douglas Library Archives, Queen's University, Kingston, Ontario, has business and personal correspondence.

Hugh MacLennan

(20 March 1907-   )

Elspeth Cameron
University of Toronto

BOOKS: *Oxyrhynchus: An Economic and Social Study* (Princeton: Princeton University Press, 1935);

Barometer Rising (New York: Duell, Sloan & Pearce, 1941; Toronto: Collins, 1941; London: Harrap, 1942);

Two Solitudes (New York: Duell, Sloan & Pearce, 1945; Toronto: Collins, 1945; London: Cresset, 1946);

The Precipice (New York: Duell, Sloan & Pearce, 1948; Toronto: Collins, 1948; London: Cresset, 1949);

Cross-Country (Toronto: Collins, 1949);

Each Man's Son (Boston: Little, Brown, 1951; Toronto: Macmillan, 1951; London: Heinemann, 1952);

Thirty and Three, edited by Dorothy Duncan (Toronto: Macmillan, 1955; London: Macmillan, 1955);

The Watch That Ends the Night (New York: Scribners, 1959; Toronto: Macmillan, 1959; London: Heinemann, 1959);

Scotchman's Return and Other Essays (Toronto: Macmillan, 1960; New York: Scribners, 1960); also published as *Scotsman's Return and Other Essays* (London: Heinemann, 1960);

Seven Rivers of Canada (New York: Scribners, 1961; Toronto: Macmillan, 1961); republished as *Rivers of Canada* (Toronto: Macmillan, 1974);

Return of the Sphinx (New York: Scribners, 1967; Toronto: Macmillan, 1967);

The Colour of Canada (Toronto: McClelland & Stewart, 1967; Boston: Little, Brown, 1967);

The Other Side of Hugh MacLennan: Selected Essays Old and New, edited by Elspeth Cameron (Toronto: Macmillan, 1978);

Voices in Time (Toronto: Macmillan, 1980; New York: St. Martin's, 1981);

On Being a Maritime Writer (Sackville, New Brunswick: Mount Allison University, 1984).

When the American critic, Edmund Wilson, first encountered the essays of Hugh MacLennan

Hugh MacLennan at McGill University, 1980 (photograph by Coshof, Atlantic Insight)

in 1960, he claimed to find in them "a point of view surprisingly and agreeably different from anything else I knew in English. . . , a Canadian way of looking at things which had little in common with either the 'American' or the British colonial one and which has achieved a self-confident detachment in regard to the rest of the world." It is for this self-conscious expression of Canada's national character that MacLennan is best known. As he theorizes in a number of his essays, he was the first Canadian novelist to attempt to set the local stage on which the nation's dramas might be played before an international audience. The success of this venture can be determined by the sales his seven novels have enjoyed inside and outside Canada, the large number of languages into which his books have been translated, and the tribute paid him by the many Canadian writers who have acknowledged his influence.

Ironically, MacLennan's foray into fictional nationalism began as a detour from his original ambitions. Both his education and his experience had conspired to foster goals of a quite different nature. The only son of Samuel John MacLennan, a stern Scots Presbyterian doctor, and Katherine Clifford MacQuarrie, a musical, artistic mother, MacLennan was born in the remote coal-mining town of Glace Bay in Cape Breton Island, Nova Scotia, on 20 March 1907. When he was eight, the family moved to Halifax, transformed by World War I from a sleepy garrison town into a bustling naval base. There, early on 6 December 1917, the accidental collision of two ships in the harbor caused the well-known Halifax Explosion which occurred just as MacLennan was getting ready for school. This event made the war an immediate reality and raised questions of great moral significance in the mind of the ten-year-old boy who saw devastation in the streets and recoiled in shock.

MacLennan's father entertained extremely high ambitions for his son. He was obsessed with the classics of Greece and Rome which he translated as a hobby. With the aid of texts from Eton College, England, he subjected MacLennan to closely regimented hours of study after school; later he made it clear that MacLennan would take Honours Latin and Greek at Dalhousie University, win a Rhodes Scholarship, and attend Oxford University. Probably with some notion of the supremacy of athletic endeavor in the classical world, Dr. MacLennan also urged his son to high achievements in tennis. Not without difficulty nor without resentment, MacLennan managed to fulfill his father's high hopes, graduating in 1928 from Dalhousie University in Halifax with numerous athletic successes, the Governor General's Gold Medal for Classics, and a Rhodes Scholarship.

At Oriel College, Oxford, a provincial among English boys much better groomed in classical studies than himself, MacLennan worked slavishly on the exceptionally difficult course of studies called Honour Moderations and Literae Humaniores. In addition he threw himself into both rugby and tennis, managing in his final year to win the Half-Blue in tennis. The determina-

tion with which he pursued tennis at Oxford can be deduced from the success he enjoyed on his return home to Halifax in the summer of 1929 where he won the Maritimes Singles Championship. During his other vacations he traveled extensively in the north of England, Scotland, and on the Continent–to France, Switzerland, Italy, Greece, and Germany. Germany appealed to him most, not only because he was preparing German as his second language at Oxford but also because he found in Freiburg a congenial family with whom he stayed on each of his three visits. From this comfortable base in those early years of the 1930s, he observed the political developments that eventually culminated in World War II. Although he worked relentlessly at Oxford to fulfill his father's ambitions, he somehow found time to indulge in a side of himself that owed much more to his mother than to his father. He began to write poetry, not just as a release but with a serious eye to having it published. Temperamentally incompatible with the modern poetry which had begun to emerge after World War I– poetry which he considered too "cynical"–he declared his own taste to be unabashedly romantic and observed in his own poems a tendency toward mysticism. Once he had written enough poems to constitute a manuscript, he tried without success to locate a publisher. He blamed this failure on the Depression and decided to try his hand at fiction. With Hemingway as a model, he began what he hoped would be a grand internationally acclaimed book about war and social change.

When he came down from Oxford in 1932, MacLennan reluctantly agreed to follow his father's advice to proceed to a graduate degree in classics at Princeton University. Once he discovered how alien to his taste and inclinations the course of study at Princeton was, drawing as it did on the meticulous Germanic school of classical scholarship and not at all resembling the wideranging philosophical discussions he had come to enjoy at Oxford, MacLennan began to rebel against his father. He abandoned both the traditional observation of Christianity and the Conservative politics which had been his legacy: he turned instead with interest and hope to the theories of Karl Marx. This rebellion was fed by his attachment to the woman he would eventually marry, a strong-spirited American named Dorothy Duncan whom he had met on a ship back from Oxford in 1932. Duncan herself had aspirations to write, saw in MacLennan a potential novel-

MacLennan with his first wife, Dorothy Duncan, in the Laurentians (courtesy of the author)

ist, and took up the role of an advising editor on his novel. Indeed, MacLennan had done his best to sidestep Princeton by finding a job so that he could marry her, but the combination of Depression conditions and a powerful colonialism in the two Canadian universities which advertised jobs in classics that summer betrayed his hopes. He recalls that even at his alma mater, Dalhousie, he was told, "After all, you're a Canadian and [the other candidate is] an Englishman. It makes a difference." In a halfhearted way he completed his Ph.D. in 1935, having reserved his best energies for his fiction. He failed to find a publisher for the novel he had begun at Oxford, but with Duncan's encouragement he had begun another to be set largely in the United States.

The only job MacLennan could locate in 1935 was one which he could readily have taken up after his B.A. from Dalhousie–that of teacher in a boys' private school in a suburb of Montreal. It was with much bitterness and a deep sense that there were forces at large over which the indi-

vidual could have no control that he took up a position at Lower Canada College. Despite extremely low pay and long hours of duty MacLennan wrote at night to fulfill his ambition to publish a novel that would bring in the money to support himself and Dorothy Duncan. Although he was finally able to marry her in 1936, having saved enough to move into a modest apartment near the school, it would be almost another decade before his literary hopes would be realized. The Canadian market was simply unripe for a national literature. In 1936 Canada was still importing approximately ninety-eight percent of the books sold, in marked contrast to Great Britain and the United States, both of which were by then producing about eighty percent of their own books. The failure of his second novel to find a publisher in 1937 was a severe blow.

It was the perspicacious Dorothy Duncan who drew her husband out of this apparent deadlock. Although he had deeply wanted to write novels on a large scale with settings located at the vortex of international events, he now came to see that there was a fictional vacuum in Canada which he might well fill. As Duncan pointed out to him on a summer trip through Nova Scotia, in the absence of a well-established school of Canadian fiction such as already existed in poetry (the Confederation Poets) and art (the Group of Seven): "Why don't you put all this part of Nova Scotia in your next book?... Nobody's ever going to understand Canada until she evolves a literature of her own, and you're the fellow to start bringing Canadian novels up to date." Duncan herself was trying to bring some money into their sparse bank account by writing a guidebook about Canada aimed at American tourists. Taking her advice to heart, MacLennan put aside his idea of writing a novel on the great themes of Europe or the United States in the manner of a Hemingway or Sinclair Lewis, plotted out a tightly knit story set in Halifax with the Halifax Explosion as its climax, and wrote the novel that marked the turning point of his career.

Barometer Rising (1941) drew on MacLennan's own personal recollections of wartime Halifax and the explosion that had so traumatically leveled the town in 1917. With World War II underway the theme was a timely one, and in using it MacLennan actually adapted his earlier concerns to a specifically Canadian locale. Although the vortex of world events was indisputably elsewhere and the traditions of English fiction and publishing located outside the country, for one blinding moment at least, the center of wartime action had been Halifax, Canada. MacLennan's story concerns a group of characters who represent different attitudes to war. To the megalomaniac Colonel Wain, war is wonderful, a thrilling "power-bananza" which he can turn to his own profit. To Neil Macrae, the novel's protagonist, it is a terrible violation of civilization. Shell-shocked and disoriented, Neil returns to Halifax to seek the woman he has left behind, Colonel Wain's daughter, the ship designer Penelope, who has meanwhile borne him an illegitimate child. Dr. Angus Murray, an older man who has been invalided home in the war in the same way MacLennan's father had been, is an outspoken pacifist who patiently courts Penelope without success. Penelope's younger brother, Roddie, is shocked by what he sees after the explosion, just as MacLennan had been at the same age. The explosion blasts all these characters into new relationships with one another and simultaneously throws Canada into a new relationship with Britain. That relationship is now no longer colonial, but "non-committal"; as Neil describes it, "if there were enough Canadians like himself, half-American and half-English, then the day was inevitable when the halves would join and his country would become the central arch which united the new order."

To Canadian readers *Barometer Rising* seemed to express, as no Canadian novel had yet done, the nationalism that had blossomed gradually over the past two decades. The Statute of Westminster in 1931 had formalized the autonomy Canada had won by her increasingly prominent role on the world stage. Now, exactly a decade later, reading this novel afforded not only Canadians but also English and American audiences their first opportunity to glimpse Canadian life in a Canadian city complete with street names and landmarks. Critics in Canada found the book, in the words of one, "as Canadian as maple sugar." In the *New York Times* a reviewer claimed, "Both in conception and workmanship it is first class. . . . Mr. MacLennan has scored a bull's eye first shot." For many readers and critics the novel has remained MacLennan's best. Edmund Wilson, for example, singled it out as "a landmark in Canadian writing but also . . . [an] authentic classic." Ironically, MacLennan had merely experimented with a national setting; for the most part, his education, experience, and interests lay elsewhere. But the advice of his American wife had been sage. Less than two months

after publication, *Barometer Rising* was doing as well in Canada as the envied Hemingway's *For Whom the Bell Tolls* (1940); in Britain and the United States it also sold well. By 1945 it had sold over 100,000 copies.

Since *Barometer Rising* had been an experiment that worked, MacLennan at once turned his attention to repeating his success in another novel. Again he wrestled with the means by which a novel could be both "Canadian" and "universal." The answer seemed to lie in the current political and social tensions in Quebec. As MacLennan saw it, if there were going to be a Canadian literature, there had to be a strong sense of Canada instead of the group loyalties he observed as typical of the different ethnic groups in the country. Just as individuals seemed ready to acknowledge allegiances to the Canadian nation rather than to the petty interests of the local group or province, so, he hoped, the nations currently at war in Europe might be persuaded to lay down their arms in the larger interests of mankind. "I see Canada as a bridge," he wrote to a friend in 1941, "a bridge with the ends unjoined. I don't believe there can be a synthesis until the ends are joined. I am trying to go ahead on the assumption that the failure of our people even to understand the necessity of joining the ends of the bridge is responsible not only for our own national schizophrenia [the French-English split], but breakdown as well. In that state of 'becoming' [a nation] I seem to detect the possibility of a universality for a writer who attempts to write out of the Canadian scene." In 1943 he obtained a Guggenheim Fellowship and spent the year in New York writing his novel, which was published in 1945.

The title *Two Solitudes* aptly implied MacLennan's aim. Taken from a letter of Rainer Maria Rilke's, the phrase was part of a definition of love: "love consists of this, that two solitudes protect, and touch, and greet each other." If French and English in Canada could manage this kind of respectful love, then perhaps the various nationalisms in Europe that had led to war could be transformed into peaceful coexistence.

MacLennan again used his characters–this time a much more varied group than in *Barometer Rising*–to dramatize his theme. His protagonist is Paul Tallard, a writer who at the novel's end sits down to write the first truly "Canadian" novel. In all that goes before–in Paul's home life and outer experience–MacLennan demonstrates a nation taking shape to the point at which a na-

*Dust jacket for MacLennan's novel that takes its title from
Rainer Maria Rilke's remark, "love consists of this, that two solitudes protect, and touch, and greet each other." The "two solitudes" of which MacLennan writes are English and
French Canada.*

tional literature becomes possible. A large part of
the novel is devoted to Paul's father, Athanase
Tallard, who is of the generation which sees the
potential for viable nationhood but which cannot
come to grips with it emotionally. For MacLennan, situated as he was in a boys' private school,
the key in the evolution of nationhood was education. Athanase, seigneur of the tiny Roman Catholic preserve of Saint-Marc in rural Quebec, is
emotionally chained by his religious upbringing,
even though he toys with an atheist manifesto.
His first wife, a devout French Catholic, has
died, leaving him a fiery French-Canadian nationalist, Marius, as a son. His second wife, the
earthy Irish Protestant Kathleen, is Paul's
mother. Athanase sees that Paul receives a "scientific" education in English to complement his
French-Canadian early childhood. The novel's villain (generally agreed to have been based
roughly on Prime Minister William Lyon MacKen-

zie King) is Huntly MacQueen, a predatory
English-Canadian industrialist who exploits the
tensions between English and French for personal gain, moving in characteristically to pur-
chase land from Athanase to set up a factory.

MacLennan's timely treatment of the conscription issue in *Two Solitudes* was one of the
many reasons for its immediate popularity. The
novel was sold out by noon of the day the first reviews appeared. Reviews were ecstatic; many Canadian critics treated the book as "the Great
Canadian Novel," while American reviewers saw
in it a sort of "case book" of many aspects of life
north of the border. As one reviewer put it:
"Here is the substance of Canada, her countryside, her cities, her conflicting cultures, and,
above all, her people. We move comfortably
among them, knowing them for our own, yet, if
it were translated into, say, Russian, it could be
read over there with something of a pleasure we
have in reading *War and Peace*."

For the rest of the year *Two Solitudes* maintained a position on best-seller lists in the United
States and Canada. Negotiations were underway
almost at once for a number of translations.
North American sales in the first year topped
50,000, and sales continued steadily after that. At
last MacLennan was able to resign his teaching position at Lower Canada College, to depend on income from writing alone.

Despite the indisputable popular success of
Two Solitudes, the novel was seriously flawed, as
later critics less dazzled by its timely content were
able to see. MacLennan had come closer to reflecting the complexity of life in this novel, having
sensed that *Barometer Rising* with its neat plot had
been too "limiting." But somehow the new novel's encyclopedic range had gotten out of hand
and its focus had blurred. On the one hand,
MacLennan had attempted a semiautobiographical "portrait of the artist as a young man"; on the
other hand, he had deliberately imitated John
Galsworthy's *Forsyte Saga* (1922) in chronicling the
interplay of history and the personal lives of a
few interrelated families. Consequently, as some
reviewers noticed and later critics confirmed, the
protagonist of the book seemed to be Athanase
Tallard, not his son Paul. Soon after the novel
was published, MacLennan confessed that he had
submitted his manuscript too soon: impatient to
free himself from his teaching duties, he did not
give the novel the final rewrite he knew it
needed. Regardless of these flaws, the book accomplished what he had hoped it would. It was a best-

MacLennan at Stone Hedge, the North Hatley (Quebec) summer cottage that he and Dorothy Duncan purchased in the mid 1940s (photograph by Brian Merrett, courtesy of the National Film Board)

seller which, as he put it, "put something like solid ground under my feet."

For his next novel MacLennan wanted above all to continue to tap the profitable market in the United States, which was still much larger than the home market, but he also wanted to keep intact the "Canadianness" for which he had become well known. As he theorized, he wished to remain a Canadian in Canada, but he wanted to avoid being "regional" by joining an "American branch cycle" of literature. "A Canadian writer, like any other artist," he wrote in "Canada Between Covers" (*Saturday Review of Literature,* 7 September 1946), "must write out of his own background . . . [but] Canadians must write for the American market because it is the cultural pattern to which they naturally belong. It is their only avenue to a world audience." Realizing that present publishing contracts, which were American based, put Canadian writers at a severe financial disadvantage, he successfully negotiated a separate Canadian contract for his next book.

The Precipice (1948) was set partly in a fictional Ontario town, Grenville, and partly in New York and Princeton. The Grenville section of the novel was directly based on the American Anthony Tudor's ballet *Pillar of Fire,* which MacLennan and his wife had seen in 1946. As in the ballet the central character in *The Precipice* is a woman whose puritanical upbringing inhibits her natural affections. It is Stephen Lassiter, the American efficiency expert who comes to Grenville to facilitate the takeover of a company, who is able to awaken her to physical and emotional experience. Their marriage and subsequent life in the United States serves as MacLennan's basis to compare the history, social mores, and geography of the two North American nations. In doing so he suggests that each nation has much to offer the other: Canadians can benefit, as Lucy does, from the forthright, guilt-free attitudes south of the border; Americans, more to the point, can learn much by tempering their monstrous drive for technological power with an emphasis on the quality of life more often found in "backward" Canada. The context provided at the novel's close by the bombing of Hiroshima stands as a sobering warning that modern man, like the

Gaderene swine in the Bible, may be racing toward a precipice beyond which lies destruction.

Carefully though this novel was planned to link American and Canadian audiences, *The Precipice* did not mark an advance in sales over *Two Solitudes*. Canadian critics were generally disillusioned that their "Canadian spokesman" was apparently turning away from Canadian subjects. "We can kiss Hugh MacLennan good-bye as a distinctly Canadian novelist," one wrote. "*Two Solitudes* . . . was . . . a promise of a potentially great Canadian novelist. *The Precipice* reduces the promise to a whisper." American critics, unencumbered by any such sense of betrayal, reviewed the novel favorably, but the condemnation of the majority of Canadian critics affected sales at home. Although MacLennan considered the book to be a marked advance over both his earlier novels, it has remained the least popular of his novels to date.

MacLennan emerged from the publication of his third novel with the aesthetic theory that the novel had a moral role to play. Despite the fact that writers such as James Jones, John Dos Passos, and Norman Mailer were reflecting a gradual breakdown of social mores, MacLennan believed that "The period we are now entering will be a period of reconstruction, both in society and in the arts. Such periods are always hard for an artist, for it is incumbent on him, not on the statesman, to discover new values."

Worried about his financial state which had induced him to take on numerous articles for American and Canadian magazines, MacLennan commenced another novel. This time he would draw back from the United States and return to his own roots in Nova Scotia. *Each Man's Son* (1951) is set in Glace Bay, Cape Breton Island, and centers on a colliery doctor like MacLennan's father. The novel is both a study in Calvinism and an examination of the use and misuse of power. Hitherto, MacLennan had embodied this theme externally, locating different points of view in separate characters. Now, he presented the conflict internally. Dr. Ainslie undergoes a crisis of conscience and guilt that he has not always tempered his powers as a medical man with sufficient love. At the novel's crisis, he senses through a mystical revelation that he can and will go on to study and practice for the greater benefit of mankind. The novel's subplot involves a former Glace Bay miner, Archie MacNeil, who has become a professional boxer. Archie has abandoned his wife, Mollie, and son, Alan, for a

number of years to batter and pummel his way to the top. Now, in his decline, he returns to find his wife with a lover. Enraged, he accidentally kills Mollie in one final act of violence and is destroyed himself. Thus, Archie also represents the misuse of power for violent destruction, much in the manner of the Greek tragedies on which MacLennan modeled this tightly constructed book. With appropriate nemesis, his son is adopted by the doctor.

Because MacLennan so successfully created an authentic atmosphere through local color and the dialogue of his characters, this novel appealed greatly to his Canadian readers. But sales did not reach the heights for which he aimed. After a year, only 10,000 copies had been sold, evidence of solid sales but not the windfall he needed to pay the debts that were rapidly mounting. Since 1948 Dorothy's health had deteriorated dramatically in a series of embolisms that were the inevitable consequence of several bouts of rheumatic fever during childhood. Her weak heart had made pregnancy too great a risk to take; now it threatened her life. In the absence of health insurance, MacLennan's medical bills were staggering. Despite his income from *Each Man's Son* and the many articles and essays he wrote, he could no longer afford to support himself as a writer. After only six years of independence, he returned to teaching, this time as a part-time English professor at McGill University. To his surprise MacLennan found that he enjoyed his new job. He no longer needed to worry about money; he found university teaching stimulating and contact with his colleagues rewarding. At a more leisurely pace he began another novel with none of the urgency with which he had written *Each Man's Son*. During the decade of the 1950s he came into his own as an essayist, writing monthly pieces for the new magazine the *Montrealer* and other articles for major journals. But during this decade his wife became seriously ill, finally dying in 1957.

The Watch That Ends the Night (1959) is in part the story of a woman with a weak heart. Catherine Martell and her husband, the surgeon Jerome, are both people of enormous will power whose lives exemplify the human choice that had fascinated MacLennan from the outset: the choice between the constructive and destructive uses of power. For Jerome, the almost mythical figure who first occurred to MacLennan in a dream, this choice involves fighting in the Spanish civil war and abandoning his wife under cir-

Dust jacket for the 1959 novel (first American edition) that won MacLennan his fifth Governor General's Award

cumstances that almost destroy her. For Catherine, it involves a continuing fight for life and creativity, since she is a painter of considerable talent. Both these characters are observed throughout by the novel's protagonist, George Stewart, who has not the explosive character of either. George, a semiautobiographical character, marries Catherine after Jerome is presumed dead in the war, though Jerome returns at a much later date. The novel's story, which like that of *Two Solitudes* is encyclopedic in scope and relates international events to the personal lives of its large cast of characters, is really George's. His closeness to both Jerome and Catherine teaches him that the power to do good and the power to do evil are inextricably linked in the human psyche. Jerome's apparently destructive force, he comes to see, is balanced by his almost mystic healing powers as a doctor: Catherine's creative exuberance has its dark underside in her vampirelike claims on his emotional strength. Reflecting his own explicit aesthetic theory that art must affirm and "within a framework of truth . . . make compensation for the human predicament," MacLennan demonstrates that ultimately the choice must be for the constructive use of power. As George comments: "There it was, the

ancient marriage of good and evil, the goodness of this day and the compulsive evil people must see and know, but the sky dominated in the end. Pale and shining, it told me that our sins can be forgiven."

Reviews of this novel revealed that at last MacLennan was appreciated as a writer, not as a specifically "Canadian" writer. Throughout Canada and the United States, reviews were the best he had yet received, praising the novel's psychological insight, its characterization, its humor, and its readability. As Robertson Davies put it in *Saturday Night* (28 March 1959), "he has gained a new mastery over the two strongest elements in his work: the storyteller and the self-explorer are one. The effect is virtually to double his stature." Sales reflected this euphoria: by the year's end *The Watch That Ends the Night* had sold 18,000 copies in Canada alone; by 1975 it had sold 700,000 copies. Numerous translations were published and at last a financial windfall came MacLennan's way through the sale of the movie rights for $70,000, although a movie was never produced.

Two years after the 1957 death of Dorothy Duncan, the same year that *The Watch That Ends the Night* was published, MacLennan remarried.

With his new bride, Frances Walker, he made a honeymoon of his research trip to the Fraser River. Claiming to feel depleted of creative energy after the massive rewriting of his last novel, MacLennan turned to nonfiction and produced, among other things, his outstanding collection of essays entitled *Seven Rivers of Canada* (1961). Many critics had noted from *Barometer Rising* onward that one of his unique characteristics was his ability to bring the Canadian landscape vividly to life. Edmund Wilson, for example, had noted in *O Canada* (1965): "The one feature of MacLennan's novels that does seem to me new and interesting is his use of the geographical and the meteorological setting. He always shows us how the characters are situated . . . in a vast expanse of land and water, the hardly inhabited space of the waste upper margin of a continent."

Eventually, however, MacLennan returned to the novel form in response to what he called "the psychic crisis" of the 1960s. Everywhere, it seemed to him, social and moral structures were disintegrating. As a writer who believed that it was the responsibility of all artists to offer direction and hope in even the most distressing of human situations, he began *Return of the Sphinx* (1967).

As the title suggests, this novel refers back to the Oedipus plays he had studied as a student of the classics. In the early 1960s he had read *Sex in History* (1953) by G. Rattray Taylor which had applied Freudian psychology–especially the theory of the Oedipus complex–to history. MacLennan adopted Taylor's theory that history moved in cycles, swinging back and forth between "patrist" periods of extreme authoritarianism and "matrist" phases of excessive libertinism. MacLennan's imagination was seized at once by Taylor's analysis–especially his assertion that the modern world was deep in the throes of a "matrist" period. The situation in Quebec–where the Quiet Revolution was afoot–seemed to demonstrate this theory on a political level as well.

The novel's protagonist, Alan Ainslie, is none other than the son of Archie MacNeil from *Each Man's Son* who had been adopted at that novel's end by Dr. Ainslie. Now minister for cultural affairs in Ottawa, he must face, from both his children, the rebellion against authority common in the 1960s. His son, Daniel, is a television host who encourages the expression of inflammatory Quebec separatist opinion and who is eventually arrested on his way to blow up a downtown Montreal building. Chantal, Ainslie's daughter, has become involved with her father's oldest friend, Gabriel Fleury. This semi-incestuous relationship is paralleled by Daniel's sexual liaison with his girlfriend's mother. "Things are falling apart, the centre cannot hold," Ainslie quotes from Yeats on one occasion, and, in an image central to the novel of a huge, impersonal tidal wave that rises out of a hurricane at sea and resembles Yeats's "great beast slouching towards Bethlehem to be born," a new cycle of human history is ushered in.

Both the obscurity of its Freudian origins and the timing of publication contributed to this novel's poor critical reception. Neither the *Oedipus at Colonus* nor Taylor's *Sex in History* were sufficiently familiar to the general public for MacLennan's allusions to be understood. Furthermore, the sheer coincidence that the book came out during the festivities that marked Canada's centennial celebrations induced reviewers to conclude that MacLennan had sat down to write a sociopolitical study of English-French relations in Quebec. Nothing could have been further from the truth. As always, MacLennan was doing his best to eschew regionalism in favor of universal themes. As he commented, "I wasn't trying to write the great Canadian novel; I took an international theme–the crack-up between generations. It could have been written about many countries, but naturally a novelist is wise to use a milieu he himself knows well." Although American critics generally reviewed the book well, noting its timely and universal nature, Canadian critics savaged it. One typically noted, "At this difficult nervous moment in Canadian history, one of our most celebrated authors has attacked our most pressing issue and produced a book that contributes nothing to politics and less than nothing to literature." Sales understandably were lower than those of *The Watch That Ends the Night*–11,000 in Canada and 16,000 in the United States in the first year. Although critics have continued to concur in this view of *Return of the Sphinx*, MacLennan himself felt it was better than his other novels.

Although he was hurt and discouraged by the Canadian reception of *Return of the Sphinx*, he slowly began to work on a seventh novel, *Voices in Time* (1980). The publication of a revised version of *Seven Rivers in Canada*, retitled simply *Rivers of Canada* (1974), stimulated him to perceive life from a wider perspective. Now in his sixties he had reached an age at which he could identify with natural history: just as Canada's river gorges

Dust jacket for MacLennan's novel set in the future after a nuclear explosion has annihilated most of the world's inhabitants

marked epochs of geological time stretching back millions of years, so too his own life seemed to him like a series of "ages" marked by violent and transfiguring transitions.

The form and scope of *Voices in Time* was bold and jagged. Set in the future after a nuclear explosion that has wiped out all but a few of the world's inhabitants, it treats one set of characters in the years spanning the two world wars, another in the October crisis of 1970 in Montreal, and a third in the "present"–the year 2039. The linking character is old John Wellfleet who as one of the few "survivors" of the holocaust is able to attain the overview of all these characters and events necessary for the young hopefuls who have been born after the "Destructions" and now struggle to create a new society on the ruins of the old. John Wellfleet's difficulty in making sense of all the "voices in time" that have also survived in the form of letters and diaries, tapes, and videotapes is analogous to MacLennan's own struggle (or that of any artist) to transform the

raw stuff of life into the coherent forms of art. Eventually he incorporates the tragic story of his German stepfather, Conrad Dehmel, who had been a conscientious objector during Hitler's rise to power, and the tale of his irresponsible, media-mad cousin Timothy Wellfleet, whose sensational television show curries disaster, into his own recollections to build a monumental pattern of human history in which affirmation is ultimately possible. *Voices in Time* is his most sophisticated treatment to date of the theme of man's use of power. Although, for the first time, American critics seemed indifferent to MacLennan, Canadian critics generally hailed *Voices in Time* as a masterpiece.

MacLennan's overall development as a writer can best be understood by remembering that he originally aimed to be a writer, not a "Canadian" writer. Behind all his successful novels on Canadian themes lay those two early unpublished manuscripts set, in the main, outside Canada. The overnight success of *Barometer Rising* encouraged him to continue in the Canadian vein, but always he struggled to find ways of avoiding regionalism in his quest to touch universal themes. Thus, his novels in succession were experimental in the sense that he tried a number of methods to make the local scene resound with wider implications. In *Two Solitudes* he used the chronicle form to lend historical authenticity to Canadian dilemma he thought was representative of the international situation in Europe; *The Precipice* specifically aimed to contrast and link the two North American nations which had much to learn from each other. *Each Man's Son* was conceived on a more modest scale, using tightly knit Greek tragedy as a model for a psychological study that he hoped might transcend parochial boundaries. In *The Watch That Ends the Night* he returned to the broad canvas like that of *Two Solitudes*, moving parts of his action out of Canada entirely and incorporating the psychological depth of *Each Man's Son*. He also tried using the first-person point of view for the first time since his early unpublished fiction. With *Return of the Sphinx* he attempted again a closely structured story modeled on Greek tragedy with deep Freudian implications. Finally, with *Voices in Time*, he set almost half of his story outside Canada in Germany as he had done with his first unpublished novel and managed to incorporate the most far-flung sets of characters and eras he had yet attempted. His enduring central theme has been the choice facing all men: whether power is to be used for constructive or destructive ends, a theme he has treated with increasing complexity and impact.

The many essays and articles MacLennan has written are not only valuable in their own right, they have contributed significantly to his development as a novelist. In them he deals with a wide variety of subjects drawn from his own experience, acquiring useful practice in expressing his humor, his intense emotions, his civilized thoughts, and his intuitions. The discipline of the essay also helped him to experiment with forms. Along with Robertson Davies, he is Canada's finest essayist.

MacLennan is widely admired for his national themes by his general public and has been regarded with deep respect by such writers as Margaret Laurence who recognize the debt their own writing owes him; professional critics, however, have varied in their opinions. Assessments of MacLennan's novels fall into three main categories: the acclaim which greeted his heroic accomplishments as the first "Canadian" writer with scant regard for his aesthetic merit; the consolidation of a critical view in the 1960s in which he was treated as important for his themes but generally outdated in his methods; and a reaction in the 1970s and 1980s to all these views in the form of careful literary analysis of his works and more thorough investigation into the context in which he wrote.

MacLennan might well be termed the Grand Old Man of Canadian Letters. He has won a Governor General's Award three times for his fiction (*Two Solitudes, The Precipice* and *The Watch That Ends the Night*) and twice for his collections of essays (*Cross-Country*, 1949, and *Thirty and Three*, 1955) along with many other awards and honorary degrees, including a Molson Award in 1984. Although he has most often been seen as a "pioneer" in Canadian literature, he is more accurately a transitional figure. Like one of his favorite Roman poets, Horace, who adapted Latin verse to Greek poetry, MacLennan has tuned a new nation's lyre to the existing measures of English fiction.

Interviews:

Naïm Kattan, "Montreal and French-Canadian Culture: What They Mean to English-Canadian Novelists," *Tamarack Review*, 40 (Summer 1966): 40-53;

Donald Cameron, "The Tennis Racket is an Antelope Bone," in his *Conversations with Cana-dian Novelists*, volume 1 (Toronto: Macmillan, 1973), pp. 30-48;

Ronald Sutherland, "Hugh MacLennan," *Canadian Literature*, 68-69 (Spring-Summer 1976): 40-48;

Alan Twigg, "Hugh MacLennan: Patricius," in his *For Openers: Conversatons with 24 Canadian Writers* (Madeira Park, British Columbia: Harbour, 1981), pp. 83-96.

References:

David Arnason, "Canadian Nationalism in Search of Form," *Journal of Canadian Fiction*, 1 (Fall 1972): 68-71;

Margaret Atwood, *Survival: A Thematic Guide to Canadian Literature* (Toronto: House of Anansi, 1972), pp. 137-138, 141, 182, 208, 241;

Hermann Boeschenstein, "Hugh MacLennan, a Canadian Novelist," *Zeitschrift fur Anglistik und Amerikanistik*, 8 (1960): 117-135;

Peter Buitenhuis, *Hugh MacLennan* (Toronto: Forum House, 1969);

Elspeth Cameron, *Hugh MacLennan: A Writer's Life* (Toronto: University of Toronto Press, 1981);

Cameron, ed., *Hugh MacLennan, 1982: Proceedings of the MacLennan Conference at University College* (Toronto: Canadian Studies Programme, University College, University of Toronto, 1982);

Robert H. Cockburn, *The Novels of Hugh MacLennan* (Montreal: Harvest House, 1971);

Roy Daniells, "Literature: I, Poetry and the Novel," in *The Culture of Contemporary Canada*, edited by Julian Park (Ithaca: Cornell University Press, 1957), pp. 1-80;

Robertson Davies, "MacLennan's Rising Sun," *Saturday Night*, 28 March 1959, pp. 29-31;

M. J. Davis, "Fathers and Sons," *Canadian Literature*, 58 (Autumn 1973): 39-50;

Dorothy Duncan, "My Author Husband," *Maclean's*, 15 August 1945, pp. 5-7;

Dorothy Farmiloe, "Hugh MacLennan and the Canadian Myth," *Mosaic*, 2 (Spring 1969): 1-9;

Paul Goetsch, *Das Romanwerk Hugh MacLennans: Eine Studie Zum literarischen Nationalismus in Kanada* (Hamburg: Cram, de Gruyter, 1961);

Goetsch, "Too Long the Courtly Muses," *Canadian Literature*, 10 (Autumn 1961): 19-31;

Goetsch, ed., *Hugh MacLennan* (Toronto: McGraw-Hill Ryerson, 1973);

Keiichi Hirano, "Jerome Martell and Norman Bethune: A Note on Hugh MacLennan's

The Watch That Ends the Night," *English Litera-ture* (English Literary Society of Japan) (1968): 37-61;

Leslie Robert Hyman, "Hugh MacLennan: His Art, His Society and His Critics," *Queen's Quarterly,* 82 (Winter 1975): 515-528;

D. G. Jones, *Butterfly on Rock: A Study of Themes and Images in Canadian Literature* (Toronto: University of Toronto Press, 1970), pp. 29, 36, 62-65, 71, 84-87, 134, 139-140, 157-162, 165, 173, 183;

Naïm Kattan, "Le Roman Canadien-Anglais," *Lettres Nouvelles* (December 1966-January 1967): 21-30;

Janice Kulyk Keefer, *Under Eastern Eyes: A Critical Reading of Maritime Fiction* (Toronto: University of Toronto Press, 1987);

Alec Lucas, *Hugh MacLennan* (Toronto: McClelland & Stewart, 1970);

T. D. MacLulich, *Hugh MacLennan* (Boston: Twayne, 1983);

W. H. Magee, "Trends in the Recent English-Canadian Novel," *Culture,* 10 (March 1949): 29-42;

Hugo McPherson, "The Novels of Hugh MacLennan," *Queen's Quarterly,* 60 (Summer 1953): 186-198;

Patricia Morley, *The Immoral Moralists: Hugh MacLennan and Leonard Cohen* (Toronto: Clarke, Irwin, 1972);

John Moss, *Patterns of Isolation in English-Canadian Fiction* (Toronto: McClelland & Stewart, 1974), pp. 9, 56, 58-62, 120, 132, 190-191, 196-197, 215-218, 222-224, 226-227;

William H. New, "The Storm and After: Imagery and Symbolism in Hugh MacLennan's *Barometer Rising,"* *Queen's Quarterly,* 74 (Summer 1967): 302-313;

Catherine Rubinger, "Two Related Solitudes: Canadian Novels in French and English," *Jour-nal of Commonwealth Literature,* 3 (July 1967): 49-57;

Ronald Sutherland, *Second Image: Comparative Studies in Quebéc/Canadian Literature* (Toronto: New Press, 1971);

Warren Tallman, "Wolf in the Snow: Part I: Four Windows onto Landscapes," *Canadian Literature,* 5 (Summer 1960): 7-20;

Jean F. Tener and others, eds., *The Hugh MacLennan Papers: An Inventory of the Archive at the University of Calgary Libraries* (Calgary: University of Calgary Library, 1986);

R. E. Watters, "Hugh MacLennan and the Canadian Character," in *As a Man Thinks,* edited by E. Morrison and W. Robbins (Toronto: Gage, 1953), pp. 228-243;

George Woodcock, "Hugh MacLennan," *Northern Review,* 3 (April-May 1950): 2-10;

Woodcock, *Hugh MacLennan* (Toronto: Copp, 1969);

Woodcock, "A Nation's Odyssey," in his *Odysseus Ever Returning* (Toronto: McClelland & Stewart, 1970), pp. 12-23;

Joseph Zezulka, "MacLennan's Defeated Pilgrim: A Perspective on *Return of the Sphinx," Jour-nal of Canadian Fiction,* 4, no. 1 (1975): 121-131.

Papers:

The Thomas Fisher Rare Book Library holds manuscripts for *Barometer Rising, The Watch That Ends the Night,* and *Seven Rivers of Canada,* as well as a few letters. A large collection of correspondence and manuscript versions for *Two Solitudes, The Watch That Ends the Night,* and two unpublished novels are at the MacLennan Library, McGill University. The University of Calgary Library has letters as well as manuscripts and galleys for *Return of the Sphinx.*

Adrienne Maillet

(10 December 1885-22 September 1963)

Dennis F. Essar
Brock University

BOOKS: *Peuvent-elles garder un secret?* (Montreal, 1937);

L'Oncle des jumeaux Pomponnelle (Montreal, 1938);

Quelle vie! Biographie d'une Canadienne-Française (Montreal: Privately printed, 1940);

Trop tard (Montreal, 1942);

Un Enlèvement (Montreal: Société des Éditions Pascal, 1944);

Amour tenace (Montreal & Ottawa: Lévrier, 1945);

La Vie tourmentée de Michelle Rôbal (Montreal, 1946);

De gré ou de force (Montreal: Editions de l'Arbre, 1948);

L'Ombre sur le bonheur (Montreal: Granger, 1951);

Coeur d'or, coeur de chair (Montreal: Granger, 1953);

L'Absent et autres récits (Montreal: Granger, 1955).

PERIODICAL PUBLICATIONS: "Les Plus Gênés," *Le Devoir*, 6 March 1930, p. 2;

Sa majesté la mode, La Tribune Postale (December 1939);

"Départ d'une grande âme," *Le Devoir*, 17 March 1957, p. 5.

Marie-Augustine-Adrienne Maillet was born in Montreal on 10 December 1885, the daughter of Ludger Maillet, a lawyer, and Sarah Larose Maillet. As a child she attended the Académie Saint-Léon in Montreal, the Slade School at Fall River, Massachusetts, and the Mont Sainte-Marie convent school in Montreal. She began studies at Montreal's *Ecole normale,* but was obliged to withdraw after completing four years of the program in order to take on additional responsibilities within her family. In 1910 she left the family home in order to administer the dental office of her brother. In 1917 she began a long career in the postal service, throughout which time she resided at a Franciscan convent in Montreal. During the period 1934-1936 she supplied three short comedies to the sisters for use in their school, and in addition she wrote seven other comedies which were staged at various locations in

Montreal, such as the Saint-Sulpice theater and the Monument National, the proceeds going to various charitable organizations. She also acted on occasion, in such plays as *L'Aiglon* by Edmond Rostand. After retiring from the postal service in 1937, she traveled extensively, visiting Egypt, Spain, and Greece. During her latter years she devoted herself to writing and produced eight novels, a collection of six short stories, and two biographies. She died in September 1963.

Maillet's literary production does not fall within the categories of what is now generally considered of significant interest in Quebec literature during the two-decade period extending from her retirement in 1937 to the appearance of her last book in 1955. Nevertheless, her work was held to be of considerable religious and moral utility and thus attracted a wide readership in a church-dominated society. To her credit, important attention is accorded in her fictional writing to certain pressing social problems of the time. However, the overabiding simplicity of plot and characterization, in addition to a persistent tendency toward the melodramatic, relegate these works unavoidably to second if not third rank.

Yves Bolduc, writing in the *Dictionnaire des oeuvres littéraires du Québec* in 1982, has pointed out with particular eloquence the fundamental principles upon which Maillet's fictional creations are based. The bipolar structures which typify the work of so many Quebec writers are indeed present in Maillet's thematic catalogue as well; in this case the bipolarity consistently pits suffering virtue, identified generally with women mistreated by dominant males in a paternalistic society, against evil that is never more than momentarily triumphant. As Bolduc points out, it is always good that has the last word. The emotionally charged atmosphere of these works is further enhanced, if somewhat artificially, by the author's frequent, evident, and openly gratuitous interventions. Lacking the sort of tight inner consistency that characterizes a higher quality of fic-

238

tional writing, these texts are frequently marked by improbable successions of chance events, coups de theatre, unforeseen meetings, and sudden shifts of plot. In obvious ways, the author betrays her presence within the fabric of the fictional discourse by frequent evaluative comments on events, by revelations of the secret thoughts of the characters, and by an unrestrained tendency toward moral observation.

Although the texts permit readers to form a more or less realistic idea of certain limited environments in Quebec during the periods portrayed (the home and the workplace of the middle and professional classes in Montreal, for example), it must be admitted that the banality of much of Maillet's dialogue and the naive simplicity evident in the psychology of her characters leave the reader somewhat dismayed. One must agree, however, with critics of the time that Maillet wrote with imagination and verve and that her denunciations of class prejudice and male chauvinism (particularly as regards the extension to women of the right to vote) must be commended. Nevertheless, the fact remains that the overall aim of much of her writing is to show that virtue is unfailingly rewarded, and that Catholic Christian faith and morality, despite adversity, are finally triumphant. It is this conviction that nourished Maillet's creative impulse and touched the largest number of her readers.

The plot of *Peuvent-elles garder un secret?* (1937), Maillet's first novel, may be cited as an example of much that typifies the melodramatic nature of her imagination. Yolande and Fernand are engaged to be married, but the fickle Fernand abandons his fiancée and seduces her sister, Madeleine. Fernand then momentarily quits the scene and is unaware of the birth of his child, Suzanne, and of the little girl's having been entrusted to a nun by Madeleine shortly before Madeleine's untimely demise. Fernand, meanwhile, undergoes a conversion experience and becomes a missionary.

In the novel's second part, Yolande's daughter and Suzanne, twenty-three years later, are in love with the same man. Suzanne is favored by the suitor, but Suzanne and Marthe, her adoptive mother who has meanwhile left the religious order, are suspected of having illicitly influenced the young man's choice. In order to secure Suzanne's honor and happiness, Marthe reveals the secret of Suzanne's origins; the principals are reconciled and Suzanne's marriage ensues.

The other novels and short stories, as well as the biographies of Michelle Rôbal and Rachel Merode (two ordinary women remarkable only for their extraordinary moral qualities), similarly turn for the most part around the moral contortions of a bourgeois society with strong church connections. Perilous situations are created from which only extreme ethical fortitude, a quality not always equally shared, can extricate the characters. Melodrama, sentimentality, and emotive Roman Catholicism combine to produce a literature of which one critic has said that the fact that it can be placed in any hands is perhaps its only merit.

Reference:

Raymond Crête, "Bio-bibliographie de Mlle Adrienne Maillet," thesis, École des Bibliothécaires, Université de Montréal, 1947.

Fletcher Markle
(27 March 1921-)

Jill Tomasson Goodwin
University of Waterloo

WORKS: *Sometime Every Summertime*, in *Radio's Best Plays*, edited by Joseph Liss (New York: Greenberg, 1947), pp. 349-365;

Brainstorm Between Opening and Closing Announcements, in *All the Bright Company: Radio Drama Produced by Andrew Allan*, edited by Howard Fink and John Jackson (Kingston: Quarry/ Toronto: CBC Enterprises, 1987), pp. 23-38.

MOTION PICTURES: *V-1: The Story of the Robot Bomb*, screenplay by Markle, British Ministry of Information, 1944;

Jigsaw, screenplay by Markle and Vincent Mc-Connor, United Artists, 1949.

TELEVISION: *Telescope*, by Markle and others, CBC, 1963-1969;

Festival, by Markle and others, CBC, 1963-1969;

That's Hollywood, by Markle and others, ABC, 1977-1978.

RADIO: *Imagine Please*, CKWX Vancouver, 1940-1941;

Action of the Tiger, Another Year, Christopher the Cricket, Postscript to a First Love, Presenting Mr. Charles, This Land Is Ours, With Heart We Sing; adaptations of: J. Jefferson Farjeon's *The Appointed Date*, W. L. George's *The Artistic Truth about Señor Pérez*, Monica Marsden's *Front Page Splash*, Peter J. Harkins's *This Was a Man*, and Rachel Reynolds's *When Charlot Comes Home*, for *Theatre Time*, CBC, 1941;

Brainstorm Between Opening and Closing Announcements, For the Love of Mike, The Gilbys of Millbrook, He and She, Journey to Eternity, One to Get Ready, Simple as ABC, There Was a Young Man (4 parts), *They Come and Go and That's the Way It Is*, and *Unfinished Blues*, for *Baker's Dozen*, CBC, 1942;

29:40, Home Is Where You Hang Your Heart, Great God Gadget, A Day in the Life, Tears, Idle Tears, The Warrior Looks Homeward, Who Do You Think You Are?, Wonderful Charlie, He and She

(enlarged version); adaptations of: Eugene O'Neill's *Ah, Wilderness!*, Prosper Mérimée's *Carmen*, Hamilton Basso's *The Great Lady*, Marcel Pagnol's *Topaze*, and Christopher Morley's *The Trojan Horse*, for *Stage*, CBC, 1944-1958;

To Be Announced, Sometime Every Summertime, Blood, Thunder and a Woman in Green, For Future Reference, Here's Harry, Illusion, Marcia, Three's Company, Midnight Town is Full of Boys, The Trouble with You, Darling, for *Radio Folio*, CBC, 1945.

During his active career Fletcher Markle was known as a "four-in-one" man, the versatile combination of actor, writer, director, and producer. Involved in both the Golden Age of Canadian radio drama and the Golden Age of American television drama, Markle worked in both countries and in three media: radio, television, and film. Markle's reputation rests on his talents as an intuitive showman and fastidious craftsman. For Markle, the writer is the crucial component of the collaborative process of modern play production, and not surprisingly, he wishes to be thought of first as a writer. With a writer's sense of symmetry in narrative, Markle began and ended his active career with his first love, radio. Markle is now in "semi-retirement," as he calls it, and is working on a number of projects, including his memoirs.

William Fletcher Markle, third son of Meta Gertrude Clarke Markle and George Wilson Markle, a well-to-do importer, was born in Winnipeg in 1921. Within a year the family moved to Vancouver, where they settled (except for a brief return to Winnipeg in 1928). At the age of ten Markle wrote his first novel, "Son of Barbarossa," a bloody tale of pirates, complete with crayon illustrations. Markle attended Point Grey High School, where his French teacher, Ruth Lynn, helped him with his severe stutter, instructing him to memorize passages from literature and to listen to different voices on the radio. One voice

Fletcher Markle

in particular captivated young Markle: that of Orson Welles, then the voice of chocolate pudding on a dessert commercial. Welles's rich and vibrant intonation and especially his flawless delivery impressed Markle, who worked for a year to overcome his speech impediment. In the process he not only learned to imitate Welles perfectly but also decided to follow his mentor into radio and the theater.

In 1939, after deciding against attending the University of British Columbia, Markle set up his own acting troupe called the Phoenix Theatre, which performed Orson Welles's modern-dress version of *Julius Caesar* and another Welles favorite, Marlowe's *Dr. Faustus*. At the same time, Markle wrote, produced, and acted in a sixty-five-week, hour-long radio drama series for CKWX in Vancouver entitled *Imagine Please*, which adapted everything from Shakespeare to fairy tales to current motion pictures. Radio drama budgets of the era generally covered the production crew's bus fare, coffee, occasional lunches, and not much more. CKWX rewarded the cast members for their enthusiasm with a twelve dollar stipend. Nonetheless, the series attracted young acting talent in Vancouver, many of whom had worked with Markle in the Phoenix troupe

and who went with him to work on CBC's *Theatre Time* with Andrew Allan, the new head of drama for CBC in Vancouver: John Drainie, Lister Sinclair, Bernard Braden, Claire Murray, Alan Pearce, John Bethune, Arthur Hill, Peggy Hassard, and Catherine Graham, among them.

In 1942 Allan was asked to fill a thirteen-week summer slot with a series of half-hour dramas for the National Network of the CBC. Allan asked Markle to write the plays, and they called the series *Baker's Dozen*. Subtitled *Original Radio Diversions*, the series experimented with genre and radio techniques; the first production was *One to Get Ready*, complete with an original musical score by Lawrence Wilson. This series marked the birth of the Golden Age of Canadian radio drama and launched, in fact, the careers of both Markle and Allan. It received such "staggering acclaim," as Allan described it, that the next year CBC made Allan national head of drama in Toronto, and he, in turn, called writers and actors together to form the nucleus of the long-running and immensely popular national radio drama series, *Stage*.

Fittingly, Markle wrote the first three scripts for the new weekly Sunday night program, *29:40* (aired 23 January 1944), an entertaining explanation of a radio drama production; *Home Is Where You Hang Your Heart* (30 January), a drama; and *Great God Gadget* (6 February), a drama and social commentary on consumerism. Canadian listeners were delighted: Canadian radio dramas produced and written by Canadians that sounded as confident and slick as those produced in the United States. In the meantime Markle had been assigned to the RCAF. Failing the physical examination for aircrew, Markle was sent to public relations, first in Ottawa and then in London, England.

Overseas Markle branched out into film work in his off-hours, acting in several films, including *Journey Together*, with Edward G. Robinson. He did some work for the BBC in 1943 and 1944, and he also wrote, edited, and narrated his first film, *V-1: The Story of the Robot Bomb* (1944), a British Ministry of Information documentary about buzz bombs, which was nominated for an Academy Award in 1944 and was named picture of the month (November 1944) by the War Activities Committee.

After the war ended Markle returned to Toronto, where in 1945 he wrote and produced *Radio Folio* for the CBC, a summer replacement series for *Stage*. The first production, *To Be An-*

nounced, was followed by *Sometime Every Summertime*, the story of a young man's discovery of his own snobbery and one of Markle's most commercially successful radio plays; it has been performed many times, published in Joseph Liss's *Radio's Best Plays* (1947), and translated into many languages, including Japanese. While he was producing *Radio Folio*, Markle received a $1,500 literary fellowship from 20th Century-Fox to expand into a novel a four-part script from *Baker's Dozen*, entitled *There Was a Young Man*. Markle never completed the book, which was sold instead as material for a film.

For some time Markle had wanted to try his hand at the American market; in 1946 he decided to create his own opportunity. Taking a *Stage 46* recording of *Life with Adam* (written by Hugh Kemp), Markle went to New York to see Orson Welles for the first time. In that production Markle played Adam, a flawless and unmistakable parody of Orson Welles. Welles was amused by the play and intrigued by Markle. He promptly aired the production on his show *Mercury Theatre of the Air* and, with equal promptness, took over Markle's career. Markle moved to New York with his wife, radio singer (Helen) Blanche Willis (whom he had married in December 1944) and their young son Stephen (born 26 September 1945). He worked for Welles and Sir Alexander Korda, helping develop screenplays for *The Lady from Shanghai*, an adaptation of Sherwood King's novel *If I Should Die Before I Wake*, starring Rita Hayworth, and for Oscar Wilde's *Salome*. However, Welles was as difficult to work for as he was famous, and Markle decided to return to Toronto.

He did not stay for long. *Columbia Workshop*, the dramatic showpiece of CBS radio, produced three of his scripts (originally broadcast on *Radio Folio*), *Sometime Every Summertime*, *Three's Company*, and *Midnight Town is Full of Boys*, an opportunity arranged for Markle by Norman Corwin, whom Markle had met and impressed. Early in 1947 CBS invited him to New York, where he wrote, directed, produced, and acted in a new, unsponsored radio drama series, which he titled *Studio One*, and which aired 29 April 1947. Using an hour-long format, the series presented contemporary novel and play adaptations and opened with a production of Malcolm Lowry's *Under the Volcano*, starring Everett Sloane, Anne Burr, Hedley Rainnie, and Joe Di Santis. Promoted by CBS as a drama series to satisfy both critics and radio listeners, *Studio One* used seasoned radio ac-

tors and solid stories. It succeeded, winning the George Foster Peabody Award for outstanding drama (1948) for *Thunder Rock* by Robert Ardrey. At twenty-six Markle was known as radio's new "boy wonder," the Canadian successor to Orson Welles and Norman Corwin.

Studio One and Markle lasted a year, at which time CBS asked Markle to take over its most prestigious sponsored drama program, *Ford Theatre*. With the highest budget in radio drama ($1,500,000, including Markle's salary of $1,000-$1,500 per week), Markle brought with him his *Studio One* script editor, Vincent McConnor, as well as his assistant producer, engineer, and soundman. Writers Brainerd Duffield and Canadian Hugh Kemp joined. Markle used Hollywood talent this time (and, having been divorced from his first wife, married someone from the Hollywood scene, Oscar-winning actress Mercedes McCambridge, in February 1950). The first production, which aired 8 October 1948, was an adaptation of Flaubert's *Madame Bovary*, starring Claude Rains, Marlene Dietrich, and Van Heflin. Though the series lasted just a season, Markle brought to the microphone such Hollywood stars as Burt Lancaster, Lucille Ball, Ingrid Bergman, Douglas Fairbanks, Jr., Ronald Colman, Edward G. Robinson, Claudette Colbert, Vincent Price, Bob Hope, Jack Benny, Bing Crosby, Charles Laughton, Montgomery Clift, Bette Davis, and Helen Hayes. The show left the air 1 July 1949.

At the same time he produced the series, Markle made his first American film for United Artists, *Jigsaw* (1949), which he directed and coauthored with Vincent McConnor. This budget film starred Franchot Tone, but Markle managed to get many others to appear as unpaid extras: Henry Fonda, Marlene Dietrich, John Garfield, Burgess Meredith, Marsha Hunt, Charles Laughton, and Everett Sloane. Two more Hollywood movies directed by Markle followed, *Night into Morning* and *The Man with a Cloak*, both released by MGM in 1951.

In 1952 CBS invited Markle, then thirty-one, to produce the television version of the Westinghouse-sponsored *Studio One* in New York, which had premiered 7 November 1949. It was modeled on the radio original, adapting contemporary novels and plays in hour-long productions. Like his assignment to *Ford Theatre* earlier, Markle took over the series after the departure of another producer and brought the series back up to popular and critical standards. Markle's premier show, a Brainerd Duffield adaptation of the Claude Houghton novel *I am Jonathan Scrivener*, was directed by Paul Nickell and starred John Forsythe, Everett Sloane, Maria Riva, and Felecia Montealegre. It aired live on 1 December 1952. Three weeks later, 22 December, Markle presented an Andrew Allan adaptation of the medieval mystery plays entitled *The Nativity*. Allan had first written it for radio in 1941 for CBC Vancouver, and the production had become an annual event on CBC *Stage*. For the *Studio One* production both Allan and Markle received the Christopher Award for outstanding television drama in 1953.

For Markle the years 1953 to 1962 were busy ones in Hollywood. He moved frequently between television films and series, both entertaining and dramatic, for CBS, NBC, and ABC. In 1953 CBS asked Markle to produce and direct the half-hour television comedy *Life With Father*, which ran until 1955. Based on the popular book and play by Clarence Day, the show aired on CBS on 22 November 1953, ran until 5 July 1955, and starred Leon Ames and Lurene Tuttle. In the summer of 1954 Markle produced, directed, and hosted *Front Row Center*, a live television drama series which included adaptations of F. Scott Fitzgerald's *Tender Is the Night* and Eugene O'Neill's *Ah, Wilderness!* From 1956 to 1962 Markle worked on projects which ranged from *Ford Theatre* and *Colgate Theatre* to *Thriller*, *Panic*, *M Squad*, *Buckskin*, and, in 1961-1962, the situation comedy *Father of the Bride*, with Leon Ames and Ruth Warwick.

In July 1963, divorced from Mercedes McCambridge, Markle married his third wife, Dorothy Conradt, and returned to Canada to direct the Walt Disney movie *The Incredible Journey* (1963), which starred John Drainie, Sandra Scott Salverson, and French-Canadian actor Emil Genest. The movie remains on *Variety*'s list of the top two hundred highest-grossing films. Shortly after the filming, Markle discovered that, at forty-two, he had diabetes and was told to slow his frenetic pace and to shorten his long days. He decided to abandon directing and to concentrate on writing and producing.

From 1963 to 1976, Markle worked on and off for CBC television, moving to Toronto. From 1963 to 1969 Markle wrote, produced, and

hosted the *Telescope* series (and in 1970 became its executive producer) and was a contributing writer for *Festival*, a performing-arts series, adapting Katherine Anne Porter's *Pale Horse, Pale Rider* and Brian Moore's *The Feast of Lupercal*, among other works. In 1970 CBC appointed Markle the head of television drama, a post from which he promoted Canadian talent and Canadian works, including the 1972 adaptation of Mazo de la Roche's *Whiteoaks of Jalna*. He was also the executive producer of *The Play's the Thing* (1974), a drama series which commissioned Canadian writers to create original television plays. Among the contributors were Morley Callaghan, Robertson Davies, Mordecai Richler, Margaret Atwood, Alice Munro, Hugh Hood, and Hugh MacLennan. In 1972 John Hirsch succeeded Markle as head of television drama.

In the last several years Markle has split his time between television and radio. In 1976 he produced *The Olympics: A Television History of the Golden Games* for CBC. Hosted by Christopher Plummer, this four-hour special included film footage from all modern Olympic summer and winter games since their inception; it was rebroadcast by PBS during the 1984 summer Olympic games in Los Angeles. In 1977-1978 Markle was a contributing writer and producer of *That's Hollywood* for ABC television. In 1979 he returned to radio as senior director and producer first of the *Sears Radio Theatre* (CBS) and then of *Mutual Radio Theatre* (MBS), two ambitious radio drama series which broadcast each season 130 original radio plays written primarily by young writers.

In semiretirement Markle has been working on television and film projects. With Robert Wise, the producer-director of *West Side Story* and *The Sound of Music*, he is setting up a television series tentatively entitled "Speaking for Myself," in which Hollywood actors give self-portraits, speaking directly to the camera. He is also planning to produce a Western based on Wallace Stegner's short story "Tenderfoot," set in a Saskatchewan winter, and he is writing his memoirs, with the working title "Sidelines."

Papers:
Fletcher Markle's radio, film, and television papers are housed in the Media Archive of the Thousand Oaks Library, Thousand Oaks, California.

Anne Marriott
(5 November 1913-   )

Hilda L. Thomas
University of British Columbia

BOOKS: *The Wind Our Enemy* (Toronto: Ryerson, 1939);

Calling Adventurers! (Toronto: Ryerson, 1941);

Salt Marsh (Toronto: Ryerson, 1942);

Sandstone and Other Poems (Toronto: Ryerson, 1945);

Countries (Fredericton: Fiddlehead, 1971);

A Swarming in my Mind, by Marriott and Joyce Moller (North Vancouver: Curriculum Services Branch, North Vancouver School District, 1977);

The Circular Coast: Poems, New and Selected (Oakville, Ontario: Mosaic Press/Valley Editions, 1981);

A Long Way to Oregon (Oakville, Ontario: Mosaic, 1984);

Letters from Some Islands (Oakville, Ontario: Mosaic, 1985).

The Wind Our Enemy (1939), Anne Marriott's first published volume, was described by Desmond Pacey as "a more incisive long poem than had appeared in Canada since [E. J.] Pratt's early 'Cachalot.'. . ." In the 1940s Marriott produced three further volumes of poems. One of them, *Calling Adventurers!* (1941), won a Governor General's Award for 1941. But there followed twenty-five years during which she published only occasional poems and short stories, and she seemed destined to be regarded as a writer whose reputation would rest on the historical importance of her early work. In the 1980s, however, Marriott's writing once more began to appear in print, in the form of a substantial number of new poems and a collection of short stories.

The daughter of Edward Guy Marriott, a civil engineer, and his wife, Catherine Heley Marriott, Joyce Anne Marriott was born in Victoria and attended private schools there. She was one of the many poets who responded to the spirit of modernism which was reinvigorating Canadian poetry in the 1930s. In Montreal and Toronto, F. R. Scott, A. J. M. Smith, Dorothy

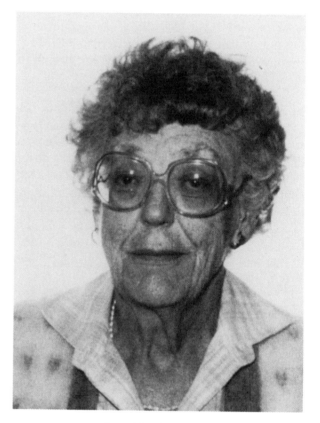

Anne Marriott in 1987

Livesay, and others were leading a rebellion against the dying romantic-Victorian tradition which had dominated Canadian poetry in the first three decades of the twentieth century. Influenced by William Butler Yeats, T. S. Eliot, the French symbolists, and the American imagists, they were developing new techniques to express the uniqueness of the Canadian experience, and, moved by the social poetry of W. H. Auden, Stephen Spender, and Cecil Day Lewis, they voiced their outrage at the suffering and misery of the Depression years.

In *The Wind Our Enemy* Marriott brought together the most vital elements of the modern tradition. The poem is episodic and documentary rather than strictly narrative in form. Using heavy alliteration and repeated sound patterns, its ten sections develop in a mosaic made up of compressed details and dramatized speech. In its colloquial rhythms and its concrete language, the poem expressed for a generation of readers the inarticulate suffering of the prairie farmer who saw his land and his hopes blowing away in a cloud of dust.

The poems in Marriott's next volume, *Calling Adventurers!*, for which she won the Governor General's Award, were originally written as a series of choruses for a CBC radio documentary, "Payload," scripted by Margaret Kennedy, with music by Barbara Pentland. The documentary, in Marriott's words, "celebrated the romance and heroism of the northern 'bush flyer' in the era leading up to World War II," and *Calling Adventurers!* was composed, Marriott said, as an "intellectual exercise." It suffers from occasional lapses into empty exhortation, and, unlike *The Wind Our Enemy*, it leans too heavily on commonplace adjectives. In its best lines Marriott's exceptional ear for natural and appropriate rhythm is fully engaged, and the northern landscape is rendered in vivid, original images. But Marriott now confesses to some embarrassment at the simplistic view of the opening up of the North expressed in *Calling Adventurers!*

Although the west coast landscape is closest to her imagination, Marriott's first works dealt with the prairies (she had spent several summers on a farm in that region) and the North. Both *Salt Marsh* (1942) and *Sandstone and Other Poems* (1945) contain some vigorous and effective lyrics inspired by prairie scenes. "Woodyards in the Rain" and "Prairie Graveyard," for example, display the intense feeling that informed *The Wind Our Enemy*. But these volumes did not meet with the critical acclaim accorded the earlier work. Both are now out of print.

In 1938 Marriott became acquainted with Dorothy Livesay. Livesay's "Day and Night," printed in the first issue of *Canadian Poetry Magazine* in January 1936, although more explicit in its political message, served as a stimulus in the writing of *The Wind Our Enemy*. It was Livesay who proposed to Marriott, Floris McLaren, and Doris Ferne that they start a poetry magazine which would serve as a vehicle for poets outside the somewhat closed Montreal circle. Alan Crawley accepted their invitation to edit the magazine, and in September 1941 the first issue of *Contemporary Verse* appeared.

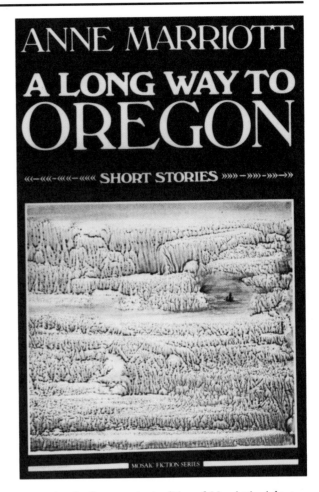

Cover for the first paperback edition of Marriott's eight-story collection published in 1984

Marriott assisted with the editing of *Contemporary Verse* until 1945, when she moved from Victoria to Ottawa to work for the National Film Board. Here she continued to write, turning out short stories and film scripts as well as poems. On 16 December 1947 she married Gerald McLellan, and in 1950 they moved to Prince George, British Columbia, where she was social editor for the local newspaper. In 1959 the couple settled in North Vancouver, where Marriott still lives.

In the 1970s Marriott began to conduct poetry workshops, chiefly for young people, in the schools and libraries of North Vancouver and the lower mainland of British Columbia. This work led to a publication, *A Swarming in my Mind* (1977), prepared in collaboration with librarian Joyce Moller for use in the district schools. But apart from *Countries*, a limited-edition volume of poems published by Fiddlehead in 1971,

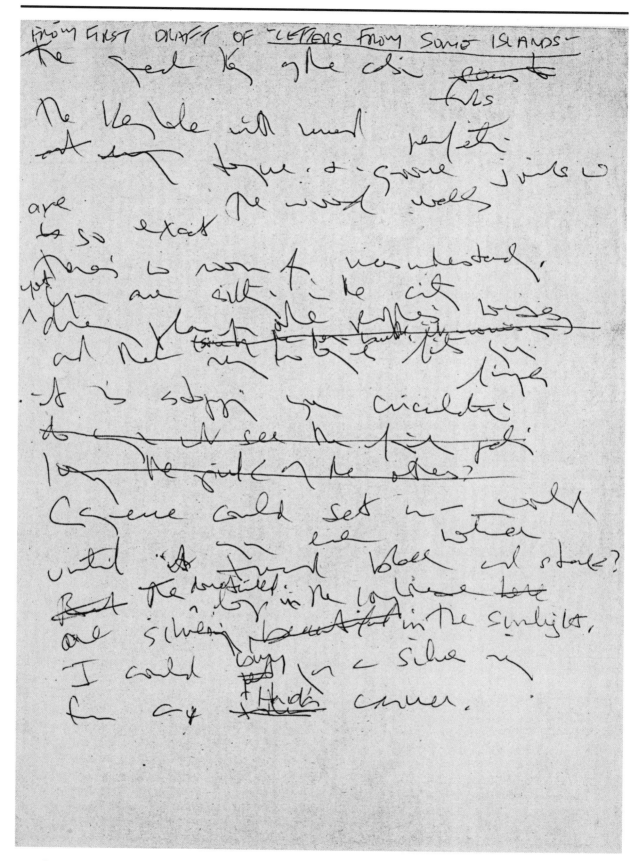

Page from the first draft of Marriott's most recent book, a collection of poems about love, loss of love, aging, separation, and death
(by permission of the author)

Marriott produced no significant new work until the 1980s.

The Circular Coast: Poems, New and Selected (1981) introduces a theme of increasing importance in Marriott's work. Here the west coast landscape is symbolically identified with the body as the poet seeks, in images which are at once precise and complex, to come to terms with the problems of aging, loneliness, and death, the central theme of her most recent published volumes.

A Long Way to Oregon (1984) is a collection of eight stories written mostly in the 1970s, although one, "Mrs. Absalom," goes back to 1954. In all of them there is a strong element of morbidity and an undercurrent of mystery reminiscent of the work of Sinclair Ross, although not as subtle. The characters are excluded from the human community by age or poverty or the cruelty of circumstance. Victims of incest, suicides, psychotics, all are isolated figures facing lonely death. In "The Death of the Cat" and "It's Alright Mr. Khan" the central character is stirred to life in the end, but this faint note of renewal comes about only through the death of a fellow creature. The stories suffer from technical naiveté. Their strength lies in the delineation of character and the binding together of character and scene through vivid and powerful images.

In *Letters from Some Islands* (1985), Marriott's most recently published work, the poems are about journeys in space and time. Landscapes both strange and familiar are here transformed into metaphors for the aging body. Trees, rivers, tides, the black rocks of Oregon, reflections of light on leaves, on water, all are triggers that release memories and feelings. These are deeply personal poems. Having chosen the physical world as a metaphor for love, loss of love, separation, and death, Marriott uses simple, descriptive language devoid of ambiguity. The persona is open, vulnerable, moved by the knowledge that if life is narrowing to a close, there are still moments of joy to be found: in friendship, in a painting by Breughel, in the "last-moment beauty" of mountains at sunset. "You have your choices," she writes; "one is of metaphors." And in spite of age, grief, the slow turning of the body toward inevitable death, she affirms life, as in "Winter Scene":

> . . . somewhere in me
> there's a stubborn pocket of warmth.
> My fingers
> fumble in the moss
> for crystalline twigs—
> encased in ice
> but dry fuel at the core.

Although Anne Marriott's reputation may rest chiefly on her first published work, the critical ledger is not yet closed. Whatever she produces in the way of new work, her contribution to *Contemporary Verse* and her energetic efforts to stimulate an interest in poetry in a new generation of readers will secure her place in the history of Canadian literature.

References:

Jan De Bruyn, "Anne Marriott, Poet of Joy," *British Columbia Library Quarterly*, 22 (January 1959): 23-29;

R. S. Philp, "Anne Marriott—Poet of Prairie and Coast," *Canadian Author and Bookman*, 58 (Spring 1983): 11-12;

Donald Stephens, "Conviction," *Canadian Literature*, 99 (Winter 1983): 157-158.

Colin McDougall

(13 July 1917-3 June 1984)

Hallvard Dahlie
University of Calgary

BOOK: *Execution* (Toronto: Macmillan, 1958; London: Macmillan, 1958; New York: St. Martin's, 1958).

PERIODICAL PUBLICATIONS: "Cardboard Soldiers," *Maclean's,* 64 (15 July 1951): 12-13, 44-47;
"The Firing Squad," *Maclean's,* 66 (1 January 1953): 6-7, 28-33;
"Love is for the Birds," *Maclean's,* 66 (15 July 1953): 14, 31-35.

Colin McDougall's reputation on the Canadian literary scene is exclusively a 1950s phenomenon: three of his most important short stories appeared early in that decade, and his only novel to date appeared in 1958. His talent, though regrettably not pursued in subsequent decades, was, however, prominently recognized; his short story "The Firing Squad" won first prize in *Maclean's* fiction contest and the University of Western Ontario President's Medal for the best Canadian short story of 1953, and *Execution* won the country's highest literary award, the Governor General's Award for fiction, as well as the Quebec Literary Prize.

Unlike many writers McDougall did not make literature a major preoccupation, and it is possible to see his writing career merely as one of many activities he pursued throughout a balanced, orderly, and fruitful life. The son of the Honorable Mr. Justice Errol McDougall and his wife, the former Mary Wynifred Rankin, McDougall was educated at Lower Canada College (1929-1936) and McGill University (B. A., 1940). He saw active service with the Princess Patricia's Canadian Light Infantry in World War II, emerging with the rank of major. He married Diana Ekers of Montreal in January 1941 and was the father of one son and three daughters. From 1946 he was associated with McGill University, first as a student counselor, then successively as director of Placement Services, registrar, and secretary general, a position he held from 1973.

Execution constitutes a complex fleshing out of his short story "The Firing Squad" and draws heavily upon his own involvement as a company commander during the Sicilian and Italian campaigns of 1943 and 1944. It is on the surface concerned with the activities of a company of Canadian officers and enlisted men, from their initial landing on the beaches of Sicily to the aftermath of the grim battles of the Adolf Hitler Line around Cassino, but its fundamental substance is philosophical and moral rather than military. The two occasions of literal executions–of the two harmless Italian deserters near the beginning of the novel and of the innocent Rifleman Jones at the end–create a realistic framework in which one can examine the ironic and tragic relationships between the title word and its human and metaphysical implications. The formal four-part structure of the novel effectively reinforces this end as well: respectively entitled "The First," "More," "And More," and "The Last," the sections allow for both the ambiguity and the inevitability that underscore the novel's resolution.

Within this perspective individual heroes and mass man tend to merge, as is characteristic of many World War II novels, but McDougall sustains the priority of realistic character by having relatively few individuals carry the burden of both the narrative and the moral unfoldings. Lieutenant Adam, Padre Philip Doorn, Private Ewart, and Captain Kildare are the major characters who survive the entire campaign, but two others who are killed late in the action, Major Bunny Bazin and Gunner Krasnick, as well as the executed Rifleman Jones, most effectively provide the novel with its ironic moral and philosophical reverberations. Bazin, Adam, and Jones are all personally implicated in the initial execution: it is Jones who discovers the deserters, Bazin who orders their interrogation, and Adam who mercifully finishes them off after the sadistic Sergeant Krebs bungles the killing.

Throughout the subsequent action Bazin and Adam attempt to exorcise their own per-

Colin McDougall (center) with officials of McGill University and John Abbott College, December 1975 (photograph by Ralph Emery, courtesy of the McGill Reporter*)*

sonal guilt and to rationalize the guilt of mass man, as represented by their company. Jones, innocent and simpleminded, carries no residue of guilt with him, and his own execution, brought on by his technical involvement in the death of an American, presumably is meant to resolve this total guilt. But he never does emerge sufficiently as a viable and credible character, as does, for example, Melville's Billy Budd, and that resolution as a result suffers on both realistic and symbolic levels. The two executions are linked by elements of injustice: the Italians are killed without any trial whatsoever, while the outcome of Jones's trial is determined solely by political expediency on the part of the Canadian and American military hierarchy.

The theme of execution is ironically articulated in the first spoken words of the novel, when the Manitoba farm boy Krasnick expresses his horror at the idea of killing horses–though

he proceeds without qualms to kill the riders of the horses. At novel's end Krasnick is dead, but Ewart's recollection that "he shot a lot of Germans–but he would never shoot horses" allows Adam to utter the novel's final irony: "Of course. None of us would." Earlier on Adam had speculated about the meaning of war with the idealistic Major Bazin, who succinctly expressed the nature of this dilemma: "What it's all about, of course, is execution. . . . Execution is the ultimate injustice, the ultimate degradation of man. . . . Perhaps it is man's plight to acquiesce. On the other hand, even recognizing execution as the evil may be a victory of sorts; struggling against it may be the closest man ever comes to victory."

Bazin, along with Adam and Padre Doorn, went through a dehumanizing stage at the first execution, a process they gradually were able to reverse. Both symbolically and literally, the force that made this reversal possible is that of love:

249

Bazin occupies himself in the gun emplacements with conjugating the Latin verb *amare;* Adam learns the Italian phrase *Io ti amo,* which elevates his sexual encounters with Elena and Toni to something higher than a mere physical act; and Doorn, however pathetically, sustains himself with what is essentially a vestigial spiritual love after the trauma brought on by those first two executions. That Bazin is the last man killed in the action of this novel is perhaps irony enough, but Adam likes to think that the German sniper who killed him was also perhaps reciting *"amo, amas, amat."*

Execution aesthetically and philosophically evokes both Stephen Crane's *The Red Badge of Courage* (1895) and Ernest Hemingway's *A Farewell to Arms* (1929) in the manner in which it isolates the dilemma of the individual caught up in the horrors that man has loosed upon himself. In other respects—in its depiction of the multiple hero, in its exploitation of the elements of absurdity and mass desensitizing, it has much in common with such World War II novels as Norman Mailer's *The Naked and the Dead* (1948), James Jones's *The Thin Red Line* (1962), and Joseph Heller's *Catch-22* (1961). It is the major World War II novel emanating from Canada, though Edward Meade's 1946 novel, *Remember Me,* achieves a degree of poignancy that is lacking in *Execution.* But at the same time McDougall's novel avoids sentimentality and didacticism, and in its blend of objective realism and carefully controlled symbolism it allows for both a credibility and an expansible interpretation that have confirmed its continuing relevance and significance.

Reference:

Ronald Sutherland, "Vital Pretense: McDougall's *Execution," Canadian Literature,* 27 (Winter 1966): 20-31.

Floris Clark McLaren

(18 December 1904-15 April 1978)

Donald A. Precosky
College of New Caledonia

BOOK: *Frozen Fire* (Toronto: Macmillan, 1937).

PERIODICAL PUBLICATION: "*Contemporary Verse:* A Canadian Quarterly," *Tamarack Review*, 3 (Spring 1957): 55-63.

Canadian poetry felt its way into modernism hesitantly over a prolonged transition period which stretched from the 1920s to the 1940s. These two decades produced a number of poets who, though not great talents, contributed to the change. One was Floris Clark McLaren.

McLaren, the daughter of Henry Clark, a farmer and horticulturist, and Marion Granger Clark, was born Floris Marion Clark in Skagway, Alaska, in 1904. After attending the public school in Skagway and the normal school at Western Washington University in Bellingham, she taught in Skagway from 1923 to 1925, the year of her marriage to John Angus McLaren. From 1925 to 1932 the McLarens lived in Whitehorse, in the Yukon, where their sons, John Angus, Jr., and Bruce Alan, were born. In 1932 the family moved to Victoria, British Columbia; McLaren remained there until her death in 1978.

In 1937 Macmillan published *Frozen Fire*, McLaren's first and only book. The poetry in it is a mélange of nineteenth- and twentieth-century techniques and attitudes. McLaren makes some attempt at free verse in this volume, but, though the irregular line lengths give the poems a modern look, the iambic meter and the rhymes make them sound old-fashioned. Many of their images would not be out of place in a Confederation poet's verse, but her poems lack the vitality of that earlier generation's work. The 1930s were a time of experimentation and radicalism for poets throughout the English-speaking world. *Frozen Fire* shows McLaren to have been untouched by these trends.

On Easter weekend 1941 McLaren, Dorothy Livesay, Anne Marriott, and Doris Ferne met in Victoria and worked out a plan for a quarterly devoted to poetry. McLaren felt that such a journal

was necessary because, as she put it in a 1957 article in *Tamarack Review*, "the chances of publication in Canada for an unknown writer, or a writer experimenting with new verse forms, or concerned with social or political themes, were almost nonexistent." The result was *Contemporary Verse*, a quarterly which appeared from September 1941 to the Fall/Winter issue of 1952. McLaren acted as business manager. The editor was Alan Crawley, in McLaren's description "a Winnipeg lawyer whose concern with poetry had begun in a London acquaintance with Harold Monro and the poetry workshop.... He had moved to British Columbia after an illness resulting in the loss of sight had forced him to retire from his profession." During its eleven-year existence *Contemporary Verse* published work by all of the major established poets of the day as well as offerings from most of the important new ones. Unlike its Montreal contemporaries, *Preview, First Statement,* and *Northern Review*, it did not have an ideologically limited editorial policy but reflected the tolerant and eclectic tastes of Alan Crawley. McLaren has summarized the aims and achievements of *Contemporary Verse* in her article in the *Tamarack Review:* "the aim was to publish, whenever possible, representative groups of poems by writers rather than collections of single pieces. This ... was one of the most valuable aspects of the magazine–tracing the threads of individual development that were forming the pattern of Canadian living." She lists Dorothy Livesay, Louis Dudek, James Reaney, Raymond Souster, P. K. Page, Miriam Waddington, Kay Smith, Anne Wilkinson, Earle Birney, A. M. Klein, Ralph Gustafson, Irving Layton, Anne Marriott, Margaret Avison, and Jay Macpherson as some of the poets published by *Contemporary Verse*.

McLaren's own poetry in *Contemporary Verse* is strikingly unlike what she wrote in *Frozen Fire*. She seems to have been thinking of the change in "No More the Slow Stream" (*Contemporary Verse*, number 2) when she contrasts two types of beauty. One is gentle and sublime, the other vio-

251

lent and powerful, and both are associated with the past:

> O the slow stream lovely, lovely no more in
>   sunlight.
> The flotsam of quiet lives turned over and over,
> The dark destructive flood; and the plan the
>   promise
> Spun in the current, swept toward no visible ocean.

The change of which she writes parallels the development of Canadian poetry in the first half of the twentieth century. Canadian poets abandoned sonnets which praised the harmony of nature in favor of less-melodious free verse which often spoke of the land's harshness.

McLaren's work in *Contemporary Verse* falls into two groups. The first contains all the works up to, but not including, those in *Contemporary Verse,* number 20. They mix personal emotion and social issues to express the poet's alienation. On the whole these poems do not succeed because they lack the ring of anger or commitment. The moral confusion which informs these poems is put clearly in "Never the Easy Answer" (*Contemporary Verse,* number 11):

> Never the easy answer, black and white
> Clear in the mind, the sharp distinction made
> The sheep and the goats divided: this is right.

There is a tendency in these poems, especially in the longer ones, such as "Figure in Shadow" (*Contemporary Verse,* number 14), to dullness and preaching.

The second group begins with *Contemporary Verse,* number 20. McLaren's work becomes retrospective and filled with descriptions of nature. She is in a sense rewriting *Frozen Fire* but with a surer control over her free verse and less obvious sentimentality. Again, the change in her own writing parallels the change taking place in Canadian poetry as a whole.

The finest poem of this second group, and her best piece in *Contemporary Verse,* is "The Stone" (number 29). It attains the fusion of self and nature which McLaren attempted and at which she failed in *Frozen Fire:*

> Cry love to the wind
> And hear the echoes go
> Around the glacier of fountains[.]

Never before was her poetry as passionate. There is none of the stale imagery of *Frozen Fire* nor the uninspiring reflection of her earlier *Contemporary Verse* work. Unfortunately, this high point also marks the virtual conclusion of Clark's career as a poet. She published only one more poem in *Contemporary Verse.* In the decades since that journal's demise McLaren did not publish a book or a substantial body of magazine verse.

Reference:

Joan McCullagh, *Alan Crawley and "Contemporary Verse"* (Vancouver: University of British Columbia Press, 1976).

Farley Mowat

(12 May 1921-   )

Eric Thompson
Université du Québec à Chicoutimi

BOOKS: *People of the Deer* (Boston: Little, Brown, 1952; Toronto: McClelland & Stewart, 1952; London: Joseph, 1952; revised, Toronto: McClelland & Stewart, 1975);

The Regiment (Toronto: McClelland & Stewart, 1955; revised, 1973);

Lost in the Barrens (Boston: Little, Brown, 1956; Toronto: Little, Brown, 1956; London: Macmillan, 1958);

The Dog Who Wouldn't Be (Boston & Toronto: Little, Brown, 1957; London: Joseph, 1958);

The Grey Seas Under (Boston: Little, Brown, 1958; Toronto: McClelland & Stewart, 1958; London: Joseph, 1959);

The Desperate People (Boston: Little, Brown, 1959; London: Joseph, 1960; revised edition, Toronto: McClelland & Stewart, 1975);

Owls in the Family (Boston: Little, Brown, 1961; Toronto: McClelland & Stewart, 1961; London: Macmillan, 1963);

The Serpent's Coil (Toronto: McClelland & Stewart, 1961; Boston: Little, Brown, 1962; London: Joseph, 1962);

The Black Joke (Toronto: McClelland & Stewart, 1963; Boston: Little, Brown, 1963; London: Macmillan, 1964);

Never Cry Wolf (Toronto: McClelland & Stewart, 1963; Boston: Little, Brown, 1963; London: Secker & Warburg, 1964; revised, Toronto: McClelland & Stewart, 1973);

Westviking: The Ancient Norse in Greenland and North America (Toronto: McClelland & Stewart, 1965; Boston: Little, Brown, 1965; London: Secker & Warburg, 1966);

The Curse of the Viking Grave (Toronto: McClelland & Stewart, 1966; Boston: Little, Brown, 1966);

Canada North (Toronto: McClelland & Stewart, 1967; Boston: Little, Brown, 1968);

This Rock Within the Sea: A Heritage Lost, photographs by John de Visser (Toronto: McClelland & Stewart, 1968; Boston: Little, Brown, 1969);

Farley Mowat (photograph by John de Visser)

The Boat Who Wouldn't Float (Toronto: McClelland & Stewart, 1969; Boston: Little, Brown, 1970; London: Heinemann, 1970);

Sibir: My Discovery of Siberia (Toronto: McClelland & Stewart, 1970); republished as *The Siberians* (Boston: Little, Brown, 1971; London: Heinemann, 1972);

A Whale for the Killing (Toronto: McClelland & Stewart, 1972; Boston: Little, Brown, 1972; London: Heinemann, 1973);

Wake of the Great Sealers, drawings by David Blackwood (Toronto: McClelland & Stewart, 1973; Boston: Little, Brown, 1974);

The Snow Walker (Toronto: McClelland & Stewart, 1975; Boston: Little, Brown, 1976; London: Heinemann, 1978);

Canada North Now: The Great Betrayal, photographs by Shin Sugino (Toronto: McClelland & Stewart, 1976); republished as *The Great Betrayal: Arctic Canada Now* (Boston: Little, Brown, 1976);

And No Birds Sang (Toronto: McClelland & Stewart, 1979; Boston: Little, Brown, 1980; London: Cassells, 1980);

The World of Farley Mowat, edited by Peter Davidson (Boston: Little, Brown, 1980);

Sea of Slaughter (Toronto: McClelland & Stewart, 1984; Boston: Little, Brown, 1984);

My Discovery of America (Toronto: McClelland & Stewart, 1985; Boston: Little, Brown, 1985);

Virunga: The Passion of Dian Fossey (Toronto: McClelland & Stewart, 1987); republished as *Woman in the Mists: The Story of Dian Fossey and the Mountain Gorillas of Africa* (New York: Warner, 1987).

OTHER: *Coppermine Journey: An Account of a Great Adventure, Selected from the Journals of Samuel Hearne,* edited by Mowat (Toronto: McClelland & Stewart, 1958; Boston: Little, Brown, 1958);

Ordeal by Ice: The Search for the Northwest Passage, edited by Mowat (Toronto: McClelland & Stewart, 1960; Boston: Little, Brown, 1961; London: Joseph, 1961); revised as volume 1 of *The Top of the World* trilogy (Toronto: McClelland & Stewart, 1973);

The Polar Passion: The Quest for the North Pole, edited by Mowat (Toronto: McClelland & Stewart, 1967; Boston: Little, Brown, 1968); revised as volume 2 of *The Top of the World* trilogy (Toronto: McClelland & Stewart, 1973);

Tundra: Selections from the Great Accounts of Arctic Land Voyages, edited by Mowat, volume 3 of *The Top of the World* trilogy (Toronto: McClelland & Stewart, 1973).

Farley McGill Mowat was born in Belleville, Ontario, on 12 May 1921, the son of Angus McGill and Helen E. Thomson Mowat. Educated in public schools in Ontario and Saskatchewan, he completed his B.A. at the University of Toronto in 1949 after serving overseas as an infantry officer with the Canadian army during World War II. Mowat had spent part of 1947-1948 working in the Northwest Territories as a student biologist for the Dominion Wildlife Service. It was this

Mowat about the time of The Serpent's Coil *(1961)*

northern experience which proved crucial to the budding forth of his writing talent, and in 1952 he published his first book, *People of the Deer.* Since then Mowat has written more than a score of books, chiefly nonfiction. The sales of his work in North America and in translation in many foreign countries testify to his widespread popularity and influence as a Canadian writer. Named as an Officer of the Order of Canada in 1982, he has won numerous important literary awards and is the recipient of several honorary degrees. First married in 1949 (to Frances Elizabeth Thornhill), Mowat was married a second time in 1961 (to Claire Wheeler). He has two sons by these marriages and now lives in Port Hope, Ontario.

According to Mowat, he began to write at the age of six or seven, or about the time he developed his lifelong interest in animals and nature. Probably the strongest early influences on him were his father and his great-uncle Frank Farley. Angus Mowat had led a peripatetic career as some-

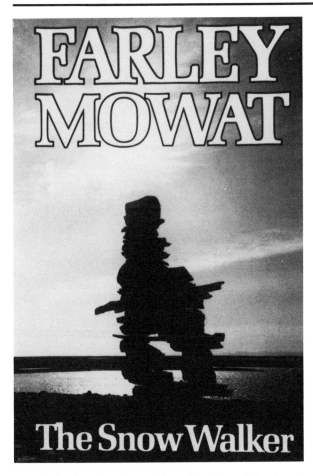

Dust jacket for Mowat's collection of stories and sketches set in the Arctic

time novelist, small-town librarian, and army officer. Mowat recalls that his father was "the most egotistical man I ever knew," but undoubtedly his bookish nature left its mark on his son. Frank Farley, a well-known ornithologist in western Canada, was responsible for introducing the author to the great northland when, in 1934, he took him to Churchill, Manitoba, for the summer. It was then that the young Mowat fell in love with the rugged tundra which, in later years, he would often describe in vivid detail.

Mowat is a man of strong opinions. He says he does not relish being at the center of the controversies he always seems to create with his books or his flamboyant behavior. He has described himself as "a chauvinist and a rampant nationalist" and as "a storyteller who is far more concerned with reaching his audience than with garnering kudos from the arbiters of literary greatness." In fact, although his work has not gone unnoticed by the critics, he is generally dismissed by them as more of a crusading journalist and would-be his-

torian than as a serious author. He has published more than one hundred articles and short stories, and a number of his television and film scripts have been produced. But it is his longer prose works which have drawn attention. Certainly, considered individually, these books contain flaws—misuse of facts, outrageous hypotheses, and the like; but taken as a whole his oeuvre reveals a depth of vision, skillful use of a range of literary forms, and liveliness of expression. Moreover, his exuberant use of what one critic called "subjective non-fiction" has permitted him to write persuasively on many diverse subjects close to his heart.

As the first of his books (and Mowat's personal favorite), *People of the Deer* launched a series of books about the North. In it and its sequel, *The Desperate People* (1959), Mowat portrayed the hardships and courage of the Ihalmiut, an inland Eskimo people, living in the Barrenlands. He did not pull his punches, blaming bureaucrats and other white officials for policies of neglect and even genocide toward the natives. Taken to task by some experts for his alleged falsifications of natural and social history, Mowat answered his critics spiritedly; subsequently, however, he tempered his views in the revised editions of these books. Still, he had revealed, as Alec Lucas put it in *Farley Mowat* (1976), a "terrible truth" about Canada's shoddy record in the North, and his books had awakened the national conscience.

In later books, particularly those eventually published in *The Top of the World* trilogy—*Ordeal by Ice* (1960), *The Polar Passion* (1967), *Tundra* (1973)—and also in *Canada North* (1967), *Sibir: My Discovery of Siberia* (1970), and *The Snow Walker* (1975), he expanded on his northern theme. The trilogy is composed of extracts from various famous and forgotten journals, all carefully edited by Mowat to show the daring (and sometimes foolhardy) achievements of high Arctic exploration. *Canada North,* written as part of a Centennial project, is an illustrated portrait of the land for which Mowat supplied an informative text. *Sibir* is an account of the author's brief journeys to Siberia in 1966 and 1969, during which he visited several remarkable communities in the great hinterland of the U.S.S.R. Part of its purpose is to show by contrast the poverty of imagination and misdirected effort which, Mowat believes, are the fruit of Canada's exploitation of its northern frontier. Lastly, *The Snow Walker* is a collection of short stories and sketches which epitomize Mowat's passionate admiration for the common

Dust jacket for Mowat's 1972 work inspired by the slaughter of a fin whale trapped in a tidal pond near Burgeo, Newfoundland

man of the North as he struggles to survive against an often hostile environment and the inroads of a modern technological civilization.

Mowat's books about Newfoundland and the sea reveal similar preoccupations. But his response to the island province and its people is hardly simple or unalloyed and ought to be seen in the context of the period he lived there (1961-1967). Claire Mowat's "fictional memoir" of their sojourn there, *The Outport People*, was published in 1984.

In the 1950s the Foundation Maritime Company had asked him to write a history of its salvage operations. The result was two books: *The Grey Seas Under* (1958) and *The Serpent's Coil* (1961). The first is virtually straight documentary, but the second is a thrilling sea-adventure, involving the suspenseful search for a derelict freighter by a hardy crew of Newfoundlanders and their oceangoing tug. A few years later Mowat's fascination with the earlier, almost legendary history of the province spurred him to write *Westviking: The Ancient Norse in Greenland and North America* (1965). Determined to prove that the Norse were the first European discoverers of North America and that the location of the Vinland settlements was on Newfoundland's northern peninsula, he made somewhat original, if controversial, use of the sagas and of archaeologi-

cal evidence. His next project, with photographer John de Visser, was a lyrical yet realistic portrayal of Newfoundland's outports. Ironically, their book, *This Rock Within the Sea: A Heritage Lost* (1968), appeared a year after Mowat's bitter departure from his erstwhile home at Burgeo.

His decision to leave Newfoundland for good was made after a tragic event in the winter of 1967. When an eighty-ton fin whale was caught in a tidal pond near Burgeo, the town sports amused themselves by shooting at the helpless creature. Some weeks later, still suffering from the gunshot wounds and starving, the whale died. Mowat had done all he reasonably could to try and save it, but to no avail. Not surprisingly then, he and the town of Burgeo were at odds over what had occurred, but–as his recounting of the incident in *A Whale for the Killing* (1972) shows–his condemnation was directed equally at politicians and scientists whose promises of aid came too late or not at all. Nonetheless, the book did arouse international attention to the plight of the whale as an endangered species, and that, more than anything else, is the true measure of its value.

If, however, as Peter Davison has written in the introduction to *The World of Farley Mowat: A Selection From His Works* (1980), the "'whale episode' . . . deepened his sense of disenchantment with his fellow men," it is probable that Mowat's "disenchantment" stems originally from his wartime experiences. His second published book, *The Regiment* (1955), is a brilliant battle history of the Ontario-based Hastings and Prince Edward outfit with whom he had served during World War II. Sober and objective, it lacks any trace of personal memoir. But, a quarter of a century later, in *And No Birds Sang* (1979), Mowat returned again to his youth and that savage conflict. This time his writing was in the first person, the memories of combat in Sicily and Italy starkly real. "For the first time" he writes, "I understood that the dead . . . were dead."

At the other end of the spectrum from Mowat's books of war are his books of humor. He is not a serious ironist in the manner of many modern novelists. Rather, he possesses intense feelings about the life he has witnessed both as observer and participant. He cannot separate himself from those feelings; and although he lacks detachment, he retains the sensitivity of a man who is genuinely puzzled by what happens and who *must* tell about it. His books of humor–*The Dog Who Wouldn't Be* (1957), *Never Cry Wolf* (1963), and *The Boat Who Wouldn't Float* (1969)–are all autobiographical in origin, no matter how farfetched the telling. And about them hovers a strangely elegiac quality, not dissimilar to the motif of the loss of innocence which is a natural element in the war books.

Lucas praises *The Dog Who Wouldn't Be* as an ingenious mixture of beast fable, tall tale, and satire. And, as Sheila Egoff notes in *The Republic of Childhood* (1967), it was "written for adults [but] adopted by children," so it is legitimate to include it with his other works for juveniles. However classified, Mutt, the puckishly eccentric dog-hero, may be seen also as a portrait of the writer as a young man. Even so, the book's humor seems forced when compared to the more sophisticated brand found in *Never Cry Wolf*. This work is vintage Mowat, uniting his talents as amateur biologist, energetic advocate of a much-slandered animal, and naturalist, with a born entertainer's sense of what makes a story interesting to readers. Finally, *The Boat Who Wouldn't Float*, winner of the 1970 Stephen Leacock Medal, is a fine example of the author's capacity for self-deprecating humor. The odyssey of the *Happy Adventure* along the Newfoundland and Maritime provinces' coastlines and its triumphant arrival at Expo '67 in Montreal is a jolly voyage in which the stubborn little schooner's caprices

are as heartily amusing as the frustrating attempts of Farley and his mates to keep her afloat.

In his genial mood, which he displays most easily as an author of children's books, Mowat can be extremely entertaining. *Lost in the Barrens* (1956), his first excursion into the world of juvenile adventure, is the most honored of his works in this genre and winner of a 1956 Governor General's Award. Drawing as much on Mowat's own reminiscences of his boyhood trip to the North as on his adult awareness of the land's terrain and mystery, it is an exciting yarn of two boys' discovery of the Arctic wilderness. A sequel, *The Curse of the Viking Grave*, was published in 1966. *Owls in the Family* (1961), also based on Mowat's childhood experience, is an affectionate tale of two pet owls. And *The Black Joke* (1963), a modern-day pirate tale, is set in the waters off Newfoundland in the days of the rumrunners. Of all of these books it should be added that Mowat's simple, lively style enhances the enjoyment children derive from reading them. Moreover, each contains a sturdy didactic element and realistic details of animal behavior and settings. Small wonder, then, that Egoff has dubbed Mowat the " 'Mr. Canada' of children books."

In recent years Mowat has continued to display the literary themes and personality traits which have endeared him to (or enraged) his readers. *Sea of Slaughter* (1984), *My Discovery of America* (1985), and *Virunga: The Passion of Dian Fossey* (1987) illustrate the point clearly. The first of these, described by Mowat as his "most important book," is a lengthy attack on man's killing of many animal species off, and on, the northeast coast of North America over the centuries. Thus its subject matter is closely linked with his previous exposés of violence against nature; and Mowat has lost none of his verve in telling the tragic story. The second work is, by contrast, slight and farcical. It tells of Mowat's celebrated contretemps with American customs officials in the spring of 1985; they denied him entry to the United States when he was about to fly to Los Angeles to promote the American edition of *Sea of Slaughter*. Apparently he was victimized as much by Canadian officialdom as by American and as a result of bungling his name turned up on a list of "undesirables." Mowat, not so much indignant as mischievous and canny, took advantage of the opportunity to cock his snoot at authority, exploit his well-known Scottish-Canadian irreverence, and write an "advertisement for myself" about the whole affair. The last of these books is

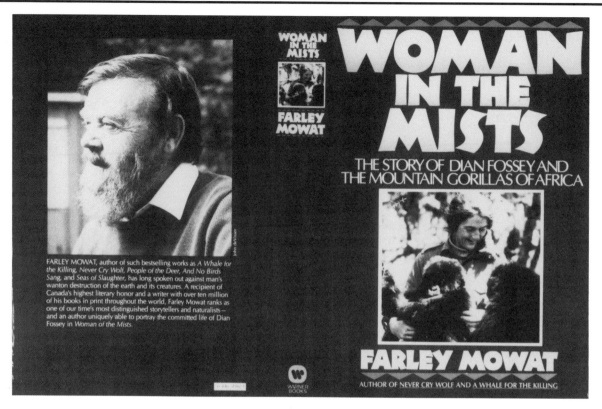

Dust jacket (first U.S. edition) for Mowat's account of the life and work of American naturalist Dian Fossey

the story of the American naturalist, Dian Fossey, and her field research among the wild gorillas living near the Virunga volcanoes of Rwanda in Central Africa. She was murdered by an unknown assailant in December 1985. Mowat bases the story on her diaries and archival records, but his narrative equally reveals his own passionate commitment to the protection and conservation of endangered species.

Mowat's achievement as a writer is impressive. Thoroughly professional, he has developed a popular style which has brought him wide exposure; moreover, he has used his popularity to champion causes in which he ardently believes. The success of the television treatment of *A Whale for the Killing* in 1981 and of the motion picture version of *Never Cry Wolf* in 1983 have solidified his reputation as an entertaining and serious-minded author.

Essentially a romantic conservative in outlook, Mowat despises the cramping influence of the modern metropolis, preferring the simpler,

older rhythms of life in small towns and traditional societies. Sometimes his nostalgia leads him into bathetic pronouncements, but more often it allows him to express something of the truth and beauty of existence as it has been known by many ordinary men and women through the ages. It is likely his future books will follow a similar path with the author himself at the center, alternately savoring and deploring the vagaries of the human adventure on this planet.

References:

Peter Davison, "Mowat Country: An Introduction," in *The World of Farley Mowat: A Selection From His Works,* edited by Davison (Toronto: McClelland & Stewart, 1980);

Sheila Egoff, *The Republic of Childhood: A Critical Guide to Canadian Children's Literature in English* (Toronto: Oxford University Press, 1967), pp. 120-123;

Alec Lucas, *Farley Mowat* (Toronto: McClelland & Stewart, 1976).

Eric Nicol
(28 December 1919-   )

David Stouck
Simon Fraser University

BOOKS: *Says We*, by Nicol, as Jabez, and Jack Scott (Vancouver: Vancouver News-Herald, 1943);

Sense and Nonsense, as Jabez (Toronto: Ryerson, 1947);

The Roving I, as Jabez (Toronto: Ryerson, 1950);

Twice Over Lightly (Toronto: Ryerson, 1953);

Shall We Join the Ladies? (Toronto: Ryerson, 1955);

Girdle Me a Globe (Toronto: Ryerson, 1957);

In Darkest Domestica (Toronto: Ryerson, 1959);

A History of Canada (Montreal: Hackett, 1959; revised edition, Toronto: Musson, 1965);

Say, Uncle: A Completely Uncalled-for History of the U.S., by Nicol and Peter Whalley (New York: Harper, 1961; London: Gollancz, 1963; Toronto: Ryerson, 1965);

A Herd of Yaks: The Best of Eric Nicol (Toronto: Ryerson, 1962);

Russia, Anyone? A Contemporary Uncalled-for History of the USSR, by Nicol and Whalley (New York: Harper & Row, 1963);

Space Age, Go Home! (Toronto: Ryerson, 1964);

100 Years of What?, by Nicol and Whalley (Toronto: Ryerson, 1966);

A Scar is Born (Toronto: Ryerson, 1968);

Vancouver (Toronto: Doubleday/Garden City: Doubleday, 1970; revised, 1978);

Don't Move! Renovate Your House & Make Social Contracts (Toronto: McClelland & Stewart, 1971);

The Clam Made a Face (Toronto: New Press, 1972);

Still a Nicol (Toronto & New York: McGraw-Hill Ryerson, 1972);

One Man's Media, and How to Write for Them (Toronto: Holt, Rinehart & Winston, 1973);

Letters to My Son (Toronto: Macmillan, 1974);

There's a Lot of it Going Around (Toronto: Doubleday/Garden City: Doubleday, 1975);

Three Plays (Vancouver: Talonbooks, 1975)—comprises *Like Father Like Fun*, *The Fourth Monkey*, and *Pillar of Sand*;

Canada Cancelled Because of Lack of Interest, by Nicol and Whalley (Edmonton: Hurtig, 1977);

Eric Nicol (photograph by Richard Savage)

The Joy of Hockey, by Nicol and Dave More (Edmonton: Hurtig, 1978);

The Joy of Football, by Nicol and More (Edmonton: Hurtig, 1980);

Golf, the Agony and the Ecstasy, by Nicol and More (Edmonton: Hurtig, 1982);

The Man from Inner Space: Plays on a Fantasy Theme (Toronto: McGraw-Hill Ryerson, 1983);

Canadide: A Patriotic Satire (Toronto: Macmillan, 1983);

Tennis: It Serves You Right! (Edmonton: Hurtig, 1984);

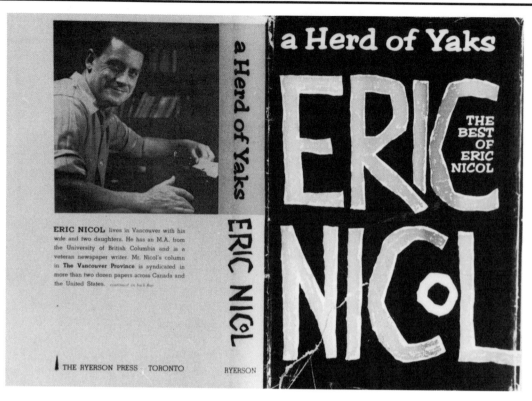

Dust jacket for Nicol's 1962 collection

How to . . . ! How to be smarter, slimmer, happier, richer, sexier–and so successful that you'll never need another how-to-book (Toronto: Macmillan, 1985);

The U.S. or US: What's the Difference, Eh?, by Nicol and More (Edmonton: Hurtig, 1986).

PLAY PRODUCTIONS: *Like Father Like Fun*, Vancouver, Playhouse Theatre, 24 March 1966; produced again as *A Minor Adjustment*, New York, Brooks Atkinson Theatre, 6 October 1967;

Beware the Quickly Who, Vancouver, Metro Theatre, 1967;

The Clam Made a Face, Vancouver, Holiday Theatre, 1968;

The Fourth Monkey, Vancouver, Playhouse Theatre, 10 October 1968;

Pillar of Sand, Ottawa, National Theatre, 1973;

Ma!, Vancouver, Waterfront Theatre, 1981.

TELEVISION: *The Bathroom*, CBC, 1964;

Borderline, CBC, 1968;

The Man From Inner Space, CBC, 1974.

RADIO: *Ratzlaff vs. The Creator*, CBC, 1986.

Eric Patrick Nicol is one of Canada's most

popular humorists, three times the recipient of the Stephen Leacock Medal for Humour. Nicol was born to William Nicol, an accountant, and his wife, Amelia Mannock Nicol, in Kingston, Ontario. He attended the University of British Columbia (B.A., 1941; M.A., 1948), served for three years (1942-1945) in the Royal Canadian Air Force, and made his home in Vancouver, where he has worked as a radio and television scriptwriter and as a syndicated columnist for the *Vancouver Daily Province*. One of his columns for the *Province*, against capital punishment, resulted in a citation for contempt and a trial that attracted national interest; another, on the assassination of John F. Kennedy, was read into *The Congressional Record*. Nicol has been married twice, to Myrl Mary Helen Heselton and to his present wife, Mary Razzell, author of fiction for young people.

In addition to his *Province* columns, Nicol has written stage plays which have had a mixed reception. *Like Father Like Fun*, which premiered in Vancouver in 1966, enjoyed full houses in its Canadian performances but failed in New York, where it was produced in 1967 under the title *A Minor Adjustment*. Nicol bounced back in characteristic good humor with a book about the experience titled *A Scar is Born* (1968).

Dust jacket for Nicol and Dave More's humorous investigation of Canadian identity

Most of Nicol's books consist of pieces collected from his newspaper column. His sketches range over the whole territory of everyday domestic concerns–pets, houseplants, cars, shopping, house parties, and so on–and include irreverent reflections on current affairs both Canadian and international. Nicol's narrator has been aptly described as "the lay sage," the easygoing man who is amused by his struggles with the complexities and idiocies of the modern world. He is uncommitted to any political or religious cause (indeed he suspects violent enthusiasms) and firmly respects the rights of his neighbors. More often than not Nicol's narrator laughs at his own folly, a form of humor which is often identified as characteristically Canadian. One of Nicol's most popular collections is *Shall We Join the Ladies?* (1955) which contains several comic observations on sexual mores. The title sketch refers to sex-change operations for men (a subject occasioned by the much-publicized case of Christine Jorgenson) and the author observes wryly: "If enough of these boys take the easy way out of baldness, tight collars, and last chance at the life-boat, the H-bomb

won't be needed. We'll be closed on account of alterations." Puns on emasculation run throughout the sketch.

As a dramatist Nicol has not been as uniformly successful as he has been as a newspaper humorist. Of his three published plays, two might be described as examples of regional theater, finding their subject and their audience in the lower mainland area of British Columbia. *Like Father Like Fun* is a play satirizing some of British Columbia's leading lumber barons. *The Fourth Monkey*, produced in Vancouver in 1968, followed hard on the failure of Nicol's first play in New York. It concerns a writer, John Tittle, who has escaped from the literary world to British Columbia's Gulf Islands; his recent play has "opened and closed on the same night, winning the United States Army Award for the Biggest Bomb of the Season." Nicol's 1973 play, *Pillar of Sand*, set in fifth century Constantinople, was inspired by the idea of civilization's decline and fall, particularly its loss of rationality. The play, staged at the National Theatre in Ottawa, was not a success from anyone's point of view. As Nicol quipped, "the reviews were mixed: bad and terrible." Nicol, the father of three children, has also written some moderately successful plays for young audiences, including *The Clam Made a Face* (produced in 1968, published in 1972), which evokes British Columbia Indian lore.

Letters to My Son (1974), an epistolary novel modeled on Lord Chesterfield's letters of advice to his bastard son in the eighteenth century, was Nicol's first sustained fiction. The letters are sent by a middle-aged Canadian drunk who is drying out in a clinic in Arizona; they are written as "fill for the generation gap" that separates the father and his worthless son living in Vancouver. Like the Chesterfield epistles, Nicol's fictitious letters tell us something about the moral values of his age, the "Swinging Seventies," but unlike the prudent earl Nicol's Canadian father assigns prime importance to matters of sex. To warn his son of the pitfalls, the older man devotes most of his letters to recounting his sexual escapades over the years, from nights of heavy "petting" in the car as a teenager to the pros and cons of masturbation for the middle-aged man. Nicol's daily newspaper readers were startled by the frank erotic nature of the book, but it was a popular success.

After *Letters to My Son* Nicol turned back to the more lighthearted purpose of his early writing. For example, in *The Joy of Hockey* (1978) and *The Joy of Football* (1980) he and coauthor Dave

More examine Canada's favorite national sports not through the eyes of a fan but from the vantage point of a rational man amazed by the manic involvement of the audience and the excessive violence of the sports. The books remain nonetheless light and humorous, to be read, one might say, with a grain of salt and a chuckle. Although Nicol is immensely popular with readers and casts back a reflection of the national character to Canadians, he is probably more accurately described as a punster and a gag writer than as a humorist with a sustained comic vision.

Reference:
Ronald J. Baker, "Eric Nicol: The Low Calling of a New Hero," *British Columbia Library Quarterly,* 23 (April 1960): 31-34.

Howard O'Hagan
(17 February 1902-18 September 1982)

Dick Harrison
University of Alberta

BOOKS: *Tay John* (London: Laidlaw & Laidlaw, 1939; New York: Potter, 1960; Toronto: McClelland & Stewart, 1974);
Wilderness Men (Garden City: Doubleday, 1958; revised edition, Vancouver: Talonbooks, 1978);
The Woman Who Got On at Jasper Station and Other Stories (Denver: Swallow, 1963; revised edition, Vancouver: Talonbooks, 1977);
The School-Marm Tree (Vancouver: Talonbooks, 1977).

Howard O'Hagan has been described as "The writer that CanLit forgot." His major novel, *Tay John*, was first published in London in 1939, where its effect was lost in the turmoil of war. It was republished in New York in 1960 but still attracted virtually no attention in Canada until it was reprinted in McClelland and Stewart's New Canadian Library in 1974, thirty-seven years after O'Hagan had completed the manuscript. It is now included regularly in courses on Canadian literature, and contemporary critics such as Margery Fee and Arnold Davidson emphasize O'Hagan's indebtedness to Tsimshian myth, his revelations of the sensibilities of a marginal people, and especially the character of the narrative strategies in the book.

Howard O'Hagan was born in Lethbridge, Alberta, in 1902 and like so many westerners,

Howard O'Hagan (photograph by Tom Gore)

spent much of his life moving. Because his father, Dr. Thomas O'Hagan, shifted from one prac-

Dust jacket for the first American edition of O'Hagan's novel about the mysterious son of a Shuswap Indian woman and a white man

tice to another, Howard O'Hagan grew up in Calgary, Vancouver, and a series of mining and railroad towns in the Rockies. In 1919 the family settled in Lucerne, a divisional point on the Canadian Northern Railway west of the town of Jasper. It was into the surrounding mountains that O'Hagan went to vacation and work as a guide and packer over the next ten years, and out of which came the settings, anecdotes, and themes of his later fiction.

Between 1920 and 1925 O'Hagan took a B.A. and an L.L.B. from McGill University, where he met Stephen Leacock and A. J. M. Smith, edited the *McGill Daily,* and decided to become a writer rather than a lawyer. Regularly he returned to the mountains, and as regularly he traveled: to England in 1924 to recruit farm laborers for the Canadian Pacific Railroad; to Australia for several months in 1926 and 1927, where, almost incidentally, he published his first story in a Sydney newspaper, and where (as he recalled in an interview with Kevin Roberts published in a 1976 issue of *Event*) he responded to the energy of the vernacular but met with violence from some Australian individuals. In 1928

he was hired as assistant to the Canadian National Railways newspaper press representative in New York. There he met the American novelist Harvey Fergusson, who later wrote an introduction to the New York edition of *Tay John.* In 1930 O'Hagan returned to Jasper to handle publicity for the CNR but soon took a publicity job with the Central Argentine Railway. From 1931 to 1934 he lived luxuriously in Buenos Aires on a salary of $20,000.

In 1934 O'Hagan returned to the Rockies intent on writing, but his friend Harvey Fergusson induced him to come to Berkeley, California, as a more congenial atmosphere for his work. There O'Hagan met his future wife, the painter Margaret Peterson (born in 1902 in Seattle, Washington), who taught art at the University of California. Refusing to take a loyalty oath in 1950, during the McCarthy era, Margaret Peterson subsequently resigned her post and moved north with her husband in 1951 to Victoria, where they initially lived in Emily Carr's old studio. Margaret Peterson's painting shows the combined influence of abstraction and native Indian art; Kevin Roberts's interview quotes her tell-

*Cover for the novel developed by O'Hagan from his 1939
short story "The Pool"*

ing one of the Coyote myths. Her interests in indigenous culture no doubt had an influence on O'Hagan's writing, but it is impossible to estimate the degree.

Until about 1956 the O'Hagans spent their winters in Berkeley and their summers in the islands off the British Columbia coast. These were productive years for O'Hagan. He wrote short stories which appeared in such magazines as *Queen's Quarterly, Tamarack Review, Story, New Mexico Quarterly,* and *Maclean's.* He wrote wilderness articles for *True, Argosy,* and other adventure magazines, and general interest articles, with titles such as "New Brunswick's New Premier, the Man," for *Maclean's* and *Saturday Night.*

Most important, O'Hagan wrote *Tay John.* The novel owes little to its namesake, the Iroquois mixed-blood called Tête Jaune who gave his name to the mountain pass west of Jasper. O'Hagan's Tay John is a Shuswap mixed-blood

born mysteriously from the grave of his mother, who had been raped by an Irish trapper-turned-evangelist. From his birth the tribe takes Tay John for the yellow-haired messiah their prophets have promised them. But Tay John refuses this responsibility and follows the other half of his blood heritage toward the coming white civilization. Among whites, however, he can find acceptance only as a picturesque embodiment of savagery. He turns finally toward nature itself and by last report appears to walk back into the earth from which he emerged.

O'Hagan's gift for strong, vivid metaphor brings out the mythic and archetypal dimensions of his story. Tay John, caught between Shuswap and white cultures, at the point of collision between civilization and the elemental power of the mountains, grows into an embodiment of the inherent dualities in man. His story, told partly in the form of an Indian legend and partly through the mouth of a white narrator, also becomes a study of the nature of story telling, of how a human life is cut and shaped to the necessities of the narrative forms through which one perceives reality. *Tay John* remains O'Hagan's greatest achievement and one of the most powerful novels in Canadian literature.

After moving to Cowichan Bay on Vancouver Island about 1956, O'Hagan continued writing for magazines and contributed columns irregularly to the Victoria *Daily Colonist.* In some of these publications can be found the anecdotes O'Hagan developed into the stories which made up his next two books. In 1958 Doubleday published *Wilderness Men,* a collection of sensitive historical re-creations of figures who, like Tay John, walked that shadowy area between the wilderness and the lives of men: Almighty Voice, Albert Johnson, John Coulter, Grey Owl, and others. In 1963 Alan Swallow of Denver published *The Woman Who Got On at Jasper Station and Other Stories,* a strong collection of eight short stories, seven of which had appeared in magazines over the previous twenty-four years.

From 1963 to 1974, while living in Lingua on the coast of Sicily, O'Hagan wrote little, but with the republication of *Tay John,* he and his wife returned to Victoria to a modest awakening of interest in O'Hagan's work. They remained there until O'Hagan's death, on 18 September 1982.

In 1977 and 1978 Talonbooks published revised versions of *The Woman Who Got On at Jasper Station* and *Wilderness Men,* and a previously unpublished novel, *The School-Marm Tree.* This second novel had a slow and difficult birth. The germ of its situation can be found in "The Pool," a story of about 3,500 words appearing in 1939 in *Story,* a journal which published work by Sherwood Anderson, Ernest Hemingway, and William Faulkner. An altered version of "The Pool" became part of "The School-Marm Tree," a story of 20,000 words included in the 1963 edition of *The Woman Who Got On at Jasper Station.* During the 1950s O'Hagan apparently expanded the story into the novel published by Talonbooks in 1977.

The School-Marm Tree has suffered by comparison with *Tay John.* Its central character is a girl in a mountain village who, in choosing her mate, must choose between the known beauties of the wilderness and the dreamed elegance of the metropolis. Again O'Hagan skillfully evokes the power of the mountains and explores themes of tension between man's primitive and civilized aspects, but the novel lacks the archetypal depth and resonance of *Tay John.*

In his later years O'Hagan earned a small but devoted following. He was made an honorary member of the Writers' Union of Canada in 1979 (at the urging of Margaret Laurence and others); he was awarded an honorary degree from McGill University in 1982; and he was awarded a Senior Arts Bursary by the Canada Council to work on an autobiographical book. This recognition came late in his career and grew only after his death.

The autobiographical book never appeared. Nor did a memorial volume, to have been edited by Gary Geddes and issued by Quadrant Press in 1983; tentatively titled "Coyote's Song," it was to have assembled many of O'Hagan's uncollected essays, together with critical pieces. As of 1987 the project remains in abeyance. What it indicates, however, is that O'Hagan's most direct influence may have been on other writers: on Geddes, Laurence, Michael Ondaatje, and Robert Harlow; and one of his most signal contributions to Canadian literature may have been the way in which he redirected critical and creative attention to the narrative and spiritual power of the indigenous myths.

References:

Arnold E. Davidson, "Silencing the Word in Howard O'Hagan's *Tay John,*" *Canadian Literature,* 110 (Fall 1986): 30-44;

Event, 5, no. 3 (1976): 41-96–comprises special section on O'Hagan;

Margery Fee, "Howard O'Hagan's *Tay John:* Making New World Myth," *Canadian Literature,* 110 (Fall 1986): 8-27;

Gary Geddes, "The writer that CanLit forgot," *Saturday Night,* 92 (2 November 1977): 84-87, 90-92;

Michael Ondaatje, "O'Hagan's Rough-edged Chronicle," *Canadian Literature,* 61 (Summer 1974): 24-31.

P. K. Page

(23 November 1916-   )

George Woodcock

BOOKS: *The Sun and the Moon,* as Judith Cape (Toronto: Macmillan, 1944; New York: Creative Age, 1944);

As Ten, as Twenty (Toronto: Ryerson, 1946);

The Metal and the Flower (Toronto: McClelland & Stewart, 1954);

Cry Ararat! Poems New and Selected (Toronto: McClelland & Stewart, 1967);

The Sun and the Moon and Other Fictions (Toronto: Anansi, 1973);

P. K. Page: Poems Selected and New (Toronto: House of Anansi, 1974);

Evening Dance of the Grey Flies (Toronto: Oxford University Press, 1981);

Five Poems (Toronto: League of Canadian Poets, 1981);

The Travelling Musicians (Victoria: Victoria Symphony, 1984);

The Glass Air: Selected Poems (Toronto: Oxford University Press, 1985);

Brazilian Journal (Toronto: Lester & Orpen Dennys, 1987).

PLAY PRODUCTION: *Silver Pennies or The Land of Honesty,* St. John, New Brunswick, Children's Theatre, 1935.

OTHER: *Unit of Five,* edited by Ronald Hambleton, includes poems by Page (Toronto: Ryerson, 1944);

Other Canadians: An Anthology of the New Poetry in Canada 1940-1946, edited by John Sutherland, includes poems by Page (Montreal: First Statement, 1947);

To Say the Least: Canadian Poets from A to Z, edited, with an introduction, by Page (Erin, Ontario: Press Porcépic, 1979).

P. K. Page, in a career that has lasted for almost half a century, has shown herself a Protean writer, continually overstepping the boundaries of genre and category. She has written a romantic novel, a number of novellas and short stories, and *Brazilian Journal* (1987), a glittering prism of a book covering three years of her life

P. K. Page (photograph by Janosz Meissner)

(1956-1959) that is both a remarkable travel book and a vivid work of autobiography. She has also acquired a reputation as a painter under her married name of P. K. Irwin; her work as a visual artist hangs in the National Gallery in Ottawa and in a number of other important public and private collections.

It is as a poet that Page has worked most consistently, even if intermittently, and that she is best known. It is well over forty years since her work began to draw attention, and she is still writing poetry. Yet the various arts she practices are strongly interactive; anyone who is familiar with her poetry, or her highly evocative prose, will

266

have sensed its strongly visual aspect, that strange white and green country of the imagination which extends beyond the mind's eye as one reads. There are times when her poetry–like that of the great T'ang masters–reads like a painting, but there are times–equally frequent–when her highly lyrical painting resonates like a poem. Some of her books–*Cry Ararat!* (1967) and *Brazilian Journal,* for example–juxtapose reproductions of her drawings or paintings with her poetry and prose, and the mingling is harmonious.

P. K. Page was born at Swanage, a coastal town in southern England, in 1916. Both her parents were English-born but her father, Lionel Frank Page, had immigrated to Alberta in 1903 where he had farmed near Red Deer, joined the Canadian militia, and volunteered for overseas service with the Canadian Expeditionary Force on the outbreak of World War I in 1914. He married Rose Laura Whitehouse in 1915 and at war's end with wife and child returned via Red Deer to Calgary where he joined the Canadian Permanent Force, ultimately attaining major-general rank. Page attended St. Hilda's School in Calgary where she was given the education then considered appropriate to girls of her class. Although she never attended a university, in later years she studied painting under the guidance of professional artists in Brazil and also at the Art Students' League in New York. She moved from the far west to the far east of Canada, and during the later 1930s she worked as a shop assistant and a radio actress in St. John, New Brunswick. Then, breaking away from the family environment, she moved to Montreal, where she became a filing clerk and subsequently a historical research worker, gaining the experience of the lower middle class that enabled her to write such evocations of the life of working women as "The Stenographers," "Typists," and "The Landlady," which are extraordinary social documents as well as poignant compositions suspended between the elegiac and the satiric.

It was in Montreal, in the highly charged wartime atmosphere of the 1940s in that divided city, that Page became associated with the writers who for a time made that bicultural community the most important center of English-language poetry in Canada. During this period she published her earliest poetry and became one of the group that founded the historic verse magazine *Preview,* whose first issue appeared in March 1942. Associated with her in this venture were F. R. Scott, Patrick Anderson, Neufville Shaw, and Bruce

Raddick, among others. Scott, who would notably influence Page, belonged to the earlier generation of the late 1920s, involved with the *McGill Fortnightly Review* and *New Provinces.* But among the younger poets of the group, it quickly became evident that Page was the most accomplished. Her poetry was first collected in a volume edited by the now almost forgotten Ronald Hambleton and called *Unit of Five* (1944). The other members of the Five, apart from Hambleton and Page, were Louis Dudek, Raymond Souster, and James Wreford, who is now as little remembered as Hambleton.

As Ten, as Twenty, which was Page's first book-length volume of verse, appeared in 1946 and, like the work of other poets in the *Preview* group (and notably the British expatriate Patrick Anderson), showed knowledge of the poetry written in England during the 1930s by W. H. Auden, Stephen Spender, and their contemporaries; indeed, Page's poetry would always retain the intellectual cast it acquired under those early influences. Given such affinities it is not surprising that the poems of *As Ten, as Twenty* also showed that, while not making the extreme political commitments of those who (like Dorothy Livesay in Canada) entered the Communist party, Page had clearly picked her side against the Anglo-Canadian establishment that then seemed to rule in Montreal, as is evident, for example, in her ironic political excursion, "Election Day":

Here in this place, the box and private privet
denote the gentleman and shut him in–
for feudally he lives and the feud on.
Colonel Evensby with his narrow feet
will cast his blue blood ballot for the Tory.

And in the polling station I shall meet
the smiling rather gentle overlords
propped by their dames and almost twins in tweed
and mark my X against them and observe
my ballot slip, a bounder, in the box.

It was not only the familiar social concerns of the 1930s that surfaced in the poems Page wrote during the following decade, recording in the process her rebellion against her class and her past. She also shared with writers such as Auden the psychoanalytic preoccupations of the time, and some of the best of her early poems were in various ways associated with neurosis, like the strange piece "Only Child," about a boy who lives browbeaten by his mother, a noted ornithologist. His knowledge is feeling; hers is information, and the conflict between them is inevitable.

> Birds were his element like air and not
> her words for them–making them statues
> setting them apart,
> nor were they facts and details like a book.
> When she said "Look!"
> he let his eyeballs harden
> and when two came and nested in the garden
> he felt their softness, gentle, near his heart.

In the end he dreams a dream in which the birds fly in multitudes around him, and as he caresses them he wrings their necks; he "placed them in her wide maternal lap/and accurately said their names aloud:/woodpecker, sparrow, meadowlark, nuthatch."

In terms of lyrical vision and technical accomplishment, the best poem in this first volume is undoubtedly, as A. J. M. Smith proposed in the 1971 article "The Poetry of P. K. Page," the haunting "Stories of Snow," in which legend and dream and child memories are mingled in–to quote Smith–"a crystal clairvoyance."

> And of the swan in death these dreamers tell
> of its last flight and how it falls, a plummet,
> pierced by the freezing bullet
> and how three feathers, loosened by the shot,
> descend like snow upon it.
> While hunters plunge their fingers in its down
> deep as a drift, and dive their hands
> up to the neck of the wrist
> in that warm metamorphosis of snow
> as gentle as the sort that woodsmen know
> who, lost in the white circle, fall at last
> and dream their way to death.

In 1946 Page went to work as a scriptwriter for the National Film Board in Ottawa. There she met William Arthur Irwin, the former editor of *Maclean's*, who had become commissioner of the NFB. In December 1950 they were married and Page left the board, having written scripts for thirty-four filmstrips. Irwin would become the Arthur of her later poems and the A. of *Brazilian Journal*.

It was at this period that Page wrote the poems that in 1954 appeared in her second volume, *The Metal and the Flower*, which earned her a Governor General's Award. In their often sharply visual presentations of concrete situations these poems seem to reflect the cinematographic knowledge she had been acquiring in recent years. Many of them concerned the plights of

Cover for Page's 1973 collection. The title work was first published in 1944 under the pseudonym Judith Cape.

lonely people or of those whom circumstances made seem contemptible or at best pitiable, and in these poems there is often a strange combination of compassion and a kind of hard surrealist perception. One example is the strange and baroque "Portrait of Marina," about the spinster daughter condemned to the service of a dotty sea-captain father who spends his old age embroidering a picture of his "lost four-master."

> Slightly offshore, it glints. Each wave is capped
> with broken mirrors.   Like Marina's head
> the glinting of these waves.
> She walked forever antlered with migraines
> her pain forever putting forth new shoots
> until her strange unlovely head became
> a kind of candelabra–delicate–
> where all her tears were perilously hung
> and caught the light as waves that catch the sun.

The high point of *The Metal and the Flower*—the most dramatic and probably the best of all Page's early poems—is the extraordinary "Photos of a Salt Mine," an elaborately patterned conceit on how in art, more than in life, reality may be concealed, but often in such a way that at the moment when the concealment seems most complete, reality is revealed with startling force.

> So all the photographs like children's wishes
> are filled with caves or winter,
> innocence
> has acted as a filter,
> selected only beauty from the mine.
> Except in the last picture
> it is shot
> from an acute high angle. In a pit
> figures the size of pins are strangely lit
> and might be dancing but you know they're not.
> Like Dante's vision of the nether hell
> men struggle with the bright cold fires of salt
> locked in the black inferno of the rock;
> the filter here, not innocence but guilt.

The image, considered in purely visual terms, is eminently cinematographic, but only the mind's, not the camera's, eye can catch the shift in moral implication that the scene contains.

Prior to the period when she was writing the poems in *As Ten, as Twenty* and *The Metal and the Flower*, Page first turned to fiction. In 1944, under the nom de plume of Judith Cape, she published a novel—or perhaps rather a romance—entitled *The Sun and the Moon*. Page has never said why she chose such a pseudonym, though Margaret Atwood has remarked on "the visions of cloak-and-dagger and Holofernes' severed head raised by the last and first names respectively," and such associations are not inappropriate in a work that deals with mysterious forces and in which the central male figure is almost destroyed. Atwood made her remark in her introduction to the 1973 volume, in which Page republished the romance under her own name, with a group of previously uncollected short stories also written during the 1940s, as *The Sun and the Moon and Other Fictions*.

The Sun and the Moon is the story of a strange girl, Kristin, who was born during a lunar eclipse and who feels with a peculiar intensity her identity with the natural world—particularly with its inanimate manifestations, such as the rocks and lakes and trees. The strength of this kinship is such that she often lapses into a kind of trance that alarms those around her. Kristin fails to realize the extent to which this affinity makes her a vehicle for forces that move outside humanly understood patterns of evil and good. She falls deeply in love with the painter Carl Bridges, whose name suggests communication with the normal world, a link she is always seeking half-consciously. But against her will she devours his talent and his identity, as the moon symbolically devours the sun in an eclipse, as the *vagina dentata* mythically consumes male potency, and in the end he can preserve himself only by flight.

The Sun and the Moon is the kind of richly textured novel of which any paraphrase must seem inadequate; so much of its appeal, like the appeal of the descriptive prose in the later *Brazilian Journal*, lies in the poet's ability to handle the heavy encrustation of suggestive visual images. Page's involvement in the processes of painting, as well as her strength of visual evocation, not only looks back to the high coloring of her early poetry but also anticipates her later career (under the name P. K. Irwin) as a painter of highly lyrical inclinations.

The Sun and the Moon is not Page's best work of fiction. Some of the stories that were written at the same time and are collected in the 1973 volume are less strained in imaginative credibility and at the same time are more tightly constructed. They also are inspired by what Atwood calls "the bizarre perspectives and the disconcerting insights" that characterize Page's best poems, and we are constantly moving through the twilight zones of the strange forests—Baudelaire's "forests of symbols," as it were—that flourish on the borderlines between states of consciousness. Some of the stories, like "The Green Bird" and "George," project a wild yet pathetic sense of comedy. Others, such as "The Glass Box," remind one of poems written during the same period—"The Landlady" and "The Stenographers," for example—in their power of conveying the infinite sadness of the existence of lonely people trying to snatch a little meaning from their lives in the unfriendly city.

From 1953 Page's husband followed a diplomatic career which led to the couple's living abroad for more than a decade. From 1953 to 1956 he was Canadian high commissioner in Australia; from 1957 to 1959 he was ambassador to Brazil, and from then to 1964 he was ambassador to Mexico. This long experience of strange and dramatic lands was eventually to have its effect on Page's poetry, but at the time she was poetically silent, suffering from a block which she has never attempted to explain, in print at least. In the *Brazilian Journal* there is a curt but poignant entry–"What to do about writing? Is it all dead?"–which indicates that already by this time her ability to call up verse had lapsed, though she had not ceased to be able to write prose, as the journal itself eloquently demonstrates. Thus her career as a poet is divided clearly–almost as if by a deep geological fault–between the early period of the 1940s and the first years of the 1950s and the later period beginning in the mid 1960s, with a long gap of unpoetic but not uncreative years between.

During these years she turned to the visual arts, drawing first and then painting, and it may well be that the reason for her silence in one art and her fertility at this time in another is one and the same: the impact of a series of exotic environments on a receptive mind which temporarily found it impossible to cope with them lyrically and so turned to the more direct transmission of impressions through images recorded by the artist's pen or brush. One might say she was still writing poems but through visual images rather than words, for when one looks at her paintings and her extremely intricate drawings, sometimes exhibited in galleries and scattered through her later books of verse and through *Brazilian Journal,* one becomes aware of how far her various arts–poetry and prose and painting–seem to reflect and interpenetrate one another. Just as her best poems are sharply visual, reflecting her interest in film first and then in paint, her best paintings call up poetic as well as aesthetic images. A good example is the painting *The Flowers of Persephone.* From a curious and intricately patterned background reminiscent of the sign language that Page learned to understand when she encountered aboriginal art in Australia, the forms of ghostly flowers do indeed emerge, suggested rather than stated, and the sense of life rising out of darkness associated with the goddess Persephone is evoked. Others work more directly in this way–the notations of Brazilian landscapes, trees, and buildings which figure in *Brazilian Journal,* for example–having the same kind of effect on the mind as the simple nature poems of, say, Andrew Young or John Clare if one could imagine these poets writing about the tropics.

P. K. Irwin has never been accorded by critics the status of a major painter, and here there is perhaps some justice, for her paintings do seem always to be illustrative and literary in their

effect: they transmit a symbol rather than a form, and so their effect is in fact more poetic than painterly; painting can in fact be regarded as P. K. Irwin's avocation rather than P. K. Page's vocation, which is certainly poetry. Perhaps that is why she chose to sign her paintings only by her acquired name and her poems by the name she received at birth.

Still, the link remains important, for one of the features that gives the poetry of her second phase its special character is in fact the visuality that connects it to her painting. That poetry appeared, rather sparingly, in two volumes, *Cry Ararat! Poems New and Selected* (1967) and *P. K. Page: Poems Selected and New* (1974), published during the decade after her return to Canada. As the titles suggest, both of these collections are made up largely of works selected from Page's first books. During the later 1960s and the early 1970s she was still writing sparingly, finding her way into a kind of poetry that reflected her understanding of new directions in Canadian writing, and she did not publish a volume consisting entirely of previously uncollected poems until her fifth book, *Evening Dance of the Grey Flies,* appeared in 1981.

In *Cry Ararat!* the presence of Page's renewed poetic persona is slight and tentative, represented by a small group of new poems with which the volume begins, entitled "Landscape with Serifs" and seven in number, and the final long piece, "Cry Ararat!" Since none of the poems is dated, it is hard to place them in terms of writing, and though some relate to Australia and one relates to Brazil, where we are led to assume Page was poetically voiceless, all may be poems of experience recollected in tranquillity. Certainly she saw the return to poetry at this time in a very tentative and uncertain way, for in "Questions and Images," an essay written in 1969 for *Canadian Literature,* she said:

> Whether or not the handful of poems written recently means that writing has "started" again, I do not know; whether there is any advance over earlier work, I shall have to let others decide. For the time being my primary concern is to remove the filters.
>
> Meanwhile the images have begun again and the questions continue.
>
> "What do I sing and what does my lute sing?"

Cry Ararat! in fact combines Page's two arts; it is illustrated with a series of designs reflecting

Dust jacket, with drawing by Page, for her 1967 poetry collection. Under her married name, P. K. Irwin, Page has won acclaim as a painter. Cry Ararat! *is one of several volumes in which she juxtaposes her writing and her art.*

the closeness of her study of Australian native art, which indeed is the subject of one poem, "Bark Drawing." Like others of the new poems, "Bark Drawing" shows an austerity of form and imagery that is in contrast to the richer texture of her earlier works, and six lines of it represent an epitome (in her practice as much as in her statement) of her own mastery of the various arts.

> (an alphabet the eye
> lifts from the air
> as if by ear
>
> two senses
> threaded through
> a knuckle bone)[.]

Not all the newer poems are so honed down as "Bark Drawing." There is both a baroque descriptiveness and a philosophic grandeur about "Cook's Mountains," for instance.

> Like mounds of ice,
> hive-shaped hothouses,
> mountains of mirror glimmering
> they form
> in diamond panes behind the tree ferns of

> the dark imagination,
> burn and shake
> the lovely light of Queensland like a bell
> reflecting Cook upon a deck
> his tongue
> silvered with paradox and metaphor.

There is the facility of conceit of the earlier poems, but Page's conceits have increased relevance, and all these poems show a moving toward verbal economy which is linked with her growing inclination toward the philosophic simplicities of Sufism. Both the philosophic and the poetic shifts are hinted at in the last verse of "After Rain," another poem evidently based on Australian experiences.

> And choir me too to keep my heart a size
> larger than seeing, unseduced by each
> bright glimpse of beauty striking like a bell,
> so that the whole may toll, its meaning shine
> clear of the myriad images that still—
> do what I will—encumber its pure line.

The purification of the line, in verse and in thought, is clearly evident. In Page's earlier poems the line is long and flowing, with the kind of full eloquence that belonged alike to the English and the Canadian 1940s, the period when the didacticism of the 1930s shifted toward the New Romanticism. In the new poems of *Cry Ararat!* there is still the old fluidity, but it is more controlled, sparser, yet totally moving, like the crystal jet that flows from a Japanese bamboo pipe into its rock basin. So has the poet's line of thought been modified and rarefied, its direction shifting from those inward-looking landscapes of the earlier poems, which were so often imaginary biographies, to look out of the self toward images–Cook's Glasshouse Mountains, Australian bark drawings, Mount Ararat itself–that suggest in Blakeian and perhaps even in Asian vision the way of liberation from the alienated, imprisoned self, as shown in the last lines of the title poem:

> The leaves that make the tree by day,
> the green twig the dove saw fit
> to lift across a world of water
> break in a wave about our feet.
> The bird in the thicket with his whistle
> the crystal lizard in the grass
> the star and shell
> tassel and bell
> of wild flowers blowing where we pass,
> this flora-fauna flotsam, pick and touch,
> requires the focus of the total I.

> A single leaf can block a mountainside;
> all Ararat be conjured by a leaf.

P. K. Page: Poems Selected and New, coming seven years after *Cry Ararat!*, was most important because it decisively reestablished Page's position in the tradition of Canadian poetry and closed the gap with the past. It was perhaps something of a disappointment in terms of the new poems it presented, few of which have the stature of such pieces as "Cry Ararat!" and "Cook's Mountains"; one that does is the sequence "Leviathan in a Pool," a poem essentially about marine mammals tortured and in captivity and by implication about man's relationship with other beings and with his own species. The reasons for the failure of human relationships can perhaps, the poem elusively suggests, be found in the failure of man's relationship with the animals, and perhaps by solving one we can solve the other: "O wise men who look/in treatise and book/for remedy/had you thought of the sea?" By including early poems not published before and poems that appeared in magazines of the 1940s and were never collected, *P. K. Page: Poems Selected and New* was a definitive reckoning with the past and a reestablishment of links over the years of silence, and

in this way it not only established what Page had achieved up to that point but also seemed to clear the way for her real second flowering as a poet in the 1970s, for the extensive reading tours she began at this time, and for the steady though never copious production of fresh work that would make *Evening Dance of the Grey Flies* her first collection including entirely new poems for twenty-seven years.

In 1985, four years after the appearance of *Evening Dance of the Grey Flies,* Page published *The Glass Air: Selected Poems*, about which perhaps the most curious fact is that the poem which in earlier volumes she called "The Glass Air" in this collection loses its title to the volume as a whole and appears, retitled but essentially unchanged, as "And We Two." As this fact suggests, *The Glass Air* is another combination of new and already collected poems, but it is by no means a "collected poems"; indeed it shows how reluctant Page is to create a *really* definitive canon of her poetry, for clearly a long process of sorting and choosing and changing is still going on in this book published in the poet's sixty-ninth year. *The Glass Air* is longer than any other of Page's books of verse, and it contains twenty poems not published before, an average of five written each year since *Evening Dance of the Grey Flies* appeared; though Page is now steadily writing poems, she is a slow perfectionist.

Ten of the poems from *Evening Dance of the Grey Flies,* published only four years before, are not included, and several more poems from earlier volumes have been discarded. One senses a desire for open entries and exits, a persistent consciousness of the tentativeness of art, its perfectibility rather than its perfection, which emerges at times in suggestions of the inadequacy not merely of particular poetic approaches but even of language itself. This consciousness is evident in one of the best poems of *Evening Dance of the Grey Flies,* entitled "Finches Feeding," in which Page describes birds coming to feed and then adds:

> Having said that, what have I said?
> Not much.

> Neither my delight nor the length of my watching is
>   conveyed
>   and nothing profound recorded, yet these birds
> as I observe them
> stir such feelings up–
> such yearning for weightlessness, for hollow bones,
> rapider heartbeat, east/west eyes

Cover for Page's collection of forty-two poems and one prose work, the futurist story "Unless the Eye Catch Fire . . ."

and such wonder–seemingly half-remembered–
  as they rise
spontaneously into air, like feathered cones.

Looking at the new poems in these last two books, which represent Page's most mature and perhaps her last phase, we see that the most recent poems are more sharply and intensely visual than ever in their sensuous evocation of shape and color and space; their imagery takes us magically beyond any ordinary seeing into a realm of imagining in which the normal world is shaken like a vast kaleidoscope and revealed in unexpected and luminous relationships.

Since *The Glass Air* comes as near to a "collected poems" as Page has produced, one can legitimately ask whether there is a thread that runs through these poems written over more than forty years and links the broken halves of Page's ca-

reer. There are obviously tonal links; the poetic voice is recognizably the same from beginning to end, though the verbal structure of the verse has loosened and become less formal without being in any real way colloquial, for Page has never aspired to "the common touch."

Take, for example, the last verse of "Stories of Snow," which was written in the 1940s and appeared in her first volume, *As Ten, as Twenty:*

And stories of this kind are often told
in countries where great flowers bar the roads
with reds and blues that seal the route to snow–
as if, in telling, raconteurs unlock
the colour with its complement and go
through to the area behind the eyes
where silent, unrefractive whiteness lies.

And compare it with the last verse of a recent poem, "The Flower Bed," also, as its title suggests, ostensibly concerned with flowers, in this case sunflowers.

And my own yellow eye, black lashed, provides
triangulation.   We enmesh
three worlds in our geometry.
I learn
in timeless Time at their green leafy school,
such silks & stares
such near-invisible straight curving lines
curving like Space itself
which merge and cross at the Omega point
and double back
to make transparent, multifoliate
Flowers of the Upper Air.

The tone of both is the same, grave with an underlying playfulness, like that of the Sufi sages Page has much admired. And in both poems she brings readers to consider the blinding reality behind the splendid appearances of the visible world. But there is a notable difference between the regular pentameters of the first selection and the broken-line form of the second, which shows how far Page has taken to heart the formal loosening of poetry in recent years; so, too, the more easy, conversational style which in the later poems she uses to make rather abstract statements reflects the movement toward making poetry viable orally as well as on paper, a process in which, over the past twenty years, she has been notably involved.

But if one seeks a deeper kind of unity in Page's poetry, it is in the perception that she is at heart, and always has been, a true metaphysical, both in the philosophic sense of being concerned to find the reality behind an appearance which she re-creates with such vivid intensity, and in the technical sense of being adept at the use of conceits. Sometimes a whole poem is a conceit as paradoxical, at once as simple and elaborate, as one by Donne; her miniature masterpiece, "Intraocular Lens Model 103G," is a good example: "This lens I look through is as clear as glass./It shows me all I saw before was false./If what *was* true is true no longer, how/now can I know the false true from true true?" And sometimes, embedded within a poem a conceit brings the leading idea into sudden focus. The poem "The Tethers," for instance, is a conceit, for the poet compares personal attachments to the guy ropes that hold a tent upright and in shape. But an internal conceit sharply inverts the image:

Think what a sail I'd make
against the blue—
flying!—for God's sake.
What a splendid din
the whip and rattle of my canvas wings
flapping me upward
ragged as a crane.

We think of tents collapsing when unsupported, not soaring, and what Page is telling us is something about the difference between spiritual and physical experiences.

Inevitably, as in all poets who grow older as their friends fall sick and die, the thought of mortality is often present, and so are the contradictions of aging, the growing gap between the outer appearance and the inner reality, as in "Masqueraders":

Worse masquerades to come:
white cane, black gaping tomb
as if we were blind, dead, lame

who, in reality, are
dark, fair and shinier
than the masks we wear or wore.

But always, in the trees or in the sky, there are the portentous intimations, natural, supernatural, or natural blending into supernatural, of forces beyond control or comprehension. One of the poems that contains such intimations on the natural level is "Visitants," which, on its more exoteric level, is a nature poem. But it also becomes, as the author watches the banded pigeons plunder her oak tree, a poem about the irreconcilabil-

ity of man's ideas of order to what happens in nature.

Through binoculars they are beautiful,
the prettiest pigeons—every feather,
each neat little head, white collar, banded tail.
But voracious, gang-despoilers of the tree-tops
they shake and thrash about in, tiny eyes
riveted upon acorns ah they are gone in a whoosh
wooden rackety twirling noisemakers
and we are left hungry in this windless hush.

In "Invisible Presences Fill the Air," the poem that follows "Visitants" in *The Glass Air*, these clumsy splendid "gang-despoilers" are elevated to the supernatural and transformed into angels of promise:

I hear the clap of their folding wings
like doors banging or wooden shutters.
They land and settle—giant birds
on the epaulettes of snowed-on statues.
....
O who can name me their secret names?
Anael, opener of gates,
Phorlakh, Nisroc, Heiglot,
Zlar.

These awarenesses of avian and angelic visitants take one far back to an early and not very much noticed poem, "Coming Home," in which the protagonist becomes, as it were, his own angel:

And as the air inflated his lungs he stood
there in the dark at his destination knowing
somewhere—to left? to right?—he was walking home
and his shoulders were light and white as though
    wings were growing.

Page's most recent volumes do not consist entirely of verse; indeed, one of them is entirely in prose. The center piece of *Evening Dance of the Grey Flies* is a striking, speculative futurist story entitled "Unless the Eye Catch Fire. . . ." Ostensibly it deals with the death of the earth as a habitation for humanity and the end of time as humankind dies. But on another level it projects a visionary perception—one need not wait for the end of time to apprehend eternity—that many of her poems also suggest.

Page has written little expository prose and has avoided the criticism which many other Canadian poets have found an appropriate complement to their more originative writings. But *The Glass Air* does contain two essays which she wrote for *Canadian Literature* about her own work, "Ques-

Covers for the 1985 volume that includes two essays in which Page explains her own work, "Questions and Images" and "Traveller, Conjuror, Journeyman"

tions and Images" and "Traveller, Conjuror, Journeyman." In the latter essay she discusses the various arts she practices and remarks that "in all essential particulars writing and painting are interchangeable. They are alternate routes to silence."

Brazilian Journal, which appeared in 1987, is her only book consisting entirely of nonfiction prose. It is also the only autobiographical work of a writer who has otherwise preferred to render experience at an imaginative distance. It is even, in its own way, an anachronism, a work appearing thirty years after it was written in day-by-day entries during the 1950s, slightly edited and clarified for publication a long generation afterward. As Page remarks in her foreword to the book, "This is a period piece. . . . In the interim, language has changed; Brazil has changed; I have changed. But for me–then–this was the way it was."

Seen within the corpus of Page's writing, *Brazilian Journal* is important for the light it throws on the rift in her poetic career that happened at the time the diary was being written. Page is reticent about her poetic block, referring to it only in passing, but she almost obsessively records her

progress in the new arts of drawing and painting, and by making so much of these compensatory exercises she discloses indirectly how deeply she was troubled by her inability to write poetry. Yet–and this is the most important revelation of *Brazilian Journal*–she did not abandon the kind of perceptions that have always been central to her poetry. She remained intent on transmuting visual experience into verbal art, and in Brazil she found a rich store of images to conserve and record. And she retained her sense of social irony, so that Brazilian social life and the parasitic social life of the diplomatic corps are recorded with as much wry faithfulness, though in a different medium, as the lives of office workers in her early poems. *Brazilian Journal* is not only the prose work that filled a long poetic silence. It is also the lode in which students of her work are likely to find the seeds of much that blossomed in her later poems. That such criticism is already forthcoming is indicated by such articles as those by Rosemary Sullivan in *Canadian Literature* and Constance Rooke in the *Malahat Review*. Like other recent commentaries, these essays reconfirm Page's position as one of the most accomplished lyricists of her generation and demonstrate how her poetic networks of image and allusion work to psychological and aesthetic purpose.

Bibliographies:

M. Preston, "The Poetry of P. K. Page: A Checklist," *West Coast Review,* 13 (February 1979): 12-17;

John Orange, "P. K. Page: An Annotated Bibliography," in *The Annotated Bibliography of Canada's Major Authors,* edited by Robert Lecker and Jack David, volume 6 (Toronto: ECW, 1985), pp. 207-285.

References:

Frank Davey, "P. K. Page," in his *From There to Here: A Guide to English-Canadian Literature Since 1960* (Erin, Ontario: Porcépic, 1974), pp. 231-235;

D. G. Jones, "Cold Eye and Optic Heart: Marshall McLuhan and Some Canadian Poets," *Modern Poetry Studies,* 5 (Autumn 1974): 175-187;

Jean Mallinson, "Retrospect and Prospect," *West Coast Review,* 13 (February 1979): 8-11;

Laurie Ricou, "Infant Sensibility and Lyric Strategy: Miriam Waddington, P. K. Page, and Dorothy Livesay," in his *Everyday Magic* (Vancouver: University of British Columbia Press, 1987), pp. 87-102;

Constance Rooke, "Approaching P. K. Page's 'Arras,'" *Canadian Poetry: Studies, Documents, Reviews,* 4 (Spring-Summer 1979): 65-72;

Rooke, "P. K. Page: The Chameleon and the Centre," *Malahat Review,* 45 (January 1978): 169-195;

Diane Schoemperlen, "Four Themes in the Poetry of P. K. Page," *English Quarterly,* 12 (Spring-Summer 1979): 1-12;

A. J. M. Smith, "The Poetry of P. K. Page," *Canadian Literature,* 50 (Autumn 1971): 17-27;

Rosemary Sullivan, "A Size Larger than Seeing: The Poetry of P. K. Page," *Canadian Literature,* 79 (Winter 1978): 32-42;

John Sutherland, "The Poetry of P. K. Page," *Northern Review,* 1 (December-January 1946-1947): 13-23.

Papers:

The P. K. Page Papers are at the Public Archives in Ottawa. There are letters from Page in The Patrick M. Anderson Papers and The Jori Smith Papers, both at the Public Archives, and in The Crawley Collection and the George Woodcock Papers, Douglas Library, Queen's University, Kingston, Ontario.

Thomas Raddall

(13 November 1903-   )

Allan Bevan
Dalhousie University

completed by

W. H. New
University of British Columbia

BOOKS: *The Saga of the "Rover,"* by Raddall, C. H. L. Jones, and T. W. Hayhurst (Halifax: Royal Print & Litho, 1931);

The Markland Sagas, by Raddall, Jones, and Hayhurst (Montreal: Gazette, 1934);

The Pied Piper of Dipper Creek and Other Tales (Edinburgh & London: Blackwood, 1939; Toronto: McClelland & Stewart, 1943);

His Majesty's Yankees (Garden City: Doubleday, Doran, 1942; Edinburgh & London: Blackwood, 1945);

Roger Sudden (Toronto: McClelland & Stewart/ Garden City: Doubleday, Doran, 1944);

Tambour and Other Stories (Toronto: McClelland & Stewart, 1945);

Pride's Fancy (Garden City: Doubleday, 1946; Toronto: McClelland & Stewart, 1946);

The Wedding Gift and Other Stories (Toronto: McClelland & Stewart, 1947);

West Novas: A History of the West Nova Scotia Regiment (Liverpool, Nova Scotia, 1947);

Halifax, Warden of the North (Toronto: McClelland & Stewart, 1948; London: Dent, 1950; Garden City: Doubleday, 1965; revised edition, Toronto: McClelland & Stewart, 1971);

The Nymph and the Lamp (Boston: Little, Brown, 1950; Toronto: McClelland & Stewart, 1950);

Son of the Hawk (Philadelphia: Winston, 1950);

Tidefall (Toronto: McClelland & Stewart, 1953; Boston: Little, Brown, 1953; London: Hutchinson, 1954);

A Muster of Arms and Other Stories (Toronto: McClelland & Stewart, 1954);

The Wings of Night (Garden City: Doubleday, 1956; London: Macmillan, 1957);

The Path of Destiny: Canada from the British Conquest to Home Rule, 1763-1850 (Garden City: Doubleday, 1957; Toronto: Doubleday, 1957);

Thomas Raddall (by permission of Sherman Hines, Ltd., Halifax)

The Rover: The Story of a Canadian Privateer (Toronto: Macmillan, 1958);

At the Tide's Turn and Other Stories (Toronto: McClelland & Stewart, 1959);

The Governor's Lady (Garden City: Doubleday, 1960; London: Collins, 1961);

Hangman's Beach (Garden City: Doubleday, 1966; Toronto: McClelland & Stewart, 1979);

277

Footsteps on Old Floors: True Tales of Mystery (Garden City: Doubleday, 1968);

This Is Nova Scotia, Canada's Ocean Playground (Halifax: The Book Room, 1970);

In My Time: A Memoir (Toronto: McClelland & Stewart, 1976);

The Mersey Story (Liverpool, Nova Scotia: Bowater-Mersey, 1979).

OTHER: Archibald MacMechan, *Tales of the Sea*, foreword by Raddall (Toronto: McClelland & Stewart, 1947);

Wallace R. MacAskill, *Lure of the Sea: Leaves from My Pictorial Log*, foreword by Raddall (Halifax: Eastern Photo Engravers, 1951);

Dudley Whitney, *The Lighthouse*, foreword by Raddall (Toronto: McClelland & Stewart, 1975);

Bruce Armstrong, *Sable Island*, foreword by Raddall (Toronto: Doubleday, 1981).

In the preface to his autobiography *In My Time* (1976), Thomas Raddall clearly and honestly describes his own writing: "In my novels and short stories I never sought to teach or to preach. My aim was intelligent entertainment, and if the reader got some information along the way I made sure that it was true. When I wrote history as such I sought to make the truth as interesting to the reader as it was to me." He adds two more statements about his place in Canadian literature: "Whatever the merit of my published works now or in the future, I may be remembered as a Canadian author who chose to stay at home, writing entirely about his own country and its people, and offering his wares in the open market of the world. I may be remembered also as one who never asked a penny of subsidy from any fund, institution or government, even when such money became easily available. From first to last I paddled my own canoe." As a novelist, short-story writer, and historian, Raddall provides his readers with true information in entertaining and interesting works, and his books re-create life in Nova Scotia from the founding of Halifax in 1749 to the twentieth century.

Thomas Head Raddall was born in Hythe, England, on 13 November 1903. His father (also Thomas Head Raddall), a Cornish Celt, was a soldier; he was a captain in the British Army and an instructor in the School of Musketry. Young Thomas Raddall "learned to walk," as he put it in *In My Time*, "in the barrack square." Captain Raddall and his wife, Ellen (Gifford) Raddall,

moved to Halifax in 1913 with their three children (young Tom Raddall had two sisters, Nellie and Winnifred); in Nova Scotia, Raddall's father was a small-arms expert and an instructor of regulars and militia. When World War I broke out the elder Raddall went overseas with the Winnipeg Rifles, and though he returned to Canada, wounded, in 1915, he insisted on going back to the front; he was promoted to the rank of lieutenant colonel overseas, but he was killed in action at Amiens in 1918. The younger Raddall, much influenced by his father's model, was, like the rest of the family, deeply marked by this death. His sisters reassessed their occupational goals, for the family needed immediate income; Thomas, leaving school at grade ten and fibbing about his age, enlisted as a wireless operator and served on various ships and coastal stations. He kept this job until 1922. One of his stations was the one on Sable Island, the setting for the 1950 novel *The Nymph and the Lamp*.

Raddall had continuing hopes of becoming a reporter, but by 1922 it was clear to him that his lack of formal education was closing opportunities, and he began to look elsewhere. In 1923 he went to Milton, Nova Scotia, on the Mersey River, to take a job as a bookkeeper in a woodpulp mill, determined to stay one year. That was more than sixty years ago; he still lives nearby, in the town of Liverpool. He had, simply, become enamored with the local wilderness, and hunting and fishing became favorite pastimes. He also met Edith Margaret Freeman at this time; she was the local music teacher. They were married on 9 June 1927, just at the time that the MacLeod Company, faced with economic pressures, was closing mills and reducing salaries. So to supplement his inadequate income, he began to write short stories. His first story appeared in *Maclean's* in 1928, earning Raddall sixty dollars—one cent per word. (His mill job paid him one hundred dollars every month.) When *Maclean's* rejected his next story, there began a feud between Raddall and the editor that was not settled for several years. Raddall turned elsewhere. He produced several serial stories for American pulp magazines, but he still sought a different audience, and in 1933 he began a successful affiliation with *Blackwood's* magazine in England, where his stories caught the eye of Rudyard Kipling and John Buchan (Lord Tweedsmuir), both of whom praised literary works that emphasized romantic plots and dramatic climaxes.

Meanwhile his life had been taking other turns. His wife nearly died in childbirth, and a child was stillborn, but on 22 November 1934 a son was born: Thomas Head Raddall III. Raddall was also seeking to free himself from the company he worked for. MacLeod had encouraged him to write–*The Saga of the "Rover,"* the story of a Liverpool privateer, had appeared in 1931, and a book of similar kind, *The Markland Sagas,* in 1934; both involved him in local history, but brought him little in the way of income or recognition. But his fascination with the eighteenth century continued, and his interest in local history ultimately led him in the direction of popular historical fiction. In 1938 he resigned his position to become a full-time writer. His first collection of short fiction, *The Pied Piper of Dipper Creek and Other Tales* (1939), won a Governor General's Award. In 1940 his frequently anthologized story "Blind MacNair" was accepted by the *Saturday Evening Post,* and he was delighted. As he put it, he had "cracked the *Post,*" and when his first novel, *His Majesty's Yankees,* appeared in 1942, he was clearly on his way.

In all of his fiction Raddall shares with his readers his knowledge of Nova Scotian life, past and present, and his own experiences often serve as the starting point for fiction. For example, the moose hunt at the beginning of *His Majesty's Yankees* was based on one of Raddall's own early hunting expeditions, and the protagonist David Strang's friendship with the Micmacs reflects Raddall's fascination with the traditions and beliefs of the Indians. The novel opens in 1774 as the deep division between the Crown and the American colonies begins to involve the Yankees in Nova Scotia, pitting brother against brother. In "At the Tide's Turn," an early short story, Raddall had touched on the painful position of the settlements in Nova Scotia during the American Revolution, when they were treated by both sides as potential enemies or dubious allies. In *His Majesty's Yankees* David Strang watches his brother John dying in the uniform of the king, fights for a time on the other side along with another brother, Mark, and eventually returns home determined to maintain the freedom of his own town. In the last action described David shoots his brother Luke, now clearly an enemy of Nova Scotia, and the neutrality of the Nova Scotian Yankees disappears. Historical figures, notably Richard John Uniacke, Jonathan Eddy, and Simeon Perkins (whose diary was an important source for Raddall's novel), fight and discuss

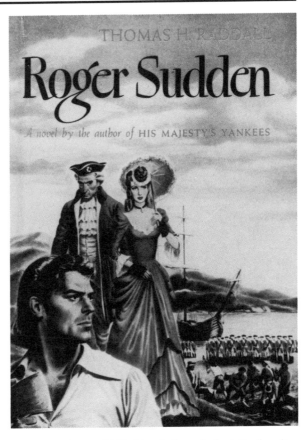

Dust jacket for Raddall's historical novel about the founding of Halifax in 1749

politics and strategies with the fictional characters, and the painful uncertainty of the times is given vivid and convincing expression. As always Raddall's research re-creates an atmosphere of a world inhabited by real people involved in real struggles. (He recast this novel in 1950 as *Son of the Hawk,* a book for young readers.)

Raddall's second historical novel, *Roger Sudden* (1944), deals with the Seven Years War and the capture of Louisbourg. The novel begins in Kent (where Raddall lived for his first ten years), switches to London, and then moves on to Nova Scotia with Cornwallis and the founding of Halifax in 1749 to counteract the French presence in the strongly fortified Louisbourg. Roger Sudden, the hero, a young disillusioned follower of Bonnie Prince Charlie, joins the expedition to escape arrest for holding up a coach. In the new world, Sudden is captured by Micmacs and lives for some time the hard life of the Indians. He is sold to the French at Louisbourg, becomes involved in intrigue against the British in Halifax, makes a small fortune as a trader, is arrested for treason, and escapes to Louisbourg just before the siege begins. Maj. James Wolfe's attack on Louisbourg and the French defenses are described in detail, with Roger Sudden present at one of the skirmishes and finding to his dismay that his real loyalty is with his countrymen. In a rather unusual ending for a historical romance, after the fighting is over Sudden is executed by the French as a traitor, leaving the beautiful Mary Johnstone, his Golden Woman, to mourn his death. Cornwallis, Wolfe, and other historical figures appear in the novel–even Roger is loosely based on the two historical figures Michael Francklin and Joshua Mauger–as Raddall again presents an authentic story of the times. The novel was popular (a radio version of it, adapted by Archibald MacMechan, was broadcast on the CBC *Tales of the Sea* program in 1947). By now, Raddall had found his form, and other novels and histories, similar in kind, followed.

Pride's Fancy (1946) is, in Raddall's words, "a romance, of course," although the background is fact. *Pride's Fancy* is Amos Pride's name for his "Fast New And Well Built Brigantine" described as a "private ship of war" with Capt. Nathan Cain, Pride's adopted son, in charge. Nathan and his crew embark on a faked treasure hunt that takes them to Hispaniola, where they are captured and released by Toussaint L'Ouverture, eventually to return–in Raddall's phrase–"Home to Nova Scotia–where else?" In this story Raddall's love of ships and his interests in the exploits of the privateersmen push the events of history into the background.

Raddall's own evaluation of *The Nymph and the Lamp* (1950) as "the best of my novels, not only for style and workmanship but also because so much of the story came out of my own observation and personal touch with life" is generally accepted as valid. Using twentieth-century Nova Scotia settings (Halifax, for example) and using the lush growth of the Annapolis Valley as a contrast to the desolate beauty and brutality of what he calls Marina (clearly Sable Island), the novel has characters with more depth and complexity than those in Raddall's historical novels, who sometimes seem to be manipulated for the sake of the plot. The central character, Isabel Jardine, is Raddall's nymph, married to a wireless operator named Matthew Carney. After an affair with Skane, another wireless operator, she runs away from Marina and makes a new life for herself in the Annapolis Valley, but then learns that Carney has gone blind and realizes that her rightful place is with him. While the novel has won many

enthusiastic readers, especially in the Maritimes, other critics have found it no more stylistically sophisticated than the earlier books.

Tidefall (1953) is another novel set in Nova Scotia; in it Capt. Saxby Nolan, with a fortune made from smuggling and other criminal acts, returns after many years to the town where he had grown up poor and despised. Determined to own the old Caraday shipping firm and attain "class" and respectability, Nolan for a time is successful. But he loses the respect of his wife, who finds love with a man he despises, and because of business losses Nolan once more resorts to foul play, overinsuring a boat that he plans to scuttle close enough to shore to allow all hands to escape. He makes a fatal error in calculating the tides and goes down with the *John C. Caraday*, to the relief of the town. Raddall's next novel, *The Wings of Night* (1956), is also about the return to Nova Scotia of one of her wandering sons. Neil Jamieson returns to a decaying town run by the corrupt Sen. Sam Quarrender and his decadent son, Steve. Neil stays longer than he had intended, builds a hunting cabin in the woods, becomes involved with his boyhood sweetheart, now Steve's wife, tries to take on the Quarrender empire, kills Steve in a hunting accident, and, after burning down his decayed mansion, leaves the town with the young teacher who had been his loyal supporter. In this novel Raddall describes the woods and the pulp and paper industry he knew well, comments on the crumbling society of the little town, and has his hero escape to a new life in the forests of Ontario.

In *The Rover: The Story of a Canadian Privateer* (1958), *The Governor's Lady* (1960), and *Hangman's Beach* (1966) Raddall returns to the past; he spent much time in 1957 in the Halifax Provincial Archives reading Sir John Wentworth's papers. In fiction as in real life, Wentworth, a Loyalist who loses everything in New Hampshire, later emerges as governor of Nova Scotia, with the help of his wife, Frances, among whose conquests was Prince William. The novel deals with the background of the unrest in the American colonies, political intrigue on both sides of the Atlantic, and the American Revolution and its aftermath. In Raddall's other historical novels the central characters are fictional; in *The Governor's Lady* they are historical figures, although they are still largely creations of the author. *Hangman's Beach* is set during the period 1803-1812, a few years after *The Governor's Lady*, and Wentworth is still governor as the novel opens. In his youth Raddall had spent happy times with his father on McNab's Island, at the entrance to Halifax Harbour, and Hangman's Beach, part of McNab's Island, was the location of the gallows where the bodies of mutinous sailors, well tarred, used to swing in their chains as a warning to restless crewmen aboard ships leaving or entering the harbor. Many tales of the McNab family continue to be told on the island, and Raddall took one of them as the basis for the new novel. Raddall's pair of lovers are a young French prisoner of war (Lieutenant Cascamond, the man who shot Nelson at Trafalgar) and the orphaned ward of Peter McNab. The novel describes the conditions of the prison camps, the brutality of officers in the Royal Navy, and the coming of war with America. The eminent merchant McNab talks with admirals and governors and other businessmen as Raddall evokes the Halifax of the Napoleonic war period.

In addition to novels and short stories–*At the Tide's Turn and Other Stories,* a 1959 paperback, selects from his life's work–Raddall has written several respected volumes of history. *Halifax, Warden of the North* (1948; revised, 1971) is, in the words of A. J. M. Smith, "a brilliantly written history of Nova Scotia's capital." This book, like Raddall's 1957 volume, *The Path of Destiny: Canada from the British Conquest to Home Rule, 1763-1850,* won a Governor General's Award for nonfiction. His 1968 work, *Footsteps on Old Floors: True Tales of Mystery,* is a volume of essays on unsolved mysteries in Nova Scotia history. An enthusiastic travel book, *This Is Nova Scotia, Canada's Ocean Playground,* followed in 1970 and a volume of local history, *The Mersey Story,* in 1979.

In addition to winning three Governor General's Awards, Raddall, a fellow of the Royal Society of Canada since 1949, has been honored with the Lorne Pierce Medal (1956), several honorary doctorates, and appointment as Officer of the Order of Canada (1971). In 1984 the Bowater-Mersey Paper Company established the T. H. Raddall prize to encourage literary and historical skills among Nova Scotia high school students. Raddall has become a highly respected figure in Maritime cultural circles. In the words of A. J. M. Smith, "He has achieved his success without compromising the rigorous standards of good writing and artistic faithfulness."

Interview:

Donald Cameron, "Thomas Raddall: The Past is Always Important," in his *Conversations with Canadian Novelists,* volume 2 (Toronto: Macmillan, 1973), pp. 99-113.

Bibliography:

Allan R. Young, *Thomas Head Raddall: A Bibliography* (Kingston, Ontario: Loyal Colonies, 1982).

Biography:

Joyce Barkhouse, *A Name for Himself: A Biography of Thomas Head Raddall* (Toronto: Irwin, 1986).

References:

Allan Bevan, Introduction to Raddall's *At the Tide's Turn and Other Stories* (Toronto: McClelland & Stewart, 1959), pp. v-ix;

Donald Cameron, "Thomas Raddall: The Art of Historical Fiction," *Dalhousie Review,* 49 (1969-1970): 540-548;

Robert Cockburn, " 'Nova Scotia is my Dwelen Plas': The Life and Work of Thomas Raddall," *Acadiensis,* 7 (Spring 1978): 135-141;

Fred Cogswell, Introduction to Raddall's *Pride's Fancy* (Toronto: McClelland & Stewart, 1974), pp. iii-x;

James Gray, Introduction to Raddall's *His Majesty's Yankees* (Toronto: McClelland & Stewart, 1977), pp. xi-xviii;

Walter John Hawkins, "Thomas H. Raddall: The Man and His Work," *Queen's Quarterly,* 75 (1968): 137-146;

John Moss, *Patterns of Isolation in English Canadian Fiction* (Toronto: McClelland & Stewart, 1974), pp. 129-138, 146-147;

Andrew Thompson Seaman, "Literature in Atlantic Canada," *Canadian Literature,* 68-69 (1976): 26-39;

John Robert Sorfleet, "Thomas Raddall: I Was Always a Rebel Underneath," *Journal of Canadian Fiction,* 2 (Fall 1973): 45-64.

Papers:

The Thomas Raddall papers are housed at Dalhousie University Archives.

James Reaney
(1 September 1926-   )

Moira Day
University of Alberta

BOOKS: *The Red Heart* (Toronto: McClelland & Stewart, 1949);

A Suit of Nettles (Toronto: Macmillan, 1958);

Twelve Letters To A Small Town (Toronto: Ryerson, 1962);

The Killdeer, and Other Plays (Toronto: Macmillan, 1962)–comprises *The Killdeer, The Sun and the Moon, One-man Masque,* and *Night-blooming Cereus;*

The Boy with an R in His Hand: A Tale of the Type-riot at William Lyon Mackenzie's Printing Office in 1826 (Toronto: Macmillan, 1965);

Colours in the Dark (Vancouver: Talonplays/ Macmillan, 1969);

Apple Butter and Other Plays for Children (Vancouver: Talonbooks, 1969)–comprises *Apple Butter, Names and Nicknames, Ignoramus,* and *Geography Match;*

Masks of Childhood, edited by Brian Parker (Toronto: New Press, 1972)–comprises *The Easter Egg, Three Desks,* and *The Killdeer,* revised version;

Listen to the Wind (Vancouver: Talonbooks, 1972);

Poems, edited by Germaine Warkentin (Toronto: New Press, 1972);

Selected Shorter Poems, edited by Warkentin (Erin, Ontario: Press Porcépic, 1975);

Sticks and Stones, part one of *The Donnellys* (Erin, Ontario: Press Porcépic, 1975);

St. Nicholas Hotel, Wm. Donnelly, Prop., part two of *The Donnellys* (Erin, Ontario: Press Porcépic, 1976);

Selected Longer Poems, edited by Warkentin (Erin, Ontario: Press Porcépic, 1976);

Baldoon, by Reaney and Marty Gervais (Erin, Ontario: Porcupine's Quill, 1976);

Handcuffs, part three of *The Donnellys* (Erin, Ontario: Press Porcépic, 1977);

14 Barrels From Sea to Sea (Erin, Ontario: Press Porcépic, 1977);

The Dismissal; or, Twisted Beards & Tangled Whiskers (Erin, Ontario: Press Porcépic, 1978);

Wacousta! (Toronto: Press Porcépic, 1979);

Gyroscope (Toronto: Playwrights Canada, 1983);

Imprecations: The Art of Swearing (Windsor, Ontario: Black Moss, 1984);

Take the Big Picture (Erin, Ontario: Porcupine's Quill, 1986).

PLAY PRODUCTIONS: *The Killdeer,* Toronto, Coach House Theatre, 13 January 1960; revised version, Vancouver, Stage Campus '70, 5 August 1970;

Night-blooming Cereus/One-man Masque, Toronto, Hart House Theatre, 5 April 1960;

The Easter Egg, Toronto, Coach House Theatre, 13 November 1962;

Names and Nicknames, Winnipeg, Manitoba Theatre Centre, 9 November 1963;

The Sun and the Moon, London, Ontario, Oasis Restaurant Theatre, 3 August 1965;

Listen to the Wind, London, Ontario, Althouse College Auditorium, 26 July 1966;

Three Desks, London, Ontario, Grand Theatre, 3 February 1967;

Colours in the Dark, Stratford, Avon Theatre, 25 July 1967;

Sticks and Stones, Toronto, Tarragon Theatre, 24 November 1973;

The St. Nicholas Hotel, Wm. Donnelly, Prop., Toronto, Tarragon Theatre, 16 November 1974;

Handcuffs, Toronto, Tarragon Theatre, 29 March 1975;

Baldoon, by Reaney and Marty Gervais, Toronto, Bathurst Street Theatre, 20 November 1976;

The Dismissal, Toronto, Hart House Theatre, 23 November 1977;

Wacousta!, Amherstburg, General Amherst High School, 20 February 1978;

King Whistle!, Stratford, Avon Theatre, 15 November 1979;

Antler River, London, Ontario, Grand Theatre, 1 October 1980;

Gyroscope, Toronto, Tarragon Theatre, 14 May 1981;

James Reaney conducting a theater workshop at the University of Windsor (photograph by Grant Black)

The Shivaree, music by John Beckwith, Toronto, St. Lawrence Centre, 3 April 1982;

I, the Parade. The Story of Professor C. F. Thiele, Waterloo, Humanities Theatre, 9 November 1982;

The Canadian Brothers, Calgary, Reeve Theatre, 24 November 1983.

OTHER: *The Canadian Brothers*, in *Major Plays of the Canadian Theatre*, edited by Richard Perkyns (Toronto: Irwin, 1984), pp. 665-725.

PERIODICAL PUBLICATIONS: "Ten Years at Play," *Canadian Literature*, 41 (Summer 1969): 53-61;

"Kids and Crossovers," *Canadian Theatre Review*, 10 (Spring 1976): 28-31;

"A Letter From James Reaney," *Black Moss*, series 2, 1 (Spring 1976): 2-10;

" 'Topless Nightmares,' being a dialogue with himself by James Reaney," *Hallowe'en*, 2 (Fall 1976): 2-10;

King Whistle!, *Brick*, 8 (Winter 1980): 5-99;

"Ontario Culture and–What?," *Canadian Literature*, 100 (Spring 1984): 252-257;

"James Reaney Looks Toward a National Repertory," *Theatre History in Canada*, 6 (Fall 1985): 218-226.

James Reaney has the distinction of being one of Canada's most talented writers and versatile men of letters. Having early in his career established a reputation as a gifted lyric poet, he has in later years made an equally important name for himself both as a powerful and innovative dramatist and as an outspoken commentator on the subjects of Canadian art and culture.

Reaney, whose frail appearance seems somewhat at odds with the vitality and sweep of his inner vision, was born on a farm in South Easthope, near Stratford, Ontario, on 1 September 1926, the son of James Nesbitt and Elizabeth Crerar Reaney. Though his mother's second marriage after the death of the elder James Reaney gave him a half brother and sister, Reaney effectively remained an only child during his formative years in Stratford.

He left his hometown in 1944 to pursue a B.A. (1948) and an M.A. (1949) in English at the University of Toronto, but Reaney's early life has made an indelible impression on the whole of his artistic career. A significant part of this heritage may be seen in Reaney's continuing focus on southwestern Ontario rural life, on orphaned or isolated child figures struggling to survive in a hostile, incomprehensible adult world, and on the family unit. However, the prime legacy of his early years lies less in subject matter than in vision—in "the belief," as he expressed it "which I held as a child that metaphor is reality." Further sophisticated and shaped by his exposure to the works of William Blake, Carl Gustav Jung, and Northrop Frye, this early belief in the power of the creative imagination to transform a dead or hostile environment into a genuinely human world of spirit and meaning has remained the backbone of Reaney's creative endeavors, the most common cipher for the striving human spirit being the child or child-man.

Though Reaney experimented with both the novel and short-story form before and during his student years at Toronto, the medium in which he seemed best able to combine vision, form, and subject matter was poetry. His first major literary success was his first book, a volume of lyric verse entitled *The Red Heart* (1949). A collection of forty-two poems written from 1944 to 1949, the book presents a cohesive portrait of a youth trying to come to terms with the harsh, incomprehensible world of experience. Portraying a psychic landscape sometimes lit to supernal beauty by flashes of the child's imagination but more often perceived as stale, brooding, and demonic, the book won praise for its intensity of feeling and richness of imagery. It also won the 1949 Governor General's Award for poetry.

In 1949 Reaney accepted a position in the University of Manitoba's English department. Though he continued to publish poetry and critical essays during the period of his tenure there, the seven years he spent in Winnipeg were perhaps more notable for the consolidation of his personal life than for the advancement of his literary career; in 1951 he married poet Colleen Thibaudeau and was soon the father of two sons: James Stewart, born in 1952, and John Andrew, born in 1954.

This period of comparative artistic calm ended with Reaney's return to the University of Toronto in 1956 to begin a doctorate under the supervision of Northrop Frye. Two years later *A Suit of Nettles* was published, winning Reaney a second Governor General's Award for poetry. Like *The Shepheardes Calendar* by Edmund Spenser (Reaney's thesis was entitled "The Influence of Spenser on Yeats"), *A Suit of Nettles* takes the form of twelve pastoral eclogues, one for each month of the year. However, in keeping with its billing as a satire, the shepherd lovers have been replaced by an anthropomorphic community of farm geese who reflect in their behavior and attitudes toward mating, religion, education, and art, much that is worthy of praise or condemnation in the Canadian community. Branwell, the main child-poet figure among the geese, avoids the crude philistinism of the worst elements of the community by virtue of his poetic powers. However, his embitterment over an unhappy love affair prevents him from reaching, even by slaughter time in December, the heights of redemptive love and vision offered by such enlightened figures as Effie. Even as Effie suggests that this failure in vision may cause one of Branwell's arms to remain a goose wing when he is reincarnated as a man, so does Reaney seem to suggest that Canadians themselves have yet to fulfill the promise of their own humanity.

Reaney must have experienced a sense of déjà vu in 1958. Once more he received a Governor General's Award for poetry, a graduate degree, and a position at the University of Manitoba. His family expanded while he was in Winnipeg, this time to include a daughter, Susan Alice Elizabeth, born in 1959. However, in contrast to the seven years of relative calm following the appearance of *The Red Heart*, the seven following the publication of *A Suit of Nettles* were an explosion of diversified creative activity.

Moving back to Ontario in 1960 to accept a position in English at the University of Western Ontario, Reaney began his own literary magazine, *Alphabet*, in September of that year. Subtitled *A Semiannual Devoted to the Iconography of the Imagination*, it ran until 1971, including not only poems, short stories, and articles by respected members of the artistic community, but many of Reaney's own theories on art and drama as well.

In the area of poetry he received a third Governor General's Award for the 1962 volume *Twelve Letters To A Small Town*. Alternating among whimsical wit, warm nostalgia, and gentle perceptive irony, *Twelve Letters To A Small Town* presents in the form of twelve lyric poems a mature poet's recollection of the geography and psychology of his hometown, Stratford.

However, the most important development of the period from 1958 to 1965 was Reaney's venture into the theater, an area that was increasingly to absorb his creative energies. He had

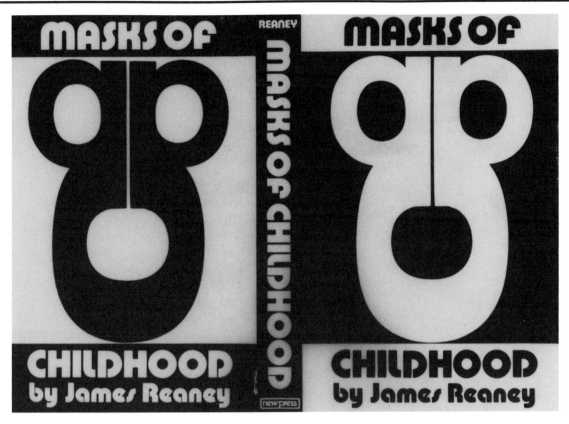

Dust jacket for Reaney's 1972 play collection comprising The Easter Egg, Three Desks, *and the revised version of* The Killdeer

begun working on a libretto for John Beckwith, *Night-blooming Cereus,* as early as 1952; similarly, rough drafts of *The Sun and the Moon* (submitted to the Toronto *Globe and Mail* play-writing competition under the title "The Rules of Joy") and *Three Desks* were in existence by 1958. However, it took the active encouragement of Pamela Terry, who directed his first two full-length stage plays, to persuade Reaney to make his debut as a playwright in 1960 with *The Killdeer.*

Reduced to its simplest terms, *The Killdeer* is a detective story. Working against time, Rebecca's own determination to shield her weakling husband, Eli, and the machinations of Eli's mother, Madame Fay, Harry Gardner must find the murderer of Eli's guardian, Clifford, before Rebecca is hanged for the crime. However, as revealed through the play's rich pattern of imagery and symbols, the workings of the mystery plot are only the outward manifestations of a greater and more deadly spiritual battle being waged for the young souls of both Harry and Eli. Thus, it is only when these two break away from the malignant or repressive psychic forces represented by their guardians and parents (Madame Fay, Mrs.

Gardner, Clifford) in order to embrace the spirit of mature love and creativity embodied in Rebecca that the mystery, born of old evil and deception, can be resolved in a new spirit of harmony and growth.

The critical reception that greeted *The Killdeer,* which opened at Toronto's Coach House Theatre on 13 January 1960, was an encouraging one for a budding playwright. While not everyone concurred with Mavor Moore's opinion (Toronto *Telegram,* 27 January 1960) that the play was a turning point in Canadian dramatic history, even the less enthusiastic reviewers, such as Nathan Cohen, who dubbed *The Killdeer* "a desperately bad play" (Toronto *Daily Star,* 14 January 1960), recognized the potential of the author to become a significant voice in the Canadian theater.

More plays soon followed. *Night-blooming Cereus* and *One-man Masque* were run as a double bill three months after the premiere of *The Killdeer.* The first, a libretto for a one-act opera originally broadcast over radio in 1959, is a gentle, romantic rendering of familiar Reaney themes, with five townspeople catching a glimpse of heaven in the once-a-century blooming of the exotic Cereus flower. By contrast, *One-man Masque,* a mosaic of satiric monologues, short prose passages, and brooding early poems acted around a circle of sixteen objects, displays the darker, more sardonic side of Reaney's art.

Though both *Night-blooming Cereus,* with its music, and *One-man Masque,* with its use of a mosaic style on a bare stage, looked forward to Reaney's future stagecraft, his next full-length ventures into the theater resembled *The Killdeer* closely in theme, characterization, and structure.

Both *The Easter Egg* (performed at the Coach House Theatre in 1962) and *The Sun and the Moon* (performed at London, Ontario's Oasis Restaurant Theatre in 1965) combine a satiric examination of the petty, provincial mentality which petrifies thought and spirit alike with a metaphysical confrontation between the powers of light and dark for the control of a child-figure's soul. In *The Easter Egg* Kenneth, whose development, like that of Eli and Harry, has been arrested in childhood through the efforts of a malignant parental figure, eventually escapes into adulthood by responding to the love, care, and teaching of his stepsister, Polly. Here the emphasis is more on the metaphysical confrontation, the action, following the unities of time and space, taking place entirely in a house which increasingly becomes a projection of the protagonist's mind. In *The Sun and the Moon* the emphasis falls more on the communal conflict. Here the spiritual powers of light and dark embodied respectively in the Reverend Francis Kingbird and Mrs. Charlotte Shade, struggle not merely for the souls of the four young people in the play, but for that of the whole town of Millbank itself.

Though the collection *The Killdeer, and Other Plays* (comprising *The Killdeer, One-man Masque, Night-blooming Cereus,* and *The Sun and the Moon*) won the Governor General's Award for drama in 1963, Reaney's reputation as a playwright still remained in dispute. His drama, like the poetry, was admired for its vital richness of language, its sharp humor, and its depth of emotion and meaning. Not quite so well admired was Reaney's stagecraft, particularly in the full-length plays. Cramming the whole of his multifarious vision into the restrictive form of a static set and linear plot line, he relied mostly on his imagery to convey to the audience the different levels of meaning simultaneously unfolding beneath the action. Unfortunately, not everyone proved as sensitive to the power of words as Reaney himself, and many an actor, audience member, and critic

found himself lost in the rapid shifting of characterization and action between the realms of social realism and romantic mysticism.

While Reaney always felt that the difficulties with the early plays stemmed more from the viewers' underuse of imaginative perception than from his own overuse of it, he began to turn his mind to the problem of form. As he suggests in "Ten Years at Play" (*Canadian Literature,* Summer 1969), two theatrical events significantly influenced his development in this direction. One, a performance by the Peking Opera in 1961, opened his mind to the possibilities of creating a whole imaginative world onstage through use of mime and a few props. The second, his writing and production of a children's play, *Names and Nicknames,* in 1963 allowed him to experiment actively with these possibilities in terms of his own child-centered artistic vision.

In 1966 he finally dared to move this experimentation to the adult stage with *Listen to the Wind,* a play that praises the powers of the creative imagination directly through its subject matter and indirectly through a stagecraft which demands that the audience and actors make extensive use of their own imaginative powers. Moving away from the earlier use of a linear plot line, *Listen to the Wind* presents two separate but interrelated worlds: the "real" 1936 farm world of Owen and his cousins, and their imaginery 1860 world of Caresfoot Court which becomes, with its murderous mothers, ineffectual guardians, and abused innocents, an archetypal expression of the same mingled forces of death, affection, and parental cruelty existing in the children's lives. Though their imaginative play can neither banish Owen's illness nor, as the children hope, bring back his runaway mother, it does allow the children to slowly rearrange their psychic patterns of reality into a more positive, redemptive vision of death and desertion both.

The audience was invited to share in this redemptive creative process of play by building with the children of the play a whole imaginative world out of an empty stage and a table of props. However, whereas the Peking Opera relied on adult actors with years of tradition and training to carry this kind of imaginative stagecraft, Reaney, as he had in *Names and Nicknames,* relied on a chorus of actual children, armed with their own natural energy, love of sound and mime, and swift improvisatory play, to achieve many of the same imaginative effects.

Cover for the first of Reaney's three plays following the fortunes of the Donnellys from their arrival in Canada in 1844 to the murder of the family in 1880

From Reaney's growing fascination with the possibilities of improvised play came yet another important development: the Listeners' Workshop (1966-1969). Consisting of young people from the cast of *Listen to the Wind* and from the greater community of London, Ontario, the Workshop gave Reaney the chance to experiment with getting real people to do what the characters in his plays did, that is, come to a spiritually redemptive vision of themselves and their world through the active play of the imagination—a concept that became increasingly important in his plays of the late 1970s. There is also evidence that the improvisational productions of the Workshop not only contributed actual material to later plays but also did much to help Reaney evolve a "playful" rehearsal, productional, and stylistic technique better suited to the expression of his child-centered vision.

Thus, while *Colours in the Dark,* written and performed in 1967, only a year after *Listen to the Wind,* is also based on the theme of a sick boy coming to terms with himself and his life through the use of his imagination, it is a much different play by virtue of Workshop-influenced changes. Moving the action of the play directly into the child's mind, the structure of *Colours in the Dark,* like creative thought itself, is infinitely faster, more fluid and complex than the two-tiered creative play world of *Listen to the Wind.* Building on Reaney's surer grasp of an imaginative shorthand built on puppetry techniques, music, chanted word litanies and verse, and an evocative aural and visual mime, *Colours in the Dark* presents, like the mind itself, a startling array of times, people, and realities—past and present, real and mythic—flashing by in a continuous overlapping stream of images, scenes, and sounds that register sharply on the audience before dissolving. Out of the whirling mosaic emerges a protagonist, who like the play itself is simultaneously many things: he is, like Owen, a real boy using his imagination and crayons to challenge the sickroom's darkness; like the protagonists of the early plays, he is the universal figure of the child-man redeeming a fallen world through the humanizing power of words, love, and faith; and, like the imaginatively participating audience, he is a representative Canadian coping with the mingled forces of land, history, and culture which is Canada.

Though *Colours in the Dark,* commissioned by the Stratford, Ontario, festival for the centennial year, won Reaney both the praise of the critics and a standing ovation on opening night, it was the last wholly new play Reaney was to write until 1973. (*Three Desks,* performed in 1967, a realistic play about the tensions existing in the academic life at a small Manitoban college, and a second version of *The Killdeer,* performed in 1970, are reworkings of earlier scripts.)

Much of the reason for this prolonged silence was Reaney's total absorption with a project he had been considering since the 1940s: an artistic rendering of the story of the infamous Donnelly family massacred by a mob of their neighbors at Lucan, Ontario, in 1880. Though sessions with the Listener's Workshop helped shape some of the research material Reaney had gathered over a period of nearly eight years, it was not until 1972 that he found, in the form of Keith Turnbull and what was to become the NDWT Company, an artistic commodity he desperately needed: a professional director and group of actors, as willing as the young Workshop participants to work "at-a-play-the-way-children-would-play-it-as-if-it-were-a-big-game." Working closely with the company over a three-year period (1972-1975) that included intensive workshopping with the actors themselves and

through your speech at four o'clock at the Academy of the Sacred Heart.

BISHOP JOHN My dear children. I have assisted at this annual distribution of prizes with much gratification. Mahony, weren't our chimneys just swept?

SECRETARY TOM Your Lordship, the bird, the wild bird that has been trapped in the fire place chimney here for three or four days now. Making oh such much whispy whispery noises that we had to move your writing table into the second parlour. The chimney sweeps are coming to settle with this trouble making bird, your Lordship.

BISHOP JOHN Ah yes. Mahony *(Mahony)*. _Pause_ It's not making much of a sound this morning, is it? The child when brought to school is not only an ignorant being, but it is also a being inclined to evil. How important, therefore ...

SECRETARY TOM Your Lordship, I beg your pardon. I forget that Mr Coughlin is already here. He scuttles out to let Coughlin in; the latter kneels to kiss the Bishop's ring.

BISHOP JOHN Michael Coughlin. May I congratulate you, Mr Michael Coughlin, on your victory at the polls yesterday. We Conservatives who are Catholics are marching forward to greater and greater strengths.

M.P. M2 Your Lordship, there is

BISHOP Who says this is not an age for miracles, Mr Coughlin? Sir John A. Macdonald waves his magic wand -- good Catholics everywhere vote for Orange Protestant Conservative candidates. He waves another magic wand -- it must be some sort of club and Protestant Orangemen voted for you, didn't they, Mr Coughlin. You whom they would privately call a Papist and worse. But whom Sir John A. Macdonald reminds -- yes, Mr Coughlin is a Catholic, but he is a fellow Conservative. I am

M.P. M2 Your Lordship, there has been a final tally of the votes. I did not get in by as wide a margin as we thought last night.

Page from the manuscript for Handcuffs, *part three of* The Donnellys *(by permission of the author)*

with actors and children together, Reaney produced the three incredibly rich and complex dramas, which taken together form the Donnelly trilogy: *Sticks and Stones* (performed in 1973), *The St. Nicholas Hotel, Wm. Donnelly, Prop.* (performed in 1974, winner of the Chalmers Award for best new drama), and *Handcuffs* (performed in 1975).

Following the fortunes of the Donnelly family from their arrival in Canada in 1844 to the murder of the family in 1880, the plays, taken separately as well as together, examine the extensive historical, political, social, and religious reasons for the family's persecution and death, within the overall mythic context of the eternal battle between the powers of spiritual light and dark in the lives of men and in nature alike. As summer passes into winter, so does the warm, fertile spiritual force of the Donnellys and the new land itself succumb to the cold, dark forces of sterility and hatred in the Biddulph community. No less impressive than the complex mix of the documentary and the mythic in the plays is the complex blending, influenced to a large extent by his close work with the NDWT Company, of all Reaney's previous lines of improvisational experimentation into a definitive style, which at its finest is a highly effective stage poetry of sound, words, and mime.

A nationwide tour of the trilogy in 1975 (described by Reaney in his 1977 book *14 Barrels From Sea to Sea*) excited considerable attention and praise throughout Canada as much for the plays' innovative style and production values as for the richness of the themes. Though occasionally criticized as overly long and somewhat cluttered and confusing in its details, as a whole the trilogy was hailed as one of the most beautiful, original, and powerful pieces of theater seen on the Canadian stage.

The Donnelly trilogy bequeathed a great deal to Reaney's plays that followed in the late 1970s, leaving them with both a definitive "play" style welded out of Reaney's various lines of dramaturgical experimentation, and a company of professional actors enthusiastically committed to this particular style of "play" theater. At the same time there was every indication that far from being simply variations on the dramaturgical theme sounded by the trilogy, the plays of the late 1970s formed the prelude to yet a new line of dramatic experimentation: the expansion of the earlier Listener's Workshop ideal of a redemptive "play" theater for adults into a comprehensive community theater in which a playwright,

company of actors, and community members at large could come together to produce a life-giving story of themselves as a community. To this end Reaney's five plays of the late 1970s— *Baldoon* (1976), a collaboration with Marty Gervais; *The Dismissal* (1977); *Wacousta!* (1978); *King Whistle!* (1979); and *Antler River* (1980)–all deal specifically with stories or incidents arising from the culture and history of southwestern Ontario.

Even more important, Reaney increasingly extended the workshop-rehearsal process, developed with the NDWT Company, to take in the general public. Whereas the *Baldoon* and *The Donnellys* tour workshops encouraged the participants to create poetry and skits out of the rough materials of their own environment, the *Wacousta!* workshops actually produced a rough draft of the final play, and the *King Whistle!* workshops culminated in a final production featuring over one hundred members of the Stratford community onstage and an additional sixty-eight behind the scenes. *Antler River*, a similar experiment involving the community of London, Ontario, in an exploration of its own past, followed the year after.

The critical response to the late-1970s plays was mixed. Some felt that Reaney's increasing emphasis on process made the plays less successful as lasting stage or literary works. Moreover, the large casts, local flavor, and stylistic complexity of the plays inhibited other professional companies from reviving them. However, as the failure of *Gyroscope* (1981) indicated again, Reaney's craft does not adapt itself well to the more popular genre of intimate domestic drama.

The dissolving in 1982 of the NDWT Company, Reaney's major dramatic interpreters for nearly a decade, marked a hiatus in Reaney's dramatic career. Both *The Shivaree* (1982), written for composer John Beckwith in the 1960s, and *The Canadian Brothers* (1983), the second half of Reaney's dramatization of novelist John Richardson's *Wacousta!* saga, mark the completion of old projects rather than the beginning of new ones. However, the warm response accorded *The Shivaree*, a comic operetta in the same mode as *Night-blooming Cereus*, has prompted Reaney to re-explore the possibilities of music in interpreting his vision. Future projects, in conjunction with composers Beckwith and Harry Somers, include two operas ("Serinette" and "Crazy to Kill") based on southwestern Ontario life or sources and a musical play about the Brontë children ("The House by the Churchyard").

In review it is possible to see that the story of Reaney's evolving and changing literary career is that of a constant experimentation with form aimed at bringing to ever fuller expression his imaginative vision of human redemption through the transforming powers of the creative imagination. Thus, while it remains true that at its best his work reveals the deepest, most complex, and transcendent of meanings through the simplest of means, it is work that has moved increasingly outward from the personal to the social scope. The introspective lyric poet of the 1950s has become the extroverted dramatist of the 1980s, constantly experimenting with new ways of changing "our whole nation" into a kind of theater "where we ourselves, with just our bodies and the simplest of props (albeit in abundance) available to everyone, create a civilization where it finally seems true that to be wise is to know how to play."

References:

Geraldine Anthony, *Stage Voices: Twelve Canadian Playwrights Talk About Their Lives and Works* (Toronto: Doubleday, 1978), pp. 139-164;

Stan Dragland, *Approaches to the Work of James Reaney* (Downsview, Ontario: ECW, 1983);

Alvin A. Lee, *James Reaney* (New York: Twayne, 1968);

James Stewart Reaney, *James Reaney* (Agincourt, Ontario: Sage, 1977);

Ross G. Woodman, *James Reaney* (Toronto: McClelland & Stewart, 1971).

Ringuet
(Philippe Panneton)

(30 April 1895-28 December 1960)

Antoine Sirois
Université de Sherbrooke

BOOKS: *Littératures . . . à la manière de . . .* , by Ringuet and Louis Francoeur (Montreal: Edouard Garand, 1924);

30 Arpents (Paris: Flammarion, 1938; Montreal: Editions Variétés, 1942); translated by Felix and Dorothea Walter as *Thirty Acres* (Toronto: Macmillan, 1940; New York: Macmillan, 1940);

Un Monde était leur empire (Montreal: Editions Variétés, 1943);

L'Héritage et autres contes (Montreal: Editions Variétés, 1946);

Fausse Monnaie (Montreal: Editions Variétés, 1947);

Le Poids du jour (Montreal: Editions Variétés, 1949);

L'Amiral et le facteur ou comment l'Amérique ne fut pas découverte (Montreal: Dussault, 1954);

Confidences (Montreal & Paris: Fides, 1965).

Ringuet was one of the first major novelists in French Canada. During a period when literature, and the novel in particular, was considered an instrument for propagating a nationalist ideology, he published a book that is still considered a classic: *30 Arpents* (1938), translated to English under the title *Thirty Acres* (1940). It has at the same time a documentary value and an aesthetic quality.

Ringuet was born Philippe Panneton in Trois-Rivières, Quebec, on 30 April 1895. The son of Ephrem-François Panneton, a doctor, and Eva Ringuet Panneton, he took his mother's family name as a pseudonym. After his third year of college, in 1914 he undertook studies in medicine in Quebec and then in Montreal and went to

Paris to specialize in otorhinolaryngology from 1920 to 1923. While practicing in Montreal, he carried on research and published articles in his field. By 1935 he was an associate professor at the University of Montreal, but he always remained interested in literature.

In 1924 he published, in collaboration with his friend Louis Francoeur, *Littératures ... à la manière de ...* , a series of parodies of important French-Canadian writers and politicians. Then he started writing his major work, *30 Arpents,* published by Flammarion in Paris in 1938. It was an immediate success and won him wide acclaim: in his own province the Prix de la Province de Québec; in Canada a Governor General's Award; and in France an award from the Académie Française as well as the Prix des Vikings. By 1940 it had been translated into German as well as into English.

Ringuet produced an unexpected work in 1943, *Un Monde était leur empire,* on the prehistory of America. *L'Héritage et autres contes* appeared in 1946, *Fausse Monnaie* in 1947, *Le Poids du jour* in 1949, and, finally, *L'Amiral et le facteur ou comment l'Amérique ne fut pas découverte* in 1954. He married, that same year, France Leriger de Laplante. In 1956 he became Canadian ambassador to Portugal, where he died in 1960. A posthumously published book appeared in 1965: *Confidences,* a collection of talks Ringuet had given on Radio-Canada. In addition to the prizes he received for *30 Arpents,* he won many other prizes and decorations, among these a "prix de la langue française" from the Académie Française (1947) and the Lorne Pierce Medal given by the Royal Society of Canada (1959). He was a cofounder and twice president of the Académie Canadienne-Française, the most important literary society in Quebec at that time. Ringuet is best known for his two major novels, *30 Arpents,* about rural life in French Canada, and *Le Poids du jour,* about the movement of farmers to the city.

30 Arpents deals with Euchariste Moisan and his family, who live on thirty acres of land, from 1887 to 1932. The main characters are Moisan, the owner of the farm; Etienne, his eldest son; Ephrem, his favorite son; and finally the land itself, mother and mistress. Moisan manages his farm well and progresses gradually in wealth and reputation in his parish. But, growing old, he becomes careless occasionally and is forced to give the use of his land to Etienne, who has been impatiently coveting the thirty acres and pushing his fa-

ther aside. Etienne finally manages to send the aging man for a period of time to live with Ephrem, who has abandoned the land, seeking an easy life with a regular salary in the factories of New England. Because of the Depression and the unwillingness of the eldest son, Moisan never comes back to his farm but becomes a janitor in a garage. The land, Mother Earth, a hard mistress, remains unchanged, while the aging father has to leave her, giving up the care of his thirty acres to a new generation.

Time is an important theme in this novel. The names of the four seasons are the titles of the four parts, which correspond to the phases in the farmer's life: spring and summer to his rise, a period of control over his children, of wealth and prestige; fall and winter to his decline, a period of loss of all possessions. His life spans a well-defined period from before World War I up to the Depression, a period of change in the province of Quebec from an agricultural society to an industrialized one. Also related to the time motif is the cyclical nature of the agricultural era, regulated by the unfailing return of the seasons, in contrast to the linear evolution associated with progress and illustrated in its technical aspects in *30 Arpents* by the advent of the tractor and the automobile.

Space is a second important theme of this novel. Physical space is divided into concentric areas, from the outer limits of the province of Quebec to the inner circles of the parish, the farm, the house, the kitchen, and the warming stove around which the family gathers. Social space is determined, in the community, by the parochial family of the church and, within the farmer's family, by the wife's managing the inside of the house and the farmer in charge outside. Nature, as a part of the physical space, and especially the land, becomes a theme, a character, and is elevated to a mythical level: "From the ancient times, there remained within him [Moisan] an obscure feeling which personified the earth; it was always the Daughter of Heaven and the Spouse of Time, the good and fruitful Goddess to whom one offers the first fruits and the first born." "She" becomes for him more important than his wife (whose death is only a minor incident in the novel) or than himself. He gives his whole life to the land and she takes everything from him until he becomes too old to fertilize her.

In the French-Canadian novel before 1938 land had been portrayed as a Garden of Eden but in *30 Arpents* Ringuet showed the other side of the story. Although farmers felt enveloped and secure in the familiar physical and social environments, they also felt threatened by three outside forces: technology, exoticism, and the city. New mechanical inventions, such as the tractor, readily accepted by the younger generation, are seen by the older generation as obstacles between themselves and the earth. Foreigners, represented in *30 Arpents* by Albert, the French hand, and the cousins from the United States, give the children, especially Ephrem, a taste of the foreign lands, and he revolts against life on the farm. The city attracts three of the children, dazzled by the lights and the promise of a regular salary. In previous novels those who left the farm for the diabolical city came back to the blessed spaces of the country or were severely punished. Here neither happens.

Traditionally in novels about the land, characters had been stereotypes and their inner personalities were not developed. The individual characters in *30 Arpents* are not developed in depth, the author being more interested in describing larger elements, but in this novel the farmer is less idealized, his actions are more plausible. He is, however, led by fate, represented by nature: "He is tied to this same land by a very old servitude." "Things have decided for him, and people run by things." He has a tragic destiny.

The use of the image of the four seasons is not new in *30 Arpents,* but the author's use of some elements of this image is interesting. Heat accompanies the happier period of the rise of the hero: the kitchen and the stable are warm. The melting snow and the cold rain and mud of the early spring accompany him when he goes away to the States and is "drowned in the ocean of the big city."

30 Arpents is better written than most comparable novels of the pre-1938 period. The author has used appropriate language for the narrator and other characters: a classical French with a few Canadianisms for the narrator, a peasant dialect of the beginning of the century for the farmers, a franglais (a mixture of popular French and English) for the Franco-Americans of New England. Nobody before Ringuet had done this. The novel is meticulously built, in the tradition of Flaubert or Zola whom the author admired. Every development is justified and plausible, and the references to the historical and social situations are accurate. In successfully describing the transitional period in Quebec from the agricultural era to the industrial one, Ringuet demonstrates a personal aesthetic approach and world view. He frees himself of the extremely idealistic and ideological approach of his predecessors and, beyond and within the localized destiny of a simple farmer, he expresses more universally the fate of the man of the land, subjugated to the elements, whose life is ephemeral compared to the permanency of the earth. This novel is the crowning achievement of a literary genre inaugurated in 1846 with *La Terre paternelle* of Patrice Lacombe.

30 Arpents, first published in Paris, drew the attention of the foremost French critics of the period. André Billy of the *Figaro Littéraire,* Robert Brasillach of the *Action Française,* and André Thérive of the *Feuilleton du Temps* gave generous reviews. Thérive wrote that this novel was until further notice the "pièce maîtresse" of the Canadian novel. In Canada the novel was also well received. Louis Dantin, one of the most prominent critics before World War II, greeted the arrival of a first-class novelist. Critics saw this work as a turning point in the tradition of the French-Canadian novel.

If *30 Arpents* is primarily concerned with life on the land, *Le Poids du jour* is mainly centered on life in the city where the majority of French-Canadians (sixty-three percent in 1941) lived. World War II had taken place between the writing of the two novels, and the author's attitude in 1949 reflects a change in mentality that had come about because of the war, even though the period covered by this last novel is largely the same as that treated in the first one, the last part of the nineteenth century and the first part of the twentieth. A new trend in literature had emerged, beginning with *Au pied de la pente douce* by Roger Lemelin in 1944 and especially with *Bonheur d'occasion* by Gabrielle Roy in 1945. The city had become a real presence, an important character in the novel.

Le Poids du jour is the story of a city "conqueror." Michel Garneau, born in 1889, grows up in a small town, Louiseville, protected by the love of his mother and of his godfather, and distant from his alcoholic father. After working for some time in a local bank, he decides to go into business in Montreal. There he learns by accident that his godfather is his real father. Astounded, he tries to enlist in the armed services during World War I but is considered unfit. He decides vengefully to reject his past, to conquer the city through business, and finally he becomes the owner of a factory. Although he successfully overcomes the stock-market crash, he is lonesome and unhappy, and he resolves, before the beginning of World War II, to sell everything and go back to the country. He settles amid the apple orchards where he regains his peace of mind, in the company of his daughter.

The novel is divided into three parts: "Michel et Hélène" (mother and son); "The Antipodes" (city versus country and childhood); "The Submission of Man" (acceptance of the past). This division indicates the psychological development of the hero but also corresponds to the author's great interest in the physical and social spaces which were important during the period between the wars. For Michel these spaces are Louiseville, a peaceful small rural community with its craftsmen and traditional professionals; Montreal with its working class in the East End and its middle class in the more fashionable quarters of the West End; and Mont Saint-Hilaire, a fruit-growing region. Two parts represent the old Quebec before World War II and the middle one, the new Quebec, with its rising social classes in the city, which are abundantly described. The farmers, like those who appeared in *30 Arpents*, are shown here adapting to an urban situation upon the breaking up of the old order. Time again appears as a theme and the young hero tires of the routine of an era ruled by nature and is eager to move into the more progressive industrial era. Many other themes are evident, such as the quest for happiness, solitude in the city, the problem of aging, the maternal role of nature.

The development of the hero is more thoroughly described in this novel; Ringuet's characters are becoming more complex. Michel Garneau is an extremely sensitive child. He wants to become a musician, but he is also proud and determined. When, after an overprotected childhood, he learns about the mystery of his birth, he is shocked and rebels against his mother and his whole past. Michel Garneau changes his name to Robert M. Garneau. He hardens himself and becomes violent with others: "Overcome things. Overcome men ... overcome himself to wrest from his heart compassion and kindness which make one weak." He takes vengeance by dominating the city environment, aiming for money and power. But he does not find happiness. His wife dies and his son, wanted for cigarette traffic, flees to the United States. With the help of his daughter he eventually settles in the countryside and slowly rediscovers in this maternal nature, through his daughter and grandson, tenderness

he had known at his mother's knee. Even though Ringuet was open to change in Quebec society, he was not sure that the urban man would find happiness in his quest. In *Le Poids du jour* there is a nostalgia for Mother Nature seen in many French-Canadian novels.

Although this novel is well constructed, the author intervenes too often and has difficulty integrating his social portraits, so that the narrative drags at times. The reviews of the critics were divided. Some were disappointed, some moderately favorable; one considered it a masterpiece of national literature. Guy Sylvestre of the Royal Society of Canada, writing in *Panorama des lettres canadiennes-françaises* (1964), thought that the author was unable to master such complex subject matter, but he stated appropriately that the novel was "the most important undertaking in French Canada to express the individual and collective drama of migration from the country to the city."

As for Ringuet's other works, they are less important than the two novels but of some interest. *Un Monde était leur empire*, written after a trip to Mexico, is concerned with the pre-Columbian civilizations. The author recounts the story of the first inhabitants of the Americas, the invasions by the Europeans, and the collapse of the Incan and Mayan empires. In the last chapter he describes how the natives were treated after the conquest, condemning, in his biased account, attitudes of the conquerors. *L'Héritage et autres contes* regroups nine stories that had been published in the *Revue Moderne* from 1940 to 1946. The title story, in which a young man of the city attempts to come back to the land, is the most interesting and recalls the pessimism of *30 Arpents*. In 1959 the National Film Board of Canada made the story into a film. The novel *Fausse Monnaie* relates a brief encounter of a young man and a young woman who spend a weekend in nature in the Laurentians and are temporarily carried away. The last of Ringuet's books published during his lifetime, *L'Amiral et le facteur ou comment l'Amérique ne fut pas découverte*, expresses the author's view that Amerigo Vespucci was the real discoverer of America, not Columbus, as tradition has it.

An interesting account of Ringuet's life is still unpublished. He kept a diary, begun in 1920, that numbers 2,390 pages. From it he extracted what he called "Le Carnet d'un cynique" that contains his thoughts in his earlier years on religion, love, politics, philosophy, and literature, but he decided not to publish it, perhaps fearing public reaction. As the "carnet" shows, while his contemporaries were influenced by the French seventeenth-century writers, he was marked by those of the eighteenth. In fact, the diary and the "carnet," like his published works, reflect one of his main character traits: not to live according to accepted ideas. He was at variance with his religious and conservative milieu, and he felt the urge to take issue with it in his writing. In his historical novels he did not accept the traditional idea that the Europeans brought civilization to the Americas, as he rejected Columbus as the discoverer of America in *L'Amiral et le facteur*. With his masterpiece, *30 Arpents*, he cut himself off from the mainstream of his period as a novelist because he considered the novel a work of art, not an instrument of nationalist propaganda.

Another of Ringuet's characteristics is his rather fatalistic approach to the destiny of man. In their quests Euchariste Moisan and Robert M. Garneau are disillusioned. They think they can dominate their natural and their human environments, but they are finally dominated, as is the young hero in "l'Héritage." This attitude of Ringuet is rather different from the idealistic current found in the typical novel of the land, in which the hero conquers by the strength of his will. As an author in a period of historical transition in Quebec, Ringuet seems to have been torn between the reality of industrialization and urbanization, which he described and accepted, and the nostalgia for nature which remains a haven of peace and beauty.

References:

Pierre Angers, "Trente Arpents," *Le Roman canadien-français* (Montreal: Fides, 1964), pp. 123-132;

René Dionne, "La Terre dans 'Trente Arpents' de Ringuet," *Collège et Famille*, 25 (October 1968): 133-157;

Claude-Henri Grignon, "Les 'Trente Arpents' d'un Canayen," *Pamphlets de Valdombre*, third year, 3 (February 1939): 93-145;

H. Hoekema, "The Illusion of Realism in *Thirty Acres*," *Essays on Canadian Writing*, 17 (Spring 1980): 102-112;

Jean Le Moyne, "Ringuet et le contexte canadien-français," *Revue Dominicaine*, 56 (February 1950): 80-90;

Gilles Marcotte, *Une Littérature qui se fait* (Montreal: HMH, 1962), pp. 33-37;

Jean Panneton, *Ringuet* (Montreal: Fides, 1970);

Réjean Robidoux and André Renaud, "Trente Arpents," *Le Roman canadien-français du vingtième siècle* (Ottawa: Editions de l'Université d'Ottawa, 1966), pp. 44-48;

Jean-Noël Samson, ed., *Philippe Panneton*, Dossier de Documentation de la Littérature canadienne-française, no. 6 (Montreal: Fides, 1970);

Antoine Sirois, "Grove et Ringuet," *Canadian Literature*, 49 (Summer 1971): 20-27;

Sirois, "Le Mythe de la terre-mère et *Trente Arpents*," *Revue de l'Université de Sherbrooke*, 4 (December 1962): 67-72;

Paul Socken, "The Narrative Structure of *Trente Arpents*," *Canadian Literature*, 86 (Autumn 1980): 152-156;

Michel van Schendel, "*Le Poids du jour* ou l'échec du roman de la ville," *La Presse*, arts and letters supplement (3 April 1965): 10;

Jacques Viens, "*La Terre*" de Zola et "*Trente Arpents*" de Ringuet (Sherbrooke: Cosmos, 1970).

Robert de Roquebrune
(Robert Laroque de Roquebrune)

(29 July 1889-4 July 1978)

Patricia Merivale
University of British Columbia

BOOKS: *L'Invitation à la vie, suivie de Paysages et autres proses* (Montreal: Privately printed, 1916);

Les Habits rouges (Paris: Monde Nouveau, 1923);

D'un océan à l'autre (Paris: Monde Nouveau, 1924);

La Banque en détresse, by Roquebrune and Fernand Préfontaine, as Dick Berton (Paris: Monde Moderne, 1926);

Les Dames Le Marchand (Paris: Monde Moderne, 1927);

Contes du soir et de la nuit (Montreal: Bernard Valiquette, 1942);

Testament de mon enfance (Paris: Plon, 1951); translated by Felix Walter as *Testament of My Childhood* (Toronto: University of Toronto Press, 1964);

La Seigneuresse (Montreal: Fides, 1960);

Les Canadiens d'autrefois, 2 volumes (Montreal: Fides, 1962, 1966);

Quartier Saint-Louis (Montreal & Paris: Fides, 1966);

Cherchant mes souvenirs, 1911-1940 (Montreal: Fides, 1968).

Joseph-Robert-Hertel, seventh son of Louis-René-Hertel Larocque and Marie-Anne-Cordélia-Lilia d'Irumberry de Salaberry, was born at Manoir de l'Assumption, Quebec, in 1889. The family moved to Montreal at a date variously given, but in any case considerably earlier than *Testament de mon enfance* (1951), the first volume of his fictionalized memoirs, would lead one to suppose. He studied at Mont Saint-Louis, Montreal, from 1902 to 1905. The period begun by the move to Montreal, from 1893(?) to his marriage, is covered in *Quartier Saint-Louis* (1966), his second volume of memoirs. In 1911 he married Marie-Louise-Joséphine Angers; they went to France for the next ten months. At this time he added the geographical suffix, "de Roquebrune," to his name; by 1918 he had dropped, for liter-

ary purposes, the (variously spelled) family name, Larocque. The couple returned to Montreal in 1912, intending to save enough money to go back to France in August 1914–an ominous date, it turned out; they did not in fact return to France until 1919.

During the period in Montreal he published a slim (thirty-one-page) volume of prose poems, *L'Invitation à la vie* (1916), and wrote the first version of his most popular novel, *Les Habits rouges* (rewritten and finally published in Paris in 1923). But most significant, in 1918 he joined with two friends (the architect Fernand Préfontaine and the pianist Léo-Pol Morin) who had been members, along with several other young Montreal intellectuals, of a "cénacle" devoted to conversation about literary and cultural matters of the day, especially in Paris, to publish a literary magazine, *Le Nigog.* It ran for twelve issues, from January through December 1918. While never heavily subscribed to (maximum circulation: 500), it was influential out of all proportion to its circulation, being perhaps the first avant-garde periodical in Quebec; it also–perhaps a greater marvel–managed almost to break even financially while arousing a significant and gratifying degree of opposition among members of the establishment. In 1919 the Roquebrunes returned to France, where they were to remain until another war again made them Quebec residents; their enforced departure from France just ahead of the invading German armies is well told in the third volume of Roquebrune's memoirs, *Cherchant mes souvenirs, 1911-1940* (1968). Roquebrune worked at the Archives Publiques du Canada in Paris for the twenty years between the two wars, first as paleographer, then from 1921 as assistant and associate archivist. He worked at the Public Archives in Ottawa from 1940 to 1946. After World War II he returned to Paris as director of the Archives, a post he retained until his retirement in 1958. The death of his wife Josée in 1964 affected him deeply: if his first published work had been a mildly daring epithalamium inspired by their marriage, his last one, the final book of memoirs, was a memorial to her and to that marriage. The last ten years of his life he lived in Quebec, dying at Cowansville in 1978. He had no children.

In addition to his historical work, his novels, and his three volumes of memoirs (though history, fiction, and memoir are not perhaps as self-evidently distinct in his works as they usually are), Roquebrune contributed actively to periodicals, both in Quebec and in France. Several of these contributions were collected, eight (not very memorable) short stories in *Contes du soir et de la nuit* (1942) and twenty-three historical essays in the two volumes of *Les Canadiens d'autrefois* (1962, 1966). The essays are notable for their re-creations of customs and atmosphere, for bringing the past to life, rather than for accuracy of detail or for a critical re-interpretation of history. Like the works of Philippe Aubert de Gaspé, on which they are partly modeled, these books are for general readers rather than for historians. Their readable, anecdotal, personal histories show French Canadians as they liked to see themselves and provides a useful introduction, not to Quebec history per se but to a rose-colored legend of Quebec. Many of the anecdotes come from the family histories of the long lineages of Larocques and Roquebrunes (there were shifts in these two names as early as 1504, Roquebrune notes, clearly finding therein a model for his own self-made nom de plume).

His novels were greeted with approval by reviewers, sold well, and were each republished at least once—with the exception of the collaboratively pseudonymous melodramatic mystery story à la Wilkie Collins, *La Banque en détresse* (1926), only recently rediscovered and attributed to Roquebrune and Fernand Préfontaine by Jean-Guy Hudon. *Les Habits rouges* was the most popular of his novels, but even its success was eclipsed by that of his first volume of memoirs, *Testament de mon enfance;* it appears to be generally agreed that this work constitutes his single unequivocal claim to a significant place in Quebec literature. He received the Prix David and the Prix d'Action Intellectuelle for *Les Habits rouges* in 1923, the Prix d'Action Intellectuelle, again, for *D'un océan à l'autre* in 1925, the Prix Duvernay in 1954, three years after the publication of *Testament de mon enfance,* and the medal of the Parisian Académie Canadienne-Française (in 1967) for the whole body of his work.

His four historical novels—all stylish and readable but far from profound and certainly neither experimental nor even up-to-date in style or technique—deal with watersheds of Quebec history. *La Seigneuresse* (1960) centers upon the English Conquest (with a central episode adapted from Philippe Aubert de Gaspé's 1862 work *Les Anciens Canadiens*): the French and Scottish heroes, earlier rivals for the hand of the eponymous heroine, duel upon the Plains of Abraham to the death of the Frenchman, her husband; he appears nobly to bequeath "her" ("épousez-la . . .") to the Scottish victor, who discovers that the pronoun actually refers to the nearly grown daughter of the couple, rather than to the careworn, and in any case faithful, heroine herself. The Rebellion of 1837 is the setting for *Les Habits rouges,* in which much the same sort of story is told, varied by the presence of some Walter Scottish eccentrics and by subplots of collaboration, treason, and the final suppression of Quebec nationalism. Westward expansion (the building of the Canadian Pacific Railway and the attendant rebellion of Louis Riel and the Métis) is, as the title suggests, the central theme of *D'un océan à l'autre* (1924), set in 1869 and 1885. Closest to the present, set in the final decades of the nineteenth century, the last gasp, by Roquebrune's estimate, of the seigneurial aristocracy of French Canada, is *Les Dames Le Marchand* (1927), which is, incidentally, the most "realistic" of these four romances; with its occasional Balzacian and Flaubertian echoes, it is almost a novel of "moeurs de province."

Roquebrune's passion for genealogy, particularly that of his own family, along with his life-long work in the historical archives of Quebec, gave him much of his material. His novels are, like his essays, a turning of the actual historical personages of his extended family into the fictional characters who comprise his microcosm of Quebec history. Conversely, the fictions of *La Seigneuresse* shadow proleptically the "autobiographical" recollections of *Testament de mon enfance.* Roquebrune sees each of these historical moments elegiacally; whatever love interests, sentiments, or adventures form the woof of his historical romances (done in the manner of a blander, more "realistic" Dumas père, or of Prosper Mérimée, whose works, as one might surmise from reading his own "contes," he particularly admired), the warp of all of them is his strong, archival sense of the historical anecdote or detail, highlighting the culminating moments of a civilization (a word used frequently in his writing) now sunk into the past and only recuperable by the effort of memory.

Even his childhood memoir, *Testament de mon enfance*, which has often been called Roquebrune's finest history *and* his finest novel, is no Proustian endeavor of recuperation but rather an exercise in nostalgia, a praise of times past seen ideally, though never as idyllically as in the "roman du terroir," the Quebec novel against which he was consciously rebelling. Yet, although Roquebrune is far more skillful with plot and characterization than his predecessors, he still seems an anachronism, a lesser Mérimée or Hugo, rather than a modernist (in the 1920s of Gide and Proust), let alone a postmodernist (in the 1960s and 1970s of Réjean Ducharme, or of Hubert Aquin, whom he actually outlived by a year). That he was no pathbreaker in fiction, and that even his first memoir, said to be (in 1959–it may still be true) among the best of its kind in Quebec fiction, is not a striking example of that familiar genre of (literary) childhood recollection, is not to his discredit; every literature has need of the competent minor author.

But the five hundred readers of *Le Nigog* might have puzzled over the paradox of a writer so "advanced" in his cultural awareness and interests in 1918 (when he was no Rimbaud or Nelligan, but a man of twenty-nine), who became so anachronistic, in theme, style, and attitude, for the rest of his literary career. Jean-Guy Hudon, along with Roger Duhamel the most knowledgeable critic of Roquebrune (see especially Hudon's entries in the *Dictionnaire des œuvres littéraires du Québec* for Roquebrune's separate works, and his chronology, found in the 1979 Fides edition of *Testament de mon enfance*), quotes him as saying that he intended no rebellion in *Le Nigog*–but, in context (in *Cherchant mes souvenirs*), Roquebrune goes on to say, a mite rebelliously, that the vacuum of Montreal cultural life at that time left nothing to rebel against. However, it hardly seems as if the distinct possibility that his share in the founding and editing of *Le Nigog*, plus his writing of one-fifth of its text (eighty pages out of its 408), may prove his most enduring contribution to Quebec literature would have struck Roquebrune as either likely or appropriate. But so it may prove, *Testament de mon enfance* notwithstanding, even though from a present-day perspective *Le Nigog* does not seem nearly as avant-garde as it once appeared to be. The vacuum in Montreal cultural life must have been extreme for the mild here-

sies of *Le Nigog,* and of its founders, to have caused the faintest ripple of alarm.

It is not so much that *Le Nigog* provided an up-to-date view of cultural life in Paris, although Roquebrune's two collaborators, in some of their essays on music, art, and architecture, were perhaps more provocatively up-to-date than Roquebrune himself was. Of all the avant-garde possibilities operative or noteworthy in the Paris of 1918, Roquebrune mentions in any emphatic way only Apollinaire. He does, however, make the claim for the Frenchness of French Canada, with its cultural ties to the motherland, as a standard by which to judge two of the crushing limitations of its cultural regionalism, the idyllicism of the "roman du terroir" and the weakness of any purely local French. He claimed that to be French-Canadian (*québécois* is never Roquebrune's term), is "être français avec [l'] aspect spécial" of having *two* of the world's greatest cultures at one's doorstep: a position very far from attitudes of recent times, to be sure, but one that may yet have a future. He championed, among Quebec writers, only Emile Nelligan, but him repeatedly and vigorously, while attacking such once intimidating Parisian literary lions as Paul Bourget, Maurice Barrès, Charles Maurras, and others even more completely forgotten. Much of this work appears in his contributions (in ten of the twelve issues) to "Mare aux grenouilles," the editorial column printed at the end of each issue, along with other more trivial reviews and items of cultural news, and, in later issues, choice selections from the letters to the editor, with editorial replies by Roquebrune and others. Their most welcome piece of "fan mail" was a postcard from Apollinaire himself; in his own column of miscellaneous literary comment, not unlike "Mare aux grenouilles" in form ("Echos," in *L'Europe Nouvelle*, 13 April 1918), he described *Le Nigog* as "un témoignage du chemin que font par le monde ... les idées modernes françaises" (evidence of the path that modern French ideas are making in the world). *Le Nigog* cartoons and comically platitudinous conversations satirized the middlebrows of Montreal, while poems and short fiction (including a story and four prose poems by Roquebrune) made the journal literary as well as critical. Jean-Guy Hudon (in *La Protée*, 1987) assesses these four prose poems, along with those collected in *L'Invitation à la vie*, as noteworthy, indeed path-breaking, antecedents of the prose poem in Quebec and seriously regrets that the poet in Roquebrune so soon gave way to the novelist. For all its limitations, *Le Nigog* was an important event in Quebec cultural history, one only now receiving a thorough study of its place at the forefront of Quebec modernism; the brief studies in *La Protée* (1987) will be followed shortly by a volume of *Archives des lettres canadiennes* (no. 7), to be devoted entirely to a reassessment of *Le Nigog,* and thus, in part, to a reassessment of Robert de Roquebrune.

The further, perhaps more easily resolvable, paradox is that of his continual commitment to Quebec history, to the celebration of French-Canadian civilization at its various plateaus of achievement, while largely resident in France. It seems as if separation in space demanded expression in terms of separation in time, with spatial expatriation turned into temporal nostalgia. Chiasmically, his French-Canadian works were designed, at least in part, to explain Quebec to the French, as, earlier, *Le Nigog* had been designed to bring France to the Quebecois. Roquebrune was an inspired amateur, suggests Duhamel, a man of cultivation, refinement, and great charm, memorable above all as "un Français du Canada" who refused to cut the thread tying him to France. Perhaps one may feel some nostalgia for him, as a last representative of the French Canada he celebrated.

References:

André -G. Bourassa, *Surréalisme et littérature québécoise* (Montreal: Herbes Rouges, 1986), pp. 60, 90, 114, 117;

Robert Charbonneau, *Romanciers canadiens* (Quebec: Presses de l'Université Laval, 1972), pp. 99-105;

Pauline Collet, "Robert de Roquebrune aux yeux du souvenir," *Livres et Auteurs Canadiens* (1968): 220-227;

Roger Duhamel, "Robert de Roquebrune," *Cahiers de l'Académie Canadienne-Française* (Montreal), 14 (1972): 5-18;

Armand Guilmette, "*Le Nigog* et la modernité," *Protée* (Chicoutimi), 15, no. 1 (1987): 63-66;

Jean-Guy Hudon, "De la modernité poétique de Roquebrune," *Protée* (Chicoutimi), 15, no. 1 (1987): 67-80;

Hudon, "Robert de Roquebrune: Entre la fiction et l'autobiographie," Ph.D. thesis, Université Laval, 1981;

Maurice Lemire, *Les Grands Thèmes nationalistes du roman historique canadien-français* (Quebec: Presses de l'Université Laval, 1970), pp. 214-216.

Papers:
The Fonds Robert Laroque de Roquebrune are at the Public Archives, Ottawa.

Gabrielle Roy

(22 March 1909-13 July 1983)

Helen Hoy
University of Lethbridge

BOOKS: *Bonheur d'occasion*, 2 volumes (Montreal: Société des Editions Pascal, 1945); translated by Hannah Josephson as *The Tin Flute* (Toronto: McClelland & Stewart, 1947; New York: Reynal & Hitchcock, 1947; London: Heinemann, 1948); French version revised (Paris: Flammarion, 1947); translated by Alan Brown (Toronto: McClelland & Stewart, 1980);

La Petite Poule d'eau (Montreal: Beauchemin, 1950); translated by Harry Lorin Binsse as *Where Nests the Water Hen* (Toronto: McClelland & Stewart, 1951; New York: Harcourt, Brace, 1951; London: Heinemann, 1952);

Alexandre Chenevert (Montreal: Beauchemin, 1954); translated by Binsse as *The Cashier* (Toronto: McClelland & Stewart, 1955; New York: Harcourt, Brace, 1955; London: Heinemann, 1956);

Rue Deschambault (Montreal: Beauchemin, 1955); translated by Binsse as *Street of Riches* (Toronto: McClelland & Stewart, 1957; New York: Harcourt, Brace, 1957);

La Montagne secrète (Montreal: Beauchemin, 1961); translated by Binsse as *The Hidden Mountain* (Toronto: McClelland & Stewart, 1962; New York: Harcourt, Brace & World, 1962);

La Route d'Altamont (Montreal: HMH, 1966); translated by Joyce Marshall as *The Road past Altamont* (Toronto: McClelland & Stewart, 1966; New York: Harcourt, Brace & World, 1966);

La Rivière sans repos (Montreal: Beauchemin, 1970); abridged edition, translated by Marshall as *Windflower* (Toronto: McClelland & Stewart, 1970);

Cet Eté qui chantait (Quebec: Editions Françaises, 1972); translated by Marshall as *Enchanted Summer* (Toronto: McClelland & Stewart, 1976);

Un Jardin au bout du monde (Montreal: Beauchemin, 1975); translated by Brown as *Garden in the Wind* (Toronto: McClelland & Stewart, 1977);

Ma Vache Bossie (Montreal: Leméac, 1976);

Ces Enfants de ma vie (Montreal: Stanké, 1977); translated by Brown as *Children of My Heart* (Toronto: McClelland & Stewart, 1979);

Fragiles Lumières de la terre: Ecrits divers, 1942-1970 (Montreal: Quinze, 1978); translated by Brown as *The Fragile Lights of Earth: Articles and Memories, 1942-1970* (Toronto: McClelland & Stewart, 1982);

Courte-Queue (Montreal: Stanké, 1979); translated by Brown as *Cliptail* (Toronto: McClelland & Stewart, 1980);

De quoi t'ennuies-tu, Eveline? (Montreal: Editions du Sentier, 1982); enlarged as *De quoi t'ennuies-tu, Eveline? Suivi de Ely! Ely! Ely! Récits* (Montreal: Boréal Express, 1984);

La Détresse et l'enchantement (Montreal: Boréal Express, 1984); translated by Patricia Claxton as *Enchantment and Sorrow: The Autobiography of Gabrielle Roy* (Toronto: Lester & Orpen Dennys, 1987);

La Pékinoise et l'Espagnole (Montreal: Stanké, 1987).

In 1945 novelist Gabrielle Roy helped create a new direction for francophone literature in Canada with *Bonheur d'occasion* (translated as *The Tin Flute*, 1947), a frank and uncompromising examination of urban misery. Her subsequent works of fiction are characterized by simplicity, compassion, a bittersweet tone, and a concentration on those Roy called "the gentle people." The muted delicacy of her work suggests the watercolor, to use Gérard Tougas's image; at the same time her themes are substantial, exploring one's place in the human family, in the natural world, and in relation to oneself.

In an interview with Donald Cameron (published in his *Conversations with Canadian Novelists*, 1973), Roy said, "I have no sooner seen the splendour of life than I feel obliged, physically obliged, to look down and also take notice of the

Gabrielle Roy

sad and of the tragic in life." The same duality is revealed in another of her comments, reported by Joan Hind-Smith in *Three Voices* (1975): "indeed without hope life would not be a tragedy." Her works, particularly her early ones, alternate dramatically between a poignant sense of individual isolation, social injustice, the power of time, loss, and the pathos of human resilience, and the same world seen through more childlike eyes, with hope and joy. So, a novel of playfulness, lyrical nostalgia, and affectionate irony may follow one of social protest or personal anguish. (Several photographs of Roy capture this same ambivalence: either something truly amusing has just caught her fancy or she has only momentarily been distracted from a brooding sorrow.)

Gabrielle Roy, born 22 March 1909 in Saint-Boniface, Manitoba (now part of Winnipeg), was the youngest of eleven children, eight of whom survived. Both her parents had come from Quebec, and her mother, the former Mélina Landry, kept the dream of Quebec alive with stories of the gentle hills and trees of St. Alphonse. Roy's father, Léon, from the village of Beaumont, became an agent for the federal Department of Colonization in Manitoba and Saskatchewan. The tranquillity and security of village life in Saint-Boniface and the beckoning immensities of prairie sky and land had an equally strong effect on the young Gabrielle's imagination.

Financial stringencies precluded university, and so, in 1927, the year of her father's death, Roy enrolled at the Winnipeg Normal Institute. When her studies were completed she took first a one-month summer teaching position in Marchand (inspiration for "L'Enfant morte" in the 1972 story collection *Cet Eté qui chantait*), then in the fall a teaching post in Cardinal, near Somerset (commemorated in "Gagner ma vie" in the 1955 *Rue Deschambault*). From 1930 to 1937 she taught boys at the Institut Collégial Provencher in Saint-Boniface. Having arranged passage to Europe, despite her mother's uncomprehending objections, and with several free months before the trip, Roy traveled in June of 1937 to the remote Little Water Hen district of Manitoba for two months' teaching, a revelatory but lonely experience which ten years later found expression in the 1950 collection *La Petite Poule d'eau*. Roy sailed to London in September of 1937 and studied acting for six months at the Guildhall School of Music and Drama. Deciding she preferred creative to interpretive art, she traveled in England and France and began writing articles on Europe and on Canada for newspapers in Saint-Boniface and Paris.

On her return to Canada before the war in 1939 Roy chose, despite the pull of home, to settle in Montreal, which became the center for her travels through Quebec and Canada, her investigations into Quebec society and urban and industrial growth, and her journalism, often on such subjects, for *Le Jour*, *La Revue Moderne*, and later *Le Bulletin des Agriculteurs*. (Her journalism and her uncollected short stories are listed in Paul Socken's bibliography in the first volume of *The Annotated Bibliography of Canada's Major Authors*, 1979, while several of her articles–on Canada's immigrant peoples, on Manitoba, Quebec, and France, on her writings, and on Expo '67–are published in *Fragiles Lumières de la terre*, 1978.) Moved by her walks through the working-class district of Saint-Henri in Montreal and convinced that the tale inspired by the place was so obvious someone else might tell it first, Roy began work on *Bonheur d'occasion* in 1941.

Although the book appeared too late to be the gift it was intended to be for Mélina Roy (who died in 1943, two years before the novel's publication), *Bonheur d'occasion* met with a startling success, welcomed for its innovative subject matter (breaking with the tradition of the soil), its manner (unflinchingly honest rather than sentimental), and its language (the vernacular of the street). In his 1958 introduction to the English translation, Hugo McPherson wrote, "I remember a year in that exciting decade that followed the Second World War when people kept asking each other: 'Have you read *The Tin Flute*? It's Canada's most devastating novel,'" and it remains Roy's best-known novel. Gérard Bessette characterized it, in his *Une Littérature en ébullition* (1968), as the first urban novel worthy of the name in a fiction predominantly regional and rural, and François Ricard (in *Gabrielle Roy*, 1975, the best early study of Roy's works) described it as transcending the sterile alternative of regionalism and exoticism and inaugurating the contemporary period for the Quebecois novel. Roy became the first Canadian to win the French Prix Fémina and, in 1947, the year of her marriage to Dr. Marcel Charbotte, the first woman to be made a fellow of the Royal Society of Canada. Her novel, in the English version, became the May 1947 selection for the Literary Guild of America and won a Governor General's Award as well as the Royal Society of Canada's Lorne Pierce Medal. *Bonheur d'occasion* was translated into at least eight languages, and within twenty years it had sold over a million copies.

By Roy's account the driving force behind *Bonheur d'occasion* was indignation, indignation at the waste of human energy and hope observed in Saint-Henri. The novel's function in impelling social change is underlined in her 1947 address "Retour à Saint-Henri" (included in *Fragiles Lumières de la terre*), in which she describes the sense of futility for the author who observes the repetition of those miseries which earlier demanded documentation. (By the time of her early 1970s interview with Donald Cameron and in accord with a shift in her own emphasis, Roy stressed the novel's concern with the human condition rather than just with social desperation.)

Bonheur d'occasion focuses on two lives: that of Rose-Anna Lacasse, gentle, harassed, and determined mother of ten, scheming to manage a cramped and impoverished household and expecting yet another child, and that of her oldest daughter, Florentine, febrile, moody, determined to escape her mother's lot but, failing to win the ambitious Jean Lévesque who could free her from Saint-Henri and pregnant with his child, settling for the "bonheur d'occasion" ("bargain-basement happiness") of marriage to the idealistic Emmanuel Letourneau. Interwoven with these stories is detailed description of street life in the district and particularly discussions, at neighborhood gathering places, of work, war, unemployment, and social inequity. The central irony around which the novel revolves is that war offers the only salvation for the men of Saint-Henri.

The manuscript for *Bonheur d'occasion*, 800 pages in all, was longer than the text printed in the 532-page, two-volume first edition. Among the deletions were discussions of the war which Roy wisely decided were repetitive and overly explicit. The novel benefits from Roy's experience in journalism in its painstaking documentation of the sights, sounds, and smells of the district. In addition Roy introduces a new realism in her use of the distinctive Quebecois *joual*, the language of the street, with its native expressions, anglicisms, and English turns of phrase, colloquialisms, and original pronunciations. So, in the dialogue, one finds "chiquer la guenille" for "to grumble," "faire le train" for "to make a racket," "à boutte" for "finished off," "ben" for "bien," "icitte" for "ici," "cout' " for "écoute," "astheur" (or "nowadays") as a corruption of "à cette heure," anglicisms such as "au party," "l'overtime," and "c'est swell," and such exclamations as "vinguienne." The same *joual* appears, but much less frequently, in her next few works, and Roy subsequently expressed concerns about the danger of "le language 'canayen' " in fiction. The freshness of the language, however, is one of the strengths of *Bonheur d'occasion* and stimulated interest especially in critics in France.

Structurally, *Bonheur d'occasion*, employing omniscient narration, moves regularly among three equally important settings–homes, the streets (the characters do a considerable amount of walking), and public establishments. Chapters are unified in several different ways: by place, as the reader surveys the thoughts of several different characters gathered together; by point of view, as he or she follows an individual from place to place; and by a process of transfer, as the reader shifts from one center of consciousness to another after two characters have met. The constant shift of setting and the amount of action set outside the home convey the degree to which the characters are socially and psychologically dispossessed. The characters do possess their district in a sense, and it can be seen as an extension of the home, but this situation is double-edged. Except during the Lacasses' abortive trip to Saint-Denis and some ironic glimpses of prosperous Westmount, the novel never leaves the district. The parade of soldiers tramping off to war and death signifies one of the few paths of escape, and the surrounding mountain and spires suggest entrapment. Ironically the repeated images of trains and ships have realistic significance in the acrid smoke, the noise, the soot they discharge, but they do not fill their conventional function as symbols of freedom, except as a grim joke. The penultimate image of the novel, of "un arbre, dans un fond de cour, qui poussait ses branches tordues entre les fils électriques et un réseau de cordes à linge. Ses feuilles dures et ratatineés semblaient à demi mortes de fatigue avant même de s'être pleinement ouvertes" ("a tree in a backyard, its branches tortured among electric wires and clotheslines, its leaves dry and shrivelled before they were fully out") symbolizes, a little heavy-handedly, both the tragedy and the limited triumph of these characters, in a social environment in which they cannot flourish and from which they cannot flee.

Thematically, Roy illustrates the emotional impoverishment caused by financial hardship. In their own need to survive, the characters have become indifferent to universal suffering as exemplified by the war. Even Rose-Anna, temperamentally the most compassionate of the characters, has learned to be sparing of her sympathy, preserving it for the many demands of her immediate family and, even there, forced to look first to physical rather than emotional needs. Florentine, more tragically, feels that gentleness, in the shape of her beloved but unreliable father, has blighted their lives, and she has resolved to expunge such emotion from her life. Roy reveals, in place of sentimental notions of the ennobling effect of poverty, how need makes Rose-Anna momentarily mean and calculating and how, once money is lacking, the strong ties between her and her husband Azarius are strained.

There is no escape for the reader from what Roy called the essential bitterness of this world. The characters often indulge in dreams of past and future, but, as Gérard Bessette has pointed out in *Une Littérature en ébullition*, the dream is undercut by an abrupt return to reality, for the reader and often for the character–for Azarius, for instance, who reawakens from fantasies of adventure to the overflowing rusty laundry basin. The few idyllic interludes are associated with the past or with the country and prove to be illusory. The most significant idyll is the one Rose-Anna anticipates in preparing to revisit the maple bush at her home in Saint-Denis, and the dream leads only to humiliation, disappointment, and fresh disasters.

There are a few slightly hopeful notes, indications of human strength, near the novel's end. Rose-Anna, after imagining death as a kind of release, is buoyed up once more by the urgent claims on her love, after the birth of her latest child, and Florentine, newly married, enjoys for the first time the comfort of doing what is wise and right in resisting the temptation to display herself in front of Jean Lévesque. (Ironically, this moral victory seems to grow out of her greater financial security.) On the larger social level, Florentine's husband, Emmanuel, receives the hope that there is some purpose to the war, that it is fought to end wars. The final effect of the novel, though, is its insistence on the unpleasant reality of what life is for the people of Saint-Henri, rather than on the more alluring possibilities of what was or could be or is somewhere else. What hope grows out of *Bonheur d'occasion* lies, really, outside the novel, in the impetus for change it may provide for the reader.

On the psychological level, the novel reveals a certain naturalistic tendency in its portrayal of the cycle of the generations. Although Florentine's youthful dreams may be contrasted with Rose-Anna's fatigued litany of troubles, the contrasts (of Florentine's grim wedding day and Rose-Anna's joyous one, for instance) more often heighten the disadvantages with which Florentine enters the same course of existence. Their simultaneous pregnancies symbolize their shared subjection to inexorable processes. Florentine's face with its "faiblesse héréditaire, la misère profonde qu'elle perpétuait" ("hereditary weakness, the deep misery of which she was an extension") already reveals the stupefied image of the old woman she will become, while Rose-Anna, in spite of herself, falls into the warnings and maxims of her mother, even into the resigned and helpless gesture of stroking the edge of her chair, and, like her own mother during the visit to Saint-Denis, fails to provide support for her daughter when it is most needed.

This interest in familial relations and emotional complexities continues in Roy's later works; what is distinctive about *Bonheur d'occasion* is the degree of socioeconomic analysis. Although not Roy's only somber novel, it is the only one which functions in large part as a social critique, implying at least a direction for change. (In later works suffering seems to be a product more of human nature than of social organization and so to be less easily resolvable. In addition, in the later Cameron interview, Roy warns of the dangers, for the writer's judgment, of political involvement, and chooses the role of the bird who sings at the prison bars rather than that of the activist fighting for the prisoner.) The political pondering of the male characters in *Bonheur d'occasion* (rather obtrusive in its expository function) exposes the depressed wages, the unemployment, and the priority given oak, brass, and stone over human limbs and lives. Emmanuel–who serves rather too blatantly to carry the novel's social commentary–formulates the central issue, the moral question underlying the economic criticism, when he asks, "De la richesse, de l'esprit, qui donc devait encore se sacrifier?" ("Which of the two, wealth or spirit, should sacrifice itself ?").

An urgent and moving portrayal of ordinary people caught in an inhospitable urban, industrial society, *Bonheur d'occasion* succeeds be-

cause it embodies its theme in fresh, accurately observed, sensory details. The novel does have weaknesses. While the women characters are convincing in their complexity, some male characters are less successful, with Emmanuel idealized and Jean methodically constructed. Furthermore, the omniscient narration, here as in later works, involves what Gérard Bessette has called "le brouillage," or interference, a confused mingling of narrator's and character's perspectives. The structuring of the novel is conservative, occasionally mechanical. On the whole, however, *Bonheur d'occasion* has retained its emotional power over the years. It is better served by Alan Brown's 1980 translation (which has been quoted here) than by Hannah Josephson's earlier one, which was stilted and inaccurate at times and which failed to capture the flavor of the Quebecois dialogue. Roy requested a Canadian translator for her next work and, fluent in English, began to work closely with her translators.

In 1947 Roy met and married Dr. Marcel Charbotte and with him traveled to France where they spent the next three years, with excursions to other parts of Europe. Near the beginning of this visit, Roy established a friendship with French paleontologist and theorist Pierre Teilhard de Chardin, whose belief in the human future she drew on for her own philosophy. In a 1956 preface to *La Petite Poule d'eau* (republished in *Fragiles Lumières de la terre*), Roy tells readers that it was amid signs of civilization's triumphs and failures, the Cathedral at Chartres and the ruins of the war, that her imagination turned to the simple, peaceful world of her second book in what is a dramatic shift from the mood of her first novel.

Particularly with her early writing, but to a lesser extent throughout her career (*La Montagne secrète*, 1961, is the notable exception), Roy's works alternate in a pendulum movement between two poles that Hugo McPherson has called the cage and the garden, the world of experience and the world of innocence. The alternation is also one between the settings of the city and the country; between (in Roy's words to Donald Cameron) "solidarity, life with others, and primitivism, or life with the God-given universe"; between the settings of Quebec and Manitoba; between present and past; between, in François Ricard's distinction, alienation and reconciliation; between loss and hope. In untraditional fashion, perhaps, Roy began in the world of experience with *Bonheur d'occasion* and, while alternating regularly between the two modes of vision, showed an overall shift in emphasis toward the world of innocence. The former mode, in its careful documentation of social complexities and personal impasses, might be called realistic, while the latter somewhat more clearly suggests the pastoral.

Roy revealed that in her second book, *La Petite Poule d'eau* (1950; translated as *Where Nests the Water Hen*, 1951), she created not so much a piece of regional realism as the simple ideal world of the imagination, distanced in time and place, the world of pastoral, when she said to Donald Cameron, "it's . . . a dream-like sort of story; it's life such as it might have been, or could have been, or could be. It's *at the beginning of all time*," and, in her preface to the work, "hélas. . . . ce n'est que très loin, *au bout du monde*, dans une très petite communauté humaine, que l'espoir est encore vraiment libre" ("only at that distance, *at the world's end*, in a tiny human community, could hope still move and breathe" [italics added]). *La Petite Poule d'eau*, set in the isolated reaches of northern Manitoba (and significantly, as far as pastoral goes, on a sheep farm), is composed of three connected but self-contained segments: a relatively short account of the annual excursion of Luzina Tousignant, mother of eight, from the family's remote island to give birth to her latest child; the crucial story of the school and sequence of three teachers that the Tousignants manage to obtain for their children; and the story of Father Joseph-Marie, the Capuchin priest of the district, and of his visit to the Tousignants. Simplicity and affection are both the subject matter and the tone of this work.

In structure *La Petite Poule d'eau* rejects a linear development, since the final episode, of the Capuchin's visit, belongs, chronologically, in the midst of the second segment, during the sojourn of the first teacher, Mlle Côté, at Little Water Hen. The work also seems to violate notions of symmetry and proportion in following up two segments on the Tousignant family with an abrupt focus on the hitherto unintroduced figure of Father Joseph-Marie, relegating the Tousignants to the background for the duration of the book. The explanation for the apparent disunity may be in the return it allows to the pastoral world of artlessness and human harmony, to the period before that world begins to succumb to the forces of the outside world and before "l'ancienne maladie" ("the ancient illness"), the desire for knowledge and wider horizons brought by Mlle Côté, has begun its depredations of the

Tousignant household. There is symmetry then in that two images of the world of innocence (dominated by its two major representatives, Luzina and Father Joseph-Marie) surround and contain the account of challenges to that world.

In the opening narrative the ingenuous tone of the narrator, playfully withholding the true purpose of Luzina's "congé" ("holiday") and the nature of "son paquet le plus precieux" ("her most fragile gift"), is as important as Luzina's own childlike benevolence and good humor in establishing the sense of a serene and natural world. *La Petite Poule d'eau* is populated with innocents: Luzina, welcoming the government's "cadeaux" ("gifts") for the school; Hippolyte, meditating as he navigates his rocking chair at full speed around the kitchen, enveloped in pipe smoke and weighed down with children; and Father Joseph-Marie, delighting in the good joke he has played on his Protestant friend in having her illness cured by Saint Joseph. The natural setting and repeated imagery of birds, whose circumstances often parallel those of the characters (made explicit in the Capuchin's simple-hearted sermon on the birds), reinforce one's sense of an untainted world. Central to the story is the conviction of Luzina and Father Joseph-Marie (inspired in large part by their own happy effect on people) that human nature is excellent, that the various races can come together in harmony. Ironically, human community is possible here because of the solitude, whereas in *Bonheur d'occasion* personal alienation accompanies the crowded conditions of the city. The idyllic nature of life at Little Water Hen is made explicit when Luzina, anticipating God's annual visit to the island (through the offices of the Capuchin), wonders, "Que demander de plus vraiment, à moins de souhaiter le ciel sur terre!" ("What more could you ask, truly, unless it were to wish for Heaven upon earth!").

Seen without the generous vision of the protagonists, situations—especially the loneliness—and characters—calculating Abe Zlutkin, aloof Nick Sluzick, stingy Isaac Boussorvsky—could be judged in a much harsher light. Inflexible Miss O'Rorke, the malcontent in Arcadia, even questions whether sheep are compatible with tranquillity. But the narrator adopts the affectionate simplicity of tone of her characters so that the reader is able to enjoy the humor and irony which grow out of their naivete while sharing and appreciating the good will and serenity they have achieved. One experiences what William

Gabrielle Roy, circa 1950 (courtesy of Kenneth Landry)

Empson in *Some Versions of Pastoral* (1950) calls "the double attitude . . . of the complex man to the simple one," of being in one way better, in another not so good. The possibilities of the simple life which Little Water Hen represents are affirmed (along with Roy's recurring theme of conflicting human needs for adventure and security) in the symbolic departure of the third teacher, M. Dubreuil, from the contentment of the island: "Si le bonheur n'était pas si facile, est ce qu'on lui tournerait ainsi le dos, tout calme, en sifflotant?" ("If this happiness were not so easy, would you thus casually leave it behind, calmly and whistling some little tune?").

Complexities are hinted at in this passage, and, in true pastoral tradition, *La Petite Poule d'eau* does allude to the world of experience which encircles and gives value to the island ideal. From the first humbling letter of Mlle Côté, Luzina's position as authority and as center of her family is challenged until finally she is figuratively and literally left behind by her children. The much-treasured education, along with the pressure of time itself, means irrevocable changes. The Capuchin's dealings with the mer-

chant Bessette on behalf of the Métis expose injustices, and their squandering of the money the Capuchin has won for them suggests to him that "sans doute, n'était-il pas au pouvoir des hommes de faire le bonheur des autres, ni même de corriger l'injustice" ("it was not in men's power to create the happiness of others or even to allay injustice"). Similarly the rectitude of Luzina and others, revealed in the confessional, oppresses Father Joseph-Marie with the "l'inépuisable somme de bonté dans le monde, la tragique, parfaite bonne volonté de tant d'humains et qui n'arrivait quand même pas â changer le monde" ("inexhaustible sum of goodness on earth, the tragic, perfect good will of so many human beings, which all the same did not succeed in changing the world"). Happiness in itself can paradoxically be a source of pain. Characters, in this book as in others, appreciate best what they have left behind. The more sated with joy they are, the more insatiable they become. Father Joseph-Marie, in an interesting anticipation of Alexandre Chenevert in Roy's next novel, is grieved by his very inability to convey how easy happiness can be. The world's pain, epitomized by an anxious and agonized childbirth the Capuchin has witnessed, remains inexplicable, as inexplicable as joy and love.

Without reducing life's arbitrariness and suffering, Roy counters with the characters' confiding trust in God: "peut-être, avec Dieu, fallait-il se passer d'explications. Quel mérite y aurait-il, autrement, à la confiance!" ("perhaps with God we had to do without explanations. Otherwise, what merit would there be in trusting Him!"). The narrative depicts the acceptance of inequity; whereas other novels of Roy's stress inequity, *La Petite Poule d'eau* focuses on and cherishes the acceptance. This curious ability on Roy's part to shift anguish from foreground to background and back to foreground from one work to the next may be explained by a passage in the later *Rue Deschambault*: "nos pensées ont un grand et curieux pouvoir sur les choses; elles peuvent certains jours faire paraître belle une vieille bicoque grise; mais il leur arrive aussi de rendre très laid quelque chose qui ne l'est peut-être pas en soi" ("our thoughts have a great and curious power over things; on certain days they can make seem beautiful some wretched grey hovel; yet it can also happen that they make very ugly something that is not such in itself"). There are dark touches in the last two segments of the work, realities symbolized perhaps by the hawks and other birds of prey whose power of flight is not acknowledged in the Capuchin's metaphor of the birds. Like the sermon, however, *La Petite Poule d'eau* downplays the tragic, ending with the social joy of the square dance and with Father Joseph-Marie's conclusion, after giving the gracious old civilization its due, that "plus il était monté haut dans le Nord, et plus il avait été libre d'aimer" ("the farther he had gone into the North, the more he had been free to love"). *La Petite Poule d'eau* defines one of the two poles of human possibility in Roy's work, as *Bonheur d'occasion* does the other.

Alexandre Chenevert (1954; translated as *The Cashier*, 1955), story of "l'âme captive" ("the captive soul") of a bank clerk, was begun in France and finished in Canada, to which the Charbottes returned in 1950. From 1952 until her death in 1983, Roy and her husband lived in Quebec City with a summer home at Petite-Rivière-Saint-François, the place of the enchanted summer commemorated in *Cet Eté qui chantait*.

Alexandre Chenevert provides a dyspeptic view of many of the realities presented genially in *La Petite Poule d'eau*. Set, like *Bonheur d'occasion*, in downtown Montreal (although emphasizing less the poverty and more the anonymity, overcrowding, and frenetic bustle of urban life), the novel returns to a purgatorial world. Since it is an internal purgatory in this case, *Alexandre Chenevert* tends toward psychological realism rather than the social realism of Roy's first work.

"Un petit homme sans dons particuliers" ("a small man without any special gifts") but affected with a hypersensitivity to the world's problems and to the incongruence between his intellectual-spiritual existence and the body with which he is encumbered, the protagonist is living demonstration that "les hommes n'étaient pas tous doués pour le bonheur" ("not all men were endowed for happiness"). Chenevert is plagued by an awareness of life's complexity: the stevedores' strike in the news wastes food while people elsewhere starve, yet the workers need the kind of leverage the strike provides to achieve their rights; Chenevert's taxes oppress him but he does not wish to deprive the widow Mathieu of her social assistance; life is both too short and too long. The small happinesses of others, his wife Eugénie's joy at his gift of flowers, for instance, reproach him with reminders of how cheaply such happiness can be bought. And even his own unhappiness is an added source of torment since he realizes that, in the context of world misery,

he has no right to be unhappy. Alexandre Chenevert scrupulously assures his doctor that most of the world's people are decent, but, in contrast with *La Petite Poule d'eau*, the conviction is a theoretical rather than deeply felt one for most of the novel. With an omniscient narrator, the reader stands outside Chenevert's experience, sees him, as his friend Godias does, as "un homme aigre, contrariant" ("a sharp, contentious man"), and realizes that his gloomy vision is colored by his physical ailments and his morose frame of mind. This does not, however, alleviate the unpleasantness of the world depicted, any more than is the sunniness of the previous novel reduced by the awareness there that the characters themselves elicit or magnify the goodwill they admire in others. In both cases, the narrator stays very close to the characters' vision.

There is a pastoral interlude in the midst of Chenevert's distress, a true respite and not simply a mirage like that pursued in *Bonheur d'occasion*. This interlude forms the central segment of the novel's tripartite structure, each segment ending with a significant departure, from the city, from the country, and ultimately, for Chenevert, from life. The idyll is anticipated (and its end foreshadowed) by the coming of spring. So brief and so welcome, the Montreal spring is described as suggesting man's infinite possibilities, communicating the Creator's love, and forging strange fragile links of kindness. Chenevert sees himself as a "réfugié" awaiting "un rapatriement" ("a return to [his] native soil") and, at Lac Vert under the protection, significantly, of a family named Le Gardeur, finally experiences "la plus belle journée de son existence" ("the most beautiful day of his life"). To settle at Lac Vert is less important than to have known it: "Croire au Paradis terrestre, voilà ce qui avait été indispensable" ("To believe in an earthly paradise—that is what he so deeply needed"). In this prelapsarian world, it is as if God has "eût pardonné à Alexandre toutes les fautes commises depuis le commencement des siècles" ("forgiven Alexandre all the sins committed since the beginning of the centuries"). As it is lifted, one sees the full measure of the excessive burden Alexandre has assumed, and, more important and ironic, Alexandre is able to forgive God the suffering of the world. As in pastoral, the escape is only temporary, a preparation for return to complex realities.

The last section of the novel records Alexandre's attempts, particularly after he discovers that he is dying of cancer, to harmonize the two aspects of life demonstrated earlier, as represented now by the intense suffering God proves capable of inflicting and the kindliness of others which Chenevert suddenly experiences in abundance. It is, ironically, the latter which reconciles him to the former: "Si Dieu avait autant de coeur qu'un homme, déjà ce serait beau" ("If God had as much heart as a man, that would already be a fine thing"). At the same time, Roy suggests that the heaven on earth Chenevert discovers in human fellowship is possibly only because his imminent death heightens feelings toward him and that the pleasure is mingled with anguish, in Eugénie and Alexandre's distressed, almost unwelcome, discovery, so late, that they love each other, for example.

The final affirmation of the novel is a mixed one. Alexandre attempts to see, in the chain of transmitted anguish running from his mother through himself to his daughter and her son, God's means of ensuring human connectedness. And the gentleness on his dying face seems to say that "la seule assurance, sur terre, vient de notre déraisonnable tendresse humaine" ("the only assurance on earth comes from that tenderness for human beings which goes furthest beyond the bounds of reason"). We are left less with a resolution, though, than with Chenevert's tortured, hopeless struggle, as a reflective and conscientious man, to take responsibility for and to understand the principles underlying everything from the future financial well-being of his family to peace in the world. The title of the novel is appropriate because what the book presents, above all, is the troubled person who is Alexandre Chenevert.

Roy's first two novels are best known to the general public; her first and third, her most somber, have received perhaps the greatest critical attention.

In 1954 Roy's somewhat reluctant drafting of "Souvenirs du Manitoba" at the request of the Royal Society of Canada reopened for her the world of her childhood in Saint-Boniface. ("Souvenirs" was published in *Mémoires de la Société Royale du Canada,* June 1954.) From these memories eventually came two linked collections of first-person short stories centering on the semi-autobiographical heroine, Christine. The first of these, *Rue Deschambault* (1955; translated as *Street of Riches,* 1957), published the year before Roy was awarded the Prix Duvernay for her work, contains almost a score of separate sketches spanning

Christine's life from early childhood through adolescence and emphasizing themes of human desire and vulnerability. The stories are basically arranged chronologically, with a substantial leap in time occurring between the very young Christine presenting strawberries to her neighbor in "L'Italienne" and the high-school-age Christine receiving her first suitor in the subsequent story, "Wilhelm." The gap is minimized by the expanded time frame of the story that precedes "L'Italienne," "Ma Tante Thérésina Veilleux," and by the double perspective in time of "L'Italienne," which employs the adolescent Christine's memories of an earlier event. There is nevertheless a certain choppiness or discontinuity about the collection if viewed as a single narrative. In addition, some stories–"Les Deux nègres" or "Les Bijoux," for instance–are considerably slighter than others.

The incidents recounted in *Rue Deschambault* are often far from idyllic: the attempt to prevent the marriage of a sister links permanently (in Christine's mind) the idea of love with fear for human vulnerability; after a dangerous fever, Christine's sister Alicia retreats in despair at human suffering into the impenetrable recesses of her mind; the effervescent Italian neighbor, who brings a joy like the sun, is killed; aspiring to be a writer, Christine is warned that the future is always something of a defeat. The stories involving Christine's father, Edouard, are particularly dark (and moving) in their examination of a man who has become a stranger to joy while, like Alexandre Chenevert, painfully alert to manifestations of suffering. In "Le Puits de Dunrea" the destruction by fire of Edouard's Edenic Ruthenian settlement and, worse, his experience of a nihilistic indifference inspired by the nearness of death contribute to an infernal vision.

Yet the desolation of that story is encapsulated and kept at a distance, set in the past and narrated at thirdhand as Christine's narrative of her sister Agnès's account of their father's story. Basically the reader experiences the child's eye view of these realities, with the security heightened, not destroyed, by reminders of vulnerability and impermanence. "Tous les voyages de ma vie, depuis," Christine remarks, "n'ont été que des retours en arrière pour tâcher de ressaisir ce que j'avais tenu dans le hamac et sans le chercher" ("All my life's voyages ever since," Christine remarks, describing the beauties of nature and the languorous peace of a childhood recuperation, "have merely been going back to try to recapture what I had possessed in that hammock–and without seeking it"). Emotionally, one dwells more with the child in the hammock or with the child attempting to comprehend the sinking of the *Titanic* (as Christine does in "Le *Titanic*") than, figuratively speaking, with the distraught passenger of the *Titanic* recalling with longing the innocence and safety of childhood. Although readers are warned that the happiness of the warm and loving classroom protected from the winter gales has a rarity which Christine, as a young schoolteacher, fails then to recognize, still *Rue Deschambault* concludes with her youthful confidence: "Est-ce que le monde n'était pas un enfant? Est-ce que nous n'étions pas au matin? . . ." ("Was not all the world a child? Were we not at the day's morning? . . ."). The English version of this work won Roy her second Governor General's Award, in 1958.

One might expect, in keeping with Roy's alternation of dark and light, that her next work, *La Montagne secrète* (1961; translated as *The Hidden Mountain*, 1962), would be a realistic novel of experience, but here Roy breaks with previous patterns. The novel, the story of an artist's development in the wilderness of northern Canada, was inspired by painter René Richard, whom Roy had met as early as 1943 and with whom she kept in contact during her summers in Charlevoix, Quebec. There are elements of pastoral innocence in *La Montagne secrète* in that the protagonist Pierre Cadorai is identified as a natural genius, ninety percent life and ten percent theory, and strongly associated with nature rather than with society. His self-portrait, late in the novel, even contains a suggestion of antlers. At the same time, though, the account is not idealized by being set in the past nor in childhood. In Pierre's gaining of experience, there is much that might remind one of Roy's "realistic" novels: the physical difficulties, Pierre's discovery that the suffering of animals is limitless and beyond acceptance, his painful identification with the caribou he must kill, the reproach that his art has failed to capture the mountain (his greatest challenge), and the concluding death not only of Pierre but also, and more significant, of "ce qui meurt d'inexprimé, avec une vie" ("that which dies unexpressed within a soul"). And yet, the stages of Pierre's progress are too clearly representative (allegorical, some have said), and the details of his physical adventure parallel and symbolize aspects of his spiritual or artistic adventure too closely, as

Jack Warwick has illustrated in *The Long Journey* (1968), for the term "realistic" to apply.

La Montagne secrète can perhaps best be seen as a romance, the story of a heroic quest with its three stages, the perilous journey, the climactic struggle, and the exaltation of the hero. Like the romantic hero, Pierre faces dangers in unexplored regions, figuratively as well as literally; adventures alone except occasionally for a faithful companion (Steve and later Stanislas); and yet delivers others: "lorsque lui-même se libérait . . . est-ce que du même coup il ne libérait pas aussi d'autres hommes, leur pensée enchaînée, leur esprit souffrant?" ("whenever he himself set himself free, did he not, by that very fact, also set other men free, set free their imprisoned thought, their suffering spirit?"). After the initiatory trials of part one, in part two Pierre, confronting the resplendent mountain which challenges his skill as an artist, triumphs and succeeds in freeing the captive bird imprisoned within his breast. The antagonist Pierre has taken on is a mighty one, nothing less than awe-inspiring, beautiful, but implacable reality; Roy once remarked to Gérard Bessette that the mountain could symbolize God, "si on entend par là tous les envoûtements, la création le grand jeu magnifique et tragique de la création" ("if you understand by that all magic, creation, the great magnificent and tragic game of creation"). In a parallel death-struggle in the next chapter, Pierre overcomes the caribou while armed only with a hatchet. These chapters of crisis may mark not only a triumph for the hero but also the point of his ritual death and disappearance since Pierre returns to find the glory of the mountain changed to threat and his paintings torn to pieces by a bear. He "goût[e] cet anéantissement proche" ("savor[s] the sweet closeness of annihilation"), of despair, and of death, and disappears temporarily from the focus of the narrative. His struggle is still heroic but less purely triumphant.

The recognition of *La Montagne secrète* as romance helps explain the curious shift of part three, when Pierre travels to Paris to see the painting of the masters and to study his craft. Although the section remains weak, with Pierre the flat figure of the untutored genius, its function is that of the third stage of the romantic quest, the discovery or recognition of the hero, qualified by Roy's concern for plausibility and (in Pierre's untimely death) by her insistence on human limitation. Pierre's role as romantic hero explains, too, why he is not shown in complex relationships with others, why his character remains somewhat abstract and his emotions symbolic, why readers are not drawn into close involvement with him as a human being as they are with other Roy characters.

The reception of *La Montagne secrète* was not particularly warm. Critics have responded to it mainly as a source of information on Roy's artistic theories: Pierre's attempts to develop skill with oils when his talent lies in pencil sketches, Jack Warwick speculates provocatively, may be a commentary on Roy's own change of direction with this work. While intriguing as an exploration, in terms of artistic development, of the same dilemmas of freedom and community and of the suffering bound up with beauty which is evident in Roy's other works, *La Montagne secrète* lacks the emotional richness of Roy's realistic novels and the charm and humor of her pastoral ones.

La Route d'Altamont (1966; translated as *The Road past Altamont*, 1966), one of Roy's most substantial later works, returns to the world of Christine's childhood. The four stories are more fully developed and more unified one with another than are those in *Rue Deschambault*. They use the passage of time and the image of the journey to explore the essential unity of youth and age, the mixed blessing of the revival of one generation, within the next, and the need for, but cost of, fresh destinations, wider aspirations. In "Ma Grand-mère tout-puissante," Christine discovers both the godlike creativity and physical vulnerability of her grandmother, while the vastness of the lake visited in "Le Vieillard et l'enfant" opens to her the mysteries of exploration and love as well as of unsatisfied aspiration and death. "Le Déménagement," the least integrated or powerful of the stories, explores the passion for new experiences in Christine's forbidden participation in the excitement of moving day and her disillusioned discovery of an urban shabbiness and hopelessness reminiscent of *Bonheur d'occasion*. And, finally, the important title story, in which Christine's mother, Eveline, chances upon the Altamont hills which restore her youthful joy and later, distraught over her daughter's approaching desertion, is unable to find them again, examines the fruits of love "c'est le seul chemin ... pour avancer un peu hors de soi" ("it's the only way ... to get a little outside one's self ") and the release of solitude. Here Roy presents, too, the sad astonishment and joy of acquiring and understanding, too late to share this discov-

ery, some of the characteristics of one's parents. Together the stories provide a concise formulation of Roy's recurring concerns and of her vision of the interpenetration of human possibilities and limitations. Christine's impression of "la splendeur triste et étrange" ("the splendor and the strange sadness") of her first trip to Lake Winnipeg sums up Roy's view of life and the emphasis of the stories here. The same doubleness is expressed in Eveline's happy reassurance that the hills are real, reassurance which "se teintait d'une tendre mélancolie comme si elle en était un peu, en les trouvant si vraies, à leur dire aussi une sorte d'adieu" ("was tinged with a tender melancholy, perhaps because, finding them so real, she would have to say to them as well a sort of good-by").

La Route d'Altamont begins with the vision of the child; in fact, since the stories are told in retrospect, the narrator's ingenuousness is sometimes overplayed. The final story though moves Christine and the reader firmly and irrevocably into the painful world of experience. As part of the structural unity of the work, the stories, from first to last, cover one full generation, and Christine at the end is part of the adult world, reliving her mother's youthful independence, just as, in the opening story, from the protection of childhood, she has observed the relations of her mother and grandmother.

The year after publication of *La Route d'Altamont*, Roy was elected Companion of the Order of Canada. In 1968 she received an honorary degree from Université Laval and the Medal of the Canada Council.

In 1961 Roy had traveled as guest of a geologist friend to Ungava in northern Quebec and spent a week at the Eskimo settlements of Fort Chimo and Old Fort Chimo. Nine years later, in 1970, *La Rivière sans repos* appeared, composed of three short stories (omitted in the 1970 English translation, *Windflower*) and the title novella, all set in this region. "Les Satellites," the longest of the stories, presents the thrilled introduction of an Eskimo woman, Deborah, to the luxuries of the south where she has been taken for cancer treatment, her subsequent longing for her own people, and her discovery, once back home, that one's needs are never satisfied. The story presents sympathetically her decision to choose death with dignity (on an ice floe) rather than follow the whites' tradition of prolonging her life simply in order to prolong it. More comically, "Le Téléphone" traces simple Barnaby's delight in using his new telephone as a plaything to torment his friends and village officials and ends on a touching note. In "Le Fauteuil roulant" Deborah's aged father, Isaac, in a donated wheelchair, incapable of speech and dependent on the capricious attentiveness of children for his mobility, suffers from being denied the opportunity to end his life as his daughter has.

"La Rivière sans repos" tells the poignant story of an Eskimo girl, Elsa, her attempts to provide her half-white child, Jimmy, with the benefits of civilization, and her eventual loss of him to the other culture. Beginning with the assault by the white soldier which sets the story in motion, the novel exposes, though less emphatically than *Bonheur d'occasion*, the problems of a community (here Fort Chimo) as a result of social change. Central to the story is the pursuit of order and possessions which preoccupies Elsa and alienates her from her indolent and contented family. The cemetery at Old Fort Chimo speaks of the cruel life of the old days but speaks also, "comme pen d'endroits au monde de fraternel accord" ("as do few places in the world, of brotherly accord"). Roy is looking not just at a particular society undergoing change but also at the larger question of progress. Human life is a struggle to go beyond one's limits, says the pastor at the funeral of Elsa's mother, Winnie, and, he adds, it is difficult to determine what carries people forward or not.

As in *Alexandre Chenevert*, Roy portrays, in the middle section of the novel, an attempt to abandon society for the old life of simplicity, as Elsa flees first to Old Fort Chimo and then, at the threat of compulsory schooling for Jimmy, toward Baffin Island. Elsa's father formulates Elsa's dilemma and Roy's sense of the human dilemma as "ce choix trop difficile entre la vie au grand large, fière et imdomptable, ou avec les autres, dans la cage" ("that too difficult choice between life in the great outdoors, proud and self-sufficient, or with the others, in the cage"). In contrast with *Alexandre Chenevert*, the return to the community is presented as less desirable than merely inevitable, as illness necessitates what to Jimmy's imagination is the abandonment of a beautiful, unattained Eden. The advances of civilization exact their price.

The ending of "La Rivière sans repos" has the touch of pessimism found in Roy's earlier novels, while the absence of struggle on Elsa's part in later life makes her story more pathetic. There is a naturalistic sense of determinism when Elsa

sees herself "relayant un jour Winnie dans cette interminable et toujours solitaire procession des generations" ("taking Winnie's place in the interminable and always solitary procession of the generations"). And she does become strikingly like her aimless, roving mother in appearance and attitude. Love, of a sort, does make its unforeseeable reappearance when Elsa, apparently, receives a radio greeting from the absent Jimmy as he flies in a plane overhead. The prevailing image, though, is that of Elsa, dreaming, oblivious, and prematurely aged, scattering the down of a flower, like the fragments of her life, to the wind.

As these details suggest, "La Rivière sans repos" shares with *Bonheur d'occasion* and *Alexandre Chenevert* an emphasis on the restrictions of human existence. Like *La Route d'Altamont*, "La Rivière sans repos" ends in the world of experience while belonging in many ways to the innocent world of *La Petite Poule d'eau* and *Rue Deschambault*. So, too, here, Roy brings the two modes, the realistic and the pastoral, into close contact. Through the remoteness and relative simplicity of the life portrayed and especially through the artlessness of the characters (Elsa's earnest attempt to write a letter to her friend Mme Beaulieu reminds one of Luzina's similarly innocent and comical letter to the schoolteacher), Roy is able to reveal the issues of life's complexity in simpler terms and, in that sense, draw on the techniques of pastoral. The year after publication of *La Rivière sans repos*, Roy was honored by the Quebec government with the Prix David.

"Every writer must eventually write his Ninth Symphony or give in to despair," Roy once wrote to Joan Hind-Smith, and *Cet Eté qui chantait* (1972; translated as *Enchanted Summer*, 1976) is her ode to joy, a series of lyrical sketches epitomizing the lightheartedness and radiance at one end of her spectrum of human possibilities. The incidents on which the delicate, whimsical sketches are based are slight: the presence of M. Toung the bullfrog in his pond, Jeannot the crow's triumphant ride at the swinging tip of a cherry tree, the brilliant flowering of some unreclaimable land after a cow has trampled and fertilized it, Wilbrod the Simple's conversation with himself: "Pis tu te laveras le corps. Pis tu changeras de linge. . . . Pis tu diras tu prière . . ." ("Then you'll wash all over. Then you'll change your underwear. . . . Then you'll say your prayers . . ."). There is no plot although the sketches are structured by a cumulative growth in the complexity of the emotions revealed.

The enchanted summer is not a period of un-alloyed bliss. The fretful killdeer in "Ames en peine" with their song of fear and happiness, dread and trust, are identified with "nous tous, les enfants de la Terre" ("all of us, children of this Earth"). Furthermore, the image of summer it-self implies the presence of other, less beneficent seasons. The enchanted summer, however, is as close to idyllic as is possible on earth. When the narrator wonders why all killdeer cannot find the protected and tranquil spot one pair has, the birds' song provides the concluding words to the volume: "when everyone is happy together, it will be paradise." The simplicity and joy of this idyll are reinforced by the tone of humility which is a characteristic mark of pastoral.

Several details imply that the delight cap-tured here is not the first bloom of innocence but a wiser innocence hard won after tribula-tions. (Interestingly, this is the only one of Roy's "pastoral" works which is set in Quebec rather than in Manitoba and in a time period close to the author's present.) The story "L'Enfant morte" serves this function, reminding readers of the development which has taken place since an earlier naivete. The story belongs to neither the time nor place of the enchanted summer but is evoked by the smell of roses, "parfum que je n'aime plus guère depuis ce juin lointain où j'allai dans le plus pauvre des villages acquérir, comme on dit, de l'expérience!" ("a scent I have not much liked since the long ago June when I went to that poorest of villages–to acquire, as they say, experience!"). Similarly, with aged Martine's much-anticipated trip to the river, life's bitterness is not glossed over but helps enhance the rapture which can accommodate such reali-ties: "Elle se tenait au seuil de l'immensité, avec le regret de ses enfants morts et le souvenir des peines endurées . . . avec la mémoire de l'attente sans fin de ce retour au fleuve. Et tout était pesé dans une mystérieuse balance: l'attente cruelle et cet instant radieux d'aujourd'hui. Et qui sait si ce n'était pas l'instant qui l'emportait!" ("She stood there on the threshold of immensity, with her re-gret for her dead children and the recollection of the troubles she had endured . . . with the mem-ory of her endless waiting for this return to the river. And it was all being weighed in a mysteri-ous balance: the cruel waiting and this radiant in-stant today. And who can say that the instant did not tip the scales!"). The insubstantial subject mat-

ter of *Cet Eté qui chantait* demands a greater-than-usual leap of faith, a suspension of the doubt that this is merely sentimentality and simple-mindedness. Passing references to other, grim-mer realities and, above all, Roy's delicacy of touch and control of tone help counter such reservations.

The simple exuberance of *Cet Eté qui chantait* would be hard to sustain, and Roy does, in fact, return to a less enchanted world in her next work, *Un Jardin au bout du monde* (1975; trans-lated as *Garden in the Wind*, 1977). This is a strangely mixed collection: two stories had been published (one in an earlier version) in 1945 and 1946 and thus seem to belong more, in setting, subject matter, and character, with the stories of *Rue Deschambault*. One of these, "Un Vagabond frappe à notre porte," explores the theme of love and faith through a tramp who poses as the Que-bec relative of a Manitoba family and brings first a return of family love and then, on his second visit, bitter disillusionment to the narrator's fa-ther. "La Vallée Houdou" shows a group of melan-cholic, idealistic Doukhobor immigrants who reject possible settlements until captivated by a blazing copper sunset and the mirage of a river and mountains in the thorny Hoodoo Valley. Again Roy creates a sense of human needs be-yond the rational.

The two longer stories, the heart of the book, contain greater affirmation than her "realis-tic" novels, although they do provide it within the world of experience. The characters, Chinese immigrant Sam Lee Wong and Ukrainian-born farm wife Martha Yaramko, are gentle people who manage to sustain some hope, but they do so in an environment hostile to them in some way. In "Où iras-tu Sam Lee Wong?," with lonely patience Wong builds a life in the middle of Sas-katchewan where the hills remind him of home, and then, in the Depression, when he is uninten-tionally driven out of Horizon after twenty-five years, he builds again, sustained by the same hills seen now from the other side.

The title of "Un Jardin au bout du monde" (a perceptive, delicate, and moving story) sug-gests a romantic remoteness like that of Little Water Hen, and the central image developed in the story, a mass of flaming flowers in an empty, inhospitable plain, might seem paradisal. But the garden is a triumph of hope in the midst of de-spair. Martha herself, old and ill, estranged from the worlds of her parents and children, no longer on speaking terms with her bitter hus-

Dust jacket for the English translation of Ces Enfants de ma vie, *the 1977 story collection that won Roy her third Governor General's Award*

band, Stépan, questions why she has had her life. Feeling no connection even with God, she wonders, "Qui s'était retiré? Dieu, oubliant ses créatures perdues au fond des terres canadiennes? Ou eux-mêmes, les êtres humains, par manque d'imagination?" ("Who had withdrawn? God, forgetting his creatures lost in the depths of the Canadian waste? Or they themselves, the humans, through a failure of the imagination?"). The garden itself leads her to ask angrily why a small life as tranquil as a flower's should have so many enemies. But the flowers' will to live, the association of summer with hope, tenderness, and youth (though a reminder too of the injustice of time), the unexpected sight of a grumbling Stépan protecting her plants when she is no longer able to, and especially the placid solitude of wind and prairie grasses permit Martha to entrust herself if not to God then to "cette humble immortalité de l'air, du vent et des herbes" ("this humble immortality of air and wind and grasses").

Roy's 1977 work of fiction, *Ces Enfants de ma vie* (translated as *Children of My Heart*, 1979), win-

ner of her third Governor General's Award, turns back to early innocence, although, as in *La Route d'Altamont*, the last and most important story explores a banishment from the kingdom of childhood. The stories celebrate the "joies un peu sauvages" ("savage joys") of childhood (to borrow a phrase from *Rue Deschambault*), the spontaneous affection and joyful release possible for children even in poverty and hardship, as observed by a young teacher. There are tender vignettes of sensitive Clair, whose need to give his beloved teacher a Christmas present torments him; the littlest Demetrioff, whose perfect alphabet, fervently formed, wins from his violent father a rare gesture of pride and love; and gentle André, who at ten must manage an entire household. In the early part of the book, the narrator confesses her own inexperience: "J'étais encore trop jeune moi-même, je suppose, pour comprendre ce qu'est un coeur allégé" ("I suppose I was too young myself to know what a lightened heart was"). In "De la Truite dans l'eau glacée," though, the story of the restless and passionate Meredic (himself like a timid trout momentarily tamed in the icy water) and of his unrecognized, budding love for his schoolteacher, Roy observes and relives the confusing, distressing, irremediable loss of childhood innocence. The bouquet of wild flowers he tosses through the train window on her departure expresses Roy's understanding of the splendor but also the tragedy of life: "Il disait le jeune été fragile, à peine est-il né qu'il commence à en mourir" ("It spoke of the young and fragile summer, barely born but it begins to die").

Roy spoke, in an interview for *Le Roman canadien-français* (Archives des Lettres Canadiennes, number 3, 1964), of the influence on her of the atmosphere of tender melancholy in Chekhov's *The Steppe*. That poignant tone, the "note plaintive et non point sans douceur triste" ("plaintive note, yet not without its sad sweetness") of the water hen's call, is, similarly, the distinctive note of her own fiction, as suggested by the title of the posthumously published autobiography of her first thirty years, *La Détresse et l'enchantement* (1984; translated as *Enchantment and Sorrow*, 1987). There are times when one may find this gentle sensitivity to life's contradictions lacking in substance. Phyllis Grosskurth, in her *Gabrielle Roy* (1972), has criticized the absence of passion and evil in the works, arguing that Roy's characters, never having eaten from the Tree of Knowledge of Good and Evil in Eden, are "bewildered, innocent exiles banished by a capricious God." Compassionate understanding rather than a sense of tragic struggle does, for the most part, dominate Roy's fiction, but there is emotional power in these works, heightened by their simplicity, tender ironies, descriptive vividness, and clear style. Roy varies, sometimes markedly, in her emphasis on the bitter or on the sweet, but all her fiction is characterized by a bittersweet vision, moving in its sensitivity.

Interviews:

Dorothy Duncan, "Le Triomphe de Gabrielle," *Maclean's* (15 April 1947): 23, 51, 54;

Léon Dartis, "La Genèse de *Bonheur d'occasion*," *Revue Moderne*, 29 (May 1947): 9, 26;

Rex Desmarchais, "Gabrielle Roy vous parle d'elle et de son roman," *Bulletin des Agriculteurs* (May 1947): 8-9, 36-39, 43-44;

Francis Ambrière, "Gabrielle Roy, écrivain canadien," *Revue de Paris*, 54th year (December 1947): 136-139;

Emilia B. Allaire, "Notre grande romancière: Gabrielle Roy," *Action Catholique*, 5 June 1960, p. 16;

John J. Murphy, "Visit with Gabrielle Roy," *Thought*, 38 (1963): 447-455;

"Gabrielle Roy," in *Le Roman canadien-français*, Archives des Lettres Canadiennes, no. 3 (Montreal: Fides, 1964), pp. 302-306;

Alice Parizeau, "Gabrielle Roy, grande romancière canadienne," *Châtelaine* (April 1966): 44, 118, 120-122, 137, 140;

Pauline Beaudry, "Gabrielle Roy: Répondre à l'appel intérieur . . . ," *Terre et foyer*, 27 (December 1968-January 1969): 5-8;

Donald Cameron, "Gabrielle Roy: A Bird in the Prison Window," in his *Conversations with Canadian Novelists*, volume 2 (Toronto: Macmillan, 1973), pp. 129-145;

Alain Houle, "Les Voyageries de Gabrielle Roy et de René Richard," *North/Nord*, 24 (December 1977): 36-43;

Paula Gilbert Lewis, " 'The Last of the Great Storytellers': A Visit with Gabrielle Roy," *French Review*, 55 (December 1981): 207-215.

Bibliography:

Paul Socken, "Gabrielle Roy: An Annotated Bibliography," in *The Annotated Bibliography of Canada's Major Authors*, volume 1, edited by Robert Lecker and Jack David (Downsview, Ontario: ECW, 1979), pp. 213-263.

References:

Jacques Allard, "Le Chemin qui mène à *La Petite Poule d'eau*," *Cahiers de Sainte-Marie*, 1 (May 1966): 57-69;

Alexandre L. Amprimoz, "Fonction gestuelle: *Bonheur d'occasion* de Gabrielle Roy," *Présence Francophone*, 24 (Spring 1982): 123-137;

Amprimoz, "L'Homme-arbre de *La Montagne secrète*," *Canadian Literature*, 88 (Spring 1981): 166-171;

Ellen R. Babby, "Alexandre Chenevert: Prisoner of Language," *Modern Language Studies*, 12 (Spring 1982): 22-30;

Babby, *The Play of Language and Spectacle: A Structural Reading of Selected Texts by Gabrielle Roy* (Toronto: ECW, 1985);

Babby, "*La Rivière sans repos*: Gabrielle Roy's 'Spectacular' Text," *Québec Studies*, 2 (1984): 105-117;

Ekitike Behounde, *Dialectique de la ville et de la campagne chez Gabrielle Roy et Mongo Beti* (Montreal: Qui, 1983);

Gérard Bessette, "*Bonheur d'occasion*," *Action universitaire*, 18 (July 1952): 53-74;

Bessette, "French-Canadian Society as seen by Contemporary Novelists," *Queen's Quarterly*, 69 (Summer 1962): 177-197;

Bessette, "Gabrielle Roy," in his *Une Littérature en ébullition* (Montreal: Editions du Jour, 1968), pp. 217-308;

Bessette, "Gabrielle Roy," in his *Trois Romanciers québécois* (Montreal: Editions du Jour, 1973), pp. 185-237;

Jacques Blais, "L'Unité organique de *Bonheur d'occasion*," *Etudes Françaises*, 6 (February 1970): 25-50;

E. D. Blodgett, "Gardens at the World's End or Gone West in French," *Essays on Canadian Writing*, 17 (Spring 1980): 113-126;

André Brochu, "Gabrielle Roy: *Ces Enfants de ma vie*," *Livres et Auteurs Québécois* (1977): 39-43;

Brochu, "*La Montagne secrète*: Le Schème organisateur," *Etudes Littéraires*, 17 (Winter 1984): 531-544;

Brochu, "La Structure sémantique de *Bonheur d'occasion*," *Revue des Sciences Humaines*, 173 (1979): 37-47;

Brochu, "Thèmes et structures dans *Bonheur d'occasion*," *Ecrits du Canada Français*, 22 (1966): 163-208;

Lee Brotherson, "Alexandre Chenevert: An Unhappy Sisyphus," *Essays in French Literature*, 18 (November 1981): 86-99;

Alan Brown, "Gabrielle Roy and the Temporary Provincial," *Tamarack Review*, 1 (Autumn 1956): 61-70;

Richard Chadbourne, "Essai bibliographique: Cinq ans d'études sur Gabrielle Roy, 1979-1984," *Etudes Littéraires*, 17 (Winter 1984): 597-609;

Chadbourne, "The Journey in Gabrielle Roy's Novels," in *Travel, Quest, and Pilgrimage as a Literary Theme: Studies in Honor of Reino Virtanen*, edited by Frans C. Amelinckx and Joyce N. Megay (Manhatten, Kans.: Society of Spanish and Spanish-American Studies, 1978), pp. 251-260;

Chadbourne, "Two Visions of the Prairies: Willa Cather and Gabrielle Roy," in *The New Land: Studies in a Literary Theme*, edited by Chadbourne and Hallvard Dahlie (Waterloo, Ontario: Wilfrid Laurier University Press, 1978), pp. 93-120;

Roland-M. Charland and Jean-Noël Samson, eds., *Gabrielle Roy*, Dossiers de Documentation sur la Littérature Canadienne-Française, no. 1 (Montreal: Fides, 1967);

Brandon Conron, Introduction to Roy's *Street of Riches*, translated by Harry Lorin Binsse, New Canadian Library, no. 56 (Toronto: McClelland & Stewart, 1967), pp. vii-xii;

Arnold E. Davidson, "Gabrielle Roy's *Where Nests the Water Hen*: An Island beyond the Waste Land," *North Dakota Quarterly*, 47, no. 4 (1979): 4-10;

Annette Décarie, "La Petite Poule d'eau," *Revue Dominicaine*, 57 (February 1951): 79-91;

Anne Srabian de Fabry, "A la Recherche de l'ironie perdue chez Gabrielle Roy et Flaubert," *Présence Francophone*, 11 (1975): 89-104;

Margaret Fairley, "Gabrielle Roy's Novels," *New Frontiers*, 5 (Spring 1956): 7-10;

Barbara Fiand, "Gabrielle Roy's *The Hidden Mountain*: A Poetic Expression of Existential Thought," *Malahat Review*, 52 (October 1979): 77-85;

Marie Francoeur, "Portrait de l'artiste en pédagogue dans *Ces enfants de ma vie*," *Etudes Littéraires*, 17 (Winter 1984): 545-562;

Gabrielle Roy: Dossier de presse, 1945-1980 (Sherbrooke, Quebec: La Bibliothèque, 1981);

Marc Gagné, "*La Rivière sans repos* de Gabrielle Roy: Etude mythocritique incluant 'Voyage en Ungava' (extraits) par Gabrielle Roy," *Revue de l'Université d'Ottawa*, 46 (January-March 1976): 83-107; (April-June 1976): 180-199; (July-September 1976): 364-390;

Gagné, *Visages de Gabrielle Roy* (Montreal: Beauchemin, 1973);

Michel-Lucien Gaulin, "Le Monde romanesque de Roger Lemelin et Gabrielle Roy," in *Le Roman canadien-français*, Archives des Lettres Canadiennes, no. 3 (Montreal: Fides, 1964), pp. 133-151;

Gaulin, "*La Route d'Altamont*," *Incidences*, 10 (April 1966): 27-38;

Monique Genuist, *La Création romanesque chez Gabrielle Roy* (Montreal: Le Cercle du Livre de France, 1966);

J. Godbout, "Gabrielle Roy: Notre-dame des bouleaux," *Actualité*, 4 (January 1979): 30-34;

Sherrill E. Grace, "Quest for the Peaceable Kingdom: Urban/Rural Codes in Roy, Laurence, and Atwood," in *Women Writers and the City: Essays in Feminist Literary Criticism*, edited by Susan Merrill Squier (Knoxville: University of Tennessee Press, 1984), pp. 193-209;

Mary Jean Green, "Gabrielle Roy and Germaine Guèvremont: Quebec's Daughters Face a Changing World," *Journal of Women's Studies in Literature*, 1 (1979): 243-257;

Marie Grenier-Francoeur, "Etude de la structure anaphorique dans *La Montagne secrète* de Gabrielle Roy," *Voix et Images*, 1 (April 1976): 387-405;

Phyllis Grosskurth, *Gabrielle Roy* (Toronto: Forum House, 1972);

Grosskurth, "Gabrielle Roy and the Silken Noose," *Canadian Literature*, 42 (Autumn 1969): 6-13;

David Hayne, "Gabrielle Roy," *Canadian Modern Language Review*, 21 (October 1964): 20-26;

François Hébert, "Gabrielle Roy: *Ces Enfants de ma vie*," *Liberté*, 20, no. 115 (1978): 102-105;

M. G. Hesse, *Gabrielle Roy* (Boston: Twayne, 1984); translated by Michelle Tisseyre and enlarged as *Gabrielle Roy par elle-même* (Montreal: Stanké, 1985);

Hesse, "Le Portrait de l'enfance et de jeunesse dans l'oeuvre de Gabrielle Roy," *Action nationale*, 62 (February 1973): 496-512;

Hesse, " 'There Are No More Strangers': Gabrielle Roy's Immigrants," *Canadian Children's Literature*, 35-36 (1984): 27-37;

Joan Hind-Smith, "Gabrielle Roy," in her *Three Voices: The Lives of Margaret Laurence, Gabrielle Roy, Frederick Philip Grove* (Toronto: Clarke, Irwin, 1975), pp. 62-126;

Terrance Hughes, *Gabrielle Roy et Margaret Laurence: Deux chemins, une recherche* (Saint-Boniface, Manitoba: Editions du Blé, 1983);

S. K. Jain, "Gabrielle Roy: A French-Canadian Novelist," *Culture,* 32 (March 1971): 391-399;

R. Jones and F. G. Howlett, "*Rue Deschambault:* Une Analyse," *Canadian Modern Language Review,* 24, no. 3 (1968): 58-63;

Eva Kushner, "De la réprésentation à la vision du monde," *Québec Français,* 36 (1979): 38-40;

René Labonté, "Gabrielle Roy, journaliste: Au fil de ses reportages (1939-1945)," *Studies in Canadian Literature,* 7, no. 1 (1982): 90-108;

Michele Lacombe, "The Origins of *The Hidden Mountain,*" *Canadian Literature,* 88 (Spring 1981): 164-166;

Guy Laflèche, "Les Bonheurs d'occasion du roman québécois," *Voix et Images,* 3 (1977): 96-115;

Jacques Lafleur, "Gabrielle Roy," *Ecriture Française dans le Monde,* 2, nos. 1-2 (1980): 74-77;

Irma Larouche, "Présentation du fonds Gabrielle Roy, 1909-1983," *Etudes Littéraires,* 17 (Winter 1984): 589-593;

Albert Le Grand, "Gabrielle Roy ou l'être partagé," *Etudes Françaises,* 1 (June 1965): 39-65;

Maurice Lemire, "*Bonheur d'occasion,* ou le salut par la guerre," *Recherches Sociographiques,* 10 (January-April 1969): 23-35;

Paula Gilbert Lewis, "Gabrielle Roy and Emile Zola: French Naturalism in Quebec," *Modern Language Studies,* 11 (Fall 1981): 44-50;

Lewis, "The Incessant Call of the Open Road: Gabrielle Roy's Incorrigible Nomads," *French Review,* 53 (1980): 816-825;

Lewis, *The Literary Vision of Gabrielle Roy: An Analysis of Her Works* (Birmingham, Ala.: Summa, 1984);

Lewis, "The Resignation of Old Age, Sickness and Death in the Fiction of Gabrielle Roy," *American Review of Canadian Studies,* 11 (Autumn 1981): 46-66;

Lewis, "*Street of Riches* and *The Road past Altamont:* The Feminine World of Gabrielle Roy," *Journal of Women's Studies in Literature,* 1 (1979): 133-141;

Lewis, "The Themes of Memory and Death in Gabrielle Roy's *La Route d'Altamont,*" *Modern Fiction Studies,* 22 (Autumn 1976): 457-466;

Lewis, "Tragic and Humanistic Visions of the Future: The Fictional World of Gabrielle Roy," *Québec Studies,* 1 (Spring 1983): 234-245;

Lewis, "Unsuccessful Couples, Shameful Sex, and Infrequent Love in the Fictional World of Gabrielle Roy," *Antigonish Review,* 12 (Winter 1982): 49-55;

Dorothy Livesay, "Two Women Writers: Anglophone and Francophone," in *Language and Literature in Multicultural Contexts,* edited by Satendra Nandan (Suva, Fiji: University of the South Pacific, 1983), pp. 234-239;

W. C. Lougheed, Introduction to Roy's *The Cashier,* translated by Binsse, New Canadian Library, no. 40 (Toronto: McClelland & Stewart, 1970), pp. vii-xiii;

Gilles Marcotte, "En relisant *Bonheur d'occasion,*" *Action Nationale,* 35 (March 1950): 197-206;

Joyce Marshall, "Gabrielle Roy 1909-1983," *Antigonish Review,* 55 (Autumn 1983): 35-46;

Marshall, "Gabrielle Roy, 1909-1983: Some Reminiscences," *Canadian Literature,* 101 (Summer 1984): 183-184;

Marshall, Introduction to Roy's *The Road past Altamont,* translated by Marshall, New Canadian Library, no. 129 (Toronto: McClelland & Stewart, 1976), pp. vii-xi;

Lorraine McMullen, Introduction to Roy's *Windflower,* translated by Marshall, New Canadian Library, no. 120 (Toronto: McClelland & Stewart, 1975);

Hugo McPherson, "The Garden and the Cage: The Achievement of Gabrielle Roy," *Canadian Literature,* 1 (Summer 1959): 46-57;

McPherson, Introduction to Roy's *The Tin Flute,* translated by Hannah Josephson, New Canadian Library, no. 5 (Toronto: McClelland & Stewart, 1958), pp. v-xi;

Carole Melançon, "Evolution de la réception de *Bonheur d'occasion* de 1945 à 1983 au Canada français," *Etudes Littéraires,* 17 (Winter 1984): 457-468;

Allison Mitcham, "Gabrielle Roy's Children," *Antigonish Review,* 36 (Winter 1979): 95-99;

Mitcham, *The Literary Achievement of Gabrielle Roy* (Fredericton: York, 1983);

Mitcham, "The Northern Innocent in the Fiction of Gabrielle Roy," *Humanities Association Bulletin,* 24 (Winter 1973): 25-31;

Mitcham, "Roy's West," *Canadian Literature,* 88 (Spring 1981): 161-163;

Brian Moore, "The Woman on Horseback," in *A Century of Achievement: Great Canadians* (To-

ronto: Canadian Centennial Library, 1965),
pp. 95-99;

John J. Murphy, "Alexandre Chenevert: Gabrielle Roy's Crucified Canadian," *Queen's
Quarterly*, 72 (Summer 1965): 334-346;

Murphy, "The Louvre and Ungava," *Renascence*,
16 (Fall 1963): 53-56;

K. O'Donnell, "Gabrielle Roy's Portrait of the Artist," *Revue de l'Université d'Ottawa*, 44
(January-March 1974): 70-77;

Suzanne Paradis, *Femme fictive, femme réelle: Le
Personnage féminin dans le roman féminin
canadien-français 1884-1966* (Quebec: Garneau, 1966), pp. 44-62;

G. Pascal, "La Femme dans l'oeuvre de Gabrielle
Roy," *Revue de l'Université d'Ottawa*, 50 (January-March 1980): 55-61;

Pascal, "Le Roman et la recherche du sens de la
vie. Vocation: écrivain," in *Mélanges de civilisation canadienne-française offerts au professeur
Paul Wyczynski*, Cahiers du Centre de Recherche en Civilisation Canadienne-française,
10, edited by Pierre Savard (Ottawa: Editions de l'Université d'Ottawa, 1977), pp.
225-235;

Marguerite A. Primeau, "Gabrielle Roy et la
prairie canadienne," in *Writers of the Prairies*,
edited by Donald G. Stephens (Vancouver:
University of British Columbia Press, 1973),
pp. 115-128;

Julia Randall, "Gabrielle Roy: Granddaughter of
Quebec," *Hollins Critic*, 14, no. 5 (1979):
1-12;

François Ricard, *Gabrielle Roy* (Montreal: Fides,
1975);

Ricard, "Gabrielle Roy ou l'impossible choix,"
Critère, 10 (January 1974): 97-102;

Ricard, "Gabrielle Roy: 'Refaire ce qui a été
quitté,'" *Forces*, 44 (1978): 37-41;

Ricard, "Gabrielle Roy: 30 ans d'écriture: Le
Cercle enfin uni des hommes," *Liberté*, 18
(January-February 1976): 59-78;

Ricard, "La Métamorphose d'un écrivain: Essai
biographique," *Etudes littéraires*, 17 (Winter
1984): 441-455;

Walter Riedel, "Variationen der Wandlung:
Gabrielle Roys Roman *Alexandre Chenevert*
und die Dramen Georg Kaisers *Von morgens
bis mitternachts* und Elmer Rices *The Adding
Machine*," *Canadian Review of Comparative Literature*, 11 (June 1984): 205-215;

Réjean Robidoux, "Gabrielle Roy: Au lendemain
du grand départ," *Lettres Québécoises*, 32 (Winter 1983-1984): 17-19;

Robidoux and André Renaud, *Le Roman canadien-
français du vingtième siècle* (Ottawa: Editions
de l'Université d'Ottawa, 1966), pp. 75-91;

Gordon Roper, Introduction to Roy's *Where Nests
the Water Hen*, translated by Binsse, New Canadian Library, no. 25 (Toronto: McClelland & Stewart, 1961), pp. vi-x;

Malcolm Ross, Introduction to Roy's *The Hidden
Mountain*, translated by Binsse, New Cana-
dian Library, no. 109 (Toronto: McClelland
& Stewart, 1975);

R. P. Paul-Emile Roy, "Gabrielle Roy ou la
difficulté de s'ajuster à la realité," *Lectures*,
new series, 11 (November 1964): 55-61;

Catherine Rubinger, "Actualité de deux contes-
témoins: *Le Torrent* d'Anne Hèbert et *Un
Jardin au bout du mondé* de Gabrielle Roy,"
Présence Francophone, 20 (1980): 121-126;

Annette Saint-Pierre, *Gabrielle Roy: Sous le signe
du rêve* (Saint-Boniface, Manitoba: Editions
du Blé, 1975);

Ben-Zion Shek, "*Bonheur d'occasion* à l'écran:
Fidélité ou trahison?," *Etudes Littéraires*, 17
(Winter 1984): 481-497;

Shek, "L'Espace et la description symbolique
dans les romans 'montréalais' de Gabrielle
Roy," *Liberté*, 13, no. 1 (1971): 78-96;

Shek, "The Jew in the French-Canadian Novel,"
Viewpoints, 4 (Winter 1969): 29-35;

Shek, "The Portrayal of Canada's Ethnic Groups
in Some French-Canadian Novels," in *Slavs
in Canada: 3. Proceedings of the Third National
Conference on Canadian Slavs* (Ottawa, 1970),
pp. 269-280;

Shek, *Social Realism in the French-Canadian Novel*
(Montreal: Harvest House, 1977), pp. 65-
111, 173-203;

Antoine Sirois, "Costume, maquillage et bijoux
dans *Bonheur d'occasion*," *Présence Francophone*, 18 (1979): 159-163;

Sirois, "Gabrielle Roy et le Canada anglais,"
Etudes Littéraires, 17 (Winter 1984): 469-479;

Sirois, "Le Mythe du nord," *Revue de l'Université
de Sherbrooke*, 4 (October 1963): 29-36;

Paul Socken, "Art and the Artist in Gabrielle
Roy's Works," *Revue de l'Université d'Ottawa*,
45 (July-September 1975): 344-350;

Socken, *Concordance de "Bonheur d'occasion" de
Gabrielle Roy* (Waterloo, Ontario: University
of Waterloo Press, 1982);

Socken, "Les Dimensions mythiques dans
Alexandre Chenevert," *Etudes Littéraires*, 17
(Winter 1984): 499-529;

Socken, "Gabrielle Roy as Journalist," *Canadian Modern Language Review,* 30, no. 2 (1974): 96-100;

Socken, "L'Harmonie dans l'oeuvre de Gabrielle Roy," *Travaux de linguistique et de littérature publiés par le Centre de Philologie et de Littératures Romanes de l'Université de Strasbourg,* 15, no. 2 (1977): 275-292;

Socken, "In Memoriam: Gabrielle Roy (1909-1983)," *Canadian Modern Language Review,* 40 (October 1983): 105-110;

Socken, " 'Le Pays de l'amour' in the Works of Gabrielle Roy," *Revue de l'Université d'Ottawa,* 46 (July-September 1976): 309-323;

Socken, "Use of Language in *Bonheur d'occasion:* A Case in Point," *Essays on Canadian Writing,* 11 (Summer 1978): 66-71;

Adrien Thério, "De l'Atlantique au Pacifique, le gout de la liberté. *De Quoi t'ennuies-tu, Eveline?,*" *Lettres Québécoises,* 31 (Autumn 1983): 31-33;

Thério, "Le Portrait du pére dans *Rue Deschambault* de Gabrielle Roy," *Livres et Auteurs Québécois* (1969): 237-243;

W. B. Thorne, "Poverty and Wrath: A Study of *The Tin Flute,*" *Journal of Canadian Studies,* 3, no. 3 (1968): 3-10;

Gérard Tougas, *Historie de la littérature canadienne-française* (Paris: Presses Universitaires de France, 1960);

Jeannette Urbas, "Equations and Flutes," *Journal of Canadian Fiction,* 1 (Spring 1972): 69-73;

Urbas, "Gabrielle Roy et l'acte de créer," *Journal of Canadian Fiction,* 1 (Fall 1972): 51-54;

Urbas, "A Universal Theme," in her *From "Thirty Acres" to Modern Times: The Story of French-Canadian Literature* (Toronto: McGraw-Hill Ryerson, 1976), pp. 45-63;

G. A. Vachon, "L'Espace politique et social dans le roman québécois," *Recherches Sociographiques,* 7, no. 3 (1966): 261-273;

André Vanasse, "Vers une solitude désespérante (La Notion d'étranger dans la littérature canadienne, V)," *Action Nationale,* 55 (March 1966): 844-851;

Jack Warwick, *The Long Journey: Literary Themes of French Canada* (Toronto: University of Toronto Press, 1968), pp. 86-100, 140-144;

Agnes Whitfield, "*Alexandre Chenevert:* Cercle vicieux et évasions manquées," *Voix et Images du Pays,* 8 (1974): 107-125.

Oscar Ryan

(27 June 1904-)

Rose Adams

BOOKS: *Deported!* (Toronto: Canadian Labour Defence League, 1932);

The Story of the Trial of the Eight Communist Leaders (Toronto: Canadian Labour Defence League, 1932);

The "Sedition" of A. E. Smith (Toronto: Canadian Labour Defence League, 1934);

Tim Buck: A Conscience for Canada (Toronto: Progress Books, 1975);

Soon To Be Born (Vancouver: New Star Books, 1980).

PLAY PRODUCTIONS: *Unity*, Toronto, Hygeia Hall, 1 May 1933;

Eight Men Speak, by Ryan, Ed Cecil-Smith, Frank Love as H. Francis, and Mildred Goldberg, Toronto, Progressive Arts Club at the Standard Theatre, 4 December 1933.

OTHER: *Unity*, by Ryan, and *Eight Men Speak*, by Ryan, Ed Cecil-Smith, Frank Love, and Mildred Goldberg, in *Eight Men Speak and Other Plays from the Canadian Workers' Theatre*, edited by Richard Wright and Robin Endres (Toronto: New Hogtown Press, 1976).

Although Oscar Ryan has been known for over fifty years as a theater critic, it is as playwright and social activist that he has earned a unique place in Canadian cultural history. His importance extends beyond his writing to include his role as cofounder of the Canadian workers' theater movement during the late 1920s and 1930s. This movement was responsible for creating and promoting an indigenous working-class theater of protest. In addition, he has been a biographer, novelist, reporter, poet, editor, activist, and organizer.

Ryan was born 27 June 1904 on St. Urbain Street in Montreal (opposite the Hotel Dieu Hospital). His parents were of Jewish descent and had immigrated to Canada. His mother, Sarah Rein, was born in Russia and came to Canada as a child with her parents. She had only an elementary education but spoke and read English fluently. Adolph Weinstein, his father, was Rumanian and immigrated to Canada as a youth. A casual reader, he was at home in Rumanian, French, Yiddish, and English. He struggled to make a meager living as bookkeeper and peddler of small wares and religious sundries in the countryside of Catholic Quebec. Ryan's mother worked in a tobacco factory and, later, in Montreal clothing factories. Ryan grew up in respectable poverty in French-Canadian neighborhoods.

When he was six the family moved to Calgary where his father opened a dry-goods store that went broke within a year, causing the family to return to Montreal. Their lot did not improve. When Ryan was about fifteen his father, broke and depressed, left his family. His mother returned to work in the needle trades. By now Ryan had a five-year-old sister. He worked after school and on weekends in grocery stores and in factories during school vacations, spending one summer as kitchen-boy in the posh Beaconsfield country club at Pointe Claire.

Ryan was educated in Montreal public schools and went to high school on a four-year scholarship as top boy in his final elementary year. During high-school days he read widely and was deeply influenced by Upton Sinclair, Jack London, Jakob Wassermann, and, most notably, Romain Rolland, whose novel *Jean-Christophe* (1904-1912) had a profound effect. He read American and British radical publications and attended public lectures and study courses in Montreal.

After his graduation the family moved again, this time to Winnipeg, where Ryan worked in a fur-pelt warehouse, at fur auctions, in a supply house for trappers, and as hotel help. When the family moved back to Montreal he worked as a shipper. Though he had done well in school, his hopes for university education had vanished by the time he moved to Toronto in 1926, where he has lived since, holding varied jobs: in a woodworking shop, with pulp-magazine publishers, and, until retirement, in free-lance advertising and copy-writing for retail stores.

Oscar Ryan

It was during the 1920s that he became politically active, working for civil rights in Canada and writing to express concerns engendered by the political struggles of the day. He wrote poetry for various leftist publications and from the 1920s through the 1930s edited the *Young Worker*, *Always Ready* children's magazine, *Canadian Labour Defender*, and the Winnipeg *Voice of Labour*. During the 1930s this editorial work expanded to include becoming a cofounder and editorial board member of *Masses* and a staff member of the *Worker* and *Daily Clarion*, all based in Toronto. While working on the *Clarion*, Ryan introduced a column called "Footlight Footnotes," offering stage news and commentary. The column was revived in 1983 by the *Canadian Tribune* and is still written by Ryan.

His political education continued as he worked with the Young Communist League. In 1928 he delivered a speech on behalf of the YCL at Toronto's Standard Theatre to celebrate the eleventh anniversary of the Russian Revolution. In 1928 and 1929 he spoke at numerous rallies and mass meetings; he was also arrested and charged with "vagrancy," an episode which furthered his commitment to free speech and the

right of people to join political parties of their choosing. He subsequently became publicity director for the Canadian Labour Defence League, an organization dedicated to the repeal of Section 98 of the Criminal Code of Canada (on unlawful assembly), and a leader of free-speech campaigns across Canada.

His political views were not held without cost; on 1 March 1931 Tom Ewen, national secretary of the Workers Unity League, and Ryan began a fifteen-day sentence in Toronto's Don Jail for "obstructing traffic" at a street corner while holding an election meeting. Their arrest included severe beatings by the police.

Ryan's working-class background, his political activism, and his widespread media involvement gave a foundation to his plays and spurred his commitment to organize workers in the Progressive Arts Club and workers' theater movement. In 1929, with the crash of the stock market, the plight of the working class in Canada worsened and Ryan and other artists saw a need to respond creatively to the deteriorating social situation.

The Progressive Arts Club was founded in 1931 by a small group of thirty-five writers, art-

Dust jacket for Ryan's biography of Tim Buck, general secretary of the Canadian Communist party who was arrested in 1931

ists, and theater workers, gathered by Ryan. Their aim was to provide support for the development of vigorous working-class art forms and to respond to social and political crises through their art. Recognizing the cultural dependency of Canada on Britain and the United States, the group also dedicated itself to providing a genuinely Canadian voice in the arts. In addition they felt that too few artists were engaged in social questions and that many ignored their role as cultural workers in relation to social struggles. The Progressive Arts Club succeeded in attracting such members as Dorothy Livesay, poet; Stanley Ryerson, historian; Ed Cecil-Smith, who later went on to command the MacPaps (the MacKenzie-Papineau Battalion) in Spain; and Toby Gordon, the actress who became Ryan's wife in 1949 and who was a cofounder of Workers' Theatre, Theatre of Action, and the Toronto

Play Actors. Toby Gordon's account of these experiences may be found in her memoir, *Stage Left: Canadian Theatre in the Thirties* (1981).

The organ of the Progressive Arts Club was *Masses*, of which twelve issues were published from April 1932 to 1934. As cofounder Ryan stayed on the editorial board until fall 1933. *Masses* united the Progressive Arts Clubs across Canada and disseminated information on how to form a club or a workers' theater group; it also offered criticism, short stories, poems, original plays, and woodcut illustrations by such artists as AVROM (Avrom Yanovsky), who was active in the Workers' Theatre group with Ed Cecil-Smith and Richard Taylor.

The Workers' Theatre group was formed under the auspices of the Progressive Arts Clubs and Toby Gordon was very much involved. Initially it was called Workers' Experimental Theatre but later shortened to Workers' Theatre. This organization drew its membership from the newly formed University of Toronto Students League and from unemployed workers eager to participate in the production of the plays. The writers of the Progressive Arts Club, including Ryan, offered to write scripts for the troupe to perform on picket lines and at mass rallies, union meetings, and so on.

Ryan wrote a one-act play entitled *Unity* to be performed by this group at a mass meeting of labor and socialist organizations at Hygeia Hall in Toronto on May Day 1933. The script was published in *Masses* and was also distributed as a mimeographed booklet in 1933 by International Labor Defense, New York; more recently it has been collected in *Eight Men Speak and Other Plays from the Canadian Workers' Theatre* (1976). *Unity* is important as a Canadian example of agitprop, a form of theater overtly political, agitational, often speaking directly to the audience and produced with the expressed purpose of promoting political action. The conflict in agitprop is between social classes or representatives of those classes rather than between individuals. Hence, characterizations are often played as caricatures. *Unity* is classic agitprop. It represents a conflict between capitalists and workers, ending in a roaring call for Canadian workers to unite and join in unity with the working classes of Germany, Great Britain, China, and the Soviet Union. *Unity* is not without its humor, as when the 2nd Capitalist blames the Soviet Union for the Depression because the Russians have "dumped goods" on Canadian soil: "Do you know that some of our best Canadians are being buried in coffins made of SO-VIET lumber? That every time you chew a toothpick, you may be chewing SOVIET lumber? That every time you light a match you may be unpatriotic, by lighting up a RED flare, instead of encouraging home industries such as Mr. Bennett's Eddy Match?"

Capitalists in *Unity* come complete with white spats, canes, silk hats, and white gloves, while the workers wear black clothing with red scarves (the official outfit of the mobile theater troupe), thus providing a strong contrast on stage. The staging of *Unity*, perhaps unprecedented in Canadian theater, consisted of three levels, used metaphorically for levels in status. The critic for *Masses* hailed *Unity* as having "tremendous propaganda value," but the events surrounding the play's opening also served to make the public aware of efforts against promoting unity among the working class. Two of the unemployed men who were actors in the play were picked up by the police on their way home from the afternoon rehearsal before the first performance. The "Red Squad" had no charges to lay, but they were determined to keep the performance from occurring that evening. The Canadian Labour Defence League rallied to the support of the actors and had them released just in time to perform.

Ryan's aims to promote a militant working-class culture through the Progressive Arts Club and his efforts to fight for free speech with the Canadian Labour Defence League found a synthesis in Canada's most ambitious and effective agitprop production, *Eight Men Speak* (1933). He cowrote this full-length play (six actors, twenty-one scenes) with Ed Cecil-Smith, Frank Love, and Mildred Goldberg. The political events which preceded the writing of the play are important to an understanding of the plot, intent, and effectiveness of *Eight Men Speak*. In 1931 Richard B. Bennett's government had revived Section 98 of the Criminal Code of Canada in an effort to outlaw the Communist party. On 11 August 1931 eight Canadian Communist leaders, including Tim Buck, general secretary of the Communist party of Canada, were simultaneously arrested across the country and charged under Section 98 with bail set at $20,000 each. They were tried, given lengthy sentences, and sent to Kingston Penitentiary in Ontario. The prisoners in Kingston led a strike for better conditions which turned into a riot. Buck was brought to trial and charged with instigating the riot. During the uprising a shot had been fired into his cell, and although there was said to be sufficient evidence against a prison guard, he was never brought to trial for the attempted assassination.

Ryan was working for the Canadian Labour Defence League when it took on the legal cases for the Kingston 8 and he was active in the Section 98 repeal campaigns. He was present at Buck's trials (the first a result of the initial Section 98 charge and the second regarding the prison riots) as a reporter. Thus, it was he who conceived of *Eight Men Speak* as a mock trial drama, enlisting the three collaborators in this effort to rouse public opinion for the repeal of Section 98 and to fight for the release of the jailed men.

The plot of *Eight Men Speak*, however, goes much further than the actual circumstances of the trials in the range of issues that it succeeds in addressing. *Eight Men Speak* talks about workers'

Dust jacket for Ryan's novel about Montreal working-class life from the turn of the century to World War II

history, the unemployed, and immigrants in Canada (including the moving story of Nick Zynchuk, killed by the police in Montreal during an eviction). *Eight Men Speak* exposes the media as a source of distortion and accuses government of being removed from the lives of ordinary people.

The play is compelling and engages its audience through its use of many different styles and techniques. It opens with a realistic garden scene, but shifts to incorporate traditional agitprop techniques of mass recitation, monologues spoken directly to the audience, stylized movements, pantomime, and melodrama. When a worker describes in court how he was brutally beaten, shadows against the backdrop serve as an ominous reminder. Vignettes are highlighted on stage in a quick, punctuated movement to represent public opinion, and characters range from realistic portrayals to such comic burlesques as the attorney named Capitalism who works for "Capitalism, Capitalism, and Exploitation."

The production had a cast of thirty-five,

mostly unemployed men with little or no acting experience. Rehearsals began in October and the performance premiered 4 December 1933 at the Standard Theatre on Spadina Avenue before an enthusiastic Toronto audience of 1,500. Audience reaction was ecstatic, with cheers, boos, and wild applause. The final curtain brought a sustained ovation.

Reviews of the play in the mainstream press were scant, while its success with its intended audience was unmistakable. Consequently, the importance of its subject matter did not go unnoticed. The Toronto Police Commission threatened to cancel the license of any theater offering to rent its hall to the Progressive Arts group. This caused the cancellation of a second performance in Toronto, and a performance in Winnipeg was prevented by a similar edict. Prime Minister Bennett is said to have received an R.C.M.P. stenographer's report of the script and to have strongly approved of banning the play. The Progressive Arts Club continued to organize mass protests against Section 98 as public opinion gradually shifted in their favor. In the federal election campaign of 1935, William Lyon Mackenzie King promised to repeal Section 98 if he became prime minister. In June 1936, with Mackenzie King in office, the law was finally repealed and the Kingston 8 were released. *Eight Men Speak* had played an active role, true to the aims of agitprop, in the class politics of its country.

Ryan appeared in the original performance and thus saw *Eight Men Speak* for the first time in 1982 when it was revived by Popular Projects Society in Halifax, Nova Scotia. The 1982 production was a collective endeavor like that of 1933, but instead of thirty-five actors the cast was reduced to eight, playing multiple roles. As agitprop *Eight Men Speak* was tied to the events of the 1930s; in 1982 its revival spoke of a period in Canadian history often ignored.

In the 1930s Ryan also wrote several topical booklets which were distributed across Canada by the Labour Defence League. These include *Deported!* (1932), *The Story of the Trial of the Eight Communist Leaders* (1932), and *The "Sedition" of A. E. Smith* (1934). He continued writing for various publications throughout the 1930s and 1940s, often under the pseudonym Martin Stone. As reviewer for the *Worker* and *Daily Clarion*, he followed and publicized the projects of the Theatre of Action (1935-1939), successor of the Workers' Theatre, and the Toronto Play Actors. While working for the *Clarion* Ryan also focused on stage reviews. During World War II Ryan was enrolled in the Queen's Own Rifles (reserve battalion) in Toronto. Since 1955 he has reviewed Toronto theater as well as the Shaw Festival and the festivals at Stratford and Charlottetown; he has also reviewed the occasional book. During the last twelve years he has visited the Soviet Union twice and written some twenty reviews and articles about the leading Russian theaters for the *Canadian Tribune*.

In 1975 he produced the biography *Tim Buck: A Conscience for Canada*. In 1980 New Star Books of Vancouver published Ryan's novel *Soon To Be Born*, about working-class life from the turn of the century, through the Depression, leading up to World War II. Ryan is currently revising a second novel. He and his wife live in Toronto. They have one daughter, Sandy Ellen.

Oscar and Toby Ryan played formidable roles in the development of Canadian working-class culture and in the founding of an indigenous workers' theater movement which operated in both urban and rural areas. Oscar Ryan's commitment to civil rights has made his work a lasting memoir of Canadian cultural history.

Reference:

Toby Gordon Ryan, *Stage Left: Canadian Theatre in the Thirties* (Toronto: CTR, 1981).

Félix-Antoine Savard

(31 August 1896-24 August 1982)

H. R. Runte
Dalhousie University

BOOKS: *Menaud, maître-draveur* (Quebec: Garneau, 1937; revised, 1944); translated by Alan Sullivan as *Boss of the River* (Toronto: Ryerson, 1947); French version revised twice (Montreal: Fides, 1960, 1964); translated by Richard Howard as *Master of the River* (Montreal: Harvest House, 1976);

L'Abatis (Montreal: Fides, 1943; revised, 1960);

La Minuit (Montreal: Fides, 1948);

Le Barachois (Montreal & Paris: Fides, 1959);

Martin et le pauvre (Montreal & Paris: Fides, 1959);

La Folle (Montreal & Paris: Fides, 1960);

La Dalle-des-Morts (Montreal & Paris: Fides, 1965);

Symphonie du Misereor (Ottawa: Editions de l'Université d'Ottawa, 1968);

Le Bouscueil (Montreal: Fides, 1972);

La Roche Ursule (Quebec: S. Allard, 1972);

Journal et souvenirs I: 1961-1962 (Montreal: Fides, 1973);

Aux Marges du silence (limited edition, Châteauguay, Quebec: Michel Nantel, 1974; trade edition, Quebec: Garneau, 1975);

Journal et souvenirs II: 1963-1964 (Montreal: Fides, 1975);

Discours (Montreal: Fides, 1975);

Carnet du soir intérieur I (Montreal: Fides, 1978);

Carnet du soir intérieur II (Montreal: Fides, 1979).

PLAY PRODUCTION: *La Dalle-des-Morts*, Montreal, Théâtre du Nouveau Monde at Théâtre Orpheum, 20 March 1966.

PERIODICAL PUBLICATIONS: "Les Devoirs de l'écrivain et de l'éditeur," *Lectures*, 1 (November 1946): 129-131;

"L'Ecrivain canadien et la langue française," *Journal de l'Instruction Publique*, 4 (May 1960): 723-726;

"Le Théâtre que je rêve," *Revue de l'Université Laval*, 15 (January 1961): 427-429.

Novelist, poet, playwright, folklorist, and memorialist, Félix-Antoine Savard was for a long time the dean of Quebec literature. Born in Quebec City, the son of Louis-Joseph and Ida-Geneviève Gosselin, he was educated by the Marist Brothers and at the Grand Séminaire in Chicoutimi. He was ordained on 4 June 1922 and taught Latin and French at his alma mater from 1919 to 1926. After a brief stay in a Benedictine monastery, he devoted fifteen years almost exclusively to the establishment and administration of rural parishes (Bagotville, Charlevoix, La Malbaie, and in the Abitibi region).

His profound knowledge of the land and the people of Quebec gained during these years determined his literary preoccupations, just as his familiarity with the literature of antiquity and of France shaped his style. In his masterwork, *Menaud, maître-draveur* (1937; translated as *Boss of the River*, 1947), usually associated with the *roman de la terre* genre, Menaud, a log-runner in the service of English-Canadians, almost loses his daughter Marie to the treacherous Délié after having already lost his son Joson on the Noire River. With the help of Alexis Tremblay, alias Le Lucon, Menaud mounts a campaign of vengeance and revolt against English Canada's exploitation of Quebec's natural resources, in the name of patriotism, freedom, and justice. Savard's lyricism, his rigorous structuring of the narrative, and his forceful application of a universal theme to Quebec have from the beginning saved *Menaud* from being categorized as an example of regional literature. However, the work, which was extensively rewritten by Savard for the 1944 edition and revised twice more, in 1960 and 1964, has not always been unanimously applauded. Early critics praised its ideology but were confused as to whether it is a novel, an epic poem, or a drama. Formal aspects were foremost in the minds of critics of the antinationalist period after World War II. Recent criticism has, however, seen *Menaud* in its masterful unity of form and content.

Félix-Antoine Savard (photograph by Kèro)

In 1941 Savard was appointed professor and folklorist at Université Laval; he was dean of the Faculté des Lettres from 1950 to 1957. In 1944 he founded the Laval Archives de Folklore with Luc Lacourcière, whom he accompanied on research trips throughout Charlevoix County, to the Gaspé Peninsula, and to Acadia. *Le Barachois* (1959), a collection of poems, stories, and remembrances, is a direct result of this research and celebrates in poeticized form the promise of a better future for those who remain faithful to nature. Savard's study of popular traditions and his pioneer and missionary work in the Abitibi made of him a convinced nationalist and an articulate social critic. *L'Abatis* (1943), a lyric account of his life in the North, is an appeal to return to the soil and to colonize Quebec's unexplored vastness. In *La Minuit* (1948), a novel-poem, Savard deplores and denounces the helplessness of all those who cannot shake off the yoke of poverty and misery. A similar theme underlies *Martin et le Pauvre* (1959), a poetic rendering of the legend of Saint Martin.

In 1960 Savard went into semiretirement (he was research associate at the University of Ot-

tawa from 1970 to 1973), a period during which he turned to the theater. *La Dalle-des-Morts* (1965), his major play set around 1830, pits mythical feminine forces of stability, embodied in Délie, against the powerful call for the conquest of Canada's wilderness which her fiancé, Gildore, in his thirst for freedom from English domination, cannot resist. *La Folle* (1960), a dramatic text, and the poem *Symphonie du Misereor* (1968), both set in Acadia, are reflections on the miracle of religious faith, on death and the fear of death, and on the consoling certainty of life after death. Savard's memoirs, *Journal et souvenirs* (two volumes) and *Carnet du soir intérieur* (two volumes), appeared from 1973 to 1979.

Despite his fundamental traditionalism and a tendency toward the glorification and folklorization of Quebec, Savard, as a patriot, a stylist, and a historiographer, was, on the basis of both his creative writings and his lyric and reflective memoirs, one of the early prophets of modern Quebec. He was a member of the Académie Canadienne-Française and the Royal Society of Canada; the literary prizes he received include the Médaille de l'Académie Française (1945), the

From the manuscript for Savard's Symphonie du Misereor. *In the 1968 University of Ottawa edition the manuscript and printed text appear on facing pages (photograph courtesy of Kenneth Landry).*

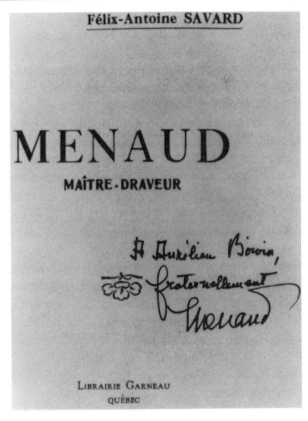

Inscription by Savard on the title page for his first and best-known work

Lorne Pierce Medal (1945), the Prix Duvernay (1948), a Governor General's Award (1960), the Prix du Grand Jury des Lettres (1961), and the Prix David (1968).

Bibliography:
Sister Thérèse-du-Carmel, *Bibliographie analytique de l'oeuvre de Félix-Antoine Savard* (Montreal & Paris: Fides, 1972).

References:
Yvon Daigneault, *"Menaud, maître-draveur* devant la critique 1937-1967," *Livres et Auteurs Québécois* (1969): 248-262;

Félix-Antoine Savard: Dossier du presse, 1937-1980 (Sherbrooke, Quebec: Bibliothèque du Séminaire, 1981);

André Major, *Félix-Antoine Savard* (Montreal & Paris: Fides, 1968);

"Monseigneur F.-A. Savard," *Incidences*, 13 (Winter 1968);

François Ricard, *L'Art de Félix-Antoine Savard dans "Menaud, maître-draveur"* (Montreal: Fides, 1972);

Jean-Noël Samson and Roland-M. Charland, *Félix-Antoine Savard* (Montreal: Fides, 1969);

Donald Smith, "Félix-Antoine Savard ou l'enchantement de la nature," in his *L'Ecrivain devant son oeuvre* (Montreal: Québec/Amerique, 1983), pp. 18-33; translated by Larry Shouldice as "Félix-Antoine Savard: The Wonders of Nature," in his translation of Smith, *Voices of Deliverance: Interviews with Quebec and Acadian Writers* (Toronto: Anansi, 1986), pp. 14-30.

Patrick Slater
(John Mitchell)

(1 April 1880-18 October 1951)

Elizabeth Waterston
University of Guelph

BOOKS: *The Kingdom of America, the Canadian Creed*, as John Mitchell (Brampton, Ontario: Privately printed, 1930);

The Yellow Briar: A Story of the Irish on the Canadian Countryside (Toronto: Allen, 1933; New York: Minton, Balch, 1934);

The Water-Drinker (Toronto: Allen, 1937);

Robert Harding: A Story of Every Day Life (Toronto: Allen, 1938);

The Settlement of York County (Toronto: Municipal Corporation of the County of York, 1952).

In the 1930s, when Canada faced depression and labor struggles, shadowed by European fascism, Canadian readers made a best-seller of a gentle story set a hundred years earlier in an unaggressive rural Ontario. *The Yellow Briar* (1933) is presented from the point of view of an outsider named Patrick Slater, one of the Irish orphans adrift in Ontario after the famine and cholera of the 1840s. The strange revelation that the Irish "Paddy" was in fact the mask of Toronto WASP lawyer John Mitchell added to the attraction of the book. Mitchell used the pseudonym for three subsequent publications but never recaptured the runaway popularity of his loving, moving, subtly Canadian version of the archetypal story of the orphan in an alien world.

John Wendell Mitchell, born on the family farm near Mono, Ontario, was the surviving son of a strong-willed mother and a bookish, restless father. His father, William Mitchell, left the Mono Mills farm to study veterinary medicine and eventually became chief surgeon, R.C.M.P., at Prince Albert. He had tacitly left his family responsibilities. Mitchell's mother, Clara Henderson Mitchell, moved to a Toronto boardinghouse near Harbord Collegiate. There, and at Victoria College of the University of Toronto, Mitchell established a brilliant academic record, with gold medals and double first-class honors. In 1897 he lectured at the University in political science,

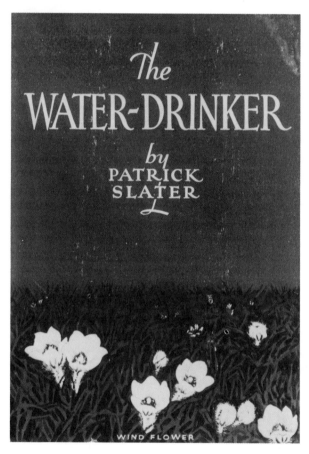

Dust jacket for Mitchell's second pseudonymous volume, written while he was imprisoned at the Langstaff, Ontario, farm-jail

then went to England and Ireland before returning to study at Osgoode Hall Law School. Called to the bar in 1907, he settled into twenty-eight years of legal practice in Toronto.

Erratic and quixotic, the young lawyer increasingly accepted clients from Chinese and Jewish communities, and his perspective on Ontario life took an unusual twist through this exposure to "outsiders." Still another aspect of Ontario society opened to him when he moved to Port

328

Credit, Ontario, with his mother and his twenty-year-old cousin Clara. Lounging around the harbor, he listened to shipmen's tales, sharpening his sense of dialects and developing a relish for yarns of the old days. After World War I Mitchell, now in his forties, bought a home, Inglewood, a farm at the Forks of the Credit, where he could raise pheasants, bring in crops, and restore his sense of the rhythms of rural life. His experiences there were an indirect apprenticeship for the writing of *The Yellow Briar*.

In 1926 Canada, after the Balfour report, reasserted its independence from British authority. Mitchell wrote a long essay, a "national creed" entitled *The Kingdom of America*, which was published at his own expense in 1930. Mitchell went on with his writing, shaping the story of an orphan who moves from chaotic Toronto to a Mono Mills farm, loves but rejects the bright, self-willed daughter of the farmer, then lives as a sailor and wanderer before returning to the derelict homestead.

The Yellow Briar: A Story of the Irish on the Canadian Countryside appeared in 1933, presented as autobiography, Patrick Slater having died in 1924. When Mitchell's hoax was revealed, however, reviewers continued to lavish praise on the book. Contemporaries who testified to its power included painter A. Y. Jackson, novelist Robertson Davies, and Frederick Banting, the Nobel Prize-winning physician who developed insulin. Canadian schools today continue to use *The Yellow Briar* as a doorway to the past: superstitions, feuds, pranks, politics. Readers of the 1930s appreciated the sad ending, as well as the jaunty Slater persona re-creating a regional past. In 1934 there were three printings; Mitchell basked in popularity.

The next year brought a total reversal. Mitchell accused himself of misusing clients' funds and wrote to the attorney-general of Ontario, asking to be arrested. Horrified clients refused to testify against him: he had in fact been shifting bits of cash, inefficiently, from one account to another. Friends, including E. J. Pratt and William Arthur Deacon, collected money to compensate; the judge, however, had no alternative but to sentence Mitchell to six months' imprisonment and the Law Society was obliged to disbar him.

Mitchell served his term at the farm-jail at Langstaff. The immediate literary result was a volume of verse, *The Water-Drinker* (1937). A whimsical introduction, on the difficulties and values of

writing poetry while in prison, leads to a sequence on French voyageurs, another on Indian life on the Chinquacousy, another on the love of an Indian girl, some formal nature poetry, and one ironic monologue by a city capitalist.

The second result of Mitchell's prison experience was *Robert Harding* (1938), the story of an ex-convict. It begins as a near-documentary account of a criminal trial and of prison conditions. Details are convincing, though unpleasant. The author adds to the discomfort of his readers by heavily ironic commentaries. The second half is an affecting romance. Again it is the beautiful girl who proposes, but this time the lonely outsider, the jailbird, accepts and settles into a long happy ending. Readers and reviewers, however, found the book disjointed.

The 1940s were hard times for Mitchell. He lost Inglewood in 1942 and moved to a shack in Streetsville, raising chrysanthemums and fighting bad health. Finally, dogged by arteriosclerosis, he moved back to the Toronto boardinghouse district of his high-school days. One bright spot was the republication of *The Yellow Briar* by Macmillan in 1945. In 1950 Mitchell was commissioned to write a book celebrating the centenary of York County's incorporation. He spent the last year of his life in research at the Toronto Public Reference Library, an eccentric, shy recluse. In 1951 he died, penniless. *The Settlement of York County* (1952), published posthumously, unedited, and without critical apparatus, remains a readable, chatty local history.

"Regional idyll" its first reviewers had called *The Yellow Briar*. Dorothy L. Bishop, who wrote a biographical introduction to a 1970 edition of the novel, uses a more accurate phrase—"regional glossary." The dialect exemplifies the blend of accuracy and charm: "I upped and inned," says Paddy, "and later I upped and outed." *The Yellow Briar* uses folktale materials and is itself a folktale with a genuinely Canadian flavor. Sad divisions keep "outsiders" from rooting in older communities; rewards do not accord with gifts; the fight for civility may fail. These Canadian twists to the archetypal story of orphan apprenticeship are also the hallmark of the sad, strange life of the author.

Reference:
Dorothy L. Bishop, "The Story of John Mitchell," in Mitchell's *The Yellow Briar* (Toronto: Macmillan, 1970).

John Sutherland

(21 February 1919-1 September 1956)

W. H. New
University of British Columbia

BOOKS: *The Poetry of E. J. Pratt: A New Interpretation* (Toronto: Ryerson, 1956);
John Sutherland: Essays, Controversies and Poems, edited by Miriam Waddington (Toronto: McClelland & Stewart, 1972).

OTHER: *Other Canadians: An Anthology of the New Poetry in Canada, 1940-1946,* edited by Sutherland (Montreal: First Statement Press, 1947).

John M. A. Sutherland is remembered as an editor and critic, one whose voice spoke out forcefully and forthrightly in the 1940s, calling for greater attention to specific literary texts and less tolerance of literary generalizations. That he was also an anthologist, essayist, and poet testifies to the range of his literary application. He remains an important figure in the history of Canadian poetry.

He was born 21 February 1919, in Liverpool, Nova Scotia, to Frederick McClae Sutherland (later the vice president and manager of the New Brunswick Light, Heat and Power Company) and the former Lois Parker. Childhood was marked by the death of his mother (from tuberculosis) when Sutherland was seven; his father (who married again four years later) remained concerned about his son's health, for the boy seemed to have inherited a susceptibility to disease. Bed rest was deemed the appropriate preventive medicine, or the cure. During one period of enforced rest, Sutherland began to write.

Later, during a year at Queen's University in Kingston, Ontario (1936-37), Sutherland developed renal tuberculosis, and one kidney was removed. Another (this time extended) period of convalescence followed at his father's home in Saint John. But he bridled at the protracted treatment and in 1941 enrolled in an arts course at McGill University in Montreal; within a few months, he withdrew and got a job as night clerk at the Windsor Hotel. He was also writing.

Dissatisfied with current publishing trends and tastes, however–and unhappy when the newly founded Montreal little magazine *Preview* rejected his poems–he decided to start publishing himself. Aided by Audrey Aikman (who married him on 27 November 1943), by his sister, Betty Sutherland (who later married the poet Irving Layton), and by other McGill undergraduates, he founded a magazine called *First Statement* in September 1942. He was friends with Mavis Gallant, William McConnell, and other fledgling writers. Layton and Louis Dudek joined the editorial board of *First Statement* a year later. Together they declared themselves to favor social realism in literature and to champion honest, direct language as the method of modern poetry. In 1943 also, the group acquired a printing press–the first issue of *First Statement* was six pages long and mimeographed–and First Statement Press produced a series of influential poetry chapbooks, the first of which was Layton's *Here and Now* (1945).

In his later years Sutherland was also involved in editing another journal, entitled *Index*, but it is for the several transformations of *First Statement* that he is mainly remembered. *First Statement* sustained a lively and sometimes waspish relationship with *Preview*, but in late 1945 the two journals merged as *Northern Review*. Sutherland became managing editor, a position he held until his death (from cancer, complicated by tuberculosis) in 1956. Neil Fisher has analyzed Sutherland's role as editor in *First Statement 1942-1945: An Assessment and An Index* (1974). Robert Weaver has commented on his role in a 1957 article for *Tamarack Review*, as has Hilda Vanneste in her 1982 book, *Northern Review, 1945-1956: A History and An Index.*

Even more barbed was the relationship between Sutherland and A. J. M. Smith, who had been one of the rebels of the preceding generation but was now considered an establishment voice. When Smith published his influential 1943 anthology, *The Book of Canadian Poetry,* Suther-

Covers for the posthumously published collection edited by Miriam Waddington, one of the first contributors to Sutherland's magazine First Statement

land took exception to both the selection and the critical categories outlined in Smith's introduction. The result was *Other Canadians* (1947), a 113-page First Statement anthology of the new poets of the 1940s–especially Layton, Dudek, and Raymond Souster–who Sutherland felt had been ignored in Smith's book and were not read as individual writers.

The introduction took Smith to task for opposing the terms "native" and "cosmopolitan" as though they were meaningful in the first place and mutually exclusive in the second. Sutherland castigated the older "nature poets" (Sir Charles G. D. Roberts and others) for their provincialism; and while acknowledging the creative energies

and social and psychological commitments of some of his contemporaries, he was at pains to point out that their so-called cosmopolitanism did not free them from provinciality: "the movement of the forties does not alter the colonial basis of our poetry. We have found it difficult to admit this because we are faced with some rather paradoxical facts. One of them is the deceptive front of the new poetry, which, being Marxist in outlook, is committed to a society in which colonies, like colonial attitudes, will cease to exist. Another fact is the poetic achievement of the new school, which, taken as a whole, reaches a level attained only by isolated figures in the past. . . . [W]e should not make the mistake of identifying 'colonial' with what is bad in the literary sense, or . . . of assuming that poetry in Canada has achieved an individuality of its own and that the impediment to its free development has now been removed. The poets of the forties are English by origin and birth, and the new poetry is predominantly English in tone. James Wreford, Ronald Hambleton, P. K. Page, Patrick Anderson, were all born in England or educated there: what they produce must seem strange and alien to those who, in a way still undefined, feel themselves Canadian. . . . There is no doubt that the English poet will find it difficult to deal with Canadian themes and Canadian material, certainly to deal with them in a way that is felt to be Canadian; he will lack the convincing reality which is increasingly demanded of our poets as Canada begins to grow up. It is this division between the poet and his audience which is of crucial importance today."

Moreover, Sutherland praised Layton, Dudek, and Souster for what they implied about poetic change: "Judged by the pure aesthetic standard, the English colonial poets are producing the best work: the writers I refer to are achieving something of more significance for the future. They are not middle class but proletarian in origin. . . . They have followed American literary models rather than English ones. . . . In their work one finds a more Canadian point of view. . . ." As for Smith's critical terms, Sutherland met them with a series of trenchant commentaries on the critical presuppositions that underlay them:

> What is significant about the nature poets is their isolation in the midst of an alien environment, and their inability to express the environment except with borrowed instruments and from a colonial point of view.
>
> . . . the critic has a penchant for the word tradition, and welcomes the wide field of speculation which it throws open to him.
>
> We could only use the word tradition if we believed that the poetry was so blended with the life of the country that it was able to reach into the present and influence its course.

What he called for to refute such critical inexactitude was a close and particular analysis of text—of text as distinct from personality—and the logical critique of criticism itself.

In his essays, reviews, and comments—collected in *John Sutherland: Essays, Controversies and Poems* (1972), edited by his friend from the

1940s and onetime *First Statement* poet, Miriam Waddington—he reiterated these views. He dismissed sentimental poetry; he championed the irritant role of coterie little magazines (though acknowledged that they inevitably therefore led precarious existences); he praised anything that seemed to him innovative and exact in language (some of Earle Birney, much of W. W. E. Ross and Anne Marriott, most of E. J. Pratt—"he may do more than anyone to clear the cobwebs out of our literature"); he got himself into a legal cause célèbre when, operating by his own principles and examining poetic texts, he elucidated what he read as the sexual implications of Patrick Anderson's verse; and he was capable of broad ironic gestures when dismissing what he did not like, as in his attack upon the awarding of the 1946 Governor General's Award for poetry to Robert Finch:

1. Respectability. Finch is a professor of French at the University of Toronto.
2. Precedent. The award has a habit of going to the sturdy Western farmer type or the etherialized academician . . .
3. Naive wonder. Mr. Finch kept his first book up his sleeve for twenty years.
4. Fairness. Ryerson Press had won many times and Oxford never had.
5. Respect for age. Mr. Finch was old enough: the other candidates were not.
6. Sanctimoniousness. Mr. Finch was morally correct and sounded religious.
7. Hypocrisy. The politics of the younger writers was "out of place" in poetry.
8. Snobbery. Finch was billed as a talented musician and painter.
9. Credulity. The judges accepted Finch's verdict on his own work. . . .
10. Ignorance. The judges knew of, but had not read, Louis Dudek, P. K. Page or Patrick Anderson.
11. Ignorance. The judges had not read Finch. None of these reasons entirely satisfy me, but the thing is hard to explain.

Many of Sutherland's poems took up similar causes, issues, and stances, as in his praise for the poet in "E. J. Pratt" (about whom he also wrote a 1956 critical volume entitled *The Poetry of E. J. Pratt: A New Interpretation*) or his ironic versions of Smith and others in "Guide to the Canadian Poets." Part seven of the latter poem, subtitled "Cynic," is a mordant unrhymed quatrain:

The times, as he observes,
Pay him no compliments at all:
Therefore, why should he
Pay compliments to the times?

In the one article to have paid any critical attention to Sutherland's poetry, "All Nature into Motion" (*Canadian Literature*, Summer 1969), Miriam Waddington notes that loneliness and fear of a loss of identity recurrently underlie his metaphors; she quotes from "The Face":

One day, in shock or indecision, all
The particles will riot in the face:
They'll crack the bony haloes of his cheeks;
Or tear at one another till they roll
In sudden harmony like smoke that seethes
About a hollow eye, then pours away.

Equally effective is "Three Prose Poems," originally published in *First Statement*.

During his lifetime Sutherland published only about twelve poems altogether, most in *First Statement*, four in *Poetry* (Chicago). At his death he left a manuscript of forty-three poems, titled "First Poems." But by the time of his death, much had changed. He had converted to Roman Catholicism and given up much of the Nietzschean stance of his earlier criticism. (Catholicism even colored his 1956 reading of the lapsed Methodist Pratt.) Following his 1947 attack on Robert Finch, moreover, the former *Preview* writers who were on the editorial board of *Northern Review* resigned; Dudek had already gone, to study in New York; Layton left in 1948. As *Northern Review* continued with Sutherland alone in the editorial chair, it became more conservative. When Souster established *Contact* magazine in Toronto in 1952, it was partly in reaction to the change in Sutherland's inclinations. Souster continued to champion the power of the American speaking voice, and with his enthusiasm in *Contact* for the work of Cid Corman, Charles Olson, and Robert Creeley, the impetus for continuing change in Canadian poetry in what remained of the 1950s moved away from Montreal.

References:

Neil H. Fisher, *First Statement 1942-1945: An Assessment and An Index* (Ottawa: Golden Dog Press, 1974);

Wynne Francis, "Montreal Poets of the Forties," *Canadian Literature*, 14 (Autumn 1962): 21-34;

Hilda M. C. Vanneste, *Northern Review, 1945-1956: A History and an Index* (Ottawa: Tecumseh, 1982);

Miriam Waddington, "All Nature into Motion," *Canadian Literature*, 41 (Summer 1969): 73-85;

Waddington, Introduction to *John Sutherland: Essays, Controversies and Poems*, edited by Waddington (Toronto: McClelland & Stewart, 1972), pp. 7-18;

Robert Weaver, "John Sutherland and *Northern Review*," *Tamarack Review*, 2 (Winter 1957): 65-69.

Miriam Waddington
(23 December 1917-   )

Laurie Ricou
University of British Columbia

BOOKS: *Green World* (Montreal: First Statement, 1945);
The Second Silence (Toronto: Ryerson, 1955);
The Season's Lovers (Toronto: Ryerson, 1958);
The Glass Trumpet (Toronto: Oxford University Press, 1966);
Say Yes (Toronto: Oxford University Press, 1969);
A. M. Klein (Toronto: Copp Clark, 1970);
Dream Telescope (London: Anvil, 1972);
Driving Home: Poems New and Selected (Toronto: Oxford University Press, 1972; London: Anvil, 1973);
The Price of Gold (Toronto: Oxford University Press, 1976);
Mister Never (Winnipeg: Turnstone, 1978);
The Visitants (Toronto: Oxford University Press, 1981);
Summer at Lonely Beach and Other Stories (Oakville, Ontario: Mosaic Press/Valley Editions, 1982);
Collected Poems (Toronto: Oxford University Press, 1986).

OTHER: *Call Them Canadians*, poems by Waddington, edited by Lorraine Monk (Ottawa: Duhamel, 1968);
John Sutherland: Essays, Controversies and Poems, edited, with an introduction, by Waddington (Toronto: McClelland & Stewart, 1972);
"Literary Studies in English," in *Supplement to the Oxford Companion to Canadian History and Literature*, edited by William Toye (Toronto: Oxford University Press, 1973), pp. 204-210;
The Collected Poems of A. M. Klein, compiled, with an introduction, by Waddington (Toronto: McGraw-Hill Ryerson, 1974).

PERIODICAL PUBLICATIONS: "Exile," *Maclean's*, 87 (March 1974): 40-43;
"Form and Ideology in Poetry," *Laurentian University Review*, 10 (February 1978): 111-119.

Miriam Waddington's memories of childhood embrace adventurous rambles across the

Miriam Waddington (photograph copyright © Ellen Tolmie)

prairie in an early Ford, jokes and folk songs around the dinner table, and growing in a family of enthusiastic gardeners. Happiness dominates despite her sense of being an "outsider": "The message that had come through to me in public school in Winnipeg, and again in high school in Ottawa, was that to be a Canadian was to be English, to have your mother in the IODE [Imperial Order of Daughters of the Empire] and your father in the Rotarians. . . . But I was Jewish, and the child of Russian immigrants who were so critical of the economic system that the conductor on the streetcar near where I lived was once moved to ask, 'Your daddy is a Bolshevik, isn't he, little girl?'" This composite image of the freely singing outsider defines Waddington's position among Canadian writers: for forty years she has written intense and subtle lyrics, the equal, certainly, of the much better known poetry of Dorothy Livesay, yet her work has received little critical attention. The standard view of her as an interesting peripheral figure may, indeed, stem, in part, from the poet's own cultivating of the role of outsider: for example, her autobiographical article published in *Maclean's* in 1974 is titled, starkly, "Exile."

Waddington was born Miriam Dworkin to Yitzhak and Mussia Dobrusin Dworkin in Winnipeg, a city which, she enthuses in "Exile," "stays in my mind like a poem and its rhythms linger in my blood like snow songs." Waddington's early formal education was "permissive"; she was taught by European intellectuals, many of whom were or became writers, in a Yiddish school which encouraged students to question their teachers. Summer vacations "at the OBU [One Big Union] camp in Gimli" deepened the young girl's political consciousness. In grade five Waddington was transferred to Machray School, where she came under the contrasting influence of "a structured, rigid, conservative school system" governed by "Scots Tories." Lemoine FitzGerald was one of her teachers in Saturday morning classes at the Winnipeg School of Art. Such diverse educational experiences intensified the "kaleidoscopic" cultural contacts of an immigrant family in Winnipeg: Waddington recalls the Ukrainian farmers, a strict Mennonite housekeeper, and Métis children near the weekend farm in St. Vital, which her father bought when she was about ten.

In the 1930s Waddington's family moved to Ottawa, extending her cultural contacts more widely. But a Winnipeg childhood had established the pattern for Waddington's career and her poetry. The many languages which surrounded her gave her great sensitivity to the sounds, rhythms, and meanings of words. Folk motifs, concern for the oppressed, and a child's eye for growing things are central to her work.

At the University of Toronto, while studying for her B.A., which she received in 1939, Waddington published several stories and poems in undergraduate publications. On 5 July 1939 she married Patrick Waddington, a journalist. During the war she began to publish poems, stories, and reviews in a variety of literary periodicals, while studying for a diploma in social work

(awarded by Toronto in 1942) and an M.S.W. (given by the University of Pennsylvania in 1945); she also worked as a social services caseworker. The ugliness of what she saw as a social worker in a big city became the theme for many of the poems in Waddington's first book, *Green World* (1945). But from the beginning her strength was the lyric celebrating the physical, growing world; in one of the first reviews of *Green World* Northrop Frye wrote that the poet has "a lyrical gift of great beauty and subtlety, and her work has a uniform level of excellence both in technique and expressive power" (*Canadian Forum*, September 1946). Waddington's title is deliberately chosen to declare her rejection of the wasteland, the fragmentation, and the grayness in modern poetry. Although unwilling to be aligned with particular movements and schools, Waddington, in a 1978 article for *Laurentian University Review*, places herself "outside ... the main stream of modernism" in terms consistent with her first title: "In poetry I disliked rhetoric, intellectual word-play, and T. S. Eliot, which made me native rather than cosmopolitan (according to A. J. M. Smith's famous classification); and realist-physical rather than metaphysical."

With her move to Montreal in 1945 Waddington became associated firsthand with the poetic revival centered in that city during the 1940s and early 1950s. She raised two sons and worked as an instructor for the McGill School of Social Work and later as a caseworker in the Montreal Children's Hospital, the John Howard Society, and the Jewish Family and Child Service. Much of the poetry which she published steadily during the period was brought together in *The Second Silence* (1955). The collection is in four sections: "Poems of Love," "Poems of Children," "Poems of Work," and "Poems of Living." Although in this book there is more narrative, more local description, and a more bitter view of society's ugliness, the poems most impressive for careful structure, use of repetition, and sustained metaphor, such as "Thou Didst Say Me" and "Catalpa Tree," are poems with singing rhythms that are heard above the somber notes. But, as Waddington later commented, ruefully, the book provoked little interest: "*The Second Silence*—an ironic title because there certainly was a silence after that. The book didn't sell. If people see a book on the shelf, they might buy it. My book is never anywhere."

The Season's Lovers (1958), again concentrating on the city's life and on Waddington's experi-

Angels who sweep   m waddington

11

The messengers
with the suffering eyes
& shaved hands
will come from the north   the moths, the lunar distance
they will sit in the cold
in cold classrooms
pretending to learn
Set their tongues will be tied
their heads will be bound
They will lean weightlessly   sometimes
towards remembered earth   they will glimpse
and are in the airless space   the flush haired lantern
the echoes of
for Jerusalem .

The traces of hands   the sound of
and birds, mother Jerusalem   broken sentences, prayers
& the touch of mother Jerusalem
hardly believe there were angels & mothers   all brush past them
They remember   & goodnight kisses
angels and the last faint
Their goodnight kiss
of mother Jerusalem

(they/we await the resurrection)

Manuscript for a poem by Waddington (by permission of the author)

ences as social worker and concluding with a section of varied poems of love, met with less silence. One reviewer concluded, grudgingly (and wrongly), that it would win a Governor General's Award. More significantly, Ian Sowton, writing for *Dalhousie Review* (Summer 1959), greeted the book's appearance with a serious examination of Waddington's metaphysical lyrics and rhythmical idioms. Sowton's article, though it is the only extended discussion of Waddington before 1978, marks a recognition that Waddington is no occasionally felicitous versifier but a serious, committed artist: "The movement of her poetic self is almost invariably responsive. The situations she projects are of the sensitive and intelligent self in the various attitudes of response from ecstatic to revulsive.... There is in Miss Waddington's work a peculiarly direct relation between the lyric form and its content: her content is almost lyricism itself."

When Waddington moved to Toronto in 1960 after separation from her husband (they were divorced in 1965), she worked as a casework supervisor in the North York Family and Child Service. But perhaps as the sensitive self more certainly recognized the intelligent self Waddington gradually returned, first as part-time lecturer at Atkinson College, to the academic life. Beginning as a full-time lecturer in York University's English department in 1964, Waddington became a professor in that department in 1973. With the recognition of a Canada Council Senior Arts Fellowship in 1962 and Borestone Mountain Poetry awards in 1964 and 1966, she began to publish almost a book a year. *The Glass Trumpet* (1966) marks a new association with Oxford University Press and introduces her most noticeable technical development, the short line (usually two to six syllables); the less-regular short line reflects a greater interest in the rhythms of the speaking voice and in the simpler language of folk song. *The Glass Trumpet* also shows a greater interest in her Winnipeg and prairie childhood. She learned there, she writes in "Things of the world," a "blazing innocence," a phrase which expresses the passionate *commitment* to the innocence of her best poetry.

Waddington wrote poems to accompany photographs for the National Film Board centennial publication *Call Them Canadians* (1968). The next year *Say Yes* appeared, broadening Waddington's subject matter to include Europe and the Near East where she spent a sabbatical in 1968-1969. By this time a good deal of her attention was de-

Waddington in 1972 (photograph by John Reeves)

voted to critical writing on other poets. She published a critical study of A. M. Klein in 1970 and edited Klein's collected poems in 1974. She also edited the work of John Sutherland, her associate from Montreal days, for publication in 1972 in the New Canadian Library.

A slim book of poems, *Dream Telescope*, was published in London in 1972. Several of its best poems also appeared that same year in the substantial collection *Driving Home: Poems New and Selected*. The book contains over thirty new poems and an intelligent selection of the best from Waddington's earlier volumes. The book continues the move to a sparer simplicity; her new poems show greater interest in landscape and in her Canadian identity, yet she finds herself, again, outside the new fashions: "There are many/ things I must learn/in order to write/better in Canada./I must learn to/write & for *and*/and *wll* for *will*:/to put *:* at the/beginning of a line/instead of at the end."

The Price of Gold (1976) is an important major collection. The first section, "Rivers," draws on some of the poet's travels, literal and

Cover for Waddington's 1978 chapbook of love poems

emotional; the second section, "Living Canadian," continues *Driving Home*'s more explicit interest, often wryly and maturely humorous, in her country; the last section, "The Cave," consists of reflections on aging and death. Perhaps the sense of the poet's not taking herself too seriously leads to a note in many of the reviews that, perhaps, Waddington is a poet who has been too long overlooked. Frank Watt, while noting an "awkward honesty and directness," concluded that Waddington is "a fine poet who takes the game of poetry too seriously to cheat us" (*Canadian Forum*, May 1977). Another reviewer, more colloquially, said "Miriam Waddington is one of the best things Can-Lit has going for it" (*Last Post*, March 1977). John Robert Colombo was perhaps most representative of the new respect for Waddington's contribution to Canadian letters, finding that *The Price of Gold* "puts the reader on an intimate footing with its author, who emerges not just as a craftsman but as a human being, full of warmth and wonder, maturity and experience" (Toronto. *Globe and Mail*, 4 September 1976).

Mister Never (1978) is a chapbook of love poems, or more exactly, as Waddington describes

them, poems of "absence, of unreturned love," most written between 1968 and 1972 and some republished from earlier volumes. *Summer at Lonely Beach and Other Stories* (1982) is a collection of fourteen of Waddington's short short stories which, with tentatively didactic simplicity, describe the emotional lives of characters usually outside the homogeneity of the Anglo-Saxon middle-class. The volume of poetry *The Visitants* (1981) is especially pleasing for the wry crankiness of its middle section, "How Old Women Should Live": "Old women/should live like worms/under the earth,/they should come out/only after a good rain." In these three later books the image of Waddington–as poet, as lover, as woman, as aging– on the outside continues. But there is also shown a writer who has recognized that outside one can grow, one's energies can expand, one can dream. The title poem of Waddington's first collection tells what happens when the poet "step[s] out." It still, perhaps, serves, as I wrote in *Essays on Canadian Writing* (Fall 1978), to sum up the fundamental direction and lyric strength of her poetry: "not anecdotal, but slightly elusive in its playing with correspondences; . . . not colloquial, but charged with alliterative rhythms; its images are relatively general, and do not serve to locate a specific experience or landscape; it begins with 'I' and ends with 'me', emphasizing the contours of the personal response."

Bibliography:

L. R. Ricou, "Miriam Waddington: An Annotated Bibliography," in *The Annotated Bibliography of Canada's Major Authors*, edited by Robert Lecker and Jack David, volume 6 (Downsview, Ontario: ECW, 1985), pp. 237-388.

References:

Maria Jacobs, "The Personal Poetry of Miriam Waddington," *CV/II*, 5 (Autumn 1980): 26-33;

Cathy Matyas, "Miriam Waddington," in *Profiles in Canadian Literature 4*, edited by Jeffrey M. Heath (Toronto: Dundurn Press, 1982), pp. 9-16;

L. R. Ricou, "Into My Green World: The Poetry of Miriam Waddington," *Essays on Canadian Writing*, 12 (Fall 1978): 144-161;

Ian Sowton, "The Lyric Craft of Miriam Waddington," *Dalhousie Review*, 39 (Summer 1959): 237-242;

Peter Stevens, "Miriam Waddington," in *Canadian Writers and Their Works Poetry Series*, edited by Robert Lecker, Jack David, and Ellen Quigley, volume 5 (Downsview, Ontario: ECW, 1985), pp. 277-329.

Papers:
The Miriam Waddington Collection at the Public Archives, Ottawa, includes manuscripts, typescripts, galleys, page proofs, notes, printed material, and some correspondence.

Ethel Wilson

(20 January 1888-22 December 1980)

Margaret E. Doyle
Wilfrid Laurier University

BOOKS: *Hetty Dorval* (Toronto: Macmillan, 1947; London: Macmillan, 1948);

The Innocent Traveller (London: Macmillan, 1949; Toronto: Macmillan, 1949);

The Equations of Love (London: Macmillan, 1952; Toronto: Macmillan, 1952);

Swamp Angel (London: Macmillan, 1954; Toronto: Macmillan, 1954; enlarged, New York: Harper, 1954);

Love and Salt Water (London: Macmillan, 1956; Toronto: Macmillan, 1956; New York: St. Martin's, 1957);

Mrs. Golightly and Other Stories (Toronto: Macmillan, 1961; London: Macmillan, 1962);

Ethel Wilson: Stories, Essays, and Letters, edited by David Stouck (Vancouver: University of British Columbia Press, 1987).

PERIODICAL PUBLICATIONS:

FICTION

"The Surprising Adventures of Peter," *Vancouver Province*, 1 March-13 June 1919;

"The Cigar and the Poor Young Girl," *Echoes* (Autumn 1945): 11, 46;

"Simple Translation," *Saturday Night*, 76 (23 December 1961): 19;

"A Visit to the Frontier," *Tamarack Review*, 33 (Autumn 1964): 55-65.

NONFICTION

"A Cat among the Falcons: Reflections on the Writer's Craft," *Canadian Literature*, 2 (Autumn 1959): 10-19;

"The Bridge or the Stokehold?: Views of the Nov-

elist's Art," *Canadian Literature*, 5 (Summer 1960): 43-47;

"Reflections in a Pool," *Canadian Literature*, 22 (Autumn 1964): 29-33;

"Series of Combination of Events and Where is John Goodwin?," *Tamarack Review*, 33 (Autumn 1964): 3-9;

"Young Vancouver Seen through the Eyes of Youth," *Habitat*, 10, nos. 3-6 (1967): 138-139.

The fiction of Ethel Wilson occupies a special place in Canadian literature. Because she was born in the late nineteenth century but did not publish her first novel until almost mid twentieth century, her writing reflects both the religious and cultural values of her past and the uncertainties of the present in which she wrote. Thus in her novels the British Columbia landscape–the usually indifferent or hostile world of the present in which her characters must make their way– is enriched by the perspectives of time and place her upbringing provides.

Ethel Davis Bryant Wilson was born in Port Elizabeth, South Africa, of English parents. Her father, Robert William Bryant, was a Methodist minister; her mother, Eliza Lila Davis Malkin Bryant, came from a staunch Methodist family. In 1890, after her mother's death, she was taken to England by her father, and in 1898, following her father's death, she moved to the then-new city of Vancouver to live with her maternal grandmother and family, themselves recent emigrants

Ethel Wilson (photograph by Stanley Read, courtesy of Special Collections, University of British Columbia Library, Vancouver)

from England. The three women of the family—the grandmother and her unmarried daughter and sister—provided a strict but loving home for the orphan. In reminiscences such as "Young Vancouver Seen through the Eyes of Youth" (published in a 1967 issue of *Habitat*), Wilson describes the ordered life of the cultured and pious household: twice daily family prayer, evenings of music or reading (but not cards), Sunday tea with the married sons and their families.

Wilson's education reflects this tradition. From 1898 to 1902 she attended a private girls' school in Vancouver where, she recalled in the "Young Vancouver" reminiscence, "the atmosphere of England, our former home, was with us, and so was the love and surprise of our new country." In 1902 she traveled to England to spend four years at a Wesleyan boarding school after which, she explained in a partly autobiographical essay, "A Cat among the Falcons" (*Cana-*

dian Literature, Autumn 1959), "my education became unorthodox, eclectic, spotty, and ceaselessly interesting," highlighted by a lifetime of reading. Back in Vancouver she attended normal school for a year, then taught in various Vancouver elementary schools from 1907 to 1920.

Her marriage on 4 January 1921 to Wallace Wilson (1888-1966), a Vancouver doctor, removed her from the strict Methodism of her grandmother's family, as she acknowledged in an article in *Mayfair* following the 1947 publication of *Hetty Dorval,* her first novel: "It was not until I was married that I learned it was possible to enjoy life without first passing a moral judgment on it." Two of the pleasures she and her husband shared were reading and travel. A summer trout-fishing trip to Lac le Jeune in the British Columbia interior soon after their marriage was a frequently repeated event over the next thirty-five years. In addition the Wilsons traveled regularly to England, and in 1930 they spent a year in Vienna preceded by a trip to the Middle East. All these settings were to find a place in her work.

But the role of doctor's wife involved numerous social responsibilities which Wilson did not enjoy and from which she increasingly turned to the privacy of her writing. Although according to "A Cat among the Falcons" it was not until 1937-1938, when she was almost fifty, that she found it "imperative to write," she had been making up stories for others almost all her life and writing since at least 1930. As a schoolgirl in Vancouver she had composed stories while on school walks; a serial adventure tale for children appeared in a Vancouver newspaper in 1919, and after her marriage she used to write in the evenings in the car, waiting while her husband was making house calls. In 1937 her first short story, "I Just Love Dogs," appeared in the *New Statesman and Nation,* to be followed by others in both English and Canadian magazines and periodicals, and during the war when her husband was serving with the Canadian army she edited a Red Cross magazine. Then in 1946-1947, when she was nearly sixty, and while helping her husband with his administrative duties as newly elected president of the Canadian Medical Association, she wrote her first published novel, *Hetty Dorval.*

The epigraphs from John Donne, "No man is an Ilande" and "Good is as visible as greene," which preface *Hetty Dorval* introduce recurrent themes in Wilson's fiction—the need for human community and moral values. But narrator

Dust jacket for Wilson's second published novel, an episodic portrait of two families, developed by the author from some of her early short stories

Frankie Burnaby's encounters with the enigmatic Hetty Dorval, which begin in the small town of Lytton, British Columbia, and end several years later with Hetty's disappearance into prewar Vienna, do not reflect the religious confidence of Donne. Instead, they emphasize human vulnerability, since each woman has the power to destroy the other's happiness. Similarly, the visibility of good is blurred by the deceptiveness of Hetty's "two-faced" appearance: the purity of her profile and the indolence and sensuality of her full face. The divided critical opinion as to whether Hetty is a "good" or "bad" woman reflects Wilson's sense of life's moral ambiguity.

Frankie Burnaby's growth from schoolgirl to young woman is marked by her changing attitude toward Hetty, from adolescent awe to recognition of Hetty's evasion of the ties of love and family whereby Wilson's characters often assume adult responsibility and find self-identity. While critics point to the novel's melodramatic ending and inconsistency of narration, they also praise

the portrayal of the British Columbia interior, the beautiful but potentially dangerous world where human values are tested.

In the *Mayfair* article Wilson revealed that for years she had been composing stories for young relatives about older members of her family who had impressed her strongly as a child; after publishing some of these stories in periodicals, she expanded them into a novel, *The Innocent Traveller*, which, although written before *Hetty Dorval*, was not published until 1949. The detailed and episodic portrait of the Edgeworth-Hastings families over the hundred years of the relatively uneventful life of Topaz Edgeworth, the "innocent traveller" of the title, contains some of Wilson's best writing and most memorable characters. Both the rewards and the dangers of human community are apparent; the family provides a form of self-definition for Topaz, as she is successively daughter, sister, aunt, and great-aunt, but it also keeps her forever "the youngest," dependent on others for survival. In the novel's water imagery, derived from Donne, her life is a canal, she herself a water-glider, her superficiality suggested by her incessant chatter.

The depths beneath the surface over which Topaz skims so innocently are provided by the other women of the family: Topaz's saintly elder sister Annie Hastings; Annie's practical daughter Rachel; and Topaz's great-niece Rose, Wilson's fictional self. As the self-contained Rose grows in the second half of the novel from child to married woman, her life stands in implicit contrast to Topaz's, so that it is through her and the omniscient narrator that the reader sees the cumulative effects of time and place (from mid-nineteenth-century England to mid-twentieth-century Vancouver) on Topaz's lifelong journey.

Wilson's next book, *The Equations of Love* (1952), explores the lives of working-class characters in two stories, "Tuesday and Wednesday" and "Lilly's Story." The former covers two days in the lives of Mort and Myrtle Johnson, ending with Mort's death in a drowning accident; the latter covers about thirty years in the life of Lilly Waller who, after successfully raising her illegitimate daughter, Eleanor, finally marries a kindly widower. While the idea for "Lilly's Story" grew out of a reference in *The Innocent Traveller*, the characters in both stories come from observation, as Wilson explained to Canadian poet Dorothy Livesay: "I have *seen* them—coming out of a hotel, a beer parlor, a bus; but once having seen the face, then

the character and life of these people has un-
rolled before me."

The book's title and its epigraph from
Dickens's *Bleak House* ("what is this Terewth") introduce the theme of the relativity of such moral
values as truth and love. One equation of love in
"Tuesday and Wednesday," for example, is that
which prompts Myrtle's lonely cousin Victoria
May Tritt to tell her false story of Mort's heroism
and thereby enable Myrtle to think of him with
pride instead of anger. And in "Lilly's Story"
Lilly's love for Eleanor and the lies she tells to fab-
ricate a respectable background for them both
transform her over the years from a materialistic
and pleasure-loving girl into a devoted and selfless mother. The powerful central scene in the latter story in which Lilly observes a crow and gull
harassing an eagle stalking a kitten stalking a
robin catching a snake graphically renders the
ruthless and amoral world outside human
morality.

Even at the height of her career Wilson remained somewhat apart from the Canadian literary scene. Since Macmillan published each of her
books in turn both in England and in Canada to
generally favorable reviews, she found from the
outset an appreciative if modest audience sufficient to make her a notable and articulate exception to Canadian man of letters George Woodcock's assertion at a writers' conference in the
1950s that Canadian writers had little hope of English publication. As he later recalled in an appreciation, "Ethel Wilson," in *Canadian Fiction
Magazine* (Autumn 1974), "a woman whom I remember as tall and very self-possessed, with clear-
cut jawlines and well-cut clothes, stood up and in
very precise diction remarked that . . . English
publishers and editors had always been kind and
considerate to her and she felt I was doing them
a notable injustice. She spoke without obvious arrogance, yet there was a patrician assurance in
her manner to which at the time I reacted rather
acerbically. I was mortified later in the day when
I learnt that she was Ethel Wilson, whose *Equations of Love* I had just been reading with
admiration."

During the decade when all her novels were
published, from the late 1940s to the late 1950s,
she continued to travel both in Canada and Europe, even when illness began to circumscribe
her life. But even the painful arthritis which neces-
sitated her use of a wheelchair in later life could
not keep her from the trout fishing at Lac le
Jeune, near Kamloops, British Columbia, a set-

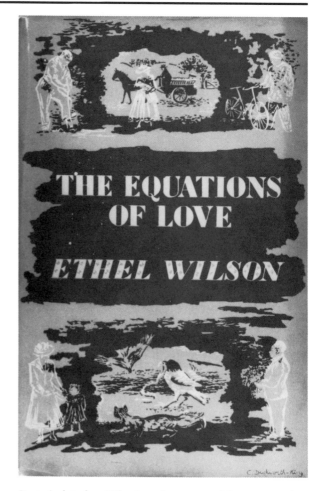

Dust jacket for Wilson's volume comprising two stories—
"Tuesday and Wednesday" and "Lilly's Story"—about the lives
of working-class characters

ting integral to her best-known and most impressive novel, *Swamp Angel* (1954).

Swamp Angel, the story of Maggie Lloyd,
who abandons a disastrous marriage and makes a
new life for herself as cook at a fishing lodge in
the British Columbia interior, embodies Wilson's
most intensive use of place to reveal theme and
character. Three Loon Lake is a powerfully realized symbol of life's ambivalences: although beautiful, the lake is potentially dangerous, capable of
drowning the unwary and foolhardy. Thus while
Maggie's swimming in the lake is equated with
her ability to swim around or overcome the obstacles in her life, the narrative voice comments:
"She could never sink, she thinks (but she
could)." On the lakeshore Maggie witnesses a playful encounter between a fawn and a kitten; over
the lake, a battle between an eagle and an osprey
for a fish.

The theme of "the miraculous interweaving
of creation," articulated in the novel by the re-

tired circus juggler Nell Severance–a friend whom Maggie leaves behind in Vancouver–is centered in Maggie, Wilson's finest character. Maggie embodies the human capacity for acts of compassion whose "operative grace" (in the words of the omniscient narrator) may, or–given the unpredictability of life–may not serve others. Thus while she rescues an elderly fisherman stranded on the lake, her attempts to help Vera Gunnarsen, the suicidal wife of the lodge owner, are less successful. Further, her refusal to burden herself with pointless self-recriminations about her past is in contrast to Nell's absorption with the "swamp angel," the gun she used in her circus act. At the end of her life Nell sends Maggie the gun: it is both a symbol and a message. By throwing the gun in the lake at the end of the novel Maggie displays both the humanity and the divine grace needed to face the conflicting and often irreconcilable claims of self and others, past and present.

Love and Salt Water (1956), Wilson's last published novel, is the story of Ellen Cuppy who, although suffering a series of traumatic events, beginning with her mother's death and ending with the near-drowning of her nephew Johnny in a boating accident, survives to marry and live a "happy chequered life." The title expresses the recurrent theme of the need for human love in a hostile or indifferent universe, represented by the sea in which a young sailor drowns and Johnny almost does. But many critics found the novel disappointing, particularly compared with *Swamp Angel*. The writing is uneven and the sense of place and the characterization are less powerful; the sea lacks the symbolic force of Three Loon Lake, and Ellen is a far less convincingly realized quester than Maggie.

A selection of short stories and sketches makes up the last book Wilson published in her lifetime, *Mrs. Golightly and Other Stories* (1961). The book's epigraph from Edwin Muir, "Life . . . is a difficult country and our home," conveys Wilson's view of the world whose unpredictability makes human actions and beliefs both difficult and necessary. The deceptiveness of appearances is a recurrent theme in stories ranging from the comedy of "I Just Love Dogs," in which an apparently dead dog gets up and walks away, to the terror and near-violence of "The Window," in which a window looking out on the world is really a wall that cuts the viewer off, as he belatedly realizes. With settings and atmosphere ranging from the fog of Vancouver to the heat of

Egypt and the constriction of a railway compartment en route to Vienna, the best stories reveal the isolation and even helplessness of characters for whom the world is, in Muir's phrasing, much more "difficult country" than "home."

By the time Wilson's contributions to Canadian literature were recognized by awards–a Canada Council Medal in 1961 and the Lorne Pierce Medal in 1964–her writing career was almost over. She published a few essays and short stories in the early 1960s, but then she suffered a stroke, and in 1966 her husband died. Devastated by this latter blow, she stopped writing. In 1971 she entered a Vancouver nursing home where in 1980 she died. A selection of her stories, essays, and unpublished letters was edited by David Stouck in 1987.

Thematically Wilson's fiction explores the need for love and community in a world characterized more by ambiguity and chaos than by moral certainty. Also discernible in Wilson's work is an increasing preoccupation with violence and death. *Love and Salt Water* originally ended with the deaths of Ellen and Johnny; a late story, "Fog," in which two young hoodlums rob and kill an elderly Chinese shopkeeper, reveals her interest in juvenile delinquency, the subject of a novel she left unfinished, "The Vat and the Brew." In "A Visit to the Frontier," published in *Tamarack Review* in 1964, death is a lonely and fatiguing experience.

While Wilson's fiction stands somewhat apart from other mid-century Canadian literature it has maintained a certain local popularity and has attracted considerable critical attention, much of it focusing on the blend of traditionalism and modernism, regionalism and universality that gives her work its characteristic voice. The traditionalism of her English literary and cultural heritage and the modernism of her portrayal of women searching for meaning and identity in the beautiful but uncertain world of British Columbia are important contributions to Canadian literature and assure her position in it.

Bibliography:
Bonnie Martyn McComb, "Ethel Wilson: An Annotated Bibliography," in *The Annotated Bibliography of Canada's Major Authors*, edited by Robert Lecker and Jack David, volume 5 (Downsview, Ontario: ECW, 1984), pp. 415-477.

References:
Dorothy Livesay, "Ethel Wilson: West Coast Novel-

ist," *Saturday Night*, 67 (26 July 1952): 20, 36;

Constance MacKay, "Vancouver's New Novelist," *Mayfair* (November 1947): 67, 101;

Lorraine McMullen, ed., *The Ethel Wilson Symposium* (Ottawa: University of Ottawa Press, 1982);

Beverley Mitchell, "Ethel Wilson," in *Canadian Writers and Their Works*, edited by Robert Lecker, Jack David, and Ellen Quigley, volume 6 (Downsview, Ontario: ECW, 1985), pp. 181-238;

Desmond Pacey, *Ethel Wilson* (New York: Twayne, 1967);

George Woodcock, "Ethel Wilson," *Canadian Fiction Magazine*, 15 (Autumn 1974): 44-49.

Papers:
The Ethel Wilson Collection and the Macmillan papers at the University of British Columbia Library contain unpublished material–essays, speeches, poems, short stories, and a novel–manuscripts of most published novels and stories, and letters, photographs, and miscellaneous papers.

Supplementary Reading List

Atlantic Provinces Literature Colloquium. Saint John, New Brunswick: Atlantic Canada Institute, 1977.

Margaret Atwood. *Survival: A Thematic Guide to Canadian Literature.* Toronto: Anansi, 1972.

Avis, Walter, and others. *A Concise Dictionary of Canadianisms.* Toronto: Gage, 1973.

Bailey, A. G. *Culture and Nationality: Essays.* Toronto: McClelland & Stewart, 1972.

Baillargeon, Samuel. *Littérature canadienne-française*, third edition, revised. Montreal & Paris: Fides, 1960.

Bélisle, Louis-Alexandre. *Dictionnaire général de la langue française au Canada.* Quebec: Bélisle, 1957.

Bélisle. *Dictionnaire nord-américaine de la langue française.* Montreal: Beauchemin, 1979.

Beraud, Jean. *350 Ans de théâtre au Canada français.* Montreal: Cercle du Livre de France, 1958.

Berger, Carl. *The Writing of Canadian History: Aspects of English-Canadian Historical Writing.* Toronto: Oxford University Press, 1976.

Bessette, Gérard. *Une littérature en ébullition.* Montreal: Editions du Jour, 1968.

Bhabha, Homi. "Representation and the Colonial Text: A Critical Exploration of Some Forms of Mimeticism," in *The Theory of Reading*, edited by Frank Gloversmith. Brighton, Sussex: Harvester, 1984, pp. 93-122.

Blais, Jacques. *De l'ordre et de l'aventure. La Poésie au Québec de 1934 à 1944.* Quebec: Presses de l'Université Laval, 1975.

Blodgett, E. D. *Configuration: Essays on the Canadian Literatures.* Toronto: ECW, 1982.

Bonenfant, Joseph, and others, eds. *A l'ombre de DesRochers: Le Mouvement littéraire des Cantons de l'est 1925-1950.* Sherbrooke, Quebec: Editions de l'Université de Sherbrooke, 1985.

Bonheim, Helmut. *The Narrative Modes: Techniques of the Short Story.* Cambridge: Brewer, 1982.

Brown, E. K. *Responses and Evaluations: Essays on Canada.* Toronto: McClelland & Stewart, 1977.

Brunet, Berthelot. *Histoire de la littérature canadienne-française.* Montreal: L'Arbre, 1946.

Cameron, Donald. *Conversations with Canadian Novelists*, 2 volumes. Toronto: Macmillan, 1973.

The Canadian Encyclopedia, 3 volumes. Edmonton: Hurtig, 1985.

Canadian Literature Index, quarterly index to book and periodical publications, with annual cumulations, edited by Janet Fraser. Toronto: ECW, 1985- .

Capone, Giovanna. *Canada: il villaggio della terra*. Bologna: Pàtron Editore, 1978.

Cappon, Paul, ed. *In Our House: Social Perspectives on Canadian Literature*. Toronto: McClelland & Stewart, 1978.

Caron, Anne. *Le Père Emile Legault et le théâtre au Québec*. Montreal: Fides, 1978.

Chaudhury, Uta. *Der Frankokanadische Roman de la terre: eine Entwicklungsstudie*. Bern & Frankfurt/Main: Herbert Lang & Peter Lang, 1976.

Cloutier-Wojciechowska, Cécile, and Réjean Robidoux, eds. *Solitude rompue*. Ottawa: Editions de l'Université d'Ottawa, 1986.

Codignola, Luca, ed. *Canadiana*. Venice: Marsilio, 1978.

Collet, Paulette. *L'Hiver dans le roman canadien français*. Quebec: Laval, 1965.

Collin, W. E. *The White Savannahs*. 1936; republished, Toronto & Buffalo: University of Toronto Press, 1975.

Colombo, John Robert. *Colombo's Canadian Quotations*. Edmonton: Hurtig, 1974.

Colombo, comp. *Colombo's Canadian References*. Toronto, Oxford & New York: Oxford University Press, 1976.

Colombo, and others, comps. *CDN SF & F: A Bibliography of Science Fiction and Fantasy*. Toronto: Hounslow, 1979.

Craig, Terrence. *Racial Attitudes in English-Canadian Fiction, 1905-1980*. Waterloo: Wilfrid Laurier University Press, 1987.

Cude, Wilfred. *A Due Sense of Differences: An Evaluative Approach to Canadian Literature*. Lanham, Md.: University Press of America, 1980.

Daymond, Douglas. *Towards a Canadian Literature*, volume 2. Ottawa: Tecumseh, 1985.

Daymond, and Leslie Monkman, eds. *Canadian Novelists and the Novel*. Ottawa: Borealis, 1981.

De Leon, Lisa. *Writers of Newfoundland and Labrador*. St. John's: Jesperson, 1985.

Dooley, D. J. *Moral Vision in the Canadian Novel*. Toronto: Clarke, Irwin, 1981.

Ducrocq-Poirier, Madeleine. *Le Roman canadien de langue française de 1860 à 1958*. Paris: Nizet, 1978.

Duffy, Dennis. *Gardens, Covenants, Exiles: Loyalism in the Literature of Upper Canada/Ontario*. Toronto: University of Toronto Press, 1982.

Duhamel, Roger. *Manuel de littérature canadienne-française*. Montreal: Editions du Renouveau Pédagogique, 1967.

Eggleston, Wilfrid. *The Frontier and Canadian Letters*. 1957; republished, Toronto: McClelland & Stewart, 1977.

Egoff, Sheila. *The Republic of Childhood: A Critical Guide to Canadian Children's Literature in English*, second edition. Toronto: Oxford University Press, 1975.

Fairbanks, Carol. *Prairie Women: Images in American and Canadian Fiction*. New Haven & London: Yale University Press, 1986.

Falardeau, Jean-Charles. *Imaginaire social et littérature*. Montreal: Hurtubise HMH, 1974.

Frick, N. Alice. *Image in the Mind: CBC Radio Drama, 1944-1954*. Toronto: Canadian Stage and Arts Publications, 1987.

Frye, Northrop. *The Bush Garden: Essays on the Canadian Imagination*. Toronto: Anansi, 1971.

Frye. *Divisions on a Ground*. Toronto: Anansi, 1982.

Frye. *The Modern Century*. Toronto: Oxford University Press, 1967.

Gagnon, Serge. *Quebec and Its Historians*, 2 volumes, translated by Jane Brierly. Montreal: Harvest House, 1982, 1985.

Gauvin, Lise, and Laurent Mailhot. *Guide culturel de Québec*. Montreal: Boréal Express, 1982.

Gnarowski, Michael. *A Concise Bibliography of English-Canadian Literature*, revised edition. Toronto: McClelland & Stewart, 1978.

Grandpré, Pierre de. *Histoire de la littérature française du Québec*, volume 2, 1900-1945. Montreal: Beauchemin, 1967.

Gross, Konrad, and Wolfgang Klooss, eds. *English Literature of the Dominions*. Würzburg: Verlag Königshausen & Neumann, 1981.

Guillaume, Pierre, Jean-Michel Lacroix, and Pierre Spriet, eds. *Canada et canadiens*. Bordeaux: Presses Universitaires de Bordeaux, 1984.

Hall, Roger, and Gordon Dodds. *Canada: A History in Photographs*. Edmonton: Hurtig, 1981.

Hancock, Geoff. *Canadian Writers at Work: Interviews*. Toronto: Oxford University Press, 1987.

Harper, J. Russell. *Painting in Canada: A History*. Toronto: University of Toronto Press, 1970.

Harrison, Dick. *Unnamed Country: The Struggle for a Canadian Prairie Fiction*. Edmonton: University of Alberta Press, 1977.

Harrison, ed. *Crossing Frontiers*. Edmonton: University of Alberta Press, 1979.

Heath, Jeffrey M., ed. *Profiles in Canadian Literature*, volumes 1-4. Toronto & Charlottetown: Dundurn, 1980-1982.

Innis, Mary Quayle, ed. *The Clear Spirit: Twenty Canadian Women and Their Times*. Toronto: University of Toronto Press, 1966.

Johnson, Harry G. *The Canadian Quandary: Economic Problems and Policies*. Toronto: McClelland & Stewart, 1977.

Jones, D. G. *Butterfly on Rock.* Toronto: University of Toronto Press, 1970.

Jones, Joseph. *Terranglia.* New York: Twayne, 1965.

Kallmann, Helmut, and others. *The Encyclopedia of Music in Canada.* Toronto: University of Toronto Press, 1981.

Keefer, Janice Kulyk. *Under Eastern Eyes: A Critical Reading of Maritime Fiction.* Toronto: University of Toronto Press, 1987.

Keith, W. J. *Canadian Literature in English.* London & New York: Longman, 1985.

Keith, W. J., and B. -Z. Shek, eds. *The Arts in Canada: The Last Fifty Years.* Toronto, Buffalo & London: University of Toronto Press, 1980.

Keitner, Wendy, ed. *"Surveying the Territory"* and *"Staking Claims,"* Canadian issues of *Literary Criterion.* 19, 3-4 (1984) and 20, 1 (1985).

Klinck, Carl F., ed. *Literary History of Canada*, 3 volumes, second edition. Toronto: University of Toronto Press, 1976.

Kline, Marcia B. *Beyond the Land Itself: Views of Nature in Canada and the United States.* Cambridge: Harvard University Press, 1970.

Laflamme, Jean, and Rémi Tourangeau. *L'Eglise et le théâtre au Québec.* Montreal: Fides, 1979.

Lafortune, Monique. *Le Roman québécois.* Quebec: Mondia, 1985.

Lecker, Robert, and Jack David, eds. *The Annotated Bibliography of Canada's Major Authors*, 6 volumes, ongoing. Downsview, Ontario: ECW, 1979- .

Lecker and David, eds. *Canadian Writers and Their Works.* 6 volumes, ongoing. Toronto: ECW, 1983- .

Léger, Jules. *Le Canada français et son expression littéraire.* Paris: Nizet & Bastard, 1938.

Legris, Renée, and Pierre Pagé. *Répertoire des dramatiques québécoises à la télévision.* Montreal: Fides, 1977.

Lemieux, Louise. *Pleins feux sur la littérature de jeunesse au Canada français.* Montreal: Leméac, 1972.

Lemire, Maurice. *Les Grands Thèmes nationalistes du roman historique canadien-français.* Quebec: Presses de l'Université Laval, 1970.

"Letters in Canada." Annual review. *University of Toronto Quarterly.* 1936- .

Lewis, Paula Gilbert, ed. *Traditionalism, Nationalism, and Feminism: Women Writers of Quebec.* Westport, Conn. & London: Greenwood Press, 1985.

Lochhead, Douglas, comp. *Bibliography of Canadian Bibliographies*, second edition, revised and enlarged. Toronto: University of Toronto Press, 1972.

MacDermott, Doireann, ed. *Autobiographical and Biographical Writing in the Commonwealth.* Sabadell, Spain: Editorial AUSA, 1984.

Mailhot, Laurent. *La Littérature québécoise*. Paris: Presses Universitaires de France, 1974.

Major, Jean-Louis. *Le Jeu en étoile: Etudes et essais*. Ottawa: Editions de l'Université d'Ottawa, 1978.

Mandel, Eli, ed. *Contexts of Canadian Criticism*. Chicago & London: University of Chicago Press, 1971.

Marcotte, Gilles. *Une Littérature qui se fait. Essais critiques sur la littérature canadienne-française*, second edition. Montreal: HMH, 1968.

Marcotte. *Le Roman à l'imparfait: essai sur le roman québécois d'aujourd'hui*. Montreal: La Presse, 1976.

Marshall, Tom. *Harsh and Lovely Land: Major Canadian Poets and the Making of a Canadian Tradition*. Vancouver: University of British Columbia Press, 1979.

Mathews, Robin. *Canadian Literature: Surrender or Revolution*. Toronto: Steel Rail, 1978.

Maugey, Axel. *Poésie et Société au Québec (1937-1970)*. Quebec: Presses de l'Université Laval, 1972.

May, Cedric. *Breaking the Silence: The Literature of Quebec*. Birmingham, U.K.: University of Birmingham, 1981.

McConnell, R. E. *Our Own Voice: Canadian English and How It Is Studied*. Toronto: Gage, 1979.

McCourt, E. A. *The Canadian West in Fiction*. Toronto: Ryerson, 1949.

McGregor, Gaile. *The Wacousta Syndrome: Explorations in the Canadian Langscape*. Toronto, Buffalo & London: University of Toronto Press, 1985.

McKillop, A. B., ed. *Contexts of Canada's Past: Selected Essays of W. L. Morton*. Toronto: Macmillan, 1980.

McLeod, A. L., ed. *The Commonwealth Pen: An Introduction to the Literature of the British Commonwealth*. Ithaca: Cornell University Press, 1961.

Moisan, Clément. *L'Age de la littérature canadienne*. Montreal: Edition HMH, 1969.

Monkman, Leslie. *A Native Heritage: Images of the Indian in English-Canadian Literature*. Toronto: University of Toronto Press, 1981.

Moritz, Albert and Theresa. *The Oxford Illustrated Literary Guide to Canada*. Toronto: Oxford University Press, 1987.

Moss, John. *Patterns of Isolation in English Canadian Fiction*. Toronto: McClelland & Stewart, 1974.

Moss. *A Reader's Guide to the Canadian Novel*. Toronto: McClelland & Stewart, 1981.

Moss. *Sex and Violence in the Canadian Novel*. Toronto: McClelland & Stewart, 1977.

Moss, ed. *Future Indicative: Literary Theory and Canadian Literature*. Ottawa: University of Ottawa Press, 1987.

Moss, ed. *Modern Times: A Critical Anthology*. Toronto: NC Press, 1982.

Narasimhaiah, C. D., ed. *Awakened Conscience*. New Delhi: Sterling, 1978.

New, W. H. *Among Worlds: An Introduction to Modern Commonwealth and South African Fiction.* Erin, Ontario: Press Porcépic, 1975.

New. *Articulating West.* Toronto: New Press, 1972.

New. *Dreams of Speech and Violence: The Art of the Short Story in Canada and New Zealand.* Toronto: University of Toronto Press, 1987.

New, comp. *Critical Writings on Commonwealth Literatures: A Selective Bibliography to 1970, With a List of Theses and Dissertations.* University Park: Pennsylvania State University Press, 1975.

New, ed. *Dramatists in Canada: Selected Essays.* Vancouver: University of British Columbia Press, 1972.

New, ed. *A Political Art.* Vancouver: University of British Columbia Press, 1978.

Nicholson, Colin, and Peter Easingwood, eds. *Canadian Story and History, 1885-1985.* Edinburgh: Edinburgh University Centre of Canadian Studies, 1985.

Northey, Margot. *The Haunted Wilderness: The Gothic and Grotesque in Canadian Fiction.* Toronto & Buffalo: University of Toronto Press, 1976.

OKanada. Ottawa: Canada Council, 1982.

O'Leary, Dostaler. *Le Roman canadien-français.* Montreal: Cercle du Livre de France, 1954.

Pacey, Desmond. *Creative Writing in Canada,* second edition, revised. Toronto: Ryerson, 1961.

Pacey. *Essays in Canadian Criticism 1938-1968.* Toronto: Ryerson, 1969.

Pache, Walter. *Einführung in die Kanadistik.* Darmstadt: Wissenschaftliche Buchgessellschaft, 1981.

Paradis, Suzanne. *Femme fictive, femme réelle: Le Personnage féminin dans le roman féminin canadien-français, 1884-1966.* Quebec: Garneau, 1966.

Park, Julian, ed. *The Culture of Contemporary Canada.* Ithaca: Cornell University Press, 1957.

Paul-Crouzet, Jeanne. *Poésie au Canada.* Paris: Didier, 1946.

Petrone, Penny, ed. *First People, First Voices.* Toronto: University of Toronto Press, 1983.

Pierce, Lorne. *An Outline of Canadian Literature.* Toronto: Ryerson, 1927.

Press, John, ed. *Commonwealth Literature: Unity and Diversity in a Common Culture.* London: Heinemann Educational, 1965.

Racine, Claude. *L'Anticléricalisme dans le roman québécois, 1940-1965.* Montreal: Hurtubise HMH, 1972.

Rashley, R. E. *Poetry in Canada: The First Three Steps.* Toronto: Ryerson, 1958.

Reid, Dennis. *A Concise History of Canadian Painting.* Toronto, Oxford & New York: Oxford University Press, 1973.

Rhodenizer, V. B. *A Handbook of Canadian Literature.* Ottawa: Graphic, 1930.

Ricou, Laurence R. *Everyday Magic: Child Languages in Canadian Literature*. Vancouver: University of British Columbia Press, 1987.

Ricou. *Vertical Man/Horizontal World*. Vancouver: University of British Columbia Press, 1973.

Riedel, Walter E. *Das Literarische Kanadabild*. Bonn: Bouvier, 1980.

Riedel. *The Old World and the New: Literary Perspectives of German-speaking Canadians*. Toronto: University of Toronto Press, 1984.

Riemenschneider, Dieter, ed. *The History and Historiography of Commonwealth Literature*. Tübingen: Gunter Narr Verlag, 1983.

Rièse, Laure. *L'Ame de la poésie canadienne-française*. Toronto: Macmillan, 1955.

Robidoux, Réjean and André Renaud. *Le Roman canadien-français du vingtième siècle*. Ottawa: Editions de l'Université d'Ottawa, 1966.

Ross, Malcolm. *The Impossible Sum of Our Traditions: Reflections on Canadian Literature*. Toronto: McClelland & Stewart, 1986.

Ross, Malcolm, ed. *The Arts in Canada*. Toronto: Macmillan, 1958.

Ross, ed. *Our Sense of Identity: A Book of Canadian Essays*. Toronto: Ryerson, 1954.

Roy, Camille. *Manuel d'histoire de la littérature canadienne de langue française*, tenth edition. Montreal: Beauchemin, 1945.

Ryan, Toby Gordon. *Stage Left: Canadian Theatre in the Thirties: A Memoir*. Toronto: CTR, 1981.

Sarkonak, Ralph, ed. "The Language of Difference: Writing in QUEBEC(ois)," special issue of *Yale French Studies*, no. 65 (1983).

Schoeck, Richard J., ed. "Canada," special issue of *Review of National Literature*, 7 (1976).

Servais-Maquoi, Mireille. *Le Roman de la terre au Québec*. Quebec: Presses de l'Université Laval, 1974.

Shek, Ben-Zion. *Aspects of Social Realism in the French-Canadian Novel*. Montreal: Harvest House, 1977.

Sirois, Antoine. *Montréal dans le roman canadien*. Montreal: Didier, 1970.

Smith, A. J. M. *On Poetry and Poets*. Toronto: McClelland & Stewart, 1977.

Smith. *Towards a View of Canadian Letters*. Vancouver: University of British Columbia Press, 1973.

Smith, ed. *Masks of Fiction: Canadian Critics on Canadian Prose*. Toronto: McClelland & Stewart, 1961.

Smith, ed. *Masks of Poetry*. Toronto: McClelland & Stewart, 1962.

Staines, David, ed. *The Canadian Imagination*. Cambridge: Harvard University Press, 1977.

Stephens, Donald G., ed. *Writers of the Prairies*. Vancouver: University of British Columbia Press, 1973.

Stevenson, Lionel. *Appraisals of Canadian Literature*. Toronto: Macmillan, 1926.

Story, G. M., and others, eds. *Dictionary of Newfoundland English*. Toronto: University of Toronto Press, 1982.

Stouck, David. *Major Canadian Authors*. Lincoln: University of Nebraska Press, 1984.

Stratford, Philip. *Bibliography of Canadian Books in Translation: French to English and English to French. Bibliographie de livres canadiens traduits de l'anglais au français et du français à l'anglais*. Ottawa: CCRH, 1977.

Stuart, E. Ross. *The History of Prairie Theatre: The Development of Theatre in Alberta, Manitoba, and Saskatchewan*. Toronto: Simon & Pierre, 1984.

Stuewe, Paul. *Clearing the Ground: English Canadian Literature After Survival*. Toronto: Proper Tales, 1984.

Sutherland, Ronald. *The New Hero: Essays in Comparative Quebec/Canadian Literature*. Toronto: Macmillan, 1977.

Sutherland. *Second Image*. Toronto: New Press, 1971.

Tallman, Warren. *Godawful Streets of Man*, special issue of *Open Letter*. 3, no. 6 (1976-1977).

Taylor, Charles. *Six Journeys: A Canadian Pattern*. Toronto: Anansi, 1977.

Thomas, Clara. *Our Nature—Our Voices: A Guidebook to English-Canadian Literature*. Toronto: New Press, 1972.

Tougas, Gérard. *Histoire de la littérature canadienne-française*. Paris: Presses Universitaires de France, 1960. Translated by Alta Lind Cook as *History of French-Canadian Literature*. Toronto: Ryerson, 1966.

Toye, William, ed. *The Oxford Companion to Canadian Literature*. Toronto: Oxford University Press, 1983.

Trudel, Marcel. *L'influence de Voltaire au Canada*, 2 volumes. Montreal: Fides, 1945.

Turnbull, Jane-M. *Essential traits of French-Canadian poetry*. Toronto: Macmillan, 1938.

Urbas, Jeannette. *From "Thirty Acres" to Modern Times; The Story of French-Canadian Literature*. Toronto & New York: McGraw-Hill Ryerson, 1976.

Véronneau, Pierre, ed. *Histoire du cinéma du Québec*, 2 volumes. Quebec: Musée du cinéma, 1979.

Viatte, Auguste. *Histoire littéraire de l'Amérique française des origines à 1950*. Quebec: Presses Universitaires Laval, 1954.

Wagner, Anton, ed. *The Brock Bibliography of Published Canadian Plays in English 1766-1978*. Toronto: Playwrights, 1980.

Walsh, William. *A Manifold Voice: Studies in Commonwealth Literature*. London: Chatto & Windus, 1970.

Wardhaugh, Ronald. *Language & Nationhood: The Canadian Experience*. Vancouver: New Star, 1983.

Warwick, Jack. *The Long Journey: Literary Themes of French Canada.* Toronto: University of Toronto Press, 1968.

Waterston, Elizabeth. *Survey: A Short History of Canadian Literature.* Toronto: Methuen, 1973.

Watters, R. E. *A Check List of Canadian Literature and Background Material 1628-1950,* revised edition. Toronto: University of Toronto Press, 1972.

Wilson, Edmund. *O Canada: An American's Notes on Canadian Culture.* New York: Farrar, Straus & Giroux, 1965.

Woodcock, George. *Canada and the Canadians.* Toronto: Oxford University Press, 1970.

Woodcock. *Northern Spring.* Vancouver: Douglas & McIntyre, 1987.

Woodcock. *Odysseus Ever Returning: Essays on Canadian Writers and Writing.* Toronto: McClelland & Stewart, 1970.

Woodcock. *The World of Canadian Writing.* Vancouver: Douglas & McIntyre, 1980; Seattle: University of Washington, 1980.

Woodcock, ed. *The Canadian Novel in the Twentieth Century.* Toronto: McClelland & Stewart, 1975.

Woodcock, ed. *A Choice of Critics.* Toronto: Oxford University Press, 1966.

Woodcock, ed. *Poets and Critics.* Toronto, Oxford & New York: Oxford University Press, 1974.

Wyczynski, Paul, and others. *Archives des lettres canadiennes.* Montreal: Fides. No. 2 (*Ecole littéraire de Montréal,* 1972); no. 3 (*Roman,* 1971); no. 4 (*Poésie,* 1969); no. 5 (*Théâtre,* 1976).

Contributors

Rose Adams ....*Dartmouth, Nova Scotia*
Alexandre L. Amprimoz...*Brock University*
Geraldine Anthony..*Mount Saint Vincent University*
Ivor A. Arnold ....*University of Western Ontario*
Michael Benazon...*Champlain College-Lennoxville*
Neil Besner ....*University of Winnipeg*
Allan Bevan ....*Dalhousie University*
Diana Brydon..*University of British Columbia*
Elspeth Cameron ....*University of Toronto*
Anne Cimon ....*Montreal, Quebec*
Hallvard Dahlie ....*University of Calgary*
Gwendolyn Davies ....*Mount Allison University*
Moira Day..*University of Alberta*
D. M. Daymond ....*University of Guelph*
Robert D. Denham...*Modern Language Association*
Margaret E. Doyle ....*Wilfrid Laurier University*
Dennis Duffy..*University of Toronto*
William Dunn ....*Birmingham, Michigan*
Dennis F. Essar ....*Brock University*
Richard Giguère ....*Université de Sherbrooke*
Susan Gingell..*University of Saskatchewan*
Terry Goldie..*Memorial University of Newfoundland*
Jill Tomasson Goodwin..*University of Waterloo*
Michael Greenstein ....*Université de Sherbrooke*
Dick Harrison ....*University of Alberta*
Helen Hoy ....*University of Lethbridge*
David Jackel ....*University of Alberta*
J. Kieran Kealy ....*University of British Columbia*
W. J. Keith ....*University of Toronto*
Kenneth Landry..*Université Laval*
Louis K. MacKendrick ....*University of Windsor*
Catherine McLay..*University of Calgary*
Patricia Merivale ....*University of British Columbia*
W. H. New ....*University of British Columbia*
Barbara Pell ....*Trinity Western University*
Donald A. Precosky ....*College of New Caledonia*
Valerie Raoul ....*University of British Columbia*
James Reaney ....*University of Western Ontario*
Laurie Ricou ....*University of British Columbia*
Malcolm Ross ....*Dalhousie University*
H. R. Runte ....*Dalhousie University*
Phyllis M. Senese ....*University of Victoria*
B.-Z. Shek ....*University of Toronto*
Linda Shohet ....*Dawson College*
Antoine Sirois ....*Université de Sherbrooke*
M. W. Steinberg..*University of British Columbia*

David Stouck ....*Simon Fraser University*
Clara Thomas ....*York University*
Hilda L. Thomas ....*University of British Columbia*
Eric Thompson...*Université du Québec à Chicoutimi*
Lee Briscoe Thompson ....*University of Vermont*
J. A. Wainwright ....*Dalhousie University*
Elizabeth Waterston ....*University of Guelph*
Lorraine Weir..*University of British Columbia*
George Woodcock..*Vancouver, British Columbia*
J. M. Zezulka ....*University of Western Ontario*

Cumulative Index

Dictionary of Literary Biography, Volumes 1-68
Dictionary of Literary Biography Yearbook, 1980-1987
Dictionary of Literary Biography Documentary Series, Volumes 1-4

This index lists authors who are the subjects of *DLB* entries, appendices to *DLB* volumes, and titles of articles in *DLB Yearbooks.*

Cumulative Index

DLB before number: *Dictionary of Literary Biography*, Volumes 1-68
Y before number: *Dictionary of Literary Biography Yearbook*, 1980-1987
DS before number: *Dictionary of Literary Biography Documentary Series*, Volumes 1-4

A

Abbey Press DLB-49

The Abbey Theatre and Irish
    Drama, 1900-1945 .... DLB-10

Abbot, Willis J. 1863-1934................... DLB-29

Abbott, Jacob 1803-1879 ....DLB-1

Abbott, Robert S. 1868-1940 .... DLB-29

Abelard-Schuman DLB-46

Abell, Arunah S. 1806-1888 .... DLB-43

Abercrombie, Lascelles 1881-1938............ DLB-19

Abrams, M. H. 1912- DLB-67

Abse, Dannie 1923- DLB-27

Academy Chicago Publishers DLB-46

Ace Books DLB-46

Acorn, Milton 1923-1986 .... DLB-53

Actors Theatre of Louisville DLB-7

Adair, James 1709?-1783? DLB-30

Adamic, Louis 1898-1951.....................DLB-9

Adams, Alice 1926- Y-86

Adams, Brooks 1848-1927.................... DLB-47

Adams, Charles Francis, Jr. 1835-1915 .... DLB-47

Adams, Douglas 1952- Y-83

Adams, Franklin P. 1881-1960 .... DLB-29

Adams, Henry 1838-1918 ....DLB-12, 47

Adams, Herbert Baxter 1850-1901 .... DLB-47

Adams, J. S. and C. [publishing house]........ DLB-49

Adams, James Truslow 1878-1949............ DLB-17

Adams, John 1735-1826..................... DLB-31

Adams, John Quincy 1767-1848............... DLB-37

Adams, Léonie 1899- DLB-48

Adams, Samuel 1722-1803 ....DLB-31, 43

Adams, William Taylor 1822-1897 .... DLB-42

Adcock, Fleur 1934- DLB-40

Ade, George 1866-1944 ....DLB-11, 25

Adeler, Max (see Clark, Charles Heber)

Advance Publishing Company................ DLB-49

AE 1867-1935 .... DLB-19

Aesthetic Poetry (1873), by Walter Pater DLB-35

Afro-American Literary Critics:
    An Introduction DLB-33

Agassiz, Jean Louis Rodolphe 1807-1873........DLB-1

Agee, James 1909-1955.....................DLB-2, 26

Aiken, Conrad 1889-1973 ....DLB-9, 45

Ainsworth, William Harrison 1805-1882....... DLB-21

Aitken, Robert [publishing house]............. DLB-49

Akins, Zoë 1886-1958 .... DLB-26

Alain-Fournier 1886-1914 .... DLB-65

Alba, Nanina 1915-1968...................... DLB-41

Albee, Edward 1928- DLB-7

Alcott, Amos Bronson 1799-1888................DLB-1

Alcott, Louisa May 1832-1888 ....DLB-1, 42

Alcott, William Andrus 1798-1859...............DLB-1

Alden, Isabella 1841-1930 .... DLB-42

Alden, John B. [publishing house]............. DLB-49

Alden, Beardsley and Company DLB-49

Aldington, Richard 1892-1962..............DLB-20, 36

Aldis, Dorothy 1896-1966 .... DLB-22

Aldiss, Brian W. 1925- DLB-14

Aldrich, Thomas Bailey 1836-1907 .... DLB-42

Alexander, Charles Wesley
    [publishing house] DLB-49

Alexander, James 1691-1756 .... DLB-24

Alexander, Lloyd 1924- DLB-52

Alger, Horatio, Jr. 1832-1899 .... DLB-42

Algonquin Books of Chapel Hill.............. DLB-46

359

B

Butler, Juan 1942-1981 .... DLB-53

Butler, Octavia E. 1947- DLB-33

Butler, Samuel 1835-1902 .... DLB-18, 57

Butterworth, Hezekiah 1839-1905 .... DLB-42

B. V. (see Thomson, James)

Byars, Betsy 1928- DLB-52

Byatt, A. S. 1936- DLB-14

Byles, Mather 1707-1788 .... DLB-24

Bynner, Witter 1881-1968 .... DLB-54

Byrd, William II 1674-1744 .... DLB-24

Byrne, John Keyes (see Leonard, Hugh)

C

Cabell, James Branch 1879-1958 ....DLB-9

Cable, George Washington 1844-1925 .... DLB-12

Cahan, Abraham 1860-1951 ....DLB-9, 25, 28

Cain, George 1943- DLB-33

Caldwell, Ben 1937- DLB-38

Caldwell, Erskine 1903-1987 ....DLB-9

Caldwell, H. M., Company DLB-49

Calhoun, John C. 1782-1850 ....DLB-3

Calisher, Hortense 1911- DLB-2

Callaghan, Morley 1903- DLB-68

Callaloo Y-87

Calmer, Edgar 1907- DLB-4

Calverley, C. S. 1831-1884 .... DLB-35

Calvert, George Henry 1803-1889 ....DLB-1, 64

Cambridge Press DLB-49

Cameron, Eleanor 1912- DLB-52

Camm, John 1718-1778 .... DLB-31

Campbell, James Edwin 1867-1896 .... DLB-50

Campbell, John 1653-1728 .... DLB-43

Campbell, John W., Jr. 1910-1971 ....DLB-8

Campbell, Roy 1901-1957 .... DLB-20

Campion, Thomas 1567-1620 .... DLB-58

Candour in English Fiction (1890),
   by Thomas Hardy DLB-18

Cannan, Gilbert 1884-1955 .... DLB-10

Cannell, Kathleen 1891-1974 ....DLB-4

Cannell, Skipwith 1887-1957 .... DLB-45

Cantwell, Robert 1908-1978 ....DLB-9

Cape, Jonathan, and Harrison Smith
   [publishing house] DLB-46

Capen, Joseph 1658-1725 .... DLB-24

Capote, Truman 1924-1984 .... DLB-2; Y-80, 84

Carey, M., and Company...................... DLB-49

Carey, Mathew 1760-1839 .... DLB-37

Carey and Hart.............................. DLB-49

Carlell, Lodowick 1602-1675 .... DLB-58

Carleton, G. W. [publishing house]........... DLB-49

Carossa, Hans 1878-1956..................... DLB-66

Carr, Emily 1871-1945 .... DLB-68

Carrier, Roch 1937- DLB-53

Carlyle, Jane Welsh 1801-1866 .... DLB-55

Carlyle, Thomas 1795-1881 .... DLB-55

Carroll, Gladys Hasty 1904- DLB-9

Carroll, John 1735-1815 .... DLB-37

Carroll, Lewis 1832-1898 .... DLB-18

Carroll, Paul 1927- DLB-16

Carroll, Paul Vincent 1900-1968............... DLB-10

Carroll and Graf Publishers DLB-46

Carruth, Hayden 1921- DLB-5

Carryl, Charles E. 1841-1920................. DLB-42

Carswell, Catherine 1879-1946 .... DLB-36

Carter, Angela 1940- DLB-14

Carter, Henry (see Leslie, Frank)

Carter, Landon 1710-1778 .... DLB-31

Carter, Lin 1930- Y-81

Carter, Robert, and Brothers DLB-49

Carter and Hendee........................... DLB-49

Caruthers, William Alexander 1802-1846 ....DLB-3

Carver, Jonathan 1710-1780................... DLB-31

Carver, Raymond 1938- Y-84

Cary, Joyce 1888-1957....................... DLB-15

Casey, Juanita 1925- DLB-14

Casey, Michael 1947- DLB-5

Cassady, Carolyn 1923- DLB-16

Cassady, Neal 1926-1968 .... DLB-16

Cassell Publishing Company DLB-49

D

E

G

H

J

K

L

Cumulative Index

M

O

P

Q

S

T

411

U

Y

Dictionary of Literary Biography